BOLLINGEN SERIES LXXX

The Divine Comedy

Inferno

2. Commentary

DANTE ALIGHIERI

The Divine Comedy

TRANSLATED, WITH A COMMENTARY, BY

CHARLES S. SINGLETON

Inferno

2. Commentary

BOLLINGEN SERIES LXXX

PRINCETON UNIVERSITY PRESS

Library of Congress Catalogue card no. 68-57090

ISBN 0-691-09855-7

Printed in the United States of America

by Princeton University Press, Princeton, New Jersey

Second printing, with corrections, 1977

CONTENTS

ILLUSTRATIONS

PLATES

FIGURES

MAPS

ACKNOWLEDGMENTS

The sources for published material that has been quoted in the present commentary will be found in the List of Works Cited. The translations most frequently used include those of the Latin classics taken from the Loeb Classical Library, the translations of the works of Dante provided by the Temple Classics, the Confraternity-Douay translation of the Vulgate, and the translation of Aquinas' *Summa theologica* by the Fathers of the English Dominican Province. Translations for which no published source was used have been provided in most cases by Professor Mario Domandi of Vassar College (Italian and Latin), Father Edwin A. Quain, S.J., of Fordham University Press (Latin), and Neil M. Larkin of the University of Rochester (Old French and Provençal).

References to the Bible are to the Vulgate; if the corresponding citation to the King James Bible differs, it is given in brackets following the Vulgate citation.

The Latin version of Aristotle that both Dante and Thomas Aquinas are assumed to have known has been quoted from the Parma edition of the *Opera omnia* of Thomas Aquinas; this "Antiqua Translatio" is the only Aristotle text quoted in the present work. Marietti editions of the Aquinas commentaries on Aristotle, which also contain the text of Aristotle in Latin, are suggested in the notes and included in the List of Works Cited for the general convenience of the reader. Bekker numbers are used in citations to the works of Aristotle to facilitate reference to any edition of Aristotle the reader may have, since Bekker numbers are not provided in the Aquinas *Opera omnia* itself; chapter numbers are those of the Loeb Classical Library.

All maps and figures were prepared for this book by the Clarendon Press, Oxford University. Maps 1 and 2, and Figures 5, 6, and 7, are based on drawings by Pauline Manning Batchelder. Maps 3 and 4 are after material in Paget Toynbee, *A Dictionary of Proper Names and Notable*

Matters in the Works of Dante, revised by Charles S. Single-
ton (Oxford, 1968). Figures 1 through 4 were prepared after
illustrations in *La Divina Commedia di Dante Alighieri*,
edited and annotated by C. H. Grandgent (Boston, 1933).

Commentaries on the *Divine Comedy*, both early and
modern, are cited by the commentator's name alone, with no
specific reference to page or verse number, because commen-
taries ordinarily follow the canto and verse number of the
Comedy. For modern authors other than commentators, the
author's name and date of publication serve as citation.

Inferno

Commentary

CANTO I

1. *Nel mezzo del cammin di nostra vita*: In the fictional time of the journey (the year 1300, as will be disclosed later in the poem), Dante, who was born in 1265, is literally midway in the journey of his life—on good scriptural authority (Ps. 89[90]:10): "Dies annorum nostrorum in ipsis septuaginta anni." ("Seventy is the sum of our years.") The Biblical life span of seventy years had become a part of accepted medical and philosophical opinion; see B. Nardi (1930), pp. 123–53. See *Conv.* IV, xxiii, 9: "Là dove sia lo punto sommo di questo arco [de la vita] . . . è forte da sapere; ma ne li più io credo tra il trentesimo e quarantesimo anno, e io credo che ne li perfettamente naturati esso ne sia nel trentacinquesimo anno." ("It is hard to say where the highest point of this arch [of life] is . . . but in the majority I take it to be somewhere between the thirtieth and the fortieth year. And I believe that in those of perfect nature it would be in the thirty-fifth year.") See also (this being the journey to Hell that it soon proves to be) Isa. 38:10: "Ego dixi: In dimidio dierum meorum vadam ad portas inferi." ("I said: In the midst of my days I shall go to the gates of hell.")

The importance of "nostra" is not to be overlooked. This is "our" life's journey, and we are necessarily involved

3

in it. Thus, in its first adjective, the poem is open to the possibility of allegory.

2. *mi ritrovai*: The form with *ri-* (*ritrovai* instead of *trovai*) stresses inwardness, awareness ("I came to myself"). Here it registers the dawning of light in the conscience. *una selva oscura*: See *Aen*. VI, 6–8:

> . . . quaerit pars semina flammae
> abstrusa in venis silicis, pars densa ferarum
> tecta rapit silvas, inventaque flumina monstrat.

Some seek the seeds of flame hidden in veins of flint, some pillage the woods, the thick coverts of game, and point to new-found streams.

See also *Aen*. VI, 179, 185–88:

> itur in antiquam silvam, stabula alta ferarum;
>
> . . . .
>
> atque haec ipse suo tristi cum corde volutat,
> aspectans silvam immensam, et sic forte precatur:
> "si nunc se nobis ille aureus arbore ramus
> ostendat nemore in tanto! . . ."

They pass into the forest primeval, the deep lairs of beasts . . . . And alone [Aeneas] ponders with his own sad heart, gazing on the boundless forest, and, as it chanced, thus prays: "O if now that golden bough would show itself to us on the tree in the deep wood!"

See T. Silverstein (1932), pp. 81–82, for a discussion of *Aen*. VI, 179–89, and the following glosses on the passage by Bernard Sylvestris:

In silvam, in collectionem temporalium bonorum. *Umbrosam* [*sic*] et *immensam*, quia non est nisi umbra. *Antiquam*, ab inicio temporis natam. . . . Vocat enim philosophia luxuriosos sues, fraudulentos vulpes, garrulos canes, truculentos leones, iracundos apros, rapaces lupos, torpidos asinos. Hii omnes temporalia bona inhabitant.

In silvam (in the woods), in the totality of the things of this world. *Umbrosam* (shadowy) and *immensam* (immense), because the shadows are everywhere. *Anti-*

quam (ancient), born in the beginning of time. . . .
Philosophy calls those who are immoderate, pigs; the
fraudulent, foxes; the garrulous, dogs; the truculent,
lions; the irascible, boars; the rapacious, wolves; the
torpid, asses. All of them dwell amidst the things of
this world.

In the *Convivio* (IV, xxiv, 12), Dante refers to "la selva
erronea di questa vita" ("the wandering wood of this life").
See also Augustine, *Conf.* X, 35: "tam immensa silva plena
insidiarum et periculorum" ("so vast a wilderness, so full
of snares and dangers").

On the darkness of the wood, Benvenuto comments: "Et
dicit *oscura* propter ignorantiam et peccatum, quae obcae-
cant, et obscurant, et tenebras petunt, quia qui male agit,
odit lucem." ("And he says *oscura* [dark] because of ig-
norance and sin, which blind us and make things dark.
Ignorance and sin seek darkness, for those who do evil hate
light.")

3. *la diritta via*: See Prov. 2:13-14: "qui relinquunt iter
rectum, at ambulant per vias tenebrosas, qui laetantur cum
malefecerint, et exsultant in rebus pessimis" ("who leave
the straight paths to walk in ways of darkness, who delight
in doing evil, rejoice in perversity"), and Prov. 4:18-19:
"Iustorum autem semita quasi lux splendens procedit, et
crescit usque ad perfectam diem. Via impiorum tenebrosa;
nesciunt ubi corruant." ("But the path of the just is like
shining light, that grows in brilliance till perfect day. The
way of the wicked is like darkness; they know not on what
they stumble.") See also II Pet. 2:15: "Derelinquentes
rectam viam erraverunt." ("They have forsaken the right
way and have gone astray.")

5. *esta = questa.*

6. *rinova = rinnova.   la paura*: Fear, which always be-
sets the sinful life and enslaves the sinner (in theology, *timor
servilis*), proves to be the main impediment at the start of
the journey. See vss. 15, 19, 44, 53, and n. to vs. 53.

7. *Tant' è amara che poco è più morte*: For the "bitter" wood and the comparison with death, see Eccles. 7:27[26]: "amariorem morte" ("more bitter than death"); Ecclus. 41:1: "O mors, quam amara est memoria tua" ("O death! how bitter the thought of you"); and Augustine, *In Ioan*. XVI, 6: "Amara silva mundus hic fuit" ("A bitter wood was this world").

8. *del ben ch'i' vi trovai*: This "ben" will be the wayfarer's rescue by Virgil after the she-wolf thrusts him back into the dark wood.

11. *pien di sonno*: The "sleep" is the sinful life in its forgetfulness of the good. See Rom. 13:11–12: "Et hoc scientes tempus, quia hora est iam nos de somno surgere . . . . Nox praecessit, dies autem appropinquavit. Abiiciamus ergo opera tenebrarum, et induamur arma lucis." ("And this do, understanding the time, for it is now the hour for us to rise from sleep . . . . The night is far advanced; the day is at hand. Let us therefore lay aside the works of darkness, and put on the armor of light.")

12. *la verace via*: The "diritta via" of vs. 3, the way of virtue, of righteousness and justice. See Ps. 22[23]:3: "Animam meam convertit. Deduxit me super semitas iustitiae." ("He refreshes my soul. He guides me in right paths.")

13–18. *Ma poi ch'i' fui . . . per ogne calle*: The wayfarer now again sees the "true way," the way of virtue and righteousness, which leads up the hill before him and from which he had strayed. The hill is the *mons Domini* of the Scriptures (Ps. 23[24]:3): "Quis ascendet in montem Domini?" ("Who can ascend the mountain of the Lord?") The poem gradually will disclose the full significance and true nature of this mountain, as well as the more exact meaning of the sun that now strikes the summit. The imagery and phraseology here remain essentially Biblical. See Pss. 14[15]:1–2; 120[121]:1; and especially Ps. 42[43]:3: "Emitte lucem tuam et fidelitatem tuam: ipsae me ducant, adducant me in montem sanctum tuum et in tabernacula

tua." ("Send forth your light and your fidelity; they shall
lead me on and bring me to your holy mountain, to your
dwelling-place.")

The meaning of the sun here is suggested in *Conv.* III, xii,
6–7: "Ora è da ragionare, per lo sole spirituale e intelligibile,
che è Iddio. Nullo sensibile in tutto lo mondo è più degno
di farsi essemplo di Dio che'l sole." ("We are now to dis-
course of the spiritual sun, accessible to the intellect, that
is God. No object of sense in all the universe is more worthy
to be made the symbol of God than the sun.") Dante is
using an ancient and well-established similitude. In the con-
text of these verses, particularly vs. 18, the "Sol iustitiae"
of the Scriptures is definitely a part of the intended meaning,
and justice—or sin as injustice—is the keynote. See Mal.
4:2: "Et orietur vobis timentibus nomen meum Sol iustitiae."
("But unto you that fear my name the Sun of justice shall
arise.")

17. *pianeta*: In the astronomy of Dante's time, the sun was
one of the planets that circle the earth. It is typically pre-
sented here, both as the real sun and as symbol (*res et
signum*), in keeping with the other properties and features
of this first scene.

18. *ogne* = *ogni*. On the basis of his MSS Petrocchi has
generally preferred "ogne" as the form Dante probably used.

20. *lago del cor*: The "lake of the heart" was understood
in Dante's time to mean a concavity or "ventricle" in which
the blood gathered. (For medieval ideas about the circula-
tion of the blood, see G. Boffito, 1932.) Beyond its physio-
logical meaning, however, this "lake" was identified as the
location of fear in the human body. Commenting on this
verse, Boccaccio observes that "è quella parte ricettacolo di
ogni nostra passione: e perciò dice che in quella gli era
perseverata la passione della paura avuta." ("That part is
the reservoir of all our passions. Therefore, [Dante] says that
the passion of fear he had felt perdured there.") The phrase
appears elsewhere. See Dante, *Rime dubbie* III, vss. 7–9:

Ver è ch'ad ora ad ora indi discende
una saetta, che m'asciuga il lago
del cor pria che sia spenta.

True it is that now and again a fiery bolt thence de-
scendeth that dryeth up a lake from my heart ere it be
quenched.

See also *Vita nuova* II, 4: "In quello punto dico veracemente
che lo spirito de la vita, lo quale dimora ne la secretissima
camera de lo cuore, cominciò a tremare." ("At that point I
verily declare that the vital spirit which dwelleth in the
most secret chamber of the heart began to tremble.")

22–27. *E come . . . persona viva*: The full import of this
first simile of the poem cannot be appreciated until much
later, when the whole figure of the Exodus is seen as the
governing image, which on this scene requires the presence
of water, the "dangerous waters" (i.e., something corre-
sponding to a Red Sea wherein many perish, as the whole
Egyptian army perished). Thus the "pelago," here, later
termed a "fiumana" (*Inf.* II, 108), corresponds even if its
full meaning in this sense cannot be seen yet. Here it is a
well-established symbol of the sinful life, harmonizing with
the other features of a landscape that is essentially spiritual
and moral. For the significance of Exodus as the master
pattern of the poem's prologue action, see C. S. Singleton
(1965a).

26–27. *lo passo . . . viva*: The "pelago" is now named the
"pass that never left anyone alive," since, as an image of
the sinful life, it can be said to sweep all sinners (i.e., all
who remain in it) to their damnation and the "second
death" (vs. 117) of Hell. See Prov. 12:28: "In semita iusti-
tiae vita, iter autem devium ducit ad mortem." ("In the
path of justice there is life, but the abominable way leads
to death.")

28. *èi = ebbi. il corpo lasso*: The mind that was still
fleeing but turned back to gaze (vss. 25–26) is no disem-
bodied vision. The wayfarer is a living man. He moves here

in the flesh, and his body is tired from its struggle to flee from the sinful life.

29. *la piaggia diserta*: "Piaggia" can mean "slope" or "shore," or, as here, it may have both meanings at once (see A. Schiaffini, 1937a; M. Barbi, 1934b, pp. 200–201). The presence of water—if only in simile—makes possible the meaning of "shore" in this passage, as the poem viewed as a whole in retrospect easily confirms. Similarly, recognition of the Exodus pattern reveals the full significance of the adjective "diserta."

30. *sì che 'l piè fermo sempre era 'l più basso*: This famously obscure verse is given its sufficient gloss by J. Freccero (1959). A long tradition applied the metaphor of feet to faculties of the soul. As this metaphor merged with Aristotle's dictum that all motion originates from the right, it was said that the first step is taken by the right foot while the left remains stationary. The left foot was seen as the *pes firmior*, the firmer or less "agile." Later, in a Christian tradition, there came about a more specific identification of the "two feet of the soul." According to Bonaventura and others, the "foot" or power that moves first is the *apprehensivus*, or the intellect, and therefore is the right. The other or left "foot" is the *affectus* or *appetitivus*—i.e., the will. In Adam's sin, wherein all men sinned, it was the intellect or right "foot" that suffered the wound of ignorance, while the left "foot," the *affectus* or will—the *pes firmior*—suffered the wound of concupiscence. As a result, postlapsarian man is a limping creature (*homo claudus*). He limps especially in his *left* foot, because it is wounded by concupiscence, the chief *vulneratio* of original sin.

In this opening scene of the poem, the wayfarer, as he strives to climb toward the light at the summit, has to discover that he bears within him the weaknesses of *homo claudus*. He can see the light at the summit (seeing, in this case, is a function of the intellect or right "foot"). At best, however, he can only limp toward the light he sees because in his other power, his will—the left "foot" or *pes firmior*—

he bears the wound of concupiscence. Thus, the "piè fermo" is the *pes infirmior*, as Freccero (1959) fully documents.

In this whole figure of conversion, or turning toward the light, as it is staged here in Canto I, the wayfarer learns that he is wounded in the power of his will and cannot advance effectively toward the apprehended goal. In fact, the sinful dispositions he thought he had left behind him in the darkness now appear before him in the form of the three beasts blocking his way.

Several features of the scene later find their further elucidation and confirmation in connection with *Purg.* I.

31–60. *Ed ecco . . . tace*: In the moral allegory, the three beasts that now appear before the wayfarer and impede his ascent are best understood as sinful dispositions. As the poem unfolds, it reveals the true names and natures of the beasts. Of the three, the she-wolf proves to be the most troublesome; this fact in itself suggests rather clearly, even without ulterior confirmations, that the beast's name in allegory is *cupiditas*, "the root of all evils" (see n. to vss. 94–101). *Concupiscentia* ("the chief *vulneratio* of original sin") would serve equally well as the wolf's allegorical name. The three beasts, as such, are plainly reminiscent of Ier. 5:6: "Idcirco percussit eos leo de silva, lupus ad vesperam vastavit eos, pardus vigilans super civitates eorum: omnis qui egressus fuerit ex eis capietur, quia multiplicatae sunt praevaricationes eorum, confortatae sunt aversiones eorum." ("Wherefore a lion out of the wood hath slain them, a wolf in the evening hath spoiled them, a leopard watcheth for their cities: every one that shall go out thence shall be taken, because their transgressions are multiplied, their rebellions are strengthened.")

31. *quasi al cominciar de l'erta*: The wayfarer has already begun to climb the slope. The meaning is "soon after the beginning of the climb."

32. *una lonza*: OFr *lonce*. This animal is mentioned in the medieval bestiaries. The description in the *Bestiario toscano* (M. S. Garver and K. McKenzie, 1912, p. 86) indicates a

rather special animal: "Loncia (var. *lonza*) è animale crudele
e fiera, e nasce de coniungimento carnale de leone con lonça
o vero de leopardo con leonissa." ("The *loncia* or *lonza* is a
vicious, ferocious animal, born of the carnal union of a lion
with a leopardess or of a leopard with a lioness.") Some
insist that the *lonza* is the female of the *pardus*, an identifi-
cation that fits the requirements of Ier. 5:6. Benvenuto says:
"Istud vocabulum florentinum *lonza* videtur magis im-
portare pardum, quam aliam feram." ("This Florentine
word *lonza* seems to signify the leopardess, rather than any
other wild beast.") And Buti mentions "la lonza, che è la
femina di quello animale che si chiama pardo" ("the *lonza*,
which is the female of that animal called the leopard"). On
the whole question of the identification of this beast, see
P. Chistoni (1903); E. Proto (1907); T. Casini (1895).

33. *pel macolato*: See "maculosae tegmine lyncis" ("a
dappled lynx's hide") in *Aen.* I, 323.

35. *anzi 'mpediva = anzi impediva.* On elisions of this
kind, see n. to vs. 96.

37–43. *Temp' era . . . la dolce stagione*: No more precise
time than this is given here for the beginning of the journey.
It was believed that at the moment of creation, when God
first set the heavenly bodies ("quelle cose belle," vs. 40) in
motion, the sun was in the sign of Aries (which it enters
at the vernal equinox, about March 21). It is spring, there-
fore, traditionally a "season of good hope"—the more so in
that it is also the time of the Incarnation (March 25). See
Macrobius, *Comm. in somn. Scip.* I, xxi, 23: "Aiunt enim
incipiente die illo qui primus omnium luxit . . . qui ideo
mundi natalis iure vocitatur, Arietem in medio caelo fuisse."
("According to them, at the beginning of that day which
was the first of all days . . . the day which is rightly called
the birthday of the universe, Aries was in the middle of the
sky.") Benvenuto comments: "Dicunt enim astrologi et
theologi quod Deus ab initio saeculi posuit solem in ariete,
in quo signo facit nobis ver." ("Indeed, the astrologers and
theologians say that at the beginning of the world, God
placed the sun in Aries, in which sign He gives us spring.")

37. *dal principio = al principio.*

44–48. *ma non sì che paura . . . tremesse*: In its furious
advance the lion manifests the violence that it later proves
to represent in the allegory. In its hunger it would devour
the wayfarer. Fear again is stressed as the prevailing emo-
tion.

45. *la vista che m'apparve*: The visionary quality of this
first scene and, accordingly, its primary significance in the
moral allegory are emphasized by such recurring words as
vista and *parere* (here, *apparere*). For *vista* in the sense of
"image" or "figure," see M. Barbi (1934b), pp. 268–69.

46. *Questi*: Masculine singular demonstrative pronoun, cor-
responding to *quei* (vs. 22). *venisse*: Petrocchi chooses,
in this case as in others, to leave what is derived from the
so-called Sicilian rhyme, i.e., *-isse* in rhyme with *-esse*, since
he is persuaded, on the basis of his MSS, that such was still
Dante's usage. For a discussion of this, see his vol. I, *Intro-
duzione*, p. 470, where he also refers to an example of this
rhyme in Boccaccio's *Teseida* (IX, 30).

47. *rabbiosa fame*: See *Aen.* VI, 421, where Cerberus opens
his triple throat "fame rabida" ("in ravenous hunger").

48. *parea che l'aere ne tremesse*: See Ovid, *Metam.* XIII,
406: "externasque novo latratu terruit auras" ("and with
strange barking affrighted the alien air"). *tremesse*:
Vandelli and Casella both have "temesse." For Petrocchi's
justification of "tremesse," see his n. to this verse and his
discussion of the point in his vol. I, *Introduzione*, pp. 165–66.
Either reading makes sense, but "tremesse" seems finally
the better.

50. *sembiava = sembrava.* *carca = carica.*

51. *fé = fece.*

53. *la paura ch'uscia di sua vista*: Again, fear is the sub-
jective impediment of the ascent up the mountain, a fear
that finally causes despair. See Sapien. 11:20: "Sed et

aspectus per timorem occidere [poterat]." ("But also the very sight might kill them through fear.") It is to be noted, however, that "uscia di sua vista" says that fear "came from sight of her." The construction is common in Dante; see *Purg.* I, 28: "Com' io da loro sguardo fui partito." See also Shakespeare, *Romeo and Juliet*, Act I, sc. 1, ll. 176-77: "Alas, that love, so gentle in his view, / should be so tyrannous and rough in proof!"

53. *uscia* (pronounced *uscìa*) = *usciva.*

55–60. *E qual . . . tace*: This figure amounts to a pseudo-simile, common enough in the poem: the "one" of the first term of the comparison actually is not distinguishable from the "other" of the second term, except that the former is given as the generic instance and the latter as the particular. The wayfarer here is precisely such a one, in that he eagerly advances up the slope until he encounters the beast.

56. *face* = *fa.*

58. *sanza* = *senza.*

60. *là dove 'l sol tace*: The darkness. The wayfarer is thrust back toward the dark wood, but not into it, since when help comes he is still on the "piaggia diserta" (vs. 29). In fact, in the next canto he will be seen as one struggling over the "fiumana" or flood (*Inf.* II, 108) to which the wolf had driven him (and again the presence of water will make the "piaggia"—*Inf.* II, 62—a "shore" as well as a "slope").

The figurative merging here of the visual ("the sun") and the auditory ("is silent") anticipates a similar device in vs. 63.

61. *rovinava*: Some MSS read "ruvinava." Vandelli had adopted "rovinava," whereas Casella had preferred "ruinava." In any case the noun *rovina* or *ruina* should not be lost sight of. The meaning is "falling back and down," with the moral connotation of "ruin."   *in basso loco*: Back toward the valley and the dark wood.   *loco* = *luogo.* See n. to vs. 66 on "omo."

63. *chi per lungo silenzio parea fioco*: The verse seems deliberately ambiguous, since "fioco" can mean "faint" either to the eye or to the ear, and "silenzio" can have meaning with respect both to space and to time. If the one who comes is faint to the eye, then he appears dim because he is seen "through long silence," i.e., "nel gran diserto" of the following verse; if faint to the ear, then it is because Virgil's voice, as the voice of reason, had not reached the wayfarer for a long time—for as long, in fact, as he had wandered from the path of virtue. The voice of reason contributes to the temporal meaning of the "long silence," and the "gran diserto" to its spatial meaning.

64. *gran diserto*: A reason that the desert slope-shore ("piaggia diserta," vs. 29) is also termed a "gran diserto" will become clear many cantos later in the poem. See C. S. Singleton (1965a), pp. 104-9.

66. *sii = sia. omo = uomo.* Characteristically in Tuscan usage, the single *o* displaces the diphthong *uo* when it bears the tonic stress (as also in *loco, foco*).

68. *li = i.*

69. *mantoani = mantovani.* Mantua, near which Virgil was born, was considered to be a city of Lombardy in Dante's day.

70. *sub Iulio, ancor che fosse tardi*: "Under Julius," i.e., in the time of Julius Caesar, "though late," since Caesar was assassinated in 44 B.C., when Virgil was only twenty-five years old and had not begun to write the works that were to bring him fame *sub Augusto*.

72. *li dèi falsi e bugiardi*: For Augustine (see *De civ. Dei* II, 2; II, 10; II, xxix, 1-2, *et passim*), as for the Middle Ages, the pagan gods were actually demons intent on deceiving and ensnaring mankind; hence they were said to be not only "false" but "lying" gods, and an enlightened Virgil can now so see them.

73-74. *quel giusto figliuol d'Anchise*: Aeneas, the "just" king. See *Aen.* I, 544-45: "Rex erat Aeneas nobis, quo

iustior alter / nec pietate fuit, nec bello maior et armis."
("Our king was Aeneas: none more righteous than he in
goodness, or greater in war and deeds of arms.")

74. *di*: Both Vandelli and Casella have "da." See Petrocchi's
justification of "di" in his n. to this vs. and his reference to
further instances in *Inf.* V, 85; VIII, 54; XIII, 11, 43; XV,
43, 62; and *passim*.

75. *superbo Ilión*: See *Aen.* III, 2–3: "ceciditque superbum /
Ilium et omnis humo fumat Neptunia Troia" ("after proud
Ilium fell, and all Neptune's Troy smokes from the
ground"). In *Purg.* XII, 61–63, the fall of Troy will be
seen as the prime example of pride laid low. / For the ac-
cent on the last syllable of "Ilión," see n. to *Inf.* V, 4.

    combusto: Past participle of *comburere*, "to burn." See
Ovid, *Metam.* XIII, 408: "Ilion ardebat." ("Ilium was in
flames.")

77–78. *il dilettoso monte . . . tutta gioia*: Virgil's words
refer to the *summit* of the mountain, of course, and what
awaits the wayfarer there if he should reach it. This is a
mountain to be climbed and the goal lies at its summit, now
illuminated by the sun. Thus, the summit, the goal, is the
final "cause" of the action that leads to it. See *De mon.* I, ii,
7: "Rursus, cum in operabilibus principium et causa omnium
sit ultimus finis." ("Again, in the case of anything that is
done it is the ultimate end which constitutes the first prin-
ciple and cause of the whole thing.") And at the summit of
the mountain, as will be seen, it is true "happiness" that
awaits the wayfarer.

79. *Or se' tu quel Virgilio*: The poet Virgil (Publius Ver-
gilius Maro) was born in 70 B.C. near Mantua in Cisalpine
Gaul. His ten pastoral poems, the *Eclogues* (*Bucolica*), on
which Dante closely modeled his *Eclogae*, were published
ca. 37 B.C.; and his four books on agriculture, the *Georgics*,
were published seven years later. The last eleven years of
his life were spent in the composition of the *Aeneid*. He
died in 19 B.C. in Brundisium.

83. *vagliami = mi vaglia*. Dante frequently uses a singular verb with a plural subject.

84. *cercar*: "To pore over."   *lo tuo volume*: The *Aeneid*.

85. *autore*: In *Conv.* IV, vi, 5, Dante notes that the word *author* "si prende per ogni persona degna d'essere creduta e obedita" ("is understood of every person worthy of being believed and obeyed"); hence, an *auctor* is an authority.

87. *stilo = stile*. This seems to mean the "illustrious" or "tragic" style that Dante distinguishes from two other styles, the comic and the elegiac (see *De vulg. eloqu.* II, iv, 5–8). Before 1300, the fictional date of his journey to the other-world, Dante already had composed a number of *canzoni* in the style referred to as "bello," which he claims here to have learned from Virgil. Dante proposed to give and expound allegorically a number of these *canzoni* in the *Convivio*. These are the poems and this is the style, then, that have done him honor.

88. *la bestia*: The she-wolf (see vs. 58).

89. *saggio = savio*. For Dante, as for his time, the ancient poets are *savi*, men of wisdom and learning, poetry itself being a form of wisdom. Thus, Dante designates as sages Homer, Virgil, Horace, Ovid, and Lucan (*Inf.* IV, 110), Statius (*Purg.* XXIII, 8), and his own contemporary Guido Guinizelli (*Vita nuova* XX, 3).

90. *e i polsi*: A standing phrase (see *Inf.* XIII, 63).

94–101. *questa bestia . . . e più saranno ancora*: The she-wolf is seen here as *cupiditas* or *concupiscentia*, one of the three major categories of sins, as we are to learn later in the poem. There is good reason for the she-wolf's being, of the three beasts, the most troublesome and for her mating with many creatures and causing many to live in sorrow: "Radix enim omnium malorum est cupiditas; quam quidam appetentes erraverunt a fide, et inseruerunt se doloribus multis"—"For covetousness is the root of all evils, and some in their eagerness to get rich have strayed from the faith and have involved themselves in many troubles" (I Tim. 6:10).

94. *gride = gridi.*

96. *lo 'mpedisce = lo impedisce.* In the older usage, as witnessed by the MSS, it was customary to elide the initial vowel of the word following a definite article or other preceding word ending in a vowel, rather than to elide the vowel of the article or other preceding word itself as in *l'impedisce.*

100. *Molti son li animali a cui s'ammoglia*: See Apoc. 18:3: "De vino irae fornicationis eius biberunt omnes gentes, et reges terrae cum illa fornicati sunt." ("All the nations have drunk of the wrath of her immorality, and the kings of the earth have committed fornication with her.")

101–2. *infin che 'l veltro verrà*: Dante never lost hope in the advent of a temporal monarch as is so obscurely predicted here by Virgil. Dante earlier had written of such a monarch in similar terms and specifically with regard to cupidity (*De mon.* I, xiii, 7):

> Cum ergo Monarcha nullam cupiditatis occasionem habere possit vel saltem minimam inter mortales . . . quod ceteris principibus non contingit, et cupiditas ipsa sola sit corruptiva iudicii et iustitie prepeditiva, consequens est quod ipse vel omnino vel maxime bene dispositus ad regendum esse potest, quia inter ceteros iudicium et iustitiam potissime habere potest.

> Since, then, the monarch cannot have any occasion for greed, or at any rate can of all men have least occasion thereto . . . which is not the case with the other princes, and since greed, in its turn, is the sole corrupter of judgment and impeder of justice, it follows that the monarch is capable either of the absolutely good disposition for governing, or at least of a higher degree thereof than others; because he amongst all others is capable of the highest degree of judgment and justice.

For the long and continuing debate over the identity of

the "veltro," see M. Barbi (1938), pp. 29–39; V. Cian (1945); R. E. Kaske (1961); E. Moore (1903), pp. 253–83; E. G. Parodi (1920), pp. 367–532; A. Vallone (1955; 1961, pp. 85–87).

103. *non ciberà terra né peltro*: The Hound will seek neither land nor money. The eating of earth as a sign of greed is enacted later when ravenous Cerberus is quieted by Virgil's tossing earth into his three greedy throats (*Inf.* VI, 25–27). *peltro*: Literally, "pewter."

105. *sua nazion sarà tra feltro e feltro*: The prophecy is deliberately obscure. If "nazion" means "birth," which seems probable, the phrase "tra feltro e feltro" could well indicate that the time of the expected advent will be under the constellation of Gemini—i.e., the twins Castor and Pollux, the Dioscuri, who were commonly represented as wearing felt caps and were, accordingly, known as the *pilleati fratres*. To be sure, such an indication does not actually make the oracular pronouncement much clearer in its meaning. Dante thought Gemini one of the best constellations to be born under, however—it was his own. For this theory of the meaning of "tra feltro e feltro," see L. Olschki (1949). For the many other interpretations advanced over the centuries, see the references cited in n. to vss. 101–2.

106. *Di quella umile Italia fia salute*: The adjective "umile" (pronounced *umìle*) intentionally echoes Virgil's use of "humilem" in *Aen.* III, 522–23, "cum procul obscuros collis humilemque videmus / Italiam," which R. M. Haywood (1959), in a new interpretation, translates as "when from afar we saw the dim hills of Italy lying low on the horizon." Since here in Dante's poem it is Virgil who utters this prophecy, the echo from the *Aeneid* is rich in suggestion: an Italy glimpsed now in the distance of time, rather than of space, as a kind of promised land to be restored to peace by the "veltro."

107–8. *morì . . . di ferute*: Of the four slain warriors named by Dante here, two fought on the side of the Trojan Aeneas and two fought against him.

107. *Cammilla*: Camilla, daughter of King Metabus of the Volscian town of Privernum, assisted Turnus in his war against Aeneas. She was ambushed and killed by Arruns. See *Aen.* XI, 759–831.

108. *Eurialo e . . . Niso*: Euryalus and Nisus, Trojan youths famous for their close friendship, accompanied Aeneas to Italy and died together after a night attack on the Rutulian camp. See *Aen.* IX, 176–449. *Eurialo*: Pronounced *Eurìalo.* *Turno*: Turnus was king of the Rutulians at the time of Aeneas' arrival in Italy. In the war that ensued, Turnus was killed by Aeneas in single combat. See *Aen.* XII, 887–952. *ferute = ferite.*

111. *là onde 'nvidia prima dipartilla*: See Sapien. 2:24: "Invidia autem diaboli mors introivit in orbem terrarum." ("But by the envy of the devil, death entered the world.") *onde 'nvidia = onde invidia.* On elisions of this kind, see n. to vs. 96. *dipartilla = la dipartì.*

112. *me' = meglio.*

113. *segui = segua.*

114. *trarrotti = ti trarrò* (future of *trarre*). Note that in older usage, conjunctive pronouns may be appended to certain finite forms of the verb, as in "dipartilla" (past absolute), in vs. 111. In such cases, the initial consonant of the pronoun is doubled if the verb form itself bears the tonic stress on its final syllable or if it is monosyllabic. That is, the doubling of the pronoun's initial consonant simply means that the verb keeps its usual tonic stress. *per loco etterno*: Hell—as distinguished from Purgatory (vss. 118–20), which will not exist eternally.

117. *ch'a la*: Both Vandelli and Casella prefer "che la," but Petrocchi has felt justified on the basis of his MSS to adopt the preposition. See his note to this vs. *la seconda morte*: See Apoc. 20:14: "Et infernus et mors missi sunt in stagnum ignis: haec est mors secunda." ("And hell and death were cast into the pool of fire. This is the second death.") See

also Apoc. 21:8: "Pars illorum erit in stagno ardenti igne et sulphure: quod est mors secunda." ("Their portion shall be in the pool that burns with fire and brimstone, which is the second death.")

119. *nel foco*: The purifying fire of Purgatory. Later, the whole purgative process of the second realm will be referred to as "il temporal foco" (*Purg.* XXVII, 127), distinguished from "l'etterno foco" of Hell, even though fire proves to be but one of several forms of cleansing punishment in that "temporal" abode. *foco = fuoco*; see n. on "omo," vs. 66.

122. *fia = sarà*.

124. *quello imperador che là sù regna*: It seems most fitting that Virgil, poet of empire, should speak thus of God, whose empire is everywhere and whose kingdom is the tenth heaven, the Empyrean, where He dwells.

125–26. *perch' i' fu' ribellante . . . si vegna*: As the poem is to make abundantly clear, Virgil died a pagan, with no burden of actual or personal sin, but only with that of original sin. This is true also of the other virtuous pagans of antiquity soon to be met in Limbo: "They did not sin . . . and if they were before Christianity, they did not worship God aright" (*Inf.* IV, 34, 37–38). Only in this sense can Virgil mean that he rebelled against God's law. It was not given to such pagans as Virgil to believe in the Christ who was to come; hence, they are forever denied the blessedness of Heaven. See vs. 131, where Virgil is said not to have known the Christian God.

126. *non vuol che 'n sua città per me si vegna*: Literally, "does not will that there be any coming into His city by me." This impersonal construction occurs frequently in the poem.
  città: See Apoc. 22:14: "Beati qui lavant stolas suas in sanguine Agni, ut sit potestas eorum in ligno vitae, et per portas intrent in civitatem." ("Blessed are they who wash their robes [in the blood of the Lamb,] that they may have the right to the tree of life, and that by the gates they may

enter into the city.") See also Heb. 11:10: "Expectabat enim fundamenta habentem civitatem, cuius artifex et conditor Deus." ("For he was looking for the city with fixed foundations, of which city the architect and the builder is God.")

Dante's image of the city here suggests specifically a heavenly Rome. See *Purg.* XXXII, 102—and, of course, Augustine's *De civitate Dei.*

130. *richeggio = richiedo.*

132. *questo male e peggio*: The evil of being in the dark wood of sin, which is so bitter, and eternal damnation, which is worse.

134. *veggia = veda.*   *la porta di san Pietro*: In Purgatory, as will be seen.

135. *color cui tu fai cotanto mesti*: The damned of Hell. *fai*: "Make," in the sense of "designate" or "term."

136. *li = gli.*

CANTO II

1. *Lo giorno se n'andava*: See *Aen.* III, 147: "Nox erat et terris animalia somnus habebat." ("It was night and on earth sleep held the living world.") See also *Aen.* VIII, 26–27; IX, 224–25. The "dark air" of evening is now here; the wayfarer has spent the whole day, from sunrise to sunset, in his attempt to climb the mountain.

2. *animai* = *animali*, i.e., all animate creatures, including man—a common use of the term both in Latin and in Dante. See Virgil's use of "animalia" (n. to vs. 1, above). See also *Inf.* V, 88, where Dante is addressed as "animal grazioso e benigno."

3. *io sol uno*: Dante can be said to be alone, since Virgil is a shade. See *Inf.* I, 67: "Non omo, omo già fui."

4. *guerra*: The "battle" or "ordeal."

5. *la pietate*: The "pity" that the living man knows he will feel for the tormented souls of the damned.

6. *ritrarrà la mente che non erra*: "Mente" is used here in the sense of *memoria*, a frequent meaning of *mente* in Dante (and of *mens* in Latin). See *Rime* L, 1; LXVII, 59.
    Memory will now faithfully retrace the real event of the journey, exactly as it took place. This most extraordinary

journey through the three realms of the afterlife is repre-
sented, never as dreamed or experienced in vision, but as a
real happening, involving—as is made evident in Canto
I—a living man who goes in the body and who moves al-
ways through real space. It is now the poet's arduous task
to go back over the entire course of the event as it actually
occurred and to give, in verse, a true report. Here, then,
and in the following invocation, the poet's voice is heard
for the first time as it speaks of his task as poet.

7–9. *O muse . . . la tua nobilitate*: The invocation is in the
epic style (see, for example, *Aen.* VI, 264–67). Similar in-
vocations are made at the beginning of the other two
cantiche. For that of the *Paradiso* see Dante's own remarks
in his *Letter to Can Grande* (*Epist.* XIII, 46–48). That the
invocation of the *Inferno* is made here in Canto II declares
that this second canto is actually the first of the *Inferno*
proper (which then, like the other two *cantiche*, consists
of thirty-three cantos). *Inferno* I thus figures as an intro-
ductory canto or prologue to the whole poem and brings
the total number of cantos to the perfect number of one
hundred.

7. *alto ingegno*: The poet's own genius, his *virtù* as poet,
whereas the Muses are invoked to give inspiration. Such a
distinction is traditional. See *De vulg. eloqu.* II, iv, 9–10,
where, after discussing the selection of the poet's *materia*
and the choice of style, Dante writes:

> Caveat ergo quilibet et discernat ea que dicimus; et
> quando tria hec pure cantare intendit, vel que ad ea
> directe ac pure secuntur, prius Elicone potatus, tensis
> fidibus, adsumptum secure plectrum tum movere in-
> cipiat. Sed cautionem atque discretionem habere sicut
> decet, hoc opus et labor est, quoniam nunquam sine
> strenuitate ingenii et artis assiduitate scientiarumque
> habitu fieri potest. Et hii sunt quos Poeta, Eneidorum
> sexto, dilectos Dei et ab ardente virtute sublimatos ad
> ethera Deorumque filios vocat, quanquam figurate
> loquatur. Et ideo confutetur eorum stultitia, qui, arte
> scientiaque immunes, de solo ingenio confidentes, ad

summa summe canenda prorumpunt; et a tanta pre-
sumptuositate desistant; et si anseres natura vel desidia
sunt, nolint astripetam aquilam imitari.

Let every one therefore beware and discern what we
say; and when he purposes to sing of these three subjects
simply [the three matters for poetry in the tragic style],
or of those things which directly and simply follow
after them, let him first drink of Helicon, and then,
after adjusting the strings, boldly take up his *plectrum*
and begin to ply it. But it is in the exercise of the need-
ful caution and discernment that the real difficulty lies;
for this can never be attained to without strenuous
efforts of genius, constant practice in the art, and the
habit of the sciences. And it is those (so equipped)
whom the poet in the sixth book of the *Aeneid* describes
as beloved of God, raised by glowing virtue to the sky,
and sons of the Gods, though he is speaking figura-
tively. And therefore let those who, innocent of art and
science, and trusting to genius alone, rush forward to
sing of the highest subjects in the highest style, confess
their folly and cease from such presumption; and if in
their natural sluggishness they are but geese, let them
abstain from imitating the eagle soaring to the stars.

8. *mente che scrivesti*: Latent is the metaphor of a Book
of Memory, a figure that controls the whole form of the
Vita nuova after it is presented there in the opening words
(see C. S. Singleton, 1949, pp. 25–54). This metaphor will
be used more than once in the *Commedia*. See *Par.* XXIII,
54, where memory is called the "libro che 'l preterito
rassegna." By virtue of this same figure the poet also speaks
of himself as "scriba" (*Par.* X, 27). Here in the *Inferno*,
however, it is "memory" itself that "wrote down" what
the poet saw.

9. *la tua nobilitate*: See *Conv.* IV, xvi, 4: "Per questo
vocabulo 'nobilitade' s'intende perfezione di propria natura
in ciascuna cosa." ("This word 'nobleness' means the per-
fection in each thing of its proper nature.")

10. *Io cominciai . . .* : The prologue and invocation completed, the canto's *pars executiva*—as Dante terms it in his *Letter to Can Grande* (*Epist.* XIII, 43)—begins with this verse.

12. *l'alto passo*: The "deep way" that lies ahead, the "guerra del cammino" of vss. 4–5. Note in "passo" the suggestion of a "passing" or "crossing over" (into the world of the dead), and a certain figurative correspondence with "lo passo che non lasciò già mai persona viva" (*Inf.* I, 26–27).

13. *Tu dici che di Silvio il parente*: The passing touch of "Tu dici che" recognizes that Aeneas' journey to the world of the dead as related in the *Aeneid* was poetic fiction. (For a similar touch, see *Par.* XV, 26: "se fede merta nostra maggior musa," referring, of course, to Virgil's *Aeneid.* Also see *Inf.* XIII, 46–48.) In contrast, no such "reservation" is made when Paul's journey is mentioned (*Inf.* II, 28: "Andovvi").   *Silvio*: Dante follows Virgil in making Silvius not the son of Ascanius (Livy, I, iii, 6–7), but the late-born son of Aeneas and Lavinia (*Aen.* VI, 763–66):

> Silvius, Albanum nomen, tua postuma proles,
> quem tibi longaevo serum Lavinia coniunx
> educet silvis regem regumque parentem,
> unde genus Longa nostrum dominabitur Alba.

> Silvius of Alban name, thy last-born child, whom late in thy old age thy wife Lavinia shall bring up in the woodland, a king and father of kings; from him shall our race have sway in Long Alba.

According to Servius (on *Aen.* VI, 760), at the death of Aeneas, Lavinia took refuge in the woods for fear of Ascanius (Aeneas' son by Creusa) and there gave birth to Silvius. Ascanius, the founder of Alba Longa, eventually was succeeded by Silvius.

14. *corruttibile ancora*: Still mortal.

14–15. *ad immortale secolo*: Cf. the Latin *saeculum* in this sense. "Mortale secolo" means "this world," of course.

"Immortale secolo" refers to "the otherworld," and is general enough to include both Hades and Paradise. It is possible that Dante knew the *Visio Sancti Pauli*, a very old and widely known account of Heaven and Hell in which Paul is represented as going to Hell. Nevertheless, "immortal world" here in Canto II clearly suggests Heaven as well as Hell: Paul went to the former, Aeneas to the latter. Dante would have expected his readers to remember that Paul had been "caught up into paradise" (see n. to vs. 29); moreover, the *vi* in "Andovvi" (vs. 28) indicates Paradise, included in the "immortale secolo." Paul's rapture will be recalled again when Dante's own ascent to the heavenly Paradise begins, and it is touched on in Dante's *Letter to Can Grande* (*Epist.* XIII, 79). / On the *Visio Sancti Pauli* and other popular accounts of the otherworld known in the Middle Ages, see T. Silverstein (1937).

15. *sensibilmente*: In his bodily senses.

17. *i = gli.* *pensando*: The subject understood may be either "God" or "one" in a kind of ablative absolute. "If one considers the high effect . . ." seems the more probable interpretation. *l'alto effetto*: As stated in vss. 20–24.

18. *e 'l chi e 'l quale*: Cf. the scholastic phrase *quis et qualis*. / Aeneas was noble by birth, by character, and by marriage. See *De mon.* II, iii, 6: "Nam divinus poeta noster Virgilius per totam Eneidem gloriosissimum regem Eneam patrem Romani populi fuisse testatur in memoriam sempiternam." ("For our divine poet Virgil, throughout the *Aeneid* testifies, for an everlasting memorial, that the glorious king Aeneas was the father of the Roman people.") And Romulus, the legendary founder of Rome, was descended from Aeneas (*Aen.* VI, 777–79). Some interpreters would refer the phrase to the "alto effetto" (vs. 17) rather than to Aeneas, but this seems less satisfactory; the focus here appears to be on Aeneas himself, as it continues to be in vss. 20–21. For yet another interpretation, see A. Pagliaro (1961), pp. 190, 231–36, and Petrocchi's note.

Petrocchi has followed Pagliaro in having no comma after "quale"; however, many other editors have a comma there, and this seems more in accord with the meaning that the translation has rendered.

20. *e' = ei (egli)*.

21. *l'empireo ciel*: The Empyrean heaven, the tenth and outermost sphere, God's abode and "kingdom," as it is called in *Inf.* I, 127. See *Conv.* II, iii, 8, 10:

> Veramente, fuori di tutti questi [cieli], li cattolici pongono lo cielo Empireo, che è a dire cielo di fiamma o vero luminoso. . . . E quieto e pacifico è lo luogo di quella somma Deitade che sola [sè] compiutamente vede. Questo loco è di spiriti beati, secondo che la Santa Chiesa vuole, che non può dire menzogna.

> But beyond all these [heavens] the Catholics assert the empyrean heaven, which is as much as to say the heaven of flame, or the luminous heaven. . . . But still and tranquil is the place of that supreme deity, which alone completely perceiveth itself. This is the place of the blessed spirits, according as holy Church, which may not lie, will have it.

21. *eletto*: For Dante, the Roman Empire is directly ordained by God as part of His providential plan for man's redemption and was established in order to prepare the way for the Advent of the Saviour and the foundation of His Church on earth—a conception that emerges time and again in the course of the poem. See C. S. Singleton (1958), pp. 86–100. Also see F. Torraca (1925), who quotes several documents of Henry VII in support of this idea, and N. Zingarelli (1927), pp. 91–94.

22–23. *la quale e 'l quale . . . fu stabilita*: "Roma e suo impero" (vs. 20) are the antecedents. A compound subject governing a singular verb is common in Dante. / The reading "stabilita" instead of "stabilito" seems preferable since it singles out the first subject (Rome) as the "holy place." Thomas Aquinas (*De reg. prin.* I, 14) refers to Rome as the city "quam Deus praeviderat christiani populi principalem sedem futuram" ("which God had foreseen as the chief abode of the Christians"). Also see *Conv.* IV, iv, 13: "E che ciò sia, per due apertissime ragioni vedere si può, le quali mostrano quella civitade imperatrice, e da Dio avere spezial nascimento, e da Dio avere spezial processo." ("And that this is so may be seen by two most manifest reasons, which show that this city [of Rome] was imperial, and had special birth and special progress from God.")

24. *u' = ubi (ove)*.   *maggior Piero*: Probably no comparison is intended here; the adjective may simply mean "great" (see M. Barbi, 1934b, p. 237). Possibly, however, some comparison might be implied in the sense that Peter is thus singled out as the first and greatest of the popes. See *Par.* XXXII, 136, where Adam is styled the "maggior padre di famiglia."

25. *onde li dai tu vanto*: Again, the particular turn of phrase implies that Aeneas' journey was poetic fiction. See n. to vs. 13.   *li = gli.*

27. *di sua vittoria e del papale ammanto*: Aeneas' victory led to the establishment of the Roman Empire, which was, in turn, a preparation for the establishment of the Church— the "alto effetto" (vs. 17) that was to come of Aeneas' journey. See n. to vs. 21.

28. *Andovvi = vi andò*, i.e., "ad immortale secolo," which is Heaven in this case (see n. to vss. 14–15).   *lo Vas d'elezione*: Paul. See Actus 9:15: "Dixit autem ad eum Dominus: Vade, quoniam vas electionis est mihi iste, ut portet nomen meum coram Gentibus et regibus et filiis Israel." ("But the Lord said to him, 'Go, for this man is a chosen vessel to me, to carry my name among nations and kings and the children of Israel.'")

29. *per recarne conforto a quella fede*: Paul, "caught up into paradise," saw by direct vision (II Cor. 12:2–4), not *per speculum*, as faith must see in this life. His was a seeing that transcended faith, and the report of it is a "conforto" to faith.

30. *principio a la via di salvazione*: See Heb. 11:6: "Sine fide autem impossibile est placere Deo." ("Without faith it is impossible to please God.") See also Thomas Aquinas, *Summa theol.* II-II, q. 2, a. 3, resp.: "Ad hoc quod homo perveniat ad perfectam visionem beatitudinis, praeexigitur quod credat Deo, tamquam discipulus magistro docenti." ("In order that a man arrive at the perfect vision of heavenly happiness, he must first of all believe God, as a disciple believes the master who is teaching him.")

31-33. *io . . . io . . . io . . .* : In Italian, the subject pronoun is always emphatic, and it becomes the more so here by its repetition.

31. *venirvi*: The *vi* continues to refer to the "immortale secolo" (vss. 14-15), including both Heaven and Hell, but the shift from the "going" of Aeneas and Paul ("andata," vs. 25) to the "coming" of Dante ("venuta," vs. 35) brings in Virgil and his point of view. This shift is sustained throughout the rest of the canto.

32. *Enea . . . Paulo*:   Aeneas at the start of his journey to Hades also names two who had been there (*Aen.* VI, 122-23): "Quid Thesea magnum, / quid memorem Alciden?" ("Why speak of great Theseus, why of Alcides?")

33. *né altri 'l crede*: Neither Vandelli nor Casella has the pleonastic pronoun "'l" ($= il$). Petrocchi argues convincingly for its inclusion in the verse; see his note.

34. *se del venire io m'abbandono*: "If I allow myself to come."

35. *folle*: "Folly"—with the touch of a suggestion that for him to undertake such a journey would be an act of *hubris*.

36. *me' = meglio.*

37-40. *E qual . . . tal mi fec' io*: Again, a pseudo-simile (see n. to *Inf.* I, 55-60).

38. *cangia = cambia.*   *proposta = proposito*   (cf. "pro-posto," vs. 138).

39. *tolle = toglie* (from Latin *tollere*). The meaning here is "si distoglie."

40. *oscura costa*: Like "piaggia" (see n. to *Inf.* I, vs. 29), "costa" can mean either "shore" or "slope," or, as here, it may have both meanings. It is dark because night has fallen, but it is dark also in a moral sense, as the "piaggia" is "diserta" in both a physical and a moral sense.

41. *la 'mpresa = la impresa.*

44. *del magnanimo quell' ombra*: Virgil might be so named in any case, but "magnanimo" here, with "viltade" (vs. 45) applied to the wayfarer, suggests a struggle between magna-nimity and pusillanimity. See *Conv.* IV, xxvi, 7, 9:

> Questo sprone si chiama Fortezza, o vero Magnanimi-tate . . . . Quanto spronare fu quello, quando esso Enea sostenette solo con Sibilla a intrare ne lo Inferno a cercare de l'anima di suo padre Anchise, contra tanti pericoli.

> This spur is called courage, or consciousness of great-ness . . . . How great spurring was that when the same Aeneas hardened himself to enter alone with the Sibyl into hell and search for the soul of his father Anchises, in the face of so many perils.

Virgil's *exhortatio* to Dante as they stand before the gate of Hell will be a direct reminiscence of this passage in the *Aeneid*. See *Inf.* III, 14–15 and the note.

46. *fiate = volte*, of frequent occurrence in Dante.

47. *onrata = onorata.*

48. *quand' ombra = quando s'adombra.*

49. *solve = solva*, present subjunctive of *solversi.*

50. *io 'ntesi = io intesi.*

51. *dolve = dolse*, archaic past absolute of *dolere* in an impersonal construction, "it grieved me for you."

52. *sospesi*: Literally, "suspended." The meaning will become clear when the reader learns more (see *Inf.* IV, 28–42) about the condition of those in Limbo, of Virgil and the other virtuous pagans whose punishment it is to live in desire but without hope. The adjective "sospesi" (both here and again in *Inf.* IV, 45) indicates not only this spiritual condition, but also the actual physical position of Limbo; outside of Hell proper, it nevertheless is counted as the first circle.

55. *Lucevan li occhi suoi più che la stella*: See *Vita nuova* XXIII, 25 and *Conv.* III, ix, 11–12.   *la stella*: Singular for the plural, as elsewhere in Dante.

56. *a dir soave e piana*: Both adjectives function here as adverbs modifying "dir." See M. Barbi (1934b), p. 203.

57. *in sua favella*: "In her speech" or mode of speaking (as E. G. Parodi, 1957, p. 338, explains).

58–60. *O anima . . . lontana*: Beatrice's words to Virgil have a rhetorical amplitude and formal development that follow recognized models, with an exordium in the manner of a *captatio benevolentiae* ("gaining the good will [of another]"). We may note here the first of the many appeals in the *Inferno* to enduring fame in the world of the living—a survival after death that is desired by many of the damned of Hell, as if it were their only "immortality."

61. *l'amico mio, e non de la ventura*: "Ventura" is synonymous with "Fortuna" and, accordingly, bears in this context some suggestion of a personification, as if two ladies, Beatrice and Lady Fortune, were contending for this man's affections. Behind the term "amico," in this context, lies the current phrase "nemica Fortuna" as well as "nemico della Fortuna." / See Boccaccio, *Decam.* III, 9 (vol. I, p. 254, ll. 17–18): "Madonna, el mi pare che voi siate delle nemiche della fortuna come sono io" ("My lady, it appears to me

that you are one of Fortune's enemies, as I am"); VIII, 7 (vol. II, p. 149, l. 36): "Ma anche questo l'aveva la sua nemica fortuna tolto" ("But this, too, her enemy Fortune had taken from her"). See also X, 8 (vol. II, p. 285, l. 11): "amato dalla fortuna" ("beloved of Fortune"). (See Plate 1, facing.)

62. *la diserta piaggia*: The "gran diserto" and the "loco selvaggio" of *Inf*. I (vss. 64 and 93). See also "la piaggia diserta," *Inf*. I, 29. In support of the meaning "shore" for "piaggia" here in *Inf*. II, 62, a metaphorical "fiumana" will appear in vs. 108.

63. *vòlt' è = è volto.   paura*: In fact, throughout the preceding account of this same scene, fear (see *Inf*. I, vss. 6, 15, 19, 44, 53, 90) was stressed as the chief obstacle to the ascent of the mountain. Now fear is explicitly said to be what caused the wayfarer finally to turn back. Virgil's question to Beatrice (*Inf*. II, 82–84) will continue to underline fear.

64. *smarrito*: The word echoes "smarrita" (*Inf*. I, 3) and suggests that the wayfarer may be in danger of again losing the "diritta via," as indeed he is in his "ruining down to the depth" (*Inf*. I, 61).

68. *mestieri = mestiere.*

70. *I' son Beatrice*: Virgil had referred to Beatrice in vss. 122–23 of the preceding canto as a soul worthier than he to take over as guide and lead the wayfarer to Paradise, but he did not explicitly name her. Now Virgil tells how she descended to Limbo and declared herself to him. But we may well wonder how Virgil, who died in 19 B.C., could be expected to recognize Beatrice, and his immediate recognition of her takes on a greater interest. See n. to vss. 76–78.

72. *amor mi mosse*: As is evident from Beatrice's whole account of the prologue action in Heaven, the love she speaks of is a love *de sursum descendens* ("descending from on high"), the blessed Virgin Mary's love and, in the

1. Imago Mundi, showing Fortune (left) and Sapience (right)

last analysis, God's love. Beatrice in the *Commedia* is no Pre-Raphaelite "Blessed Damozel."

76–78. *O donna di virtù . . . li cerchi sui*: These words of recognition to Beatrice are most important as a first focus on her allegorical meaning. See C. S. Singleton (1956). / Some editors place a comma after "virtù"; and since "donna" is the antecedent of "cui," this seems preferable.

78. *sui = suoi.*

81. *è uo' = è uopo* (cf. Latin *opus est*). For a justification of this reading see Petrocchi's note.

82. *la cagion che = la cagione per la quale.*

83. *in questo centro*: In this context the phrase bears a strong pejorative connotation, which stems from the well-established view that the earth's position at the center of the universe is the most ignoble—because it is farthest from God and His angels. The cavity of Hell is, of course, even farther from the "ampio loco" (vs. 84) of the Empyrean heaven. See Fra Giordano da Rivalto, *Prediche* VI (1739 edn., p. 22):

> La terra . . . è il centro di questo mondo; imperocch'ella è nel mezzo di tutti i cieli, e di tutti gli elementi. Ma il diritto centro si è appunto quel miluogo della terra dentro, ch'è in mezzo della terra, come la granella è in mezzo del pome. Quello è il diritto centro, ove noi crediamo, che sia il ninferno.

> The earth . . . is the center of this world, for it is in the midst of all the heavens and of all the elements. But the true center is precisely that point within the earth which is in its midst, as the core is in the midst of the apple. We believe that Hell is located there, at the true center.

84. *l'ampio loco*: The Empyrean heaven, the outermost sphere, which contains the whole universe. It is a spiritual heaven where the saints abide with God.   *ardi*: Latent in the verb is the metaphor of fire or a flame which, in

33

Dante's physics as in Aristotle's, seeks ever to rise to its "proper" place, i.e., the sphere of fire, the highest of the elemental spheres, as to its resting place. So Beatrice "burns" to return to her "proper" place. (See Figs. 1 and 2.)

85. *saver = sapere.*

86. *dirotti = ti dirò.*

88. *dee = deve.*

89. *altrui*: A dative here, although it should be noted that *altrui*, invariable in form, also can be accusative or possessive, according to the context.

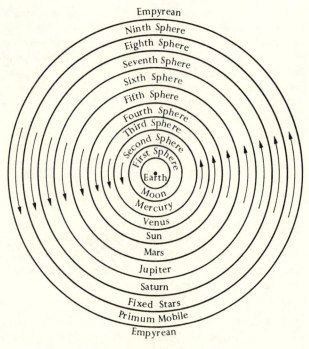

Figure 1. The Heavenly Spheres

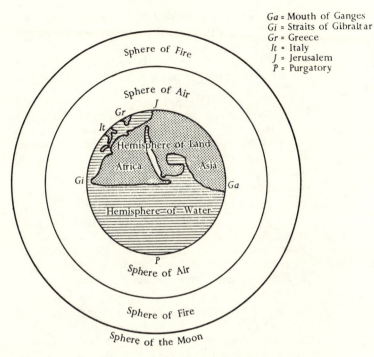

Ga = Mouth of Ganges
Gi = Straits of Gibraltar
Gr = Greece
It = Italy
J = Jerusalem
P = Purgatory

Figure 2. Earth surrounded by air and fire

91–93. *I' son fatta . . . non m'assale*: This lack of com-
passion toward the damned in Limbo and Hell is the char-
acteristic attitude shown by the saints in Paradise. As
Thomas Aquinas summarizes it (*Summa theol.* III, Suppl.,
q. 94, a. 2, resp.): "Et ideo beati qui erunt in gloria nullam
compassionem ad damnatos habebunt." ("Therefore the
blessed in glory will have no pity on the damned.") On
this matter of the saints' immunity to compassion, see C. H.
Grandgent (1926).

92. *la vostra miseria*: Readers of this translation, which
does not use the second person singular "thou" but only
"you," except when the Deity is addressed, should remark
the shifts from singular to plural that take place in the orig-

inal Italian. In making the shift here, Beatrice refers to the misery of all the damned of Hell. *tange*: See Sapien. 3:1: "Iustorum autem animae in manu Dei sunt, et non tanget illos tormentum mortis." ("But the souls of the just are in the hand of God, and the torment of death shall not touch them.")

93. *né fiamma d'esto 'ncendio non m'assale*: Fire stands for all the torments of Hell, even though it actually proves to be the instrument of punishment in only two of the several circles (the seventh and the eighth). Among the many Biblical references to the fire of Hell, see especially Ecclus. 28:25–27:

> Mors illius mors nequissima, et utilis potius infernus quam illa. Perseverantia illius non permanebit, sed obtinebit vias iniustorum, et in flamma sua non comburet iustos; qui relinquunt Deum incident in illam, et exardebit in illis et non extinguetur, et immittetur in illos quasi leo, et quasi pardus laedet illos.

> The death [inflicted by an evil tongue] is a most evil death: and hell is preferable to it. Its continuance shall not be for a long time, but it shall possess the ways of the unjust: and the just shall not be burnt with its flame. They that forsake God shall fall into it, and it shall burn in them, and shall not be quenched, and it shall be sent upon them as a lion, and as a leopard it shall tear them.

93. *d'esto 'ncendio = d'esto incendio*.

94–96. *Donna è gentil nel ciel . . . là sù frange*: As is made clear later (but may well be taken for granted), the blessed Virgin Mary is "our advocate" in Heaven. Her intercession, in fact, makes this journey to God possible—"stern judgment is broken thereabove." The sinner otherwise would have remained in the darkness of sin and finally have been swept down to the "second death" of Hell. Dante's own great devotion to the Virgin Mary is evident throughout the poem. How the Divine Will may be affected or changed by love is described in *Par.* XX, 94–99. See also, in the prayer addressed to Mary at the end of the poem (*Par.* XXXIII, 16–18), what may be applied to her intercession here at the beginning:

> La tua benignità non pur soccorre
> a chi domanda, ma molte fiate
> liberamente al dimandar precorre.

97–102. *Questa chiese Lucia . . . l'antica Rachele*: No reader will miss the courtly atmosphere of this prologue scene in Heaven, the gracious manner in which one "lady" turns or comes to another, with due observance of station and degree. Indeed, this is the court of the "Emperor who reigns thereabove," to whom Virgil referred (*Inf.* I, 124).

97. *Lucia*: This doubtless is St. Lucy of Syracuse, the third-century virgin martyr regarded as patron saint of those who suffer from eye ailments. Early commentators consider her as the symbol of illuminating grace. The meaning of Lucy's role in this first relay of grace will become clearer as the poem unfolds.

98. *il tuo fedele*: There were two churches in Florence dedicated to St. Lucy of Syracuse. Commentators frequently point out that Dante may have placed himself under Lucy's protection while he was suffering from a temporary eye affliction (*Vita nuova* XXXIX, 4; *Conv.* III, ix, 14–16). This can hardly be intended as any part of the meaning here, however, where seeing is a matter, above all, of an inner light.

100. *nimica di ciascun crudele*: The phrase is similar to "l'avversario d'ogne male" in vs. 16. "Crudele" is an adjective used substantively, and the meaning is "all who are cruel."

101. *si mosse*: Mary does not leave her seat, as Lucy does; a higher and a lower rank thereby are implied.

102. *con l'antica Rachele*: Beatrice has her seat in Heaven beside Rachel, as the poem states both here and again at the end (see *Par.* XXXII, 8–9). / Rachel, according to the ac-

37

count in Genesis, was the younger sister of Leah. Jacob first married Leah, and then finally won Rachel.

103. *loda di Dio vera*: See *Vita nuova* XXVI, where Dante recounts that all who watched Beatrice pass along the way praised God for her. In her earthly life, and now in her heavenly life, Beatrice is such a wondrous being that she is a living praise of the Creator.

104. *ché* = *perché*.

105. *ch'uscì per te de la volgare schiera*: A familiar tenet of the doctrine of courtly love is expressed here: by his love for his lady the poet is lifted above the vulgar. The past tense points back to the experience described in the *Vita nuova*, where Beatrice appears not as a disembodied allegory but as a real lady, as here.

107. *la morte*: Spiritual death, primarily, but also physical death (see *Purg.* I, 58–60). / What is seen here from Heaven connects with the first simile of the poem (*Inf.* I, 22–27).

108. *su la fiumana ove 'l mar non ha vanto*: This river or "flood" is essentially the same water as the "pelago" of *Inf.* I, 22–27. It is not a river that flows into the sea; hence, the sea rightly can be said to have no vaunt over it. On the imagery and meaning of this verse, see C. S. Singleton (1948).

109. *fur* = *furono*.   *ratte* = *rapide*.

111. *cotai* = *cotali*.   *fatte*: The verb *fare* often replaces the more specific verb *dire*.

116. *li occhi lucenti lagrimando volse*: Beatrice turns her tearful eyes to Virgil (not toward Heaven, as some commentators understand). *Volgere* often is used to signify a turning of the attention rather than a bodily movement. Beatrice was looking at Virgil before, as she spoke to him; it is only now that her eyes fill with tears, as she continues to face toward him and urges him to proceed to the rescue of the wayfarer on the dark slope. It is this that makes Virgil more eager to do her command.

118. *volse = volle*, past absolute of *volere*.

119. *quella fiera*: The she-wolf, the most troublesome of
the three beasts and the one that was causing the wayfarer
finally to ruin back into the darkness of sin.

120. *il corto andar*: The phrase clearly implies that there is
a longer way up the mountain. What that longer path is
the poem will make clear in due course.

121. *restai = ristai*. "Why do you stay" or "Why do you
hold back" from entering upon this journey? *Restare* fre-
quently means "to stay" or "to leave off."

122. *allette = alletti*.

124. *tai = tali*. Cf. "cotai," vs. 111.

126. *'l mio parlar*: All that Virgil had said (*Inf.* I, 112–
20).   *ben*: Cf. *Inf.* I, 8.

135. *porse*: Past absolute of *porgere* (literally, "to proffer").

138. *proposto = proposito*. Cf. "proposta," vs. 38.

141. *li = gli.   fue = fu*.

142. *cammino alto e silvestro*: "Alto" echoes what was said
of the way or crossing to the otherworld ("alto passo,"
Inf. II, 12), while the adjective "silvestro" clearly connects
with "selva" in "selva oscura" of the poem's opening verses
(*Inf.* I, 2). Thus, Virgil leads the wayfarer from the desert
strand of this prologue scene into the way through Hell.
This way will be described as savage, "silvestro" (*Inf.* XXI,
84). In metaphor, then, the savage way ("cammino sil-
vestro") of Hell corresponds to the dark wood ("selva
oscura") of the sinful life. The journey beyond always
remains potentially our journey here. Not only through
metaphor, but primarily through allegory this transition
is achieved, so that in the dimension of the literal journey
through Hell the dimension of our own journey in "our
life" is constantly recalled and developed.

CANTO III

1–3. *Per me*: The famous inscription has the portal speaking, even as later (*Inf.* XI, 8–9) an inscription will speak for a tomb. / The entrance to Hell is always wide open. See *Aen.* VI, 127: "Noctes atque dies patet atri ianua Ditis." ("Night and day the door of gloomy Dis stands open.")

1. *città*: Hell in general is meant, and more particularly the city of Dis. As the description of this city develops, it can be seen as an exact imitation in reverse of the heavenly city of Paradise.

4. *Giustizia*: Hell and its torments are the supreme example of God's justice. From this point on, the inscription speaks not simply for the gate but for Hell in its entirety.

5–6. *podestate . . . sapienza . . . amore*: These are the established terms for the three persons of the Holy Trinity. When God the Creator is mentioned, it is most often in His triunity. For Dante's use of the terms, see *Conv.* II, v, 8: "Chè si può contemplare de la potenza somma del Padre . . . la somma sapienza del Figliuolo . . . la somma e ferventissima caritade de lo Spirito Santo." ("For the supreme power of the Father may be contemplated . . .

the supreme wisdom of the Son . . . the supreme and most burning love of the Holy Spirit.")

7. *fuor = furono*.

8. *se non etterne*: On the first day, God created the heavens, the angels, and primal matter; all three are eternal, being made directly by God (see *Par.* XXIX, 22–48). Then, when almost immediately Satan and his rebellious band fell (*Par.* XXIX, 49–51), God made Hell to receive them; Hell, too, is eternal. See Matt. 25:41: "Tunc dicet et his qui a sinistris erunt: Discedite a me, maledicti, in ignem aeternum, qui paratus est diabolo et angelis eius." ("Then he will say to those on his left hand, 'Depart from me, accursed ones, into the everlasting fire which was prepared for the devil and his angels.' ")   *etterno = etternamente*.

12. *il senso lor m'è duro*: *Duro* means "hard to understand," but it also may mean "harsh," "ominous," "fearful." The meaning of *accorto* as applied to Virgil in the following verse will vary accordingly. For *duro* in the first sense, see Ioan. 6:61[60]: "Durus est hic sermo." ("This is a hard saying.")

14–15. *Qui si convien . . . morta*: These verses echo the Cumaean Sibyl's words to Aeneas when they are on the point of entering into the netherworld (*Aen.* VI, 261): "Nunc animis opus, Aenea, nunc pectore firmo." ("Now, Aeneas, thou needest thy courage, now thy stout heart!") See *Conv.* IV, xxvi, 7, 9 (quoted in n. to *Inf.* II, 44).

16. *i' t'ho detto*: See *Inf.* I, 114–17.

18. *il ben de l'intelletto*: Truth is the good of the intellect (echoing a statement by Aristotle), and the supreme truth is the highest good of the intellect, which is God. The saints in Heaven enjoy the direct vision of God forever. The damned of Hell, by their sinful and unrepented deeds, are forever denied the knowledge of God, and thus have lost the possibility of this highest "good." / On Aristotle's statement, see *Conv.* II, xiii, 6: "Per l'abito . . . potemo la

veritade speculare, che è ultima perfezione nostra, sì come dice lo Filosofo nel sesto de l'Etica, quando dice che'l vero è lo bene de lo intelletto." ("By the habit [of the sciences] we can speculate concerning the truth, which is our distinguishing perfection, as saith the Philosopher in the sixth of the *Ethics*, when he says that truth is the good of the intellect.") The reference is to *Eth. Nicom.* VI, 2, 1139^a.

21. *le segrete cose*: Things "hidden" to the living, few of whom travel through this world of the dead. This canto is full of reminiscences of Aeneas' descent to Hades. See *Aen.* VI, 264–67 (closely following the *exhortatio* to Aeneas quoted in n. to vss. 14–15):

Di, quibus imperium est animarum, umbraeque silentes
et Chaos et Phlegethon, loca nocte tacentia late,
sit mihi fas audita loqui; sit numine vestro
pandere res alta terra et caligine mersas.

Ye gods, who hold the domain of spirits! Ye voiceless shades! Thou, Chaos, and thou, Phlegethon, ye broad, silent tracts of night! Suffer me to tell what I have heard; suffer me of your grace to unfold secrets buried in the depths and darkness of the earth!

22. *Quivi*: The vestibule of Hell. (See Fig. 4, p. 44.)

23. *sanza stelle*: (See *Aen.* VI, 534: "tristis sine sole domos," "sad, sunless dwellings.") It is the absence of the stars that first is felt in Hell. Likewise, when the wayfarer emerges from Hell, he sees before anything else the stars, the "beautiful things" of *Inf.* I, 40.

27. *suon di man*: As will be seen, the damned smite themselves and each other with their hands.   *con elle*: In early Italian, forms of this pronoun can be used in the oblique case; for one of many occurrences, see vs. 42.

29. *aura* = *aria*.   *sanza tempo*: As the words of the inscription over the portal declare, Hell is an eternal place and in this sense is "outside of time." Hell is "without time" in another sense: the sun, stars, and planets are not visible in Hell, and their movements about the earth are what constitute time.

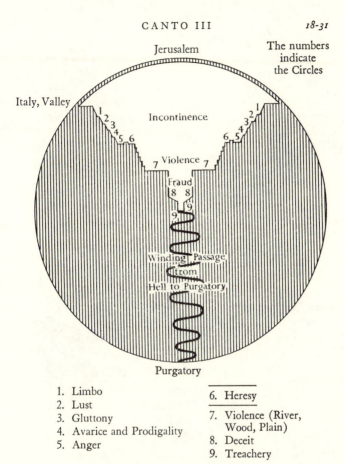

Figure 3. Cross section of Earth

1. Limbo
2. Lust
3. Gluttony
4. Avarice and Prodigality
5. Anger

6. Heresy

7. Violence (River, Wood, Plain)
8. Deceit
9. Treachery

31. *d'error la testa cinta*: On Petrocchi's preference for "error" instead of "orror," see his note to this verse; also see his vol. I, *Introduzione*, pp. 168–69. Many editors have preferred the reading "orror" and have quoted in support of it *Aen.* II, 559: "At me tum primum saevus circumstetit horror." ("Then first an awful horror encompassed me.") *cinta*: Past participle of *cingere*.

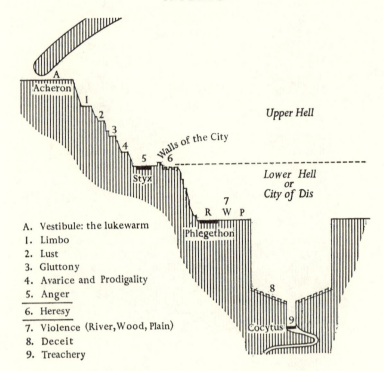

A. Vestibule: the lukewarm
1. Limbo
2. Lust
3. Gluttony
4. Avarice and Prodigality
5. Anger
6. Heresy
7. Violence (River, Wood, Plain)
8. Deceit
9. Treachery

Figure 4. The slope of Hell

35. *triste*: Here, as often in Dante's usage—especially in the *Inferno*—this adjective means "sorry," "base," "vile," "contemptible."

36. *sanza 'nfamia = sanza infamia*.

37–39. *quel cattivo coro de li angeli . . . per sé fuoro*: Although no mention of neutral angels is made in the Bible, the notion of moral neutrality stretches back into very early legends. The long tradition is represented in the many versions of Brendan's voyage, in Wolfram von Eschenbach's *Parzival*, Walter Map's *De nugis curialium*, and the epic poem *L'image du monde*, as well as, among the patristic writings, in Clement of Alexandria's *Stromata*. On the legend's origins and medieval forms, see J. Freccero (1962).

The theological problem of the angels' neutrality has been studied by J. Freccero (1960), who says (pp. 13–14):

> [The neutral angels] simply did not act [as did those who rebelled with Satan], but remained frozen in a state of aversion from God. It is pointless to ask whether they were better or worse than the lowest of sinners, for they do not fit into any category, after the initial division of heavenly light from infernal dark. With the aversion from God, the bond of charity was smashed; with the abstention from action, they deprived themselves of the one positive element which could win them a place in the cosmos. They are as close to nothing as creatures can be and still exist, for by their double negation, they have all but totally removed themselves from the picture. To be deprived of action is to be deprived of love, and love is the law of Dante's cosmos, determining all classifications. There remains nothing for them but the vaguely defined vestibule of hell, and they merit no more than a glance from the pilgrim before he passes on to the realm of love perverted.

39. *fur = furono.*

40. *Caccianli = li cacciano.   i ciel per non esser men belli*: The heavens are the special domain of angels—hence the plural here. The Empyrean or outermost heaven is, of course, the abode of the blessed; it certainly would be "less beautiful" if "that base band of angels" (vss. 37–38) and these "sorry souls" (vs. 35) were to be admitted.

41–42. *né lo profondo inferno . . . d'elli*: As the poem later reveals, Satan and the other fallen angels (now devils), as well as the worst human souls, are relegated to lower Hell ("profondo"). Both the devils and the wicked souls ("i rei"), being greater in wickedness than these, the lukewarm, might on that account boast or glorify themselves in their own eyes. Thus, the lukewarm and the neutral angels are seen here from the projected point of view of the denizens of lower Hell. Doubtless there is an echo of Apoc. 3:15–16, about the church of Laodicea: "Scio opera tua, quia neque frigidus es neque calidus; utinam frigidus esses aut calidus! Sed quia tepidus es, et nec frigidus nec calidus, incipiam te evomere ex ore meo." ("I know thy works; thou art neither cold nor hot. I would that thou wert cold or hot. But because thou art lukewarm, and neither cold nor hot, I am about to vomit thee out of my mouth.")

42. *alcuna = qualche.*

44. *a lor*: All the spirits here, both neutral angels and human souls, but especially the latter, as is evident from vss. 46–48.

45. *Dicerolti = te lo dirò.* The relative position and order of conjunctive pronouns is not fixed in early Italian, so that the direct object often precedes the indirect object.

46. *Questi non hanno speranza di morte*: None of the damned in Hell can hope for the cessation of punishment or pain that death might be thought to afford. But there is a terrible irony in these souls' living the "second death" (*Inf.* I, 117) with no hope for its cessation either. The explicit statement that "these have no hope of death" clearly suggests that the lukewarm, particularly, desire cessation of their condition just as they desire the nothingness that would ensue. This death being denied them, they so hate their next-to-nothingness that they envy every other condition. For the desire of death in this sense, see Apoc. 9:6: "Et in diebus illis quaerent homines mortem et non invenient eam, et desiderabunt mori et fugiet mors ab eis." ("And in those days men will seek death and will not find it; and they will long to die and death will flee from them.") The punishment of the lukewarm related in vss. 65–66 may be a reminiscence of the locusts that "in those days" came forth "to harm mankind" (Apoc. 9:3–10).

48. *che 'nvidiosi = che invidiosi.*

49. *Fama di loro il mondo esser non lassa*: Throughout Hell, the damned, or at least many of them, will be seen to

hope for enduring fame in the world above—the only
kind of "immortality" they can ever expect. Such a hope
was appealed to in Beatrice's words to Virgil in *Inf.* II,
59–60. But even this is denied these wretches, the luke-
warm. The poet's contempt here reaches its highest pitch.
lassa = lascia.

50. *misericordia e giustizia li sdegna*: By God's mercy, man
is saved; by His justice, man is condemned. In the preced-
ing verse, the world's judgment on these souls was given;
here, God's judgment. Thus, as these verses have it,
the lukewarm are despised by God and by the world, even
as they are rejected by the heavens and by lower Hell. And
it might be said that with the following verse Virgil adds
his own rejection of them.

52–54. *vidi una 'nsegna . . . indegna*: The punishment of
those who refused to follow any banner, either in Heaven
(the neutral angels) or on earth (the lukewarm), observes
the law of retribution. Termed the *contrapasso* in *Inf.*
XXVIII, 142, this law is the basis of all the punishments,
purgations, and rewards of "souls in the afterlife"—what
Dante in his *Letter to Can Grande* termed the "status
animarum post mortem" (*Epist.* XIII, 33). Thus, it is an
example of God's justice that these souls should run forever
after this aimless and nameless banner, which "might never
have any rest."

52. *una 'nsegna = una insegna.*

54. *indegna*: The term generally means "incapable," also
"unworthy" or "alien to."

59–60. *colui che fece per viltade il gran rifiuto*: Pope Celes-
tine, according to most of the early commentators. Celestine
V (Pietro Angeleri da Isernia) was called Pietro da Mor-
rone, from Monte Morrone where he established a monas-
tery later declared the seat of the Order of Celestines. He
was elected pope at the age of nearly eighty, in July 1294,
and abdicated some five months later. Describing the cir-
cumstances of Celestine's election, Villani (VIII, 5) says:

I cardinali . . . furono in concordia di non chiamare niuno di loro collegio, e elessono uno santo uomo, ch'avea nome frate Piero dal Morrone d'Abruzzi. Questi era romito e d'aspra vita e penitenzia, e per lasciare la vanità del mondo . . . . Questi eletto e fatto venire e coronato papa, per riformare la Chiesa fece di Settembre vegnente dodici cardinali . . . ma perchè egli era semplice e non litterato, e delle pompe del mondo non si travagliava volentieri, i cardinali il pregiavano poco, e parea loro che a utile e stato della Chiesa avere fatta mala elezione. Il detto santo padre avveggendosi di ciò, e non sentendosi sofficiente al governamento della Chiesa, come quegli che più amava di servire a Dio e l'utile di sua anima che l'onore mondano, cercava ogni via come potesse rinunziare il papato.

The cardinals . . . agreed not to choose anyone of their college. Instead they elected a holy man called Frate Pietro da Morrone d'Abruzzi, a hermit who had lived a harsh life of penitence, leaving behind the vanities of this world . . . . When he was elected, he came and was crowned pope. The following September he created twelve cardinals, to reform the Church . . . but because he was a simple, uneducated man, heedless of worldly pomp, the cardinals held him in little esteem. It seemed to them that they had served the welfare and power of the Church very poorly when they elected him. The Holy Father became aware of this. Being a man who loved God and the welfare of his own soul more than he did worldly honors, and feeling unequal to the task of governing the Church, he sought every possible way to renounce the papacy.

Dante shared the current belief (see *Inf.* XIX, 56–57) that Celestine's abdication was brought about by the crafty Benedetto Caetani, who secured his own election as pope a few days later (December 24, 1294) and succeeded Celestine as Boniface VIII. As to Boniface himself, Villani (VIII, 5) continues:

Intra gli altri cardinali della corte era uno messer

Benedetto Guatani d'Alagna molto savio di scrittura, e delle cose del mondo molto pratico e sagace, il quale aveva grande volontà di pervenire alla dignità papale, e quello con ordine avea cercato e procacciato col re Carlo e co' cardinali, e già aveva da loro la promessa, la quale poi gli venne fatta. Questi si mise dinanzi al santo padre, sentendo ch'egli avea voglia di rinunziare il papato, ch'egli facesse una nuova decretale, che per utilità della sua anima ciascuno papa potesse il papato rinunziare, mostrandogli l'esemplo di santo Clemente, che quando santo Pietro venne a morte, lasciò ch'appresso lui fosse papa; e quegli per utile di sua anima non volle essere . . . e così come il consigliò il detto cardinale, fece papa Celestino il detto decreto; e ciò fatto, il dì di santa Lucia di Dicembre vegnente, fatto concestoro di tutti i cardinali, in loro presenza si trasse la corona e il manto papale, e rinunziò il papato, e partissi della corte, e tornossi ad essere eremita, e a fare sua penitenzia. E così regnò nel papato cinque mesi e nove dì papa Celestino.

Among the cardinals of the court was one Benedetto Caetani of Anagni, a man very learned in Scripture, and practiced and wise in the ways of the world. He wanted very much to attain the papal dignity, and he pursued that end with great strategy in his dealings with King Charles and the cardinals. He got their promise, which was, in fact, subsequently fulfilled. Having heard that Celestine was inclined to renounce the papacy, he went before the Holy Father and urged him to put out a new decree declaring that for the welfare of his soul any pope might renounce the papacy. He gave the example of St. Clement, whom the dying St. Peter wanted as his successor, and who refused for the welfare of his own soul . . . and thus, Pope Celestine put out the decree, just as the cardinal advised. That done, on the day of St. Lucy [the 13th] in the following December, he called a consistory of all the cardinals. In their presence, he removed his crown and the papal robe, renounced the papacy, and left the court, to become a

49

hermit once again and to do penance. The reign of Pope Celestine lasted for five months and nine days.

The *Cronica fiorentina* (*s.v.* year 1294, p. 142) describes Cardinal Caetani's deception of the old pope:

Per suo trattato e per molta moneta che spese al patrizio, rinchiudevasi la notte nella camera del Papa, ed avea una tronba lunga, e parlava nella tronba sopra il letto del Papa, e dicea:—Io sono l'angelo che tti sono mandato a parlare, e comandoti dalla parte di Dio grorioso, che ttue inmantanente debi rinunziare al papato, e ritorna ad essere romito.–E così fece iij notti continue; tanto ch'elli crette alla boce d'inganno, e rinunçiò il papatico, del mese di dicenbre, e con animo diliberato, co li suo' frati cardinali, dispose se medesimo, ed elesse papa uno cardinale d'Anangna ch'avea nome messer Benedetto Gatani, e suo nome papale Bonifazio ottavo.

Through various machinations, and by spending large amounts of money on the [pope's] attendants, [Caetani] succeeded in hiding himself at night in the pope's chamber. He placed a long tube just above the bed of the pope, and spoke through it, saying: "I am the angel sent to speak with you, and I command you, in the name of glorious God, to renounce the papacy immediately, and return to being a hermit." He did this for three nights in a row, so that the pope believed in the deceitful voice, and renounced the papacy, in the month of December. With his mind made up, he deposed himself before his brother cardinals, who elected to the papacy the cardinal of Anagni, whose name was Messer Benedetto Caetani, and whose papal name was Boniface VIII.

To prevent any attempt at opposition, Boniface ordered Celestine confined to a monastic cell in a castle near Alatri. There, about a year and a half after his abdication, the old pope died. He was canonized, in 1313, as St. Peter Celestine.

The identification of Celestine as the spirit described by Dante in vss. 59–60 cannot be certain. But Pietro di Dante, the poet's son who (probably *ca.* 1340) began a commentary on the *Commedia*, wrote with assurance: "Inter quos nominat fratrem Petrum de Murrono, ut credo, qui dictus est Papa Coelestinus V.; qui possendo ita esse sanctus et spiritualis in papatu sicut in eremo, papatui, qui est sedes Christi, pusillanimiter renuntiavit." ("I believe he places among them Frate Pietro da Morrone, who is known as Pope Celestine V. He could have led as holy and as spiritual a life in the papacy as he had in his hermitage: and yet, he pusillanimously renounced the papacy, which is the seat of Christ.")

Other early commentators are almost unanimously of the same opinion, although most of them mention Esau as a possible alternative. Benvenuto, however, maintains that Dante could not have meant Celestine, since the pope's abdication was an act not of cowardice but of noble self-renunciation. Benvenuto believes that the reference in vss. 59–60 is to Esau, but he adds that if Dante did intend Celestine, he did so without knowledge of the old man's sanctity; Celestine, says Benvenuto, willingly made way for Boniface.

In a work written before 1360, Fazio degli Uberti—evidently alluding to this passage—places Celestine "in Inferno" (see *Dittamondo* IV, xxi, 37-40):

> Tra lor così cattivo si danna
> il misero Giovanni lor Delfino,
> che rifiutò l'onor di tanta manna,
> com'è in Inferno papa Celestino.

Among those damned for wickedness is the wretched Giovanni, their dauphin. Like Pope Celestine, who is in Hell, he too refused the honor of so great a blessing.

Identifications other than Celestine have been suggested by modern commentators. Among the candidates mentioned are Diocletian, the Roman Emperor who abdicated in the year 305; Romulus Augustulus, the last Roman Emperor in the West; Pilate; Vieri de' Cerchi, incapable head of the Florentine Whites (see n. to *Inf.* VI, 61); and Giano della Bella, leader of the popular faction in Florence and author of the Ordinances of Justice. For a review and bibliography, see

G. Padoan (1961); on the canonization of Celestine, see
U. Cosmo (1898).

61. *Incontanente intesi e certo fui*: This verse serves to heap
even greater contempt on the figure of "him who made the
great refusal" (vss. 59–60); to see and know (vs. 59) him
in this vestibule of Hell is to understand and know that
these are indeed the base souls of those "who never were
alive" (vs. 64).

62. *d'i = dei.   cattivi*: The substantive use of this ad-
jective is frequent in the *Inferno*. The term here echoes the
"cattivo coro," the "base band" of neutral angels, of vs. 37.

63. *sui = suoi*. Forms like this are common in early Ital-
ian, in prose as well as in verse.

64. *sciaurati = sciagurati*. The meaning is close to the
"cattivi" of vs. 62, but this is even stronger in its expression
of contempt.

65–69. *erano ignudi . . . ricolto*: The ignominious and com-
paratively trivial punishment of the lukewarm reflects the
nature of these souls and thus is right and just for them.
See n. to vs. 46.

70. *E poi . . .* : From this point on, much of the detail is
reminiscent of Aeneas' descent to Hades (*Aen.* VI, 295ff.).

71–78. *genti a la riva . . . d'Acheronte*: Virgil calls Acheron
"amnis" (*Aen.* VI, 318); Dante calls it "fiume" (*Inf.* III,
71, 81) and "rio" (*Inf.* III, 124). For Virgil's description
of Acheron and the throng on its banks, see *Aen.* VI, 295–
330. Aeneas questions the Sibyl (vss. 318–20):

"dic," ait, "o virgo, quid volt concursus ad amnem?
quidve petunt animae? vel quo discrimine ripas
hae linquunt, illae remis vada livida verrunt?"

[Aeneas] cries: "Tell me, O maiden, what means the
crowding to the river? What seek the spirits? or by
what rule do these leave the banks, and those sweep
the lurid stream with oars?"

71. *genti*: Dante often uses this plural to suggest different groups of people, as here.

76. *Le cose ti fier conte*: This promise is kept in vss. 121–29.   *fier* (pronounced *fier*) = *fiero*, i.e., *saranno*.

80. *temendo no*: Cf. Latin *timens ne*.   *li* = *gli*.

81. *del parlar mi trassi*: *Trarsi di* means, literally, "to withdraw from."

83. *un vecchio*: Charon ("Caron," vs. 94), son of Erebus, is the ferryman who transports the shades of the dead across the rivers of the lower world. Dante represents him as having shaggy cheeks ("lanose gote," vs. 97) and fiery eyes ("occhi di fiamme rote," vs. 99; "occhi di bragia," vs. 109), in imitation of Virgil's description (*Aen.* VI, 298–304):

> portitor has horrendus aquas et flumina servat
> terribili squalore Charon, cui plurima mento
> canities inculta iacet, stant lumina flamma,
> sordidus ex umeris nodo dependet amictus.
> ipse ratem conto subigit velisque ministrat
> et ferruginea subvectat corpora cumba,   .
> iam senior, sed cruda deo viridisque senectus.

A grim warden guards these waters and streams, terrible in his squalor—Charon, on whose chin lies a mass of unkempt, hoary hair; his eyes are staring orbs of flame; his squalid garb hangs by a knot from his shoulders. Unaided, he poles the boat, tends the sails, and in his murky craft convoys the dead—now aged, but a god's old age is hardy and green.

88–93. *E tu che se' costì, anima viva . . . ti porti*: Charon recognizes at once that Dante is alive, and he also appears to know that after death Dante will not go to Hell but will cross to the shore of the mountain of Purgatory, and in a much lighter craft—a matter made clear later in the poem (see *Purg.* II, 10–51). This passage in Canto III is the first of several, throughout the poem, in which Dante causes his own salvation to be predicted.

88. *costì*: See the corresponding "cotesti" in vs. 89, indicating a position near the person addressed. Charon's words closely resemble those (*Aen*. VI, 388-91) addressed to Aeneas when he entered the lower world, even in this detail: in "costì" is heard the "iam istinc" of *Aen*. VI, 389.

92. *piaggia*: For the meaning "shore," see n. to *Inf*. I, 29.

94. *lui*: A dative here, common in Dante's usage.

95-96. *vuolsi così . . . non dimandare*: This formula, a sort of password, will be used more than once by Virgil—when the passage through Hell is challenged. In a certain sense it corresponds to Aeneas' golden bough (see *Aen*. VI, 405-10).

95. *vuolsi = si vuole.   colà*: There, in Heaven, the abode of God.   *si puote = si può*.

98. *livida palude*: Acheron, the "vada livida" ("lurid stream") of *Aen*. VI, 320, is both a river and a marsh.

101. *cangiar = cangiarono (cambiarono).   dibattero* (pronounced *dibattèro*) *= dibatterono (batterono)*.

102. *ratto che*: The meaning is *tosto che*. Cf. "ratta" (vs. 53).
   inteser = intesero.   le parole crude: Charon's fierce utterance in vss. 84-87.

103-5. *Bestemmiavano Dio . . . nascimenti*: See Iob 3: 3-26; Ier. 20:14-18.

104-5. *'l seme . . . di lor nascimenti*: Their parents are cursed as well as their forefathers.

106. *Poi si ritrasser tutte quante insieme*: See *Aen*. VI, 305: "Huc omnis turba ad ripas effusa ruebat." ("Hither rushed all the throng, streaming to the banks.")

109. *occhi di bragia*: Charon's "ember eyes" smolder with wrath as he herds the souls into his boat.

111. *batte col remo qualunque s'adagia*: The detail is worthy of some sculptor's work on the west portal of a medieval

cathedral—the damned on Christ's left being driven into Hell.

112–17. *Come d'autunno . . . richiamo*: The simile of the leaves of autumn was directly inspired by *Aen.* VI, 309-12, a passage describing the throng of spirits:

> quam multa in silvis autumni frigore primo
> lapsa cadunt folia, aut ad terram gurgite ab alto
> quam multae glomerantur aves, ubi frigidus annus
> trans pontum fugat . . .

> thick as the leaves of the forest that at autumn's first frost dropping fall, and thick as the birds that from the seething deep flock shoreward, when the chill of the year drives them overseas . . . .

And yet Dante has introduced strikingly new elements. The bough "sees" its leaves fall away till it is finally bare, and this, in simile, is the "evil seed of Adam." Moreover, while the shift to falcon imagery may have been prompted by Virgil's birds ("aves," vs. 311), Dante's bird descends with desire as to its lure. Departure (from the bough) and arrival (at the lure) complete the movement that corresponds to the movement of the souls.

It should be noted that a tree was also given vision and a point of view by Virgil in *Georg.* II, 80–82:

> . . . nec longum tempus, et ingens
> exiit ad caelum ramis felicibus arbos,
> miraturque novas frondes et non sua poma.

> And in a little while, lo! a mighty tree shoots up skyward with joyous boughs, and marvels at its strange leafage and fruits not its own.

117. *augel = augello.   richiamo*: The "call," "recall," or, metaphorically, the lure that serves to call down the falcon. The lure's calling the falcon, in the simile, corresponds to Charon's beckoning ("loro accennando," vs. 110).

118. *sen = se ne.*

119. *sien = siano.*

120. *anche = ancora.   s'auna = s'aduna.*

121. *disse 'l maestro cortese*: Virgil's courtesy at this point is evidenced by his answering Dante's questions of vss. 72–75 without again being asked.

124–26. *pronti sono a trapassar . . . disio*: The desire of these shades, although it is prompted in them by Divine Justice, has its correspondence in Virgil's netherworld; see *Aen.* VI, 313–14.

127. *Quinci non passa mai anima buona*: See *Aen.* VI, 563: "Nulli fas casto sceleratum insistere limen." ("No pure soul may tread the accursed threshold.")

129. *omai = ormai.   che = ciò che.*

132. *la mente di sudore ancor mi bagna*: Cf. *Inf.* I, 6.

133. *La terra lagrimosa diede vento*: It was thought that earthquakes were caused by windy vapors imprisoned within the earth; see *Purg.* XXI, 55–57. Here the wind is said to have caused the red flash of light.

136. *cui*: Petrocchi finds justification for "cui," direct object, relative pronoun, in place of "che," which both Vandelli and Casella have. *Cui* as a direct object is common in Old Italian.

CANTO IV

1. *Ruppemi = mi ruppe.*

2. *truono = tuono*, literally, "thunder." The form in this meaning is frequent in early Italian.

4. *l'occhio riposato*: "Rested" by his deep sleep.

5. *dritto levato*: "Having risen upright to my feet." Dante had fallen (*Inf.* III, 136).   *fiso = fisamente.*

7. *Vero è*: The phrase indicates something to be wondered at (cf. English "verily")—that the poet has been mysteriously transported across Acheron while he was in a deep sleep. Such miraculous happenings will not continue; instead, the normal or natural conditions of the real world will prevail in the otherworld.

9. *che 'ntrono = che introno*. See Petrocchi's note on this form.

11. *per ficcar lo viso a fondo*: "However intently I thrust my gaze into the depths."

13. *qua giù*: These words (repeated in vs. 20) register Virgil's sense of return now to the dark place that is his eternal abode, even as his pallor bears witness to the com-

passion he feels for those who share his fate. *cieco mondo*: Hell is "blind" or dark, in both a physical and a spiritual sense.

17. *verrò*: Dante continues to see the journey from Virgil's point of view (see *Inf.* II, 31).

18. *che suoli al mio dubbiare esser conforto*: "Comfort" has been given by Virgil already (see *Inf.* I, 91–129 and *Inf.* II, 43–126).

22. *ne = ci*, as very often in the poem.

23. *fé = fece.*

25. *secondo che per ascoltare*: "For all I could hear." In the darkness here the eye can make out very little, and the ear must be depended on.

26. *non avea = non vi era.   mai che*: Cf. Latin *magis quam.*

27. *aura = aria.*

28. *avvenia = avveniva.   duol*: The direct object of "avean," vs. 29.

30. *viri*: A Latinism for *uomini.* See *Aen.* VI, 306–7: "matres atque viri . . . / pueri innuptaeque puellae" ("mothers and men . . . boys and unwedded girls").

31. *Lo buon maestro a me*: Virgil, in not waiting for Dante to ask, reveals a touching eagerness to explain to his charge the condition of souls in this his own circle.

33. *vo' = voglio.   andi = vada.*

34. *ei = elli (essi).   peccaro = peccarono.* Virgil's affirmation regards only personal sin, not original sin. Here, as elsewhere in the poem, it will be noted that Virgil's understanding of a specifically Christian truth—even one such as this, by which he himself is judged—is veiled and dim.

36. *porta*: Many MSS read *parte.* Petrocchi in his vol. I, *Introduzione*, pp. 170–71, notes other references to baptism

as the door of faith. Among others, he cites Augustine, *Conf.* XIII, 21: "Non enim intratur aliter in regno caelorum ex illo." ("For there is entrance into the kingdom of heaven no other way.")

37. *e' = ei.*

38. *non adorar debitamente a Dio*: See Thomas Aquinas, *In Ioan. evangel.* III, iii, 5:

> Sed numquid omnes infideles habent mala opera? Videtur quod non: nam multi gentiles secundum virtutem operati sunt; puta Cato, et alii plures. Sed dicendum, secundum Chrysostomum, quod aliud est bene operari ex virtute, aliud ex aptitudine et dispositione naturali. Nam aliqui ex dispositione naturali bene operantur, quia ex eorum dispositione non inclinantur ad contrarium; et hoc modo etiam infideles potuerunt bene operari: . . . Vel dicendum, quod licet infideles bona facerent, non tamen faciebant propter amorem virtutis, sed propter inanem gloriam. Nec etiam omnia bene operabantur, *quia Deo cultum debitum non reddebant.* [Italics added.]

> But is it true that the works of infidels are always evil? It seems not, because many of the gentiles have walked in the ways of virtue, as, for instance, Cato and many others. But, with Chrysostom, we must say that it is one thing to do good works out of virtue and quite another merely out of one's natural tendency and disposition. Some people do good works simply because their natural disposition is not at all inclined to evil; in this fashion even infidels can do good works. . . . Or we might say that even though infidels may have done good works, it was not out of love for virtue that they did so, but rather for the sake of empty renown. Nor were they wont to do all things well *because they did not pay due honor to God.*

See also Ioan. 3:19: "Lux venit in mundum, et dilexerunt homines magis tenebras quam lucem; erant enim eorum mala opera." ("The light has come into the world, yet men have loved the darkness rather than the light, for their works were evil.")

A more essential statement of the matter would be that the pagans did not have sanctifying grace or the three theological virtues that attend such grace, and without these "Deo cultus debitus" is impossible.

41. *semo = siamo.*

43. *lo 'ntesi = lo intesi.* The pronoun refers to Virgil.

44. *però che = per ciò che.*

45. *sospesi:* As in *Inf.* II, 52, the adjective indicates the physical position of Limbo (outside of Hell proper) as well as the spiritual condition of the souls confined there.

49. *uscicci = ci uscì. Ci* meaning "hence" occurs frequently in the poem; e.g., see vs. 55, "trasseci."

50. *o per altrui:* "Altrui" is a possessive here. With this turn of phrase, the question evidently concerns the souls of children who died before they reached the age of responsibility and personal choice (a matter treated at some length in *Par.* XXXII, 40–84). Only the souls of those "infanti" who had merit, either through the faith of their parents or through circumcision or through baptism, were taken from Limbo.

52. *Io era nuovo in questo stato:* Virgil died in 19 B.C. and therefore was newly come to Limbo when Christ harrowed Hell. The wayfarer's awareness of this fact prompted his question.

53. *un possente:* Christ is never named in the *Inferno*; moreover, in speaking of such a "Christian" event as the harrowing of Hell, Virgil would veil his words.

54. *con segno di vittoria coronato:* Wearing the cruciform nimbus. (See Plate 2, facing.)

55. *Trasseci = ci trasse.* See vs. 49 and the corresponding note.   *primo parente:* Adam. Eve is not named, nor

2. Christ delivering the souls in limbo. An example of a cruciform nimbus

is any Old Testament woman except Rachel, but it is under-
stood that many other Hebrew women were taken with
Rachel from Limbo at this time and were "made blessed."
Both of our "first parents," after their sin, were privileged—
through grace—to have implicit faith in the advent of a
Redeemer. This same faith merited salvation for the other
great figures of the Old Testament. As to Abel and Noah,
named in vs. 56, see Heb. 11:4, 7.

57. *ubidente*: Moses was called the "servant of God" (see
Iosue 1:1–2, 7).

59. *Israèl*: The name means "soldier of God" and it was
given to the patriarch Jacob after he had wrestled with the
angel at Peniel (Gen. 32:28). Jacob was the grandson of
Abraham and the younger son of Isaac and Rebekah. He
bought the birthright of his twin brother, Esau, whom he
thus deprived of their father's blessing. *con lo padre*:
Isaac, son of the patriarch Abraham and Sarah.

60. *Rachele, per cui tanto fé*: Rachel was given in marriage
to Jacob only after he had served her father Laban for twice
seven years (Gen. 29:9–30). *fé = fece.*

61. *feceli = li fece. beati*: "Blessed" here means uplifted
to the vision of God, which is the supreme "ben de l'intel-
letto" (see *Inf.* III, 18 and the note).

64. *Non lasciavam l'andar perch' ei dicessi*: Literally, "we
did not leave going because he spoke," i.e., "we continued
on our way the while he spoke." *dicessi = dicesse.*

68. *di qua dal sonno*: Literally, "on this side of the sleep,"
the "sonno" of vs. 1.

69. *vincia = vinceva.* This fire is said to drive back the
darkness and form a (celestial) hemisphere of light, sym-
bol of the natural light of reason. Natural reason was ac-
cessible to the worthy pagans, and it was through this
reason or intellect that they won honor in their endeavors.
In the darkness before the Advent of Christ, these pagans
had no other light than this; hence, their condition in

Limbo is as it was on earth. This is the justness or justice of their state in the afterlife. / On the allegorical pattern of meaning in the three kinds of light—natural light, light of grace, and light of glory—see C. S. Singleton (1958), pp. 15–38.

72. *orrevol* = *onorevole.* *possedea* = *possedeva.* The wayfarer cannot see the worthy folk yet, but surmises that they must dwell apart from the others.

74. *onranza* = *onoranza.* Forms of *onore* are repeated insistently throughout this passage: see vss. 72, 73, 74, 76, 80, 93, and 100. (Dante had affirmed in the *De monarchia*—II, iii, 3—that "honor is a reward of virtue.") Honor, or fame in the world, is given in the *Commedia* as the dominant aspiration of the pagans (see, for example, *Inf.* II, 59–60). Needless to say, in conceiving that such fame would win merit in Heaven, Dante is venturing beyond established doctrine—as he is generally in his conception of Limbo, for that matter. Augustine, to be sure, had thought there would be a certain attenuation of suffering in Hell for such good deeds as these pagans were able to perform even without sanctifying grace. Dante here appears to have made a positive appraisal of so negative a concession.

77. *Sù ne la tua vita*: "In the world above."

79. *per me* = *da me.*

83. *quattro grand' ombre*: Here, as elsewhere in the *Commedia* as well as in medieval painting and sculpture, moral greatness is denoted by great physical stature.

84. *né trista né lieta*: The phrase expresses the characteristic "state of souls after death" as conceived in ancient pagan thought. The justice of this condition for them is apparent, since these virtuous souls thus attain a state that is as good as they themselves had imagined.

88. *Omero*: Homer. Dante did not know Greek and had no direct knowledge of Homer, since no complete or direct translation of Homer's works existed in the Middle Ages.

The *Iliad* and the *Odyssey* were known only through quotations by classical authors and by way of a narrative on the Trojan War in Latin verse, known variously as *Homerus Latinus*, *Homerus minor*, or *Pindarus Thebanus* (supposedly a translation by Pindar of the *Iliad*). See E. Moore (1896), pp. 164–66; P. Toynbee (1902), pp. 204–15.

89. *Orazio*: Horace (Quintus Horatius Flaccus), the Roman poet, was born at Venusia (mod. Venosa) in 65 B.C. and died in 8 B.C. Dante's reference to him as "Orazio satiro" has been supposed to be an allusion to Horace as author of the *Satires* (or *Sermones*). E. Moore (1896, p. 205) has suggested, however, that the word "satiro" in this case means "moralist" rather than "satirist," and therefore does not refer exclusively to the *Satires*. Nevertheless, in the *Ars poetica*, with which Dante is known to have been familiar, Horace speaks of himself in vs. 235 as a writer of satire (as Grandgent notes). On Dante and Horace, see E. Moore (1896), pp. 197–206.

90. *Ovidio*: Ovid (Publius Ovidius Naso) was born in 43 B.C. and died in exile in A.D. 17 or 18. His chief work, the *Metamorphoses*, was Dante's main authority for mythology. On Dante's acquaintance with Ovid, see E. Moore (1896), pp. 206–28. *Lucano*: Lucan (Marcus Annaeus Lucanus), born in Córdoba, Spain, in A.D. 39, was educated in Rome. Like Seneca, he was forced to commit suicide (in the year 65) because of his implication in the conspiracy of Piso against the Emperor Nero. Of his works there is extant only the epic called *De bello civili*, or *Pharsalia*, whose subject is the civil war between Caesar and Pompey. Lucan was widely known and frequently quoted by medieval writers; in fact, among Dante's main historical sources is the *Pharsalia*. On Dante's obligations to Lucan in general, see E. Moore (1896), pp. 228–42.

91. *Però che = per ciò che.*

95. *altissimo canto*: Epic poetry, traditionally the noblest "style" or genre. The *Aeneid* is referred to as "alta tragedia" (*Inf.* XX, 113).

96. *che sovra li altri*: Grammatically, the antecedent of "che" could be, in the preceding verse, either "canto" or "quel segnor" (Homer). The latter seems preferable since "altissimo canto" refers specifically to epic poetry, and not all the poets mentioned wrote epics.

98. *volsersi = si volsero.*

100. *fenno = fecero.*

102. *senno*: Again it is stressed that poets are wise, as in vs. 110 where they are called sages ("questi savi").

103. *la lumera*: The hemisphere of light (see vss. 68–69) surrounding the noble castle.

106–11. *un nobile castello . . . fresca verdura*: The entire episode of this "noble castle" is given in a focus of allegory that is unusual in the poem, and the meaning of this castle is never entirely clear. The walls surrounding the castle are seven, a number surely intended to be significant—but what exactly is the meaning? Such a feature is not supported by any strong literal sense, and this is precisely what makes the instance rare as allegory, now that we have left the prologue scene, with its special requirements in allegory, and move upon the "real" scene of the afterlife.

Probably the noble castle is best understood as the Castle of Fame, special dwelling of those whose "honored name" has won them a privileged place in Limbo. In that case the seven circles of walls, each with its gate leading to the castle, may well represent the seven liberal arts, and perhaps also the seven virtues, moral and intellectual, so well known to the pagans. Dante's conception of the "status animarum post mortem" becomes as shadowy and unsubstantial here as Virgil's in the sixth book of the *Aeneid*, and clearly Dante is much influenced by Virgil in this passage. See *Aen.* VI, 477–78, where Aeneas comes to the "farthest fields" and meets the souls of famous warriors. See also vss. 660–64, where Aeneas sees in the Elysian fields those who died fighting for their country and those who were priests and poets, as well as those who, as philosophers, "ennobled life" by their speculations.

110. *per sette porte intrai*: Each wall has its own gate.

111. *prato di fresca verdura*: Echoes of the *Aeneid* continue. See *Aen.* VI, 638: "locos laetos et amoena virecta" ("a land of joy, the green pleasaunces").

115-17. *Traemmoci . . . tutti quanti*: For the corresponding detail in the *Aeneid*, see VI, 752-55, where Anchises leads Aeneas and the Sibyl to a mound from which they can view the throng of souls.

115. *Traemmoci = ci traemmo*.

117. *potìen = potevano*.

119. *fuor = furono*.

121. *Eletra*: Electra—daughter of Atlas and mother of Dardanus, the founder of Troy (see *Aen.* VIII, 134-37)— is called Aeneas' "most ancient ancestress" in the *De monarchia* (II, iii, 11).

123. *Cesare . . . con li occhi grifagni*: Caesar is described by Suetonius (*De vita Caesarum* I, xlv, 1) as having "keen black eyes" ("nigris vegetisque oculis").

124. *Cammilla*: See n. to *Inf.* I, 107.·   *la Pantasilea*: Penthesilea, daughter of Mars and queen of the Amazons, was famous for her beauty, youth, and valor. After the death of Hector, she came to the assistance of the Trojans, but was slain by Achilles. She is mentioned twice by Virgil (*Aen.* I, 490-93 and, in connection with Camilla, *Aen.* XI, 661-63).

125-26. *Latino . . . Lavina sua figlia*: Latinus, king of Latium and husband of Amata, and their daughter Lavinia, who, though once betrothed to Turnus (see n. to *Inf.* I, 108), married Aeneas and by him had one son, Silvius (see n. to *Inf.* II, 13).

127–28. *Vidi quel Bruto . . . Tarquino, Lucrezia*: This is the Brutus (Lucius Junius Brutus) who, according to tradition, roused the Romans to revolt against the tyrant Tarquin (last of the legendary kings) after the rape of Lucretia and her consequent suicide. The story is told by Livy (I, lvii–lx). Brutus and Lucretia's husband were chosen as first magistrates or consuls of the Roman Republic when it was established after Tarquin's expulsion (510 B.C.).

128. *Iulia*: Julia, daughter of Julius Caesar, married Pompey in 59 B.C., a political expedient that she accepted for the sake of her father's career. Lucan (*Phars*. I, 111–20) refers to the death of Julia and laments that she did not live to reconcile her husband and her father. *Marzia*: Marcia was the wife of Cato of Utica (see *Phars. II, 326–49*).

Corniglia: Cornelia, daughter of the elder Scipio Africanus, was the mother of the Gracchi.

129. *Saladino*: Saladin (Salāḥ-al-Dīn Yūsuf ibn-Ayyūb), sultan of Egypt and Syria, founder of the Ayubite dynasty in Egypt, was born *ca.* 1138 and died at Damascus in 1193. His father was a native of Kurdistan. Saladin early distinguished himself as a soldier. Sent to Egypt by Nureddin, sultan of Damascus, he became vizier. On the death of the Fatimite caliph in Egypt (1171), Saladin established himself as successor, and on the death of Nureddin three years later, he took possession of Damascus and much of Syria. He extended his campaigns, and in 1187, after inflicting a crushing defeat upon the Christian army in a battle near Tiberias, he besieged and captured Acre, Jerusalem, and other towns. Subsequently he was defeated several times by Richard Coeur de Lion, with whom he concluded a truce in 1192. See H. A. R. Gibb (1962), pp. 91–107. The generosity and magnanimity of Saladin, as of Alexander the Great, were a commonplace in the Middle Ages. Saladin's great act of clemency toward the prisoners taken at Tiberias won him universal admiration. The earlier commentators lay special stress on his liberality and munificence. Boccaccio in his *Comento* notes that Saladin "fu pietoso signore e

maravigliosamente amò e onorò i valenti uomini" ("was a compassionate ruler, and one who deeply cherished and honored worthy men"). He is also mentioned in two tales of Boccaccio's *Decameron*—I, 3 (vol. I, pp. 44–46); X, 9 (vol. II, pp. 291–308)—and in several of the *Novelle antiche*. On Saladin and Dante's view of him, see P. Toynbee (1902), pp. 144–45; G. Paris (1893); and J. Hartmann (1933).

130–32. *Poi . . . filosofica famiglia*: Two groups have been seen so far: poets, represented by the four who came forward to greet Virgil; and warriors, represented—with the exception of Saladin—by those who had a part in the founding of the Roman Empire. Now the wayfarer raises his eyes to see a third group: philosophers, with Aristotle sitting highest.

131. *'l maestro di color che sanno*: This is Aristotle, whose influence in Dante's time was so pervasive that he was called simply "the Philosopher." Aristotle was born in 384 B.C. in Stagira, a Greek colony on the Aegean Sea. He studied under Plato in Athens. After Plato's death, Aristotle returned to Macedonia, where he became tutor to Alexander the Great. He returned to Athens in 335 and taught there as head of the Peripatetic school of philosophy. From this period, until his death in 322, come "the Philosopher's" major works. Aristotle's treatises, consisting primarily of lectures delivered to his students, are classified as studies in logic, metaphysics, the natural sciences, rhetoric, poetics, ethics, and politics.

Until the twelfth century, Aristotle was virtually unknown in the Christian West. In the twelfth and thirteenth centuries, however, his major works were recovered by means of translations into Latin—through Arabic translations from the Greek and Latin translations from the Arabic, sometimes with intermediate translations into Syriac and Hebrew. Aristotle strongly influenced medieval science, philosophy, and theology. Thomas Aquinas apparently counted among his greatest achievements the merging of the whole of Aristotle's philosophy into Christian belief.

Dante himself, profoundly influenced by Aristotelian as well as Thomistic thought, quotes or refers to Aristotle's works more than any other body of writing with the exception of the Bible. On this and Dante's obligations in general to Aristotle, see E. Moore (1896), pp. 92–156; also see pp. 307–18 for Moore's discussion of the Aristotle translations used by Dante. In *Conv.* II, xiv, 7, Dante mentions two Latin translations of Aristotle; he calls these the "new" and the "old." Moore concludes that Dante's "new" translation of Aristotle corresponds to the Greek-into-Latin version now known as the "Antiqua Translatio" printed in the works of Thomas Aquinas (and used in the present work as the source for all Aristotle quotations). What Dante called the "old" translation probably corresponds to the still earlier Arabic-into-Latin version of Aristotle.

134. *Socrate*: Pronounced *Sòcrate*. *Socrate e Platone*: Socrates and Plato now take "second seats" and, like the others, look up to Aristotle and honor him.

135. *li = gli* (as in vs. 133 also).

136. *Democrito*: Pronounced *Demòcrito*. Democritus, a contemporary of Socrates, was born in Thrace, *ca.* 460 B.C., and died *ca.* 370. He adopted and extended the atomistic theory. *che 'l mondo a caso pone*: An allusion to Democritus' theory of creation, for which Dante probably was indebted to Cicero (see *De nat. deor.* I, xxiv, 66) or to Albertus Magnus (see *Phys.* II, ii, 11).

137. *Diogenès*: According to the early commentators, this is Diogenes the Cynic, born *ca.* 412 B.C. in Asia Minor, and died 323. *Anassagora*: Pronounced *Anassàgora*. Anaxagoras, philosopher of the Ionian school, was born *ca.* 500 B.C. and died *ca.* 428. He is believed to have been the friend and teacher of Euripides and Pericles. Dante's knowledge of Anaxagoras probably was derived from Cicero (e.g., see *Academica* I, xii, 44; II, xxxi, 100; II, xxxvii, 118; *Tusc. disp.* I, xliii, 104; III, xiv, 30; V, xxxix, 115). *Tale*: Thales of Miletus, one of the Seven Wise Men, was born *ca.* 640 B.C. and died *ca.* 546.

138. *Empedoclès*: Empedocles, philosopher and statesman of Acragas (Agrigentum), Sicily. Knowledge of his dates is uncertain except that he was active at Acragas after 472 B.C. and died later than 444. Dante may have learned of him from Aristotle's *Metaphysics* and from Cicero (see *Academica* I, xii, 44; II, v, 14; II, xxiii, 74; *De nat. deor.* I, xii, 29; I, xxxiii, 93). Aristotle (*Eth. Nicom.* VIII, 1, 1155ᵇ) mentions Empedocles together with Heraclitus.

Eraclito: Pronounced *Eràclito*. Heraclitus, philosopher of Ephesus who flourished *ca.* 500 B.C., held that fire was the primary form of all matter. Dante's knowledge of him probably was derived from Cicero (see *Academica* II, xxxvii, 118; *Tusc. disp.* V, xxxvi, 105; *De fin.* II, v, 15; *De nat. deor.* III, xiv, 35).

139–40. *e vidi . . . Diascoride*: Pedanius Dioscorides, of Anazarba, in Cilicia, was a Greek physician of the first or second century A.D. He was the author of a work on botany and *materia medica* that had a great reputation and was translated into Arabic. See the *Ottimo Commento*: "Questo Dioscoride compose uno libro delle virtudi dell'erbe, e la materia in che nascono, cioè che radice, che fusto (o vero gambo), che foglia, che fiore, che frutto fanno, e il libro delle semplici medicine." ("This Dioscorides wrote a book on the properties of herbs, and the manner in which they grow, that is, what roots, stem [or stalk], leaf, flower, fruit they produce; and [he wrote] the book on medicinal herbs.") He appears to have been a soldier in his youth and to have collected the materials for his work, *De materia medica*—which covers between five and six hundred plants and their medicinal qualities—while following his profession in Greece, Italy, Gaul, and Asia Minor.

140. *Diascoride*: Pronounced *Diascòride*. *Orfeo*: Orpheus was the mythical Greek poet who, according to the legend, played so divinely on the lyre given him by Apollo that he charmed not only the wild beasts, but even the trees and rocks on Olympus so that they moved from their places and followed him. Dante's probable source for Orpheus is Ovid (see *Metam.* XI, 1–66).

141. *Tulio*: Marcus Tullius Cicero, the great Roman orator, philosopher, and statesman (106–43 B.C.), is often alluded to and quoted by Dante, who characteristically refers to him as "Tully."   *Lino*: Linus, a mythical Greek poet. Varying legends about Linus prevailed in different regions. In Argos he was believed to be the son of Apollo and Psamathe and to have been slain by dogs (see Statius, *Theb.* I, 557–668). However it was the Linus of Thebes, Helicon, and Olympus who (with either Apollo, Mercury, Amphimarus, or Oeagrus as his father and one of the Muses as his mother) was regarded as a great poet, the inventor of melody and rhythm and of the Linus song, and as the teacher of Thamyris and Orpheus (who killed Linus because of jealousy). Later he is described as a great musician (the son of Ismenius and one of the Muses), the teacher of Orpheus and Hercules (who killed Linus with a lyre). Dante probably got the name from Virgil, who described Linus (*Eclog.* VI, 67) as a "divino carmine pastor" ("shepherd of immortal song")—i.e., the founder of pastoral poetry—and coupled him with Orpheus (*Eclog.* IV, 55–57):

> non me carminibus vincet nec Thracius Orpheus,
> nec Linus, huic mater quamvis atque huic pater adsit,
> Orphei Calliopea, Lino formosus Apollo.

> Not Thracian Orpheus, not Linus shall vanquish me in song, though his mother be helpful to the one, and his father to the other, Calliope to Orpheus, and fair Apollo to Linus.

As Benvenuto points out, Augustine mentions Linus together with Orpheus and Musaeus as among the first "theological" poets (*De civ. Dei* XVIII, 14 and 37).   *Seneca*: Lucius Annaeus Seneca, Roman philosopher and tragedian, was born at Córdoba, *ca.* 4 B.C. He was appointed tutor to the youthful Domitius Nero, and was for a time practically the administrator of the Empire. He committed suicide by command of Nero, who charged him with being involved in the conspiracy of Piso, A.D. 65. Seneca was a voluminous writer. His philosophical works consist of formal treatises on ethics, moral letters, and discussions of natural philosophy from the point of view of the Stoical system.

142. *Euclide*: Euclid, the Greek mathematician, lived in Alexandria *ca.* 300 B.C. The most famous of his extant works is the *Elements of Geometry.*   *Tolomeo*: Ptolemy (Claudius Ptolemaeus), the Alexandrian mathematician, astronomer, and geographer, was born near the end of the first century A.D. He is known to have observed at Alexandria between the years 127 and 151. His two most famous works are the *Geography*, in eight books, and his mathematical treatise, in thirteen books, commonly known as the *Almagest* (a hybrid name derived from the Arabic article *al* and the Greek superlative μεγίστη). The *Almagest* lays out a system of astronomy and geography according to the theory that the sun, stars, and planets revolve around the earth. Dante's concept of the cosmos derives from this Ptolemaic system. A Latin translation of the *Almagest* is said to have been made by Boethius, but this has not been preserved. An Arabic translation of the *Almagest* was made in the ninth century, and in 1175 a translation from Arabic into Latin was made by Gerard of Cremona (who also translated Alfraganus). A translation from Greek into Latin was made *ca.* 1160 and another in 1451 by George of Trebizond. Although the cosmography of the *Commedia* closely follows Ptolemy's system, Dante's knowledge of Ptolemy probably came not from the *Almagest* itself but from Alfraganus' *Elementa astronomica*, which is based to a great extent on Ptolemy's treatise.

143. *Ipocràte*: Hippocrates, the most famous physician of antiquity, known as the father of medicine and thought to be a descendant of Asclepius. He was born on the island of Cos (one of the Dodecanese in the Southern Sporades), *ca.* 460 B.C., and died at Larissa in Thessaly, *ca.* 377. In addition to practicing and teaching at home, he traveled in Greece. His writings, held in high esteem from early times, became the nucleus of a collection of medical treatises by various authors. These works were long attributed to him and still bear his name. The most famous of them is

the *Aphorisms*.   *Avicenna*: Avicenna (abu-'Ali al-Ḥusayn ibn-Sīna)—also known as ibn-Sina—was an Arab philosopher and physician of Isfahan in Persia. He was born near Bokhara in 980 and died in 1037. Called the greatest of the early Moslem thinkers, Avicenna was a voluminous writer; among his works are commentaries on Aristotle and Galen ("Galieno"). Avicenna is said to have remarked that Galen, the famous physician whose writings he condensed and arranged, knew a great deal about the branches of medicine but very little about its roots.

144. *Averoìs*: Averroës, also known as ibn-Rushd, was a Spanish-Arabian scholar of the twelfth century whose commentaries on Aristotle had tremendous influence on the history of Western philosophy. Born at Córdoba, Spain, in 1126, Averroës was a physician and lawyer as well as a philosopher; he died in Morocco in 1198. Known in the Middle Ages as "the Commentator"—just as Aristotle was called "the Philosopher"—Averroës wrote commentaries or summaries of all of Aristotle's major works with the exception of the *Politics*. In its place, there is a commentary by Averroës on Plato's *Republic*. Latin translators (among them Michael Scot) began to work on Averroës' commentaries in the second and third decades of the thirteenth century, but not all of the commentaries were translated into Latin during this period. Averroës' commentaries on Aristotle were of three types: the short (synopsis or summary), the intermediate or middle, and the long or "magna." Not all types of commentaries exist for all the titles covered. For this, and the complete inventory of Averroës' Aristotelian commentaries, see H. A. Wolfson (1931). / Averroës, last to be named in the school of the philosophers here in Canto IV, matches the figure of Saladin, last named among the warriors, each being a modern among these ancients.   *feo = fece*.

147. *al fatto il dir vien meno*: That the "telling falls short of the fact" again points to the journey as a real journey, not a dream or vision.

148. *La sesta compagnia in due si scema*: Dante and Virgil leave the other four and proceed on their way.

149–51. *per altra via . . . luca*: The wayfarer and his guide quit the still "air" by a way other than that by which they had entered (nor is any allegorical significance implied by this) and again come into the air that trembles with sighs (vs. 27). Then they descend into the deeper darkness of the second circle.   *luca*: Present subjunctive of *lucere*.

CANTO V

1. *Così*: Proceeding through the darkness with Virgil.
primaio = primo. Limbo is reckoned as the first of the nine circles of Hell, even though in another sense it lies outside of Hell proper. Perhaps Limbo is best regarded as "marginal," as the name itself ("hem," "border") implies. The presence of Minos as judge of sins "at the entrance" (vs. 5) clearly marks the beginning of Hell proper, where actual sin is punished.

2. *men loco*: Since Hell is funnel-shaped, each successive circle in the descent is smaller in circumference than the one above it.

3. *punge a guaio*: "Goads to pain" that causes the spirits to wail, in contrast to those in Limbo who only sigh (*Inf.* IV, 26). For "guaio," see *Inf.* III, 22; IV, 9.

4. *Stavvi = vi sta.* *Minòs*: Minos in legend and myth was a king of ancient Crete, son of Zeus and Europa, and brother of Rhadamanthus. In assigning to Minos the office of judge in Hell, Dante imitates Virgil (*Aen.* VI, 432–33): "Quaesitor Minos urnam movet; ille silentum / conciliumque vocat, vitasque et crimina discit." ("Minos, presiding, shakes the urn; 'tis he calls a court of the silent, and learns men's lives and misdeeds.")

74

In Dante's usage, Greek proper names are regularly stressed on the last syllable, since this was thought to be the standard Greek accentuation. See "Semiramìs" (vs. 58) and "Parìs" (vs. 67).   *ringhia*: "Snarls." The word is often used of dogs and implies a show of fangs.

7. *mal nata*: The term, applied repeatedly to the damned in Hell, suggests that "it would be better for them not to have been born" (see Matt. 26:24). In the *Vita nuova* (XIX, 8), the souls of Hell are addressed, "O, malnati." The contrary term "bene nato" (*Par.* V, 115) is addressed to one assured of salvation.

8. *li = gli.*

9. *le peccata*: A type of collective feminine plural (originally neuter plural) not uncommon in Italian.

11. *cignesi = si cigne (cinge)*. Minos wraps his tail about himself as many times as the number of the level down to which the damned soul is to be sent. From the phraseology in the poem it is not clear whether Minos' tail is long enough to be wrapped around himself continuously in nine convolutions, or whether he twines it around himself a first time, then a second, and so on. The early illustrators do not reveal any certainty of interpretation, nor does *Inf.* XXVII, 124–29 clear up the matter.

15. *dicono e odono*: They confess their sins and then hear sentence pronounced on them.

18. *cotanto offizio*: The importance of Minos' function is stressed: he is the sole judge of all the souls who enter Hell, and he sentences each to its just place of punishment.

19. *cui = chi.   fide = fidi.*

20. *l'ampiezza de l'intrare*: Since the entrance to Hell proper is here where Minos stands as judge and there is, in fact, no portal at all, the "entrance" is very wide indeed. See Matt. 7:13: "Intrate per angustam portam, quia lata porta et spatiosa via est quae ducit ad perditionem, et multi sunt

qui intrant per eam." ("Enter by the narrow gate. For wide is the gate and broad is the way that leads to destruction, and many there are who enter that way.") See also *Aen.* VI, 126–27.

21–24. *Perché pur gride? . . . e più non dimandare*: "Pur" implies persistence ("why do you persist in shouting these challenges") and recalls Charon's shout to the way-farer (*Inf.* III, 88–93), and now Virgil repeats to Minos the same formula he had used there with the boatman (*Inf.* III, 95–96).

22. *fatale andare*: The journey of Aeneas to the nether-world was also "by decree of the gods"; see *Aen.* VI, 461–62.

25. *Or incomincian*: Shifts to the vivid present are common in the narrative style of the poem.

27. *mi percuote*: The phrase anticipates the buffeting of the wind in this circle.

28. *d'ogne luce muto*: Deprived ("mute") of all light. For a similar merging of the visual and the auditory, see *Inf.* I, 60: "dove 'l sol tace."

34. *Quando giungon davanti a la ruina*: The reader must wait for clarification of this matter. Why is there a "ruin" (which seems to mean a breakdown in the rock structure of Hell) in this circle? And why should the lamentation of the damned souls be louder here as they pass before the ruin? The point at which the poem throws light on this will be duly noted. Meanwhile a sense of mystery prevails.

36. *la virtù divina*: "The Divine Power" that condemns them to such torment.

38. *enno = sono.*

39. *talento*: "Desire," "appetite"; specifically, "carnal ap-petite," since this is the circle of *lussuria* or lust.

40–49. *E come li stornei . . . E come i gru . . .* : The two similes comparing the souls to birds are strictly functional:

the first conveys the helter-skelter movement of the "wide flight" of souls; the second disposes them in single file so that they may pass in review and be noted and named.

40. *stornei = stornelli*. Grammatically, "ali" is the subject of the verb and "stornei" is the object, thus paralleling the second part of the simile where "fiato" (vs. 42) is the subject of the verb and "spiriti" the object.

41. *nel freddo tempo*: In late autumn, birds such as starlings are seen gathering in great flocks, wheeling about in flight (see M. Barbi, 1927, pp. 126–27). The suggestion of autumn and of winter's coming continues (see *Inf*. III, 112) and extends here into the simile of the cranes (vss. 46–47), contributing the tone of sadness and melancholy commonly associated with these seasons. Indeed, the cumulative effect of such touches as these establishes for the *Inferno* a mood that is impressively different from that of the *Purgatorio* or the *Paradiso*.

44–45. *nulla speranza . . . di minor pena*: The object of greater desire is rest or peace ("posa"), and peace is precisely what is forever denied these souls. Francesca's own words will reveal her longing for peace (see n. to vs. 99).

46. *lai*: The term entered the Romance languages with the Breton *lais* but commonly implied a lament by Dante's time (see A. Schiaffini, 1937b).

48. *traendo guai*: The phrase *trarre guai* ("to utter wails") is common in early Italian.

52–60. *La prima di color . . . corregge*: Semiramis is the Greek name of a queen of ancient Assyria. She was famous for her beauty and licentiousness as well as for her prowess in war. According to legend, she was married to Ninus, succeeded to his power, and ruled the Assyrian empire for forty-two years. During her reign she is said to have founded many cities, including Babylon, and to have conquered many others. Her reputation for beauty, charm, and sexual excesses supports the view that she was identified in some legends with the goddess Ishtar. / The description of

Semiramis in the poem is taken directly from Paulus
Orosius, one of Dante's chief historical sources. See Orosius,
Hist. I, iv, 4, 7–8:

> [Nino] mortuo Samiramis uxor successit. . . . haec,
> libidine ardens, sanguinem sitiens, inter incessabilia et
> stupra et homicidia, cum omnes quos regie arcessitos,
> meretricie habitos concubitu oblectasset occideret, tan-
> dem filio flagitiose concepto, impie exposito, inceste
> cognito privatam ignominiam publico scelere obtexit.
> praecepit enim, ut inter parentes ac filios nulla delata
> reverentia naturae de coniugiis adpetendis ut cuique
> libitum esset liberum fieret.

> [Upon the death of Ninus,] his wife Semiramis suc-
> ceeded him on the throne. . . . Burning with lust and
> thirsty for blood, Semiramis in the course of continu-
> ous adulteries and homicides caused the death of all
> those whom she had delighted to hold in her adulterous
> embrace and whom she had summoned to her by royal
> command for that purpose. She finally most shamelessly
> conceived a son, godlessly abandoned the child, later
> had incestuous relations with him, and then covered
> her private disgrace by a public crime. For she pre-
> scribed that between parents and children no reverence
> for nature in the conjugal act was to be observed, but
> that each should be free to do as he pleased.

Dante obviously has borrowed several phrases from Orosius.
Dante's words "libito fé licito" (vs. 56)—which were bor-
rowed in turn by Chaucer and applied to Nero: "His lustes
were al lawe in his decree" (*Monk's Tale*, vs. 2477)—are
an exact translation of Orosius' "ut cuique libitum esset
liberum fieret." The statement "si legge / che succedette a
Nino e fu sua sposa" (vss. 58–59) points directly to Orosius'
words "[Nino] mortuo Samiramis uxor successit." In the
De monarchia, Dante also mentions the careers of Semira-
mis and Ninus (Orosius—*Hist.* II, iii, 1—put their com-
bined reigns at more than ninety years), and cites Ovid's
allusion to them in the story of Pyramus and Thisbe
(*Metam.* IV, 58, 88). See *De mon.* II, viii, 3–4.

60. *tenne la terra che 'l Soldan corregge*: Egypt, in Dante's time, was under the Sultan's rule. Apparently Dante confused Babylonia, a kingdom of the Assyrian empire, with Babylon (Old Cairo), a fortified city on the Nile. Dante's confusion of Babylonia and Babylon is not unique. Boccaccio, for example, describes Saladin as "il soldano di Babilonia"; see *Decam.* I, 3 (vol. I, p. 44, ll. 27-28) and X, 9 (vol. II, p. 292, l. 16). Benvenuto, in his commentary on the *Commedia*, takes notice of Dante's confusion of the two places, but suggests the poet meant to imply that Semiramis extended her empire to include Egypt as well as Assyria. For other theories, see E. G. Parodi (1957), pp. 343-47.

61-62. *L'altra è colei . . . Sicheo*: Dido, also called Elissa, was a daughter of Belus, king of Tyre, and the sister of Pygmalion. She married Sichaeus, who later was murdered by Pygmalion for his wealth. When the shade of Sichaeus revealed Pygmalion's crime to Dido, she fled from Tyre and sailed across to Africa where, according to legend, she founded Carthage. In the *Aeneid*, Virgil makes Dido a contemporary of Aeneas, with whom she falls in love despite her vow to remain faithful to her dead husband. When Aeneas leaves Carthage for Italy, Dido, in despair, stabs herself and dies on a funeral pyre of her own making. Dante's reference to the unfaithful Dido is an evident reminiscence of *Aen.* IV, 552: "Non servata fides cineri promissa Sychaeo." ("The faith vowed to the ashes of Sichaeus I have not kept.")

63. *Cleopatràs*: Cleopatra, queen of Egypt, mistress of Julius Caesar and of Mark Antony, was famous for her beauty and seductive ways. Lucan (*Phars.* X, 60-62) compares her to Helen of Troy.

64. *Elena*: Helen, wife of Menelaus, the Spartan king. Her abduction by Paris led to the long Trojan War. Like Dante, Benoît de Sainte-Maure (*Roman de Troie*, vss. 28426-33) also blames Helen:

> Par cui li monz a trait tel peine,
> Par cui Grece est si apovrie
> De la noble chevalerie,
> Par cui li siegles est peior,
> Par cui li riche e li meillor
> Sont mort, vencu e detrenchié,
> Par cui sont li regne eissillié,
> Par cui Troie est arse e fondue.

Because of her, the world has had such trouble; because of her, Greece is so impoverished of her noble knighthood; because of her, the world is worse; because of her, the rich and best are dead, vanquished, and cut to pieces; because of her, kingdoms have been devastated; because of her, Troy is burned and destroyed.

65–66. *Achille*: Achilles, Greek hero of the Trojan War. Dante's allusion to his death refers not to the Homeric story but rather to the accounts of the Trojan War current in the Middle Ages. According to this medieval version of the story, Achilles was killed by treachery in the temple of Apollo Thymbraeus in Thymbra, to which Paris lured him by the promise of a meeting with Polyxena, with whom Achilles was in love (see Dictys Cretensis, *Ephemeris belli Troiani* IV, 11; and Dares Phrygius, *De excidio Troiae* XXXIV).

67. *Parìs*: Paris, son of Priam and Hecuba, known in Greek mythology as most handsome of all mortal men, was appointed umpire to decide who was the fairest of the three goddesses, Juno, Minerva, or Venus. He chose Venus, who had promised to reward him with Helen, most beautiful woman in the world. His abduction of Helen led to the Trojan War, during which he killed Achilles and, later on, received the wound from which he ultimately died. Benvenuto points out the special propriety of the position Dante assigns to Paris in Hell:

> Hic autor immediate post Achillem locat Paridem occisorem eius. Hic certe potest dici miles Veneris, potius quam Martis . . . adiudicavit pomum Veneri,

spreta Pallade et Iunone. Sic iuvenis amorosus, neglecta
sapientia et opulentia, ponit pomum, idest summum
bonum, in venerea voluptate.

Here, immediately after Achilles, the author places
Paris, his murderer. Surely, Paris may be called a
soldier of Venus rather than of Mars . . . he awarded
the apple to Venus, spurning Pallas and Juno. Thus
amorous youth, disdaining wisdom and opulence,
places the apple, which is the highest good, in sensual
pleasure.

The coupling of Paris and Tristan—and of Helen and
Isolde—as typical instances of lovers whose woes were
wrought by love was a poetic commonplace in the Middle
Ages. Chaucer, for instance, in the *Parliament of Fowls* (vss.
290–91), couples "Tristram, Isaude, Paris, and Achilles, /
Eleyne, Cleopatre, and Troylus," and in the *Prologue* to
the *Legend of Good Women* (vss. 254–55) he says: "Hyde
ye youre beautes, Ysoude and Eleyne: / My lady cometh,
that al this may disteyne." In the *Roman de Renart*, Paris
and Tristan are similarly coupled, as are Helen and Isolde
in a work by Eustache Deschamps, the contemporary and
friend of Chaucer. All four lovers are introduced together
in the following passage from a thirteenth-century manu-
script belonging to the Ashburnham collection:

> Li corteis Tristam fu enginné
> De l'amor et de l'amisté
> Ke il out envers Ysolt la bloie.
> Si fu li beau Paris de Troie
> De Eleine e de Penelopé.

The courteous Tristan was deceived by the love and
friendship he bore Isolde the fair, just as the handsome
Paris of Troy was by Helen and Penelope.

67. *Tristano*: Tristan, lover of Isolde. There are several
medieval versions of the Tristan story in both poetic and
prose forms dating from the late twelfth and early thir-
teenth centuries. The death of Tristan as Dante probably
was familiar with it is told in the OFr prose romance,

Roman de Tristan.   *mille*: Often used, as here, to denote an approximate number, "a great many," "a multitude"; see also *Inf.* VIII, 82.

68. *mostrommi = mi mostrò.*   *nominommi = mi nominò.*

69. *ch'amor di nostra vita dipartille*: This whole encounter with those "who died of love" is reminiscent of Aeneas' visit in the underworld (see *Aen.* VI, 440–76) to the lovers in the Mourning Fields and the myrtle grove, "quos durus amor crudeli tabe peredit" ("those whom stern Love has consumed with cruel wasting," vs. 442).   *dipartille = le dipartì.* The relative "che" is the direct object, and "le" is redundant.

71. *nomar = nominare.*

75. *e paion sì al vento esser leggieri*: This suggests that these two spirits are more violently tossed by the wind than the others are. According to the principle of just punishment, the heightened violence of the wind signifies that the love, which led them in life and leads them now, was, and is, most passionate.

78. *i = li.*   *ei = elli.*

81. *s'altri nol niega*: In Hell the name of God is avoided, or is uttered only in blasphemy.

82–84. *Quali colombe . . . portate*: The simile in its main features seems derived from the *Aeneid*, but in other respects is strikingly altered. See *Aen.* V, 213–17:

> qualis spelunca subito commota columba,
> cui domus et dulces latebroso in pumice nidi,
> fertur in arva volans plausumque exterrita pinnis
> dat tecto ingentem, mox aere lapsa quieto
> radit iter liquidum celeris neque commovet alas.

Even as, if startled suddenly from her cave, a dove whose home and sweet nestlings are in the rocky coverts, wings her flight to the fields and, frightened from her home, flaps loudly with her wings; soon, glid-

ing in the peaceful air, she skims her liquid way and
stirs not her swift pinions.

83. *al dolce nido*: See Virgil, *Georg.* I, 414: "dulcisque
revisere nidos" ("to see once more their sweet nests").

85. *la schiera ov' è Dido*: This second mention of Dido—this
time by name—invites us to remember Virgil's heroine and
her tragic love, as we listen to Dante's "heroine" tell of
her own. In a sense Dante is vying with Virgil here.

88. *animal*: "Living creature," as in *Inf.* II, 2.

89. *perso*: See *Conv.* IV, xx, 2: "Lo perso è uno colore misto
di purpureo e di nero, ma vince lo nero, e da lui si dino-
mina." ("Perse is a colour mingled of purple and of black,
but the black predominates, and it is called after it.")

90. *tignemmo = tingemmo* (from *tingere*).

94. *vi piace*: The shift to the plural is significant. Fran-
cesca begins to address both Dante and Virgil now.

95. *voi*: On the admissibility of such imperfect rhymes as
voi-fui (see vs. 97), see Petrocchi, vol. I, *Introduzione*, p.
471.

96. *mentre che 'l vento, come fa, ci tace*: The function of
"ci" here is uncertain, since it can be the pronoun meaning
"to us" and, by implication, "within us," or it can be the
adverb meaning "here." Thus, either the wind could hush
"for us," i.e., for Francesca and her lover, and so allow them
to hover before Dante and Virgil while she tells her story
(see C. Schick, 1955), or the wind could hush "here," i.e.,
in this place before Dante and Virgil where Francesca and
her lover have been given a brief respite that makes it pos-
sible for her to speak (see M. Barbi, 1934b, pp. 263–64).
Essentially the meaning is the same in either case. Divine
Providence may cause the wind to "be silent" for the spe-
cial benefit of the wayfaring Dante, so that he may hear of
this sinful and tragic love; or Divine Providence may allow
this pair to come out of the wind to where Dante and Virgil
stand unassailed by the blast.

97. *la terra*: Ravenna, a city on the Adriatic coast of Emilia
between the Po and the Rubicon. Although originally it
was only about a mile from the coast, the city now is about
five miles inland, owing to the retreat of the sea. *dove
nata fui*: The soul that speaks is not named until vs. 116,
where she is addressed simply as Francesca. Francesca da
Rimini, as she is known, was the daughter of Guido da
Polenta the elder, lord of Ravenna (d. 1310), and the aunt
of Guido Novello, Dante's host at Ravenna; Francesca
married—possibly *ca.* 1275—Gianciotto (see n. to vs. 107).
No contemporary chronicle or document mentions the love
between Francesca and Paolo (see n. to vs. 101) or their
death, as Dante has Francesca relate it. The earlier commen-
tators merely give the names of the three. For Boccaccio's
account of the story, see below. E. G. Parodi (1920, p. 63)
notes that even the date of the tragic event is uncertain, with
estimates ranging from 1283 to 1286.

According to the accepted story, Francesca, betrothed to
Gianciotto for political reasons, fell in love with his younger
brother Paolo, who had acted as his proxy at the betrothal,
and shortly after the marriage was surprised with him by
Gianciotto, who immediately killed them both. In reality,
however, at the time of their tragic death—if it took place
ca. 1285—Francesca had a nine-year-old daughter by Gian-
ciotto, and Paolo, who was about forty and had been mar-
ried some sixteen years, was the father of two sons.

The story of the two lovers as told by Boccaccio, in his
Comento, is greatly expanded and embroidered nicely to
exculpate Francesca as much as possible:

È adunque da sapere che costei fu figliuola di messer
Guido Vecchio da Polenta, signor di Ravenna e di
Cervia; ed essendo stata lunga guerra e dannosa tra lui
e i signori Malatesti da Rimino, addivenne che per certi
mezzani fu trattata e composta la pace tra loro. La
quale acciochè più fermezza avesse, piacque a ciascuna
delle parti di volerla fortificare per parentado; e 'l pa-
rentado trattato fu che il detto messer Guido dovesse
dare per moglie una sua giovane e bella figliuola,
chiamata madonna Francesca, a Gianciotto, figliuolo di

messer Malatesta. Ed essendo questo ad alcuno degli
amici di messer Guido già manifesto, disse un di loro
a messer Guido:—Guardate come voi fate, perciochè,
se voi non prendete modo ad alcuna parte, che in
questo parentado egli ve ne potrà seguire scandolo.
Voi dovete sapere chi è vostra figliuola, e quanto ell'è
d'altiero animo: e, se ella vede Gianciotto, avanti che il
matrimonio sia perfetto, nè voi nè altri potrà mai fare
che ella il voglia per marito. E perciò, quando vi paia, a
me parrebbe di doverne tener questo modo: che qui non
venisse Gianciotto ad isposarla, ma venisseci un de' fra-
tegli, il quale come suo procuratore la sposasse in
nome di Gianciotto.—Era Gianciotto uomo di gran
sentimento, e speravasi dover lui dopo la morte del
padre rimanere signore; per la qual cosa, quantunque
sozzo della persona e sciancato fosse, il disiderava messer
Guido per genero più tosto che alcuno de' suoi frategli.
E, conoscendo quello, che il suo amico gli ragionava,
dover poter avvenire, ordinò segretamente che così si
facesse, come l'amico suo l'avea consigliato. Per che, al
tempo dato, venne in Ravenna Polo, fratello di Gian-
ciotto, con pieno mandato ad isposare madonna Fran-
cesca. Era Polo bello e piacevole uomo e costumato
molto; e, andando con altri gentiliuomini per la corte
dell'abitazione di messer Guido, fu da una damigella
di lá entro, che il conoscea, dimostrato da un pertugio
d'una finestra a madonna Francesca, dicendole:—Ma-
donna, quegli è colui che dee esser vostro marito;—e
così si credea la buona femmina; di che madonna Fran-
cesca incontanente in lui pose l'animo e l'amor suo.
E fatto poi artificiosamente il contratto delle sponsalizie,
e andatane la donna a Rimino, non s'avvide prima
dell'inganno, che essa vide la mattina seguente al dì
delle nozze levare da lato a sè Gianciotto: di che si dee
credere che ella, vedendosi ingannata, sdegnasse, nè
perciò rimovesse dell'animo suo l'amore già postovi
verso Polo. Col quale come ella poi si giugnesse, mai
non udii dire, se non quello che l'autore ne scrive; il che
possibile è che così fosse. Ma io credo quello essere più

tosto fizione formata sopra quello che era possibile ad
essere avvenuto, chè io non credo che l'autore sapesse
che così fosse. E perseverando Polo e madonna Fran-
cesca in questa dimestichezza, ed essendo Gianciotto
andato in alcuna terra vicina per podestà, quasi senza
alcun sospetto insieme cominciarono ad usare. Della
qual cosa avvedutosi un singulare servidore di Gian-
ciotto, andò a lui, e raccontògli ciò che della bisogna
sapea, promettendogli, quando volesse, di fargliele toc-
care e vedere. Di che Gianciotto fieramente turbato,
occultamente tornò a Rimino, e da questo cotale, avendo
veduto Polo entrare nella camera da madonna Fran-
cesca, fu in quel punto menato all'uscio della camera,
nella quale non potendo entrare, chè serrata era dentro,
chiamò di fuora la donna, e die' di petto nell'uscio. Per
che da madonna Francesca e da Polo conosciuto, cre-
dendo Polo, per fuggire subitamente per una cateratta,
per la quale di quella camera si scendea in un'altra,
o in tutto o in parte potere ricoprire il fallo suo; si
gittò per quella cateratta, dicendo alla donna che gli
andasse ad aprire. Ma non avvenne come avvisato avea,
perciochè, gittandosi giù, s'appiccò una falda d'un co-
retto, il quale egli avea indosso, ad un ferro, il quale
ad un legno di quella cateratta era; per che, avendo
già la donna aperto a Gianciotto, credendosi ella, per
lo non esservi trovato Polo, scusare, ed entrato Gian-
ciotto dentro, incontanente s'accorse Polo esser ritenuto
per la falda del coretto, e con uno stocco in mano cor-
rendo là per ucciderlo, e la donna accorgendosene,
acciochè quello non avvenisse, corse oltre presta, e
misesi in mezzo tra Polo e Gianciotto, il quale avea
già alzato il braccio con lo stocco in mano, e tutto si
gravava sopra il colpo: avvenne quello che egli non
avrebbe voluto, cioè che prima passò lo stocco il petto
della donna, che egli aggiugnesse a Polo. Per lo quale
accidente turbato Gianciotto, sì come colui che più che
se medesimo amava la donna, ritirato lo stocco da capo,
ferì Polo e ucciselo: e così amenduni lasciatigli morti,
subitamente si partì e tornossi all'uficio suo. Furono poi

li due amanti con molte lacrime, la mattina seguente,
seppelliti e in una medesima sepoltura.

You must know that she was the daughter of Guido
da Polenta the elder, lord of Ravenna and Cervia. A
long, harsh war had raged between him and the
Malatesta, lords of Rimini, when through certain in-
termediaries, peace was treated and concluded. To make
it all the more firm, both sides were pleased to cement
it with a marriage. Whereupon it was arranged that
Messer Guido was to give his beautiful young daughter,
called Madonna Francesca, in marriage to Gianciotto,
son of Messer Malatesta. When this became known to
some friends of Messer Guido, one of them said to him:

"Be careful how you proceed, for if you do not take
precautions, this wedding may bring scandal. You know
your daughter, and how high-spirited she can be. If she
sees Gianciotto before the marriage is concluded, neither
you nor anyone else can make her go through with it.
And so, by your leave, it seems to me that you ought
to go about it in this way. Do not let Gianciotto come
here to marry her, but rather one of his brothers who,
as his representative, will marry her in Gianciotto's
name."

Gianciotto was a very capable man, and everyone
expected that he would become ruler when his father
died. For this reason, though he was ugly and de-
formed, Messer Guido wanted him rather than one of
his brothers as a son-in-law. Recognizing that what his
friend had told him was true, he secretly ordered that
his advice be carried out. So that, at the agreed-upon
time, Paolo, Gianciotto's brother, came to Ravenna with
a full mandate to marry Francesca in Gianciotto's name.

Paolo was a handsome, pleasing, very courteous man.
As he was walking together with some other gentlemen
about the courtyard of Messer Guido's home, he was
pointed out through a window to Madonna Francesca
by a young handmaiden inside, who recognized him
and said to her: "Madonna, that is the man who is to
be your husband." The good woman said it in good

faith. Whereupon Madonna Francesca immediately fell completely in love with him.

The deceptive marriage contract was made, and the lady went to Rimini. Nor did she become aware of the deception until the morning after the wedding day, when she saw Gianciotto getting up from beside her. Whereupon she realized she had been fooled, and, as can well be believed, she became furious. Nor did the love she had conceived for Paolo disappear. I have never heard tell how they then got together, other than what [Dante] writes; and it is possible that it did happen that way. But I believe that that is probably a fiction constructed upon what might possibly have happened; and that the author did not know what really took place.

In any case, the feelings of Paolo and Francesca for each other were still very much alive when Gianciotto went off to some nearby town as *podestà*. With almost no fear of suspicion, they became intimate. But a certain servant of Gianciotto found them out, went to Gianciotto, and told him all he knew, promising to give him palpable proof should he want it. Gianciotto, completely enraged, returned secretly to Rimini. When the servant saw Paolo entering Francesca's room, he immediately went to get Gianciotto and brought him to the door of the room. Since it was bolted from within and he could not enter, he shouted to her and began to push against the door.

Paolo and Francesca recognized him immediately. Paolo thought that if he fled quickly through a trapdoor that led to a room below, he might conceal his misdeed, in whole or in part. He threw himself at it, telling the woman to go open the door. But it did not happen as he had planned. As he jumped through, a fold of the jacket he was wearing got caught on a piece of iron attached to the wood. Francesca had already opened the door for Gianciotto, thinking she would be able to make excuses, now that Paolo was gone. Whereupon Gianciotto entered and immediately noticed Paolo caught by the fold of his jacket. He ran, rapier in hand, to kill him. Seeing this, Francesca quickly ran between them, to try to prevent it; but Gianciotto had already raised his rapier, which he now brought down with all his weight behind it.

And thus happened what he would not have wanted: before reaching Paolo, the blade passed through Francesca's bosom. Gianciotto, completely beside himself because of this accident—for he loved the woman more than himself—withdrew the blade, struck Paolo again, and killed him. Leaving them both dead, he left, and returned to his duties. The next morning, amidst much weeping, the two lovers were buried in the same tomb.

99. *per aver pace co' seguaci sui*: Peace (see "posa," vs. 45), the condition most longed for by these souls eternally tossed on the infernal wind is that which, in punishment, is eternally denied them. Francesca expresses her longing for peace in the circumlocution by which she indicates the city of her birth. Does the river seek peace of its tributaries ("seguaci") as if they were so many pursuers? In the whole turn of phrase there is a rich ambiguity, which the internal "rhyme" (*pace . . . seguaci*) serves to reinforce. / It should be remembered that the she-wolf of the first canto (*Inf.* I, 58) was a "bestia sanza pace."

100–108. *Amor . . . Amor . . . Amor . . .* : The anaphora frames and sets off two fateful laws of love and their tragic consequences. "Love kindles quickly in the gentle heart"; accordingly, Paolo cannot escape feeling the fire of love in his own heart. "Love absolves no loved one from loving in return"; accordingly, Francesca must love him who loves her. In declaring these ineluctable laws, Francesca speaks the language of the cult of courtly love, whose god, Love, is all-powerful. In adducing the ineluctability of love, moreover, Francesca pleads her own excuse: neither she nor Paolo was responsible, for, as she implies, none may withstand Love's power. The perverseness of such love (cf. the "mal perverso" of vs. 93) from the point of view of Christian doctrine is evident.

100. *Amor, ch'al cor gentil ratto s'apprende*: Francesca's language, and especially her reference to the "cor gentil," is indeed that of courtly love. The verse recalls the famous *canzone* of Guido Guinizelli that begins (see G. Contini, 1960, vol. II, p. 460): "Al cor gentil rempaira sempre amore / come l'ausello in selva a la verdura." ("Love always repairs to the gentle heart, as the bird in the wood to the verdure.") *s'apprende*: "Catches fire." The term frequently had this meaning; see Boccaccio, *Decam*. III, 10 (vol. I, p. 262, l. 2): "Avvenne che un fuoco s'apprese in Capsa." ("It came to pass that a fire broke out in Capsa.")

101. *costui*: Paolo Malatesta, who is not named here or elsewhere in the poem. He was the third son of Malatesta da Verrucchio; Malatestino and Gianciotto (see n. to vs. 107) and Pandolfo were his brothers. Paolo, said to have been handsome and attractively mannered, was married in 1269 to Orabile Beatrice, by whom he later had two sons. On Paolo's tragic love for Francesca, see n. to vs. 97.

102. *e 'l modo ancor m'offende*: Gianciotto apparently surprised the two lovers and killed them immediately, leaving them no time for repentance; hence, the "manner" of her death still offends Francesca (cf. "anime offense," vs. 109). Another interpretation (see A. Pagliaro, 1953, pp. 333–53) would refer the phrase not to the manner of the murder but to the intensity of Paolo's passion, suggested by Francesca's words (vss. 100–101): "Amor . . . / prese costui de la bella persona." However, this view seems farfetched and this meaning extremely unlikely in the context, despite the apparent correspondence of "ancor m'offende" (vs. 102) and "ancor non m'abbandono" (vs. 105) cited in support of it.

103. *Amor, ch'a nullo amato amar perdona*: Francesca's second law of love echoes a dictum which the cult of courtly love characteristically had taken over from Christian doctrine. See I Ioan. Apos. 4:19: "Nos ergo diligamus Deum, quoniam Deus prior dilexit nos." ("Let us therefore love, because God first loved us.") Thus Fra Giordano da

Rivalto sermonizes (*Prediche* XLV, 1831 edn., vol. II, p. 78): "Non è nullo che, sentendosi che sia amato da alcuno, ch'egli non sia tratto ad amar lui incontanente." ("There is no one who, feeling himself loved, will not immediately feel drawn to love in return.") See also Andreas Capellanus, *De amore* II, 8 (p. 311): "Amor nil posset amori denegare." ("Love can deny nothing to love.")

104. *mi prese*: With this echo of the "prese costui" of vs. 101, the parallel application of the two laws of love becomes most evident.   *del costui piacer = del piacer di costui.* "Costui" is the genitive form here. "Piacer" probably is intended to correspond to the "bella persona" of vs. 101. Thus, Paolo falls in love with the beautiful Francesca, and Francesca falls in love with the handsome Paolo. *Piacer*, like the Provençal *plazer*, often means "charm," "attraction." See M. Barbi (1932), pp. 10–11. It would corroborate this second law of love more precisely, however, if "piacer" here meant instead Paolo's "pleasure" in Francesca, his love for her, the pleasure he took in her charm. Neither meaning can be ruled out, since the poetic ambiguity can support one or the other.

106. *Amor condusse noi ad una morte*: The third verse of the anaphora fatefully seals the doom of the two lovers, as if Love himself had pronounced the decree; "una morte" seems to unite these lovers in that moment of death and forever thereafter.

107. *Caina attende chi a vita ci spense*: Gianciotto is awaited in Caina (or so Francesca believes and even hopes), but the reader must wait to learn the meaning of that place in lower Hell. / Gianciotto (*Gian ciotto* = "crippled John"), husband of Francesca, was Giovanni Malatesta, second son of Malatesta da Verrucchio, lord of Rimini (called "il mastin vecchio" in *Inf.* XXVII, 46). Gianciotto appears to have been a man of brutish exterior, but was valiant and able. He died in 1304, before both his father and his older brother, Malatestino ("il mastin nuovo"). On Gianciotto's tragic marriage to Francesca, see n. to vs. 97.

108. *ci fuor porte = ci furono portate.* Truncated past participles (*porte = portate*) are common in Italian.

109–20. *Quand' io intesi . . . disiri*: The "interruption," focusing on the wayfarer as a pensive and compassionate listener, and then the further question, momentarily relax the pitch of the sentiment so that it can attain an even higher climax.

109. *quell' anime offense*: The adjective in the context of the wayfarer's compassion would mean "wretched," "suffering"; yet it is Divine Justice that punishes or "offends" these sinners, and Divine Justice scarcely can be said to "do offense." Thus, there is a meeting here of two perspectives, human and divine, which adds a dramatic dimension to this episode and to the *Inferno* as a whole.

111. *pense = pensi.*

114. *al doloroso passo*: To their death. "Passo" in a similar though more metaphorical sense appears in *Inf.* I, 26; see also "alto passo" in *Inf.* II, 12, where "passo" refers to the passage from the world of the living to the world of the dead.

116. *Francesca*: She is named only now, and her lover is not named at all—true indications that the poet is presenting a *cause célèbre.*

118. *d'i = dei.*

119. *a che e come concedette amore*: The questioner Dante has entered into the spirit of Francesca's words and joins her in speaking the language of courtly love. It was Love, as she had said, that brought the lovers to "one death"; and it is Love, he therefore assumes, who allows the lovers to manifest their desire.

120. *conosceste*: The verb is plural; the question concerns both souls. *i dubbiosi disiri*: Given the context of the two perspectives, human and divine, this adjective, like "offense" in vs. 109, is rich in ambiguity. *Dubbioso*, referring

to the desire of lovers, can mean "hesitant," "not yet manifested," i.e., desire of which neither lover is wholly conscious (see M. Barbi, 1932, p. 16). But *dubbioso* can also mean "dangerous," "that which is to be feared"; cf. the verb "dubbiar" in *Purg.* XX, 135.

121–23. *Nessun maggior dolore . . . miseria*: A number of antecedents to Francesca's words have been noted. See, for example, Augustine, *Conf.* X, 14: "Aliquando et e contrario tristitiam meam transactam laetus reminiscor, et tristis laetitiam." ("Sometimes on the contrary, in joy do I remember my forepassed sorrow, and in sadness my joy.") See also Thomas Aquinas, *Summa theol.* II-II, q. 36, a. 1, ad 4: "Memoria praeteritorum bonorum, inquantum fuerunt habita, delectationem causat: sed inquantum sunt amissa, causant tristitiam." ("Recollection of past goods in so far as we have had them, causes pleasure; in so far as we have lost them, causes sorrow.") But much closer is Boethius, *Consol. philos.* II, iv, ll. 3–6: "Sed hoc est quod recolentem vehementius coquit. Nam in omni adversitate fortunae infelicissimum est genus infortunii fuisse felicem." ("But this is that which vexeth me most, when I remember it. For in all adversity of fortune it is the most unhappy kind of misfortune to have been happy.")

123. *e ciò sa 'l tuo dottore*: Virgil's "misery" is his confinement to Limbo without hope of attaining the "good of intellect."

124–26. *Ma s'a conoscer . . . dice*: See *Aen.* II, 10, 12-13:

sed si tantus amor casus cognoscere nostros
. . . .
quamquam animus meminisse horret luctuque refugit,
incipiam. . . .

Yet if thou hast such longing to learn our disasters . . .
though my mind shudders to remember, and has recoiled in grief, I will begin.

127. *Noi leggiavamo un giorno per diletto*: Stories of King Arthur and the Arthurian heroes were very popular in

Dante's time; see P. Rajna (1920). Other allusions in Dante's writings include *De vulg. eloqu.* I, x, 2: "Arturi regis ambages pulcerrime" ("the exquisite legends of King Arthur"), and the "prose di romanzi" of *Purg.* XXVI, 118. See also *Par.* XVI, 14–15, which is, in fact, a reminiscence of *Lancelot du Lac*.

128. *Lancialotto*: Lancelot of the Lake, the hero of the romance *Lancelot du Lac*, in which he is styled "la flor des cheualiers del monde" ("the flower of the knighthood of the world"). At the court of King Arthur the famous knight became enamored of Arthur's queen, Guinevere; in consequence of this guilty love, Lancelot failed in his quest for the Holy Grail. For the OFr manuscript version of the *Lancelot du Lac*, see P. Toynbee (1902), pp. 10–37.

129. *sanza alcun sospetto*: It is possible to understand this to mean "without reason to fear that anyone might surprise us," thus reinforcing the "soli"; but it seems better, given the context, to understand "knowing nothing," i.e., "unaware of the love we already felt for one another." It is the *reading* itself that reveals their love to them and in this sense is their "go-between": hence the book as "Gallehault" (see n. to vs. 137).

133. *il disiato riso*: Guinevere's lips, her smiling mouth. Note the corresponding but impressively stark "bocca" of vs. 136.

134. *basciato = baciato*.

135. *questi, che mai da me non fia diviso*: As if the kiss had sealed their doom and had bound them together for eternity.
  fia = sarà.

136. *basciò = baciò*.

137. *Galeotto*: Gallehault (not to be confused with Galahad) was one of the characters in the OFr *Lancelot du Lac*. Called "Roy d'outre les marches" ("king from beyond the marshes"), he made war on King Arthur, but by the intervention of Lancelot was induced to come to terms. During

Gallehault's residence at King Arthur's court a warm friend-
ship developed between him and Lancelot, who confided his
love for Queen Guinevere. Gallehault arranged for the two to
meet. In the course of this interview, Gallehault urged the
queen to kiss Lancelot—and so began the guilty love be-
tween those two. From the part he played on this occasion,
the name of Gallehault ("galeotto"), like that of Pandarus
("pander"), became a synonym for "go-between."

141. *morisse = morissi.*

CANTO VI

1. *la mente*: "My senses."   *si chiuse*: "Closed" to any sensation.

2. *la pietà*: See *Inf.* II, 4–5: "la guerra / . . . de la pietate." *d'i = dei*.

3. *trestizia = tristizia*.

5. *mi veggio intorno*: With this vivid use of the present tense, the wayfarer faces a new circle of Hell. The manner of his passage from the circle above, like his mysterious crossing of Acheron (see n. to *Inf.* IV, 7), remains unexplained. These miraculous ways of passing from one circle to another are characteristic of the beginning of the poem.

11. *si riversa*: The use of a singular verb with a plural subject is not uncommon in the poem. Apart from the requirements of meter, *versare* rather than *riversarsi* might have been used for the downpouring of hail, rain, and snow. The use of "si riversa" to describe the punishment of gluttons is significant, therefore, since *riversarsi* and *riversare* are used of a liquid such as soup spilled upon oneself. (Compare the expression *riversare la broda addosso ad alcuno*.)

12. *che questo riceve*: "Questo" is especially expressive here, suggesting that the whole downpour is one stinking slop.

13-17. *Cerbero, fiera crudele . . . unghiate le mani*: Again Dante has drawn one of the guardians of Hell's circles from classical sources but has transformed him to suit the requirements of the creature's infernal office. The incident follows *Aen.* VI, 417-23:

> Cerberus haec ingens latratu regna trifauci
> personat, adverso recubans immanis in antro.
> cui vates, horrere videns iam colla colubris,
> melle soporatam et medicatis frugibus offam
> obicit. ille fame rabida tria guttura pandens
> corripit obiectam, atque immania terga resolvit
> fusus humi totoque ingens extenditur antro.

> These realms huge Cerberus makes ring with his triple-throated baying, his monstrous bulk crouching in a cavern opposite. To him, seeing the snakes now bristling on his necks, the seer flung a morsel drowsy with honey and drugged meal. He, opening his triple throat in ravenous hunger, catches it when thrown and, with monstrous frame relaxed, sinks to earth and stretches his bulk over all the den.

The Cerberus of the *Inferno* has his traditional three heads and throats, but Dante has made the brute more grotesque by giving him distinctly human attributes: hands, and three faces (each with a greasy beard). Moreover, the beast's three ravening gullets are silenced with handfuls of earth (vss. 25-33) instead of with honey cake. / Can an early tradition that had Cerberus as one of the devourers of the dead have any part in Dante's conception of the demon's role here? See H. E. Butler (1920), p. 171:

> In popular superstition and early legend Cerberus has far more terrible functions than merely guarding the gates of Hades: he is one of the devourers of the dead. Cp. SERVIUS (ad *Aen.* 6.395) *Cerberus terra consumptrix omnium corporum. unde et Cerberus dictus est quasi* κρεόβορος ["Cerberus, the devourer of all the bodies in the earth. Hence he is called Cerberus, as if κρεόβορος,

the eater of flesh"]. . . . Vergil ignores the grosser and more horrible features of legend, and makes him but the guardian of the gate, though in *Aen.* 8.297 we have an allusion to the more terrible aspects of the superstition: *te ianitor Orci / ossa super recubans antro semesa cruento* ["before thee, the warder of Hell, as he lay on half-gnawn bones in his bloody cave"].

13. *Cerbero*: Pronounced *Cèrbero*.　　*diversa*: "Strange," "monstrous."

15. *sommersa*: The souls wallow in the filth; the adjective or past participle connotes "swinish" and "sodden," "soaked."

18. *iscoia = scuoia.*　　*isquatra = squatra.*

19. *come cani*: Matching the "caninamente latra" used in vs. 14 to describe Cerberus.

21. *volgonsi = si volgono.* The verb suggests "turning oneself over" in bed—here, in the mire. These gluttons are having a bad night of it, so to speak.　　*i miseri profani*: M. Barbi (1934b, p. 265) reads the two adjectives as synonyms and gives examples to support his view. There is a significant echo of Biblical usage in "profani." See Heb. 12:16: "ne quis fornicator aut profanus, ut Esau, qui propter unam escam vendidit primitiva sua" ("lest there be any immoral or profane person, such as Esau, who for one meal sold his birthright"). Especially note the "profane broth" of Isa. 65:4, where the prophet scornfully refers to the people "qui comedunt carnem suillam, et ius profanum in vasis eorum" ("that eat swine's flesh, and profane broth is in their vessels"). Thomas Aquinas in discussing gluttony cites these verses and quotes the *Glossa ordinaria* on them (see *De malo* q.14, a. 2, obj. 1, and ad 1).

22. *il gran vermo*: Since in the Bible the worm often symbolizes decay, the name is most appropriately applied here to Cerberus who stands in the midst of so much putrefaction. "Vermo" is used for Satan himself later in the poem (see *Inf.* XXXIV, 108).

23. *mostrocci = ci mostrò.   sanne = zanne,* "fangs," as also in *Inf.* XXII, 56.

26–27. *prese la terra . . . canne*: The fact that the sop thrown to Cerberus is earth rather than honey cake emphasizes that earth can satisfy Cerberus, a detail worth connecting with *Inf.* I, 103, where it was said that the "veltro" to come "will not feed on earth." By implication, the she-wolf, which is to be driven back into Hell by this Hound, craves and eats earth, even as Cerberus does here.

28. *agogna*: "Desires," "craves." M. Barbi (1934b, pp. 265–66) cites Fra Giordano and Bono Giamboni for some very suggestive examples of the use of this verb in the context of eating or greed for worldly things. See Fra Giordano da Rivalto, *Prediche* XXXVI (1739 edn., p. 157): "Questa è *hora epulandi,* cioè da mangiare; imperocchè allora la natura hae digesto e smaltito, e agogna." ("This is the *hora epulandi,* that is, the time to eat; for nature has digested and eliminated, and now craves.") See also Bono Giamboni, *Trattati morali*, pp. 49–50: "[Chi pone l'amore suo nelle cose mondane] non s'empie per quello che trova, anzi rimane vuoto, e agogna; e dilungasi dal sovrano bene, cioè Iddio, per lo quale empiere si puote." ("[He who loves things of this world] will not be fulfilled by what he finds; in fact, he will remain empty, and will crave. And he will move away from the Highest Good, which is God, Who could fulfill him.")

Here, in the context of the *Commedia*, the verb "agogna" suggests the straining or lurching forward of a dog on a chain or leash, a meaning reinforced by the rhyming "pugna" (vs. 30), which also suggests struggle. Grandgent has noted this sense of "pugna" in a chapter heading of the *De animalibus* of Albertus Magnus (VIII, i, 2): "De pugna animalium pro cibo et domo et pullis" ("On the struggle of animals for food, shelter, and their young").

32. *lo demonio Cerbero*: The term "demonio" emphasizes once more the grotesquely transformed figure of Cerberus,

dog and devil. *'ntrona = introna*, "deafens" as by thunder; cf. "truono" in *Inf.* IV, 2.

34. *adona*: "Beats down," "subdues." Cf. Provençal *adonar*, and see *Purg.* XI, 19.

35. *ponavam = ponavamo.*

36. *sovra lor vanità che par persona*: This verse can serve as an index of the relative "substantiality" of the souls in the various levels of Hell. Here in upper Hell, the souls of the gluttons are "empty" and insubstantial; they have only "the appearance of bodies." Farther down, the wayfarer will encounter souls that are much more substantial and corporeal.

38. *una ch'a seder si levò*: This is the soul of the Florentine Ciacco, about whom little is known beyond what is learned in this canto. There has been some attempt to identify him with one Ciacco dell'Anguillaia, a poet of the thirteenth century, but no substantiating documents have been found. Boccaccio's tale—*Decam.* IX, 8 (vol. II, pp. 220–23)—has almost no value in this regard, since its representation of Ciacco as a glutton is probably derived from this very canto of the *Commedia.*

40. *tratto*: "Drawn," "led" (past participle of *trarre*).

43. *a lui*: To the soul (*anima*) as yet unidentified but already recognized to be that of a man, as evident in the use of "disfatto," vs. 42.

48. *maggio = maggiore.* Cf. the Via Maggio (i.e., Via Maggiore), a street in Florence.

49. *La tua città*: The city of Florence, which figures so prominently in Dante's poem, here makes its first appearance.

50. *già trabocca il sacco*: In order to understand Ciacco's "prophecies" and his pronouncements on past events in Florence, the reader must remember that in the fictional time of the poem this encounter takes place in late March

or early April of the year 1300, when trouble was already brewing between the two Guelph factions—the one headed by the Cerchi, the other by the Donati.

52. *Voi cittadini mi chiamaste Ciacco*: "Ciacco" as a nickname means "hog," but it also is an abbreviation for the name Giacomo. This verse, then, is a striking instance of the doctrine expressed by the dictum *nomina sunt consequentia rerum*, Ciacco being both *Ciacco* (Giacomo) and *ciacco* ("hog" or "glutton"). For another example of this, see the note on the name Beatrice (*beatrice*) in C. S. Singleton (1949), p. 119.

57. *fé = fece*.

58. *li = gli*.

60–63. *ma dimmi . . . assalita*: Ciacco is asked three questions, which concern the future, the present, and the past, respectively. (Later on, in Canto X, the wayfarer will be told how it is that souls in Hell can see into the future.) Ciacco replies to the questions in the order in which they are asked, so that vss. 64–72 are the "prophetic" answer to the first question.

61. *la città partita*: Florence was "divided" between the two Guelph factions, which took the names "Bianchi" (Whites) and "Neri" (Blacks) from a similar political division in the neighboring city of Pistoia.

64–72. *E quelli a me . . . n'aonti*: These verses concerning the future of the "divided city" were written while Dante was enduring an exile brought about by the events Ciacco here predicts.

64–65. *Dopo lunga tencione verranno al sangue*: By the spring of 1300, the two Guelph factions had been quarreling for some twenty years. Finally, during the *Calendimaggio* of 1300 (the May Day festivities) in the Piazza di Santa Trìnita, there was bloodshed between the two factions. This (as I. Del Lungo, 1908, pp. 29–30, has observed) solidified the enmity between the Bianchi and the Neri, and soon each party was seeking to gain control of the city and to banish the other.

65–66. *la parte selvaggia caccerà l'altra*: The Bianchi will drive the Neri from the city. The Bianchi were termed the "parte selvaggia" because their leading family, the Cerchi, had come to Florence from the country and therefore were commonly called "rustic"; the Donati were a much older urban family. In June 1301 the Bianchi, then in political control of the city, took advantage of a conspiracy against them and had the Neri banished from Florence.

66. *con molta offensione*: Del Lungo (1908, p. 30) understands the phrase to refer not to the Neri but to the Bianchi, and to mean "passing from the defensive to the offensive."

67–68. *Poi appresso convien . . . l'altra sormonti*: The exiled Neri, led by Corso Donati, turned to Pope Boniface VIII for aid, and by conniving with him and his so-called peacemaker, Charles of Valois, managed to regain control of Florence and to pass severe sentences against some six hundred Bianchi. Among those exiled at this time was Dante himself. Ciacco predicts these events as taking place within three solar years.

69. *con la forza di tal che testé piaggia*: The "one who is temporizing now"—in 1300—is Pope Boniface; he played his ambiguous political game with both factions and finally sent to Florence the ostensible *paciaro*, Charles of Valois, who proceeded to side with the Neri. / On "piaggia" Boccaccio comments:

> Dicesi appo i fiorentini colui "piaggiare," il quale mostra di voler quello che egli non vuole, o di che egli non si cura che avvenga: la qual cosa vogliono alcuni in questa discordia de' Bianchi e de' Neri di Firenze aver fatta papa Bonifazio, cioè d'aver mostrata igual tenerezza di ciascuna delle parti.

> The Florentines use the word *piaggiare* for someone who pretends to desire something which he really does not desire at all, or which he does not want to see

happen. Some people claim Pope Boniface did this in
the conflict between the Whites and the Blacks of
Florence; that is to say, that he displayed equal con-
cern for both sides.

And Buti says: "[Bonifazio] ora si sta di mezzo et in-
differente; cioè non dà vista d'essere da l'una parte, nè
dall'altra, perchè piaggiare è andare fra la terra e l'alto
mare." ("[Boniface] now remains in the middle, indiffer-
ent; that is to say, he pretends to favor neither side. For
piaggiare means walking between the land and the high
sea.") For "piaggia" meaning "shore," see *Inf.* I, 29 and
the note.

70. *lungo tempo*: For as long as Dante had suffered exile
by the time he was writing these verses. (The date of com-
position, however, is not known.)

71. *l'altra*: The Bianchi.

72. *aonti = adonti.*

73. *Giusti son due*: The wayfarer's second question to
Ciacco, whether any in Florence be just (vs. 62), has a
distinctly Biblical flavor. See Ezech. 14:15–16; also see
Abraham's questions to the Lord concerning the destruc-
tion of Sodom (Gen. 18:24): "Si fuerint quinquaginta iusti
in civitate . . ." ("if there be fifty just men in the city . . .").
It is clearly impossible to identify the two just men of
Ciacco's reply, since his pronouncement keeps something
of the obscurity and mystery of its Biblical origin. Who-
ever they are, the two are not heeded in a city corrupted
by "pride, envy, and avarice" (vs. 74).

77–84. *Ancor vo' che mi 'nsegni . . . attosca*: The way-
farer now asks Ciacco about men who were great political
figures in Florence before the Bianchi and Neri had arisen
to divide the city. All except Arrigo will be encountered
later in the poem "among the blackest spirits" of Hell (see
vs. 85), and will be discussed as they appear.

Little is known about Arrigo; even his historical iden-
tity is uncertain. Benvenuto comments: "Istum numquam

nominabit amplius; debet tacite poni cum Musca, quia fuit
secum in eadem culpa; fuit enim nobilis de Sifantibus."
("[The poet] never says any more about him. He is prob-
ably put tacitly with Mosca because they shared the same
fault. He was a nobleman of the Fifanti family.") Boccac-
cio calls him Arrigo Giandonati and says merely: "Furono,
questi, cinque onorevoli e famosi cavalieri e cittadini di
Firenze." ("These five were honorable, famous knights,
and citizens of Florence.") Some identify him with Odar-
rigo de' Fifanti—who might be the person Boccaccio called
Arrigo Giandonati, since the Giandonati and Fifanti fam-
ilies were closely related and had their houses together. This
Odarrigo was implicated in the murder in 1215 of the
Guelph leader, Buondelmonte de' Buondelmonti. For a
review of the various identifications advanced, see P. Santini
(1923), pp. 40–44, who suggests yet another Arrigo, the
judge Arrigo di Cascia, but concludes: "Fino a che da
qualche parte non vengano fuori altri dati di fatto, la
figura di quest'Arrigo dantesco è destinata a rimaner nella
penombra." ("Until such time as other facts are uncovered,
the figure of this Dantesque Arrigo will remain enveloped
in shadows.")

78. *facci = faccia*.

79. *fuor = furono*.

81–84. *e li altri . . . attosca*: The wayfaring Dante asks his
question from the human point of view and judges these
figures by the criteria of the *polis*, the city-state of Florence.
But his question, as he continues, recognizes that Divine
Justice does not judge by any such standards and that those
"who set their talents to good works" (vs. 81) may be in
Hell (where in fact they are). The meeting of the human
and divine perspectives, which we have already noted in
the episode of Paolo and Francesca (see n. to *Inf.* V, 109),
is evident here in the way Dante phrases his question.

86. *grava*: Again, a singular verb with a plural subject
("colpe").

87. *i = li.*

89. *priegoti = ti prego.*

91–93. *Li diritti occhi torse . . . li altri ciechi*: Ciacco's
cross-eyed look, as he sinks back with the other blind souls,
represents the state of *hebetudo*, a condition regularly dis-
cussed by the theologians in connection with gluttony. See
Thomas Aquinas, *Summa theol.* II-II, q. 148, a. 6, resp.:

> Et quantum ad hoc ponitur filia gulae *hebetudo sensus
> circa intelligentiam*, propter fumositates ciborum per-
> turbantes caput . . . . Secundo, quantum ad appetitum,
> qui multipliciter deordinatur per immoderantiam cibi
> et potus quasi sopito gubernaculo rationis . . . .
>
> In this respect we reckon as a daughter of gluttony,
> *dullness of sense in the understanding*, on account of
> the fumes of food disturbing the brain . . . . Secondly,
> as regards the appetite, which is disordered in many
> ways by immoderation in eating and drinking, as
> though reason were fast asleep at the helm . . . .

92. *guardommi = mi guardò.*

94–99. *Più non si desta . . . rimbomba*: The verb *destarsi*
means "to awaken" and catches something of the implica-
tion in the preceding rhyme word "ciechi." All these glut-
tonous souls will lie "blind" and "asleep" in their mire
until the Last Judgment when the angel's trumpet will
sound and each soul will return to its tomb (cf. *Purg.* XXX,
13–14) and resume its "flesh and form." This declaration
applies to all the damned of Hell, and thus raises the gen-
eral question which is now put by the wayfarer to his guide
as they move on, talking of "the future life" (vs. 102). / On
the second coming of Christ (who is referred to here, al-
though not by name—see n. to vs. 96) and the sound of
the angel's trumpet, see Matt. 24:27–31. On the resurrection
of the flesh, see I Cor. 15:51–53:

> Ecce mysterium vobis dico: omnes quidem resurgemus,
> sed non omnes immutabimur. In momento, in ictu
> oculi, in novissima tuba; canet enim tuba, et mortui

resurgent incorrupti, et nos immutabimur. Oportet enim corruptibile hoc induere incorruptionem, et mortale hoc induere immortalitatem.

Behold, I tell you a mystery: we shall all indeed rise, but we shall not all be changed—in a moment, in the twinkling of an eye, at the last trumpet. For the trumpet shall sound, and the dead shall rise incorruptible and we shall be changed. For this corruptible body must put on incorruption, and this mortal body must put on immortality.

See also I Thess. 4:14-16, where the notion of awaking is more evident.

96. *la nimica podesta*: Christ is never named in Hell. Here, for the damned, he is the "enemy judge," the "hostile Power." / The form *podèsta* is derived from the Latin nominative *potestas* (cf. *pièta* from the Latin *pietas*), while the more common form *podestà* is from the Latin accusative *potestatem*. / M. Bardi (1934b, p. 238) notes also that in Dante's time *la podestà* and *messer la podestà* were more common than *il podestà*.

100-101. *sozza mistura de l'ombre e de la pioggia*: The stress on filth and on the punishment of the rain continues.

103. *Esti = questi*.

105. *fier* (pronounced *fìer*) = *fiero*. This form, now obsolete, is clearly interchangeable with *saranno*, as is evident in this verse.

106-7. *Ritorna a tua scienza . . . perfetta*: This "science" is Aristotelian philosophy as developed in the scholastic teachings. Aristotle had held that the soul is the form of the body, and that the human person is essentially a composite of body and soul; see, for example, *De anima* II, i, 412ª–413ª. Following Aristotle, Thomas Aquinas held that the soul does not have its natural perfection unless it is united with the body. (In his *Summa theol.* I, q. 90, a. 4, resp., Aquinas argued: "Anima autem, cum sit pars humanae naturae, non habet naturalem perfectionem, nisi secundum

quod est corpori unita"—"Now the soul, as part of human
nature, has its natural perfection only as united to the
body"; see also his *Summa contra Gentiles* II, 83.) It fol-
lows, therefore, that on Judgment Day when the souls of
the dead will have returned to their bodies, the soul re-
united with the body will be "more perfect" than the soul
is alone. This is the principle to which Virgil refers here
in his command to the wayfaring Dante. On this principle
and its historical elaboration and significance in Thomistic
philosophy, see E. Gilson (1921), pp. 109–24.

CANTO VII

1. *Pape Satàn, pape Satàn aleppe!* If we may assume
from what is said in vs. 3 that Virgil understands Plutus'
angry words, we must conclude that these words have some
meaning and are not simply a senseless expression of rage.
Yet, the exact meaning of the strange words remains ob-
scure. Most of the early commentators construe "pape"
(like the Latin exclamation *papae*, or the Greek παπαî)
as an *interiectio admirantis*, an interjection expressing great
marvel, and "aleppe" as an exclamation of dismay or grief,
identified by some as the first letter of the Hebrew alphabet,
aleph. Thus, to take the *Ottimo Commento*'s gloss as repre-
sentative:

> *Pape* . . . è . . . una parte di grammatica, che ha
> a dimostrare quella affezione dell'animo, che è con
> stupore, e maravigliarsi; e due volte il disse, per più
> esprimere quello maravigliarsi: *Satan* è il grande
> Demonio: *Aleppe* è una dizione, che ha a dimostrare
> l'affezione dell'animo quando si duole; sicchè in somma
> puoi dire, che questo Padre di ricchezze gridasse,
> maravigliandosi, e chiamandosi, e dolendosi, l'aiutorio
> del suo maggiore.

> *Pape* . . . is . . . a form that expresses the state of mind
> called astonishment and marvel. And he said it twice,

to express the marvel more strongly. *Satan* is the great demon; *aleppe* is a form of speech intended to express the state of pain. In sum, we may say that this father of riches cried out in marvel, in succor, and in pain, for the aid of his superior.

Boccaccio's *Comento* suggests a similar meaning for the opening words of the canto:

> Maravigliasi adunque Plutone, sì come di cosa ancora più non veduta, cioè che alcun vivo uomo vada per lo 'nferno; e, temendo questo non sia in suo danno, invoca quasi come suo aiutatore il suo maggiore; e, acciochè egli il renda più pronto al suo aiuto, si duole.

> Pluto marvels, then, for this is something never seen hitherto: that a living man should be walking through Hell. Fearing that this might redound to his harm, he invokes the aid of his superior. And, in order to render him more disposed to help, he laments.

This meaning nicely fits the context: Plutus, as one of the guardians of Satan's realm, does well to call upon his chief, now that he sees a living man entering Hell. / For a full discussion of this verse, see D. Guerri (1904); see also B. M. Marti (1952).

2. *Pluto*: Dante may have meant his "Pluto" to be Pluto, the god of the netherworld (who, in Greek mythology, was also called Hades, son of Cronus and Rhea and brother of Zeus and Poseidon), or Plutus, the god of wealth (son of Iasion and Demeter). Probably Dante made no clear distinction between Pluto and Plutus, since even in classical times the two divinities had been identified with each other. There clearly is a connection between the name Pluto, as an epithet for the god Hades, and the name Plutus. The Greek word for wealth is πλοῦτος ("plutus"), and grain—the chief wealth of early times—was thought to be sent by the god Hades, husband of Demeter's daughter. From earliest times, by the Greeks as well as the Romans, Pluto as identified with Plutus was considered to be the god of riches as well as the ruler of the under-

world. / Modern readers call Dante's guardian of the fourth circle Plutus, the god of wealth. Most early commentators thought that Dante meant Pluto, the god of the underworld, but even they went on to connect their "Pluto" with the idea of wealth. Pietro di Dante (whose source might have been Cicero, *De nat. deor.* II, xxvi, 66) comments on these opening verses of Canto VII as follows:

> Et sicut in aliis circulis finxit [auctor] adesse et praeesse unum Daemonem repraesentantem motum diabolicum ipsius vitii, ita fingit nunc se pro eo invenire Plutonem, quem Poetae dicunt fuisse filium Saturni et Cybelis, quae ponitur pro elemento terrae, et dicitur *Dis* seu *Dites*, eo quod divitiae in terra et ex terra nascuntur, et ab eis, seu propter eas, per consequens avaritia.

> And just as [Dante], in the other circles, depicted a demon who presides there and symbolizes the diabolical drive itself, so he now depicts himself encountering just such a demon in Pluto. The poets say Pluto was the son of Saturn and Cybele, who represents the element earth. He is called *Dis* or *Dite*, because riches are born of or in the earth; and consequently from them, or because of them, comes avarice.

Benvenuto comments further that "quia ex terra nascitur omnis opulentia divitiarum ex quibus nascitur avaricia, ideo autor per Plutonem regem terrenarum et mundanarum diviciarum repraesentat in generali universale vicium avaritiae." ("Because the earth gives birth to all the opulence of wealth, from which is born avarice, the author represents the universal vice of avarice in general through Pluto, the king of earthly and worldly riches.")   *chioccia*: The term will be used in *Inf.* XXXII, 1 to describe the style by which the poet seeks to represent lowest Hell, where Satan, the greatest enemy and Plutus' chief, abides.

3. *che tutto seppe*: An all-understanding Virgil must know the meaning of Plutus' clucking words; see n. to vs. 1, above.

6. *questa roccia*: Their path goes down the embankment of rock that divides the third circle of Hell from the fourth.

7. *'nfiata = enfiata.   labbia*: "Face," a form not uncommon in early Italian and used elsewhere by Dante (see *Inf.* XIV, 67; XIX, 122).

11. *vuolsi ne l'alto*: Virgil's words here are a variant of the formula addressed to Charon (*Inf.* III, 95) and to Minos (*Inf.* V, 23).   *vuolsi = si vuol.*

11–12. *là dove Michele . . . strupo*: See Apoc. 12:7–9:

> Et factum est proelium magnum in caelo: Michael et angeli eius proeliabantur cum dracone; et draco pugnabat et angeli eius: et non valuerunt, neque locus inventus est eorum amplius in caelo. Et proiectus est draco ille magnus, serpens antiquus qui vocatur diabolus et Satanas, qui seducit universum orbem; et proiectus est in terram, et angeli eius cum illo missi sunt.

> And there was a battle in heaven; Michael and his angels battled with the dragon, and the dragon fought and his angels. And they did not prevail, neither was their place found any more in heaven. And that great dragon was cast down, the ancient serpent, he who is called the devil and Satan, who leads astray the whole world; and he was cast down to the earth and with him his angels were cast down.

12. *fé = fece.   strupo = stupro* (by metathesis), from the Latin *stuprum*, meaning "defilement," "dishonor," "disgrace." (The form *strupum* is frequent in medieval Latin.) Here, given the context, the meaning of "violence" or "rebellion" is uppermost. (See E. G. Parodi, 1911a, p. 69; 1957, pp. 242–43, 347.)

14. *fiacca = si fiacca.* See E. G. Parodi (1957), p. 280.

16. *lacca*: Dante will use the term twice again in the poem (*Inf.* XII, 11; *Purg.* VII, 71) and with much the same meaning of "slope" or "hollow."

19. *stipa*: "Piles in," phrasing in another way the "insacca" of the preceding verse.

20. *viddi = vidi*. The form was common in early Italian; see E. G. Parodi (1957), p. 259.

21. *scipa*: "Spoils"; see *Inf.* XXIV, 84.

22. *l'onda là sovra Cariddi*: Charybdis, the famous whirl-pool in the Strait of Messina, was regarded by navigators as peculiarly dangerous because in their endeavor to avoid it they risked being wrecked upon Scylla, a rock on the Italian coast. Homer described the spot in the *Odyssey* (see XII, 85–110, 235–59), but more important for Dante is Virgil's description in *Aen.* III, 420–23:

> dextrum Scylla latus, laevum implacata Charybdis
> obsidet, atque imo barathri ter gurgite vastos
> sorbet in abruptum fluctus rursusque sub auras
> erigit alternos, et sidera verberat unda.

Scylla guards the right side; Charybdis, insatiate, the left; and at the bottom of her seething chasm thrice she sucks the vast waves into the abyss, and again in turn casts them upwards, lashing the stars with spray.

On the "warring winds" (see *Inf.* V, 30) that produce the clash of waves in the strait, Pietro di Dante comments:

> [Comparat] eorum percussiones illi brachio maris quod dividit Calabriam a Sicilia, ubi perpetuo undae impulsae ab Euro orientali, et ubi impulsae a ventis occidentalibus se invicem percutiunt, juxta illud: *dextrum Scylla latus, laevum implicata* [sic] *Charybdis.*

[The author compares] their reciprocal blows to that arm of the sea which divides Calabria from Sicily, where the waves driven by the east wind and those driven by the west wind constantly strike each other, according to the verse that reads: *Scylla [guards] the right side; snakelike Charybdis, the left.*

See also *Aen.* III, 558–59; VII, 302; Ovid, *Metam.* VII, 63–65; Lucan, *Phars.* IV, 459–61.

24. *riddi*: The verb *riddare* is based on the noun *ridda*, a round dance performed by a group. There is a derisive note in the use of such a term for the eternal clash, the "joust" (vs. 35), of these souls.

25. *più ch'altrove troppa*: "Far more numerous than elsewhere." See *Aen.* VI, 611: "quae maxima turba est" ("the largest number this"), said of those (vs. 610) "qui divitiis soli incubuere repertis" ("who brooded in solitude over wealth they had won").

27. *voltando pesi*: See *Aen.* VI, 616: "Saxum ingens volvunt alii." ("Some roll a huge stone.")

28. *Percoteansi 'ncontro = si percotevano incontro.   pur lì*: This odd rhyme is one of the several harsh and clucking forms the poet introduces into this canto to express the eternal clash of the two groups.

30. *tieni*: "Grasp," as in the common expression *tener il denaro* ("to grasp money"); also see vs. 58, "Mal dare e mal tener."   *burli*: From *burlare*, "to throw away"; cf. the Provençal *burlar* in this meaning. See E. G. Parodi (1957), pp. 278, 347-48, for examples of this usage in early Italian.

37. *mi dimostra = dimostrami.*

38. *fuor = furono*, as again in vss. 40 and 46.   *cherci = chierici.*

39. *chercuti = chiericuti.   a la sinistra nostra*: These, as explained in vss. 46-48, are the avaricious; they are on the left to indicate that avarice is a worse sin than prodigality. Benvenuto, alluding to Aristotle, comments: "Et avaricia est magis insanabilis et plus nocet . . . probat philosophus Libro Ethicorum." ("And avarice is more incurable and more damaging . . . as the Philosopher proves in his Book of Ethics.")

42. *spendio* (pronounced *spèndio*) = *spesa*. The sinfulness is expressed in terms of dispensing riches. See Thomas Aquinas (*Summa theol.* II-II, q. 119, a. 1, ad 1): "Ille qui

superabundat in dando, vocatur *prodigus*; qui autem deficit
in dando, vocatur *avarus*." ("He who exceeds in giving is
said to be *prodigal*, while he who is deficient in giving is
said to be *covetous*.")   *ferci = ci fecero*.

51. *furo = furono*.

53. *i = li*.

57. *col pugno chiuso*: "Tight-fisted."   *coi crin mozzi*:
"Cropped hair" as a symbol of wasting one's substance—as
the prodigal does—is brought out again in *Purg*. XXII, 46.

58-59. *Mal dare e mal tener . . . ha tolto*: Again, a com-
pound subject governs a singular verb.

58. *lo mondo pulcro*: "Heaven" (in this construction, the
direct object).

60. *appulcro*: "Adorn," "make pretty," "embellish"; the
verb may have been coined by Dante, perhaps on the model
of *abbello, abbellare*.

61. *buffa*: A synonym of *beffa* and cognate of *buffo, buffone*
(see E. G. Parodi, 1957, p. 278).

62. *d'i = dei*.

63. *si rabuffa = si rabbuffa*. Parodi (1957, p. 275) calls at-
tention to verses (credited to Jacopone da Todi but pos-
sibly apocryphal) in which the expression is found in much
the same sense: "In Jacopone, in the canticle *Udite nova
pazzia* ['Harken to this new madness'], we read, in the old
editions, vss. 4 ff.: 'This world is a swindle, and everyone in
it squabbles' ('Questo mondo è una truffa,—dove ogni homo
se rabuffa')."

64. *tutto l'oro ch'è sotto la luna*: The whole sublunar world
is Fortune's realm. See also *Inf*. II, 61 and the note.

66. *non poterebbe farne posare una*: This is said particu-
larly of the souls of the avaricious and applies to them as if
they were still among the living. On man's thirst for riches,
see *Conv*. IV, xii, 2-10. See also Eccles. 5:9[10]: "Avarus

non implebitur pecunia." ("The covetous man is never satisfied with money.")

68. *tocche = tocchi.*

69. *branche*: "Claws," here in a strongly pejorative sense, as if Dante were indulging in the common complaint against Fortune. This prompts Virgil's "Oh creature sciocche" in the following verse, addressed to all men who make such complaint.

72. *ne 'mbocche = ne imbocchi*, "take into the mouth," "swallow," as a spoon-fed child might do. The use of the term here continues Virgil's pitying tone.

74. *fece li cieli e diè lor chi conduce*: See *Conv.* II, iv, 2: "È adunque da sapere primamente che li movitori di quelli [cieli] sono sustanze separate da materia, cioè intelligenze, le quali la volgare gente chiamano Angeli." ("Be it known, therefore, firstly, that the movers [of the heavens] are substances sejunct from matter, to wit, Intelligences, which are vulgarly called Angels.") In the course of the poem, particularly in the *Paradiso*, the reader will hear much about these Intelligences, who preside over the revolving heavens and actually turn the heaven assigned to them. Similarly, Fortune turns her own sphere—that of "worldly splendors" (vs. 77). *diè = diede.*

78. *ministra*: See *Purg.* XXX, 18, where angels are called "ministri . . . di vita etterna." In applying the term to Fortune here in *Inf.* VII, the poet is already beginning to represent Lady Fortune as an angelic creature or Intelligence assigned to a sphere.

80. *di gente in gente*: Gmelin notes that Thomas Aquinas (*Summa contra Gentiles* III, 80), in treating of angels or Intelligences, says of the order known as *Principati*: "Et sic dispositio regnorum et mutatio dominationis de gente in gentem ad ministerium huius ordinis pertinere oportet." ("And so, the arrangement of kingdoms and the changing of domination from one people to another ought to belong to the ministry of this order.")

81. *oltre la difension d'i senni umani*: Vs. 85 serves as a gloss to this verse. Also see Boethius, *Consol. philos.* II, i, ll. 59–62: "Tu vero voluentis rotae impetum retinere conaris? At, omnium mortalium stolidissime, si manere incipit, fors esse desistit." ("Endeavourest thou to stay the force of the turning wheel? But thou foolishest man that ever was, if it beginneth to stay, it ceaseth to be fortune.")

d'i = dei.

84. *occulto come in erba l'angue*: See Virgil, *Eclog.* III, 93: "Latet anguis in herba." ("A snake lurks in the grass.")

85. *contasto = contrasto*, i.e., "power to withstand."

86. *provede = prevede.*

87. *li altri dèi*: The Intelligences commonly referred to as gods and goddesses. See *Conv.* II, iv, 4–6 (which follows the passage cited above in n. to vs. 74):

> Altri furono, sì come Plato, uomo eccellentissimo, che puosero non solamente tante Intelligenze quanti sono li movimenti del cielo, ma eziandio quante sono le spezie de le cose . . . . E volsero che sì come le Intelligenze de li cieli sono generatrici di quelli, ciascuna del suo, così queste fossero generatrici de l'altre cose ed essempli, ciascuna de la sua spezie; e chiamale Plato "idee," che tanto è a dire quanto forme e nature universali. Li gentili le chiamano Dei e Dee.

> Others were there such as Plato, a man of supreme excellence, who laid down not only as many Intelligences as there are movements of heaven, but just as many as there are kinds of things . . . . And they would have it that as the Intelligences of the heavens are the generators of the same, each of his own, so those others were the generators of the other things, and the exemplars each one of his own kind; and Plato calls them Ideas, which is as much as to say Forms, and Universals. The Gentiles called them gods and goddesses.

See also "l'altre dee" in *Par.* XXVIII, 121, and the description of the "three divinities" that follows.

90. *sì spesso vien chi vicenda consegue*: The turning of Fortune's wheel is implicit in the phraseology, "vicenda" meaning a "change" or "turn."

92. *dovrien = dovrebbero*.

94. *ma ella s'è beata*: The reflexive pronoun in this usage often is called pleonastic or redundant, but it is far from that, for it serves to set apart or "distance" the subject. In fact, this verse is an excellent example of the reflexive used in this "distancing" function, since it refers to the goddess Fortune as transcending men and their purposes and turning her sphere blissfully so far beyond their reach. See vs. 96 for another example of this same so-called "pleonastic" reflexive: "e beata si gode."

97. *a maggior pieta*: See *Inf.* I, 21.

98–99. *già ogne stella cade . . . mi mossi*: It is now a little after midnight; the stars, which were rising when Virgil set out (see *Inf.* II, 141) at sunset, are beginning to decline. On this and other time references, see E. Moore (1887); on these verses, see his p. 42.

101. *una fonte*: This spring, mysterious and nameless, is not mentioned again in the poem. When it is explained, however, that bodies of water such as Acheron and Styx (which are circular, covering a whole level of Hell) are all connected, this spring or fountain and the channel leading from it take on significance as parts of what is sometimes referred to as the "hydraulic system" of Hell (see n. to *Inf.* XIV, 121–38).

103. *buia assai più che persa*: For the color "perse," see n. to *Inf.* V, 89. This means that the water from the spring is almost black.

106–7. *In la palude . . . questo tristo ruscel*: In classical mythology, Styx is one of the five rivers that surround Hades (see, for example, *Aen.* VI, 134, 323). / It is significant that this stream, flowing from the fountain into Styx, should be styled "tristo ruscel" in view of Servius' gloss on

Aen. VI, 134: "A tristitia Styx dicta est." ("The Styx is named from sadness.") This interpretation of Styx is repeated by Uguccione da Pisa (see P. Toynbee, 1902, p. 105) and by Boccaccio in his *Comento*: "Questo nome Stige è interpretato 'tristizia.'" ("The name Styx is interpreted to mean 'sadness.'")

108. *piagge*: *Piaggia* can mean "slope" or "shore," or the word may have both meanings at once, as here (see A. Schiaffini, 1937a; M. Barbi, 1934b, pp. 200–201). Also see *Inf.* I, 29.

109–16. *E io . . . l'ira*: The "muddy people" are the wrathful, as vs. 116 makes clear, and in this "second death" of Hell they continue to act the part as they assail and rend each other in their furious anger.

117–26. *e anche . . . integra*: The souls who are entirely submerged in the mire constitute a special problem. By their own declaration, they were "sullen" in life and harbored "a sluggish smoke" within themselves. Moreover, as vss. 125–26 declare, they can only "gurgle" their words and are unable to utter them with unbroken speech. As Gmelin and others point out, Thomas Aquinas (*Summa theol.* I-II, q. 35, a. 8, obj. 3) cites Gregory of Nyssa's view that "acedia est tristitia vocem amputans." ("Torpor is sorrow depriving of speech.") In the response of this same article, moreover, Aquinas comments:

> Si vero intantum procedat talis aggravatio, ut etiam exteriora membra immobilitet ab opere, quod pertinet ad *acediam*, sic erit extraneum quantum ad utrumque, quia nec est fuga, nec est in appetitu. Ideo autem specialiter *acedia* dicitur vocem amputare, quia vox inter omnes exteriores motus magis exprimit interiorem conceptum et affectum, non solum in hominibus, sed etiam in aliis animalibus, ut dicitur in 1 Politic.

> If, however, the mind be weighed down so much, that even the limbs become motionless, which belongs to *torpor*, then we have the foreign element affecting both, since there is neither flight, nor is the effect in the

appetite. And the reason why torpor especially is said
to deprive one of speech is because of all the external
movements the voice is the best expression of the in-
ward thought and desire, not only in men, but also in
other animals, as is stated in [Aristotle, *Polit.* I, 1,
1253ᵃ].

Aquinas also observes (*Summa theol.* I-II, q. 46, a. 8, resp.):
"Philosophus in 4 Ethic., cap. 5, quosdam irascentium vocat
acutos quia cito irascuntur; quosdam *amaros*, quia diu
retinent iram; quosdam *difficiles,* quia numquam quiescunt,
nisi puniant." ("Hence the Philosopher [in *Eth. Nicom.*
IV, 5, 1126ᵃ] calls some angry persons *choleric*, because they
are easily angered; some he calls *bitter*, because they retain
their anger for a long time; and some he calls *ill–tempered*,
because they never rest until they have retaliated.") These,
then, are the three classes of the wrathful: the choleric or
hot-tempered, the bitter or sullen, and the ill–tempered or
vengeful. In *Summa theol.* II-II, q. 158, a. 5, Aquinas
again discusses the three types, remarking (ad 2) on the
sullen: "Nam *amari* habent iram permanentem propter
permanentiam tristitiae, quam inter viscera tenent clausam"
("for a *sullen* person has an abiding anger on account of an
abiding displeasure, which he holds locked in his breast"),
whereas the *vindictive* harbor wrath because of their intense
desire for vengeance, "et ideo tempore non digeritur, sed
per solam punitionem quiescit" ("so that it does not wear
out with time, and can be quelled only by revenge"). In the
light of these categories, founded on the great authority of
Aristotle and undoubtedly known to Dante, it is now gen-
erally assumed that the wrathful who are not entirely sub-
merged are the hot-tempered (and perhaps the vengeful),
while the completely submerged are the sullen. On these
distinctions and Dante's moral system in general, see E.
Moore (1899), pp. 173–76; W.H.V. Reade (1909), pp.
398–403.

120. *u' che = ovunque.*

125. *Quest' inno si gorgoglian ne la strozza*: The derisive

tone evident here in both "inno" and "strozza" appears more frequently as the descent through Hell continues.

128. *mezzo*: "Soft," "wet"; also used to refer to fruit that is overripe and beginning to decay. The word here describes the wet, soft mire of Styx. *Mézzo* (closed "e") is distinguished, by the quality of the "e," from *mèzzo* (open "e"), meaning "middle" or "half"; see vs. 35.

CANTO VIII

1–2. *Io dico, seguitando . . . al piè de l'alta torre*: This is a unique canto beginning, for it retrogresses to take up the narrative before the point reached in the last verse of Canto VII. Benvenuto comments here that the poet "retrocedit ordine artificiali" ("turns back in an artificial order"). In fact, this beginning is so extraordinary that it seems to have inspired a legend—accepted by two of the early commentators, Boccaccio and the *Anonimo fiorentino*—that Dante composed the first seven cantos of the *Comedy* before his exile and left them behind in Florence, and then in 1306, when the cantos were sent to him at the Malaspina court in Lunigiana, took up the work where he had interrupted it and began Canto VIII with the phrase "Io dico, seguitando." H. Hauvette (1922, pp. 1–64) has defended the authenticity of the story, but his arguments are not persuasive and lack documentary support.

3. *n'andar = ne andarono*, "went thence," i.e., from the foot of the tower.

4–5. *due fiammette . . . cenno*: Setting lights as signals in towers (referred to as "cenni di castella" in *Inf.* XXII, 8) constituted a common practice in warfare at the time. Boccaccio comments:

Far si suole per le contrade nelle quali è guerra, che, avvenendo di notte alcuna novità, il castello o il luogo, vicino al quale la novità avviene, incontanente per un fuoco o per due . . . il fa manifesto a tutte le terre e ville del paese.

In regions where there is a war going on, it is customary, when something happens during the night, for the castle or the place near which the event happened, to make it known immediately by means of one signal fire or two . . . to all the towns and villages of the region.

4. *i* = *ivi*.

6. *tanto*: Modifies "da lungi" (vs. 5).   *a pena il potea l'occhio tòrre*: Vandelli compares Virgil's use of *capio* in the following expression in *Georg.* II, 230: "Locum capies oculis." ("You must look out a place.")

7. *al mar di tutto 'l senno*: See *Inf.* VII, 3: "quel savio gentil, che tutto seppe."

8–9. *Questo che dice . . . fenno?* The meaning of the fire signals may be surmised from what follows, but the wayfarer's last question remains unanswered.

9. *fenno* = *fecero*, "made" or set the signal of the answering fires.

11. *quello che s'aspetta*: "What is awaited," "what will come," which Virgil knows, who knows all.

13. *Corda non pinse mai da sé saetta*: The figure of the arrow sped from the bowcord gives us the boatman of Styx departing (from some unspecified place in the swamp). Then with "com' io vidi" (vs. 15) the point of view changes, and we see him speeding toward the wayfarer and his guide. For a similar change in point of view, see *Inf.* III, 115–17. For Virgil's use of the figure of the bow and arrow, see *Aen.* X, 247; XII, 855; *Georg.* IV, 313. Also see Ovid, *Metam.* VII, 776–78.

16. *in quella*: "In that instant," "at that moment."

17. *galeoto* = *galeotto*; on such changes between single and double consonants in early Italian, see E. G. Parodi (1957), pp. 235–41. / The "oarsman" of Styx, whom Virgil soon addresses by name (vs. 19), is Phlegyas. According to the ancient myths, Phlegyas was the son of Mars and Chryse. He was the father of Ixion and of Coronis, who was violated by Apollo and became the mother of Aesculapius. Phlegyas in fury set fire to the temple of Apollo at Delphi, and for this sacrilege was slain by the god and condemned to eternal punishment in Tartarus, the region in the lower world reserved for those who sin against the gods. See *Aen.* VI, 618–20:

> . . . Phlegyasque miserrimus omnis
> admonet et magna testatur voce per umbras:
> "discite iustitiam moniti et non temnere divos."

And Phlegyas, most unblest, gives warning to all and with loud voice bears witness amid the gloom: *Be warned; learn ye to be just and not to slight the gods!*

See also Statius, *Theb.* I, 712–15, where Phlegyas' eternal punishment is described:

> . . . ultrix tibi torva Megaera
> ieiunum Phlegyan subter cava saxa iacentem
> aeterno premit accubitu dapibusque profanis
> instimulat, sed mixta famem fastidia vincunt.

To avenge [Apollo] grim Megaera holds fast the starving Phlegyas, who lies ever pressed beneath the cavernous rocks, and tortures him with the unholy feast, but mingled loathing defeats his hunger.

Here in the *Inferno*, however, Phlegyas is made boatman of the fifth circle, the swamp of Styx, and guardian of the wrathful variously immersed there; he does not himself undergo punishment.

18. *Or se' giunta, anima fella!* The meaning of *giungere* here could be either "to arrive" or "to be seized," but the latter seems preferable in the context. (See M. Barbi, 1934b, p. 206, and cf. *Inf.* XXII, 126.) Phlegyas' cry, freely trans-

lated, is "I have you now!" The boatman, in his fury, seems unaware that not one but two—a soul and a living man—stand on the shore. If Phlegyas' angry cry is his customary form of greeting, we may surmise that he usually comes to seize each soul as it arrives here. Perhaps the signal of the two flames on the tower was meant to indicate something unusual: that two "souls" were standing on the shore instead of one. If so, Phlegyas evidently paid no attention to the signal.   *fella*: The adjective imputes malicious intent, as if Phlegyas expected to find the soul still wrathful and bent on vengeance.

19. *vòto* = *vuoto*. The literal meaning of the phrase is "emptily."

20. *a questa volta* = *per questa volta*.

21. *più non ci avrai che sol passando il loto*: The exact role of Phlegyas as "galeoto" is not clear, but the boatman's sense of deception upon hearing these words suggests that he usually comes in his boat to seize the soul and carry it to some point or other in the marsh, while wreaking his wrath upon it. Thus, the phrase "sol passando il loto" points to an exceptional assignment for him, and he is obliged to suppress his rage ("l'ira accolta," vs. 24) over this.   *il loto*: The muddy swamp of Styx.

23. *li* = *gli*.   *rammarca* = *rammarica*.

24. *fecesi* = *si fece*.

27. *sol quand' io fui dentro parve carca*: The boarding of the Stygian boat is described similarly in *Aen.* VI, 413–14: "Gemuit sub pondere cumba / sutilis et multam accepit rimosa paludem." ("The seamy craft groaned under [Aeneas'] weight, and through its chinks took in a marshy flood.")   *carca* = *carica*.

28. *'l duca e io nel legno fui*: Again, a singular verb with a plural subject.

30. *più che non suol con altrui*: The wayfarer, by the weight of his body, causes the craft to draw more water than usual

(literally, "more than with another"). "Altrui" may refer either to the souls usually taken into the boat by Phlegyas, or to Phlegyas himself. On the interpretation of the boatman's role here, see F. Mazzoni (1951), p. 286.

31. *corravam = correvamo*; cf. "leggiavamo" in *Inf.* V, 127.   *la morta gora*: Since the swamp now serves as a way of passage, it is called a stagnant "channel" or "slough."

32. *un pien di fango*: This is Filippo Argenti (see vs. 61), one of the Cavicciuli branch of the Adimari family of Florence. The early commentators say that Filippo got the nickname Argenti because he was wont to have his horse shod with silver. They also remark that he had a savage temper. Boccaccio, for example, comments:

> Fu questo Filippo Argenti . . . de' Cavicciuli, cavaliere ricchissimo, tanto che esso alcuna volta fece il cavallo, il quale usava di cavalcare, ferrare d'ariento, e da questo trasse il sopranome. Fu uomo di persona grande, bruno e nerboruto e di maravigliosa forza e, più che alcuno altro, iracundo, eziandio per qualunque menoma cagione.

> This Filippo Argenti was . . . of the Cavicciuli family. He was a very rich knight—so rich that he sometimes had his horse shod in silver, and hence the nickname. He was a large man, dark and muscular, and of prodigious strength. He was more irascible than any other man, even at the slightest provocation.

See *Decam.* IX, 8 (vol. II, pp. 220–23) for the story of Filippo's dealings with a certain Biondello, who at the instigation of Ciacco had ventured to trifle with him. According to this story, Filippo was Dante's contemporary, since he is represented as living in the time of Messer Vieri de' Cerchi.

33. *Chi se' tu che vieni anzi ora?* The words are an insult to the wayfarer, implying that he was so wicked in life that he has been dispatched to the swamp of the wrathful before his death.   *vieni*: In this word there seems to be further support of the view that Phlegyas' function is to

carry the wrathful soul to some point in the swamp and drop it there in the mire. Dante seizes upon the word and, in the next verse, throws it back at Filippo Argenti, even as he does with "piango" (see vss. 36, 37).

36. *Vedi che son un che piango*: The words, concealing the identity of the soul, have something of the tone, "Don't you see that I am one who suffers torment here? And isn't that enough?"

37–42. *Con piangere . . . cani*: The language grows more violent and reaches a climax with Virgil's "Away there, with the other dogs!"

38. *ti rimani*: An imperative: "Stay right where you are," i.e., "You suffer the punishment you deserve." / For the distancing effect of the pleonastic reflexive (in this verse, "ti"), see n. to *Inf.* VII, 94.

39. *ancor*: "Although."

40. *distese al legno ambo le mani*: The soul of Filippo Argenti tries to lay violent hands on the wayfarer. / The reader might pause to consider that the souls and other things in Hell are becoming more substantial, losing their "emptiness" (see n. to *Inf.* VI, 36).

42. *Via costà con li altri cani!* It is fitting that the souls of the wrathful should be called "dogs," since violent rage characterizes that animal. Thomas Aquinas, for example, remarks (*Summa theol.* I-II, q. 46, a. 5, ad 1) that animals "naturaliter disponuntur ad excessum alicuius passionis, ut leo ad audaciam, canis ad iram, lepus ad timorem, et sic de aliis" ("are naturally disposed to some excess of passion, such as the lion in daring, the dog in anger, the hare in fear, and so forth"). Also see Aquinas' statement in *De malo* q. 12, a. 1, obj. 2: "Praeterea, sicut Dionysius dicit (in 4 cap. de div. Nomin.), ira est naturalis cani, innaturalis autem homini." ("Besides, as Dionysius tells us in *De divinis nominibus*, chapter IV, anger is natural to a dog but unnatural in a man.")

44. *basciommi* = *baciommi*.

45. *benedetta colei che 'n te s'incinse*: Virgil's blessing—which echoes Luc. 11:27: "Beatus venter qui te portavit" ("Blessed is the womb that bore thee")—is a most solemn approval of the wayfarer's righteous indignation (*bona ira*). / For *incingersi in* in this sense, see Boccaccio's comment: "Cingonsi sopra noi le madri nostre nel mentre nel ventre ci portano." ("Our mothers gird themselves around us while they carry us in the womb.") See also the *Anonimo fiorentino*, who suggests the expression: "Ella è incinta in . . . ."

47. *fregi*: From *fregiare*, "to ornament."

48. *così s'è l'ombra sua qui furiosa*: "Si" is the pleonastic reflexive, distancing the subject—the shade of Filippo Argenti—and placing it in Styx as in its proper place.

49. *gran regi*: Meaning, figuratively, "great and important people."   *regi* = *re*.

53. *attuffare*: "To thrust under," "to dip."   *in questa broda*: "Broth," designating the mud of Styx, is obviously derisive and strikes a note that will become more familiar as the journey progresses through Hell.

55. *la proda*: The landing place.

57. *convien*: *Convenire* often expresses necessity, Heaven's Will, or what is otherwise destined or fated. Here the word apparently suggests the working of the Divine Will, since God is then praised for the satisfaction of the wayfarer's desire.

59. *a le* = *da le*.

61. *A Filippo Argenti!* "Have at him! Let's get Filippo Argenti!"

62. *bizzarro*: Boccaccio comments on the connotations of the word:

Credo questo vocabolo "bizzarro" sia solo de' fioren-
tini, e suona sempre in mala parte; perciochè noi te-
gnamo bizzarri coloro che subitamente e per ogni piccola
cagione corrono in ira, nè mai da quella per alcuna
dimostrazione rimuover si possono.

I believe this word *bizzarro* is uniquely Florentine, and
is always used in a pejorative sense. We call those
people *bizzarri* who are quickly angered, even for the
slightest reason, and cannot be persuaded to calm down.

63. *in sé medesmo si volvea co' denti*: A typical gesture of
the wrathful. Rage drives the Minotaur in *Inf.* XII, 14-15,
to bite himself, and Minos in *Inf.* XXVII, 124-26, to gnaw
his own tail. See also Giotto's conception of *Ira* (Plate 6,
facing p. 502).

65-66. *mi percosse . . . sbarro*: Dante frequently shifts from
the past absolute to the present in the same sentence.

65. *un duolo*: The wailing comes from the whole city of
Dis, or lower Hell, and contrasts with the strange silence
of the irascible in the swamp; for the souls of the hot-
tempered (the *acuti*) are not said to utter any sound as they
rend each other, and the sullen (the *amari*) cannot be heard
—except by Virgil "who knows all." (On the wrathful and
the sullen, and their lack of speech, see n. to *Inf.* VII,
117-26.)

66. *l'occhio . . . sbarro*: Literally, "I unbar my eye."

68. *la città c'ha nome Dite*: Dis was the name given by the
Romans to Pluto, god of the netherworld; see, for ex-
ample, *Aen.* VI, 127, "atri ianua Ditis" ("the door of gloomy
Dis"), and *Aen.* VI, 541, "Ditis magni sub moenia" ("under
the walls of great Dis"). "Dite" is one of the names of
Satan in the *Commedia*, but here it is assigned to the city
which looms in the distance with its fiery ramparts. These
walls of Dis are the outermost line of fortification and
defense, now that the portal to Hell is broken down and
remains perpetually unbarred (vss. 125-26). / On the name
of the city, see Augustine's discussion of a *civitas diaboli* in
Enar. in Ps. IX, 8.

69. *gravi cittadin*: The sinners of lower Hell (vs. 75).

grande stuolo: The demons, Satan's band, who have re-treated within the fortified city of Dis and have thrown up their defenses there.

70. *le sue meschite*: "Mosques," as if Dis were a city of Saracens or Turks—that is, of Moslems and treacherous infidels.

71. *la valle*: The land glimpsed ahead, distinct from the swamp itself, but apparently on equally low ground.

73. *Il foco etterno*: This is not merely a figure of speech, since there actually are flames and fires just within the city's walls (see *Inf.* IX, 118–19).

75. *basso inferno*: Lower Hell, as the poem will make clear later on. For a similar use of terms, see Ps. 85[86]:13: "Et eruisti animam meam ex inferno inferiori." ("And thou hast delivered my soul out of the lower Hell.")

76. *Noi pur giugnemmo*: "Pur" stresses the notion of pro-ceeding onward.

77. *vallan*: The verb is based on "vallo," a rampart or barri-cade.   *terra*: "City."

78. *le mura mi parean che ferro fosse*: The verb "fosse" agrees with the singular predicate nominative "ferro." / See *Aen.* VI, 554: "Stat ferrea turris ad auras." ("There stands the iron tower, soaring high.") Indeed, the city that the wayfarer now makes out in the distance is strongly reminis-cent of Tartarus and its castle as seen by Aeneas (*Aen.* VI, 548–50):

> Respicit Aeneas subito et sub rupe sinistra
> moenia lata videt, triplici circumdata muro,
> quae rapidus flammis ambit torrentibus amnis . . .

> Suddenly Aeneas looks back, and under a cliff on the left sees a broad castle, girt with triple wall and en-circled with a rushing flood of torrent flames.

See also *Aen.* VI, 630–31: "Cyclopum educta caminis / moenia" ("the ramparts reared by Cyclopean forges").

79. *grande aggirata*: The defenses of the moats apparently make this circuitous approach necessary.

80. *forte*: Phlegyas shouts in rage.

81. *"Usciteci," gridò*: G. Vandelli (1921a) defended this reading against the alternative " 'Uscite' ci gridò," and Petrocchi agrees. For *ci* meaning *di qui*, see *Inf.* IV, 49 and 55.

83. *da ciel*: With certain nouns, the definite article often is omitted in early Italian. *piovuti*: See Luc. 10:18: "Videbam Satanam sicut fulgur de caelo cadentem" ("I was watching Satan fall as lightning from heaven"), and Apoc. 12:9: "Et proiectus est in terram, et angeli eius cum illo missi sunt" ("And he was cast down to the earth and with him his angels were cast down").

87. *lor parlar segretamente*: The leader's advancing alone to parley secretly with the citizens of the besieged city continues the military aspect of the whole episode.

88. *chiusero*: "Put down," "repressed."

90. *sì ardito*: But the reader will recall how timid the wayfarer was at the start, when he said to his guide (*Inf.* II, 35): "Temo che la venuta non sia folle," words which seem to find an echo here in "la folle strada" (vs. 91).

91. *si ritorni*: "Si" is a pleonastic reflexive here (see n. to *Inf.* VII, 94).

93. *li = gli. iscorta = scorta*, past participle of *scorgere*, "to guide." *contrada*: The term is applied to the "regions" or "country" around a fortified town or castle (see, for example, Boccaccio's usage in the passage quoted above in n. to vss. 4–5); hence it is most appropriately used here before the walls of Dis.

94. *Pensa, lettor*: The poet invites the readers to put themselves in his place at that moment.

96. *ritornarci*: The particle *ci* ("here") refers to the world of the living, where the poet is as he writes his poem.

97–98. *più di sette volte*: Seven is used here as an indefinite number, as frequently in the Bible. See, for example, Prov. 24:16: "Septies enim cadet iustus et resurget; impii autem corruent in malum." ("For the just man falls seven times and rises again, but the wicked stumble to ruin.")

102. *ratto = rapido* (here used adverbially).

105. *da tal*: By God, as Beatrice explained in Limbo.

108. *nel mondo basso*: Again there is the suggestion that the two travelers now have reached lower Hell.

111. *sì e no nel capo mi tenciona*: "Yes and no" with respect both to the success of Virgil's parley and to the wayfarer's own chances of returning to the world above without his guide.   *tenciona = tenzona*.

112. *potti = potei*.   *quello ch'a lor porse*: What Virgil proposed to the demons.

114. *a pruova*: *A gara*, vying with each other in their haste to run back into the city.

117. *rivolsesi = si rivolse*.

118–19. *le ciglia avea rase d'ogne baldanza*: This was an established phrase. (*Rase* is the past participle of *radere*.)

120. *Chi m'ha negate*: This is more of an exclamation than a question.   *le dolenti case*: Cf. the "tristis domos" ("sad dwellings") of *Aen.* VI, 534.

121. *perch'*: "Although."

123. *qual ch'a la difension dentro s'aggiri*: Freely translated, "regardless of the defense that may be made within." However, "qual" may be a personal pronoun in this construction, in which case the meaning would be "no matter who sets up the defense within."

124–26. *Questa lor tracotanza . . . ancor si trova*: Christ broke down the first and outer portal of Hell when He came to Limbo (see *Inf.* IV, 52–63), for Satan and his band tried to oppose Him at the outer entrance. That "less hidden gate" was never bolted again and is always open.

See Ps. 106[107]:16: "Contrivit portas aereas, et vectes ferreos confregit" ("He shattered the gates of brass and burst the bars of iron"), and Matins of the Office of Holy Saturday: "Hodie portas mortis et seras pariter Salvator noster disrupit" ("Today our Saviour shattered the gates and likewise the bolts of death"). See also Matt. 16:18:

> Et ego dico tibi, quia tu es Petrus, et super hanc petram aedificabo Ecclesiam meam, et portae inferi non praevalebunt adversus eam.

> And I say to thee, thou art Peter, and upon this rock I will build my Church, and the gates of hell shall not prevail against it.

The open door to Hell also figures in *Aen.* VI, 127: "Noctes atque dies patet atri ianua Ditis." ("Night and day the door of gloomy Dis stands open.")

125. *usaro = usarono.*

127. *vedestù = vedesti tu.*   *la scritta morta*: The inscription over the portal of Hell (*Inf.* III, 1–9), "dead" because it is over the door to the world of the dead and to the "second death" (*Inf.* I, 117).

128. *di qua da*: "This side of." Virgil knows that the one who is to come has already entered through the portal ("lei").   *l'erta*: The slope of Hell.

130. *tal*: "Such a one."   *ne = ci.*   *fia = sarà.*   *terra*: "City," as in vs. 77.

CANTO IX

1-3. *Quel color che viltà . . . ristrinse*: The wayfarer is again seized by cowardice (see *Inf*. II, 45: "viltade") and his pallor shows it. Seeing this, Virgil represses "his own new color"— a flush of vexation and anger (*Inf*. VIII, 121)—in order not to cause his follower greater dismay.

1. *di fuor*: "On my face."   *pinse = spinse*.

3. *il suo novo*: *Colore* is understood.

4-9. *Attento si fermò . . . giunga*: Virgil has his own moment of misgiving, as he listens intently, anxiously awaiting the one who is to open the city for them.

5. *a lunga*: For the adverbial phrase "a lunga," see E. G. Parodi (1957), p. 262.

7. *Pur a noi converrà*: "Yet it behooves us."   *punga = pugna*. See E. G. Parodi (1957), pp. 231, 348.

8. *Tal ne s'offerse*: "Such did she [Beatrice] offer herself to us"—when she came to Limbo and sent Virgil to guide the wayfarer on this journey which is vouchsafed from Heaven. Virgil's confidence in the successful accomplishment of the journey through Hell has found its expression repeatedly in

some variation of the formula "vuolsi così colà dove si puote ciò che si vuole" (see *Inf.* III, 95–96; V, 23–24: VII, 11-12).

9. *altri*: The one ("tal," *Inf.* VIII, 130) who is expected.

12. *fur = furono*.

13. *dienne = ne diede*, literally, "gave to us," but meaning "gave to me," as is evident from the context. The "ne" in Virgil's words "Tal ne s'offerse" (vs. 8) has the same meaning.

14. *la parola*: "Discourse," "words."

16–18. *In questo fondo . . . cionca?* The pilgrim's circumspect question refers to all the souls in Limbo.

17. *primo grado*: Limbo.

18. *che sol per pena ha la speranza cionca*: Cf. *Inf.* IV, 41–42: "We are lost, and only so far afflicted that, without hope, we live in longing." *cionca = cioncata*, past participle of *cioncare*, "to cut off."

20. *incontra*: Present indicative of *incontrare*, "to occur."

21. *per qual = per il quale*.

22. *Ver = vero.*   *Ver è ch'*: In its particular context, the phrase has the value of "however."

23. *Eritón*: Erichtho, a Thessalian sorceress, who, according to Lucan (*Phars.* VI, 507–830), was employed by Pompey's son Sextus to conjure up the spirit of one of his dead soldiers on the eve of the battle of Pharsalia, so that he could learn what was to be the outcome of the campaign. The story Dante tells about Erichtho's sending Virgil into the nethermost Hell is of unknown authority. It probably was suggested to Dante by one of the numerous legends associated with Virgil in the Middle Ages, when the Roman poet was universally regarded as a magician. Boccaccio, for instance, in his comment on *Inf.* I, 71, calls Virgil "solennissimo astrolago" ("a very great astrologer") and gives a list of his wonderful performances. (On this aspect of Virgil's

reputation in the Middle Ages, see D. Comparetti, 1955, pp. 266–67; also see E. Moore, 1896, pp. 234–37.) Referring specifically to Dante's story about Erichtho and Virgil, Boccaccio admits in his *Comento* that he cannot "recall ever having read or heard just what this story was." Benvenuto was of the opinion that Dante invented the tale: "Ista est simpliciter fictio nova." ("This is simply a new fiction.") But the "fiction" is, in a sense, not so new: the Sibyl who guided Aeneas through the nether regions declared that she had been there once before and had seen all (*Aen.* VI, 562–65).   *cruda*: Lucan calls the sorceress "effera" (fierce) and "tristis" (cruel) in *Phars.* VI, 508, 640.

24. *sui = suoi*. Such forms of the possessive pronoun (see "noi," vs. 20) are common in early Italian prose as well as verse.

29. *dal ciel che tutto gira*: This can mean the Primum Mobile, outermost of the nine revolving heavens, which, as its name implies, does turn ("gira") all the other spheres ("tutto"); or it can designate the Empyrean, which neither revolves nor turns the other heavens in any physical sense, but does "encircle" or enclose them (see Fig. 1, p. 34). The Empyrean seems the more appropriate meaning here, since it is the tenth sphere and as such is most remote from Hell. In this antithetical sense, the circle in Hell that is farthest from Heaven would contain the greatest evil and the worst sinners, as indeed Judecca (*Inf.* XXXIV, 117), the "circle of Judas," will be seen to do. Thus, Virgil not only has journeyed to Hell before but has journeyed to the very bottom of Hell, and therefore qualifies as an experienced guide through the whole nether region.

30. *però = per ciò*.   *ti fa = fatti*, an imperative.

32. *la città dolente*: The whole city of Dis, the entire area of lower Hell (see Fig. 4, p. 44).

33. *u' = ove* (see *Inf.* II, 24).   *potemo = possiamo*.

37. *furon dritte = furon diritte*. Thus, they are already risen when the wayfarer sees them.

38–48. *tre furie infernal . . . nel mezzo*: The Furies, also
known as the Erinyes or Eumenides, were represented as
the daughters of Earth or of Night, dwelling in the depths
of the nether regions and dreaded alike by gods and men.
Dante's description of them is traditional and could be
derived from such writers as Virgil, Ovid, or Statius. See,
for example, *Aen.* VI, 555–56, 570–72; VII, 324–29; XII,
845–48; Ovid, *Metam.* IV, 451–54, 481–96. See especially
Statius' description of Tisiphone in *Theb.* I, 103–7, 112–16:

> centum illi stantes umbrabant ora cerastae,
> turba minax diri capitis; sedet intus abactis
> ferrea lux oculis, qualis per nubila Phoebes
> Atracia rubet arte labor; suffusa veneno
> tenditur ac sanie gliscit cutis; . . .
> tunc geminas quatit ira manus: haec igne rogali
> fulgurat, haec vivo manus aera verberat hydro.
>
> Ut stetit, abrupta qua plurimus arce Cithaeron
> occurrit caelo, fera sibila crine virenti
> congeminat . . .

A hundred horned snakes erect shaded her face, the
thronging terror of her awful head; deep within her
sunken eyes there glows a light of iron hue, as when
Atracian spells make travailing Phoebe redden through
the clouds; suffused with venom, her skin distends and
swells with corruption. . . . Then both her hands are
shaken in wrath, the one gleaming with a funeral torch,
the other lashing the air with a live water-snake.

She halted, where the sheer heights of vast Cithaeron
rise to meet the sky, and sent forth from her green locks
fierce repeated hisses . . . .

38. *di sangue tinte*: See Virgil's description of Tisiphone,
guardian of the infernal gates, in *Aen.* VI, 555–56: "Ti-
siphoneque sedens, palla succincta cruenta, / vestibulum
exsomnis servat noctesque diesque." ("And Tisiphone, sitting
girt with bloody pall, keeps sleepless watch o'er the portal
night and day.")

39. *avieno* (pronounced *avìeno*) = *avevano*. The form is
repeated in vs. 41.

40. *con idre*: The hydra, according to Pliny (*Nat. hist.* XXIX, xxii, 72), is one of the most poisonous of all snakes.

41. *ceraste*: Cerastes, horned snakes. Boccaccio comments: "E sono 'ceraste' una spezie di serpenti, li quali hanno o uno o due cornicelli in capo." ("*Ceraste* is a species of snake that has one or two little horns on its head.")

43. *meschine*: Servants or "handmaids" (from Arabic *meskin*, meaning "poor one"). See Boccaccio's *Comento*: " 'le meschine,' cioè le damigelle" (" 'the *meschine*,' that is, the handmaids").

44. *la regina de l'etterno pianto*: This is Hecate or Persephone, also known as Proserpina, the wife of Pluto, king of the netherworld. See *Aen.* IV, 609–10, where the Furies are named in the company of Hecate.

46. *Megera*: Megaera, according to Servius (on *Aen.* VI, 575), sits at the door of Dis.

47. *quella che piange dal destro è Aletto*: See *Aen.* VII, 324, where Virgil describes Alecto as *luctifica* ("baleful").

48. *Tesifón è nel mezzo*: See *Aen.* X, 761: "Pallida Tisiphone media inter milia saevit." ("Pale Tisiphone rages amid the thousands of men.")

50. *battiensi* (pronounced *battìensi*) = *si battevano*.   *a palme* = *con le palme*. *Battersi a palme* was a standing expression, referring to this common mourning gesture of the time; see M. Barbi (1934b), p. 267. On the "suon di man" of *Inf.* III, 27, Boccaccio comments: "come soglion far le femmine battendosi a palme" ("as women are wont to do, beating themselves with their palms").

52. *Medusa*: Youngest of the three sisters known as the Gorgons, Medusa alone was mortal and was at first a beautiful girl. According to Ovid (*Metam.* IV, 794–803), after she was ravished by Neptune in one of Minerva's temples, her hair was changed into serpents by the goddess. This gave Medusa's head so fearful an appearance that everyone who looked upon it was changed to stone.   *smalto*: Lit-

erally, "mortar," "cement," made of sand and slaked lime, thus referring to a stone that is indeed "made." Buti comments: "Lo smalto è pietra: però che di pietra si fa." ("*Smalto* is stone, since it is made from stone.")

54. *mal non vengiammo in Teseo l'assalto*: Theseus, legendary hero of Athens, accompanied by his friend Pirithoüs descended to the underworld and tried unsuccessfully to abduct Proserpina, Pluto's queen. According to the version of the story accepted by Dante, Pirithoüs and Theseus were kept prisoners in Hell until Theseus alone was released through the efforts of Hercules. Both Virgil and Statius represent Theseus, however, as a prisoner in the infernal regions to eternity; see *Aen.* VI, 617–18 and *Theb.* VIII, 52–56. Also see *Aen.* VI, 391–97, where Charon mentions Theseus' crossing of Styx.   *vengiammo in = vengiammo contra*.   *Teseo*: Pronounced *Tèseo*.

56. *'l Gorgón*: The masculine form serves to indicate more precisely the head of the Gorgon Medusa, which Perseus had used as a weapon to turn adversaries to stone. See Ovid, *Metam.* V, 178–80.

58. *stessi = stesso*; see E. G. Parodi (1957), pp. 250–51.

60. *chiudessi = chiudesse*.

61. *'ntelletti sani*: See *Conv.* IV, xv, 10–11:

Dico adunque che, per quello che detto è, è manifesto a li sani intelletti che i detti di costoro sono vani, cioè sanza midolla di veritade. E dico sani non sanza cagione. Onde è da sapere che lo nostro intelletto si può dir sano e infermo.

I affirm, then, that it is plain to "sound intellects" by what has been said, that these utterances of theirs are vain, that is to say without the marrow of truth. And I say "sound" not without cause. Wherefore be it known that our intellect may be spoken of as sound or sick.

67-72. *non altrimenti fatto . . . li pastori*: For the simile of the wind, see *Aen.* II, 416-19:

> adversi rupto ceu quondam turbine venti
> confligunt, Zephyrusque Notusque et laetus Eois
> Eurus equis; stridunt silvae saevitque tridenti
> spumeus atque imo Nereus ciet aequora fundo.

> . . . even as at times, when a hurricane bursts forth, diverse winds clash, West and South and East, proud of his orient steeds; the forests groan and Nereus, steeped in foam, storms with his trident, and stirs the seas from their lowest depths.

Dante has introduced many new elements into the figure and has personified the wind in a new way.

68. *impetuoso per li avversi ardori*: The phrase "conflicting heats" has reference to accepted scientific opinion as to the cause of hurricanes. Landino comments:

> I venti son generati da vapori caldi, e secchi, e elevati dalla terra insino alla region dove consistono le nuvole, e quivi ripercossi da gli ardori superiori son spinti per lato, e ripercuotono l'aria, e la parte percossa ripercuote l'altra, e quell'altra di mano in mano; perchè il vento non è altro che aria ripercossa, e quanto gli ardori sono più adversi tanto il ve[n]to è più impetuoso.

> Winds are generated by hot and dry vapors, rising from the earth up to the region of the clouds. There they are struck by the superior heats and pushed sideways, whereupon they beat the air. The part [of the air] that is hit beats against the next, and that against the next, and so on. For wind is nothing but beaten air; and the more the heats are in conflict, the greater the impetus of the wind.

69. *fier = fiere (ferisce).*   *rattento = rattenimento.*

70. *fori = fuori*, "outside." The meaning here is "forth from the wood."

73-74. *il nerbo del viso*: Cf. the Latin *acies oculorum*.

75. *più acerbo*: Literally, the "bitterest," i.e., most offensive to the eyes.

76–78. *Come le rane . . . s'abbica*: See Ovid, *Metam.* VI, 370–81, a passage that Dante drew upon several times in the *Commedia*.

78. *s'abbica*: The verb is based on *bica*, a "shock" (or "cock"), and suggests sheaves of wheat or other grain stacked in the fields in a conical shape, to shed the rain and protect the grain. Accordingly, *abbicarsi* indicates the triangular outline of the frightened frog sitting motionless on the bottom, head erect. The figure could have been suggested by Ovid's description (*Metam.* VI, 379): "Turpe caput tendunt, colla intercepta videntur" ("They stretch their ugly heads, the necks seem to have disappeared"), but Dante's graphic image of the *bica* is strikingly his own.

83. *menando la sinistra*: The angel holds the "verghetta" (vs. 89) in his right hand.

85. *da ciel messo*: For the omission of the article with *cielo*, see *Inf.* VIII, 83 and the note. / "Messo" can be either the past participle of *mettere*, "to send," or the noun meaning "messenger," as angels were styled. See *Purg.* XV, 30.

86. *volsimi = mi volsi*.

89. *con una verghetta*: The little wand is carried as a scepter.

91. *dispetta*: On the use of this adjective in the sense of "despised," see E. G. Parodi (1957), p. 273.

93. *s'alletta*: See *Inf.* II, 122.

94. *Perché recalcitrate a quella voglia*: See Actus 9:5: "Durum est tibi contra stimulum calcitrare." ("It is hard for thee to kick against the goad.") This is repeated in Actus 26:14.

95. *mozzo = mozzato*, "cut off."

96. *più volte v'ha cresciuta doglia*: What these "several times" are we are not told, though the harrowing of Hell, when Satan and his band tried to oppose Christ at the main portal of Hell (see *Inf*. VIII, 125-26), surely is intended as one.

97. *Che giova ne le fata dar di cozzo?* "Le fata" (on the model of a Latin neuter plural) here, as elsewhere in a Christian context, must mean "that which is ordained by God." See Thomas Aquinas, *Summa contra Gentiles* III, 93.

98. *Cerbero vostro*: The last and most difficult of the twelve labors of Hercules was to bring Cerberus into the upper world, which he accomplished by putting a chain on the monster and hauling him forth (see *Aen*. VI, 391-97).

99. *pelato*: "Peeled," the hair being rubbed off by the chain. This touch is Dante's own.

102. *altra cura stringa e morda*: See *Aen*. VII, 402: "si iuris materni cura remordet" ("if care for a mother's rights stings [your souls]") and *Aen*. IX, 294: "atque animum patriae strinxit pietatis imago" ("and the picture of filial love touched his soul"). The angel's sole concern now is to return to Heaven.

105. *appresso = dopo*.

106. *li = vi*, the unemphatic adverb.   *'ntrammo = intrammo*.

112. *Sì come ad Arli*: The reference is to the famous Aliscamps, ancient Roman cemetery at Arles in Provence, near the place where the Rhone forms its delta ("stagna") before entering the Mediterranean Sea. Many sarcophagi are still to be seen there. (See Plate 3, facing p. 142, in which the exact type of tomb intended by Dante is shown; also see C. Cipolla, 1894, p. 409.)

113. *Pola*: A fortified seaport near the southern tip of the Istrian peninsula, Pola (now Pulj, Yugoslavia) is cele-

brated for its Roman remains. Of the sepulchers there Benvenuto says: "Iuxta Polam civitatem est etiam magna multitudo arcarum; audio quod sunt quasi septingentae numero, et fertur quod olim portabantur corpora de Sclavonia in Histria sepelienda ibi iuxta maritimam." ("Near the city of Pola there are a great number of tombs. I hear that they are almost seven hundred in number; and it is said that once bodies were conveyed from Slavonia to Istria, to be buried there by the sea.")   *Carnaro*: The Gulf of Quarnero (now Veliki Kvarner, Yugoslavia), at the head of the Adriatic Sea, on the eastern side of the Istrian peninsula.

115. *varo = vario*. The tombs variegate or diversify the terrain.

118. *tra li avelli fiamme erano sparte*: These flames or fires should be thought of as being outside the tombs and close to each of them, making them "red hot."

121. *sospesi*: Precisely what is intended by "suspended" here is not clear. Are the lids literally (and mysteriously) raised above each tomb, leaving it open, or are they laid back? They are open, no doubt, to admit the souls of heretics yet to come. But are they said to be "sospesi" to suggest that they are only temporarily open in this way and will be lowered upon the tombs, to close them, after the Judgment Day (*Inf.* X, 10–12)? A further reference ("già son levati / tutt' i coperchi," *Inf.* X, 8–9) does not help to clear up the matter, nor does *Inf.* X, 52.

127. *eresiarche*: Plural of *eresiarca*. On the use of this form, see E. G. Parodi (1957), p. 248.

129. *più che non credi*: The phrase implies what the reader already knows to be true: the wayfarer's thoughts can be read by his guide.

131. *più e men caldi*: The sepulchers vary in temperature according to the gravity of the sin involved in the several kinds of heresy punished in this circle.

3. The Aliscamps, the ancient Roman cemetery at Arles

132. *a la man destra si fu vòlto*: This turn to the right is more than a literary reminiscence (see *Aen.* VI, 540–42). It is particularly striking here because the two wayfarers have always turned to the left and—with a minor exception to be noted later and easily explained for literal reasons—will continue to do so. This unusual turn in Hell is thrown into sharper relief by the fact that through Purgatory the pilgrim and his guide always turn to the right as they climb. On a possible significance of this exceptional turn to the right here in the circle of heresy, see J. Freccero (1961a), p. 179:

> This apparent exception to Dante's rule will help in reality to prove it. Heresy, unlike all other sins in hell, attacks the True, and not the Good; which is to say, in the words of St. Thomas, that its *subiectum* is not *voluntas* but rather *intellectus*. Here is the only instance in Dante's moral system where an error of the speculative intellect is punished in hell, a fact which no pagan, neither Cicero, nor Aristotle, nor Virgil would have been able to understand. It is for this reason that the pilgrim must perform his retrograde movement to the right, in order to deal with an aberration of the intellect in the realm of perverted will.

CANTO X

1. *un secreto calle*: The path is recessed or withdrawn, since it passes between the walls and the tombs. "Secreto" may also indicate that the path is narrow, obliging the two wayfarers to go in single file. Cf. the "secreti calles" ("withdrawn walks") of *Aen.* IV, 405.

2. *martìri*: "Torments," as in *Inf.* IX, 133.

3. *dopo = dietro.*

4. *O virtù somma*: These words suggest Virgil's meaning in allegory: reason, the supreme virtue in human nature.

5. *mi volvi . . . com' a te piace*: The phrase further stresses Virgil's deliberate turn to the right (see *Inf.* IX, 132: "a la man destra si fu vòlto," and the note).

6. *sodisfammi a' miei disiri*: See the same construction in vs. 126. The indirect conjunctive pronoun is both a dative of person and a reinforcement of the possessive.   *miei disiri*: His hidden desire is to speak with Farinata, as is more clearly revealed in vs. 18 and what follows. Ciacco's assurance (*Inf.* VI, 85–87) that Farinata is indeed farther down in Hell, together with Farinata's apparent reputation as a heretic, might well lead the wayfarer to look for him here in this circle.

8. *potrebbesi = si potrebbe.*

9. *nessun guardia face*: The Furies and the devils all have disappeared, nor is there any guardian here like Cerberus or Plutus. *face = fa.*

11. *Iosafàt*: The Valley of Jehoshaphat, a common name for the Kidron valley, source of the stream that separates Jerusalem from the Mount of Olives. According to a tradition common both to Jews and Moslems, it is in this valley that the Last Judgment is to take place. See Ioel 3:2; also 3:12: "Consurgant et ascendant gentes in vallem Iosaphat, quia ibi sedebo ut iudicem omnes gentes in circuitu." ("Let them arise and let the nations come up into the valley of Josaphat: for there I will sit to judge all nations round about.") Also see Matt. 25:31–32. Thomas Aquinas (*Summa theol.* III, Suppl., q. 88, a. 4) cites Actus 1:11 to support a literal interpretation of Joel's words. Since Christ ascended from the Mount of Olives, which overlooks the Valley of Jehoshaphat, He will descend in the same place and there judge the world.

13. *Suo = loro.*

14–15. *Epicuro tutti suoi seguaci . . . fanno*: Epicurus, the famous philosopher, born *ca.* 342 B.C., died 270. The philosophical school named after him taught that pleasure, i.e., the absence of pain, is the highest good. See *Conv.* IV, vi, 11–12, where Dante summarizes Epicurean beliefs; also see Cicero, *De fin.* I, 9–11. In *Conv.* II, viii, 8, Dante strongly condemns disbelief in a future life:

> Dico che intra tutte le bestialitadi quella è stoltissima, vilissima e dannosissima, chi crede dopo questa vita non essere altra vita; però che, se noi rivolgiamo tutte le scritture, sì de' filosofi come de li altri savi scrittori, tutti concordano in questo, che in noi sia parte alcuna perpetuale.

> I say that of all stupidities that is the most foolish, the basest, and the most pernicious, which believes that after this life there is no other; for if we turn over all

the scriptures both of the philosophers and of the other sage writers, all agree in this that within us there is a certain part that endures.

Disbelief in this basic idea was traditionally characterized as Epicurean; it was also, of course, heretical. In the Christian view, then, Epicurus can be seen as an archheretic.

16. *Però* = *per ciò*, "hence."   *faci* = *fai.*

17. *satisfatto sarà*: An impersonal construction; Sapegno compares the Latin expression *satisfactum erit.*

18. *al disio ancor che tu mi taci*: Virgil can read the wayfarer's thoughts and knows his unexpressed desire to see Farinata (see n. to vs. 6).

20. *dicer* = *dire.*

21. *non pur mo*: "This is not the first time." See *Inf.* III, 76–78, and perhaps *Inf.* IX, 86–87.   *mo* (from Latin *modo*) = *ora.*

22. *Tosco*: The form, used frequently in the poem, means "toscano."   *città del foco*: The whole city of Dis, but more particularly this sixth circle of fiery tombs just inside the walls.

23. *parlando onesto*: Having overheard the wayfarer's courteous words to the guide, Farinata now speaks courteously himself: "piacciati di restare" (vs. 24).

24. *piacciati* = *ti piaccia.*

25. *La tua loquela ti fa manifesto*: Dante's speech is plainly Florentine. See Matt. 26:73: "Nam et loquela tua manifestum te facit." ("For even thy speech betrays thee.")

28. *uscìo* = *uscì.*

29. *però* = *per ciò*, "wherefore."

32. *Farinata*: This is the great Ghibelline leader of Florence —Manente, son of Jacopo degli Uberti. Known as Farinata, he was inquired about by the wayfarer previously (see *Inf.*

VI, 79) among the worthy Florentines. According to the early biographer Filippo Villani (*Le vite*, p. 50), Farinata was "di statura grande, faccia virile, membra forti, continenza grave, eleganza soldatesca, parlare civile, di consiglio sagacissimo, audace, pronto e industrioso in fatti d'arme" ("of large stature, virile countenance, strong limbs, grave bearing, military elegance, and civil speech; he was wise in counsel, and bold, ready, and able in feats of arms"). Farinata was born in Florence at the beginning of the thirteenth century, and as a boy witnessed the introduction into the city of the Guelph and Ghibelline factions. In 1239 he became the head of his house, the leading Ghibelline family, and in 1248 took a prominent part in the expulsion of the Guelphs. The Guelphs returned to Florence a few years later, and in 1258 expelled the Ghibellines. Farinata, by this time the acknowledged head of his party, took refuge with the rest of the Ghibelline exiles in Siena (for the account of a Florentine chronicler, see Villani, VI, 65). With the help of the Sienese and others, Farinata actively engaged in organizing measures which led to the crushing defeat of the Florentine Guelphs and their allies at Montaperti (September 4, 1260) and left the Ghibellines masters of Tuscany. After this victory the Ghibellines held a council at Empoli, about eighteen miles from Florence. According to Villani, VI, 82:

> Nel detto parlamento tutte le città vicine . . . e tutti i baroni d'intorno proposono e furono in concordia per lo migliore di parte ghibellina, di disfare al tutto la città di Firenze, e di recarla a borgora, acciocchè mai di suo stato non fosse rinomo, fama, nè podere. Alla quale proposta si levò e contradisse il valente e savio cavaliere messer Farinata degli Uberti . . . dicendo . . . com'era follia di ciò parlare, e come gran pericolo e danno ne potea avvenire, e s'altri ch'egli non fosse, mentre ch'egli avesse vita in corpo, colla spada in mano la difenderebbe. Veggendo ciò il conte Giordano, e l'uomo, e dell'autoritade ch'era messer Farinata, e il suo gran seguito, e come parte ghibellina se ne potea partire, e avere discordia, sì si rimase, e intesono ad

altro; sicchè per uno buono uomo cittadino scampò la nostra città di Firenze da tanta furia, distruggimento, ruina. Ma poi il detto popolo di Firenze ne fu ingrato, male conoscente contra il detto messer Farinata, e sua progenia e lignaggio.

At this meeting [at Empoli] all the nearby cities . . . and all the barons of the surrounding area proposed and agreed that, for the good of the Ghibelline faction, the city of Florence be completely destroyed, and reduced to the status of a village. No trace of the fame, reputation, and power of the former state was to survive. When this proposal was made, the valiant and wise knight, Messer Farinata degli Uberti, arose and opposed it . . . saying . . . that such talk was madness, and might well bring about great danger and harm. So long as there was life in his body, he said, he would defend the city with sword in hand, even if he had to do it alone. Count Giordano [Manfred's vicar-general in Tuscany] knew the sort of man Farinata was, and what authority and great following he enjoyed. Fearing that the Ghibelline faction might break up in discord, he gave in, whereupon another course was taken. And thus did a good citizen save our city of Florence from great fury, destruction, and ruin. But the people of Florence later proved to be ungrateful, bearing ill will toward Messer Farinata, his offspring, and his lineage.

After Montaperti and Empoli, Farinata returned to Florence, where he died in 1264 (see M. Barbi, 1924a, p. 89), the year before Dante's birth. In 1267, when an attempt was made to reconcile the two factions in Florence by means of matrimonial alliances, a daughter of Farinata was betrothed to the Guelph Guido Cavalcanti, and the marriage subsequently took place. The bitter and vindictive hatred toward Farinata remained, however; in 1283 he and his wife Adaleta were posthumously condemned as heretics by the inquisitor Fra Salomone of Lucca, and two surviving nephews were deprived of their inheritance (see N. Ottokar, 1921, pp. 159–63).

33. *da la cintola in sù*: This was a standing phrase in Dante's time; see M. Barbi (1924a), pp. 93–94.   *tutto 'l vedrai*: On the meaning of "tutto," see M. Barbi (1924a), pp. 92–93. The touch heightens the total effect of a towering Farinata.

34. *già*: Even before Virgil has finished urging him to turn and look, the wayfarer sees Farinata rising in his tomb.

36. *dispitto = dispetto (disprezzo)*. See *Inf.* IX, 91.

38. *pinser = spinsero.*

39. *conte*: For examples of the word meaning "appropriate," and therefore used in a sense different from that of *Inf.* III, 76, see E. G. Parodi (1957), p. 279. See also M. Barbi (1934b), p. 206.

41. *guardommi = mi guardò.*

42. *Chi fuor li maggior tui?* Since Farinata died just before Dante was born, he asks about the poet's ancestors—whom he could have known. Were they friends or foes of the Uberti?   *fuor = furono*.   *tui = tuoi*; see *Inf.* IX, 20, 24.

44. *non gliel celai, ma tutto gliel' apersi*: In the emphatic redundancy of this affirmation and in the use of the word "tutto," Dante's pride in his ancestry is unmistakable.

45. *ond' ei levò le ciglia un poco in suso*: Thereby showing even greater disdain.

46. *furo = furono*.   *avversi*: Dante's ancestors were Guelphs.

48. *due fiate*: The Guelphs were expelled from Florence for the first time in 1248 with the aid of the Emperor Frederick II, and again in 1260 following the battle of Montaperti.   *li dispersi*: The haughty leader of the Ghibellines makes the declaration in the first person as if, single-handed, he had driven from the city all the Guelphs, not Dante's ancestors alone.

49. *fur = furono.*   *tornar = tornarono.*   *d'ogne parte*: From the various places where they were living in exile.

50. *l'una e l'altra fiata*: The Guelphs returned first in 1251, after the defeat of the Ghibellines at Figline (see Villani, VI, 38), and again in 1266, after the defeat and death of Manfred at Benevento (see Villani, VII, 9, 14–15; Dino Compagni, I, 3, n. 2). The Ghibellines were not so "skilled"; after they were expelled in 1267, they never returned to Florence as a party, and in the peace of 1280 the most powerful Ghibelline families, among them the Uberti, were excluded from the terms of the agreement.

51. *i vostri*: The wayfarer addresses Farinata with the respectful *voi*.   *arte*: Clearly there is irony in the use of such a term in this context.

52–54. *Allor surse . . . in ginocchie levata*: Cavalcante appears on his knees and is visible only down to the chin as he peers over the edge of the tomb beside the towering Farinata. The scene exemplifies a familiar mode of medieval art, in which greater physical size signifies greater moral stature.

52. *la vista scoperchiata*: The uncovered opening of the tomb (all the lids are raised or laid back; see *Inf.* IX, 121). For "vista" in this meaning, see also *Purg.* X, 67.

53. *un'ombra*: This unnamed shade is the spirit of Guido Cavalcanti's father, Cavalcante de' Cavalcanti, on whom Boccaccio comments: "Fu . . . leggiadro e ricco cavaliere, e seguì l'opinion d'Epicuro in non credere che l'anima dopo la morte del corpo vivesse, e che il nostro sommo bene fosse ne' diletti carnali; e per questo, sì come eretico, è dannato." ("He was . . . a graceful and wealthy knight. He followed Epicurus in that he did not believe in the life of the soul after the death of the body, and in that he believed our highest good to consist in carnal pleasure. For these beliefs, he is damned as a heretic.") Benvenuto comments on the figure of Cavalcante as follows:

Iste omnino tenuit sectam epicureorum, semper credens, et suadens aliis, quod anima simul moreretur cum corpore; unde saepe habebat in ore istud dictum Salomonis: *Unus est interitus hominis et iumentorum, et aequa utriusque conditio*. . . . Iste cum audisset autorem conferentem multa cum Farinata de novitatibus Florentiae . . . surrexit statim libenter ad videndum autorem, qui ita mordaciter tangebat ghibelinos, quia ipse Cavalcante erat guelphus cum suis. . . . Et sic vide quod autor ponit duos epicureos simul de parte contraria, unum ghibelinum, alterum guelphum.

In all matters, he agreed with the Epicureans. He always believed and tried to persuade others that the soul dies simultaneously with the body. Wherefore he so often cited that saying of Solomon [Eccles. 3:19]: "The lot of man and beast is one, and their condition is the same." . . . When he heard [Dante] discussing at length with Farinata the recent events in Florence . . . he quickly and eagerly got up to see the author, who was just making a biting remark about the Ghibellines. Cavalcante himself was a Guelph, as was his family. . . . Observe, then, that the author places together two Epicureans of opposite parties, one a Ghibelline, the other a Guelph.

55. *talento*: "Desire," as in *Inf.* V, 39.

56. *altri*: The singular form, meaning "anyone."

57. *sospecciar*: "Surmise," hopeful at first, then disappointed.

58–59. *cieco carcere*: Hell might be so called by any of the damned, since they are forever imprisoned in its darkness. But when we learn (vss. 100–105) that these souls cannot see present things in the world above and that Cavalcante, therefore, cannot know that his son is alive, the phrase takes on special meaning. See *Aen.* VI, 733–34: "Hinc metuunt cupiuntque, dolent gaudentque, neque auras / dispiciunt clausae tenebris et carcere caeco." ("Hence their

fears and desires, their griefs and joys; nor discern they the
light, pent up in the gloom of their dark dungeon.")

60. *mio figlio*: Guido Cavalcanti, famous Florentine poet,
was born probably *ca.* 1255, but not later than 1259. In
1267, he was betrothed by his father to Beatrice degli Uberti,
daughter of Farinata (see Villani, VII, 15). His friendship
with Dante dates from 1283; the *Vita nuova* (see III, 14)
is dedicated to him as Dante's "first friend." He was an
ardent Guelph, and when the Guelph party in Florence
split into Bianchi and Neri factions, headed by the Cerchi
and the Donati respectively, Guido supported the Bianchi
and distinguished himself by his violent opposition to the
Donati. There were continued hostilities between the two
factions, and on June 24, 1300, the priors of Florence
decided to put an end to these disturbances. The leading
Neri were banished to Castel della Pieve in Perugia, and
the leading Bianchi, including Guido, were exiled to Sar-
zana in Lunigiana. Among those who approved this de-
cision were Dante in his capacity as prior (June–August)
and Dino Compagni, who, as he informs us in his *Cronica*
(see I, 21), belonged to the council: "I Signori, sdegnati,
ebbono consiglio da più cittadini, e io Dino fui uno di
quelli." ("The angered priors took counsel with many
citizens, and I, Dino, was one of them.")

It thus came about that Dante was instrumental in
sending his own friend into exile—and to his death, as it
proved, for though the exiles were soon recalled to Flor-
ence, Guido never recovered from the effects of the malari-
ous climate of Sarzana. He died shortly after his return
home, and was buried in the cemetery of the cathedral of
Santa Reparata (which was replaced by Santa Maria del
Fiore) on August 29, 1300, as is attested by an entry in the
church *Registro*, still preserved in Florence. Chronicling
Guido's exile and death, Villani says (VIII, 42):

Questa parte vi stette meno a' confini, che furono
revocati per lo infermo luogo, e tornonne malato Guido
Cavalcanti, onde morìo, e di lui fu grande dammaggio,

perocchè era come filosofo, virtudioso uomo in più cose,
se non ch'era troppo tenero e stizzoso.

This faction [the Bianchi] remained in exile a shorter
time, for when the location proved to be unhealthy,
they were recalled. Guido Cavalcanti was ill when he
returned, and died soon afterward. It was a great pity,
for he was a philosopher and an able man in many
respects, though, to be sure, much too sensitive and
irritable.

In the whole exchange here between Guido's father and the
wayfaring Dante, there are distinct reminiscences of Aeneas'
encounter with Andromache in *Aen.* III, 310–13 (italics
added):

"verane te facies, verus mihi nuntius adfers,
nate dea? vivisne? *aut si lux alma recessit,*
Hector ubi est?" dixit lacrimasque effudit et omnem
implevit clamore locum. . . .

"Art thou a real form, a real messenger, coming to me,
goddess-born? Art living? or if kindly light has fled,
where is Hector?" She spake, and shedding a flood of
tears filled all the place with her cries.

Also see *Aen.* VI, 339: "Quid puer Ascanius? *superatne et*
vescitur aura?" ("What of the boy Ascanius? Lives he yet
and feeds he on the air of heaven?")

63. *cui*: Connects with "colui" of the preceding verse.
"Colui" is to be understood as the first part of a compound
relative pronoun; the second part, "cui," is the direct object
of "ebbe a disdegno."   *Guido vostro*: The wayfarer ad-
dresses Cavalcante, as he does Farinata, with the respectful
voi.

64. *Le sue parole*: His question about his son.   *'l modo*
de la pena: Since Cavalcante was a notorious Epicurean.

65. *m'avean . . . letto il nome*: Literally, "had read me
his name," i.e., "had taught it to me," "had told me who
he was."

66. *però = per ciò*.

67. *Di sùbito drizzato*: Since Cavalcante was on his knees at first, this can only mean that he has risen to his feet.

67–68. *Come? dicesti "elli ebbe"*? On the whole point here, hinging on the meaning of "ebbe," see C. S. Singleton (1962). As to punctuation for the phrase, see M. Barbi (1924a), p. 101.

69. *lo dolce lume*: H. Kuen (1940) has argued that Dante may have used the quite special form *lome* here instead of "lume" because in Guido Cavalcanti's famous poem, "Donna me prega," *lome* rhymes internally with *come* and *nome*— as it would here in Canto X. See "Donna me prega" in E. Monaci (1955), p. 574, vss. 15–20:

> In quella parte   dove sta memora
> prende suo stato   sì formato,   come
> diafan da lome,   d'una scuritate,
> la qual da Marte   vene, e fa demora.
> Elli è creato   ed ha sensato nome,
> d'alma costume e de cor volontate.

In that part where memory resides it takes shape; just as transparent things receive their form from light, so love is formed by a dark ray that comes from Mars, and dwells there (in the mind). It is a created thing, and has sensibility, a name, a spiritual habit, and strength of will.

It should be noted that another editor—see G. Contini (1960), vol. II, p. 525—gives *lume* instead of *lome* in vs. 17 of Guido's poem. Petrocchi, however, argues persuasively for the rhyme *come/lume*. Whatever reading is accepted, however, it is significant that in this very *canzone* Guido expresses his disdain of the supernatural. On Guido's disdain, see C. S. Singleton (1962).

72. *supin ricadde*: With the clear suggestion that the souls lie in the tombs, face up, like corpses.   *parve = apparve* (*ricomparve*).   *fora = fuori*.

73. *a cui posta*: "At whose request."

74. *m'era*: A pleonastic reflexive; see n. to *Inf.* VII, 94.

76. *e sé continuando*: The phrase has been punctuated variously by modern editors: *e "Se" continuando*, and *"E se," continuando*. But on the reading *e sé continuando* as the most probable, see G. Vandelli, 1921b. / This touch vividly emphasizes the haughtiness of Farinata, who in no way stoops to the small talk between his tomb companion and the wayfarer—even though Guido, on whom that "small talk" turns, was Farinata's own son-in-law.

77. *quell' arte*: The "art" of returning from exile. In continuing his words, Farinata picks up the thrust of the wayfarer's "i vostri non appreser ben quell' arte" (vs. 51) and twice throws it back at him (vss. 77, 81).

79–80. *Ma non cinquanta volte . . . qui regge*: Before fifty months have passed, Dante is to learn the difficulty of returning from exile. E. Moore (1903, p. 372)—assuming that in the fictional time of the poem the encounter with Farinata takes place on April 9, 1300—points out that the forty-ninth new moon would fall about March 5, 1304, and the fiftieth about April 4, 1304, and that precisely between these two dates (on March 10) began the unsuccessful mission of Cardinal Niccolò da Prato, who was sent to Florence by Benedict XI to reconcile the Neri and the Bianchi and secure the recall of the Bianchi, including Dante, from exile.   *fia = sarà*.

80. *la donna che qui regge*: Hecate, also called Proserpina, goddess of the moon and queen of Hades. See *Inf.* IX, 44.

82. *se tu mai nel dolce mondo regge*: This formula of entreaty will be used frequently in the poem. The speaker entreats the person addressed by something most dear to him (such as the wayfarer's presumed hope to return to the world above) to say or to do something. The clause with *se* always takes the subjunctive in such a construction.   *mai*: "As you hope ever to return."   *regge*: Present subjunctive of *redire* (*riedere*), from the Latin *redeo* (here, from *redeas*); see E. G. Parodi (1957), p. 257.

83. *quel popolo*: The Florentines.

83–84. *sì empio incontr' a' miei in ciascuna sua legge*: Each time exiled Ghibellines were allowed to return to Florence, the Uberti were excluded, denounced as enemies of the state, and sentenced to decapitation if captured.

86. *l'Arbia*: A small stream which rises a few miles south of Siena and flows into the Ombrone at Buonconvento. On its left bank is the hill of Montaperti, where the Ghibellines overwhelmingly defeated the Florentine Guelphs in 1260.

87. *tal orazion fa far nel nostro tempio*: M. Barbi (1924a, p. 104) has pointed out that this is a purely figurative expression, in which "far orazion" requires the complementary "nel nostro tempio" for a unified image. Barbi says that the verse simply means: "causes Florence to take these measures."

89. *A ciò = a far ciò*, i.e., to take part in the battle of Montaperti.

90. *sanza cagion*: His motive was to return to Florence from exile once the Florentine Guelphs could be defeated.
    con li altri: With the other Ghibellines.   *sarei mosso*: "Would I have taken part," "would I have joined in the battle."

91–93. *Ma fu' io solo, là dove . . . a viso aperto*: At the council of Empoli (see n. to vs. 32).

92. *per = da*.

94. *Deh, se riposi mai*: Again, as in vs. 82, the formula of entreaty or adjuration.

95. *quel nodo*: The wayfarer's perplexity, as stated in the verses that immediately follow.

97. *El = egli*, "it."   *El par che voi veggiate*: The "voi" refers to the damned of Hell, as does the "noi" (vs. 100) of the reply. Since both Farinata (vss. 79–81) and Ciacco (see *Inf.* VI, 64–72) have predicted events to come, the wayfarer has good reason to believe that souls in Hell can see the future.

98. *dinanzi*: "Ahead."   *quel che 'l tempo seco adduce*:
Future things, which time is yet to bring with it—as if time
were a river.

99. *e nel presente tenete altro modo*: "And yet, with respect
to the present, you follow another way," i.e., "you have no
knowledge of present things"—for example, Guido's father
does not know that his son is still living.

100–105. *Noi veggiam . . . stato umano*: Although Ciacco
(*Inf.* VI, 73) had some knowledge of present things,
Farinata's statement that "unless another bring report to
us, we know nothing of your human state" appears never-
theless to apply to all the damned of Hell. They can see
dimly into the future and can therefore prophesy future
events.

The question *De cognitione animae separatae* had en-
joyed a long tradition in theological speculation by Dante's
time, as is amply reflected in Thomas Aquinas' *Summa
theol.* I, q. 89, which bears precisely this heading. For a
searching review of the question in its main doctrinal as-
pects, see E. G. Parodi (1912); Parodi demonstrates here
that the poet adapted to his needs a tradition that was
vague enough to allow such liberty. Thus, as doctrinal back-
ground for the statement "e s'altri non ci apporta, / nulla
sapem di vostro stato umano," one may compare Aquinas'
statement (*Summa theol.* I, q. 89, a. 8, ad 1) that "sepa-
rated" souls "possunt etiam facta viventium non per seipsos
cognoscere, sed vel per animas eorum qui hinc ad eos
accedunt." ("Moreover, the affairs of the living can be
made known to [separated souls] not immediately, but [by]
souls who pass hence [thither].")

100. *come quei c'ha mala luce*: Literally, "as one who has
poor light," hence "dimly." Their light, which is said to
come from God, is "poor" only in the sense of being in-
sufficient.

101. *ne = ci*, as again in the following verse.

102. *cotanto ancor ne splende il sommo duce*: As E. G. Parodi (1912, p. 178) has pointed out, the damned see not by the light of grace but by natural light, a possibility allowed by Thomas Aquinas (*Summa theol.* I, q. 89, a. 1, ad 3): "Nec tamen propter hoc cognitio vel potentia non est naturalis: quia Deus est auctor non solum influentiae gratuiti luminis, sed etiam naturalis." ("Nor is this way of knowledge unnatural, for God is the author of the influx both of the light of grace and of the light of nature.") *il sommo duce*: God, who sees past, present, and future things simultaneously. He is never named in Hell—except in blasphemy.

103. *Quando s'appressano*: "When they draw near," but we are not told exactly how near. Cavalcante, for example, cannot foresee the death of his son Guido, which took place in August 1300, about five months after the fictional date of this encounter.

104. *s'altri non ci apporta*: Some soul ("altri" is singular) coming from the world of the living. "News" or "report" is understood as the object of "apporta."

105. *sapem = sappiamo.*

106. *Però = per ciò.*

107. *fia = sarà*, as again in the following verse.

108. *del futuro fia chiusa la porta*: Time itself will end at the Last Judgment; there will be no future after that.

111. *'l suo nato*: His "offspring."

113. *fate i = fategli.* For "i" as a dative form, see *Inf.* II, 17.   *fei*: Replaces the verbal *fui muto.*

113–14. *pensava già ne l'error*: This perplexity, which was called a "nodo" in vs. 95, is now called an "error," since when the wayfarer spoke with the soul of Cavalcante he assumed (mistakenly, as he now knows) that souls in Hell see present things.

116. *avaccio*: This obsolete adjective (derived from the Latin *vivacius*) is used here as an adverb modifying "dicesse" in vs. 117.

117. *chi con lu' istava*: The wayfarer asks Farinata who is with him there in this part of the cemetery where the Epicureans have their tombs (cf. "da questa parte" in vs. 13). Thus, in Farinata's reply, "Qui" (vs. 118) and "qua dentro" (vs. 119) have the same meaning.

119. *il secondo Federico*: The Emperor Frederick II, grandson of Frederick Barbarossa, son of Henry VI and Constance of Sicily, was known to his contemporaries as Stupor Mundi, "the wonder of the world." Born in 1194, he was head of the Holy Roman Empire from 1215 until his death in 1250. In placing Frederick among the Epicurean heretics, Dante followed the contemporary estimate. Salimbene da Parma, thirteenth-century chronicler, says (vol. I, p. 510): "Erat enim Epycurus, et ideo quicquid poterat invenire in divina Scriptura per se et per sapientes suos, quod faceret ad ostendendum quod non esset alia vita post mortem, totum inveniebat." ("He was an Epicurean, and therefore he and his scholars tried to find anything they could in Divine Scripture which might serve to show that there is no life after death.")

A *sirventes* composed by Ugo di Sain Circ reveals a similar view of Frederick (see in N. Zingarelli, 1886, p. 250): "Ni vida apres mort ni paradis non cre: / E dis c'om es nienz despueis que pert l'ale." ("He believed neither in life after death nor in paradise, and he said that a man is nothing after he draws his last breath.")

120. *'l Cardinale*: This is Cardinal Ottaviano degli Ubaldini, known to his contemporaries antonomastically as "the Cardinal." In the words of the *Anonimo fiorentino*: "Però che questo cardinale Ottaviano fu il maggiore di veruno altro cardinale a quel tempo, per eccellenzia, dicendo il Cardinale, s'intendea di Ottaviano." ("Since Ottaviano was by far the greatest cardinal of his time, to say 'the Cardinal' sufficed to signify Ottaviano.") He had been made bishop

of Bologna in 1240, when he was under thirty, by special
dispensation of Pope Gregory IX, and in 1244 was created
cardinal by Innocent IV. Ottaviano, who died in 1273, was
a brother of Ubaldino della Pila (*Purg.* XXIV, 29) and an
uncle of Archbishop Ruggieri (*Inf.* XXXIII, 14). Ben-
venuto describes the Cardinal as a devoted Ghibelline, and
credits him (as do Lana and others) with saying he had
"lost his soul a thousand times" for that cause. Benvenuto
comments on him as follows:

> Erat multum honoratus et formidatus; ideo, quando
> dicebatur tunc: Cardinalis dixit sic; Cardinalis fecit sic;
> intelligebatur de cardinali Octaviano de Ubaldinis per
> excellentiam. Fuit tamen epicureus ex gestis et verbis
> eius; nam cum semel petiisset a ghibelinis Tusciae
> certam pecuniae quantitatem pro uno facto, et non
> obtinuisset, prorupit indignanter et irate in hanc vocem:
> si anima est, ego perdidi ipsam millies pro ghibelinis.

> He was greatly respected and feared. In those days
> when people said, "The Cardinal said this, the Cardinal
> did that," it was understood they were talking about
> Cardinal Ottaviano degli Ubaldini. Still, he was an
> Epicurean in word and deed. Once, when he asked the
> Tuscan Ghibellines for a certain sum of money he
> needed for something, and did not obtain it, he burst
> into these indignant and angry words: "If there be a
> soul, I have lost it a thousand times for the Ghibel-
> lines."

In the *Cronica* of Salimbene, who was personally acquainted
with the Cardinal, appears the following naïve account
(vol. II, pp. 30-32):

> Missus fuit in Lombardiam legatus domnus Octavianus
> diaconus cardinalis. Hic fuit pulcher homo et nobilis,
> scilicet de filiis Ubaldini de Musello in episcopatu
> Florentino. Multum reputatus fuit ex parte imperii, sed
> propter honorem suum interdum faciebat aliqua ad
> utilitatem Ecclesie, sciens quia propter hoc missus
> fuerat. . . . Cum autem redii in Lombardiam, et post
> plures annos domnus Octavianus adhuc legatus esset

Bononie, pluribus vicibus comedi cum eo; et locabat me semper in capite mense sue, ita quod inter me et ipsum non erat nisi socius frater, et ipse tertium locum mense habebat a capite. Tunc faciebam quod sapiens in Proverbiis docet XXIII *Quando sederis, ut comedas cum principe, diligenter attende que posita sunt ante faciem tuam et statue cultrum in gutture tuo.* Et hoc fieri oportebat, quoniam tota sala palatii discumbenti-bus erat plena. Verumtamen abundanter et decenter comestibilia habebamus, et *vinum abundans et preci-puum ponebatur*, et omnia delicata. Tunc cepi cardi-nalem diligere.

Lord Ottaviano, the Cardinal, was sent as papal legate to Lombardy. He was a handsome, noble man, a son of the Ubaldini of Mugello in the diocese of Florence. The imperial party set great store by him, even though on occasion his honor forced him to act in the best interests of the church, since he knew that that was the purpose of his mission. . . . And when I returned to Lombardy, after several years, and Lord Ottaviano was still legate in Bologna, I dined with him several times. He always placed me at the head of the table, so that between him and me there was no one but his brother. He himself took the third place from the head of the table. Then, I would do what the wise man in Proverbs counsels [Prov. 23:1–2]: "When you sit down to dine with a ruler, keep in mind who is before you, and put a knife to your throat." And that was sound advice, for the whole hall of the palace was full of reclining diners. And indeed, there was good food in abundance, and [Esther 1:7] "wine in abundance and of the best was served," as well as many other delicacies. I began then to like the Cardinal.

123. *nemico*: "Inimical" or "hostile" because Farinata's words contain a prophecy of exile, not because Farinata himself is hostile.

126. *li = gli*. See vs. 6 for the same construction.

129. *e drizzò 'l dito*: The familiar gesture of emphasis.

131. *quella il cui bell' occhio tutto vede*: Beatrice, who sees all things in God; not so Virgil, who sees solely by the natural light.

133. *mosse a man sinistra il piede*: They thus resume the normal directions of turns in Hell (see n. to *Inf.* IX, 132), proceeding now toward the center of this circle and the way down to the next.

135. *a una valle fiede*: So far there has been no steep descent in Hell; but now the wayfarers come to a cliff that drops sharply to a valley, the seventh circle.

CANTO XI

3. *stipa*: "Pack." See also *Inf.* VII, 19; XXIV, 82.

6–7. *ad un coperchio . . . una scritta*: Again the reader may wonder just how the lids of the tombs are raised or laid back (see n. to *Inf.* IX, 121), since here the wayfarer can read the inscription on one of them. For "scritta" meaning "inscription," see also *Inf.* VIII, 127. Another inscription expressed in the first person occurs in *Inf.* III, 1–9, where the main portal to Hell "speaks."

8–9. *Anastasio papa . . . de la via dritta*: A certain tradition seems to have confused Anastasius II, pope from 496 to 498, and his namesake and contemporary Anastasius I, emperor from 491 to 518. Emperor Anastasius is said to have been led by Photinus, a deacon of Thessalonica (not to be confused with the better-known Photinus, bishop of Sirmium), into the heresy of Acacius, patriarch of Constantinople (d. 488). Acacius denied the divine origin of Christ, holding that He was naturally begotten and conceived in the same way as the rest of mankind. Dante was following the accepted medieval tradition concerning Pope Anastasius' heretical persuasion, as related by the *Anonimo fiorentino* in these words:

Fu costui papa Anastagio secondo, nato di Fortunato cittadino Romano, che sedette nella sedia apostolica anni due et mesi undici et dì XXIIJ. Questi constituì che niuno cherico, nè per ira nè per rancore nè per simile accidente, pretermettesse o lasciasse di dire l'ufficio suo. Scomunicò Anastagio imperadore; et però che in quel tempo molti cherici si levorono contro a lui, però ch'egli tenea amicizia et singulare fratellanza et conversazione con Fortino Diacono di Tessaglia, che poi fu Vescovo . . . et questo Fortino fu famigliare et maculato d'uno medesimo errore d'eresìa con Acazio dannato per la Chiesa Cattolica; et perchè Anastagio volea ricomunicare questo Acazio, avegna iddio ch'egli non potessi, fu percosso dal giudicio di Dio; però che, essendo raunato il concilio, volendo egli andare a sgravare il ventre ne' luoghi segreti, per volere et giudicio divino, sedendo et sforzandosi, le interiora gli uscirono di sotto, et ivi finì miserabilmente sua vita.

This was Pope Anastasius II, born of the Roman citizen Fortunatus. He sat on the apostolic seat for two years, eleven months, and twenty-three days. He decreed that no cleric was to omit or neglect to say his office for any reason whatsoever, be it ire, rancor, or anything else. He excommunicated the Emperor Anastasius. Many clerics at that time rose against him, because he was a very intimate friend of Photinus, deacon of Thessalonica who later became bishop . . . and this Photinus was familiar with and tainted by the same heretical error as Acacius, who was condemned by the Catholic Church. Anastasius wanted to accept this Acacius back into the fold, and was unable to do so. But because he had tried, he was struck by the judgment of God. When the council was convened, he went out to some private place to relieve himself. While he sat forcing himself, his insides, by Divine Will and Judgment, came out from below, and his life ended miserably right there.

For further discussion of Anastasius, see B. Nardi (1955), pp. 6–7; F. Tocco (1899), pp. 20–21. On the heresy of

Photinus, see Thomas Aquinas, *Summa contra Gentiles* IV, 4 and 28.

9. *la via dritta*: "The true faith."

11. *s'ausi = s'adusi.*

12. *i = vi* or (with the same sense) *gli.   fia = sarà.*

14. *lui = a lui.*

16. *cotesti sassi*: The "pietre rotte" of vs. 2. These broken rocks frame the whole valley comprising the seventh circle, below which lie the eighth and ninth circles.

17. *tre cerchietti*: The "three lesser circles" are the seventh, eighth, and ninth. They are smaller in circumference than those already traversed; hence the diminutive suffix. (See Fig. 4, p. 44.)

18. *come que' che lassi*: Refers to the phrase "di grado in grado."   *lassi = lasci.*

21. *costretti*: "Impounded," continuing the sense of "stipa," vs. 3.

22. *D'ogne malizia*: For the specific meaning of the term "malice" in this context, see Thomas Aquinas, *Summa theol.* I-II, q. 78. *Malizia* is a covering key term for the sins of lower Hell, as is soon made plain in Virgil's exposition.   *ch'odio in cielo acquista*: See Ps. 44:8 [45:7], and Ps. 5:7 [5:5–6]: "Odisti omnes qui operantur iniquitatem, perdes omnes qui loquuntur mendacium; virum sanguinum et dolosum abominabitur Dominus." ("You hate all evil-doers; you destroy all who speak falsehood; the bloodthirsty and the deceitful the Lord abhors.") Also see *Conv.* IV, i, 4: "Ciascuna cosa per sè è da amare, e nulla è da odiare se non per sopravenimento di malizia." ("Everything is lovable in itself, and nought is to be hated save for the evil superinduced upon it.")

23. *ingiuria è 'l fine*: "Ingiuria" is a technical term in this context, having here the meaning of the Latin *iniuria*, "in-

justice," and can be viewed in both its subjective and objective aspects. In this statement, the "fine" is the intended end or goal, the object aimed at by the will: *obiectum voluntatis est finis*. Thus, injustice in its subjective aspect is in the will (*sicut in subiecto*) and pertains to the sins of both upper and lower Hell. Sins of incontinence are punished in upper Hell because they are not *ex electione*, but *ex infirmitate* or *ex passione*. Sins of malice are punished in lower Hell, however, since they are always *ex intentione* and *ex electione* (or, in the words of Thomas Aquinas [*Exp. Eth. Nicom.* V, lect. 17, n. 1104]: "non solum voluntarie, sed ex electione"—"not only voluntarily but by choice"). Also see *Summa theol.* I-II, q. 78, a. 3, resp.: "Sed tunc solum ex certa malitia aliquis peccat, quando ipsa voluntas ex seipsa movetur ad malum." ("For then alone does anyone sin through certain malice, when his will is moved to evil of its own accord.")

23–24. *ogne fin . . . altrui contrista*: The focus now is on the "fine" in its objective aspect, as on that which is intended and done. See Thomas Aquinas, *Summa theol.* II-II, q. 59, a. 4, resp.: "Et ideo cum iniustitia semper consistat in nocumento alterius, manifestum est quod facere iniustum, ex genere suo est peccatum mortale." ("And so since injustice always consists in an injury inflicted on another person, it is evident that to do an injustice is a mortal sin according to its genus.") And since all sins of malice are sins that involve both deliberate intention and deliberate choice of means (*ex intentione* and *ex electione*), the means used to inflict injury on others here becomes the distinguishing element, i.e., force or fraud.

23. *cotale = cotale che.*

28. *Di violenti il primo cerchio è tutto*: It is pointed out by W. H. V. Reade (1909) that the concept expressed here presents difficulties in the light of Aristotle's *Nicomachean Ethics* and of Thomas Aquinas' adoption and adaptation of Aristotle's thought on the matter. The sins of the seventh circle (vss. 28–51) are proper to man alone,

since they follow from *malizia*, or injustice in the will, of which man alone is capable. See Reade's remarks, p. 421:

. . . an insinuation to the effect that violent injuries are less characteristically human than Fraud has no warrant in the systems of Aristotle, Cicero, or St. Thomas, and no support in Dante's own doctrine of *voluntas*. All injustice is *in voluntate sicut in subiecto*, and *voluntas* effectually separates man from the beasts. . . . What, then, is the explanation? To me it seems almost ludicrously plain that Dante's statement is merely an effective device (*a*) for getting *bestialitas* into the circle of *forza*, (*b*) for thrusting *frode* down into the lowest circles of all. . . . If you say that Fraud is the *proprio male* of man, what can this mean but that Force is more or less bestial? But, according to the interpretation of Aristotle favoured by St. Thomas, *bestialis malitia* is just the kind of badness in which man oversteps the bounds of humanity and comes near to the behaviour of beasts. And so, by one ingenious stroke of the pen, Dante succeeds both in recognizing the special position of *bestialitas* and in proving that *frode* must occupy the lowest circles. Once rate *forza* at the value of *bestialis malitia*, and there can be no question that *frode* is more damnable.

il primo cerchio: The seventh circle, the next ahead of the two wayfarers at this point. For the whole picture of the punitive system of Hell as expounded in this canto, see Fig. 4, p. 44.

31. *A Dio, a sé, al prossimo*: These offenses are given here in the relative order of their gravity, the worst being "to God," the next "to one's self," and the least offensive "to one's neighbor." See Thomas Aquinas, *Summa theol.* II-II, q. 118, a. 1, obj. 2: "Omne peccatum aut est in Deum, aut in proximum, aut in seipsum." ("Every sin is against either God, or one's neighbor, or oneself.")   *A Dio*: It is not literally possible for any human creature to do violence to God, but violence may be willed and attempted, as in the

act of blasphemy.   *a sé*: As W. H. V. Reade (1909, pp. 424–25) points out:

> But if Suicide is to be treated as an end deliberately willed [as it must be if it is a case of *malitia*], there is . . . no option but to count it an *iniuria*. According to Aristotle, it is an *iniuria civitati*, but Dante does not, apparently, condemn any sinners to the Inferno on the sole ground that they had offended against the State. . . . Apart from the Aristotelian view, St. Thomas was ready with a suggestion which would have converted Suicide into an *iniuria Deo*; yet Dante, even when working upon the threefold *in Deum, in se, in proximum*, insists on selecting the least legitimate class of the three. . . . To call it an *iniuria sibi* is openly to flout all respectable philosophers. . . . [Dante] imposes upon *peccata in seipsum* a sense which, in the system of St. Thomas, would be impossible.

Thus, along with bestiality and usury, suicide itself presents a special problem of classification. See vs. 40.   *pòne* = *può*. Grandgent notes: "The ending *-ne*, originally East Tuscan, Umbrian, and Roman, was often attached to verb forms ending in an accented vowel."

32. *in loro e in lor cose*: Or, as Thomas Aquinas might phrase it, *in personam et in rem*, a distinction that extends throughout the argument that follows. Aquinas himself, in discussing sins against God through the "things" of God, passes directly to the mention of suicide (*Summa theol.* I-II, q. 73, a. 8, ad 2):

> Unde non sequitur quod, si nocumentum maxime habet locum in peccatis quae sunt contra proximum, illa peccata sint gravissima; quia multo maior inordinatio invenitur in peccatis quae sunt contra Deum, et in quibusdam eorum quae sunt contra seipsum. Et tamen potest dici quod etsi Deo nullus possit nocere quantum ad eius substantiam, potest tamen nocumentum attentare in his quae Dei sunt, sicut extirpando fidem, violando sacra, quae sunt peccata gravissima. Sibi etiam aliquis quandoque scienter et volenter infert nocumentum,

sicut patet in his qui se interimunt, licet finaliter hoc referant ad aliquod bonum apparens, puta ad hoc quod liberentur ab aliqua angustia.

Hence it does not follow, supposing harm to be inflicted chiefly by sins against our neighbor, that such sins are the most grievous, since a much greater inordinateness is to be found in sins which man commits against God, and in some which he commits against himself. Moreover we might say that although no man can do God any harm in His substance, yet he can endeavor to do so in things concerning Him, e.g. by destroying faith, by outraging holy things, which are most grievous sins. [And following immediately, the suicide:] Again, a man sometimes knowingly and freely inflicts harm on himself, as in the case of suicide, though this be referred finally to some apparent good, for example, delivery from some anxiety.

See the "a sé . . . far forza" of vss. 31–32.

34. *ferute* = *ferite*; see also *Inf.* I, 108.

36. *tollette*: On the use of this form, see M. Barbi (1903), p. 4.

37. *omicide*: Plural of *omicida*. The form is the same as in *Inf.* IX, 127: "eresiarche."   *fiere* = *ferisce*.

40. *Puote* = *può*.

44–45. *biscazza e fonde . . . giocondo*: These will prove to be the class of the wantonly extravagant who wasted their own substance in the extreme. In distinguishing them, Dante is making use of Aristotle's definition of prodigality in *Eth. Nicom.* IV, 1, 1120ᵃ.

The Latin "Antiqua Translatio" of Aristotle that is often printed in the works of Thomas Aquinas is the translation of Aristotle which both Dante and Thomas Aquinas are assumed to have used. This "Antiqua Translatio" is the only text of Aristotle's works that is quoted in this commentary. Thus, for Aristotle's observations on prodigality, see in Aquinas, *Opera omnia* (vol. XXI, p. 116), the text of *Eth.*

Nicom. IV, 1, 1120ᵃ: "Prodigus enim qui propter seipsum perditus. Videtur autem perditio quaedam ipsius esse et substantiae corruptio, ut vivere per has existente." This version of Aristotle's *Ethics* is given also in R. M. Spiazzi (1964), p. 183. For an English translation, see C. I. Litzinger (1964), vol. I, p. 286: "[A spendthrift] is ruined by his own fault. The dissipation of one's substance seems to be a kind of ruin of one's being, since a man lives by means of riches." / For a discussion of the translations of Aristotle used by Dante, see E. Moore (1896), pp. 307–18.

45. *e piange là dov' esser de' giocondo*: See *Inf.* VII, 121–22. / W. H. V. Reade (1909, p. 428) calls attention to the possible influence on Dante of Aquinas' statements on sadness. See, for example, *Summa theol.* I-II, q. 37, a. 4, resp.:

> Passiones autem quae important motum appetitus cum fuga vel retractione quadam, repugnant vitali motioni, non solum secundum quantitatem, sed etiam secundum speciem motus, et ideo simpliciter nocent; sicut timor, et desperatio, et prae omnibus tristitia . . . .

> On the other hand, those passions which denote in the appetite a movement of flight or contraction, are repugnant to the vital movement, not only as regards its measure, but also as regards its species; wherefore they are simply harmful: such are fear and despair, and above all sorrow . . . .

45. *de'* = *devi*.

46. *Puossi* = *si può*.

47. *col cor negando*: See Ps. 13[14]:1: "Dixit insipiens in corde suo: Non est Deus." ("The fool says in his heart, 'There is no God.'") This reappears in Ps. 52[53]:1.

48. *spregiando natura e sua bontade*: Any sin against Nature is a sin of *ingiuria* against God, the *Ordinator naturae*. See Thomas Aquinas, *Summa theol.* II-II, q. 154, a. 12, ad 1: "Sicut ordo rationis rectae est ab homine, ita ordo naturae est ab ipso Deo. Et ideo in peccatis contra naturam, in quibus ipse ordo naturae violatur, fit iniuria ipsi Deo or-

dinatori naturae." ("Just as the ordering of right reason
proceeds from man, so the order of nature is from God
Himself: wherefore in sins contrary to nature, whereby the
very order of nature is violated, an injury is done to God,
the Author of nature.")

49. *però = perciò.*

49–50. *suggella del segno suo:* "Stamps with its seal" of
falling fire, as will be seen.

50. *Soddoma:* The sodomites. The usual name for sodomy
in theological discussions is *vitium contra naturam.* See
Thomas Aquinas, *Summa theol.* II-II, q. 154, a. 11, and
note that Aquinas refers to Augustine in a. 12, ad 1. Also
see Augustine, *Conf.* III, 8:

> Itaque flagitia, quae sunt contra naturam, ubique ac
> semper detestanda atque punienda sunt, qualia Sodomi-
> tarum fuerunt. quae si omnes gentes facerent, eodem
> criminis reatu divina lege tenerentur, quae non sic fecit
> homines, ut hoc se uterentur modo. violatur quippe ipsa
> societas, quae cum deo nobis esse debet, cum eadem
> natura, cuius ille auctor est, libidinis perversitate pol-
> luitur.

> Therefore are those crimes which be against nature, to
> be everywhere and at all times both detested and pun-
> ished; such as those of the men of Sodom were: which
> should all nations commit, they should stand all guilty
> of the same crime, by the Law of God, which hath not
> so made men, that they should this way use one an-
> other. For even that society which should be betwixt
> God and us, is then violated, when the same nature of
> which he is author, is polluted by the preposterousness
> of lust.

50. *Caorsa:* Cahors, a town in southern France, on the
river Lot. In the Middle Ages, Cahors was the capital of
the ancient province of Quercy in Guienne; it is the capital
of the modern department of Lot. It was famous in the
Middle Ages as a great center of usurers, so much so that

the term *Caorsinus* became a common synonym for usurer. Boccaccio observes in his *Comento*:

> Caorsa è una città di Proenza . . . sì del tutto data al prestare a usura, che in quella non è nè uomo nè femmina, nè vecchio nè giovane, nè piccol nè grande che a ciò non intenda; e non che altri, ma ancora le serventi, non che il lor salario, ma se d'altra parte sei o otto denari venisser loro alle mani, tantosto gli dispongono e prestano ad alcun prezzo. Per la qual cosa è tanto questo lor miserabile esercizio divulgato, e massimamente appo noi, che, come l'uom dice d'alcuno:—Egli è caorsino,—così s'intende ch'egli sia usuraio.

> Cahors is a city in Provence . . . so completely given to loans and usury that there is no one in the city, man or woman, old or young, small or great, who is not well versed in those matters. Why even servants will lend money for a price—not only their salaries, but any six or eight cents they may happen to get their hands on. Their wretched practice is so widespread, especially among us, that the phrase "he is from Cahors" means that the person is a usurer.

In the frequent edicts issued by various European sovereigns for the expulsion of usurers, the term *Caorsini* (often coupled with *Lombardi*) constantly recurs. Du Cange, under the entries "Caorcini" and "Langobardi" (vol. II, p. 110; vol. V, p. 25, respectively), quotes from an edict issued by Charles II of Naples against the Jews, dated December 8, 1289: "Praecipimus ut expulsio praedicta extendatur ad omnes Lombardos, Caturcinos, aliasque personas alienigenas, usuras publice exercentes." ("We order that the aforementioned expulsion be extended so as to include all Lombards, those from Cahors, and other foreigners who have been publicly engaged in usury.") See further G. Todeschini (1872), pp. 303–12; C. Piton (1892), pp. 23–37.

51. *chi, spregiando Dio col cor, favella*: The blasphemers, also referred to in vs. 48.

52. *La frode*: With this designation, the argument now passes to the last two circles of Hell, the eighth and ninth.

54. *non imborsa*: Literally, "pockets no trust," i.e., "places no special trust," the "fede spezial" of vs. 63.

56. *lo vinco d'amor che fa natura*: See *Conv.* I, i, 8: "ma però che ciascuno uomo a ciascuno uomo naturalmente è amico" ("but inasmuch as every man is naturally friendly to every man") and *Conv.* III, xi, 7: "la naturale amistade . . . per la quale tutti a tutti semo amici" ("the natural friendship whereby we are all friends to all"). See also Ecclus. 13:19: "Omne animal diligit simile sibi: sic et omnis homo proximum sibi." ("Every living thing loves its own kind, every man a man like himself.") Thomas Aquinas, in *Exp. Eth. Nicom.* VIII, lect. 1, n. 1541, says:

> Est etiam naturalis amicitia inter eos, qui sunt unius gentis adinvicem, inquantum communicant in moribus et convictu. Et maxime est naturalis amicitia illa, quae est omnium hominum adinvicem, propter similitudinem naturae speciei. Et ideo laudamus philantropos, idest amatores hominum, quasi implentes id quod est homini naturale.

> There is also a natural friendship between people of the same race who have common customs and social life. There is above all that natural friendship of all men for one another by reason of their likeness in specific nature. For this reason we praise philanthropists or friends of mankind as fulfilling what is natural to man.

Also see Aquinas, *Summa contra Gentiles* I, 91.

57. *cerchio secondo*: This is the eighth circle actually, second of the three lesser circles; see Fig. 4, p. 44.

58–60. *ipocresia, lusinghe . . . e simile lordura*: The eighth circle (see Fig. 6, p. 312) contains ten subdivisions, for as many kinds of sins—not all of which are identified by name. The term "simile lordura" serves to lump these sins together with a suggestion of the contempt and disgust already present in the indiscriminate way in which the sins and sinners are named.

61. *Per l'altro modo*: As described in vs. 53.

63. *cria = crea*.

64. *cerchio minore*: The ninth and last circle.   *'l punto*: The center (see Fig. 3, p. 43).

65. *Dite*: One of the names of Satan.   *siede*: Satan actually is gripped there by the ice, as in a vise.

66. *trade = tradisce*.

69. *questo baràtro*: The area of Hell still to be traversed, i.e., the three lesser circles or "cerchietti" ahead. See the reference in Gregory, *Moral.*, pars secunda, IX, lxvi, 102, to the "infinite patens inferni barathrum" ("gaping and immeasurable chasm of Hell").

70–75. *Ma dimmi . . . foggia*: The wayfarer's question directs the argument to upper Hell and the four circles of the incontinent already traversed and easily recognizable in the phrases that point to the respective punishments observed there.

73. *perché non dentro da la città roggia*: The division of Hell into two parts is stressed, the walls of the city of Dis being the dividing line. The sixth circle, where heresy is punished and where the wayfarers now stand, is passed over without any question, and heresy is not classified.   *roggia*: On this form, see E. G. Parodi (1957), pp. 227–28.

74. *se Dio li ha in ira*: The phrase goes back to Virgil's opening statement in vss. 22–23—"D'ogne malizia, ch'odio in cielo acquista, / ingiuria è 'l fine"—with "hatred in Heaven" referred to now as "wrath of God." Why are those in the circles above and outside Dis punished as they are, if God does not have them "in ira"? And if He does have them "in ira," why are they not punished within the city of Dis? The wayfarer's question arises from the latent ambiguity of "ogne malizia, ch'odio in cielo acquista," in

which the key term is *malizia*. In short, the wayfarer is asking his guide if the sins of upper Hell are not sins of malice. He has not understood and must be told or reminded that the sins punished in upper Hell are sins arising from the disposition that Aristotle terms *incontinentia*, sins that do not afflict others (see "altrui contrista," vs. 24, the further qualifying phrase of the opening statement) but do affect the sinner himself, resulting in "personal disordering."

77. *sòle* = *suole*.

80–83. *la tua Etica . . . bestialitade*: This is a specific reference to a distinction drawn by Aristotle in the *Nicomachean Ethics*. See *Eth. Nicom.* VII, 1, 1145ª: "Post haec autem dicendum, aliud facientes principium, quoniam circa mores fugiendorum tres sunt species, malitia incontinentia et bestialitas." (This Latin version of Aristotle—see n. to vss. 44–45, above—is printed in Aquinas, *Opera omnia*, vol. XXI, p. 222, and also in R. M. Spiazzi, 1964, p. 351.) For the English, see C. I. Litzinger (1964), vol. II, p. 607: "Now, making a new start, we must indicate that there are three kinds of dispositions in moral practice to be avoided, viz., vice, incontinence and brutishness."

80. *pertratta*: From the Latin verb *pertractare*, "to treat thoroughly."

81. *disposizion*: *Dispositio* and *habitus* are clearly defined terms in Aristotelian-Thomistic philosophy. Aquinas distinguishes between the two concepts as follows, clarifying the exact meaning of *dispositio* (*Summa theol.* I-II, q. 49, a. 2, ad 3):

> Dispositio autem dupliciter accipitur; uno modo secundum quod est genus habitus; nam in 5 Metaph. *dispositio* ponitur in definitione habitus. Alio modo secundum quod est aliquid contra habitum divisum; et potest intelligi dispositio proprie dicta condividi contra habitum dupliciter: uno modo sicut perfectum et imperfectum in eadem specie, ut scilicet *dispositio* dicatur retinens nomen commune, quando imperfecte

inest, ita quod de facili amittatur; *habitus* autem, quando perfecte inest, ut non de facili amittatur, et sic dispositio fit habitus, sicut puer fit vir.

Now disposition may be taken in two ways; in one way, as the genus of habit, for disposition is included in [Aristotle's] definition of habit: in another way, according as it is divided against habit. Again, disposition, properly so called, can be divided against habit in two ways: first, as perfect and imperfect within the same species; and thus we call it a disposition, retaining the name of the genus, when it is had imperfectly, so as to be easily lost: whereas we call it a habit, when it is had perfectly, so as not to be lost easily. And thus a disposition becomes a habit, just as a boy becomes a man.

For the definition of *habitus* in Aristotle, *Metaphys.* V, 20, 1022[b], see *Summa theol.* I-II, q. 49, a. 1, resp., where the Philosopher is quoted as saying:

Habitus dicitur dispositio secundum quam bene vel male disponitur dispositum aut secundum se aut ad aliud; ut sanitas habitus quidam est. Et sic loquimur nunc de habitu; unde dicendum est quod habitus est qualitas.

Habit is a disposition whereby that which is disposed is disposed well or ill, and this, either in regard to itself or in regard to another: thus health is a habit. And in this sense we speak of habit now. Wherefore we must say that habit is a quality.

81. *che 'l ciel non vole*: This phrase brings in the specifically Christian dimension that is not, of course, found in Aristotle, in whose anthropocentric *Ethics* the three dispositions are simply "mores fugiendorum," "dispositions to be avoided" (see n. to vss. 80–83, above).   *vole = vuole*.

83–84. *incontenenza men Dio offende*: Aristotle says nothing of the sort, but Christian theology readily stated it so, as regards a vertical dimension of sin, which is an offense to God. Thomas Aquinas elaborately worked out the prin-

ciples by which such a judgment is made. In the Latin
version of Aristotle's *Nicomachean Ethics* (see in Aquinas'
Opera omnia, vol. XXI, p. 91, or in R. M. Spiazzi, 1964,
p. 144), there is reference to those who are "iniustos" and
those who are "incontinentes" (III, 5, 114^a):

> Sed forsitan talis aliquis est ut non diligens sit.
>
> Sed eius quod est tales fieri ipsi sunt causa, viventes
> remisse, et eius quod est iniustos vel incontinentes esse.
> Hi quidem mala facientes. Hi autem in potationibus
> et in talibus degentes.

> Perhaps such a person is naturally not diligent.
>
> But men make themselves negligent by living care-
> lessly, and unjust and incontinent by doing evil to
> others and spending their time in drinking and such
> things.

Aquinas' commentary on this passage is found in his *Exp.
Eth. Nicom.* III, lect. 12, n. 510, which says in part (italics
added):

> Est autem considerandum quod habitus differunt, sicut
> et actus mali. Quidam enim sunt mali habitus . . . per
> quos aliquis inclinatur ad male agendum; sive hoc sit
> *in nocumentis aliorum*, sive *in propriam deordina-
> tionem*. Et quantum ad hoc dicit quod homines sibiipsis
> sunt causa quod sunt iniusti, inquantum mala faciunt
> aliis, et incontinentes inquantum vitam suam ducunt
> in superfluis potibus et in aliis huiusmodi quae ad
> delectabilia tactus pertinent.

> We must consider that evil habits differ as evil acts do.
> Some habits are evil . . . because through them a man is
> inclined to do evil, whether this brings about the *injury
> of others* or *one's own disordered condition*. With re-
> spect to these [Aristotle] says men by their own volition
> are the reason why they are unjust inasmuch as they
> do evil to others, and incontinent inasmuch as they live
> their lives in unnecessary drinking and in other things
> of this kind which pertain to the pleasures of touch.

As G. Busnelli (1907, pp. 14-15) has remarked, the phrases
(italicized above) distinguish the sins of incontinence from

those of injustice. *Malitia*, in short, is distinguished on the
basis of the *male agendum* to which the respective evil dis-
position inclines the sinner: *in propriam deordinationem* in
the case of incontinence and *in nocumentis aliorum* in the
case of malice. These Thomistic distinctions are exactly those
followed by Dante in the punitive system of Hell. For the
specific evaluation by which sins of incontinence must be
accounted less grave than sins of malice, see Thomas
Aquinas, *Summa theol.* I-II, q. 78, a. 4, resp.:

> Respondeo dicendum, quod peccatum quod est ex certa
> malitia, est gravius peccato quod est ex passione, triplici
> ratione.
>
> Primo quidem, quia cum peccatum principaliter in
> voluntate consistat, quanto motus peccati est magis
> proprius voluntati, tanto peccatum est gravius, caeteris
> paribus. Cum autem ex certa malitia peccatur, motus
> peccati est magis proprius voluntati, quae ex seipsa in
> malum movetur, quam quando ex passione peccatur,
> quasi ex quodam extrinseco impulsa ad peccandum.

> I answer that a sin committed through malice is more
> grievous than a sin committed through passion, for
> three reasons. First, because, as sin consists chiefly in an
> act of the will, it follows that, other things being equal,
> a sin is all the more grievous, according as the move-
> ment of the sin belongs more to the will. Now when a
> sin is committed through malice, the movement of sin
> belongs more to the will, which is then moved to evil
> of its own accord, than when a sin is committed
> through passion, when the will is impelled to sin by
> something extrinsic, as it were.

86. *rechiti* = *ti rechi.*

87. *sù di fuor*: Above, outside the walls of Dis.

90. *la divina vendetta*: Divine Justice, but as wrought by
a vengeful God, "in ira" (vs. 74).

91. *O sol*: The reader will do well to note that Virgil, as
guide and mentor to the wayfaring Dante, is again and

again referred to as "light" (see, for example, *Inf.* I, 82), whereby his meaning in allegory is being pointed to—though only the poem, as it unfolds, will finally disclose what that meaning is.

95–96. *là dove di' ch'usura . . . bontade*: The wayfarer is referring to what was said in vs. 48 as well as what was implied by the name "Caorsa" in vs. 50.   *di' = dici*.

97. *Filosofia*: The reference could be to Aristotelian philosophy in general, but G. Busnelli (1907, p. 128, n. 2) holds that it is to the *Metaphysics* in particular and gives six good reasons for thinking so.   *a chi la 'ntende*: See *Conv.* II, iii, 10: "Aristotile pare ciò sentire, a chi bene lo 'ntende." ("Aristotle likewise seemeth to agree hereto, to whoso rightly understandeth.")

98. *non pure in una sola parte*: G. Busnelli (1907, p. 128, n. 3) shows that the dependence of the Universe and of Nature on God is observed by Aristotle at "more than one" point in the *Metaphysics*. See, for example, *Metaphys.* XII, 7, 1072^b: "Ex tali igitur principio dependet caelum et natura." (On the Latin version of Aristotle quoted here, see n. to vss. 44–45, and Aquinas, *Opera omnia*, vol. XX, p. 636. For an English translation of this version, see J. P. Rowan, 1961, vol. II, p. 886: "It is on such a principle, then, that the heavens and the natural world depend.") Thomas Aquinas, who understands this "principle" as God, comments in his *Exp. Metaphys.* XII, lect. 7, n. 2535:

Finis autem principium est, quod postea nominat Deum, inquantum attenditur per motum assimilatio ad ipsum: assimilatio autem ad id quod est volens, et intelligens, cuiusmodi ostendit esse Deum, attenditur secundum voluntatem et intelligentiam, sicut artificiata assimilantur artifici, inquantum in eis voluntas artificis adimpletur.

The end is the principle which [the Philosopher] later calls God inasmuch as things are assimilated to God through motion. Now assimilation to a being that wills and understands (as he shows God to be) is in the line of will and understanding, just as things made by art are assimilated to the artist inasmuch as his will is fulfilled in them.

99–100. *natura lo suo corso prende dal divino 'ntelletto e da sua arte*: See *De mon.* I, iii, 2: "Deus eternus arte sua, que natura est" ("eternal God, by his art, which is nature"), and II, ii, 3: "Quicquid est in rebus inferioribus bonum . . . per prius ab artifice Deo sit et secundario a celo, quod organum est artis divine, quam naturam comuniter appellant" ("Whatsoever good there is in things below . . . must come primarily from the artificer, God, and secondarily from heaven, which is the instrument of that divine art which men commonly call nature").

101. *la tua Fisica*: Aristotle's *Physics*. See, for example, *Physica* II, 2, 194[a] ("ars imitatur naturam") and II, 8, 199[a]. Thomas Aquinas alludes to this concept in his *Exp. Phys.* VII, lect. 5, n. 917: "Et, quia ars est imitatrix naturae, et artificiatum est quaedam rei naturalis imago . . . ." ("And since art is the imitator of nature, and since an artifact is an image of a natural thing . . . .") G. Busnelli (1907, p. 129, n. 1) suggests, however, that Dante's concept of usury as something offensive to Nature and art probably came more directly from Aquinas' commentary on Aristotle's *Politics* than from the *Physics* itself. W. H. V. Reade (1909, p. 429) further observes that the notion of usury as a violation of art and Nature is nothing more than a commonplace that can be traced, if need be, to Aristotle's *Nicomachean Ethics* as well as the *Politics* and *Physics*. Reade also points out that "St. Thomas always teaches that in Usury an art is put to an unnatural purpose, and when proving [in *Summa theol.* II-II, q. 78, a. 1, ad 3] that Justice is thus outraged, he alludes to the *Politics*." (Aquinas' reference is to *Polit.* I, 3, 1258[b].)

103. *pote* = *può*.

105. *vostr' arte*: The use of the plural pronoun suggests mankind as a whole—human art, or human industry. *a Dio quasi è nepote*: Nature, daughter of God, follows Him

(His eternal ideas and His art, vs. 100) in her operation, while human industry, the daughter of Nature, follows (or ought to follow) her and her art.

106. *queste due*: Nature and human industry.

107. *lo Genesì dal principio*: Gen. 3:17, 19: "In laboribus comedes ex ea cunctis diebus vitae tuae . . . in sudore vultus tui vesceris pane." ("In toil shall you eat of it all the days of your life . . . . In the sweat of your brow you shall eat bread.") See also II Thess. 3:10: "Quoniam si quis non vult operari, nec manducet." ("If any man will not work, neither let him eat.")

107–8. *convene prender sua vita e avanzar la gente*: Grandgent translates this: "Mankind must derive its sustenance and progress." ("La gente" is the subject of the two infinitives.) The verse echoes God's command to Adam and Eve in Gen. 1:28: "Crescite et multiplicamini." ("Be fruitful and multiply.") / For the expression "prender sua vita" in the sense of *nutrirsi*, Torraca cites the following examples from *Novelle antiche* CL: "Questo destriere . . . andando per le pratora pigliando sua vita . . . pigliò questa vitalba per rodere, per pigliare sua vita." ("This steed . . . roaming through the fields to find sustenance . . . picked up this clematis to gnaw on, for sustenance.") *Prender vita* was also said of a transplanted plant, meaning "to take root." On this see G. Manuzzi (1865), p. 727, under the entry "vita," par. 92: "Arbore trasportato sovente non prende vita." ("Often, a transplanted tree will not take root.")

109. *l'usuriere altra via tene*: Aristotle, in his discussion of avarice in the *Nicomachean Ethics*, speaks of usurers in the same context with tyrants. See (in Aquinas' *Opera omnia*, vol. XXI, p. 124, or R. M. Spiazzi, 1964, p. 194) *Eth. Nicom*. IV, 1, 1121^b-1122^a:

Hi autem rursus secundum acceptionem superabundant in undique accipiendo et omne, puta illiberales operationes operantes et de meretricio pasti et omnes tales et usurarii et in parvo et in multo. Omnes enim isti unde

non oportet accipiunt et quantum non oportet. Com-
mune autem in ipsis turpis lucratio apparet. Omnes
enim gratia lucri et huius parvi opprobria sustinent.
Eos enim qui magna, non unde oportet, accipiunt,
neque quae oportet, non dicimus illiberales, puta tyran-
nos civitates desolantes et sacra praedantes; sed per-
niciosos magis et impios et iniustos.

Others again are immoderate in their taking by accept-
ing anything and from any quarter, for example, those
who engage in disreputable enterprises, those who live
from the proceeds of prostitution, and such like, and
usurers who lend small sums and at high rates. All of
these receive more than they should and from repre-
hensible sources. Common to them is sordid gain be-
cause they all become infamous for the sake of a little
money. People who wrongly take great sums from
wrong sources are not called illiberal, for instance,
usurpers who plunder cities and despoil sacred places
but rather wicked, impious, and unjust.

Thomas Aquinas (see *Summa theol.* II-II, q. 78, a. 1, ad 3)
quotes Aristotle's view that "to make money by usury is
exceedingly unnatural." See also Aquinas' remarks in *Exp.
Polit.* I, lect. 8, n. 134, where he discusses the acquisition
of money through "interest":

Unde fit quidam partus cum denarius ex denario crescit.
Et ideo etiam ista acquisitio pecuniarum est maxime
praeter naturam: quia secundum naturam est, ut denarii
acquirantur ex rebus naturalibus, non autem ex denariis.

Thus, a kind of birth takes place when money grows
from [other] money. For this reason the acquisition of
money is especially contrary to Nature, because it is in
accordance with Nature that money should increase
from natural goods and not from money itself.

110–11. *per sé natura e per la sua seguace dispregia*: The
usurer despises Nature twice over—in herself, and in her
follower, which is human industry.

113–14. *ché i Pesci . . . giace*: See M. A. Orr (1956), p.
246:

The Fishes (of the zodiac) are quivering on the horizon, and the Wain lies to the north-west. As it is the time of the vernal equinox, and the sun is in Aries, Pisces is the zodiacal sign immediately preceding the sun, and begins to rise about four in the morning. The part of Ursa Major called the Wain is somewhat less than 180° distant from Pisces; hence when the latter appears on the eastern horizon the former will be in the west (and of course always in the north). "Caurus" of the Latins was the wind from the north-west.

114. *'l Carro tutto*: According to G. Antonelli (1871, p. 86): "All'apparire della Costellazione dei Pesci sopra di un orizzonte, il quale abbia una latitudine boreale di 32 gradi, l'Orsa maggiore, e più propriamente il Carro, dee mostrarsi *tutto* da quel lato, l'estremo del timone distando circa 40 gradi dal Polo." ("At the appearance of the constellation of the Fishes over a horizon that has a northern latitude of 32 degrees, the Great Bear, or, more properly speaking, the Chariot should be *completely* visible on that side, the end of the tongue [of the Chariot] being about 40 degrees from the pole.") See further E. Moore (1887), p. 43.

CANTO XII

1. *la riva*: The "ripa" of *Inf*. XI, 1, both words denoting the steep edge of the "balzo" mentioned in *Inf*. XI, 115. These two verses are the first and last of the preceding canto, in which Virgil has paused to expound the system of Hell.

2. *alpestro*: "Mountainous" is the literal meaning; the word refers back to the "great broken rocks" of *Inf*. XI, 2. The place where the wayfarers might find a way down the cliff to the first *girone* of the seventh circle was said at the end of Canto XI (vs. 115) to be some distance farther on. They have apparently proceeded to the left, around the rim of broken rocks, and have reached the spot.   *e, per quel che v'er' anco*: The vagueness of the phrase creates suspense and, with the qualification that follows, a sense of horror as well. "What was there" (the Minotaur) is termed the "infamia di Creti" (vs. 12).

4–6. *Qual è quella ruina . . . manco*: Dante is understood by most of the early commentators to be comparing this "ruina," which the wayfarers are beginning to descend, to the Slavini di Marco, a vast fall of rocks due to an enormous landslide some twenty miles south of Trent. Benvenuto points out that "istud praecipitium vocatur hodie slavinum ab incolis et ibi est unum castellum quod vocatur Marcum."

("This precipice is today known by the inhabitants as Slavini and by it is a castle called Marco.") He notes that Albertus Magnus mentions the ruin in his treatise *De meteoris* (III, ii, 18) and there discusses its probable causes. Dante's familiarity with this work may account for his ascription of a similar cause to the landslide of the seventh circle. According to Albertus Magnus:

> Aliquando autem, eo quod multum elevantur, siccantur et in sublimi scinduntur: in quas fixuras ingredientes aquae currentes cum impetu deiiciunt partem scissam a reliqua parte montis: et cadit magna pars vel modica secundum proportionem scissurae illius: et hoc modo cecidit mons magnus in montibus qui sunt inter Tridentum et Veronam civitates, et cecidit in fluvium qui dicitur Athesis, et super ripam eius oppressit villas et homines ad longitudinem trium vel quatuor leucarum.

> However, it sometimes happens that [large masses of rock] dry up and split near the top, because they are so high; and, when water gets into the cracks, they move with great force and one part of the mountain breaks loose. Depending on the size of the fissure, a large or a small part falls. In this way, a great mountain fell on the hills between Trent and Verona. Falling into the river known as the Adige, it demolished houses and buried people for a distance of three or four leagues along its banks.

On the Slavini di Marco and Dante's allusion to it, also see E. Lorenzi (1896, 1897) and A. Bassermann (1902), pp. 651–52.

5. *di qua da Trento*: South of Trent.   *Adice = Adige.*

6. *per sostegno manco*: Undermined by erosion from the water.   *manco = mancato.*

7. *onde si mosse*: The subject is "ruina."

8. *discoscesa*: To be construed as a past participle of *discoscendere* rather than as an adjective.

10. *burrato*: The term is used again in *Inf.* XVI, 114.

11. *lacca*: Dante uses this word three times in the poem and with much the same meaning; see also *Inf.* VII, 16; *Purg.* VII, 71.

12. *l'infamia di Creti*: Dante has so far failed to identify what "every eye would shun" (vs. 3). He continues to withhold the Minotaur's name, designating it here only by the infamy it witnesses. *Creti = Creta.* *distesa*: "Stretched out," as a quadruped might be. The word implies what the simile in vss. 22–25 confirms: that Dante imagined the Minotaur as having a bull's body and a human head, rather than a human body and a bull's head in accordance with another tradition. For the source of Dante's conception and a discussion of earlier figurations, see G. Mazzoni (1906), p. 14.

13. *concetta = concepita.* *falsa vacca*: The legendary wooden cow by means of which the Minotaur was conceived. According to the legend, Pasiphaë, wife of King Minos of Crete, was inspired with an unnatural passion for a snow-white bull. The artisan Daedalus built her a wooden cow covered with cowhide and placed it over her. The bull mounted the "counterfeit cow," and from this intercourse Pasiphaë later gave birth to the Minotaur. See n. to vs. 25; also *Purg.* XXVI, 87. Dante may have taken the story from Virgil (see *Eclog.* VI, 45–60; *Aen.* VI, 24–26, 447) or from Ovid (see *Metam.* VIII, 131–37; *Ars amat.* I, 289–316).

14. *sé stesso morse*: The characteristic gesture of rage; see the descriptions of Filippo Argenti turning on himself with his teeth (*Inf.* VIII, 63) and of Minos biting his own tail (*Inf.* XXVII, 124–26). See also Giotto's conception of *Ira* (Plate 6, facing p. 502).

15. *come quei cui l'ira dentro fiacca*: "Fiacca" is used in like manner to describe the self-consuming rage of the guardian of another circle: see the simile by which the effects of Plutus' rage are likened to a broken mast (*Inf.* VII, 14). Note that in both cases "fiacca" is rhymed with "lacca."

16–21. *Forse tu credi . . . le vostre pene*: This taunting reminder to the monster of its death at the hands of Theseus is successfully calculated to enrage the beast. See n. to vs. 25.

17. *'l duca d'Atene*: Theseus (see *Inf.* IX, 54 and the note), to whom Dante, like other writers (Boccaccio, Chaucer, Shakespeare), anachronistically gives a medieval title.

20. *la tua sorella*: Ariadne (see n. to vs. 25).

21. *vassi = si va. Si* is the pleonastic reflexive which sets off the subject in the usual way (see n. to *Inf.* VII, 94).   *le vostre pene*: This shift to the plural pronoun is a further taunt; by including the guardian of the seventh circle with the damned of Hell in this phrase, Virgil speaks as if it, too, were among those being punished there.

22–24. *Qual è quel toro . . . saltella*: *Aen.* II, 223–24 is often cited as a possible source for this simile: "qualis mugitus, fugit cum saucius aram / taurus et incertam excussit cervice securim" ("like the bellowings of a wounded bull that has fled from the altar and shaken from its neck the ill-aimed axe"). In Dante's figure, however, the bull is understood to have been struck on the head with a sledge hammer (the usual prelude to slaughter—then as now), and this detail conveys far more aptly the stunned, crazed effect Dante intended; the monster standing guard at the entrance to the circle of the violent represents insensate bestiality itself. If the creature literally had been dealt such a blow, the hammer would have struck its human forehead.

25. *lo Minotauro*: At last the monster is named. The Minotaur, offspring of the intercourse of Pasiphaë, wife of King Minos of Crete, and a bull (see n. to vs. 13), was kept in a labyrinth constructed by Daedalus. Every year it devoured a tribute of seven youths and seven maidens, whom Minos exacted from the Athenians in satisfaction for their murder of his son, Androgeos. The monster eventually was slain by Theseus with the assistance of Ariadne—Minos' daughter by Pasiphaë—who supplied him with a sword and a clew to the labyrinth.   *far cotale*: This may

be understood as the equivalent of either *farsi tale* or *fare lo stesso.*

26. *varco = valico*; the place of descent to the next, or seventh, circle (see n. to vs. 1), provided by the "ruina," or "scarco di pietre" as it is called in vss. 28–29, and guarded by the Minotaur.

27. *mentre ch'e' 'nfuria = mentre che egli è in furia.* With his stinging insult concerning Theseus, Virgil has provoked this fit of rage in the Minotaur, who, like the bull in the first term of the simile above (vss. 22–24), now jumps here and there half-paralyzed "and cannot go." *è buon = è bene.* *ti cale = ti cali (scenda).*

28. *scarco = scarico*; literally, "dump."

29. *moviensi = si movevano.* As E. G. Parodi (1957, p. 235) points out, the word must be read as *moviènsi* for the sake of the rhyme.

30. *lo novo carco*: The unusual weight (for this place) of a living body.

31. *gia* (pronounced *gìa*) *= giva (andava)*. *pensando*: "Pensive," thinking about this breakdown in the rock structure, which Virgil now terms a "ruina."

32. *questa ruina*: Repeating the term from the simile in vs. 4 and anticipating what will now be explained and related to the "ruina" of *Inf.* V, 34.

33. *quell' ira bestial = quella bestia irosa.* It is, however, most effective to make "passion" the noun. *spensi*: Literally, "extinguished," but here meaning "rendered innocuous" (cf. "fiacca," vs. 15).

34. *l'altra fiata*: See *Inf.* IX, 22–27, where Virgil explains the circumstances of his other journey here.

35. *nel basso inferno*: Again the line of division between an upper and a lower Hell.

36–45. *questa roccia . . . fece riverso*: Christ is always re-
ferred to in Hell by circumlocution. Virgil, who died before
the birth of Christ, has seen Him come to Limbo (here
called the "cerchio superno") and has spoken of Him (see
Inf. IV, 53–54) as "un possente, / con segno di vittoria
coronato." At the moment of Christ's death on the cross
(Matt. 27:51) "terra mota est, et petrae scissae sunt" ("the
earth quaked, and the rocks were rent"), and soon there-
after He descended to Hell and "took the great spoil." But
Virgil, being a pagan, understands such matters dimly at
best, as his phrase, "se ben discerno" (vs. 37), suggests.

39. *Dite*: Here Satan himself, not Satan's city, which con-
stitutes the entire area of lower Hell. When Christ came
to Limbo, Satan's devils attempted in vain to withstand
Him at the main upper entrance to Hell, which now re-
mains forever unbarred. (See *Inf.* VIII, 124–26 and the
note.)

40. *feda*: Cf. the Latin *foeda*, "vile."

42. *è chi creda*: Cf. the Latin *est qui credat*. The reference
is to Empedocles' theory of the alternate supremacy of hate
and love as the cause of periodic destruction and construc-
tion in the scheme of the universe, a theory to which
Aristotle refers in *Metaphys.* III, 4, 1000^{b}, and on which
Thomas Aquinas comments in *Exp. Metaphys.* III, lect. 11,
n. 478:

> Dicebat enim quamdam transmutationem esse in rebus
> odii et amicitiae, ita scilicet quod amor quandoque
> omnia uniebat, et postmodum omnia odium separabat.
> Sed causam, quare sic transmutabatur, ut quodam
> tempore dominaretur odium, et alio tempore amor,
> nullam aliam dicebat, nisi quia sic aptum natum est
> esse.

> For Empedocles said that there exists in the world
> a certain alternation of hate and friendship, in such a
> way that at one time love unites all things and after-
> wards hate separates them. But as to the reason why
> this alternation takes place, so that at one time hate

predominates and at another time love, he said nothing more than that it was naturally disposed to be so.

43. *caòsso* =*caòs.*   *converso = convertito.*

44. *vecchia*: Almost as old as the creation, as the inscription over the main portal of Hell declares (see *Inf.* III, 7–8): "Dinanzi a me non fuor cose create / se non etterne."

45. *qui e altrove*: So far in the poem there has been only the passing suggestion (through the repetition of the word "ruina") of a breakdown in the rock structure of Hell (see *Inf.* V, 34). Another such collapse lies ahead in the eighth circle.   *tal fece riverso = fece tal riverso.*

46. *a valle*: "Yonder below."   *s'approccia*: A Gallicism, which Dante uses elsewhere also in rhyme; see E. G. Parodi (1957), pp. 228, 273.

47. *la riviera del sangue*: The circular ditch of boiling blood is only later (*Inf.* XIV, 116) identified as Phlegethon. / "Riviera" is also a Gallicism, as A. Schiaffini (1937c, p. 183) notes.

48. *qual che = chiunque.* The whole verse serves as a reminder of what the wayfarer has been told about the seventh circle in *Inf.* XI, 28 and especially 37–39: namely, that it contains the souls of the violent and that this "first ring torments homicides and every one who strikes in malice, spoilers, robbers, in different troops."

49–51. *Oh cieca cupidigia e ira folle . . . c'immolle*: Cupidity and rage are the two passions which, more than others, prompt deeds of violence against one's neighbor and against his property—rage being responsible for the former, cupidity for the latter. Macrobius refers to the river of blood (Phlegethon) in terms of cupidity and rage (*Comm. in somn. Scip.* I, x, 11): "Phlegethontem ardores irarum et cupiditatum putarunt." ("They thought that Phlegethon was merely the fires of our wraths and passions.")

51. *immolle* = *immolli*, subjunctive of *immollare*, "to bathe," "to steep." The two subjects are twice served by a singular verb: "sproni," "immolle."

52-53. *un'ampia fossa . . . 'l piano abbraccia*: The wayfarer, knowing that the seventh circle contains the souls of the violent, now realizes that the ditch before him must be the first of what in Virgil's exposition (hence, "secondo ch'avea detto la mia scorta") were called the three *gironi* ("rings") of this circle. Judging from the arc made by the part of the ditch that he can actually see, he concludes that it describes a complete circle, enclosing and framing the plain.

55. *tra 'l piè de la ripa ed essa*: Between the rock wall of the precipice and the ditch.   *traccia*: "Troop"; see vs. 99.

56. *corrien*: Pronounced *corrìen*.   *centauri*: Centaurs, a mythical race of creatures, half horse and half man, notorious for their gluttony and violence. See also *Purg.* XXIV, 121–26.

57. *solien* = *solevano*.

60. *con archi e asticciuole prima elette*: See Lucan (*Phars.* VII, 141–42): "Tendunt nervis melioribus arcus, / Cura fuit lectis pharetras inplere sagittis." ("Bows were strung with better cords, and care was taken to fill the quivers with picked arrows.")

63. *costinci*: "From where you are." See Charon's challenge to Aeneas (*Aen.* VI, 388–89): "Quisquis es, armatus qui nostra ad flumina tendis, / fare age, quid venias, iam istinc, et comprime gressum." ("Whoso thou art that comest to our river in arms, O tell me, even from there, why thou comest, and check thy step.")

65. *Chirón*: Saturn, enamored of Philyra and fearing the jealousy of his wife, Rhea, changed himself into a horse and in this shape begat Chiron, who took the form of a centaur. Chiron educated Achilles, Aesculapius, Hercules, and many other famous Greeks, and Virgil knows at once that, because he is the wisest, he must be the leader of the

band.   *costà*: The word implies, "When we have come
to Chiron there beside you." With this reversal of the psy-
chological position of "costinci" (vs. 63), the offensive passes
from the centaurs to the wayfarers.

66. *mal fu la voglia tua sempre sì tosta*: A reference to
Nessus' attempted rape of Deianira (see n. to vss. 67–68).

67. *mi tentò*: Nudging him with his elbow.

67–68. *Nesso . . . la bella Deianira*: Deianira was the wife
of Hercules, whose death she unwittingly caused. Hercules
killed the centaur Nessus with a poisoned arrow for having
attempted to violate her; but before Nessus died, he gave
Deianira a robe dipped in his blood, telling her it would
act as a charm to preserve her husband's love. Later, jealous
of Hercules' love for Iole, Deianira gave him the robe; and
when he put it on, the poison in Nessus' blood maddened
him. To put an end to his agony, he burned himself on a
funeral pyre, and Deianira in remorse hanged herself. The
story is elaborated by Ovid (*Metam.* IX, 127–33, 152–62,
166–69), Dante's probable source; on the resemblance be-
tween Dante's and Ovid's accounts, see E. Moore (1896),
p. 214.

69. *e fé di sé la vendetta elli stesso*: Ovid has Nessus say
(*Metam.* IX, 131): "Neque enim moriemur inulti." ("I
shall not die unavenged.")

70. *ch'al petto si mira*: Chiron's bowed head may be in-
tended to suggest wisdom or an attitude of meditation, as
most commentators believe, since he was considered to be
the wisest of all the centaurs; but it also serves to direct the
reader's gaze to the creature's breast, where its two natures,
human and bestial, are joined. This emphasis is repeated
in vss. 84 and 97.

72. *Folo*: While Pholus, one of the centaurs, was entertain-
ing Hercules during the latter's expedition against them,
he met his death when he accidentally dropped one of his
guest's poisoned arrows on his own foot. Pholus is men-
tioned by Ovid (*Metam.* XII, 306), Lucan (*Phars.* VI, 391),

and Statius (*Theb.* II, 564), as well as by Virgil (*Georg.* II, 456; *Aen.* VIII, 294) and Servius (on *Aen.* VIII, 294), writers whose works were familiar to Dante. The phrase "sì pien d'ira" may be an echo of *Georg.* II, 455-56, where Virgil (giving a different version of Pholus' death) says of Bacchus: "Furentis / Centauros leto domuit, Rhoetumque Pholumque." ("It was he who quelled in death the maddened Centaurs, Rhoetus and Pholus.")

74. *si svelle*: *Svellere* literally means "to uproot"; this use of the word implies violence and suggests that these souls are "rooted in blood."

75. *sortille = le sortì*. The depth to which the souls are immersed in the river of boiling blood accords with the respective gravity of their sins. On Dante's possible source for this motif, see T. Silverstein (1936), pp. 449-52.

76. *isnelle = snelle*.

78. *fece la barba in dietro*: Porena notes that *barba*, in the usage of the day, meant both "beard" and "moustache."

80. *Siete voi accorti = vi siete accorti.*   *voi*: Emphatic for *vi*.

81. *quel di retro*: Dante, who is walking behind Virgil.
    move ciò ch'el tocca: The wayfarer dislodges the stones with his feet as he descends the slope.

82. *d'i = dei*.

83-84. *che già li er' al petto . . . consorti*: This phrase suggests that Virgil's head is level with Chiron's breast as he stands before him. It also serves again to focus on the dual nature of the centaur, beast and man.

85. *soletto*: See Torraca's excellent note on Virgil's words to Chiron and the meaning of this particular touch:

> Virgilio non grida a Chirone parole sdegnose, nè dà comandi. Prima cerca di amicarselo, di entrargli in grazia: *ben è vivo* conferma l'osservazione del centauro; val quanto dirgli: Hai dato nel segno. Poi procura

d'ispirargli compassione per quel povero suo compagno, al quale, *così soletto*, egli deve mostrare la *valle*, la valle *buia*, e non *per diletto*, che a ciò lo conduca, ma per *necessità*. Con garbo, e adattando il linguaggio all'intelligenza dell'uditorio, accenna a Beatrice, *tal*, che interruppe il dilettoso canto dell'*alleluia* per scendere a commettergli quell'uffizio. E si fa piccino. *Nuovo* è l'uffizio; perciò egli ha bisogno di aiuto altrui. Ma, poi, nega con forza (*non* . . . *nè*) che il compagno sia *ladrone*, ed egli *anima* di ladro; no, essi non dovranno rimaner lì, nel sangue bollente.

Virgil does not shout disdainful words at Chiron, nor does he give commands. First he seeks to become friends with him, to enter into his favor. "He is indeed alive" confirms the observation of the centaur; it amounts to telling him: "You guessed it." Then he continues to inspire him with compassion for his poor companion, to whom "thus alone" he must show the "valley," the "dark" valley, and it is not for "pleasure" that he is leading him through this, but by "necessity." Gracefully, and by fitting his language to the understanding of his hearer, he alludes to Beatrice, the "one" who interrupted the delightful singing of the "Alleluia" to descend and commit to him this task. And he humbles himself. The task is "new"; accordingly, he needs the help of others. But, then, he denies forcefully ("not . . . neither") that his companion is a "thief" and he the "spirit" of a thief; no, they are not to remain there, in the boiling blood.

86. *li = gli.*   *la valle*: The term, here as elsewhere in the poem, signifies the whole cavity of Hell; see vs. 40 of the present canto, as well as *Inf.* IV, 8 and *Purg.* I, 45.

87. *necessità 'l ci 'nduce*: Precisely what this necessity is, in the allegory, will be clear later, in retrospect. But from Cantos I and II, the reader already understands that the wayfarer must go the "long way round" for his salvation.   *'l ci = ce lo.*

88. *Tal si partì da cantare alleluia*: Beatrice; see Virgil's account of her coming (*Inf.* II, 53–114). Though the centaurs would not know of Beatrice, they would at least understand that one who sings Alleluia must be one of the blessed of Heaven, since such is their constant activity there in their bliss.

89. *quest' officio novo*: "This most unusual office" of guiding a living man through Hell.

90. *fuia*: From Latin *fur*, "thief." Virgil here replies to the centaur's earlier question (vss. 61–62), "A qual martiro / venite voi," thus keeping his promise (vss. 64–65) to answer Chiron. He is saying, in effect, "We are not condemned to this river of blood for robbery" (the least grave of the sins punished by immersion therein) "or for any other sin"; in other words, "We are not here for the usual reasons."

91. *Ma per quella virtù*: This appeal of Virgil's to the Divine Power to explain his role corresponds to the formula he has used earlier with the guardians of other circles. See, for example, his words to Charon, the first guardian he encounters (*Inf.* III, 95–96): "Vuolsi così colà . . . si vuole."

93. *danne = dàcci.*   *siamo*: This is the subjunctive (as are "mostri," vs. 94, and "porti," vs. 95).   *a provo*: From the Latin *ad prope*, "close to," "near"—in other words, "as guide"; see E. G. Parodi (1957), p. 290.

94. *ne = ci.*

95. *che porti costui in su la groppa*: Chiron promptly assigns this duty to Nessus, since, as Ovid says (*Metam.* IX, 108), he was "membrisque valens scitusque vadorum" ("strong of limb and well acquainted with the fords"). See n. to vss. 67–68.

97. *si volse in su la destra poppa*: This phrase again focuses attention on the double nature of the centaur.

98. *Torna*: We may assume that the centaurs were coming from the left when they first saw the two strangers. The wayfarers will proceed along the ditch of blood to the left; hence Nessus, in order to act as their guide, will have to "turn back" to guide them. *e sì li guida*: Porena observes that this use of "sì" is very common in the fourteenth century, either to introduce a main clause following subordinate clauses or to emphasize the clause which has the greatest "conceptual importance," as here.

99. *fa cansar = falli cansar*, "make them stand aside" and allow you to pass. *v'intoppa*: The words suggest that another such band might attempt to prevent them from passing. For the use of *intoppare* to mean "to meet in opposition," "to clash," see *Inf.* VII, 23.

102. *facieno* (pronounced *facìeno*) = *facevano*.

105. *dier = diedero*. *Dare di piglio* means "to lay hold of," and is ordinarily used only with *avere*, "property," and not with *sangue*; but by extension, in this verse, it suggests dipping the hands in blood.

107. *Alessandro*: This might be either Alexander the Great of Macedonia (356–323 B.C.) or Alexander of Pherae, a tyrant of Thessaly (ruled *ca.* 368–359 B.C.). Alexander of Pherae was famed for his cruelty, one of his amusements being to dress up men in the skins of wild beasts and to set dogs to worry them. Alexander of Pherae is coupled with Dionysius the Elder, as possibly here (see n. to vss. 107–8), by Cicero (*De officiis* II, 7), by Valerius Maximus (*Fact. dict. memor.* IX, 13), and by Brunetto Latini (*Tresor* II, cxix, 6).

The view that the person intended is Alexander the Great is strongly supported by the fact that Orosius, whose *Historiarum adversum paganos libri VII* was one of Dante's chief authorities in matters of ancient history, describes the Macedonian conqueror (III, 7, 18, 23) as: "vere . . . gurges miseriarum atque atrocissimus turbo totius orientis . . . sanguinis inexsaturabilis . . . recentem tamen semper sitiebat cruorem" ("a veritable whirlpool of evils and a

hurricane that swept the whole East in its fury . . . in-
satiable for human blood . . . always thirsty for fresh
slaughter"). After oppressing the world for twelve years,
Orosius records, he died at Babylon (III, 120) "adhuc
sanguinem sitiens" ("still thirsting for blood"). Orosius
concludes with a long apostrophe on the ruin and misery
that Alexander had inflicted on the whole world. Lucan,
another of Dante's historical authorities, also denounces
Alexander the Great—whom he calls "the mad son of
Macedonian Philip"—as a robber and the bane of the
world (*Phars.* X, 30–36):

> Perque Asiae populos fatis urguentibus actus
> Humana cum strage ruit gladiumque per omnes
> Exegit gentes; ignotos miscuit amnes
> Persarum Euphraten, Indorum sanguine Gangen:
> Terrarum fatale malum fulmenque, quod omnes
> Percuteret pariter populos, et sidus iniquum
> Gentibus. . . .

> Driven by the impulse of destiny, he rushed through
> the peoples of Asia, mowing down mankind; he drove
> his sword home in the breast of every nation; he defiled
> distant rivers, the Euphrates and the Ganges, with
> Persian and Indian blood; he was a pestilence to earth,
> a thunderbolt that struck all peoples alike, a comet of
> disaster to mankind.

Among the early commentators, Benvenuto mentions the
theory that someone other than Alexander the Great is
intended, but dismisses it with contempt. This Alexander
must be understood, he says, first, "per excellentiam . . .
secundo quia iste fuit violentissimus hominum" ("because
of his pre-eminence [and] second, because he was the most
ferocious of men"). He then proceeds to justify this opinion
at length, citing Orosius, Justin, Lucan, and others, and con-
cludes that Dante places Alexander "primum et principem
violentorum . . . et describit eum simpliciter et nude, quasi
dicat: cum nomino Alexandrum intellige, quod iste fuit
maximus autor violentiarum in terris" ("first and foremost
among the violent . . . and refers to him simply and baldly,

as if to say, 'When I name Alexander, understand that he was the greatest perpetrator of violent deeds in the world' ").
For a detailed review of the question, see U. Bosco (1942), pp. 131–36.

107–8. *Dionisio fero . . . dolorosi anni*: There is little doubt that Dante intends Dionysius the Elder, tyrant of Syracuse, who ruled 405–367 B.C. (in which case the "dolorosi anni" of vs. 108 are thirty-eight). Valerius Maximus says of the elder Dionysius (*Fact. dict. memor.* IX, xiii, ext. 4): "Dionysius, Syracusanorum tyrannus . . . duodequadraginta annorum dominationem . . . peregit." ("Dionysius, the tyrant of Syracuse, maintained his despotism for thirty-eight years.") Some think Dante's reference is to Dionysius the Younger, who succeeded his father as tyrant of Syracuse in 367 B.C. but was expelled in 356. He took refuge at Locri, made himself tyrant of that city, and treated the inhabitants with great cruelty. *Cicilia = Sicilia.*

109. *E quella fronte*: Since these tyrants are immersed in the boiling blood up to their brows, only their foreheads and hair are visible.

110. *Azzolino*: Ezzelino III da Romano (1194-1259), son-in-law of the Emperor Frederick II and chief of the Ghibellines in Upper Italy. During his long lordship over the March of Treviso, the city of Padua, and part of Lombardy, he committed one atrocity after another. Villani (VI, 73) says of him:

> Questo Azzolino fu il più crudele e ridottato tiranno che mai fosse tra' cristiani . . . e' cittadini di Padova molta gran parte consumò, e acceconne pur de' migliori e de' più nobili in grande quantità, e togliendo le loro possessioni, e mandogli mendicando per lo mondo, e molti altri per diversi martirii e tormenti fece morire, e a un'ora undicimila Padovani fece ardere . . . e sotto l'ombra di una rudda e scellerata giustizia fece molti mali, e fu uno grande flagello al suo tempo nella Marca Trevigiana e in Lombardia . . . .

This Azzolino was the most cruel and feared tyrant who ever existed in Christendom . . . he did away with large numbers of the citizens of Padua, and he put out the eyes of even the best and most noble in great numbers, depriving them of their possessions and sending them begging through the world. He caused many others to die by various tortures and torments and at one time had eleven thousand Paduans burned . . . and under the pretext of a rough and wicked justice, he did much evil, and during his lifetime he was a great scourge in the March of Treviso and in Lombardy . . . .

In 1255, Pope Alexander IV criticized Ezzelino severely for his infamous cruelty and proclaimed a crusade against him. After a war of three years' duration, he was defeated and captured; and he died in prison at the age of sixty-four, after a reign of thirty-four years.

111. *Opizzo*: Pronounced *Òpizzo*.

111-12. *Opizzo . . . nel mondo*: Obizzo II d'Este (1247–93). As lord of Ferrara and later of Modena and Reggio, he was an ardent Guelph and a supporter of Charles of Anjou. He is said to have wielded his power with pitiless cruelty. Obizzo was succeeded by his son Azzo VIII, by whom he was commonly supposed to have been smothered; this may have been a calumny, but Dante accepted the story, which was current in his day. Thus he speaks of Azzo as "figliastro," perhaps to indicate the unnaturalness of his crime, as Benvenuto proposes. Or, as Boccaccio suggests in his *Comento*, he may use the term in order to hint that Obizzo's wife had been unfaithful. For studies of the Este family, see A. Lazzari (1938) and L. Simeoni (1935).

113-14. *quei disse*: "*Questi ti sia . . . io secondo*": Dante apparently turns to Virgil for confirmation of the centaur's assertion, and Virgil endorses it, commanding the wayfarer to let Nessus "be first now," as guide, and himself "second." In addition, as Boccaccio interprets the verses: "Vuole in questo affermar Virgilio che al centauro sia da dar fede a quel che dice." ("With this, Virgil wishes to indicate that what the centaur says is to be believed.")

116-17. *'nfino a la gola . . . uscisse*: Those who are standing in the boiling stream up to their necks are murderers; their guilt is evidently less than that of tyrants, who are immersed up to their brows (see vss. 103-4).

117. *bulicame*: The boiling ditch. Cf. the Bulicame of Viterbo (*Inf.* XIV, 79).

118. *un'ombra da l'un canto sola*: The soul of Guy de Montfort (*ca.* 1243-98), son of Simon de Montfort, earl of Leicester (who was killed at the battle of Evesham, August 4, 1265), and Eleanor, daughter of King John of England. In revenge for his father's death and for the indignities offered his corpse, Guy murdered his first cousin, Prince Henry of Cornwall, in the church of San Silvestro at Viterbo in March 1271, during the assembly of the cardinals to elect a successor to Pope Clement IV. The crime is popularly supposed to have taken place at the moment of the elevation of the Host, when Henry was on his knees. To compound the atrocity, Guy, upon being reminded that his father's body had been trailed, seized Henry by the hair and dragged his corpse out into the open street. See Villani (VII, 39) for a detailed account; also G. Ciacci (1935), pp. 189-248, and G. Masi (1930).

119. *fesse = fendette.   in grembo a Dio*: In church and in this instance during the Mass, at the elevation of the Host.

120. *lo cor che 'n su Tamisi*: The heart of Prince Henry. Henry's body was brought to England and interred in the Cistercian abbey at Hales in Gloucestershire, which had been built by his father. Villani (VII, 39) believes that the heart was enclosed "in una coppa d'oro . . . in su una colonna in capo del ponte di Londra sopra il fiume di Tamigi, per memoria agl'Inghilesi del detto oltraggio ricevuto" ("in a gold casket . . . atop a pillar at the end of London Bridge over the Thames River, as a reminder

to the English of the aforementioned outrage"). Benvenuto, however, states that it was placed in the hand of a statue of the prince in Westminster Abbey, with an inscription appealing to Henry's cousin, Edward, for vengeance: "Cor gladio scissum, do cui consanguineus sum." ("My heart, which was pierced by the sword, I give to my cousin.") For one attempt to settle this difference, see F. Maggini (1910), p. 127.   *ancor si cola*: Some commentators interpret this verb as if it were derived from the Latin *colere*, "to venerate," but, though such a possibility should not be excluded, the usual meaning of the verb *colare*, "to flow," "to drip," seems more likely. Some also understand the "si" here as *sì* for *così*, but it makes better sense to take it as a pleonastic reflexive (see n. to *Inf.* VII, 94), in its common function of "distancing." Thus, even as the murderer's soul is "on one side alone," so the heart of the murdered man, severed from the body, is placed (whether on the bridge or in the abbey) over the Thames where it drips blood, signifying that it is still unavenged and appeals for vengeance.

121. *gente*: These, we may assume, are the "guastatori," "predoni," and "ciascun che mal fiere," named in *Inf.* XI, 37–38, those who did violence to others or their property and whose guilt thus assigns them to a lesser pain.

126. *quindi = per quivi*. The boiling blood at this point probably does not come above the centaur's hoofs.

127–38. *Sì come tu da questa parte vedi . . . tanta guerra*: The centaur actually is fording the boiling stream as he speaks, and to do this he has turned to the right. Thus, "da questa parte" indicates the direction from which the trio has come, which is clear when we remember that the blood has become progressively shallower. The three have now reached the shallowest point of all; hence, on the left ("da quest' altra [parte]") the blood gradually gets deeper, until it again reaches the depth befitting the tyrants, and is deepest "di qua" (vs. 133), where Attila and others are punished. In proceeding around to the left in this way, one comes to the two highway robbers named in vs. 137 before reaching the tyrants.

129. *credi = creda.*

131. *el*: The reference is to the "bulicame" (vs. 128).

134. *Attila*: Known as "the Scourge of God," this king of the Huns (lived *ca.* 406–53; ruled *ca.* 433–53) ravaged both the Eastern and Western Roman Empires before (according to legend) yielding to Pope Leo I, who persuaded him to evacuate Italy.

135. *Pirro*: There has been some controversy over the identity of this murderer; Dante may refer either to Pyrrhus, son of Achilles, or to Pyrrhus, king of Epirus. The first Pyrrhus, also grandson of Lycomedes, king of Skyros, was brought by Ulysses to take part in the Trojan War. He is reported to have slain the aged Priam when the city fell, killed Priam's son, Polites, and sacrificed his daughter Polyxena to the shade of Achilles (see *Inf.* XXX, 17). His violence and cruelty are recorded by Virgil (*Aen.* II, 469–559). Pyrrhus, king of Epirus (*ca.* 318–272 B.C.), whom Dante mentions several times elsewhere, made war against the Romans but was eventually defeated in 275 B.C. Among the earlier commentators, Boccaccio is in doubt on this point, but is inclined to favor the son of Achilles, who "fu e crudelissimo omicida e rapacissimo predone" ("was a most cruel murderer and a most rapacious pillager"). Benvenuto, on the other hand, is decidedly in favor of the king of Epirus, "qui fuit valentissimus et violentissimus" ("who was most powerful and most violent"). Modern commentators, for the most part, agree with Benvenuto. *Sesto*: Probably Sextus Pompeius Magnus, younger son of Pompey the Great and a notorious pirate.

135–37. *e in etterno munge . . . Rinier Pazzo*: Divine Justice is said to "milk" tears from the two robbers, to unlock from their hard hearts tears that they never shed in life when they wrought their "spietati danni" (vs. 106). The two Rinieri, robbers if not murderers, are standing with their heads above the boiling blood, whereas the tyrants are visible only from the brow up (vs. 103).

137. *Rinier da Corneto*: A notorious highway robber in Dante's day, of whom, however, little else is actually known. According to the *Anonimo fiorentino*, he was "grandissimo rubatore, tanto che mentre visse tenea in paura tutta Maremma" ("a very great bandit who, while he lived, held all the Maremma in fear of him"). *Corneto*: See n. to *Inf.* XIII, 9. *Rinier Pazzo*: Another highway robber of Dante's day (died before 1280), who was well known in the territory between Florence and Arezzo. The *Ottimo Commento* says of him:

> Rinieri Pazzo fu uno cavaliere de' Pazzi . . . questi fu a rubare li prelati della Chiesa di Roma per comandamento di Federigo II. imperadore delli Romani, circa li anni del Signore mille dugento ventotto; per la qual cosa elli, e li suoi discendenti furon sottoposti a perpetua scomunicazione, e contro a loro furon fatte leggi municipali in Firenze, le quali li privarono in perpetuo d'ogni beneficio.

> Rinier Pazzo was a knight of the Pazzi family . . . he set about robbing prelates of the Church of Rome by command of Frederick II, emperor of the Romans, around the year of our Lord 1228; because of this he and his descendants were put under perpetual excommunication and in Florence municipal laws were made against them, perpetually depriving them of any rights.

For one of these laws, see E. Regis (1912).

139. *ripassossi = si ripassò*. *Si* serves as a distancing pleonastic reflexive (see n. to *Inf.* VII, 94). Such backward glances in the poem have the effect of making the space of the otherworld more real. If this journey were given merely as a dream or vision, that space might well fade out as the wayfarer moves on, leaving no sense of its continuing existence.

CANTO XIII

1. *Non era ancor di là Nesso arrivato*: On the value of such backward glances in giving a sense of real space, see n. to *Inf.* XII, 139.

2-9. *quando noi ci mettemmo . . . i luoghi cólti*: The anaphoric device of the repeated "non" is the salient feature of these opening verses describing the second *girone* of the seventh circle, in which those who have denied (done violence to) nature are punished. The description of the wood may derive in part from a passage in Seneca's *Hercules furens*, in which Theseus describes his own journey to Hades. There near the stream Cocytus, he tells, lies a wood where (vs. 689) "horrent opaca fronde nigrantes comae" ("the leaves shudder, black with gloomy foliage") and (vs. 687) "hic vultur, illic luctifer bubo gemit" ("here the vulture, there the dole-bringing owl utters its cry"). In the wood (vss. 698-703):

> Non prata viridi laeta facie germinant
> nec adulta leni fluctuat Zephyro seges;
> non ulla ramos silva pomiferos habet:
> sterilis profundi vastitas squalet soli
> et foeda tellus torpet aeterno situ,
> rerumque maestus finis et mundi ultima.

No meadows bud, joyous with verdant view, no ripened
corn waves in the gentle breeze; not any grove has
fruit-producing boughs; the barren desert of the abysmal
fields lies all untilled, and the foul land lies torpid in
endless sloth—sad end of things, the world's last estate.

As Porena has observed, the wood of this second *girone* is
the only vegetation in the whole of Hell proper (below the
second circle, at the entrance to which Minos stands and
judges); but, he points out, unlike the "meadow of fresh
verdure" of *Inf.* IV, 111, it only adds to the impression of
horror. / As the wayfarers leave the river of boiling blood
and pass into the wood, they come upon the two groups
of sinners that are punished there: suicides and spendthrifts
(see the general exposition in *Inf.* XI, 28–45, and specifically
40–45).

3. *che da neun sentiero era segnato*: A pathless wood was
especially horrible to the medieval mind. As Boccaccio
comments: "Per questo si può comprendere il bosco dovere
essere stato salvatico e per conseguente orribile." ("From
this we can understand that the wood must have been wild,
and therefore horrible.") Later (vss. 97–99) we learn that
the "plants" take root wherever chance casts them; hence
there is no discernible order here, and this too makes the
wood more repulsive.   *neun = nessuno.*

6. *pomi*: Any kind of fruit or seed that might be pro-
duced by such shrubs as these. Edible fruit would hardly
be expected here.

7. *han = hanno.* The subject is "quelle fiere" in the fol-
lowing verse.   *sterpi*: Buti comments: "Sterpi sono pruni
et altri piccoli arbuscelli i quali sono molto folti et involti
insieme . . . che si chiamano macchie." ("*Sterpi* are very
dense and intertwined thorn bushes or other shrubs . . .
that are called thickets.") The image is one of a dense
wilderness of low-growing bushes; there are no tall trees
with clearly visible trunks. Although the word "tronco"
("trunk") does appear is vs. 33, it is used there in quite
another sense.

9. *tra Cecina e Corneto*: The Cecina River flows into the Mediterranean Sea about twenty miles south of Leghorn. The town of Corneto (see Rinier da Corneto, *Inf.* XII, 137 and the note) is situated on the Marta River, about ten miles north of Civitavecchia, and is named here probably to indicate that stream, since the Cecina and the Marta serve roughly to mark the northern and southern limits of the Tuscan Maremma, which was famous for its dense wild growth of vegetation, unrelieved by fields (see Map 3). The wild boar and other beasts that lived in the Maremma, Dante implies, must have preferred its denseness to more open, cultivated lands ("i luoghi cólti"). *Cecina*: Pronounced *Cècina*.

10–15. *le brutte Arpie . . . alberi strani*: The Harpies were loathsome monsters in the shape of birds, with clawed hands and the faces of women. Dante here alludes to an incident recounted by Virgil, in which Aeneas and his companions are driven from the Strophades (islands in the Ionian Sea) by the Harpies, who befoul their feast and prophesy their eventual starvation (see *Aen* III, 209–12, 214–18, 225–35, 242–57).

10. *Arpie*: Pronounced *Arpìe*.

11. *cacciar = cacciarono*.

16. *entre = entri*.

17. *nel secondo girone*: The second ring of the seventh circle; see the description of this circle in *Inf.* XI, 28–45.

18–19. *mentre che*: "Until."

19. *l'orribil sabbione*: Of the next, or third, *girone* of the seventh circle. The adjective generates a certain suspense.

20. *sì vederai*: On this use of "sì," see n. to *Inf.* XII, 98.

21. *torrien* (pronounced *torrìen*) *= torrebbero*. *sermone*: "Discourse." The whole verse amounts to: "things you would not believe, were I to tell them to you." See Aeneas'

words (*Aen.* III, 39): "Eloquar, an sileam?" ("Should I speak or be silent?")

22. *sentia = sentiva.   trarre guai*: See *Inf.* V, 48.

23. *persona = nessuno.*

25. *Cred' io ch'ei credette*: The first of several highly con-ceited verses in this canto, probably intended to imitate the literary style of Pier della Vigna, the first soul who ad-dresses the wayfarers in this wood (vs. 32); see F. D'Ovidio (1907), p. 206.   *credesse =credessi.*

26. *bronchi*: Large "sterpi" (see vs. 7).

27. *gente che per noi si nascondesse*: "Persons hidden from us," not, as some commentators would have it, "persons hiding from us."   *per noi = a noi.*

28. *Però = perciò.*

29. *este = queste.*

30. *monchi*: Literally, "lopped off."

31. *Allor porsi la mano un poco avante*: The verb *porgere* and the modifying phrase, "un poco," clearly suggest that the wayfarer makes a hesitant movement; the words "colsi un ramicel" in the following verse, and especially the di-minutive suffix, carry forward this impression: Dante breaks off the mere tip of a branch.

31-45. *Allor porsi la mano . . . come l'uom che teme*: In this passage Dante apparently has followed closely an epi-sode in the *Aeneid* (III, 22-48) in several respects:

>forte fuit iuxta tumulus, quo cornea summo
>virgulta et densis hastilibus horrida myrtus.
>accessi, viridemque ab humo convellere silvam
>conatus, ramis tegerem ut frondentibus aras,
>horrendum et dictu video mirabile monstrum.
>nam quae prima solo ruptis radicibus arbos
>vellitur, huic atro liquuntur sanguine guttae
>et terram tabo maculant. mihi frigidus horror

membra quatit, gelidusque coit formidine sanguis.
rursus et alterius lentum convellere vimen
insequor et causas penitus temptare latentis;
ater et alterius sequitur de cortice sanguis.
multa movens animo Nymphas venerabar agrestis
Gradivumque patrem, Geticis qui praesidet arvis,
rite secundarent visus omenque levarent.
tertia sed postquam maiore hastilia nisu
adgredior genibusque adversae obluctor harenae
(eloquar, an sileam?), gemitus lacrimabilis imo
auditur tumulo, et vox reddita fertur ad auris:
"quid miserum, Aenea, laceras? iam parce sepulto,
parce pias scelerare manus. non me tibi Troia
externum tulit, aut cruor hic de stipite manat.
heu! fuge crudelis terras, fuge litus avarum.
nam Polydorus ego. hic confixum ferrea texit
telorum seges et iaculis increvit acutis."
tum vero ancipiti mentem formidine pressus
obstipui steteruntque comae et vox faucibus haesit.

By chance, hard by there was a mound, on whose top
were cornel bushes and myrtles bristling with crowded
spear-shafts. I drew near; and essaying to tear up the
green growth from the soil, that I might deck the altar
with leafy boughs, I see an awful portent, wondrous to
tell. For from the first tree, which is torn from the
ground with broken roots, drops of black blood trickle
and stain the earth with gore. A cold shudder shakes
my limbs, and my chilled blood freezes with terror.
Once more, from a second also I go on to pluck a tough
shoot and probe deep the hidden cause; from the bark
of the second also follows black blood. Pondering much
in heart, I prayed the woodland Nymphs, and father
Gradivus, who rules over the Getic fields, duly to bless
the vision and lighten the omen. But when with greater
effort I assail the third shafts, and with my knees wrestle
against the resisting sand—should I speak or be silent?
—a piteous groan is heard from the depth of the mound,
and an answering voice comes to my ears. "Woe is me!
why, Aeneas, dost thou tear me? Spare me in the tomb

at last; spare the pollution of thy pure hands! I, born of
Troy, am no stranger to thee; not from a lifeless stock
oozes this blood. Ah! flee the cruel land, flee the greedy
shore! For I am Polydorus. Here an iron harvest of
spears covered my pierced body, and grew up into sharp
javelins." Then, indeed, with mind borne down with
perplexing dread, I was appalled, my hair stood up, and
the voice clave to my throat.

On Polydorus, see n. to *Inf.* XXX, 18.

32. *un gran pruno*: The emphasis is on "gran." Benvenuto
comments: "Et hic nota, quod hic erat inclusa anima magna
viri magni." ("And here note that there has been enclosed
here the great spirit of a great man.") The great bush ex-
emplifies a motif familiar in medieval art, in which greater
physical size denotes greater moral stature (see n. to *Inf.* X,
52–54 on towering Farinata). Although he is never named,
this is the soul of Pier della Vigna (*ca.* 1190–1249), min-
ister of the Emperor Frederick II. He appears to have been
of humble origin (his name perhaps implying that he was
the son of a vine dresser) and to have studied at Bologna,
either at the expense of a patron or supported by charity. He
soon attracted the notice of the archbishop of Palermo and
was recommended to Frederick II. Pier entered the court
ca. 1220 and rapidly rose to distinction. Between 1225 and
1247 he served variously as judge, ambassador, chancellor,
and private secretary to Frederick. In 1231, as chancellor of
the Italian realms, he revised and rearranged the whole
body of statute law. In 1234–35, he negotiated the marriage
of Frederick with Isabella, sister of Henry III of England.
Although by 1247 he was at the height of his power as
Frederick's most intimate adviser, two years later he sud-
denly fell into disgrace, and was arrested at Cremona,
thrown into prison, and blinded. The cause of his fall is
not accurately known; the most probable surmise is that he
was suspected of having intrigued with the pope and of
having attempted, at the latter's instigation, to poison the
emperor. It was a general opinion, in which both Dante
and Villani shared, that he was the victim of calumnious

accusations on the part of those jealous of his supreme in-
fluence with the emperor. Soon after his disgrace and im-
prisonment he committed suicide (it is said by dashing his
brains out against a wall). / Like his imperial master, Pier
della Vigna was a poet. Some of his poems and a number
of Latin letters have been preserved. For examples of his
poetry, see G. Contini (1960), vol. I, pp. 119–28; the letters
have been edited by A. Huillard-Bréholles (1865).

33. *'l tronco suo*: The stub or broken-off branch of the
thorn bush, not the trunk of the bush, as some commen-
tators and translators understand it.   *schiante = schianti*
(also used of breaking branches in *Inf.* IX, 70: "li rami
schianta"). See *Aen.* III, 41, quoted in n. to vss. 31–45. In
addition to the Polydorus episode of the *Aeneid*, Dante may
have had in mind in writing this passage a similar one in
Ovid's *Metamorphoses* (II, 358–66). This recounts the
transformation of the Heliades into poplar trees when they
were mourning the death of their brother, Phaëthon:

> non satis est: truncis avellere corpora temptat
> et teneros manibus ramos abrumpit, at inde
> sanguineae manant tamquam de vulnere guttae.
> "parce, precor, mater," quaecumque est saucia, clamat,
> "parce, precor: nostrum laceratur in arbore corpus
> iamque vale"—cortex in verba novissima venit.
> inde fluunt lacrimae, stillataque sole rigescunt
> de ramis electra novis, quae lucidus amnis
> excipit et nuribus mittit gestanda Latinis.

That is not enough: she tries to tear away the bark
from their bodies and breaks off slender twigs with her
hands. But as she does this bloody drops trickle forth
as from a wound. And each one, as she is wounded,
cries out: "Oh, spare me, mother; spare, I beg you. 'Tis
my body that you are tearing in the tree. And now
farewell"—the bark closed over her latest words. Still
their tears flow on, and these tears, hardened into amber
by the sun, drop down from the new-made trees. The
clear river receives them and bears them onward, one
day to be worn by the brides of Rome.

34-35. *Da che fatto fu poi di sangue bruno, ricominciò*: Later (vss. 91-92), the bleeding of the branch momentarily chokes the voice coming from it.

35. *scerpi*: Cf. the Latin *discerpere*, "to rend," "to mangle."

36. *alcuno* = *nessuno*.

40. *stizzo* = *tizzo* (*tizzone*). Clearly the form beginning with *s* contributes more to the desired effect of hissing. Either term signifies a branch or a fire log.

41. *geme*: "Drips" with sap.

42. *cigola*: "Hisses" with the escaping steam. Benvenuto comments with admiration on the appropriateness of the simile: "Comparatio est propria ex omni parte sui, quia de ramo ad ramum, de humore ad sanguinem, de stridore rami ad clamorem rami, de violentia ardoris ad violentiam doloris." ("The comparison is fitting in every respect, from the branch to the limb, from the humor to the blood, from the creaking of the branch to the cry of the limb, from the violence of the burning to the violence of the pain.")

43-44. *usciva insieme parole e sangue*: As noted before, Dante frequently uses a singular verb with a plural subject. The construction is especially effective here.

44-45. *io lasciai la cima cadere*: The tip of the branch, which the wayfarer has plucked and is still holding in his hand, he now lets fall in fright and amazement "like one who is afraid." The corresponding line in the *Aeneid* passage is vs. 48.

48. *la mia rima*: An explicit reference to the Polydorus episode in the *Aeneid*.

52. *dilli* = *digli* (imperative).

53. *tua fama rinfreschi*: Virgil does not yet know who the spirit is and merely appeals to that which is dear to so many souls in Hell, their earthly fame. But, as becomes clear in vss. 55-57, to this soul especially these are "sweet words."

54. *li lece = gli è lecito.   lece =* Latin *licet.*

55. *'l tronco:* Again, as in vs. 33, the bleeding stub of the broken branch.

55-57. *adeschi . . . inveschi:* Pier's language, anticipated by Dante's words in vs. 25, now is full of conceits. These verbs, taken from bird hunting, are appropriate to the branch. *Adescare* is based on *esca,* "lure," "bait"; and *invescare,* on *vischio,* "bird lime," a kind of glue, which is smeared on branches and is so sticky that birds, once enticed to alight, adhere to it and are taken. Thus, Virgil's words of promise to the soul of renewed fame in the world above are sweet words ("dolce dir") that lure it, as it says, by beliming it to speak, to tell its tale and so to make the request in vss. 76-78.

56. *e voi non gravi = e a voi non sia grave.* "Voi" is dative here.

58-59. *ambo le chiavi del cor di Federigo:* See Isa. 22:22: "Et dabo clavem domus David super humerum eius; et aperiet et non erit qui claudat, et claudet et non erit qui aperiat." ("And I will lay the key of the house of David upon his shoulder: and he shall open, and none shall shut: and he shall shut, and none shall open.") Sapegno quotes a letter by a friend of Pier's, one Nicola della Rocca, which refers to Pier as "tamquam imperii claviger, claudit, et nemo aperit; aperit, et nemo claudit" ("the key-bearer, so to speak, of the empire: what he shuts, none can open; what he opens, none can shut").

59. *Federigo:* The Emperor Frederick II; see n. to *Inf.* X, 119 for biographical details.

60. *soavi = soavemente.*

61. *secreto suo:* His confidence, and secret matters of state.

62. *fede:* Torraca notes that the word comes in an emphatic position.

63. *li sonni e ' polsi*: "My sleep and my health." Porena comments that the pulses ("polsi") denote the arteries, and since the pulsing of the blood through the arteries is the condition of being alive, they symbolize vitality in general.

64–65. *La meretrice*: Envy.   *l'ospizio di Cesare*: The imperial court.   *non torse li occhi putti*: The sin of envy is thought of as a movement of the eyes, first of all. Thus, in *Purg.* XIII-XIV, souls are purged of that sin by having their eyelids sewed shut. Pietro di Dante, commenting on *Purg.* XIII, says: "Invidia facit, quod non videatur, quod expedit videre; et ideo dicitur *invidia*, quasi *non visio*." ("Envy causes that which should be seen not to be seen. And therefore it is called *invidia*, almost as if to say, nonvision.") Grandgent (p. 432) quotes the *Magnae derivationes* of Uguccione da Pisa: "*Invideo tibi*, idest non video tibi, idest non fero videre te bene agentem." ("I envy you—that is to say, I do not see you; that is, I cannot bear to see you doing well.")

66. *morte comune*: See Sapien. 2:24: "Invidia autem diaboli mors introivit in orbem terrarum." ("But by the envy of the devil, death entered the world.") See also Prov. 14:30: "Vita carnium sanitas cordis, putredo ossium invidia." ("A tranquil mind gives life to the body, but [envy] rots the bones.") Envy sends forth other sins to beset us; cupidity, for one, is represented by the "lupa" in Canto I, whom the hound will drive back into Hell, "là onde 'nvidia prima dipartilla" (*Inf.* I, 111). Thus envy, as the source of other sins, is the "common ruin" of mankind and the prevailing "vice of courts."

67–72. *infiammò contra me . . . contra me giusto*: Note the many alliterations and antitheses in these verses, all suggestive of the *altus stilus* of Pier's Latin writings. Cf. vss. 25, 55–57.

68. *infiammar = infiammarono.*   *Augusto*: The Emperor Frederick II.

69. *che ' lieti onor = che i lieti onor.* Some early manu-
scripts have *che lieti*, but since the article *i* was often written
e, this actually represents *che i*, without any punctuation to
indicate the fact.   *tornaro = tornarono.*

70. *per disdegnoso gusto*: We learn the object of Pier's
scorn only in the following verse; it is a scorn "to escape
from scorn." Note also the stylistic device of the repeated
"disdegno."

71. *credendo col morir fuggir disdegno*: Seeking to flee a
life that has become unbearable, because of the scorn of
others and especially that of the emperor, Pier, like other
suicides, chooses death as the lesser of two evils.

72. *ingiusto fece me contra me giusto*: Suicide, like all other
sins in lower Hell, is a sin of malice (see *Inf.* XI, 22–24)
and intends some injustice. This injustice, considered in its
objective, or moral, aspect, consists of doing harm to an-
other, either by force or by fraud: "ed ogni fin cotale / o con
forza o con frode altrui contrista." Here in Canto XIII the
phrases "ingiusto me" and "giusto me" serve to distinguish
two persons in the suicide, so that the act of suicide may be
seen as a case of harming another, as it were, while the
means to the end, force, makes suicide a sin of violence.

73. *Per le nove radici*: After the climax of the preceding
verse, Pier's manner of speaking, which imitates his lit-
erary style, becomes straightforward and simple. The mean-
ing of "nove" may be either "new" (Pier's "bush" is little
more than fifty years old, since he took his own life in the
spring of 1249) or "strange" (as explained later, vss. 97–99,
since the roots sprouted from the soul itself as from a seed).
The latter meaning seems preferable. Accordingly, as Por-
ena observes, to swear by such roots amounts to swearing
per l'anima mia ("by my soul").

75. *che fu d'onor sì degno*: The emperor remains blameless
in the eyes of his faithful servant.

76. *E se di voi alcun nel mondo riede*: "Se" does not imply
any real doubt here. Virgil has assured Pier (vs. 54) that

it is permitted to his companion to return to the world above. Nowhere are we told whether the souls inside these bushes can see. Farther on (vs. 139), another "bush man," not perceiving that Dante is alive, takes the wayfarers to be two "souls."

77. *la memoria mia*: "The memory of me," "my fame," which Virgil has said can be renewed for Pier in the world above.

79. *Un poco attese*: The subject is "il poeta," in the following verse.

85–86. *Se l'om ti faccia . . . dir priega*: The formula of adjuration that is used so often in the poem; see, for example, *Inf.* X, 82, 94.

85. *om* = French *on*.

86. *liberamente*: "Generously," without need of promptings or entreaties.

88. *dirne* = *dirci*.   *come l'anima si lega*: The question focuses with keenest interest on the relation of the soul to the "plant body." The words "si lega" continue the suggestion of imprisonment, stressed not only by the words "spirito incarcerato" (vs. 87) but also by the opposite notion of liberation expressed in the words "si spiega" (vs. 90) of the second question.

89. *in questi nocchi*: "In these gnarled bushes."   *dinne* = *dicci*.

90. *si spiega*: Literally, "unfolds itself," frees itself from the prison of such a body.

91. *Allor soffiò il tronco forte*: While Virgil is speaking, the bleeding of the branch has somewhat obstructed the outlet for the voice in the broken end. The spirit now must puff hard to reopen it. (See this point carried forward in *Inf.* XIV, 3.)

95. *disvelta* = *divelta* (*divellere*); "to uproot" is the literal meaning. The word is doubly appropriate here, first

because it is spoken by a spirit who has put down new roots in Hell, and because it refers to a deed of violence committed by an "anima feroce" (vs. 94).

96. *Minòs la manda*: See *Inf.* V, 6: "giudica e manda secondo ch'avvinghia." *foce*: Cf. the Latin *faux*, "gullet." Porena comments that "foce" here refers to the seventh circle conceived as a gullet opened to receive the sinner. See "gola" in this sense in *Inf.* XXIV, 123.

97. *non l'è parte scelta*: This explains why the wood is trackless and devoid of plan or order. See vs. 3 and the note. *scelta = prescelta*.

98. *balestra*: Literally, "shoots," as from a crossbow (*balestra*), hence conveying violent motion.

99. *germoglia come gran di spelta*: Spelt, like wheat, barley, and other such grains, germinates by sending up first a single shoot and later many shoots, which form a clump (*cesto*; see vs. 142). Boccaccio observes in his *Comento*: "È la spelda una biada, la qual, gittata in buona terra, cestisce molto." ("Spelt is a grain which, when sown in good earth, sprouts many shoots.") Thus the bushes in this wood of Canto XIII are thick, many-branched clumps, none presenting a single, clean trunk to view.

Dante's image of the spelt seed with its many shoots corresponds to Virgil's image of the mound of the dead Polydorus (*Aen.* III, 23), "densis hastilibus horrida" ("bristling with crowded spear-shafts"). The mound still bears witness to the manner of his death (*Aen.* III, 45–46): "Hic confixum ferrea texit / telorum seges et iaculis increvit acutis." ("Here an iron harvest of spears covered my pierced body, and grew up into sharp javelins.")

100. *vermena*: The first tender sprout or shoot that the plant sends up.

102. *fanno dolore, e al dolor fenestra*: The Harpies feed upon the foliage, and in so doing produce lacerations which at one and the same time cause the imprisoned spirits pain and

create an outlet ("window") for them to express their pain. This detail now explains the wailings that the wayfarer heard at once throughout the gruesome wood (vs. 22), without being able to see who might be uttering them.

103. *Come l'altre verrem per nostre spoglie*: Virgil has asked (vss. 89–90) whether any spirit in the wood ever frees itself from its bush. This answer clearly implies that only at the Last Judgment (see *Inf.* VI, 96-98) will any of these souls be permitted to leave their plant bodies. On that day, like all other souls, they will assemble in the Valley of Jehoshaphat, but, unlike the rest, they will not reclothe themselves in their flesh. They will return, as explained in vss. 106–8, only to be reincarcerated forever, each in its own bush.

105. *ché non è giusto aver ciò ch'om si toglie*: Thus the sin of suicide, in accordance with its classification in Canto XI, is seen again as an act of injustice ("iniuria").

106. *strascineremo*: The word suggests more violence than would *trascinare*. F. D'Ovidio (1907, p. 172) remarks that the necessity for the souls of suicides to drag the "dead weight" of their own bodies is another example of *contrapasso* (see n. to *Inf.* III, 52–54).

108. *l'ombra sua molesta*: The violent and unjust soul (see n. to vs. 72); also see "anima feroce," vs. 94.

110. *ne = ci.*

112. *colui*: One of the several hunters who would be stationed, each in a different place (*posta*), where the hunt might pass. The whole episode of this wild hunt seems to owe something to Ovid's account of Actaeon, who was torn to pieces by his own hounds (*Metam.* III, 198–252).

The wood of this second *girone* already has been compared (vss. 2–9) to the Tuscan Maremma, which was famous for its wild beasts and particularly the wild boar. The presage made by such a comparison is now realized, but here the quarry is not a wild beast but a human soul. Nor should we forget that of the three dispositions named in

Canto XI (vss. 82–83), bestiality (*bestialitas*) applies to this seventh circle and has already been symbolized by the centaurs, who were also dedicated to the chase and who carried bows and arrows for their own hunt along the river of blood.

115. *da la sinistra costa*: "On the left side."

117. *rompieno* (pronounced *rompièno*) = *rompevano*.
ogne rosta: "Every branch" of the dense, pathless wood. However, since the "naked" spirits are forced to endure the torment of being chased through the wood, "rosta" here might be construed as "obstacle." For examples of *rosta* meaning "obstacle," see M. Barbi (1934b), p. 208; and see "arrostarsi," used in the sense of self-defense (against an obstacle), in *Inf*. XV, 39.

118. *Quel dinanzi*: Lano (named in vs. 120), a gentleman of Siena, said to be a member of the Maconi family. According to some of the early commentators, Lano (an abbreviation for Arcolano) belonged to the notorious Brigata Spendereccia, or "Spendthrift Club," of Siena (see *Inf*. XXIX, 130 and the note), and squandered all his property in riotous living. He appears to have taken part in an expedition against Arezzo in 1288, which ended in the defeat of the Sienese force. The Sienese fell into an ambush near Arezzo and were cut to pieces by the Aretines under Buonconte da Montefeltro. See Villani (VII, 120) for an account of the incident. *accorri, accorri, morte*: Fleeing in terror before the hounds, this soul invokes death before he is torn to pieces; but death as cessation of torment he will never have, in this his eternal "second death" (see *Inf*. I, 117).

119. *l'altro*: This is Jacopo da Santo Andrea of Padua (named in vs. 133), reported to have inherited a considerable fortune which he squandered in the most senseless acts of prodigality. Benvenuto gives the following account of him, which he claims to have had from a trustworthy source:

Debes scire, quod iste Jacobus . . . fuit de potenti civitate Paduae, vir nobilis de capella sancti Andreae,

a qua denominationem sumpsit; homo quidem ditissi-
mus omnium privatorum suae patriae in campis, villis,
pecuniis, animalibus; qui inaestimabilem epulentiam
divitiarum prodigaliter, immo proterve et insane perdi-
dit et consumpsit. Nam, ut audivi a fide dignis de terra
sua, fecit multas ridendas vanitates. Semel cum non
posset dormire, mandavit, ut portarentur plures petiae
pignolati cipriani facti cum colla, et lacerarentur a
familiaribus in camera, ut ad illum stridulum sonum
provocaretur sibi somnus; ideo digne autor facit ipsum
a canibus lacerari, non ad solatium, sed ad supplicium.
Alia vice cum iret de Padua Venetias per flumen
Brentae in navi cum aliis iuvenibus sociis, quorum
aliqui pulsabant, aliqui contabant, iste fatuus, ne solus
videretur inutilis et otiosus, coepit accipere pecuniam,
et denarios singulatim deiicere in aquam cum magno
risu omnium. Sed ne discurrendo per ista videar tibi
magis prodigus verborum quam ipse nummorum, venio
breviter ad magnam violentiam, quam insane fecit in
bona sua. Cum enim semel esset in rure suo, audivit
quemdam magnatem cum comitiva magna nobilium ire
ad prandium secum; et quia non erat provisus, nec
poterat in brevissimo temporis spatio providere, secun-
dum quod suae prodigalitati videbatur convenire, subito
egregia cautela usus est; nam fecit statim mitti ignem
in omnia tuguria villae suae satis apta incendio, quia
ex paleis, stipulis et canulis, qualia sunt communiter
domicilia rusticorum in territorio paduanorum; et veni-
ens obviam istis dixit quod fecerat hoc ad festum et
gaudium propter eorum adventum, ut ipsos magnifi-
centius honoraret. In hoc certe violentior et vanior fuit
Nerone; quia Nero fecit incendi domos urbis, iste vero
proprias . . . . Ideo bene autor induxit canes ad faciendam
venationem de eo, qui sibi et alteri violentiam misera-
bilem intulerat.

You must know that this Jacopo . . . was a citizen of
the powerful city of Padua, a nobleman of the parish
of Santo Andrea, from which he took his name. He
was in truth the richest of all the private citizens of

his country, possessing more fields, farmhouses, money, and cattle than anyone. He prodigally—or rather, wickedly and insanely—squandered and wasted an inestimable treasure of wealth. Indeed, I have heard from reliable people of his country that he committed many acts so frivolous as to be even risible. Once, when he could not sleep, he ordered several lengths of Cyprian linen, treated with rosin [to make it stiff], brought to his room. Then he had his servants tear them up, so that the strident sound might induce sleep. Thus, the author very appropriately has him torn apart by dogs; and the tearing is no longer a pleasure, but a torment.

Another time, he was going from Padua to Venice on board a boat on the river Brenta, together with some young friends, some of whom played while others sang. In order not to seem the only one who was useless and idle, this fool began to take money, and to throw a coin at a time into the water, to the great laughter of everyone.

But, lest my lengthy talk of these matters make me seem more prodigal of words than he was of money, I shall quickly come to the greatest act of violence he madly committed against his possessions. Once, when he was in his country place, he heard that a certain important person, together with a large entourage of nobles, was coming to dine with him. Since he was not prepared for them, and could not, in the short space of time, provide for them in a manner consonant with his prodigality, he immediately had recourse to an extraordinary measure. In fact, right on the spot, he had fire set to all the cottages on his estate, which were highly inflammable, being made of posts, boards, and reeds, as the dwellings of the peasants in the Paduan territory generally are. Coming forth to greet them, he said he had done this to celebrate their arrival, and to make it joyous; for he wanted to honor them magnificently. In this, surely, he was more violent and more foolish than Nero; for Nero had the houses of the city burned, but he his own . . . . The author, then, very rightly has the dogs hunt him, for he did terrible violence to him-self and to others.

Jacopo is supposed to have been put to death by order of Ezzelino III da Romano (see *Inf.* XII, 110 and the note) in 1239. On political and social changes possibly occasioned by the decadence of Jacopo and others of his class, see R. Cessi (1908); see also E. Salvagnini (1865).   *cui pareva tardar troppo*: As compared with the other, Lano, who is running faster and is out ahead of him.   *cui*: The dative, "to whom."

120-21. *sì non furo accorte le gambe tue*: The words are a taunting reminder to Lano of how fast he ran away, in fear and cowardice, from the battle (in which he never-theless lost his life; see n. to vs. 118).

120. *furo = furono*.

121. *dal*: Da more than *di* indicates the vicinity of the Toppo.   *Toppo*: The ford (apparently across a branch of the Chiana), near Arezzo, where a Sienese force was cut to pieces by the Aretines in 1288 (see n. to vs. 118).

122. *li = gli*.   *fallia = falliva*.   *lena*: See *Inf.* I, 22.

123. *di sé e d'un cespuglio fece un groppo*: Another defini-tion of "groppo" is "clump." The meaning of the phrase is made clearer by the expression "fare schermo" (vs. 134).

126. *come veltri ch'uscisser di catena*: See Dante's *Rime* LXI, 3: "e di guinzagli uscir veltri correnti" ("and fleet hounds issuing from the leash").

127. *miser = misero (mettere)*.

128. *dilaceraro = dilacerarono*.

129. *sen portar = se ne portarono (si portarono via)*. The punishment of the squanderer on the principle of *contra-passo* (see n. to *Inf.* III, 52-54) is most evident; the one who brought about his own ruin by wasting or scattering his substance is eternally torn to pieces and "scattered" by these dogs, over and over again.

130. *Presemi* = *mi prese*.

131. *menommi* = *mi menò*.

131–32. *al cespuglio che piangea per le rotture sanguinenti*:
The fact that the bush is weeping through its many bleed-
ing fractures is stressed again when Virgil addresses it in
vss. 137-38.

132. *in vano*: Modifies "piangea."

136. *fermo* = *fermato*.

137. *punte*: See *Purg.* III, 119. The word here refers to the
many bleeding tips of the branches, or "rotture sanguinenti"
of vs. 132; see M. Barbi (1934b), p. 208.

138. *sermo*: A Latinism, "speech" (see "sermone," vs. 21).

139. *O anime*: The bush is unaware that the wayfarer is
alive, yet obviously knows that the one who has spoken to
him has a companion.

140. *disonesto*: See *Aen.* VI, 497: "truncas inhonesto volnere
naris" ("his nostrils lopped by a shameful wound").

142. *cesto*: The word again stresses the image of the ger-
minating grain of spelt (see Boccaccio's use of *cestire*,
quoted in n. to vs. 99). G. Manuzzi (1859, p. 659), under
the first "cesto" entry, gives the meaning as "pianta di
frutice, e d'erba; (e propriamente dicesi di Quelle piante,
che sopra una radice moltiplicano i figliuoli in un mucchio)"
("a kind of shrub or plant—properly speaking, it designates
those plants that send a clump of many shoots off one
root").

143. *I' fui de la città*: According to some of the early
commentators, the identity of this Florentine suicide is not
known; others (Bambaglioli, Lana, and the *Anonimo fioren-
tino*) identify him as one Lotto degli Agli, a Florentine
judge who went home and hanged himself after delivering
an unjust judgment. Other commentators think the person
intended was Rocco de' Mozzi, who hanged himself in

despair at finding himself bankrupt. The *Chiose anonime*, for example, comments: "Questo cespuglio che piangea si ebbe nome Rucco de' Mozzi da Firenze; e fu molto ricco: e perchè la compagnia loro fallì venne in tanta povertà che egli s'impiccò egli stesso in casa sua." ("The name of this weeping shrub was Rocco de' Mozzi of Florence. He had been a very rich man, but when his company failed, he fell into such poverty that he hanged himself in his own house.") G. Masi (1938) discusses the question at length.

la città: Florence.

143-50. *nel Batista . . . indarno*: According to legend, recounted by the chroniclers and early commentators (see, for example, Villani, I, 42), the citizens of Florence in pagan times chose Mars to be their special patron; and in the time of Augustus, soon after the first founding of the city, they erected a great temple in his honor. They made a statue of the god as an armed knight on horseback and placed it atop a column in the middle of the temple. In the fourth century, the legend continues (see Villani I, 60), when the Florentines adopted Christianity, they substituted John the Baptist for the pagan god as patron of their city. They converted the temple of Mars into a church and dedicated it to St. John (San Giovanni); mindful of the tradition concerning the statue of Mars, they removed it to a tower near the Arno. Villani explains (I, 60):

> E nol vollono rompere nè spezzare, perocchè per loro antiche memorie trovavano, che il detto idolo di Marti era consegrato sotto ascendente di tale pianeta, che come fosse rotto e commosso in vile luogo, la città avrebbe pericolo e danno, e grande mutazione.

> They did not want to break or destroy it; for according to ancient tradition, this idol of Mars was consecrated under the ascendance of such a planet that as soon as it was broken, or moved to a vile place, the city would suffer danger and harm, and great changes would take place.

According to the legend (Villani, II, 1), the statue remained in the tower until the destruction of Florence in 450 by

Attila (confused by Villani and others with Totila), at which time it fell into the river. The church of San Gio-vanni—known as the Baptistery—was spared from the general ruin. Later, at the beginning of the ninth century, when the city was rebuilt by Charlemagne, the Florentines recovered the statue from the river and placed it on a pillar on the river bank where the Ponte Vecchio afterward was built. According to Villani (III, 1):

> Dicesi che gli antichi aveano oppinione, che di rifarla [la città] non s'ebbe podere, se prima non fu ritrovata e tratta d'Arno l'imagine di marmo, consecrata per li primi edificatori pagani per nigromanzia a Marti, la quale era stata nel fiume d'Arno dalla distruzione di Firenze infino a quello tempo; e ritrovata, la puosero in su uno piliere in su la riva del detto fiume, ov'è oggi il capo del ponte vecchio.

> The ancients, it is said, believed that it [the city] could not be rebuilt until they first found and removed from the Arno the marble statue, which the first founders had consecrated by necromancy to Mars, and which had been in the river Arno since the time of the destruction of Florence. They found it, and placed it atop a pillar on the bank of that river, in the place that today is the head of the Ponte Vecchio.

As the story goes, the statue remained on the Ponte Vecchio until the bridge was carried away by a great flood, after which it was never again seen or heard of (Villani, XI, 1).

A statue commonly believed to be of Mars did exist in Florence in Dante's time; the speaker here alludes to it in the word "vista" (vs. 147). The flood that destroyed it oc-curred in 1333, after Dante's death.

144. *ei* = *egli*.

145. *sempre con l'arte sua*: The art of the god Mars is, in this instance, civil war. Thus the dominant theme of this canto, of rending, of tearing asunder by violence (in this case, rending the body politic), is sustained. Indeed, the murder in 1215 of Buondelmonte de' Buondelmonti at the

foot of this statue of Mars on the Ponte Vecchio was the cause of a bitter feud which resulted in the introduction into Florence of the Guelph and Ghibelline factions and all the ensuing strife between these two parties. See *Inf.* XXVIII, 106–8 and n. to vs. 106.

146. *passo d'Arno*: The Ponte Vecchio.

147. *vista*: "Trace"; see M. Barbi (1934b), pp. 268–69. In *Par.* XVI, 145, this same remnant of a statue is termed a "pietra scema."

148. *rifondarno = rifondarono*.

149. *sovra 'l cener che d'Attila rimase*: Legend had it that Attila (see n. to *Inf.* XII, 134) had destroyed Florence. This tradition doubtless arose from a confusion of Attila with Totila, king of the Ostrogoths (541–52), by whose forces Florence was besieged in 542. Villani (II, 1) gives an account of the destruction of the city by "*Totile Flagellum Dei* re de' Goti e de' Vandali" ("Totila, the Scourge of God, king of the Goths and Vandals") in the year 440, thus hopelessly confounding the two. There appears to be no truth in the tradition that Florence was destroyed, either by Attila or by Totila, and rebuilt by Charlemagne, as both Dante and Villani believed.

150. *avrebber fatto lavorare indarno*: The city would have been destroyed again.

151. *fei = feci*.   *gibetto*: F. D'Ovidio (1907, pp. 330–31) points out that the word is derived from the OFr *gibet*, "gallows," and is here used more in the sense of "place of execution."   *de le mie case*: The plural indicates, as Porena observes, groups of buildings belonging to the same noble family.

CANTO XIV

1–3. *Poi che la carità . . . fioco*: A parting gesture of piety that is almost ritualistic. That the first-person protagonist is a Florentine has already been made clear in his encounters with Ciacco (*Inf.* VI, 49–52) and Farinata (*Inf.* X, 22–27). Dante's love for his native city emerges most poignantly again later. See *De vulg. eloqu.* I, vi, 3: "Florentiam adeo diligamus ut quia dileximus exilium patiamur iniuste" ("though we love Florence so dearly that for the love we bore her we are wrongfully suffering exile").

2. *mi strinse*: See *Aen.* IX, 294: "Animum patriae strinxit pietatis imago." ("The picture of filial love touched his soul.") Also see *Inf.* V, 128: "come amor lo strinse."
raunai = radunai.

3. *rende'le = le rendei.   ch'era già fioco*: Earlier the bleeding of the branch choked the passage of the voice (see n. to *Inf.* XIII, 91). Now the momentary healing of the wound, the clotting of the blood, makes the voice "faint." On "fioco" in this sense, see n. to *Inf.* I, 63.

4. *fine = confine.   si parte = si divide*.

6. *di giustizia orribil arte*: The rain of fire of vss. 28–30, called the "vendetta di Dio" in vs. 16. God is the maker of

this as of all other punishments in Hell. The words "orribil arte" echo the "orribil sabbione" of *Inf.* XIII, 19.

7. *cose nove*: "Things never seen before," "strange things." See *Inf.* VII, 20, for "novo" in the sense of "strange," as it is frequently used in the poem.

8-11. *dico che arrivammo . . . ad essa*: Compare these verses, which provide a comprehensive view of the whole of the seventh circle, with *Inf.* XII, 139 and *Inf.* XIII, 1-2. For the significance of such backward glances, see n. to *Inf.* XII, 139.

8. *landa*: A "plain," sometimes a clearing in a wood.

9. *che dal suo letto ogne pianta rimove*: The verse focuses on the *contrapasso*, or retributive, aspect of the torments. Sodomy, one of the three sins punished here, seems to have determined the mode of punishment. As sodomy is a denial of and an offense against nature, so the plain is said to reject all natural growth. "Letto" is used here in the sense of "suolo." In writing this passage (especially vss. 8-9 and 13-15), Dante evidently borrowed much from the description of the Libyan desert in Lucan's *Pharsalia* (IX, 431- 37):

> At, quaecumque vagam Syrtim conplectitur ora
> Sub nimio proiecta die, vicina perusti
> Aetheris, exurit messes et pulvere Bacchum
> Enecat et nulla putris radice tenetur.
> Temperies vitalis abest, et nulla sub illa
> Cura Iovis terra est; natura deside torpet
> Orbis et inmotis annum non sentit harenis.

But all that coast which surrounds the shifting Syrtis, as it lies flat under the scorching sun and near the parched sky, burns up corn-crops and smothers the vine with dust; and the powdery soil is bound together by no roots of plants. The temperate air that life needs is not found there, and Jupiter pays no heed to the land; Nature is inactive; the lifeless expanse, with sands that are never ploughed, is unconscious of the seasons.

12. *a randa a randa*: "Randa" derives from the German *Rand*. I. Del Lungo (1906, p. 82) points out that though the phrase "a randa" is unfamiliar to the modern ear, it was very much a part of Florentine idiom as late as 1600.

13. *spazzo = spazio* (Latin *spatium*), but with a difference of meaning. Sapegno calls attention to Vincenzo Borghini's explanation of the two words. See Borghini, "Errori," p. 248: "Noi abbiamo *spazio* e *spazzo*: diversi di dire e di significato; il primo importa *intervallum*, il secondo *solum*." ("We have *spazio* and *spazzo*, different in sound and in significance: the first means *intervallum* [interval]; the second *solum* [ground].") See also the passage from Lucan quoted in n. to vs. 9.

14. *colei*: The "rena" of vs. 13. On this use of the pronoun (nowadays a personal pronoun only) to refer to an inanimate object, see E. G. Parodi (1957), p. 250, n. 93.

15. *Caton*: Cato the Younger of Utica (95–46 B.C.), whose march through the Libyan desert shortly before his death is recounted in Lucan's *Pharsalia* (IX, 371–410). See also n. to vs. 9.

16. *vendetta di Dio*: The justice (vs. 6) meted out by a wrathful God to whom violence has been done, directly or indirectly (see *Inf.* XI, 46–48 and n. to vs. 48), by those who are punished in this circle.   *dei = devi*.

19. *anime nude*: Although all souls in Hell are nude (except the hypocrites of *Inf.* XXIII), Dante mentions the fact whenever he wishes to point up a particular great torment that is increased by a soul's going naked. See also, for example, *Inf.* XIII, 115–16.   *gregge*: Plural of *greggia*, "herd."

21. *diversa legge*: This phrase refers to the different postures of the souls under the rain of fire, as the following tercet makes clear.

22. *Supin = supino*. The adjective is used for the adverb.

22–24. *Supin giacea . . . sedea . . . andava . . .* : Each verse of the tercet refers to one of the three groups mentioned in *Inf.* XI, 49–51—blasphemers, usurers, and sodomites.

24. *continüamente*: The diaeresis is very effective.

25–27. *Quella che giva . . . sciolta*: The tercet narrows the focus to two of the three groups: those who run, the sodomites; and those who lie on their backs, the blasphemers. These are dealt with first.   *più molta =più numerosa*; the sodomites are said to outnumber the others.

27. *ma più al duolo avea la lingua sciolta*: The blasphemers, being those sinners guilty of the gravest sin in this whole seventh circle—a direct offense to God—endure the most pain. The *contrapasso* aspect of their torment is thus apparent in their supine position, for when they uttered their blasphemies they presumably turned their faces toward Heaven, and now as they utter their laments they hold their faces turned the same way, while God's punishing fire falls upon them.

28–29. *Sovra tutto 'l sabbion . . . falde*: The rain of fire is plainly reminiscent of the fire which fell upon Sodom and Gomorrah (Gen. 19:24): "Dominus pluit super Sodomam et Gomorrham sulphur et ignem a Domino de caelo." ("The Lord poured down on Sodom and Gomorra sulphur and fire from the Lord out of heaven.") See also Ezech. 38:22: "Ignem et sulphur pluam super eum." ("I will rain fire and brimstone upon him.")

30. *come di neve in alpe sanza vento*: This extremely effective verse seems to echo Guido Cavalcanti's "e bianca neve scender senza venti" ("and white snow falling without winds"), from his sonnet beginning "Biltà di donna" (in G. Contini, 1960, vol. II, p. 494, vs. 6), which names things pleasant to behold. For the rain of fire "like snow," see the quotation from Albertus Magnus in n. to vss. 31–36.   *alpe*: Dante frequently uses the word for "mountains" in a general sense.

31. *Quali*: Modifies "fiamme" (vs. 33).   *Alessandro*: See
n. to *Inf.* XII, 107.

31–36. *Quali Alessandro . . . solo*: Dante's source for this
story probably was the apocryphal *Epistola Alexandri ad
Aristotelem, magistrum suum, de itinere suo et de situ
Indiae*, a Latin version of a work by an unknown Greek
author commonly referred to as Pseudo-Callisthenes. There
is, however, a notable discrepancy between the two ac-
counts, in that Dante has Alexander bid his soldiers
trample the flames, whereas in the *Epistola Alexandri* (p.
208) they are bidden to trample the snow:

> Nam et flatus Euri ceciderat et frigus ingens vespertino
> tempore accrescebat. Cadere mox in modum vellerum
> immensae coeperunt nives. Quarum aggeratione me-
> tuens ne castra cumularentur, calcare militem nivem
> iubebam, ut quam primum iniuria pedum tabesce-
> ret . . . .

> For the southeast wind had fallen, and toward evening
> the great cold became worse. Very soon, large flakes of
> snow began to fall, like flakes of lamb's wool. Fearing
> that the camp might be buried under the heavy snow-
> fall, I ordered my soldiers to trample the snow, so that
> it would melt as quickly as possible under the blows
> of their feet.

A similar account is given in the abridged Latin version—
by the Archpriest Leo—of Pseudo-Callisthenes, commonly
known as the *Historia de preliis*. Yet another version, in
elegiacs, composed in 1236 by Quilichinus de Spoleto, had
been popular in Italy more than sixty years before the date
of the *Commedia*.

The commentators have assumed that Dante relied on
his memory of the *Epistola Alexandri* and thus confused
the details of the story. The immediate—though secondary—
source of his description, however, was almost certainly a
passage in the *De meteoris* of Albertus Magnus (a book with
which Dante was well acquainted), who, owing to a mis-
quotation of the *Epistola Alexandri*, is guilty of precisely
the same confusion as to the trampling of the flames as is

Dante. Albertus mentions the incident of Alexander in India
as an illustration of the occurrence of igneous vapors (the
same term used by Dante in vs. 35 to describe the fiery
downpour), the origin and nature of which he has been
discussing (*De meteoris* I, iv, 8): "Admirabilem autem im-
pressionem scribit Alexander ad Aristotelem in epistola de
mirabilibus Indiae, dicens: 'Quemadmodum nivis nubes
ignitae de aere cadebant, quas ipse militibus calcare prae-
cepit.'" ("Moreover, Alexander gives a remarkable descrip-
tion of it in a letter on the Wonders of India addressed to
Aristotle. He says: 'Fiery clouds fell from the sky like snow
and he ordered the soldiers to stamp them down.'") That
Dante was acquainted with this book of the *De meteoris*
(see I, iv, 9) of Albertus Magnus is borne out by the fact
that it was his authority for the quotations from Albumazar
and Seneca in the *Convivio* (II, xiii, 22).

32. *stuolo*: "Army," "host"; see *Inf.* VIII, 69.

33. *fiamme cadere infino a terra salde*: See the description
in the *Epistola Alexandri* quoted in n. to vss. 31–36.

34. *scalpitar*: "Stamp out," strongly suggesting the friction
of feet on burning ground and flakes of fire.

35. *acciò che = per ciò che*, "inasmuch as."   *vapore*:
Fire was termed *vapor igneus* ("igneous vapor") in the
science of the day.

36. *mei = meglio* (see *Inf.* II, 36).   *stingueva = estin-
gueva.   mentre ch'era solo*: See the description in the
Epistola Alexandri quoted in n. to vss. 31–36.

38–39. *com' esca sotto focile*: Again the deliberate stress on
the friction of bare feet on burning sand.

39. *a doppiar lo dolore*: The scorching of the feet by the
burning sand is added to the burning by the fire that falls
from above.

40. *la tresca*: Buti comments: "Tresca si chiama uno ballo
saltereccio, ove sia grande e veloce movimento e di molti

inviluppato." ("*Tresca* is a dance full of jumps, very fast moving, engaged in by many participants.")

42. *escotendo da sé*: The subject of this participial construction is the souls, not the hands.　*l'arsura fresca*: The fire, freshly fallen on the naked sinners.

44–45. *fuor che ' demon duri . . . uscinci*: The defense made by the devils at the walls of the city of Dis is described in *Inf.* VIII, 82–130.

44. *che ' = che i.*

45. *uscinci = ci uscinno* (*uscirono*); see E. G. Parodi (1957), p. 256.

46. *quel grande*: Capaneus, depicted as a towering giant by Statius (*Theb.* X, 872 and *passim*), was one of the seven legendary kings who besieged Thebes (see n. to vss. 68–69). As he was scaling the walls of the city, Capaneus defied Jupiter, and the god struck him dead with a thunderbolt. Dante has apparently borrowed several touches from Statius' account of Capaneus (*Theb.* X, 883–84, 897–911, 918–19, 927–30, 935–39):

Iamque Iovem circa studiis diversa fremebant
Argolici Tyriique dei . . . .
non tamen haec turbant pacem Iovis: ecce quierunt
iurgia, cum mediis Capaneus auditus in astris.
"nullane pro trepidis" clamabat, "numina Thebis
statis? ubi infandae segnes telluris alumni,
Bacchus et Alcides? pudet instigare minores.
tu potius venias—quis enim concurrere nobis
dignior? en cineres Semeleaque busta tenentur—,
nunc age, nunc totis in me conitere flammis,
Iuppiter! an pavidas tonitru turbare puellas
fortior et soceri turres exscindere Cadmi?"
　　　Ingemuit dictis superum dolor; ipse furentem
risit et incussa sanctarum mole comarum,
"quaenam spes hominum tumidae post proelia Phlegrae!

tune etiam feriendus?" ait. premit undique lentum
turba deum frendens et tela ultricia poscit,

. . . .
. . . in media vertigine mundi
stare virum insanasque vident deposcere pugnas,

. . . .

talia dicentem toto Iove fulmen adactum
corripuit: primae fugere in nubila cristae,
et clipei niger umbo cadit, iamque omnia lucent
membra viri. . . .
stat tamen, extremumque in sidera versus anhelat,
pectoraque invisis obicit fumantia muris,
ne caderet: sed membra virum terrena relinquunt,
exuiturque animus; paulum si tardius artus
cessissent, potuit fulmen sperare secundum.

Meanwhile about Jove's throne the Argive and the
Tyrian deities were clamouring in diverse factions . . . .
Yet undisturbed is the peace of Jove; and lo! their quar-
rels ceased when in mid-heaven Capaneus was heard:
"Are there no gods among you," he cries, "who stand
for panic-stricken Thebes? Where are the sluggard sons
of this accursed land, Bacchus and Alcides? Any of
lesser name I am ashamed to challenge. Rather come
thou—what worthier antagonist? For lo! Semele's ashes
and her tomb are in my power!—come thou, and strive
with all thy flames against me, thou, Jupiter! Or art
thou braver at frightening timid maidens with thy
thunder, and razing the towers of thy father-in-law
Cadmus?"
    Loud rose the gods' indignant clamour at his words;
Jove himself laughed at the madman, and shaking the
thick mass of his sacred locks: "What hope has man
after Phlegra's arrogant assault?" he says, "and must
thou too be struck down?" As he hesitates the gods
throng round him, gnashing their teeth and crying for
the avenging weapons . . . . They see the hero stand
midway in the dizzy height of air, and summon them
to insane battle . . . . Even as he spoke, the thunder-
bolt struck him, hurled with the whole might of Jove:

his crest first vanished into the clouds, the blackened shield-boss dropped, and all the hero's limbs are now illumined. . . . He stands nevertheless, and turning towards heaven pants out his life and leans his smoking breast on the hated battlements, lest he should fall; but his earthly frame deserts the hero, and his spirit is released; yet had his limbs been consumed a whit more slowly, he might have expected a second thunderbolt.

47. *lo 'ncendio = lo incendio*.   *torto*: This could mean "twisted" and refer to the giant's body as he writhes under the fire; but since Capaneus appears to scorn the fire, the adjective probably refers to the "scowling" expression on his face—an echo of the Latin *torvus* that Statius applies to the great figure as it lies dead (*Theb.* XI, 9–11):

> ille iacet lacerae complexus fragmina turris,
> torvus adhuc visu memorandaque facta relinquens
> gentibus . . .

Grasping the fragment of a shattered tower the hero lies, with a scowl yet upon his face, and leaving deeds for all the world to tell of . . . .

48. *maturi*: Some MSS have "marturi" (a form of *marturare*, akin to *martoriare*, "to torture"), and Petrocchi has accepted this form rather than the "maturi" of earlier editions. But "maturi" is surely to be preferred here (since the MS tradition allows it without question) for a *conceptual* reason: pride (as will be made clear by subsequent uses of this metaphor) is considered to be "green," "unripe," "sour" (*acerbo*). (See *Inf.* XXV, 18, where "acerbo" refers to the proud Vanni Fucci, in connection with whom Capaneus is recalled.) This rain of fire ought to "ripen" (humble) the proud Capaneus, but seems not to do so.

49–51. *E quel medesmo . . . morto*: The supine Capaneus has turned his head to observe the fact, then shouts at the wayfarers, which is what prompts Virgil to shout back so loudly (see vss. 61–62).

52–60. *Se Giove stanchi . . . allegra*: A blasphemer even now, Capaneus reviles the God he knew as the supreme deity. For Statius' description of his defiance of Jupiter, see *Theb.* X, 902–6, quoted in n. to vs. 46.

53. *aguta = acuta.*

55. *li altri*: The Cyclopes, Vulcan's assistants.   *a muta a muta*: "In relays."

56. *Mongibello*: Another name for Mount Etna, in Sicily. In the interior of Mount Etna and on one of the Lipari Islands, according to myth, Vulcan had his workshops and with the help of the Cyclopes ("li altri" of vs. 55) forged Jupiter's thunderbolts. See *Aen.* VIII, 416–22:

> Insula Sicanium iuxta latus Aeoliamque
> erigitur Liparen, fumantibus ardua saxis,
> quam subter specus et Cyclopum exesa caminis
> antra Aetnaea tonant, validique incudibus ictus
> auditi referunt gemitus, striduntque cavernis
> stricturae Chalybum et fornacibus ignis anhelat,
> Volcani domus et Volcania nomine tellus.

Hard by the Sicanian coast and Aeolian Lipare rises an island, steep with smoking rocks. Beneath it thunders a cave, and the vaults of Aetna, scooped out by Cyclopean forges; strong strokes are heard echoing groans from the anvils, masses of Chalyb steel hiss in the caverns, and the fire pants in the furnace—the home of Vulcan and the land Vulcan's by name.

58. *la pugna di Flegra*: In the battle of Phlegra Jupiter, with the help of Hercules, defeated the giants who attempted to storm Olympus. In the various versions of the story, Phlegra (literally, "the place of burning") was always localized in volcanic regions. At first it was located on the Macedonian peninsula of Pallene; later it sometimes was placed on the Phlegraean Fields (Campi Flegrei), a volcanic region west of Naples and east of Cumae. The phrase "pugna di Flegra" seems to be an echo of "proelia Phlegrae" ("Phlegra's assault") in the verses of the *Thebaid* (X,

907-9) that relate how as Jupiter makes ready to hurl his bolt at the defiant Capaneus he thinks of that other, greater battle with the giants (see n. to vs. 46).

59. *con tutta sua forza*: See Capaneus' defiant challenge to Jupiter (*Theb.* X, 904), quoted in n. to vs. 46.

63. *non s'ammorza*: The verb keeps the image of the flame (*ammorzarsi* being said of a flame that "dies down"), thereby suggesting an inner flame of pride burning in Capaneus, even in this second death of Hell; it is matched by the terrible rain of fire without, which "does not seem to ripen him."

65. *nullo = nessun*.

66. *compito* (pronounced *compìto*) = *compiuto*; past participle of *compire*.

67. *labbia*: "Aspect," "countenance"; see *Inf.* VII, 7.

68. *d'i = dei.   regi = re*.

69. *assiser = assediarono* (from *assidere, assedere*).   *Tebe*: Thebes, city of Boeotia. As a result of the dispute between Eteocles and Polynices, sons of Oedipus, over the sovereignty of Thebes, an expedition against the city on behalf of Polynices, known as the war of the Seven against Thebes, was undertaken by Adrastus, king of Argos, accompanied by his son-in-law Capaneus, Amphiaraus, Hippomedon, Parthenopaeus, Polynices, and Tydeus. The battle is the subject of the *Thebaid* of Statius.

70. *Dio*: Capaneus' blasphemy, which was aimed at the pagan Jupiter, is accounted a blasphemy against the true God.

71. *lui*: Dative here.

72. *fregi*: "Decorations," "ornaments."

73. *mi vien* (imperative) = *vienmi.   metti = metta*.

74. *ancor*: Modifies "guarda" (vs. 73); the words imply: "See that you do as you have done up to now, and do not . . ." (see vs. 12).

76. *divenimmo* (Latin *devenio*) = *giungemmo*.   *spiccia*: The verb is commonly used of blood spurting from a vein and therefore is not only appropriate and suggestive here but accounts for the wayfarer's shudder (vs. 78). See *Purg.* IX, 102: "come sangue che fuor di vena spiccia," where the word is again used in rhyme with "arsiccia."

79–81. *Quale del Bulicame . . . quello*: See "bulicame" as a common noun in *Inf.* XII, 117. Here, by antonomasia, it refers to a famous hot sulphurous spring near Viterbo, noted since Roman times. Like similar establishments, the hot spring known as the Bulicame was the resort of prostitutes (the "peccatrici" of vs. 80), who supplied the baths in their houses with water by means of conduits leading from the spring. Benvenuto says:

> Ad cuius declarationem debes scire quod apud civitatem Viterbii est quaedam mirabilis aqua calida, rubea, sulphurea, profunda, de cuius lecto exit quidam rivulus parvus, quem meretrices habitantes in illa planicie dividunt inter se; nam in qualibet domuncula meretricis est balneum ex illo rivulo ordinatum; ergo bene est comparatio propria in rubore, in calore et in foetore.

> To understand this passage, you must know that in the environs of Viterbo there is an extraordinary hot spring, which is reddish, sulphurous, and deep. From its bed rushes a brook, which the prostitutes of that area divide among them. Indeed, even in the most modest prostitute's dwelling, there is a bath that uses the water from that brook. It is therefore a good comparison, apt as to the reddish color, the heat, and the bad smell.

For a convincing rebuttal of the thesis maintained by G. Mazzoni (1941, pp. 239–66), among others, that the reading should be *pectatrici* or some variant thereof, meaning "hemp combers" (*pettinatrici di canapa*), and also for examples of *peccatrice* in the sense of "prostitute," see M. Barbi and A. Duro (1949). Also see Petrocchi's long note.

82. *le pendici*: The sloping inner banks of the conduit.

83. *fatt' era 'n pietra*: For a justification of this reading, as preferable to *fatt' eran pietra*, see Petrocchi's note. The past participle "fatto" agrees with the first subject, "lo fondo suo," according to common usage in such cases; see *Inf.* II, 23. *e ' margini = e i margini*, the tops or edges of the banks, as distinguished from the "pendici," or sloping sides.

84. *per ch'io m'accorsi*: The wayfarer makes this surmise from the observed fact that the "margini" are of stone and have no burning sand on their surface and moreover, as we are told in vs. 141, no fire falls on them: "li margini fan via, che non son arsi." *lici = lì*. The form was common in prose in Dante's time.

85. *dimostrato = mostrato*.

87. *sogliare = soglia*, the threshold of the main entrance to Hell, which is now left forever unbarred (see *Inf.* VIII, 125–26). See *Aen.* VI, 126–27: "Facilis descensus Averno: / noctes atque dies patet atri ianua Ditis." ("Easy is the descent to Avernus: night and day the door of gloomy Dis stands open.")

90. *ammorta*: "Deadens," "quenches," as is clear from the words "si spegne" in vs. 142. Dante uses the verb in rhyme in his *canzone* "Io son venuto" (*Rime* C, 35): " 'l freddo lor spirito ammorta." ("The chill has deadened their spirit.")

91. *fuor = furono*.

94–95. *In mezzo mar . . . Creta*: The opening phrase echoes Virgil's "medio ponto," and the two lines, his description of Crete (*Aen.* III, 104–6):

> Creta Iovis magni medio iacet insula ponto,
> mons Idaeus ubi et gentis cunabula nostrae.
> centum urbes habitant magnas, uberrima regna . . .

In midocean lies Crete, the island of great Jove, where
is Mount Ida, and the cradle of our race. There men
dwell in a hundred great cities, a realm most fertile . . . .

The sea is the Mediterranean, which, as its name implies,
lies at the center of an inhabited hemisphere of land; thus
Crete is truly at the center of the center. Benvenuto com-
ments:

> Est . . . hic bene notandum, quod autor per istam
> insulam figurat nobis mundum istum, sive terram
> habitabilem, quia ista insula est circumcincta mari sicut
> terra tota oceano . . . et est quasi in medio mundi, et
> quasi omnia maria et confinia partium terrae terminan-
> tur ibi; et ibi regna primo incoeperunt secundum poetas.

> It . . . must be carefully noted here that by means of
> this island, the author is representing the world—that
> is to say, the inhabited earth. For this island is sur-
> rounded by the sea, just as the entire earth is surround-
> ed by ocean . . . and it is almost at the center of the
> world. Nearly all the seas, and the outer boundaries of
> the various parts of the earth, end there. And it was
> there, according to the poets, that kingdoms first came
> into being.

The Trojan race, and therefore (according to Virgil) the
Roman race, had its beginning there, as Anchises says in
the continuation of the passage from the *Aeneid* quoted
above (*Aen.* III, 107–9):

> maximus unde pater, si rite audita recordor,
> Teucrus Rhoeteas primum est advectus ad oras
> optavitque locum regno. . . .

> . . . whence our earliest ancestor Teucer, if I recall
> the tale aright, first sailed to the Rhoetean shores, and
> chose a site for his kingdom.

Thus, in accordance with Anchises' interpretation of the
oracle's injunction in *Aen.* III, 96: "antiquam exquirite
matrem" ("seek out your ancient mother"), Aeneas and
his Trojan band first made their way to Crete.

94. *In mezzo mar = in mezzo al mar.* *siede*: See *Inf.*
V, 97. *un paese guasto*: "A wasteland." An episode in
the *Aeneid*, which occurred at a time when Aeneas and
his band had not been long in their new island home, may
have entered into Dante's conception of Crete as a ruined,
wasted land (see *Aen.* III, 137–39):

> . . . subito cum tabida membris,
> corrupto caeli tractu, miserandaque venit
> arboribusque satisque lues et letifer annus.

On a sudden, from a tainted quarter of the sky, came
a pestilence and season of death, to the wasting of our
bodies and the piteous ruin of trees and crops.

96. *sotto 'l cui rege*: For the form "rege," see *Inf.* VIII, 49.
The reference is to Saturn, mythical king of Crete, iden-
tified by the Romans with the Greek god Cronus and
hence regarded by them as the father (by Rhea) of Jupiter,
Neptune, Pluto, Juno, Ceres, and Vesta. *fu già 'l mondo
casto*: In *Par.* XXI, 26–27, Saturn again is alluded to as
the "caro duce / sotto cui giacque ogne malizia morta";
the reference, as here, is to the Golden Age that prevailed
during his reign, the first of a succession of ages, according
to the famous account of Ovid at the beginning of the
Metamorphoses (I, 89–93):

> Aurea prima sata est aetas, quae vindice nullo,
> sponte sua, sine lege fidem rectumque colebat.
> poena metusque aberant, nec verba minantia fixo
> aere legebantur, nec supplex turba timebat
> iudicis ora sui, sed erant sine iudice tuti.

Golden was that first age, which, with no one to com-
pel, without a law, of its own will, kept faith and did
the right. There was no fear of punishment, no threat-
ening words were to be read on brazen tablets; no sup-
pliant throng gazed fearfully upon its judge's face, but
without judges lived secure.

Although this first Golden Age was truly an age without
injustice (*malizia*), Ovid goes on to say (*Metam.* I, 113–15)
that, later:

> Postquam Saturno tenebrosa in Tartara misso
> sub Iove mundus erat, subiit argentea proles,
> auro deterior, fulvo pretiosior aere.

After Saturn had been banished to the dark land of
death, and the world was under the sway of Jove, the
silver race came in, lower in the scale than gold, but
of greater worth than yellow brass.

Ovid then tells of the continuing decline of human civiliza-
tion through successive ages that find their exact corres-
pondence in the metals that make up the "gran veglio" de-
scribed here in Canto XIV, vss. 103–14.

According to Virgil (*Aen.* VIII, 319–25), when Saturn
was banished by his son Jupiter from Crete, he came to
Italy and there established another Golden Age. Virgil
prophesied the return of that age (*Eclog.* IV, 6): "Iam . . .
redeunt Saturnia regna." ("Now the reign of Saturn re-
turns.")

98. *Ida*: See n. to vss. 100–102.

99. *vieta*: This word may derive either from the Latin
vetus, "old," or from the Latin *vietus*, "shrunken," "with-
ered," "decayed." The latter meaning fits the context very
well.

100–102. *Rea la scelse . . . grida*: Rhea, also called Cybele,
is the ancient goddess represented as the daughter of Heaven
(Uranus) and Earth (Gaea) and the wife of Saturn. She
was the mother of Vesta, Ceres, Juno, Pluto, Neptune, and
Jupiter. According to legend, Saturn, in order to avert the
fulfillment of the prophecy that he would be dethroned by
one of his children, devoured each one as soon as it was
born, with the exception of Jupiter, who was saved by an
artifice of his mother. When Rhea was on the point of
giving birth to Jupiter, she retired to Mount Ida in Crete.
When the infant was born, she gave Saturn a stone wrapped
in swaddling clothes, which he swallowed, supposing it to
be his child. To prevent Saturn from hearing the cries of
the infant, Rhea ordered her priests, the Curetes, to shout
and clash their swords and shields. She thus succeeded in

raising the child Jupiter without the knowledge of his
father. Eventually Saturn was forced to disgorge the children
he had swallowed and, in fulfillment of the prophecy, was
dethroned by Jupiter. The story is elaborated by Ovid (*Fasti*
IV, 197–214), Dante's probable source. See also Virgil,
Georg. IV, 150–52.

103. *Dentro dal monte sta dritto un gran veglio*: In the
context of an observed decline in the following sense, that
"cuncto mortalium generi minorem in dies fieri prope-
modum" ("with the entire human race the stature on the
whole is becoming smaller daily"), Pliny (*Nat. hist.* VII,
xvi, 73) reports: "In Creta terrae motu rupto monte in-
ventum est corpus stans XLVI cubitorum, quod alii Orionis
alii Oti esse arbitrabantur." ("When a mountain in Crete
was cleft by an earthquake a body 69 feet in height was
found, which some people thought must be that of Orion
and others of Otus.")

103–11. *Dentro dal monte . . . l'altro, eretto*: The "veglio,"
as described in these verses, clearly represents a fusion of
Ovid's ages (see n. to vs. 96) with the great image in the
dream of Nebuchadnezzar (Dan. 2:31–35):

> Tu, rex, videbas, et ecce quasi statua una grandis:
> statua illa magna et statura sublimis stabat contra te,
> et intuitus eius erat terribilis. Huius statuae caput ex
> auro optimo erat, pectus autem et brachia de argento,
> porro venter et femora ex aere, tibiae autem ferreae,
> pedum quaedam pars erat ferrea, quaedam autem fictilis.
> Videbas ita, donec abscissus est lapis de monte sine
> manibus, et percussit statuam in pedibus eius ferreis
> et fictibilibus, et comminuit eos; tunc contrita sunt
> pariter ferrum, testa, aes, argentum et aurum, et
> redacta quasi in favillam aestivae areae quae rapta
> sunt vento, nullusque locus inventus est eis; lapis
> autem qui percusserat statuam factus est mons magnus,
> et implevit universam terram.

> Thou, O king, sawest, and behold *there was* as it were
> a great statue. This statue, which was great and high,

tall of stature, stood before thee, and the look thereof
was terrible.

The head of this statue was of fine gold, but the
breast and the arms of silver, and the belly and the
thighs of brass:

And the legs of iron, the feet part of iron and part
of clay.

Thus thou sawest, till a stone was cut out of a moun-
tain without hands: and it struck the statue upon the
feet thereof that were of iron and of clay and broke
them in pieces.

Then was the iron, the clay, the brass, the silver and
the gold broken to pieces together, and became like the
chaff of a summer's thrashingfloor. And they were
carried away by the wind: and there was no place
found for them. But the stone that struck the statue be-
came a great mountain and filled the whole earth.

104. *Dammiata*: The old town of Damietta in Egypt, situ-
ated at the mouth of the easternmost of the two principal
branches formed by the Nile at its delta. During the Middle
Ages Damietta seems to have been identified with the an-
cient Memphis. The modern Damietta, situated four miles
farther inland, is built on the remains of the old town.
I. Del Lungo (1906, pp. 107–8) says:

Damiata per l'Oriente ha ragione d'esser qui nominata,
perchè, città marittima, prospetta direttamente Creta, e
di qua da Creta la penisola italica e, in essa, Roma;
occorrendo alla poetica figurazione del Veglio avere in
diritta linea i due termini correlativi, l'uno che è alle
spalle l'altro in faccia di lui . . . . Damiata, dunque, ha
nel concepimento dantesco funzione meramente geo-
grafica.

Damietta is quite properly mentioned here for the East.
Being situated on the coast, it looks directly at Crete,
and, this side of Crete, to the Italian peninsula and to
Rome. It is necessary for the poetic image of the Old
Man to have the two correlative terms in a direct line,
one in back and one in front of him . . . . Damietta,

then, has a merely geographic function in the Dantesque conception.

105. *speglio* = *specchio*.

109. *eletto*: "Chosen," "choice"; past participle of *eligere*.

114. *accolte*: "Collected" as the tears fall at the foot of the cracked figure. *grotta*: The rock of Mount Ida; see this word again in *Purg.* I, 48; III, 90; XIII, 45.

115-19. *Lor corso . . . Cocito*: Acheron, Styx, Phlegethon, and Cocytus all belong to the classical conception of the underworld (on Phlegethon, for example, see *Aen.* VI, 548-51, quoted in the n. to vs. 134; also Statius, *Theb.* IV, 520-24). The wayfarers have already encountered the first three: Acheron at the entrance to the first circle (*Inf.* III, 71), Styx outside the city of Dis (*Inf.* VII, 106), and Phlegethon in the first *girone* of this seventh circle (*Inf.* XII, 53). However, Phlegethon was not named; and the wayfarer does not realize that he has seen it, and will question his guide further. Cocytus lies ahead.

115. *valle*: Hell is so called twice again: see *Purg.* XXIV, 84 and *Par.* XVII, 137. *si diroccia*: "Flows down from rock to rock."

117. *doccia*: The "conduit" running out across the sand, termed a "fiumicello" in vs. 77.

118. *dove più non si dismonta*: The center of the earth.

119. *fanno Cocito*: The subject of "fanno" is the "tears" that flow down from the crack in the "veglio." The pond of Cocytus is the last of the four so-called infernal rivers (see n. to vss. 121-38). *e qual sia quello stagno*: See *Aen.* VI, 323: "Cocyti stagna alta vides." ("Thou seest the deep pools of Cocytus.")

121-38. *Se 'l presente rigagno . . . rimossa*: Virgil's account of what has been called the "hydraulic system" of Hell has frequently puzzled the commentators. His initial description of the four "rivers" of Hell and their derivation

from "our world" is straightforward enough, but his answer
to the wayfarer's question of vss. 121–23 is more ambiguous.
In Dante's conception Acheron, Styx, Phlegethon, and
Cocytus are none of them really rivers, for water does not
flow in them. They are all circular bodies of water and
may all, not just Cocytus, be more properly called "stagni";
that is, they all contain still or stagnant water. Styx is, in
fact, a "palude," or swamp, surrounding the city of Dis.
Phlegethon (although the wayfarer has not yet grasped the
fact) is the stream of boiling blood "that embraces the
entire plain" (*Inf.* XII, 53) and forms the first *girone* of
this seventh circle; when not viewed as a whole, but only
at one given point, it has the narrower shape of a river
and is so termed at times. The same is true, given the
conical shape of Hell, of Acheron. Cocytus has been ex-
plicitly called a "stagno" (vs. 119).

If all the waters of Hell form one system deriving from
the crack in the "veglio" and are made up of the tears that,
collected, bore their way through the rock and flow down
into the cavity of Hell, and if the above-named "rivers" are
actually "stagni" and as such do not flow down, then it
follows that there must be connecting streams or canals be-
tween them through which the water passes from one to
another. The wayfarers encountered one stream, termed a
"ruscello," near the boundary between the fourth and fifth
circles; it issued from underground and clearly fed the
swamp of Styx (see *Inf.* VII, 100–108). Looking back to
this "ruscello" flowing into Styx, we see that it must in
fact be a section of the stream that leads from Acheron to
Styx, though whether it flows underground all the way from
Acheron to the point where it comes bubbling to the sur-
face (*Inf.* VII, 101) we are not told. However, Virgil's next
remark bears the clear implication that the two wayfarers
might have encountered such a connecting stream above
ground at some other point through that upper area if, in
turning ever leftward, they had proceeded far enough
around any given circle. Thus the wayfarers' present con-
versation about the waters of Hell presupposes an aware-
ness on both their parts that they have already encountered

a connecting stream, namely the "ruscello" leading into Styx.

The wayfarer's first question concerns the stream now before them that "spurts out from the forest" (vss. 76–77), at the very edge of which they are standing, and runs out across the plain of sand. Dante now refers to the stream as a "rigagno" (it has already, in vs. 77, been termed a "fiumicello" and might be called a "ruscello"). Virgil has explained that the four named bodies of water, the traditional "rivers" of Hell, derive from a single source in "our world": Crete. This "rigagno," as the wayfarer now understands from Virgil's explanation, must have its source too in the tears that flow down from the crack in the "veglio" and that make up all the waters of Hell. But if this water, flowing so red in the channel before him, derives from "our world," why, he asks, does it appear "at this edge only"?

Not having forgotten the "ruscello" which he saw leading into Styx, the wayfarer is now wondering about the connecting canals. Virgil has told him that the stream before them flows on down to form Cocytus. Thus the wayfarer's first question, "Perché ci appar pur a questo vivagno?" (vs. 123), concerns this stream considered as a connecting stream between Styx and Cocytus. (Since, as his second question reveals, he does not yet understand where Phlegethon is, that "river" is no part of the matter at the moment.) Now, the two wayfarers have traversed the sixth circle and two thirds of the seventh, and nowhere so far have they come across any canal—and there must be one— that joins Styx and Cocytus. Does it flow across the sixth circle? Does it flow through the wood (the second *girone* of the seventh circle), on the far edge of which they now stand? Why only at this point do they meet such a connecting canal?

To answer the wayfarer's question, Virgil looks back over the whole area of Hell that they have so far traversed. He is not forgetting the stream that feeds Styx, but he makes a generalization about Hell and the manner of their descent through it. They have turned always to the left (with the notable exception in the sixth circle—see *Inf.* IX, 132—

which he chooses to overlook!), yet nowhere have they
come full circle around any of the levels, so that the con-
necting canal in question might well have traversed one or
more of the circles and been visible in any one of them
(even between Acheron and Styx) without their having
come upon it. Therefore, if "something new appears" to
them (vs. 128) in their descent through Hell, it should not
cause the wayfarer to wonder. Virgil's "cosa nova" (vs.
128) has been a major source of difficulty here; for some
commentators have taken the words to mean that he and
his charge have forgotten about the connecting stream
they encountered between Acheron and Styx, at the "edge"
of the fourth circle. But surely Virgil is not to be thought of
as having such a bad memory; neither does he impute any
such forgetfulness to his charge (and Dante can hardly have
forgotten!). The "cosa nova" is precisely the "presente
rigagno" (vs. 121) that here flows out across the sand,
viewed as one of the sections of the canal that must connect
the "stagni" named; and it is new because, since encounter-
ing the "ruscello" that bubbles up and flows into Styx, they
have seen no such canal again until now. If they had
circled far enough, on either circle six or circle seven (i.e.,
through the wood), they might have come across it before
now, Virgil's answer clearly implies. It runs above ground
through the wood.

Dante has understood this, but he has *not* understood one
very important matter. As far as he is concerned, all the
rivers of the underworld, as Virgil and the classical poets
had conceived them, have been accounted for in the to-
pography of Hell except two: Phlegethon, named by Virgil
as one of the four, and Lethe, traditionally a river of this
netherworld. Virgil is silent about the one (Lethe) and
says that the other (Phlegethon) is "formed of this rain"
of tears (vs. 132) that, in the "rigagno" before their eyes,
flows down to form Cocytus. Where, then, are these two?
Lethe is quickly disposed of. That river (and it is a true
river, a stream that flows) the wayfarer will see in Purga-
tory. As for Phlegethon, the boiling of the red stream before
them should answer that question, Virgil says. For what

else does the name Phlegethon itself imply? (See n. to vs. 134.) In short, Virgil says, "Have you not understood that the river of boiling blood that forms the first *girone* of the seventh circle is Phlegethon?" Virgil's reference to Phlegethon is to the river itself, not this stream. But the two things put together provide a final explanation: this "fiumicello" or "rigagno" that flows out across the sand before their eyes is the connecting canal that leads from Phlegethon to Cocytus. The words "esta piova" (vs. 132) refer to the churning red water that the wayfarer sees running through the canal before them; the tears from the "veglio" have turned red in the overflow from Phlegethon. And this the wayfarer had not understood, because he did not know where Phlegethon was, not having grasped the fact that the river of blood which is the first *girone* of this seventh circle *was* that river.

All is clear now. Between Acheron and Styx they had encountered a connecting canal. Would there not be one leading off from Styx to the other "stagni" named? Yes, but the wayfarers did not turn about the sixth circle (where curiously enough they went to the right!) far enough to encounter it, wherever it may run through the cemetery of the heretics. Here now is just such a canal as might have been expected, flowing across the inner *girone* of the seventh circle after spurting forth from the edge of the wood; and yet it is not the canal that leads from Styx, but that which leads from Phlegethon, since as Dante now understands, the river of blood of the first *girone* of this seventh circle is precisely Phlegethon. For other interpretations of this famous crux, see M. Barbi (1937), pp. 132–43, A. Camilli (1943), and the commentaries.

123. *vivagno*: "Border," the innermost boundary of the second *girone*, the edge of the wood where the wayfarers stand.

129. *de' = deve*.

131. *Flegetonta = Flegetonte*. See the similar form "orizzonta" in *Inf.* XI, 113.   *Letè*: See Minòs (*Inf.* V, 4,

17; XIII, 96), Semiramìs (*Inf.* V, 58), Cleopatràs (*Inf.* V,
63), Parìs (*Inf.* V, 67), Flegiàs (*Inf.* VIII, 19, 24), already
encountered, and Climenè (*Par.* XVII, 1). On the rule for
the accentuation of such names, see n. to *Inf.* V, 4; also
E. G. Parodi (1957), pp. 233-34.

132. *di' = dici.   piova = pioggia*, the tears that fall from
the crack in the "gran veglio."

134. *ma 'l bollor de l'acqua rossa*: The pointed reference
here to the meaning of the Greek name Phlegethon
(φλεγέθων)—"flaming," "fiery"—does not necessarily imply
a knowledge of Greek on Dante's part (see n. to *Inf.* IV,
88). This much Dante might have gathered from Virgil
(*Aen.* VI, 548-51):

> Respicit Aeneas subito et sub rupe sinistra
> moenia lata videt, triplici circumdata muro,
> quae rapidus flammis ambit torrentibus amnis,
> Tartareus Phlegethon, torquetque sonantia saxa.

> Suddenly Aeneas looks back, and under a cliff on the
> left sees a broad castle, girt with triple wall and en-
> circled with a rushing flood of torrent flames—Tar-
> tarean Phlegethon, that rolls along thundering rocks.

The following etymology is given in the *Magnae deriva-
tiones* of Uguccione da Pisa, with which Dante was ac-
quainted (see P. Toynbee, 1902, p. 104): "*Flegeton-ontis*,
quidam fluvius infernalis totus ardens, a *fos* quod est ignis,
vel *flegi* quod est inflammans, et totus." ("*Flegeton-ontis*,
a river of the underworld composed entirely of flame: from
fos, which is fire—or *flegi*, because it is afire—and *totus*
[all].") Also see Statius, *Theb.* IV, 523: "Fumidus atra
vadis Phlegethon incendia volvit." ("Smoky Phlegethon
rolls down his streams of murky flame.")

135. *faci = fai.*

136. *Letè vedrai, ma fuor di questa fossa*: The wayfarer
will find Lethe at the top of Purgatory (*Purg.* XXVIII,
25-35), where the meaning of vss. 137-38 will become
clearer.   *fossa*: The whole cavity of Hell.

138. *pentuta = pentita.*

140. *vegne = venga.*

142. *ogne vapor*: Every flake of falling fire, every flame.
si spegne: See vs. 90: "che sovra sé tutte fiammelle am-
morta," to which vss. 141–42 refer.

CANTO XV

1, 3. *Ora cen porta . . . sì che dal foco . . .* : These two verses constitute what are called, in Italian prosody, *versi sdruccioli*. That is, they end in words accented on the antepenult (*àrgini, màrgini*) and have one more syllable than normal (in this case, twelve instead of eleven).

2. *e 'l fummo del ruscel di sopra aduggia*: The vapor rising from the boiling stream is said to "overshade" and "shelter" the water and the banks from the fire. This was that most "notable" thing to which Virgil pointed in *Inf.* XIV, 88–89. *fummo = fumo*.

4–9. *Quali Fiamminghi . . . quali Padoan . . . il caldo senta*: The structure implied in the first term of this double comparison ("Quali Fiamminghi . . .") is this or any long dike stretching across a plain. The second term ("quali Padoan . . .") suggests more particularly a channeled stream with raised banks, and this corresponds more closely to the physical features of the seventh circle of Hell.

4. *Guizzante*: Wissant, a Flemish town between Calais and Cape Gris-Nez, in medieval times the usual embarkation point for England (the Channel there being narrowest).

4. *Bruggia*: Bruges, a town about twenty-five miles north-west of Ghent, capital of the modern province of West Flanders. Dante here uses Bruges to denote the eastern limit of the Flemish seaboard, and Wissant the western; hence they represent the two ends of the great Flemish dike.

5. *'l fiotto*: Brunetto Latini, whom the wayfarer soon encounters, describes the ocean tide in his *Tesoretto* (in G. Contini, 1960, vol. II, p. 212, vss. 1030–42):

> verso 'l mare Ucïano,
> quel che cinge la terra
> e che la cerchia e serra,
> e ha una natura
> ch'è a veder ben dura,
> ch'un'ora cresce molto
> e fa grande timolto,
> poi torna in dibassanza;
> così fa per usanza:
> or prende terra, or lassa,
> or monta, or dibassa;
> e la gente per motto
> dicon c'ha nome fiotto.

> . . . toward the oceanic sea, that encircles the earth, surrounding and enclosing it, and whose nature is most difficult to discern. At one hour it grows enormously and makes great tumult, then it declines; that is its wont: now it takes over the land, now leaves it; now it mounts, now it descends; and people call this the tide.

6. *si fuggia* = *si fugga* (*fuggire*).

7. *e quali Padoan*: The understood predicate is "fanno lo schermo" in the preceding verse.   *la Brenta*: A river of northern Italy that rises in the Tirolese Alps above Trent and flows southeast and then south past Bassano. After being joined by the Bacchiglione just below Padua, it enters the Venetian Lagoon by two mouths; the southern, near Brondolo, is now the outlet of the Brenta Canal. On the Brenta in Dante's time, see G. Dalla Vedova (1865).

9. *Carentana*: *Chiarentana* is also a common form in the early MSS. Carinthia forms the mountainous southwestern province of modern Austria and consists largely of the upper valley of the Drava, which runs east to the Danube. The medieval duchy of Carinthia was considerably more extensive than the modern province of that name, and Dante, in using the term, seems to include the upper valley of the Brenta, the Valsugana. See Petrocchi's note on "Carentana," in which he holds that Dante is referring to the Carnic Alps, or Carantania, which corresponds to the territories of Carinthia, Styria, and Carniola. On Carinthia also see C. Hardie (1964).   *il caldo*: The heat, which melts the snows and causes the river to flood.

11. *né sì alti*: The banks are actually about the height of a man, as vss. 24 and 40 clearly suggest.

12. *lo maestro*: The banks are as God willed them; but the poet, in the words "Già eravam" (vs. 13), seems to allow that they actually might have been constructed by some lesser artisan in accordance with the will of the Master Architect. See Dante's use of "maestro" in *Inf.* XXXI, 85–86.   *félli = li fece*.

13–14. *da la selva rimossi tanto*: The wayfarers are not necessarily very far from the wood; the prevailing new-moon darkness (vss. 18–19) and the vapor rising from the stream would cause both poor visibility and a feeling of distance.

16–17. *una schiera che venian*: These souls are the sodomites. Although they are not named here, we know from the exposition in *Inf.* XI, 49–51 that blasphemy, sodomy, and usury are punished in the third *girone* of the seventh circle, and from *Inf.* XIV, 22–24 that these three groups of sinners are punished in different ways. Since the sodomites "run incessantly," it follows from the present description that the approaching band is made up of sodomites, the most numerous of the three groups punished in this desert (see *Inf.* XIV, 25).

17. *venian* = *venivan*.

18–21. *come suol da sera . . . come 'l vecchio sartor*: These two similes are comparable in function to the pair in vss. 4–9. The first presents a more general scene; the second focuses on something particular, the single figure of an old tailor, who implicitly is compared to old Brunetto, the personage the wayfarer meets in the next verses.

19. *guardare uno altro sotto nuova luna*: See *Aen.* VI, 268–72, 451–54:

> Ibant obscuri sola sub nocte per umbram
> perque domos Ditis vacuas et inania regna,
> quale per incertam lunam sub luce maligna
> est iter in silvis, ubi caelum condidit umbra
> Iuppiter, et rebus nox abstulit atra colorem.
>
> . . . .
> . . . quam Troius heros
> ut primum iuxta stetit adgnovitque per umbras
> obscuram, qualem primo qui surgere mense
> aut videt aut vidisse putat per nubila lunam . . . .

On they went dimly, beneath the lonely night amid the gloom, through the empty halls of Dis and his phantom realm, even as under the grudging light of an inconstant moon lies a path in the forest, when Jupiter has buried the sky in shade, and black Night has stolen from the world her hues. . . . And soon as the Trojan hero stood nigh and knew her, a dim form amid the shadows—even as, in the early month, one sees or fancies he has seen the moon rise amid the clouds . . . .

20. *ver'* = *verso*.

24. *per lo lembo*: The wayfarer is understood to be wearing the typical Florentine gown of the day, the lower hem of which Brunetto now seizes, marveling. Brunetto, who is walking on the lower level of the sandy plain, reaches upward a little to touch the garment.

26. *ficcai li occhi*: For the justification of this reading, in preference to "ficca' i li occhi" (Casella) or "ficca' [li] li occhi"

(Scartazzini-Vandelli), see M. Barbi (1934a), pp. 36–37.

per lo cotto aspetto: Sapegno comments that the use of "per" here expresses more than just the direction of the wayfarer's glance; it also suggests an effort to penetrate beneath Brunetto's scorched features in order to make out the familiar countenance.

27. *abbrusciato* = *abbruciato*. *non difese*: See "difension," *Inf.* VII, 81.

29. *e chinando la mano*: Some late and less authoritative manuscripts read "chinando la mia [faccia]." In the context of the poem, either reading is possible, but "mano" seems preferable; see Petrocchi's note. The wayfarer cannot touch Brunetto's face, but seems to express the wish to make out his scorched features better by reaching out his hand as if he would touch them.

30. *Siete voi qui*: The wayfarer addresses Brunetto, as he does Farinata and Cavalcante (*Inf.* X, 51, 63), with the respectful "voi."   *ser*: Brunetto's title as a notary. Boccaccio observes in his *Comento*: "La sua principal facultà fu notaria." ("His principal occupation was that of notary.")

32. *Brunetto*: Brunetto Latini, philosopher and public servant, was born in Florence *ca.* 1220 and died there *ca.* 1294. He is commonly supposed (from a misunderstanding of vss. 82–85) to have been Dante's master, which in the ordinary sense of the word he cannot have been, since he was about forty-five when Dante was born. He was active in public affairs in Florence as early as 1253; and public documents notarized by him, some drawn in his own hand, date from 1254. An influential Guelph, Brunetto was returning from an embassy to Alfonso X of Castile in 1260 when he learned that the Ghibellines had decisively defeated the Florentine Guelphs at Montaperti and had expelled them from Florence. Brunetto mentions these events in his *Tesoretto* (in G. Contini, 1960, vol. II, pp. 180–81, vss. 123–28, 135–47, 152–62):

esso Comune saggio
mi fece suo messaggio
all'alto re di Spagna,
ch'or è re de la Magna
e la corona atende,
se Dio no · llil contende.

. . . .

E io presi campagna
e andai in Ispagna
e feci l'ambasciata
che mi fue ordinata;
e poi sanza soggiorno
ripresi mio ritorno,
tanto che nel paese
di terra navarrese,
venendo per la calle
del pian di Runcisvalle,
incontrai uno scolaio
su'n un muletto vaio,
che venia da Bologna,

. . . .

Io lo pur dimandai
novelle di Toscana
in dolce lingua e piana;
ed e' cortesemente
mi disse immantenente
che guelfi di Firenza
per mala provedenza
e per forza di guerra
eran fuor de la terra,
e'l dannaggio era forte
di pregioni e di morte.

This wise commune made me its messenger to the
noble king of Spain, who now is king of Germany,
and who expects to have the crown, if God does not
otherwise ordain. . . . And I went forth to Spain and
carried out the embassy entrusted unto me. Then, with-
out tarrying, I returned; and in the Navarrese, coming

by way of the plain of Roncesvalle, I met a student
riding a spotted mule, returning from Bologna I
asked him news of Tuscany in sweet and gentle words,
and he most courteously told me immediately that the
Guelphs of Florence, through lack of foresight, and by
force of arms, had had to leave the city, and that many
were dead or imprisoned.

After receiving this disastrous news, Brunetto took refuge
in France. (For views on his sojourn there, see E. J. L.
Scott, 1897; J. E. Harting, 1897; P. Toynbee, 1897.)
When the Ghibellines of Tuscany were overthrown follow-
ing the decisive battle of Benevento in 1266, Brunetto re-
turned to Florence and resumed his role in public affairs
until his death. Villani, in recording that event, speaks of
Brunetto as having introduced systematic oratory and politi-
cal science into Florence (VIII, 10):

> Nel detto anno 1294 morì in Firenze uno valente
> cittadino il quale ebbe nome ser Brunetto Latini, il
> quale fu gran filosofo, e fu sommo maestro in rettorica,
> tanto in bene sapere dire come in bene dittare. . . . e fu
> dittatore del nostro comune. Fu mondano uomo, ma di
> lui avemo fatta menzione, perocch'egli fu cominciatore
> e maestro in digrossare i Fiorentini, e farli scorti in
> bene parlare, e in sapere guidare e reggere la nostra
> repubblica secondo la politica.

> In this same year, 1294, there died in Florence a most
> worthy citizen, whose name was Ser Brunetto Latini.
> He was a great philosopher and an excellent teacher of
> rhetoric, a man who both spoke and wrote well. . . .
> He was secretary of our commune, and a very worldly
> man. We have mentioned him because it was he who
> was the initiator and the master in refining the Floren-
> tines, in making them aware of good speech, and in
> knowing how to guide and maintain our republic ac-
> cording to the art of politics.

Brunetto's two best known works are *Li livres dou Tresor*
and the *Tesoretto*, both written during his four-year stay
in France. The *Tresor*, composed in French prose, is an

encyclopedia of history, natural science, ethics, rhetoric, and political science. Of it the author says (*Tresor* I, i, 7):

> Et se aucuns demandoit pour quoi cis livres est escris en roumanç, selonc [la] raison de France, puis ke nous somes italien, je diroie que c'est pour .ii. raisons, l'une ke nous somes en France, l'autre por çou que la parleure est plus delitable et plus commune a tous langages.

> And should anyone ask why this book is written in the vernacular of France since I am an Italian, I will reply that there are two reasons: first because I am in France, second because this language is the most pleasing and the most universal.

The *Tresor* was soon translated into Italian as the *Tesoro* by Bono Giamboni. The *Tesoretto*, written in Italian, is a long didactic poem in rhymed heptasyllabic couplets.

The question has been raised as to the correct form of Brunetto's name. The form "Latini" is most commonly used, but Brunetto himself, on occasion at least, preferred "Latino," a form that occurs in rhyme in the *Tesoretto* (see G. Contini, 1960, vol. II, p. 178, vs. 70; p. 215, vs. 1133). On Brunetto's life and works, see Contini, vol. II, pp. 169–74; T. Sundby (1884).

33. *traccia*: "File," "band": see *Inf.* XII, 55.

34. *lui = a lui.*   *ven preco = ve ne prego*; cf. the Latin *precor.*

35. *m'asseggia = mi sieda (assedersi).*

36. *faròl = lo farò.*   *costui*: Once again (as in *Inf.* X, 62) Dante avoids naming Virgil and refers to him with an indefinite pronoun. In fact, the two characters never name each other explicitly in Hell. The allegorical purpose of this fact will become clearer as the poem unfolds.   *che vo seco*: On this peculiar construction, common in early Italian, see M. Barbi (1934b), p. 269.

37. *greggia*: The word is not necessarily used in a pejorative sense.

38. *cent' anni*: See *Aen*. VI, 329: "Centum errant annos volitantque haec litora circum." ("A hundred years they roam and flit about these shores.")

39. *sanz' arrostarsi quando 'l foco il feggia*: Through this verse we see that the blasphemers endure more painful punishment for a graver sin; they lie under the fire without being able to brush it off. If a sodomite stops even for an instant, he must, as a special penalty, suffer the blasphemer's punishment for a hundred years.   *arrostarsi*: Here, "to brush off" or, freely, "to defend oneself" from the falling fire; see the description of these souls under the rain of fire (*Inf*. XIV, 42): "escotendo da sé l'arsura fresca." Cf. the use of "rosta," *Inf*. XIII, 117. M. Barbi (1934b, p. 208) discusses the meanings of both "rosta" and "arrostarsi."   *il feggia = lo fieda (ferisca)*.

40. *Però = per ciò.   a' panni*: Walking below and beside the wayfarer. Brunetto's head reaches the lower hem of Dante's gown; see notes to vss. 11, 24. Benvenuto says: "Ita quod cum capite attingebat pannos autoris, et agger iste videtur esse altus per staturam unius hominis." ("So that his head reached the author's garment; thus the bank is clearly as high as a man.")

41. *masnada*: The word does not here bear the pejorative sense that it later acquired.

43. *Io non osava scender*: The wayfarer would have been burned had he done so.   *strada*: The top of the bank, which was said to provide a "path" (*Inf*. XIV, 141).

45. *tenea = teneva*.

46. *Qual fortuna o destino*: Note Virgil's use of "casus" and "fortuna" in the following passage from the *Aeneid* (VI, 531–34):

> sed te qui vivum casus, age fare vicissim,
> attulerint. pelagine venis erroribus actus
> an monitu divum? an quae te fortuna fatigat,
> ut tristis sine sole domos, loca turbida, adires?

But come, tell in turn what chance hath brought thee here, alive. Comest thou driven in thy ocean-wanderings, or at Heaven's command? Or what doom wearies thee, that thou shouldst visit these sad, sunless dwellings, this land of disorder?

49–54. *Là sù di sopra . . . questo calle*: These two tercets recapitulate the opening scene and action of the *Inferno* (Canto I). It may be noted that in the *Tesoretto* Brunetto also portrays himself as having strayed from the "gran cammino" and entered a wild wood (see G. Contini, 1960, vol. II, p. 182, vss. 186–90):

> e io, in tal corrotto
> pensando a capo chino,
> perdei il gran cammino,
> e tenni a la traversa
> d'una selva diversa.

And I, thinking of that, with bowed head strayed from the main road, and turned into a path that led through a strange wood.

50. *lui*: Dative.　*in una valle*: See *Inf.* I, 14.

51. *avanti che l'età mia fosse piena*: Before I had reached the age of thirty-five; see n. to *Inf.* I, 1. More precise information about the beginning of Dante's *smarrimento* is given in the *Purgatorio* (XXXI, 34–36), but here the date is left vague.

53. *questi*: Virgil (see n. to vs. 36).　*tornand' io in quella*: The antecedent of "quella" is "valle" in vs. 50. See *Inf.* I, 61, where Dante speaks of this return in moral terms: "Mentre ch'i' rovinava in basso loco."

54. *ca = casa*. The form was current in Tuscan usage before Dante's time. See the use of "co" for *capo* in *Purg.* III, 128; also E. G. Parodi (1957), p. 274. / Virgil has promised to lead Dante on a way that will eventually bring him to the "imperador che là sù regna" (*Inf.* I, 124), and in this allegorical journey there will be no stopping short of that point. Thus, in the light of a perspective of mean-

ing now available to the reader, "a ca" means "to God." The idea of a journey to God implies the return of the soul to God, a concept which is emphasized by the use of "reducemi." Dante discusses the idea in the *Convivio* (IV, xii, 15, 18):

> E sì come peregrino che va per una via per la quale mai non fue, che ogni casa che da lungi vede crede che sia l'albergo, e non trovando ciò essere, dirizza la credenza a l'altra, e così di casa in casa, tanto che a l'albergo viene; così l'anima nostra, incontanente che nel nuovo e mai non fatto cammino di questa vita entra, dirizza li occhi al termine del suo sommo bene . . . . Veramente così questo cammino si perde per errore come le strade de la terra.

> And like a pilgrim who is travelling on a road where he hath never been before, who believes that every house which he sees from afar is the hostel, and finding that it is not directs his belief to another, and so from house to house until he comes to the hostel; even so our soul, so soon as it enters upon the new and never-yet-made journey of life, directs its eyes to the goal of its supreme good . . . . But in truth we may lose this way in error, just as we may lose the paths of earth.

The journey to God also implies a foretaste, in this life, of the final bliss enjoyed by the blessed in Heaven. See *Inf.* XVI, 61, where Dante speaks of his goal as "dolci pomi" in the sense of happiness; also *Purg.* XXVII, 115-17.

55. *Se tu segui tua stella*: The figure is essentially nautical, as the word "porto" implies. "Stella" in this context does not imply fatality; rather it means one's goal in life if one is true to one's "own self." Achieving the goal depends both on one's *ingegno* (native intellectual gifts), which is determined by astral influences ("il cielo," vs. 59), and on one's acquired *virtù*. Brunetto does not speak, here or elsewhere, of supernatural guidance.

58. *per tempo morto*: When Brunetto died, *ca.* 1294, Dante was about twenty-nine years old.

60. *opera*: Civil and political activity. Dante did not par-
ticipate in public affairs before 1295 (see U. Bosco, 1961,
pp. 16–17), but by the time of this exchange with Brunetto
(1300, as we shall see) his "work" as he saw it was well
under way. On Dante's political activities from 1295 to
1300, see M. Barbi (1933), pp. 16–20.

61–64. *Ma quello ingrato popolo . . . nimico*: Brunetto
prophesies Dante's exile in 1302, as Farinata did (see *Inf.*
X, 79–80 and the note). In fact, the two scenes display a
striking resemblance in more than one respect.

61. *quello ingrato popolo maligno*: The judgment upon
Florence and its people is made in the bitterness of exile;
the "people" here are essentially those in power at the time
of Dante's banishment and responsible for it.

62. *Fiesole*: A city of Tuscany, situated on a hill about
four miles northeast of Florence, and commanding a view
of that city and of the valley of the Arno. In ancient times
Fiesole was one of the twelve Etruscan towns, and the
remains of Cyclopean walls are still extant, as well as the
ruins of a Roman theater and baths. / Dante here is follow-
ing the legend that the Florentine nobility was descended
from the Romans and the common people from the Fiesol-
ans. Villani (I, 38) tells how the Romans destroyed Fiesole
(the headquarters of Catiline's army) and founded Florence.
Then, he says: "[La cittade] fu popolata della migliore
gente di Roma, e de' più sofficienti . . . e accolsono con
loro quelli Fiesolani che vi vollono dimorare e abitare."
("The city was populated by the best and most capable
Romans . . . and they welcomed into their midst those
Fiesolans who wanted to stay on and live there.") Brunetto
Latini also speaks of the Romans' founding of Florence
(*Tresor* I, xxxvii, 1–2):

Quant la conjuroison fu descoverte et le pooir Catelline
fu affoibloié, il s'enfui en Toschane en une cité ki avoit
non Fiesle et la fist reveler contre Rome. . . . Aprés
ce assegerent li romain la cité di Fiesle, tant k'il le
venkirent et misent en sa subjection; et lors firent il

enmi les plains ki est au pié des hautes montaignes u
cele cités seoit une autre cité, ki ore est apelee Florence.

When the conspiracy was discovered and Catiline's
power weakened, he fled to Tuscany to a city called
Fiesole and caused it to revolt against Rome. . . . As
a result, the Romans laid siege to the city of Fiesole
until they conquered and subjugated it; they then built,
in the midst of the plains which are at the foot of the
high mountains where that city was located, another
city which is today called Florence.

Villani records a second immigration, which took place
nearly a thousand years later, after the Florentines de-
stroyed Fiesole (IV, 6):

Allora i Fiorentini patteggiarono che chi volesse uscire
della città di Fiesole e venire ad abitare in Firenze,
potesse venire sano e salvo . . . per la qual cosa in grande
quantità ne scesero ad abitare in Firenze, onde poi
furono e sono grandi schiatte in Firenze.

Then the Florentines agreed that whoever wanted to
leave the city of Fiesole and come to live in Florence
could do so in complete safety . . . . Whereupon many
came down, and subsequently became—and still are—
great families in Florence.

In the light of Brunetto's attitude toward the "Fiesolan
beasts" see Villani (I, 38):

I Fiorentini sono sempre in guerra e in dissensione tra
loro, che non è da maravigliare, essendo stratti e nati
di due popoli così contrarii e nemici e diversi di co-
stumi, come furono gli nobili Romani virtudiosi, e'
Fiesolani ruddi e aspri di guerra.

The Florentines are always in disagreement and at war
among themselves. Nor need that cause amazement,
since they descend from two so opposed, inimical, and
very different peoples—namely, the noble and virtuous
Romans and the crude, war-embittered Fiesolans.

62. *ab antico* = *ab antiquo*, a Latinism.

63. *e tiene ancor del monte e del macigno*: Boccaccio comments that Dante uses " 'del monte,' in quanto rustico e salvatico, e 'del macigno,' in quanto duro e non pieghevole ad alcuno liberale e civil costume" (*"del monte* [of the mountain], inasmuch as they are rustic and crude; *del macigno* [of the rock], inasmuch as they are rough and not amenable to gentle and civil customs").

64. *per tuo ben far*: For Dante's public service in the affairs of government. See Dante's use of "ben far" in *Inf.* VI, 81.

65–66. *tra li lazzi sorbi . . . al dolce fico*: The "lazzi sorbi" are those Florentines descended from the Fiesolans; the "dolce fico" is a Florentine—Dante himself—descended from the Romans. See Luc: 6:43–44:

> Non est enim arbor bona quae facit fructus malos, neque arbor mala faciens fructum bonum. Unaquaeque enim arbor de fructu suo cognoscitur. Neque enim de spinis colligunt ficus, neque de rubo vindemiant uvam.

> For there is no good tree that bears bad fruit, nor is there a bad tree that bears good fruit. For every tree is known by its fruit. For from thorns men do not gather figs, neither from a bramble do they harvest grapes.

Dante's metaphor, to be sure, is different; it is unfitting that the sweet fig even should bear its fruit among the sour sorbs.

67. *Vecchia fama nel mondo li chiama orbi*: There are two traditions concerning the origin of the old proverb about the "blindness" of the Florentines. According to one account, the Florentines are called blind because they allowed their foe Totila to beguile them into admitting him within their gates and thereby brought about the destruction of their city (Villani, II, 1):

> E veggendo [Totile] che per assedio non la potea avere . . . per inganno, e lusinghe, e tradimento s'ingegnò d'averla . . . Totile si rimase di guastare intorno alla città, e mandò a' Fiorentini che volea esser loro amico . . . promettendo e mostrando a loro grande amore . . . .

I Fiorentini malavveduti (e però furono poi sempre in proverbio chiamati ciechi) credettono alle sue false lusinghe e vane promessioni: apersonli le porte, e misonlo nella città lui e sua gente.

And when [Totila] realized he could not take it by siege . . . he tried to devise ways to take it by deception, by flattery, and by treachery . . . Totila desisted from laying waste the surrounding countryside, and sent word to the Florentines that he wanted to be their friend . . . promising and showing great affection for them . . . . The incautious Florentines (and thus they have been proverbially called blind) believed his false flattery and vain promises. They opened their gates to him, and allowed him and his army to enter the city.

On this legend and Dante's possible allusion to it, see G. Ferretti (1950), pp. 113–15. According to the other account, preferred by some early commentators, the proverb arose from a trick the Pisans played upon the Florentines after they conquered Majorca from the Saracens in 1117. While they were away, the Pisans had asked the Florentines to guard their city for them against the Lucchese. As Boccaccio recounts the incident in his *Comento*:

Avendo i fiorentini con grandissima onestà servata la città, e i pisani tornando vincitori, ne recarono due colonne di porfido vermiglio bellissimo, e porti, de tempio o della città che fossero, di legno, ma nobilissimamente lavorate: e di queste fecero due parti, che posero dall'una parte le porti e dall'altra le due colonne coperte di scarlatto, e diedero le prese a' fiorentini, li quali, senza troppo avanti guardare, presono le colonne. Le quali venutene in Firenze, e spogliate di quella veste scarlatta, si trovarono essere rotte, come oggi le veggiamo davanti alla porta di San Giovanni.

The Florentines guarded the city [Pisa] with the utmost probity. When the Pisans returned victorious, they brought back with them two beautiful vermilion porphyry columns, and exquisitely wrought wooden doors, either from a temple or a city. They separated this booty, with the doors on one side and the columns covered in scarlet on the other, and gave the Florentines the choice between them. Without looking very closely, the Florentines chose the columns. When they arrived in Florence and were stripped of their scarlet covering, the columns were found to be broken, just as we see them today, before the portals of San Giovanni.

Boccaccio in his *Comento* avers that this story was accepted as an explanation of the proverbial blindness of the Florentines, but is himself dubious about its validity.

68. *gent' è avara, invidiosa e superba*: See *Inf.* VI, 74–75: "superbia, invidia e avarizia sono / le tre faville c'hanno i cuori accesi."

69. *dai lor costumi*: Commenting on this verse, Gmelin recalls the title of the *Divine Comedy* as commonly given in the manuscripts: "Incipit Comedia Dantis Alagherii florentini natione, non moribus." ("Here begins the Comedy of Dante Alighieri, a Florentine by birth but not by character.")   *forbi* = *forbisca*.

70. *La tua fortuna tanto onor ti serba*: The prophecy, concerning Dante's life in exile, now seems to focus on his literary rather than his political work.

71. *l'una parte e l'altra*: The Neri and also the Bianchi, with whom Dante first found himself obliged to associate in exile, but from whom he soon separated. In the *Paradiso* (XVII, 62), he refers to the Bianchi as a "compagnia malvagia e scempia."

73–74. *Faccian le bestie fiesolane strame di lor medesme*: "Let these Fiesolan beasts consume and destroy themselves"; on *fare strame* see M. Barbi (1934b), pp. 240–41.

74. *la pianta*: Dante, the "dolce fico" (vs. 66) of the preceding figure.

75. *s'alcuna surge ancora*: See *Epist.* V, 11: "si quid de Troyanorum Latinorumque semine superest" ("and if aught of

the seed of the Trojans and the Latins remain"). *letame*: "Manure," continuing the metaphor of "bestie" and "strame."

76–77. *la sementa santa di que' Roman*: See *De mon*. II, v, 5, in which Dante refers to "populus ille sanctus, pius et gloriosus" ("that people, holy, compassionate, and glorious"). In the *Convivio* (IV, v, 12) the Romans are called "non umani cittadini, ma divini" ("not human but divine citizens").

77. *che vi rimaser*: See n. to vs. 62.

80. *lui*: Dative, as in vs. 34.

81. *de l'umana natura posto in bando*: The prophecy of Dante's exile seems to have prompted the metaphor, which simply means: "You would still be among the living, not banished from them by death." On this verse see G. Vandelli (1925).

82. *ché 'n la mente m'è fitta*: See *Aen*. IV, 4–5: "Haerent infixi pectore voltus / verbaque." ("His looks and words cling fast within her bosom.")

85. *come l'uom s'etterna*: By the attainment of earthly fame and glory. In the *Tresor* (II, cxx, 1) Brunetto says: "Glore done au preudome une seconde vie; c'est a dire que aprés sa mort la renomee ki maint de ses bones oevres fait sambler k'il soit encore en vie." ("Glory gives the wise man a second life; that is to say, after his death the reputation which remains of his good works makes it seem as if he were still alive.")

86. *in grado = in grato*.

87. *si scerna = si discerna*.

88. *mio corso*: The course of my life. *scrivo*: "I write down" in the "book of memory." See *Inf*. II, 8 and the note. See also Prov. 7:3: "Scribe illam in tabulis cordis tui." ("Write them on the tablet of your heart.")

89. *serbolo = lo serbo.* *a chiosar*: Literally, "to be glossed"; to be interpreted and explained. On the figure, see C. S. Singleton (1949), pp. 34–42. *con altro testo*: The prophecy of Dante's exile, which he has already heard from Farinata (see *Inf.* X, 79–80 and the note).

90. *a donna che saprà*: Beatrice, from whom, as Virgil has promised (*Inf.* X, 132), the wayfarer will hear "di [sua] vita il viaggio." Actually it is not Beatrice but another, Dante's great-great-grandfather, who performs this office. His words keep the figure of glossing (*Par.* XVII, 94–95): "Figlio, queste son le chiose / di quel che ti fu detto."

91. *tanto*: "This much at least"; cf. the Latin *tantum*.

92. *garra = garrisca.*

94. *arra*: Here used ironically, since it is a forecast of the hard fortune to come. Farinata has made much the same prediction; hence, the "earnest is not new."

95–96. *giri Fortuna la sua rota . . . la sua marra*: The peasant (*villano*) idly whirling his mattock is juxtaposed, in a defiant, challenging tone, to Fortune turning her wheel. The phrase "e 'l villan [giri] la sua marra" seems to echo some unknown proverb.

97–98. *Lo mio maestro . . . riguardommi*: Virgil is walking along the top of the bank ahead of his charge, while Brunetto keeps pace to the wayfarer's right. Accordingly Virgil turns his head back over his right shoulder ("cheek") to look at the two.

98. *riguardommi = mi riguardò.*

99. *Bene ascolta chi la nota*: "He who listens to this listens well," since it is well said. See Apoc. 1:3: "Beatus qui legit et audit verba prophetiae huius, et servat ea quae in ea scripta sunt." ("Blessed is he who reads and those who hear the words of this prophecy, and keep the things that are written therein.") *la*: The feminine of many idioms.

100. *Né per tanto di men = nondimeno.   vommi = mi vado.* The reflexive serves to "distance" the subject, here to set off the wayfarer from his guide as he walks along with Brunetto. On the pleonastic reflexive, see n. to *Inf.* VII, 94.

102. *più sommi: Sommo* commonly was used as a simple adjective.

103. *è buono:* See *Inf.* XII, 27.

105. *ché 'l tempo saria corto:* We are not told how many souls there are in Brunetto's "schiera," but this phrase seems to indicate that it is a numerous company.

106. *cherci = chierici.*

109. *Priscian:* Priscian, the celebrated Latin grammarian (fl. *ca.* A.D. 500), was born at Caesarea in Mauretania and taught grammar at Constantinople. The work to which he owes his fame is the *Institutiones grammaticae*, a systematic exposition of Latin grammar. It was immensely popular and the recognized authority on the subject until quite recent times. / What basis Dante had for imputing to Priscian guilt of a sexual nature is not known; there is nothing to justify the accusation in any of the scanty notices of him that have reached us. The early commentators believe he is meant to represent the whole tribe of *pedagogi* and would justify Dante's condemnation of him by the argument, *pedagogus ergo sodomiticus* ("teacher, therefore sodomite"). Thus Boccaccio says in his *Comento:*

> Non lessi mai nè udi' che esso di tal peccato fosse peccatore, ma io estimo abbia qui voluto porre lui, acciochè per lui s'intendano coloro li quali la sua dottrina insegnano; del qual male la maggior parte si crede che sia maculata, perciochè il più hanno gli scolari giovani, e per l'età temorosi e ubbidienti, così a' disonesti come agli onesti comandamenti de' lor maestri; e per questo comodo si crede che spesse volte incappino in questa colpa.

I have never read or heard that he was guilty of such a sin. Rather, I judge he put him here to represent those who teach his doctrine, since the majority of them are believed to be tainted with that evil. For most of their students are young; and being young, are timorous and obey both the proper and the improper demands of their teachers. And because the students are so accessible, it is believed that the teachers often fall into this sin.

The *Anonimo fiorentino* follows the same line of reasoning:

Perchè questo Prisciano non si truova ch'elli peccasse in questo vizio, pare che l'Auttore ponga qui Prisciano per maestri che 'nsegnano grammatica, che comunemente pajono maculati di questo vizio, forse per la comodità de' giovani a' quali elli insegnano.

Since there is no evidence to indicate that Priscian was guilty of this vice, it would appear that the author is making Priscian represent teachers of grammar, who seem to be commonly tainted with this vice—perhaps because the young men they teach are so easily accessible.

There is not much to be said for the suggestion that Dante confused Priscian with Priscillian, the heretical fourth-century bishop of Ávila who, with his followers the Priscillianists, was accused of practicing magic and engaging in free love. Benvenuto seems to have fallen into some such confusion himself, however, for he speaks of Priscian as having been an apostate monk:

Priscianus ponitur hic tamquam clericus, quia monachus fuit et apostatavit, ut acquireret sibi maiorem famam et gloriam . . . . Ponitur etiam tamquam magnus literatus in genere eloquentiae, quia fuit doctor . . . grammaticae, vir vere excellentissimus, princeps in hac arte primitiva, magnus orator, historicus, et autorista.

Priscian is placed here as a cleric. He was a monk, and an apostate who sought greater fame and glory . . . . He is also placed here as one of the great masters in the field of eloquence, for he was a doctor . . . of grammar. Indeed, he was an excellent man, the leader in this basic art; and he was a great orator, a historian, and an author.

110. *Francesco d'Accorso*: Francesco d'Accorso (1225–93) was the son of a famous Florentine jurist and law professor, Accorso da Bagnolo (commonly known by the Latin name Accursius). Born at Bologna, where his father taught at the university, Francesco also became a celebrated lawyer and professor of civil law. In 1273, when Edward I passed through the city on his way back from Palestine, Francesco accepted the monarch's invitation to accompany him to England. He lectured for some time at Oxford, where he had free quarters in Beaumont Palace. The Bolognese, in an attempt to keep the eminent jurist at their university, had forbidden Francesco to go under pain of confiscation of all his property. This threat was executed in 1274, when he was proscribed as a Ghibelline. His belongings, however, were restored to him on his return in 1281 to Bologna, where he died three years later. A sister of his is said also to have professed law at the University of Bologna.   *vedervi*: Depends on "potei" (*potevi*, used in a conditional perfect sense), vs. 112.

112. *colui*: The person indicated is Andrea de' Mozzi, member of the noble Florentine family of that name (they were Guelphs and Bianchi) and bishop of Florence 1287–95. During his episcopacy, the church of Santa Croce and the hospital of Santa Maria were founded in Florence, the latter being endowed (in 1287, reputedly at Andrea's suggestion) by Folco Portinari, the father of Beatrice. In September 1295, because of his unseemly living, Andrea was transferred by Boniface VIII to the see of Vicenza (see n. to vs. 113), where he died in February 1296. On Andrea's life and his place in the *Commedia*, see R. Davidsohn (1908), pt. 1, p. 440; pt. 2, p. 155 *et passim*; E. Palandri (1931); E. Sanesi (1938).   *servo de' servi*: The pope (*servus servorum Dei*), Boniface VIII in this case; hence the expression is not without a touch of bitter sarcasm.

113. *Bacchiglione*: A river of northern Italy, which rises in the Alps above Vicenza, through which it passes, and flows in a southeasterly direction as far as Padua, where it divides into three streams. One of these runs into the Brenta, another into the Adige, while the third, retaining the name Bacchiglione, enters the Adriatic Sea near Brondolo. Here the Bacchiglione indicates Vicenza, as the Arno indicates Florence.

114. *dove lasciò li mal protesi nervi*: Where he died, leaving the body whose muscles had been "ill stretched" in the sinful act of sodomy.

117. *là*: "Ahead," in the direction in which they are moving. *nuovo fummo*: The smoke, apparently rising from the sand, actually comes from the burning feet and scorched flesh of another band of souls.

118. *deggio = debbo (devo)*.

119. *Sieti* (pronounced *sìeti*) = *ti sia*. *il mio Tesoro*: His great encyclopedia, *Li livres dou Tresor*.

120. *nel qual io vivo ancora*: See the quotation from the *Tresor* in n. to vs. 85. *cheggio = chiedo*.

121. *Poi si rivolse*: He turns back to rejoin his band; see vs. 41. For one possible reading of "poi," see S. Debenedetti (1923b).

122–23. *che corrono . . . per la campagna*: This foot race, known as the *palio*, was run annually on the first Sunday in Lent on a course outside Verona. According to Boccaccio, the competitors ran naked, and the winner was awarded a piece of green cloth (the *palio*):

> Secondo che io ho inteso, i veronesi per antica usanza fanno in una lor festa correre ad uomini ignudi un drappo verde, al qual corso, per tema di vergogna, non si mette alcuno se velocissimo corridor non si tiene.

> I have heard that the Veronese observe an ancient tradition at one of their feasts. They have naked men run a race, and the prize is a piece of green cloth. For fear of being embarrassed, no one enters the race unless he thinks himself a very fast runner.

In fact, a "booby" prize was awarded to the runner who came in last; this was a rooster, which the loser was obliged to carry into the city before all the people. M. Barbi (1899, p. 217) has noted the mention of this prize in the Veronese statutes of Can Grande I (1328):

> Aliud vero ad quod curretur ad pedes sit unum palium et unus gallus cum uno pari cirothecarum; et prius currenti detur palium, et ultimo currenti detur gallus quem palam portare debeat usque in civitatem.

> Another prize for which the foot race was run was a banner and a rooster and a pair of gloves; the winner was awarded the banner and the last man in the race the rooster, which he had to carry openly into the city.

CANTO XVI

1. *era = ero.   onde = ove.   s'udia = s'udiva.*

2. *cadea = cadeva.   ne l'altro giro*: The eighth circle.

3. *simile a quel che l'arnie fanno rombo = simile a quel rombo che fanno l'arnie.*

4. *si partiro = si partirono*, "detached themselves."

5. *una torma che passava*: Virgil and Dante have now come some distance along the dike since leaving Brunetto; hence, this is but one of several troops passing by. Just as the sodomites described in Canto XV were primarily teachers and clerics, those now approaching, as will be seen, had been active in politics. Thus, it would appear that the sodomites are grouped in the burning desert according to profession—although nowhere is this stated in so many words.

7. *Venian ver' = venivano verso.*

8–9. *ch'a l'abito . . . prava*: Farinata recognized the wayfarer as a Florentine because of his speech (*Inf.* X, 25–26); now he is known as such from the manner of his dress. Villani (XII, 4) says with noticeable pride that the dress of the Florentines "era il più bello e nobile e onesto che di

274

niuna altra nazione, a modo di togati Romani" ("was the most beautiful, the most noble, and the most decorous of that of any nation; it was in the manner of the togaed Romans").

8. *ne = ci.*

11. *ricenti = recenti.   da le fiamme incese = incese da le fiamme.*

12. *men duol = me ne duole.   pur ch'i' me ne rimembri:* For other examples of emotion restirred by memory, see *Inf.* I, 6; XIV, 78; XXXIII, 5–6.

13–15. *A le lor grida . . . cortese:* Virgil demonstrates that he is indeed the "gentle sage who [knows] all" (see *Inf.* VII, 3) by his instant recognition of these Florentines who now come running toward him and his pupil. The latter knows them only by reputation, but he has already asked about two of them in *Inf.* VI, 79–82.

14. *ver' = verso.*

17. *la natura del loco:* The subject of "saetta" in the preceding verse.   *dicerei = direi.*

18. *stesse = si convenisse.   fretta:* Haste itself (quite apart from the ignominy of the sin here punished and the punishment itself) was, to Dante's mind, particularly undignified. See *Purg.* III, 10–11.

19. *Ricominciar = ricominciarono.   ei = essi;* see E. G. Parodi (1957), p. 250.

19–20. *Ricominciar . . . l'antico verso:* Some commentators understand "verso" here to refer to the gait of the three shades: seeing that Virgil and Dante had stopped, the three ceased to run and resumed walking. But "verso" seems rather to refer to an utterance on the part of the shades: they had interrupted their wailings to address the wayfarers; seeing that the latter had stopped, the three "resumed their former lament" (see *Inf.* XIV, 20). "Antico" also carries the meanings "wonted," "eternal."

20. *fuor = furono.*

21. *fenno = fecero.* *una rota*: As Brunetto has already explained (*Inf.* XV, 37–39), the souls must keep moving lest they suffer an even severer penalty. *trei = tre.* See E. G. Parodi (1957), p. 251.

22. *Qual sogliono i campion far nudi e unti*: Many commentators, both early and late, understand the "champions" here to be those who took part in the ancient Greek and Roman pugilistic games. See *Aen.* III, 279–82:

> . . . votisque incendimus aras
> Actiaque Iliacis celebramus litora ludis.
> exercent patrias oleo labente palaestras
> nudati socii . . .

[We] kindle the altars with offerings, and throng the Actian shores in the games of Ilium. My comrades strip and, sleek with oil, engage in their native wrestling bouts . . . .

Also see Lucan, *Phars.* IV, 613–14: "Perfundit membra liquore / Hospes Olympiacae servato more palaestrae." ("The stranger, faithful to the fashion of wrestlers at Olympia, drenched his limbs with oil.") Boccaccio explains in his *Comento*:

> E tra gli altri giuochi, usavano [gli antichi] il fare alle braccia, e questo giuoco si chiamava "lutta." E a questi giuochi non venivano altri che giovani molto in ciò esperti, e ancora forti e atanti delle persone, e chiamavansi "atlete," li quali noi chiamiamo oggi "campioni"; e, per potere più espeditamente questo giuoco fare, si spogliavano ignudi, acciochè i vestimenti non fossero impedimento o vantaggio d'alcuna delle parti; ed, oltre a questo, acciochè più apertamente apparisse la virtù del più forte, s'ugnevan tutti o d'olio o di sevo o di sapone: la quale unzione rendeva grandissima difficultà al potersi tenere, perciochè ogni piccol guizzo, per opera dell'unzione, traeva l'uno delle braccia all'altro; e così unti, avanti che venissero al prendersi, si riguardavan per alcuno spazio, per prendere, se prender si potesse, alcun vantaggio nella prima presa.

Among other games, there was a contest at grappling, and this was called *lutta* ("wrestling"). Only very expert young men, still strong and powerfully built, came to these games. They were called *atlete* ("athletes"), and today we call them *campioni* ("champions"). To be better able to play the games, they removed all their clothes, so that no garment would provide either impediment or advantage for either contestant. Furthermore, the better to prove the prowess of the stronger, they covered themselves completely with oil, tallow, or soap. This unction made them very difficult to hold, for the slightest squirm enabled the one to free himself from the arms of the other. For that reason, they would watch each other for some time before coming to grips, in order, if possible, to gain the advantage with the first hold.

Benvenuto understands the verse in much the same way and also attests to the continuation of public wrestling into Dante's day: "sicut etiam e simili videmus hodie, ad festa maxime quae fiunt in villis" ("just as we can see today from something similar that takes place especially at country feasts"). Those who hold with the view that vs. 22 refers to the ancient games point out that the verb *solere* often is used in the present with the sense of the imperfect, as in Provençal (see also "suole," vs. 68).

However, R. Davidsohn (1900, 1902) argues that the reference is not to ancient pugilistic bouts but rather to the medieval custom of trial by combat, in which "champions" were hired to do battle in order to decide some legal question; and in this connection he produces some interesting documentation concerning the practice in Dante's time. Such combatants were indeed called "campioni," but Davidsohn fails to show that the medieval fighters were ever "naked and oiled." Moreover, they probably were armed with some weapon, a detail which does not fit the comparison here, for, as Benvenuto points out, the "blows and thrusts" referred to are clearly blows and thrusts of the fists and palms. For a view opposed to Davidsohn's, see Torraca; also A. Bassermann (1932), pp. 163–65.

277

23. *avvisando lor presa e lor vantaggio*: This, as Porena suggests, is probably a hendiadys, to be understood as *la presa più vantaggiosa*, the phrase referring to the familiar preliminary sparring that takes place during such bouts and possibly suggesting that the wrestlers circle about and take hold of each other's arms before breaking away and then coming to grips. But just how the reader is to imagine the three sodomites "studying their hold and vantage" in this way is not clear, for as they are "wheeling" thus, the sole object of their concern is the wayfarer.

25. *visaggio = viso*.

26–27. *sì che 'n contraro . . . continuo viaggio*: As the three sodomites, turning about in their wheel, try to keep their eyes fixed on the wayfarer, standing on the bank above, each, at a given point in his wheeling on the sand below, must turn his neck and head back in the direction opposite to that in which his feet are moving. "Continuo viaggio" means "continually" in the sense of "repeatedly." / Other readings have been adopted by different editors; for example, Scartazzini-Vandelli prefers "sì che 'ntra loro il collo / faceva e i piè continuo viaggio."

28. *sollo*: "Soft," "yielding," here because sandy; see *Purg.* V, 18; XXVII, 40. Again the reader's attention is directed to the sodomites' feet and the contact these make with the burning sand. See vss. 32–33 and n. to *Inf.* XIV, 34.

30. *e 'l tinto aspetto*: One of the subjects of "rende" in the preceding verse.   *brollo = brullo*, "bare," "hairless," containing in one word the meanings of the two adjectives "nudo e dipelato" in vs. 35. On the use of *brollo*, see M. Barbi (1934b), p. 270.

31. *la fama nostra*: As it endures in the world above.

32. *dirne = dirci*.

33. *freghi*: Literally, "rub"; the word continues the focus on the friction of feet on scorching ground. See vs. 28.

35. *tutto che = sebbene*.

37. *la buona Gualdrada*: Gualdrada was the daughter of Bellincione Berti de' Ravignani of Florence. Through her marriage with Guido Guerra IV, the Conti Guidi traced their descent from the great Ravignani family. See *Par.* XVI, 97–98. Sapegno observes that she was known in her day as an example of domestic virtue and high morals.

38. *Guido Guerra*: A member of the illustrious Conti Guidi of the Dovadola line. Born *ca.* 1220, Guido Guerra was the eldest son of Marcovaldo, fourth son of Guido Guerra IV and Gualdrada de' Ravignani. He was a leader of the Guelphs, although his family before him appears to have belonged to the Imperial party. One of his earliest exploits— the relief of Ostina from a Ghibelline siege (1250)—gave the impulse to the reaction in favor of the Guelphs in Florence. In 1255 he expelled the Ghibellines from Arezzo, although they were later reinstated there. Guido Guerra was among those who attempted to dissuade the Florentine Guelphs from undertaking the disastrous expedition against Siena in 1260 (Villani, VI, 78) which resulted in the defeat at Montaperti and the ruin of the Guelph party in Florence. After this reverse, the Guelphs took refuge in Romagna, where Guido acted as their leader. At the battle of Benevento (1266) the Florentine and Tuscan Guelphs under his command materially contributed to Charles of Anjou's defeat of Manfred, who bitterly exclaimed: "Where are my Ghibellines for whom I have made such sacrifices?" (Villani, VII, 8). Guido Guerra died in 1272 at Montevarchi. M. Barbi (1899), pp. 211–12, and P. Santini (1923), pp. 25–28, give short but detailed accounts of his life.

40. *trita*: "Treads." *Tritare* often was used to refer to the "threshing" of grain with the feet. Once again the stress is on the painful burning of feet, as in the word "freghi," vs. 33 (see note).

41. *Tegghiaio Aldobrandi*: This Florentine Guelph of the powerful Adimari family was at one time (1256) *podestà* of Arezzo. Villani (VI, 78) describes him as "cavaliere savio e prode e di grande autoritade" ("a gallant and wise knight,

of great authority"). *la cui voce*: These words probably allude to Tegghiaio's advice to the Florentine Guelphs not to engage in the ill-fated expedition against Siena in 1260. On that occasion, according to Villani (VI, 78), Tegghiaio acted as the spokesman of the Guelph nobles headed by Guido Guerra. He survived the battle and took refuge with the rest of the Tuscan Guelphs at Lucca. On Tegghiaio see M. Bardi (1899), p. 205; I. Del Lungo (1898), p. 71; P. Santini (1923), pp. 31–40. When the wayfarer questioned Ciacco about Tegghiaio (*Inf.* VI, 79) and other worthy men, Ciacco told him that Tegghiaio was "among the blackest spirits."

42. *dovria esser gradita* = *avrebbe dovuto esser gradita*, a common use of the imperfect for the conditional perfect; for a comparable construction, see vs. 93.

44. *Iacopo Rusticucci*: According to the early commentators, Jacopo Rusticucci was socially inferior to his two companions. For example, the *Anonimo fiorentino* says: "Fu costui uno popolare di Firenze di picciol sangue, cavaliere, chiamato messer Jacopo Rusticucci, il quale fu valoroso uomo et piacevole." ("This valorous and likable knight, called Messer Jacopo Rusticucci, came from an unimportant family of the Florentine middle class.") To bear this out, it has been remarked that when the wayfarer asked Ciacco about the fate of certain Florentines (*Inf.* VI, 79–82), Rusticucci was the only one whose surname was mentioned, thereby implying perhaps that he was not especially well known or distinguished. He was, however, a close neighbor, in the Porta San Piero quarter of Florence, of Tegghiaio Aldobrandi, with whom as a Guelph he often was engaged in political and diplomatic affairs. They are mentioned together in a document of 1237. (See I. Del Lungo, 1884, pp. 203–4; 1898, p. 71; P. Santini, 1923, pp. 31–40.)

44–45. *e certo . . . mi nuoce*: The implication is that Rusticucci's "shrewish wife" drove him to sodomy. As the *Anonimo* explains: "Ebbe costui una sua moglie, diversa et spiacevole tanto, che costui la divise et seperolla da sè, et

mandolla a casa i parenti suoi." ("He had a wife who was
so odd and so disagreeable that he got rid of her, sending
her home to her relatives.") Benvenuto is more explicit:
"Habuit enim mulierem ferocem, cum qua vivere non
poterat; ideo dedit se turpitudini." ("Indeed his wife was
ferocious, and it was impossible to live with her. Thus he
gave himself over to this vice.")

46. *dal foco coperto*: "Sheltered from the fire."

48. *avria = avrebbe*. Virgil would have allowed it, be-
cause these souls are so worthy (see vss. 15–18).

49. *brusciato = bruciato*.

51. *di loro abbracciar = d'abbracciarli*.

52. *Non dispetto*: Dante's reply refers back to Rusticucci's
fear (see vss. 28–30) that the wretchedness of the place and
of their appearance might render them contemptible ("rende
in dispetto," vs. 29).

56. *parole*: Those in vss. 14–18.

57. *qual voi siete*: "Persons such as you" (i.e., persons so
worthy).

59. *ovra = opera*, in the meaning it had in *Inf.* XV, 60 (see
the note). It is the "ben far" of *Inf.* VI, 81.   *e li onorati
nomi*: This phrase echoes "la fama nostra" of vs. 31.

60. *ritrassi*: Past absolute of *ritrarre*, "to tell," "to relate."
See *Purg.* V, 32.

61–63. *Lascio lo fele . . . tomi*: In a single tercet Dante's
journey is again stated in the simplest possible terms (see
Inf. X, 61–62; XV, 49–54), yet with a meaning that ex-
ceeds the comprehension of those souls in Hell to whom
the words are addressed. However, the reader understands
that "lo fele" is the bitter wood of sin (*Inf.* I, 5–7) and
"dolci pomi" corresponds to "ca" in *Inf.* XV, 54: the goal
of the journey as promised by Virgil (*Inf.* I, 118–22).

62. *per lo = dal*.

63. *al centro*: "To the center" of the earth—namely, the bottom of Hell. *tomi*: From *tomare*: literally, "to fall," with the connotation of "fall headlong," though this hardly applies here.

64-65. *l'anima conduca le membra tue*: See *Conv.* III, vi, 12: "Manifesto è che la sua forma, cioè la sua anima, che lo conduce sì come cagione propria, riceva miracolosamente la graziosa bontade di Dio." ("It is manifest that her form, to wit her soul, which guides the body as its proper cause, miraculously receives the gracious excellence of God.")

64-66. *Se lungamente . . . luca*: A double use of the formula of adjuration, in which the person spoken to is entreated by that which is most dear to him (see *Inf.* X, 82).

67. *cortesia*: This word is used frequently by Dante to denote a complex cluster of virtuous attributes, such as nobility and generosity of character, politeness, graciousness, and refinement. See *Conv.* II, x, 7–8:

> E non siano li miseri volgari anche di questo vocabulo ingannati, che credono che cortesia non sia altro che larghezza; e larghezza è una speziale, e non generale, cortesia! Cortesia e onestade è tutt'uno: e però che ne le corti anticamente le vertudi e li belli costumi s'usavano, sì come oggi s'usa lo contrario, si tolse quello vocabulo da le corti, e fu tanto a dire cortesia quanto uso di corte. Lo qual vocabulo se oggi si togliesse da le corti, massimamente d'Italia, non sarebbe altro a dire che turpezza.

> And let not the wretched vulgar be deceived as to this word [*cortese*] also, thinking that courtesy is no other than openhandedness, for openhandedness is a special form of courtesy, and not courtesy in general. Courtesy and honour are all one, and because in courts of old time virtuous and fair manners were in use (as now the contrary), this word was derived from courts, and "courtesy" was as much as to say "after the usage of courts." Which word, if it were now taken from courts,

especially of Italy, would mean nought else than base-ness.

67–69. *cortesia e valor dì se dimora . . . fora*: The familiar use of a singular verb with a plural subject. It is clear from the feminine form of the participle *gita* that the agreement is with the first noun, which is usual—here the feminine noun "cortesia."

68. *suole*: A common use of the present tense of this verb to denote the past (see n. to vs. 22).

70. *Guiglielmo Borsiere*: Guglielmo Borsiere, according to Benvenuto, was a Florentine pursemaker who grew tired of his trade and left it to become a man of society, spending his time traveling and visiting the houses of noblemen. Boccaccio says of him:

> Questi fu cavalier di corte, uomo costumato molto e di laudevol maniera; ed era il suo esercizio, e degli altri suoi pari, il trattar paci tra' grandi e gentiliuomini, trattar matrimoni e parentadi, e talora con piacevoli e oneste novelle recreare gli animi de' faticati, e confortargli alle cose onorevoli; il che i moderni non fanno, anzi, quanto più sono scellerati e spiacevoli e con brutte operazioni e parole, più piacciono e meglio son provveduti.

> He was a knight who frequented the courts, a very well-bred man of the most laudable manners. It was his endeavor, and that of others like him, to make peace among aristocrats and gentlemen, to negotiate marriages and family relationships, and occasionally, with delightful and moral tales, to refresh the spirits of the troubled, and to spur them on to honorable deeds. Modern men no longer do these things; in fact, the more wicked and unpleasant men are, and the uglier their words and deeds, the more are they liked and the better are they rewarded.

The date of his death is not known, but the words "per poco" (vs. 71) clearly imply that he died shortly before

1300. Guglielmo is the subject of one of the tales of Boccaccio's *Decameron* (I, 8; vol. 1, pp. 60–62).

71. *per poco = da poco (tempo)*.

72. *ne = ci.*   *con le sue parole*: Guglielmo Borsiere's report that courtesy and valor are gone from the city.

73. *La gente nuova*: Those who had recently migrated to the city from the surrounding villages and countryside. See *Par.* XVI, 49–69. I. Del Lungo (1888), pp. 1–132, discusses these newcomers.

75. *ten piagni = te ne piangi*.

76. *con la faccia levata*: Various commentators take this phrase to have various meanings. Some say it implies that, in apostrophizing his native city, Dante looks up toward Florence. This is possible, since he is indeed addressing Florence. However, one can easily imagine that Dante might have raised his eyes heavenward had he pronounced such words on earth—thus also by habit here in the netherworld—such a gesture serving to invoke God or the heavens as witness to the truth of what he is affirming. Sapegno points out further that the gesture of lifting the face underscores the oratorical and prophetic tone of the discourse; and he notes the following comment by Buti: "Questo fu segno di cruccio e d'indegnazione insieme col grido: imperò che a Dante increscea delli vizi della sua città; et ancora si può intendere che significhi ardire, e che mostrava che dicesse vero: imperocchè il vero si dice con ardire." ("This, together with the shout, was a sign of anger and indignation; for Dante was grieved at the vices of his city. Or it can be interpreted to mean boldness, and to show that he was speaking the truth—for truth is spoken boldly.")

77. *ciò inteser per risposta*: The shades accept the wayfarer's words as an answer to their question, even though Dante has explicitly addressed Florence and not the shades directly.

78. *guardar = guardarono.   com' al ver si guata*: The three shades already had referred to Florence as "degenerate" ("nostra terra prava," vs. 9), and Jacopo Rusticucci had mentioned Guglielmo Borsiere's report of the city's sad decline. Now the three glance at one another with the look of men who hear confirmed something they already hold to be true. See *Aen.* XI, 120–21: "Dixerat Aeneas. Illi obstipuere silentes / conversique oculos inter se atque ora tenebant." ("Aeneas ceased: they stood dumb in silence, and kept their eyes and faces turned on one another.") Also see Statius, *Theb.* II, 173–75:

> Audierant, fixosque oculos per mutua paulum
> ora tenent, visique inter sese ordine fandi
> cedere. . . .

They heard him, and for a while held their eyes fixed in mutual gaze, seeming to yield each other place of speech.

80. *il satisfare altrui*: That is, with a reply so ready and to the point.

82. *Però = perciò.*

82–83. *se campi . . . e torni*: Again the formula of adjuration, as in vss. 64–66.

84. *quando ti gioverà dicere "I' fui"*: See *Aen.* I, 203: "Forsan et haec olim meminisse iuvabit." ("Perchance even this distress it will some day be a joy to recall.") The phrase—and especially the word "dicere" (*dire*)—clearly implies that the wayfarer, once he is back among the living, will take pleasure in recounting this most extraordinary journey.

85. *favelle = favelli.*

87. *sembiar = sembrarono.* See *Aen.* VIII, 224: "Pedibus timor addidit alas." ("Fear lends wings to his feet.") The three run to overtake their particular group again, as Brunetto had done.   *isnelle = snelle.*

88. *saria = sarebbe.   possuto = potuto.*

89. *fuoro* = *furono*.

92. *'l suon de l'acqua*: The thundering of the water at first was like the low hum that issues from a beehive (vs. 3). *n'* = *ci*.

93. *saremmo* = *saremmo stati*, another use of the imperfect for the conditional perfect. See n. to vs. 42.

94–102. *quel fiume . . . recetto*: The river to which Dante refers is the Montone, which rises as a torrent in the eastern Apennines, about six miles from the Benedictine monastery of San Benedetto dell'Alpe, near which it is joined by the torrents of the Acquacheta and Riodestro. At Forlì and Ravenna it is joined by two more streams, and enters the Adriatic above Sant'Apollinare. In Dante's day the Montone entered the Adriatic below the Po and was then the first river after the Po that, rising on the eastern slope of the Apennines, flowed into the sea (all the others flowed into the Po). Boccaccio, in his gloss on vs. 95, comments:

> E il primo fiume, il quale nasce in Appennino, senza mettere in Po, andando l'uomo da Po inver' levante, è chiamato, là dove nasce, Acquacheta; poi, divenendo al piano presso a Forlì in Romagna, cambia nome, ed è chiamato Montone, perciochè impetuosamente corre e passa allato a Forlì, e di quindi discende a Ravenna, e lungo le mura d'essa corre, e forse due miglia più giù mette nel mare Adriatico; e così è il primo che tiene "proprio cammino," appresso a quello che scende di monte Veso.

> Going from the Po eastward, the first river to rise in the Apennines without flowing into the Po is called, in the place where it rises, the Acquacheta; then, coming toward the plain near Forlì in Romagna, it changes name and is called the Montone ("Ram"), for it rushes impetuously by Forlì. From there it descends to Ravenna, running along its walls, and some two miles farther flows into the Adriatic. And thus, it is the first river after the Po that has its "own course" [see n. to vs. 95].

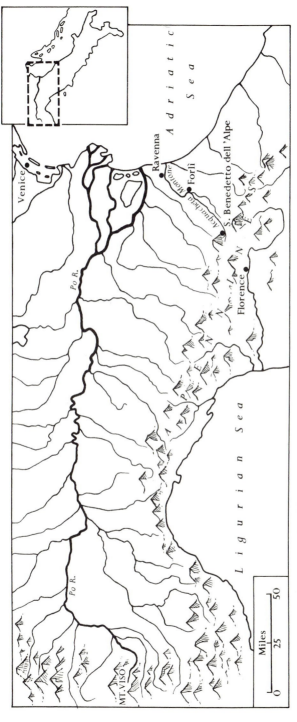

1. The course of the Po River, showing also the Acquacheta, in Dante's day, the first stream eastward whose water flowed into the sea rather than into the Po

Today the first river rising in the eastern Apennines to flow directly into the Adriatic is the Reno, which until the sixteenth century had no direct outlet to the sea. See Map 1, facing p. 286.

Dante and Boccaccio both imply that the river was known as the Acquacheta as far as Forlì and received the name of Montone only on reaching that city. In the present day, at any rate, this is not the case, the name of Montone being applied as far north as San Benedetto.

95. *prima*: This adverb modifies "ha proprio cammino," in the preceding verse; taken together they mean "is the first to have its own course." *Monte Viso*: Mount Viso or Monviso, the Mons Vesulus of the ancients (*Aen.* X, 708; Pliny, *Nat. hist.* III, xvi, 117), is forty miles southwest of Turin near the French border. Its peak (12,605 feet) is the highest of the Cottian Alps. On its slopes the Po River rises. Boccaccio explains:

> Monte Veso è un monte nell'Alpi, là sopra il Monferrato, e parte la Provenza dalla Italia, e di questo monte Veso nasce il fiume chiamato il Po. Il quale in sè riceve molti fiumi, li quali caggiono dell'Alpi dalla parte di ver' ponente, e d'Appennino di ver' levante, e mette in mare per più foci, e tra l'altre per quella di Primaro, presso a Ravenna; e questa è quella che è più orientale.

> Mount Viso is a mountain in the Alps, above Monferrato, separating Provence from Italy. On this mountain rises the river Po, into which flow many other rivers, which flow down from the Alps in the west, and from the Apennines in the east. The Po flows into the sea by various outlets, the easternmost of which is at Primaro, near Ravenna.

95. *dal Monte Viso 'nver' levante*: In counting the Montone as the first river to have its own course to the Adriatic ("'nver' levante"), Dante was starting at Mount Viso and following along the crest of the Apennine chain, which first runs in an easterly direction and then turns south.

96. *da la sinistra costa d'Apennino*: See *De vulg. eloqu.* I, x, 6:

> Dicimus ergo primo Latium bipartitum esse in dextrum et sinistrum. Si quis autem querat de linea dividente, breviter respondemus esse iugum Apennini, quod, ceu fictile culmen hinc inde ad diversa stillicidia grundat, aquas ad alterna hinc inde litora per imbricia longa distillat, ut Lucanus in secundo describit.

> In the first place, then, we say that Italy has a twofold division into right and left. But, if any should ask what is the dividing line, we answer shortly that it is the ridge of the Apennines, which like the ridge of a tiled roof discharges its droppings in different directions on either side, and pours its waters down to either shore alternately through long gutter-tiles, as Lucan describes in his second book [*Phars.* II, 396–438].

On the accepted geography of the time, see M. Casella (1927), pp. 65-68. Here in Canto XVI Dante's viewpoint is from the north looking south. Adopting the same viewpoint, Boccaccio, in his gloss to vs. 95, explains:

> E dice l'autore che egli viene dalla sinistra costa d'Appennino. Intorno alla qual cosa è da sapere che Appennino è un monte, il quale alcuni vogliono che cominci a questo monte Veso; altri dicono che egli comincia a Monaco, nella riviera di Genova . . . . Ora si chiama il lato destro di questo monte quello il quale è volto inverso il mar Tireno, e quello che è volto verso il mare Adriano è chiamato il sinistro.

> Now, the author says that it descends from the left side of the Apennines. Concerning this, you must know that the Apennines are mountains which some say begin at this Mount Viso, and others say begin at Monaco, on the Genoese Riviera . . . . The side of these mountains that faces the Tyrrhenian Sea is called the right, and that which faces the Adriatic is called the left.

97. *Acquacheta*: The Acquacheta, the upper part of the river in question, runs across a high plateau that is almost

level, so that the water is relatively quiet (*cheta, quieta*) or slow in its course. This doubtless accounts for the name.

98. *nel basso letto*: In the plain of Romagna, around Forlì.

101–2. *ad una scesa ove dovea per mille*: These are much debated lines. It is hard to see how "mille" could refer to anything except "scesa," with the meaning that the water of the Acquacheta roars down in a single cascade where "there might well have been a thousand," i.e., where it would normally require a thousand *scese* ("cascades") to contain it. Since such a description applies only in flood time, some objections have been raised to this interpretation. But Dante may be speaking of those times when the river was at its full. An observer, P. Nadiani (1894, pp. 14–16), has described the cascade at such a time:

> Nulla di nuovo e straordinario vi ha, come ho detto, in questa caduta, e solo essa riceve la sua rinomanza dalla menzione che ne fa Dante. Trovasi circa a quattro miglia al ponente di san Benedetto, sul torrente Acquacheta, ed è come il muro di divisione tra il territorio toscano ed il romagnolo, però che qui a punto si dipartono le due regioni. È alta circa 70 metri, tutta cavata nella roccia di sasso arenario o sereno, ch'è il sasso proprio di questi monti, larga in media quasi la metà dell'altezza. Non credasi ch'essa precipiti verticalmente, ma ha un pendìo assai inclinato e gli strati del macigno in linea orizzontale sporgendo alquanto in fuori formano come altrettanti gradini di una scalinata, di modo che può chiamarsi propriamente *scesa*. È bello o a dir meglio spaventoso contemplarla quando il torrente è gonfio. Allora l'acqua dal balzo precipita a mezzo della scesa, quindi al fondo, con tal fragore, che può dirsi veramente che *rimbomba*. Nel precipitare batte l'opposta riva con grande veemenza e forma tanti spruzzi d'acqua, che offendono la vista e sembra che si risolvano in minutissimo fumo o nebbia. Forse Dante la vide in questa occasione e ferì la sua immaginazione a tale, che poi la descrisse.

As I said, there is nothing new or extraordinary about this waterfall. It is famous only because it was mentioned by Dante. It is located about four miles west of San Benedetto, on the river Acquacheta, which place forms a sort of dividing wall between Tuscany and Romagna—for it is precisely at this point that the two regions meet. It is about seventy meters high, falling over sandstone, the stone peculiar to these mountains. It is almost half as wide as it is high. You must not imagine that it falls vertically; rather, it has a very inclined slope, and the layers of stone jutting forth horizontally form, as it were, the steps of a staircase, so that it may quite appropriately be called a *cascade*. It is beautiful, even awesome, to watch it when the river is full. At such times, the water rushes over the cliff, falls halfway down the cascade, and from there to the bottom with a truly *resounding* roar. In falling, it hits the opposite shore with great violence, forming many sprays that obstruct the vision, and seem to dissolve into fine smoke or fog. Perhaps Dante saw it on just such an occasion, and it so struck his imagination that he later described it.

102. *esser recetto*: Cf. the medieval Latin *esse receptus*.

104. *tinta*: "Tinged" red with blood, since it is coming from Phlegethon, the river of boiling blood.

105. *avria* = *avrebbe*.

106. *Io avea una corda*: The whole incident of the cord which the wayfarer throws over the precipice to attract the monster who then appears opens the poem to allegory (see C. S. Singleton, 1954, pp. 4–5). Up to now we have not been told that the wayfarer was wearing such a cord, nor is this a customary part of the dress by which the three sodomites had recognized him as a Florentine (vss. 8–9). Clearly, in such a context, this cord has more than literal meaning.

   intorno cinta: The cord serves, therefore, as a belt or girdle. A girdle was a symbol of strength, enabling the wearer to accomplish something, such as capturing a

leopard (vs. 108). Pliny (*Nat. hist.* XXVIII, xxvii, 93)
refers to capturing the hyena by using a girdle tied with
seven knots: "At si in laevam detorserit [hyaena], de-
ficientis argumentum esse celeremque capturam, facilius
autem capi, si cinctus suos venator flagellumque imperitans
equo septenis alligaverit nodis." ("Should however the
hyaena swerve to the left, it is a sign of failing strength and
a speedy capture; this will be easier however if the hunter
tie his girdle with seven knots, and seven in the whip with
which he controls his horse.") On the cord used to take
animals, see V. F. Hopper (1936).

107-8. *pensai alcuna volta prender la lonza*: The words
"alcuna volta" refer to the moment recounted in the first
canto (see *Inf.* I, 31-42). In this context, *prendere* means
"to catch," "to capture"; with reference to *Inf.* I, the mean-
ing is "to cope with"—in such a way as to enable the way-
farer to proceed up the mountain. This he failed to do,
and "pensai prender" has the implication of failure: "I
thought I would be able to capture [the leopard], but
failed."

108. *a la pelle dipinta = da la pelle dipinta.* See Dante's
description of the leopard's skin in *Inf.* I, 33 ("che di pel
macolato era coverta") and *Inf.* I, 42 ("a la gaetta pelle").

110. *sì come 'l duca m'avea comandato*: The clause can be
construed as modifying either the preceding or the following
verse—or both, which seems more likely.

111. *porsila = la porsi.*

112. *Ond' ei si volse inver' lo destro lato*: The wayfarer is
on his guide's left when he hands him the cord. Taking
the cord in his right hand, Virgil swings to the right in
order to cast it far out over the edge, so that it may fall
free of jutting rocks. The cliff is not sheer but, if it truly
resembles the cascade at San Benedetto, drops away sharply
with many projecting rocks against which the water breaks
to make the roar referred to in vs. 1 (see the description

by P. Nadiani in n. to vss. 101–2). The words "alquanto di lunge da la sponda" (vs. 113) further stress this point. *inver'* = *inverso*.

115. *E'* = *egli*, indefinite subject of "convien." *pur*: "Yet."

117. *seconda* = *asseconda*.

118. *dienno* = *devono*.

122. *e che il tuo pensier sogna*: "And which your thoughts are musing on," but without being able to conceive what it might be.

124–26. *Sempre a quel ver . . . vergogna*: See *Formula honestae vitae* I (also called *De quatuor virtutibus cardinalibus*), a treatise now acknowledged as the work of Martin of Dumio (Martinus Dumiensis) although believed by Dante to be by the younger Seneca:

> Nihil inexpertum affirmes quia non omne verisimile statim verum est; sicut et saepius quod primum incredibile videtur, non continuo falsum est. Crebro siquidem faciem mendacii veritas retinet. Crebro mendacium specie veritatis occulitur.

> Do not affirm anything unless you have experienced it; for not everything that seems likely is actually true. Likewise, very often it happens that things that at first seem incredible turn out later not to be false. Quite frequently, truth assumes the aspect of falsehood; and frequently, falsehood hides beneath the appearance of truth.

See S. Debenedetti (1923a), pp. 21–22, who points out that this is repeated by Brunetto Latini (*Tresor* II, lviii, 3).

125. *de'* = *deve*. *puote* = *può*.

126. *però che* = *per ciò che*.

127. *le note*: As if the poem were a song.

128. *comedìa*: Here, for the first time, Dante indicates the title of his poem, and here and in *Inf.* XXI, 2, where it ap-

pears again, it is pronounced with the medieval accent (as is "tragedìa" in *Inf.* XX, 113).

129. *s'elle non sien di lunga grazia vòte*: By a formula of asseveration paralleling that of adjuration, the poet swears by that which is most dear to him: "so may they [the notes of my Comedy] not be devoid of lasting favor."

130. *aere grosso*: Thick with the exhalations from below. See "aere grasso," *Inf.* IX, 82.

133. *colui che va giuso*: A diver.

136. *che 'n sù si stende . . . rattrappa*: In swimming upward a man reaches up with his hands and arms and pulls his feet up under him, in order to propel himself to the surface.

CANTO XVII

1-18. *Ecco la fiera . . . per Aragne imposte*: The aura of suspense generated by the figure closing Canto XVI (*Inf.* XVI, 131-36) continues here at the beginning of Canto XVII as Virgil points to the beast that emerges from the depths, "swimming" through the air. Before we see the monster in his literal shape, his allegorical significance as fraud is emphasized (vs. 7). His name, Geryon, is withheld until vs. 97.

Whereas Dante's monster has three natures—those of man, beast, and serpent—the monster Geryon of classical literature, after whom he is named, had three bodies and three heads. Thus Virgil (*Aen.* VIII, 202) refers to *tergeminus Geryon*. For Geryon's treacherous nature Dante apparently drew on the medieval tradition according to which he lured strangers into his power and then slew them. For instance, Boccaccio says of Dante's monster (*Geneal. deor. gent.* I, 21): "Et inde Gerion dicta, quia regnans apud Baleares insulas Gerion miti vultu, blandisque verbis et omni comitate consueverit hospites suscipere, et demum sub hac benignitate sopitos occidere." ("It is named after Geryon, who reigned near the Balearic Islands. With a mild face, with sweet words, using every politeness, he used to attract strangers to him; and then, having lulled them with his benignity, he would slay them.")

Certain other features of Dante's description of the monster probably were borrowed from the Bible. Geryon's reptilian form, appropriate to his role as the "foul image of fraud" (vs. 7), may have been suggested by Gen. 3:1 and II Cor. 11:3. His human face and pointed tail may derive from Apoc. 9:7, 10:

> Et similitudines locustarum similes equis paratis in proelium . . . et facies earum tamquam facies hominum . . . et habebant caudas similes scorpionum, et aculei erant in caudis earum: et potestas earum nocere hominibus . . . .

> And in appearance the locusts were like horses made ready for battle . . . and their faces were like the faces of men . . . And they had tails like those of scorpions and there were stings in their tails; and they had power to harm mankind . . . .

Dante also may have drawn on Solinus, Latin grammarian and writer probably of the third century, who gives the following description of the *mantichora*, a fabulous Indian beast, in his *Collectanea rerum memorabilium* (LII, 37–38):

> Facie hominis . . . corpore leonino, cauda velut scorpionis aculeo spiculata . . . . pedibus sic viget, saltu sic potest, ut morari eam nec extentissima spatia possint nec obstacula latissima.

> He walks about with the face of a man, the body of a lion, and his tail is spiked as is the stinging tail of a scorpion . . . . He has so much power with his feet and he is able to jump so far that neither the greatest distance nor the broadest barriers can withstand him.

On Geryon see R. T. Holbrook (1902), pp. 62–66; F. Cipolla (1894–95); A. R. Chisholm (1929); A. Sepulcri (1916); E. Proto (1900); B. Soldati (1903).

2. *che passa i monti e rompe i muri e l'armi*: No defense, either natural or man-made, can avail against the beast.

5. *accennolle = le accennò.   proda*: Literally, "shore"; see *Inf.* VIII, 55. Here in Canto XVII the word refers to the

very end of the bank, or dike ("passeggiati marmi," vs. 6), along which the two wayfarers have been walking.

6. *d'i = dei.*

7. *froda = frode;* for other occurrences of this form, see E. G. Parodi (1957), p. 244.

8. *arrivò:* "Brought ashore." The verb is transitive here; its objects are "testa" and "busto."

9. *non trasse la coda:* As it were, concealing this "weapon."

10. *era faccia d'uom giusto:* See Apoc. 9:7, quoted above in n. to vs. 1. See also *Conv.* IV, xii, 3:

> E quelle cose che prima non mostrano li loro difetti sono più pericolose, però che di loro molte fiate prendere guardia non si può; sì come vedemo nel traditore, che ne la faccia dinanzi si mostra amico, sì che fa di sè fede avere, e sotto pretesto d'amistade chiude lo difetto de la inimistade.

> And those things which at first conceal their defects are the most dangerous; because, in many cases, we cannot be on our guard against them, as we see in the instance of a traitor who in appearance shows himself a friend, so that he begets in us a confidence in him, and beneath the pretext of friendship he hides the fault of enmity.

11. *tanto benigna avea di fuor la pelle:* The subject of "avea" is "faccia" in the preceding verse. / Commenting on Apoc. 9:5, Thomas Aquinas mentions the deceptively benign face of the scorpion in *Exp. I super Apoc.* IX (p. 399):

> "Et cruciatus eorum," idest illatus ab eis, "ut cruciatus scorpii," cuius cruciatus valde gravis est, et vix potest sanari "cum percutit hominem," facie blandiens, et cauda pungens.

> "Their sting"—that is, the wound that they cause—"is like the sting of a scorpion," whose sting is very serious indeed. Nor can it be cured "when he strikes a man," with a smiling face and a sting in his tail.

12. *fusto:* "Trunk."

13. *due branche*: Boccaccio comments: "due piedi artigliati, come veggiamo che a' dragoni si dipingono" ("two clawed feet, such as we see on dragons in paintings").   *insin* = *fino a*.

14. *le coste*: The sides of the monster's body.

15. *dipinti*: Reminiscent of the "pelle dipinta" of the "lonza" (*Inf.* XVI, 108).   *rotelle*: Dragons were sometimes depicted in medieval manuscripts with little circles or rings covering their bodies; see R. T. Holbrook (1902), pp. 63, 65.

16. *sovraposte*: P. Toynbee (1902, pp. 115–18) argues from ample documentation that this word (or the variant form *sopraposte*) means "embroidered patterns."

17. *fer* = *fecero*.   *drappi*: The direct object of "fer."
   drappi Tartari . . . Turchi: The so-called Tartar cloths were in high repute during the Middle Ages. P. Toynbee (1902, p. 119) quotes Nerio Moscoli, a poet of the thirteenth century, who speaks of cloth so rich that "niun tartaresco Paregiar lo porria." ("No Tartar cloth could match it.") And Boccaccio (*Decam.* VI, 10; vol. II, p. 28, ll. 9–10) describes a garment "con più macchie e di più colori che mai drappi fossero tartereschi o indiani" ("with even more designs and more colors than the Tartar or Indian fabrics"). Turkish fabrics were also famous and highly valued in the Middle Ages.   *Tartari . . . Turchi*: Both peoples were treacherous, from the Christian point of view, as their mention here, in connection with the "foul image of fraud," suggests. See a similar reference to mosques glimpsed within the city of Dis (*Inf.* VIII, 70 and the note).
   Boccaccio's *Comento* ends abruptly midway through his observations on *Inf.* XVII, 16–17. He died, as P. Toynbee (1907, p. 103) says, almost as though with pen in hand, for his last sentence remained unfinished.

18. *fuor* = *furono*.   *Aragne*: In Greek mythology Arachne, who excelled in weaving, challenged Minerva to a competition. Unable to find fault with Arachne's work, Minerva tore it to pieces. In despair Arachne hanged herself, but the

goddess loosened the rope and changed her into a spider. Ovid tells the story in the *Metamorphoses* (VI, 5–145). Arachne has an allusive function here similar to that of the Tartars and Turks in the preceding verse: the spider's web also suggests cunning and treachery.   *imposte*: Probably "placed" upon the loom, although the term can mean "designed"; see M. Barbi (1934b), p. 241.

19. *burchi*: Plural of *burchio*, a kind of rowboat sometimes equipped with a cover. This cover may be intended as part of the image here, since it would suggest some kind of cloth, possibly colored and printed with a design.

21. *Tedeschi lurchi*: According to a tradition recorded as early as Tacitus, gluttony was characteristic of the Germans; see A. Sepulcri (1916), pp. 179–82.

22. *lo bivero*: Cf. the Latin *biber*; the commoner Italian word is *castoro*. Dante probably shared a popular belief, delineated later by his son, Pietro di Dante: "Dicitur de bivero animali, quod cum cauda piscatur mittendo ipsam in aquam et ipsam agitando, ex cuius pinguedine resultant guttae ad modum olei, et dum pisces ad eas veniunt, tunc se revolvendo eos capit." ("It is said that the beaver fishes by putting its tail in the water and agitating it; the fat in the tail squirts forth drops similar to oil and when the fish are attracted to these drops, the beaver turns around and grabs them.") In point of fact, the beaver is not a fish-eater and was notoriously confused with the otter and the badger, which do feed on fish. Moreover, while beavers abounded in Germany in Dante's time, they were not common as far south as Italy— although Benvenuto cites the contrary view: "Inveniuntur hic non longe a Ferraria in territorio Marchionum Estensium." ("They are to be found here too, not far from Ferrara, in the territory of the marquis of Este.") On ancient and medieval knowledge of the beaver, see A. Sepulcri (1916), pp. 171–72.

Dante intended the beaver—like the Tartars and Turks and Arachne—to represent craft and deception. The image of the beaver awaiting its prey fits the description of Geryon, lying in wait on the bank, his tail (armed at the point for a purpose too) thrust out into the void, which already (*Inf.* XVI, 133–36) has been compared to water.

22. *s'assetta*: "Settles itself"; see vs. 91.

24. *su l'orlo ch'è di pietra e 'l sabbion serra*: The rim of the precipice, an edge of rock, is sheltered from the fire, as are the banks of the conduit; see vss. 32–33, 43–45.

30. *corca = corica*.

31. *scendemmo a la destra mammella*: Virgil and Dante have been walking along the right bank of the conduit; they must now descend the right side of that bank, since the boiling stream lies to their left. On a possible symbolic meaning of this second turn to the right in Hell (the first turn to the right is discussed in n. to *Inf.* IX, 132), see J. Freccero (1961a), p. 180:

> As heresy is the perversion of the intellect's higher function, the speculative activity of theology and moral philosophy, so usury is a sin of its lower activity: human industry, or art. Usury for this reason is also a sin against nature and God Himself . . . . This is the only sin in Dante's *Inferno* which the poet specifically tells us is against human industry, for it is the only sin which methodically and systematically reproduces the materials it began with in a parody of productivity which is in fact sterile. It is to counter this perversion of the practical reason that the poet retrogresses for the second time "to the right."

32. *diece passi*: "Ten" is merely an approximate number and holds no evident symbolic meaning here.   *femmo = facemmo.   lo stremo*: The outer rim of the circle.

33. *cessar*: "To avoid."

34. *semo = siamo*.

35–36. *in su la rena gente seder*: These shades who sit upon the burning sand are the usurers. They are identifiable both from Virgil's exposition in Canto XI (vss. 46–51) of the three categories of sinners condemned to the seventh circle, and from Dante's description (*Inf.* XIV, 19–24) of the different postures assumed by these three groups when they are first observed on the fiery plain. Until now the usurers have not, so postured, come into the picture again. The wayfarer must hear them and note their condition more closely in order to have "full experience" (vss. 37–38) of this *girone*.

39. *mena*: The manner of their punishment.

41. *mentre che = finchè.*   *con questa*: The antecedent is "bestia" (vs. 30).

43. *ancor*: Dante has already taken "ten" steps along the rim.

44. *tutto solo*: This is the first time in the *Commedia*, and the only time in the *Inferno*, that Dante proceeds alone, without Virgil's guidance.

46. *fora = fuori.*

47. *soccorrien = soccorrevano.*

47–48. *soccorrien con le mani . . . suolo*: The usurers attempt to defend themselves by brushing off the burning flakes of fire (see "arrostarsi," *Inf.* XV, 39) and by raising themselves on their hands to relieve their burning rumps.

52. *a certi*: None prove to be Jews or moneylenders of low station; all are Christians, from distinguished Florentine and Paduan families.

54. *non ne conobbi alcun*: Except by the escutcheons on their moneybags (vs. 56)—their only real identity—the usurers are unrecognizable. Similarly, the avaricious and the prodigal had been rendered unrecognizable by their sins; see *Inf.* VII, 53–54: "la sconoscente vita che i fé sozzi / ad ogne conoscenza or li fa bruni."

55. *tasca*: A common term for a moneychanger's purse (it is also called a "borsa" in vs. 59 and a "sacchetto" in vs. 65).

300

G. Salvemini (1902, p. 115) notes the use of the same word in a document of 1299 (in Latin) which refers to the custom of moneylenders who sit "ad tabulam sive banchum cum tascha et libro" ("at a table or bench with a wallet and a book"). Here in Canto XVII the usurers sit "crouched up" (as they were described in *Inf.* XIV, 23), feasting their eyes (vs. 57) on the coats-of-arms on their moneybags.

56. *certo colore*: The background color.   *certo segno*: The design of the escutcheon.

57. *e quindi par che 'l loro occhio si pasca*: See a similar use of "eyes" ("oculi") in Eccles. 4:7–8: "Considerans reperi et aliam vanitatem sub sole: unus est et secundum non habet, non filium, non fratrem, et tamen laborare non cessat, nec satiantur oculi eius divitiis." ("Again I found this vanity under the sun: a solitary man with no companion; with neither son nor brother. Yet there is no end to all his toil, and [his eyes are not satisfied by riches].")

58. *E com' io riguardando tra lor vegno*: "As I continue to look among them."

59–60. *in una borsa gialla . . . contegno*: The arms of the Gianfigliazzi of Florence were "on a field or a lion azure." According to Villani, the family, who were Guelphs, lived in the section of Florence (which at one time was divided into "sixths") known as the Sesto di Borgo (V, 39). They were exiled from Florence with other prominent Guelph families in 1248 and again in 1260 after the battle of Montaperti (VI, 33, 80); and when the Guelph party later split into the Bianchi and Neri factions, they sided with the Neri (VIII, 39). They were still prominent in the fourteenth century (XII, 3). F. P. Luiso (1908) holds that Dante refers here to Messer Catello di Rosso Gianfigliazzi, who practiced usury in France and was made a *cavaliere* on returning to Florence. He died some time after 1283. M. Barbi (1934b), pp. 270–72) gives a fuller biography.

61. *procedendo di mio sguardo il curro*: A grammatical construction similar to the ablative absolute. *il curro* = *il corso*; some commentators understand it as *carro*.

62. *vidine* = *ne vidi*.

62–63. *un'altra come sangue rossa . . . burro*: The arms of the Florentine Ubbriachi (or Obriachi) were "on a field gules a goose argent." Villani states that the Ubbriachi were Ghibellines (V, 39; VI, 33) who lived in the Sesto d'Oltrarno and were among those expelled from Florence in 1258 (VI, 65).

64. *una scrofa azzurra e grossa*: The arms of the Scrovegni family of Padua were "on a field argent a sow azure." The usurer in question is thought to be Rinaldo (or Reginaldo) Scrovegni, who amassed one of the largest personal fortunes in Padua. The first documentary mention of him is in 1263; he died some time between March 1288 and October 1289. His son Enrico commissioned the famous chapel of the Scrovegni frescoed by Giotto. On the Scrovegni see G. Biscaro (1928).

66–67. *Che fai tu in questa fossa? Or te ne va*: This is the first of a number of angry challenges addressed to the wayfarer as he proceeds through lower Hell.

66. *fossa*: The cavity of Hell itself (see *Inf.* XIV, 136). Thus, as the next verse makes clear, the challenge is to the living man.

67. *te ne va* = *vattene*.   *anco* = *ancora*.

67–73. *e perché se' vivo . . . becchi*: Also for the first time a soul maliciously names other sinners here present in the hope that the wayfarer will report their shameful deeds to the world of the living. Unlike the souls Dante has already met among the incontinent of upper Hell and the violent of the first circle of lower Hell, some of the shades he encounters among the fraudulent punished in the lowest circles will wish not to be remembered in the "sweet world" above. This incident, taking place as it does on the verge of those circles (the eighth and ninth), seems to foreshadow that new attitude.

68. *'l mio vicin*: "My fellow townsman"; see *Purg.* XI, 140.

Vitaliano: The early commentators state that this sinner still among the living was Vitaliano del Dente, who appears to have been an important person in Padua, where he was *podestà* in 1307. He is mentioned as a moneylender in several documents of the late thirteenth century. E. Morpurgo (1865, pp. 213-15, 231) thinks the reference is to a certain Vitaliano di Jacopo Vitaliani, who is mentioned as a usurer in an old Paduan chronicle (supposedly written in 1335), in which Dante's condemnation of him to Hell apparently is alluded to: "Et unus dominus Vitalianus potens et ditissimus vitam mirabilem in peccatis duxit, quoniam maximus usurarius fuit, quem doctor vulgaris damnat ad inferos permanere." ("There was a man named Vitaliano who, with his power and wealth, led an extraordinary life of sin. He was the greatest of usurers and for this reason the doctor of the vernacular condemns him to eternal hell.")

70. *Con questi Fiorentin*: The thrust at Florence as a nest of usurers, "noble" usurers, is strong; it reaches a climax in vss. 71-72.

72. *'l cavalier sovrano*: This is the Florentine usurer Giovanni (or Gianni) Buiamonte of the Becchi family. M. Barbi (1925b) states that he was born in 1260 and died in 1310; he was of a Ghibelline family of the Sesto di Porta San Pancrazio, and his father had himself been a *cavaliere*; in 1293, Giovanni was *gonfaloniere di giustizia*, and thereafter until his death his name was frequently recorded in Florentine documents. It is uncertain precisely when Giovanni Buiamonte was made a *cavaliere*, but Barbi (1925b, pp. 67-68) cites documentary evidence to prove that the honor was conferred at some time before 1298. The souls in Hell, then, correctly address Giovanni as "the sovereign knight," since Dante's fictional journey takes place in 1300.

In 1308 Giovanni fell into disrepute with the merchant society of Florence, and was charged with having absconded with the money and property of others. Barbi (1925b, pp. 68–69) has noted a Florentine document proclaiming a sentence "contra Iannem Buiamontis tanquam contra mercatorem et artificem cessantem et fugitivum cum pecunia et rebus alienis" ("against Giovanni Buiamonte as against a merchant or artisan who has absconded and fled with money and other valuables").

73. *tre becchi*: Several of the early commentators say that the arms of the Becchi family were "on a field or three goats sable." The *Anonimo fiorentino*, for example, remarks: "Portava per arme il campo giallo et tre becchi neri l'uno sopra l'altro, come stanno i Leopardi che sono nell'arme del re d'Inghilterra." ("His coat of arms consisted of a yellow field and three goats sable, one above the other, like the leopards on the escutcheon of the king of England.")

74–75. *Qui distorse la bocca . . . lecchi*: This grotesque gesture of derision and scorn is directed, not at the wayfarer, but at the Florentine usurers now in Hell and their "sovereign knight" who will one day join them. The gesture is known in Italian as *fare le boccacce*. See Isa. 57:4: "Super quem lusistis? super quem dilatastis os et eiecistis linguam?" ("Upon whom have you jested? Upon whom have you opened your mouth wide and put out your tongue?") / The qualifying phrase, "come bue che 'l naso lecchi," adds a touch of the *bestialitas* that characterizes this seventh circle (see *Inf.* XI, 83).

76–77. *E io . . . lui*: For this construction see *Inf.* III, 80–81.

77. *lui*: Virgil.   *di poco star*: See vs. 40.   *'mmonito* = *ammonito*.

78. *torna'mi* = *mi tornai*.

81–84. *Or sie forte . . . male*: Porena acutely observes that Virgil here uses every means to encourage the wayfarer: example (he himself has "already mounted" Geryon); exhortation ("be strong and bold"); reason (there is no other means of descent to the eighth circle); protection (he bids

Dante climb on in front of him, so that he, Virgil, is "between" the wayfarer and the creature's dangerous tail).

81. *sie = sii.*

82. *Omai:* "Now," "at this point" in Hell to which we have come. The word also suggests "from this point on," "henceforward," which is in fact borne out: a giant will set Virgil and Dante down on the bottommost level of Hell.   *sì fatte scale*: Given the context, the metaphor is obviously ironic, an acknowledgment on Virgil's part, as he exhorts the wayfarer, that there might indeed have been less frightful "stairs."

83. *mezzo = medio.* See *Conv.* IV, xvii, 7: "E queste tutte sono li mezzi intra quelli." ("And they themselves are the [mean] between them.")

85. *riprezzo = ribrezzo.*

85–86. *riprezzo de la quartana*: The shivering fit that precedes the paroxysm of the quartan fever is intermittent and recurs in four-day cycles (whence the name).

87. *pur guardando*: "At the merest glimpse of."   *'l rezzo = l'orezzo.* Scartazzini-Vandelli calls attention to a comment of Vincenzo Borghini on these words. See Borghini, "Errori," p. 235: "Chiamasi in Toscana, e credo per tutto, *Rezzo*, ove *non batte sole*, e *stare al Rezzo*, ove *non sia sole.*" ("In Tuscany, and I believe everywhere else too, *rezzo* means 'a place upon which the sun does not shine'; and *stare al rezzo* means 'to be where there is no sun.'") See *Inf.* XXXII, 75.

88. *parole porte*: See the expression *porgere parole* in *Inf.* II, 135; *Inf.* V, 108.

89–90. *ma vergogna mi fé . . . forte*: Shame is here personified, as if she might shake an admonishing finger at the servant in the presence of a worthy master. See *Conv.* IV, xix, 8: "e tocca nobilitade, che bene è vera salute, essere là dove è vergogna, cioè tema di disnoranza" ("which refers to nobleness, which is indeed a truly saving thing—

to exist where there is sensitiveness to shame, that is, fear of dishonor").

92. *sì volli dir*: "Sì" modifies "volli," and the whole expression means "I did indeed wish to say."

95. *ad altro forse*: "Forse" is treated as a noun here and can mean "dubious moment" (for example, in the expression *stare in forse*) or, in this instance, "peril"; see *Purg.* XXVII, 22–23, where this moment on Geryon's back is remembered as one of greatest danger. Another moment of peril in which Virgil helped Dante was recorded in *Inf.* IX, 58–60, when he shielded his charge from the Gorgon. Other readings have been proposed, however; for example, see M. Barbi (1934a), p. 46, who argues for *alto forse*. Also see the evaluation of this problematical expression by Petrocchi in his note on this verse.

98. *le rote larghe* = *le rote siano larghe*.

99. *la nova soma*: This most unusual burden of a living man.

100. *di loco*: "From its berth." The "burchio" (vs. 19) has now become, figuratively, a larger vessel, a small ship.

102. *a gioco*: "Free" of encumbrance, "at large."

104. *e quella tesa*: Up to now the monster has kept its tail turned up; see vs. 26.

105. *con le branche l'aere a sé raccolse*: This, indeed, was the manner in which the monster came swimming upward from the void, as the image at the end of the preceding canto suggested; see especially the phrase (*Inf.* XVI, 136): "che 'n sù si stende."

107. *Fetonte*: In classical mythology Phaëthon was the son of Helios, god of the Sun, and Clymene. He persuaded Helios to let him drive the chariot of the Sun for one day; but he was too weak to hold the horses and they rushed out of their usual course, approaching so near to Earth that they almost set her on fire. Jupiter, then, in answer to the

prayer of Earth, killed Phaëthon with a thunderbolt and
hurled him down into the Po. Dante alludes to the story,
which is elaborated by Ovid (*Metam.* II, 1–328), more than
once in the *Commedia.* See, for example, *Par.* XVII, 1–3.
   abbandonò li freni: See *Metam.* II, 200: "Lora remisit."
("Down he dropped the reins.")

108. *per che 'l ciel, come pare ancor, si cosse*: This is a
reference to the Milky Way or Galaxy (termed "Galassia"
in *Par.* XIV, 99). See *Conv.* II, xiv, 5–6:

> Per che è da sapere che di quella Galassia li filosofi
> hanno avute diverse oppinioni. Chè li Pittagorici dissero
> che 'l Sole alcuna fiata errò ne la sua via e, passando
> per altre parti non convenienti al suo fervore, arse lo
> luogo per lo quale passò, e rimasevi quella apparenza
> de l'arsura: e credo che si mossero da la favola di
> Fetonte, la quale narra Ovidio nel principio del secondo
> di Metamorfoseos.

> Wherefore we are to know that concerning this milky
> way philosophers have held divers opinions. For the
> Pythagoreans said that once upon a time the sun strayed
> in his course, and passing through other portions not
> suited to his heat scorched the place along which he
> passed; and this appearance of scorching was left there.
> And I believe that they were moved thereto by the fable
> of Phaëton, which Ovid tells in the beginning of the
> second of the *Metamorphoses.*

Following this passage, Dante proceeds to discuss more sci-
entific causes of the phenomenon.

109. *Icaro*: Pronounced *Ìcaro*. Icarus was the son of Dae-
dalus, the famous artisan. Father and son were attempting
to fly from Crete on wings made by Daedalus, when Icarus
fell into the sea and was drowned. The story is related by
Ovid; see especially *Metam.* VIII, 200–209, 222–35.

111. *Mala via tieni!* The father's cry to his son is Dante's
own invention. In Ovid's story (*Metam.* VIII, 231–32) Dae-
dalus calls: "Icare . . . / Icare . . . ubi es? qua te regione

requiram?" ("Icarus, Icarus, where are you? In what place shall I seek you?")

117. *se non che al viso*: The wayfarer knows from the wind on his face that he is moving through the air and assumes that Geryon is obeying Virgil's instructions and thus is wheeling. *e di sotto mi venta*: Dante also knows, by the wind "from below," that he is descending.

118. *da la man destra il gorgo*: Geryon, who apparently is wheeling in a counterclockwise direction, or to the left, passes the cascade of boiling blood as it crashes into the pool below, which is now much nearer since already they have descended a considerable distance.

121. *stoscio*: Some editors have adopted the reading "scoscio," understanding the meaning to be "in my straddle"; but Petrocchi agrees with other editors in adopting, on good manuscript authority, "stoscio," meaning "fall," "descent," which the present translation follows. See his note on this vexed problem.

122. *però ch'* = *perciò che*.

123. *tutto mi raccoscio*: "I press in firmly with my thighs."

124–25. *E vidi poi . . . lo scendere e 'l girar*: Only now can the wayfarer *see* that Geryon is descending in a spiral; before he could only *feel* this from the wind on him.

126. *da diversi canti*: This phrase gives a measure of the "wheeling" course of the descent.

127–136. *Come 'l falcon . . . come da corda cocca*: The closing image of Geryon's arrival at the bottom of the abyss and his swift departure is most striking in its assumption of an observation post—assumed before it actually is reached. In the first term of the comparison, we are privileged to take up a position corresponding to that of the falconer, and to watch Geryon circle about, like a falcon weary from an unsuccessful hunt, and finally land, "disdegnoso e fello" (vs.

132), at some distance from this point, which in actuality does not exist. In the second term of the simile, Dante, having dismounted, assumes the position of the falconer, to watch the dragon-like monster vanish upward, as if it were initiating the flight of the falcon in the figure just completed. Geryon departs, like the falcon that "si move isnello" (vs. 130), soaring up toward some possible prey.

128. *sanza veder logoro*: The falcon is trained not to descend until it takes its quarry or is called down by the falconer, who whirls the lure ("logoro") about his head as a signal to recall it. The falconer in the simile, therefore, is dismayed that the hawk should give up the hunt and descend before it is called down by the lure. (See Fig. 5.)   *logoro*: The

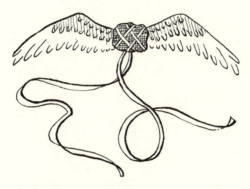

Figure 5. Falcon lure

lure was made by fastening two bird's wings to the end of a thong and baiting it with a piece of meat which the bird was allowed to eat. / *Richiamo*, literally, "signal," is sometimes used as a synonym for *logoro* (see *Inf*. III, 117).

130. *onde si move*: Some editors prefer "onde si mosse"; see M. Barbi (1934a), pp. 35–36. The present tense adopted here, however, really implies the past tense.

133. *ne puose = ci depose.*

CANTO XVIII

1. *Malebolge*: Name invented by Dante to combine the word *malo* ("evil") and *bolgia* ("pouch"). The *Anonimo fiorentino* comments: "Dice l'Auttore che questo luogo dello inferno, dove poeticamente discrive dieci cerchietti, è chiamato Malebolge, che tanto vuole dire quanto Male sacco, o veramente Male valige." ("The author says that this place in Hell, where he poetically depicts ten small circles, is called Malebolge, which means the evil sacks, or the evil bags.")

2. *pietra di color ferrigno*: "Dark stone"; see "sasso tetro" in vs. 34.

3. *la cerchia*: The "stagliata rocca" of *Inf.* XVII, 134; also called here in Canto XVIII "alta ripa" (vs. 8) and "roccia" (vs. 16). *Cerchia* was commonly used in Dante's time to designate the walls encircling a city (see *Par.* XV, 97). Such a connotation may be intended here, since the wayfarers now are entering a new area of Hell, a new "city."   *il volge*: "Surrounds it."

4. *Nel dritto mezzo*: "In the exact center."   *campo*: The whole "field" is seen as if from some vantage point above. It is the poet Dante, not the character in the poem, who knows the entire configuration.

6. *suo loco*: "In the proper place." This Latin phrase was current in Dante's day. The "place" will prove to be *Inf.* XXXI; the pit here referred to leads down into the ninth and last circle.   *dicerò = dirò*.   *l'ordigno*: "Arrangement."

7. *cinghio*: The whole circular area or band that constitutes the eighth circle, between the wall of stone and the pit.

9. *valli*: Plural of *valle*.

10–12. *Quale . . . rende figura*: This should be construed: *Quale figura* [object] *rende la parte* [subject] *dove sono i fossi che cingono un castello*. The reader was told (*Inf.* VIII, 76–77) that such concentric moats surround the walls of the city of Dis.

13. *quelli*: The "fossi" of vs. 11.

14. *sogli* (plural of *soglio*) = *soglie*.

15. *la ripa di fuor*: "The outside bank" of the moat farthest from the castle.   *ponticelli*: Little drawbridges span the moats.

16. *scogli*: Unlike the drawbridges that connect the moats surrounding a castle, the "reefs of stone" spanning the ten concentric *bolge* that constitute the eighth circle, or Malebolge, are not artificial but natural bridges. They are very rough on top, as indicated by the word "scheggia" (vs. 71) and by many later references. How many of these reefs extend from the wall of stone to the pit at the center, like spokes in a wheel, we are not told. Each spans the ten *bolge* (except for one breakdown which the reader will learn of later) and makes successive abutments of their banks. The yawning pit at the center "terminates" the reefs and "gathers them in" (vs. 18) like the hub of a wheel. (See Fig. 6, p. 312.)

17. *movien = movevano*.   *ricidien = recidevano*, "traversed."

311

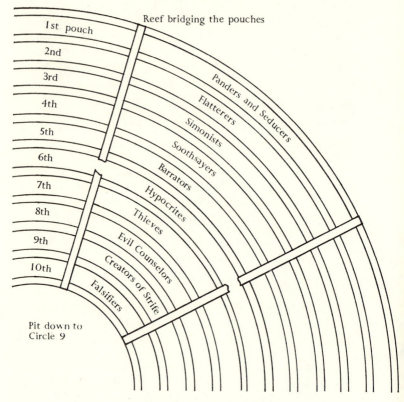

Reef bridging the pouches

1st pouch
2nd
3rd
4th
5th
6th
7th
8th
9th
10th

Pit down to
Circle 9

Panders and Seducers
Flatterers
Simonists
Soothsayers
Barrators
Hypocrites
Thieves
Evil Counselors
Creators of Strife
Falsifiers

Figure 6. a. Segment of the eighth circle of Hell

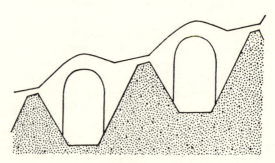

b. Cross section of two pouches
of the eighth circle

18. *i = li.   raccogli = raccoglie.* Other editors have read "racco'gli" (see E. G. Parodi, 1957, p. 242) and this is possible, taking the form *gli* to be the direct object plural *li.* See Petrocchi's note on this; also Parodi (1957), pp. 351–52.

19. *In questo luogo*: Having viewed the eighth circle panoramically, the reader is brought back to the narrative.
    scossi: The word suggests a new meaning for "discarcate," *Inf.* XVII, 135: Geryon, in his spitefulness, literally had shaken the wayfarers from his back.

20. *trovammoci = ci trovammo.*

21. *tenne a sinistra*: Virgil resumes the normal spiral direction through Hell, turning to the left. He and his charge now walk across the stone margin between the high wall and the first *bolgia*; and when they come to the first reef, which will serve them as walkway and bridge over the *bolge*, they will turn to the right as they ascend it and proceed. The right turn is necessitated by the configuration of this eighth circle and bears no symbolic meaning. See n. to *Inf.* XVII, 31.

22. *pieta*: Pronounced *pièta*; see *Inf.* II, 106.

23. *novi frustatori*: In this series of new things the "new scourgers" come with some surprise for the reader and generate a momentary suspense. These scourgers are also "novi" in the usual sense of "strange," since they are "horned demons" (see vs. 35).

24. *repleta*: A Latinism current in Dante's day and used elsewhere by him.

25. *ignudi*: As usual, whenever the pain of a particular torment is increased by a soul's going naked, this condition is emphasized (see, for example, *Inf.* XIII, 116). Such is clearly the case here, for these souls—the panders and seducers—are scourged by demons.

26–27. *dal mezzo in qua . . . di là con noi*: As the simile of vss. 28–33 at once makes clear, the first *bolgia* holds two

files of sinners, who proceed around it in opposite direc-
tions. Those in the file nearest the wayfarer ("dal mezzo in
qua")—the panders—go in a counterclockwise direction,
and so are said to come "toward us"; whereas the other
file—the seducers—keeping to the inner half of the *bolgia*,
circulates clockwise, thus moving in the same direction as
Virgil and Dante, who are still walking along between the
high wall and the first *bolgia*.

26. *venien = venivano*.

27. *ma con passi maggiori*: The phrase refers to the souls
just described as moving in the same direction as the way-
farer, who therefore can compare their pace with his own.
However, those who come toward him are also moving
faster than he is, for both groups, whipped by demons, are
driven to go faster than they might otherwise choose (see
vss. 37–39).

28–29. *come i Roman . . . giubileo*: This first Jubilee of the
Roman church was proclaimed by Boniface VIII in his bull
Antiquorum habet fidem, dated February 22, 1300, but with
retroactive force to the previous Christmas (1299). This bull
granted indulgence to all who visited the basilicas of San
Pietro and San Paolo fuori le Mura on a certain number of
days during the year and confessed and repented of their
sins. Villani (VIII, 36) gives the following account:

> Negli anni di Cristo 1300, secondo la nativitade di
> Cristo . . . papa Bonifazio ottavo che allora era aposto-
> lico, nel detto anno a reverenza della natività di Cristo,
> fece somma e grande indulgenza in questo modo; che
> qualunque Romano visitasse infra tutto il detto anno,
> continuando trenta dì, le chiese de' beati apostoli santo
> Pietro e santo Paolo, e per quindici dì l'altra universale
> gente che non fossono Romani, a tutti fece piena e
> intera perdonanza di tutti i suoi peccati, essendo con-
> fesso o si confessasse, di colpa e di pena. . . . E fu la più
> mirabile cosa che mai si vedesse, che al continuo in
> tutto l'anno durante, avea in Roma oltre al popolo
> romano, duecentomila pellegrini, sanza quegli ch'erano

per gli cammini andando e tornando, e tutti erano for-
niti e contenti di vittuaglia giustamente, così i cavalli
come le persone, e con molta pazienza, e sanza romori
o zuffe: ed io il posso testimoniare, che vi fui presente
e vidi.

In the year of Christ 1300, according to the birth of
Christ . . . Pope Boniface VIII, who then occupied
the Holy See, granted a supreme and great indulgence
in that year, to commemorate the birth of Christ. It
was to be in this manner: to Romans who, within the
space of that year, visited the churches of the Blessed
Apostles St. Peter and St. Paul for thirty consecutive days,
and to all others who were not Romans who did so for
fifteen days, a full and complete pardon of all sins would
be granted as well as remission of guilt and punishment,
provided the sins were or would be confessed. . . .
And it was the most wondrous thing ever seen, for
throughout the entire year, there were continuously two
hundred thousand pilgrims in Rome, aside from the
Romans themselves, and not counting those who were
on the roads, coming or going. All were properly and
satisfactorily provided with victuals, the horses as well
as the people; and it was done with great patience and
without uproar or arguments. And I can testify to it,
for I was present, and I saw it.

It is thought that Dante was in Rome during that year and
himself witnessed the remarkable organization here de-
scribed.

28. *essercito = esercito*, "multitude," "host."

29. *lo ponte*: The Ponte Sant'Angelo, a bridge over the
Tiber at Rome, was built by the Emperor Hadrian to con-
nect his tomb (the present Castel Sant'Angelo; see n. to
vs. 32) with the city. In Dante's day it was the only bridge
serving the Trastevere section where St. Peter's is located,
and accordingly was very crowded at the time of the Jubilee.

32. *'l castello*: The Castel Sant'Angelo, on the right bank
of the Tiber at Rome, originally the Moles Hadriani, was

erected by Hadrian as a mausoleum for himself and his successors. It owes its modern name to the tradition that Gregory the Great (pope 590–604), while leading a procession to pray for the cessation of the plague, beheld the archangel Michael sheathing his sword above the castle, in commemoration of which a chapel was subsequently erected at the summit of the building by Boniface IV (pope 608–615). (See Plate 4, facing.)

33. *'l monte*: Monte Giordano, a low hill across the Tiber from Castel Sant'Angelo.

34. *su per lo sasso tetro*: The devils walk among the sinners, on the dark stone of the bottom of the *bolgia*.

35. *demon* (pronounced *demòn*) = *demoni*, plural of "demonio" (vs. 64). *ferze* = *sferze*, "whips."

36. *battien* = *battevano*.

37. *levar le berze*: This phrase probably is one of the derisive taunts that now become more frequent in Dante's description of lower Hell. The *Anonimo fiorentino* says: "Vocabolo antico et volgare, et vuol dire le calcagna." ("This is an old and common word, and it means heels.") See "zucca" (literally, "gourd") used for "head" (vs. 124), and "broda" ("soup") for the mire of Styx (*Inf.* VIII, 53). For present-day usage of *berze* in certain North Italian dialects, see E. G. Parodi (1957), p. 352, and G. Bertoni (1933), p. 25.

38–39. *già nessuno . . . le terze*: The jeering tone of the narrative becomes more evident in this turn of phrase.

41. *furo* = *furono*. *furo scontrati* = *si scontrarono*.

42. *Già di veder costui non son digiuno*: Now the derisive note enters even into what the wayfarer says, though here he speaks mainly to himself. Grandgent translates the phrase: "I am not fasting for previous sight of him."

43. *figurarlo* = *raffigurarlo*. *affissi*: See "affisse," *Inf.* XII, 115.

4. Castel Sant'Angelo, on the right bank of the Tiber at Rome

45. *assentio = assentì.*   *gissi*: First person past subjunctive of *gire*.

46. *celar si credette*: The wish to hide oneself, to avoid being recognized, becomes more and more frequent on the part of sinners in lower Hell. See n. to *Inf.* XVII, 67–73.

47. *li = gli.*

49. *se le fazion che porti non son false*: The verse stresses the fraudulent, deceptive aspect of pandering. See the *Ottimo Commento*'s gloss on "femmine da conio" (vs. 66): "Quando uno inganna altro, quello si dice coniare; mostra uno, ed è altro. Coniare è mutare d'una forma ad altra forma, e viene a dire ingannare, fare falso conio, falsa forma." ("When one deceives the other, it is called *coniare*: he seems to be one thing, and is another. *Coniare* means to change from one form to another, and signifies to deceive, to make false coin, false form.") The thrust is aimed at one who is recognized as having been guilty, in life, of changing "from one form to another." See n. to vs. 66.

50. *Venedico . . . Caccianemico*: Venedico de' Caccianemici dell'Orso, of Bologna, was the son of Alberto de' Caccianemici, head of the Geremei, or Guelph party of Bologna. Venedico (pronounced *Venèdico*) is said to have gained the marquis of Este admittance to the bedchamber of his sister Ghisolabella for money. Venedico was at various times *podestà* of Pistoia, Modena, Imola, and Milan and was, with his father, an active opponent of the Lambertazzi, or Ghibelline party of Bologna. He was a staunch ally of the marquis of Este (Obizzo II; see n. to *Inf.* XII, 111–12), and his support of the marquis's policy with regard to Bologna appears to have led to his expulsion from his native city in 1289. He died in January 1303, although clearly Dante believed him dead by 1300. (On Venedico see C. Ricci, 1921a, pp. 10–11; G. Zaccagnini, 1914, pp. 27–47, 1915, 1934, pp. 19–40; Q. Sàntoli, 1921; G. Gozzadini, 1875, pp. 212–21.)

51. *sì pungenti salse*: Benvenuto, who knew Bologna well, comments:

Ad intelligentiam huius literae, ut videas quot sunt occulta et ignorata in isto libro, volo te scire, quod *Salse* est quidam locus Bononiae concavus et declivus extra civitatem post et prope sanctam Mariam in Monte, in quem solebant abiici corpora desperatorum, foeneratorum, et aliorum infamatorum. Unde aliquando audivi pueros Bononiae dicentes unum alteri ad improperium: Tuus pater fuit proiectus ad Salsas. Ad propositum ergo autor vult dicere: Quid ducit te ad vallem tam infamem, sicut est vallis Salsarum apud patriam tuam? Non ergo capias hic Salsas pro sapore, sicut communiter omnes exponunt, quia metaphora esset aliena a proposito, ut per se patet.

So that you may understand this word, and at the same time see how many things are hidden and unknown in this book, I want you to know that *Salse* is a certain sloping, concave place outside Bologna, just past Santa Maria in Monte. The bodies of desperate criminals, usurers, and other unspeakable persons used to be thrown there. And I have heard boys in Bologna say to each other as an insult: your father was thrown to Salse. Thus, what the author means to say is: what has brought you to a valley as infamous as the valley of Salse in your homeland? In this passage, therefore, you must not interpret "Salse" as having to do with taste, as is commonly done. For it is self-evident that such an interpretation would not correspond to the author's intention.

On the other hand, "salse," in its derisive context here, makes perfectly good sense without reference to the Salse of Bologna. M. Barbi (1934b, p. 241) quotes a passage from Fra Giordano da Rivalto which is an example of the word's metaphorical use. See Fra Giordano da Rivalto, *Prediche* XXVI (1831 edn.), vol. i, pp. 201–2:

Tu vedrai uno ricco uomo, e parratti ch'abbia tutta la gloria del mondo, e penserai che Iddio l'ami molto, ed egli n'avrà molte volte molto poca; non sapete le salse, c'hanno questi ricchi, e non sapete la mostarda, c'hanno

questi signori, no; le mostarde, e le salse, che si trovano
nel matrimonio, e nelle ricchezze, e nelle signorìe. . . .
Voi sentite pur le vostre, ma voi non sentite le loro . . . .
Ben lo ti credo, che tu no'l credi, chè tu non hai provato
delle mostarde, c'ha provato egli.

You see a rich man, and it will seem that he possesses
all the glory in the world, and you will think God must
love him very much. And very often, he will possess
but very little glory. No, you do not know what sauces
these rich men must bear, nor what mustard. The mus-
tards and the sauces that are in matrimony, in riches,
in lordship. . . . You feel your own, but you do not
feel theirs . . . . I can well believe that you do not be-
lieve it, for you have not tried the mustards he has
tried.

It seems possible that Dante has drawn on both senses of
the word, effectively increasing the sarcasm of the taunt.
The Bolognese Venedico would thus get the thrust in both
senses, but particularly in its reference to his native city;
hence perhaps his own reference to Dante's "plain speech,"
which causes him to remember the "former world."

55. *la Ghisolabella*: Sister of Venedico de' Caccianemici, who
is said to have accepted a bribe to betray her to the marquis
of Este (see n. to vs. 50). The marquis reportedly took his
pleasure and abandoned the fair lady, who nevertheless later
(in or before 1270) married Niccolò da Fontana of Ferrara.
The early commentators and editors write the name as two
words, "Ghisola bella," and assume that she was so called
because of her beauty. The *Anonimo fiorentino* says: "Per
eccellenzia, però che avanzava in bellezza tutte le donne
bolognesi a quello tempo, fu chiamata la Ghisola bella."
("She was called 'Ghisola bella' by virtue of her manifest
superiority, for she was more beautiful than any other
Bolognese woman of that time.") Ghisolabella or Ghislabella,
however, may well have been her name, as indicated by her
will, dated September 1, 1281, in which she is described as
"D. Ghislabella, filia quondam domini Alberti de Cazanimi-
tis, et uxor domini Nichollay de Fontana" ("Lady Ghisla-

bella, daughter of Signor Alberto de' Caccianemici and wife of Signor Niccolò da Fontana"). For the will, see I. Del Lungo (1888), p. 270. For Ghisolabella and a possible explanation of Dante's attitude toward Venedico, see Del Lungo (1888), pp. 235-47.

59. *anzi n'è questo loco tanto pieno*: Denunciation of particular cities of Italy for this or that sin begins here in earnest, although Florence has already come in for very severe judgment on more than one count, including usury (as did Padua in *Inf.* XVII, 70).

60. *apprese*: "Capable of," "given to" saying *sipa*.

61. *sipa*: Archaic Bolognese dialect for *sia* (modern Bolognese *sepa*), often used for "yes." *Sàvena e Reno*: These two rivers of northern Italy both rise in the Tuscan Apennines and flow north through Emilia. The Savena, the smaller stream, leaves Bologna about two miles to the west; the Reno leaves Bologna about two miles to the east. Thus the two streams roughly indicate the eastern and western limits of Bologna and her territory.

63. *seno*: "Disposition." Benvenuto comments:

> Nota quod autor capit hic avaritiam large; nam bononiensis naturaliter et comuniter non est avarus in retinendo, sed in capiendo tantum. Illi enim, qui sunt vitiosi, ibi prodigaliter expendunt ultra vires facultatis vel lucri; ideo faciunt turpia lucra, aliquando cum ludis, aliquando cum furtis, aliquando cum lenociniis, exponentes filias, sorores, et uxores libidini, ut satisfaciant gulae et voluptatibus suis.

> Note that the author here means avarice in the wide sense. Generally, and by nature, the Bolognese are not avaricious about keeping things, but only in acquiring them. In fact, those subject to this vice very often spend prodigally, far beyond their earnings and their possibilities. For that reason, they earn money in shameful ways—by gambling, stealing, or pimping, subjecting their own daughters, sisters, and wives to the lust of

others, just to satisfy their own gluttony and their own pleasures.

65. *de la = con la.   scuriada*: Also *scuriata*; literally, a "horsewhip," but also a whip for children, as Buti says in his commentary on *Inf.* XXV, 79: "Ferza e scuriata è una medesima cosa, et è lo strumento con che si batte lo cavallo, o vero li fanciulli." (*"Ferza* and *scuriata* mean the same thing, an instrument with which to whip horses or children.")

66. *femmine da conio*: I. Del Lungo (1888, pp. 199–269) made an exhaustive study of this much-debated phrase. In his commentary on the *Inferno* he concluded:

> "Da conio," da inganno, da ingannare, da corrompere con frode. I sostantivi *conio, coniello*; i verbi *coniare, coniellare*; i verbali *coniatore, coniellatore*, sono formali nel linguaggio statutale d'allora, per designare inganno di frodolenti. E distintivo del mezzano è la frode; compresivi i ruffiani di mestiere, per turpe lucro, al che è l'allusione dei vv. 59–63.

> "Da conio"—made for deception—that which deceives, which corrupts through fraud. The substantives *conio, coniello*; the verbs *coniare, coniellare*; and the nouns *coniatore, coniellatore* are all used in the statutory language of the time to designate fraudulent deception. The distinguishing characteristic of the pander is fraud. And that includes the professional pimp who does it for filthy lucre—to which vss. 59–63 allude.

Torraca cites the early Italian Aesop (fable XLIII): "i malvagi coniatori, i quali s'adornono e mostrono apparenzia di buone persone . . . acciò che meglio possino coniare e tradire e ingannare" ("the evil falsifiers [*coniatori*], who cloak themselves with the appearance of good men . . . so that they may all the better falsify, betray, and deceive").

Clearly, panders are being punished here in the first *bolgia* of the eighth circle for fraud, and this aspect of the meaning is essential. However, in the immediate context, with the reference to the "avaricious nature" of the

Bolognese, the meaning of "conio" as the steel die used in minting (Latin *cuneus*, OFr *coigne*, English *coin*) would seem to be uppermost in its reference to money. Thus on "da conio" G. Bertoni (1933, p. 28) hesitated between the meaning *da mercanteggiare* ("for purposes of trade") and *da ingannare* ("for purposes of deception"). Both meanings probably are present, the first being predominant. Venedico induced his sister to do the will of the marquis, probably on the basis of false promises, and this was a fraudulent act, but he did so for coin, for hire. For a recent discussion of the meaning of "femmine da conio," see W. Conner (1955).

67. *mi raggiunsi = mi ricongiunsi.*

68. *divenimmo = pervinimmo.* See *Inf.* XIV, 76.

69. *là 'v' uno = là ove uno.   la ripa:* "La cerchia" (vs. 3). *uscia = usciva.*

71. *scheggia:* Literally, "chip"; here used to indicate the jagged top of the stone reef.

72. *da quelle cerchie etterne:* E. Bianchi (1921) proposes that "cerchie" here refers to the custom of whipping a condemned man along a certain course through the city as he was led to the place of execution. He cites two passages from Antonio Francesco Grazzini's *Le Cene* (I, 5), pp. 115, 116. The first is: "L'altra mattina, facendo le cerchie maggiori per Pisa, fosse attanagliato e finalmente squartato vivo." ("The other morning, after first having been made to take the widest course around Pisa, he was then tortured with pincers and finally quartered alive.") The second citation is: "Lo infelicissimo Fazio, fatto per tutta Pisa le cerchie maggiori, in piazza condotto, sopra un palchetto a posta fatto . . . dal manigoldo in presenza di tutto il popolo fu squartato." ("The unhappy Fazio, after having been made to take to the widest course in Pisa, was brought to the square, placed upon a specially constructed platform . . . and was quartered by the executioner, in the presence of the entire populace.") Bianchi concludes that "cerchie etterne" refers to the "eternal circlings" of the sinners under the

demons' whiplashes. He goes on to say that the adjective "eternal" lends an unexpected and terrifying suggestion of Divine Justice.

Although Bianchi's examples are late (Grazzini died in 1584), as are those cited by M. Barbi (1921, 1924b), certainly, as G. Vandelli has observed (1932a, p. 196), the expression *cerchie*, or *cerchia*, or *cerca*, in this meaning might be as old as the custom to which it refers. Commentators have not (to my knowledge) noted that this custom figures in Boccaccio's *Decameron* in a context that further suggests that such a punishment for panders and seducers, especially the latter, applies here. In the seventh story of Day V, a certain Pietro is arrested for having got the daughter of Messer Amerigo with child and is condemned to death and forced to suffer just this punishment. See *Decam.* V, 7 (vol. I, p. 386, ll. 34–36; p. 387, ll. 7–8): "Pietro condannato, essendo da' famigliari menato alle forche frustando, passò, sì come a color che la brigata guidavano piacque, davanti ad uno albergo . . . . Era Pietro dalla cintura insù tutto ignudo e con le mani legate di dietro." ("The condemned Pietro was being led to the gallows by people, who whipped him. At the pleasure of those who were leading the group, he was made to pass before an inn . . . . Pietro was naked to the waist, with his hands tied behind his back.") This Pietro was making the *cerchie*, although Boccaccio does not use the term.

"Cerchie," in the present context, would thus appear to carry a possible double meaning comparable to that of "salse" in vs. 51 (see note). First, the word applies to the actual situation in Hell: the souls of the panders literally are circling. However, the fact that they are scourged as they go calls up the image of the condemned man being whipped through the city.

The wayfarers proceed over the bridge, turning their backs on the first file of sinners, the panders; in this sense they leave the eternal circlings of the panders behind to attend to the circlings of those who go in the opposite direction, the seducers. The demonstrative adjective in the immediate context thus takes on a special force: "We departed from *those* everlasting circlings," in order to attend to the next.

73. *el*: The "scoglio" of vs. 69, upon which the wayfarers walk as on a bridge.

75. *Attienti*: See *Inf.* XXXIV, 82.   *feggia = ferisca*.

79. *Del = dal.*   *traccia*: See *Inf.* XII, 55; XV, 33.

80. *venìa = veniva.*

86. *Iasón*: Jason was the leader of the Argonauts on their celebrated expedition to the land of Colchis in quest of the golden fleece. In the course of this adventure the Argonauts visited Lemnos, where Jason seduced and abandoned Hypsipyle. At length they arrived in the land of the Colchians, where Medea, the daughter of Aeëtes, king of Colchis, having fallen in love with Jason, helped him secure the golden fleece. When Jason and his companions sailed away, they took Medea with them. Jason married Medea, but afterward deserted her for Creusa.

The several episodes referred to in connection with Jason are elaborated by Statius and Ovid: the seduction of Hypsipyle is described in *Theb.* V, 403–85 (also in *Heroides* VI); the betrayal of Medea in *Heroides* XII. Valerius Flaccus (*Argonautica* II, 77–425) gives another version of the story of Hypsipyle. See E. R. Curtius (1950, pp. 398–428) on the ship of the Argonauts.

87. *féne = fe'* (*fece*). See the similar use of "pòne" for *pò* (*può*) in *Inf.* XI, 31.

90. *dienno = diedero.*

91. *segni*: Mute tokens of affection.

92. *Isìfile*: Hypsipyle was the daughter of Thoas, king of Lemnos. She secretly saved her father's life when the Lemnian women killed all the other men on the island. After the Argonauts landed in Lemnos, she was seduced and abandoned by Jason, by whom she had twin sons. See n. to vs. 86.

94. *Lasciolla = la lasciò.*

96. *Medea*: Daughter of Aeëtes, king of Colchis. With the help of Medea, Jason secured the golden fleece. As the condition of her assistance Jason promised to marry her. He did take her with him as his wife when he sailed from Colchis, but afterward abandoned her for Creusa (sometimes called Glauce), daughter of Creon, king of Corinth. In revenge Medea caused the death of Creusa and murdered her own two children by Jason. See Ovid, *Metam.* VII, 1–397; also n. to vs. 86.

99. *assanna = azzanna.*

101. *con l'argine secondo*: The embankment that forms the inner bank of the first *bolgia* and the outer bank of the second. The stone margin on which the wayfarers had walked before climbing onto the reef was the first embankment.

103. *si nicchia*: Benvenuto comments: "sicut facit aliquando infirmus in lecto" ("as a sick man sometimes does, in his bed"). The term could be equivalent to *si rannicchia* and mean "to nestle," but given the present context, such a meaning seems less likely. Virgil and Dante cannot see anything yet, but only hear ("sentimmo") what is in the next *bolgia*.

104. *scuffa = scuffia*. Said of one who eats so greedily that his nostrils become covered with the food and he has to snort through it in order to breathe. The exact way in which this applies to these sinners is soon made clear. Some editors would read "sbuffa" ("puffs," "blows").

106. *grommate*: "Caked." *Gromma* is the deposit of cream of tartar that wine leaves in the cask (see *Par.* XII, 114). The "exhalation" is indeed thick, to make such a deposit here.

109. *cupo*: The meaning can be either "deep" or "dark," but the latter seems preferable.

114. *che da li uman privadi parea mosso*: "Mosso" clearly suggests that the "sterco" (vs. 113) would have been trans-

ported here. Could the poet have had in mind something that must have been a common sight in his day and to which Boccaccio refers in one of his stories, namely, those ditches near the outskirts of the city into which human excrement (jestingly called, in the story, "la contessa di Civillari") was dumped for use as manure? See *Decam.* VIII, 9 (vol. II, p. 171, ll. 17–19): "Erano allora per quella contrada fosse, nelle quali i lavoratori di que' campi facevan votare la contessa di Civillari per ingrassare i campi loro." ("In that district, there were ditches into which the peasants used to empty the countess of Civillari, to fertilize the fields.")

116. *merda*: Here, as elsewhere in lower Hell, Dante's language becomes deliberately nasty, violent, derisive, and taunting, as it continues to be in the next verse.

118. *sgridò*: "Shouted angrily."   *gordo*: See "ghiotto," *Inf.* XVI, 51.

119. *brutti*: All besmeared with excrement. See *Inf.* VIII, 35.

122. *Alessio Interminei*: Of this Alessio, member of the prominent Interminei or Interminelli family of Lucca, little is known beyond the fact that he lived during the latter half of the thirteenth century. It appears from a document dated 1295 that he was alive in that year, and he must have died not long after. (See C. Minutoli, 1865, pp. 209–10.) Benvenuto says: "Iste ergo Alexius ex prava consuetudine tantum delectabatur adulatione, quod nullum sermonem sciebat facere, quem non condiret oleo adulationis: omnes ungebat, omnes lingebat, etiam vilissimos et mercenarios famulos; et ut cito dicam, totus colabat, totus foetebat adulatione." ("Well, this Alessio had a terrible habit: he was so given to flattery, that he was unable to say anything at all without seasoning it with the oil of adulation. He greased everyone, he licked everyone, even the most vile and venal servants. In short, he completely dripped with flattery and stank of it.")

123. *t'adocchio*: See *Inf.* XV, 22.

124. *zucca*: Literally, "gourd," "pumpkin." The tone of derision in such words is evident. See "berze," vs. 37, and the note. It should be noted that such terms are most often rhyme words; the rhyme doubles the derisive effect.

126. *stucca = stuccata*.

127. *pinghe* (*pinga*) = *spinga*.

129. *attinghe* = (*tu*) *attinga*.

130. *fante*: "Wench," but with the strong connotation of "prostitute"; see M. Barbi (1924c).

133. *Taide*: Thaïs, a courtesan in *Eunuchus*, a play by Terence. In the episode referred to, Thraso, her lover, has sent her a gift of a slave through a soldier named Gnatho. There is little doubt that Dante took the conversation, not from the play itself (Act 3, sc. 1, ll. 1–2), with which he probably was not acquainted, but from Cicero's *De amicitia* (XXVI, 98–99), which he knew well. Dante introduces the quotation in the same context in which Cicero does, namely in illustration of the habitual exaggeration indulged in by flatterers:

> Hos delectat assentatio, his fictus ad ipsorum voluntatem sermo cum adhibetur, orationem illam vanam testimonium esse laudum suarum putant. Nulla est igitur haec amicitia, cum alter verum audire non volt, alter ad mentiendum paratus est. Nec parasitorum in comoediis assentatio faceta nobis videretur, nisi essent milites gloriosi.
> > magnas vero agere gratias Thais mihi?
> Satis erat respondere "magnas." "Ingentis," inquit. Semper auget assentator id, quod is, cuius ad voluntatem dicitur, volt esse magnum. Quam ob rem, quamquam blanda ista vanitas apud eos valet, qui ipsi illam adlectant et invitant, tamen etiam graviores constantioresque admonendi sunt, ut animadvertant ne callida assentatione capiantur.

Such men delight in flattery, and when a compliment-
ary speech is fashioned to suit their fancy they think the
empty phrase is proof of their own merits. There is
nothing, therefore, in a friendship in which one of the
parties to it does not wish to hear the truth and the
other is ready to lie. Nor should we see any humour
in the fawning parasites in comedies if there were no
braggart soldiers.

> In truth did Thais send me many thanks?
It would have been enough to answer, "Many." "Mil-
lions of them," said the parasite. The flatterer always
magnifies that which the one for whose gratification
he speaks wishes to be large. Wherefore, although that
sort of hollow flattery influences those who court and
make a bid for it, yet even stronger and steadier men
should be warned to be on their guard lest they be
taken in by flattery of the crafty kind.

Through his undoubted ignorance of the play, Dante has
attributed to Thaïs the exaggerated reply ("ingentis") put
by Terence into the mouth of the parasite Gnatho. In the
original play this entire exchange takes place between
Thraso and Gnatho, not (as Dante supposes, from an un-
derstandable misreading of Cicero, taking his "Thais" as
a vocative) between Thraso and Thaïs directly.

134–35. *Ho io grazie grandi apo te?* For the expression
aver grazie (the equivalent of *gratias habere* in Latin), see
Thomas Aquinas, *Summa theol.* I-II, q. 110, a. 1, resp.:
"Secundum communem modum loquendi tripliciter gratia
accipi consuevit: uno modo pro dilectione alicuius, sicut
consuevimus dicere quod iste miles habet gratiam regis,
idest, rex habet eum gratum." ("According to the common
manner of speech, grace is usually taken in three ways,
first, for anyone's love, as we are accustomed to say that the
soldier is in the good graces of the king, i.e., the king looks
on him with favor.") Also see *Summa contra Gentiles* III,
150: "Unde et qui ab aliquo diligitur dicitur gratiam eius
habere." ("Consequently, he who is loved by another is said
to enjoy his grace.")

135. *apo* (Latin *apud*) = *presso*.

CANTO XIX

1. *Simon mago*: In the Bible, Simon Magus was a sorcerer of Samaria who was converted by the preaching of Philip the evangelist (see Actus 8:9-13). When he subsequently attempted to buy the power of conferring the Holy Ghost, he was severely rebuked by the apostle Peter for thinking that the gift of God might be purchased with money (see Actus 8:14-24). From the name Simon is derived the word "simony," which is applied to all traffic in sacred things, especially the buying or selling of ecclesiastical offices; those guilty of the offense are termed "simonists" or "simoniacs."

miseri seguaci: The simonists.

2. *le cose di Dio*: Spiritual goods and offices.

2-3. *di bontate deon essere spose*: "Should be married to goodness," i.e., should be assigned to the good and righteous.

3. *deon = devono*.

3. *e voi rapaci*: The "voi" singles out present practitioners of simony, the followers of Simon contemporary to Dante.

4. *avolterate*: Archaic, "adulterate."

5. *per voi suoni la tromba*: "Proclaim judgment upon you." Town criers sounded a trumpet to announce their reading of judicial sentences in public; the word here may also

suggest the sounding of the angel's trumpet on the Day of Judgment. / "Tromba" probably should be considered the subject of "suoni," although *io* (understood) might be the subject and "tromba" the object.

7-8. *Già eravamo, a la seguente tomba, montati*: Those who advocate this punctuation take "tomba" as the ditch ("fosso," vs. 9) in which the simonists are "buried"; see, for example, M. Barbi (1934b), p. 241. Other interpreters, however, have understood "tomba" to mean the bridge itself; see F. D'Ovidio (1907), pp. 342-45.

9. *sovra mezzo 'l fosso = sovra il mezzo del fosso*.

10-12. *O somma sapienza . . . comparte*: On this tercet and the "art" and "justice" here exclaimed over, see C. S. Singleton (1954), pp. 29–30.

11. *in cielo*: "In the heavens"; not "in Heaven."

12. *giusto*: The adjective is used for the adverb. *comparte*: "Metes out" or "apportions" the punishments of Hell.

14. *livida*: The color that was called "ferrigno" (see *Inf.* XVIII, 2) in the general description of the eighth circle.

15. *d'un largo = di una larghezza*. Thus there is a certain calculated regularity in the architecture here, which the simile of the Florentine Baptistery (vs. 17) emphasizes.

17. *nel mio bel San Giovanni*: The famous Baptistery of Florence, in which Dante, like most Florentine children of his time, was baptized; see *Par.* XXV, 8–9. John the Baptist is the patron saint of Florence; see *Inf.* XIII, 143-44. The present Baptistery, octagonal in form, was in Dante's time the cathedral of Florence. (The present cathedral, Santa Maria del Fiore, was begun in 1296 from plans of Arnolfo di Cambio and was not completed until the middle of the fifteenth century.) The Baptistery dates back to at least the sixth century, although its precise date is still the subject of controversy. It may have been erected on the site of an ancient temple of Mars, the original patron of Florence; see *Inf.* XIII, 144 and n. to *Inf.* XIII, 143-50.

18. *d'i = dei*.

21. *e questo sia suggel ch' ogn' omo sganni*: G. Vandelli
(1935, p. 117) asserts that the verse is designed to induce
those who interpreted the story of Dante's breaking the
baptismal font in San Giovanni's differently from the way
Dante does (i.e., as an act of sacrilege) to change their
minds. / He points (pp. 119–20) to two examples of *suggello*
used in the same sense it has in this verse, namely,
"dichiarazione scritta, debitamente munita di *suggelli*"
("written declaration, duly furnished with *suggelli* [seals]").

22. *soperchiava*: The subject is plural: "piedi" and "gambe."

24. *grosso*: The "calf" of the leg (though Porena prefers to
understand "thigh").

26. *giunte = giuntura*. If "grosso" (vs. 24) is taken to mean
the calf, then "giunte" refers especially to the ankles; how-
ever, the knees might be wriggling too without actually
being visible.

27. *averien = avrebbero*.   *ritorte e strambe*: Giovanni
Battista Gelli (*Letture* VII, 9; see p. 172) defines *ritorte* as
"quei legamenti de' rami d'arbori attorti, con che i villani
legono le fastella della stipa" ("those bands made of
twisted branches of trees, with which the peasants tie their
bundles of brushwood") and *strambe* as "quelle fune fatte
d'erbe secche e nervose, con le quali vengon legate le cuoia
di verso la Barberia" ("those ropes made of dry and sinewy
grass, used over in Barbary to tie up bundles of leather").

29. *strema = estrema*.   *buccia*: Literally, "rind."

30. *punte*: The toes, possibly the tips of the toes.

31. *Chi è colui*: Dante's opening words are similar to those
which singled out Capaneus (*Inf.* XIV, 46): "chi è quel
grande . . . ."   *che si cruccia*: "Who shows his pain"
by writhing.

33. *e cui più roggia fiamma succia*: The phrase may sug-
gest the way in which physical magnitude repeatedly is used

to signify moral stature (see *Inf.* X, 52–54 and the note; *Inf.* XIII, 32 and the note). But here there is a striking difference: it is not greater physical size but more intense punishment that singles out this sinner: the punishing flame is redder on his feet. *cui*: Accusative here. *succia* = *succhia*, "sucks," as a flame draws up oil through a wick.

35. *quella ripa che più giace*: As will be seen later (*Inf.* XXIV, 34–40), the whole field of the eighth circle slopes toward the pit at the center. If the floors of the *bolge* are fairly level (as seems to be the case), then the inner bank of each will be shorter than the outer, and will "slope less," will "have a more gradual slope." (See Fig. 6b, p. 312.)

37. *m'è bel*: "Is gratifying to me"; see *Purg.* XXVI, 140.

39. *quel che si tace*: Virgil can read Dante's thoughts and thereby divine his wishes.

40. *in su l'argine quarto*: The fourth embankment, dividing the third *bolgia* from the fourth.

41. *a mano stanca* = *a mano sinistra*. The phrase modifies "volgemmo" and "discendemmo."

42. *nel fondo foracchiato e arto*: The bottom is "narrow" (cf. the Latin *artus*) in the sense that the many holes leave only a narrow passageway between.

44. *non mi dipuose, sì* . . . : A common construction in early Italian; see vss. 127–28. *dipuose* = *depose*. *mi giunse*: "Brought me up to." *rotto*: "Crevice," the "hole" into which the sinner is thrust head down.

45. *che si piangeva*: Some editors prefer "sì piangeva," which in the present context would make perfectly good sense; "si" without the accent, on the other hand, could be the familiar pleonastic reflexive, which sets off or frames the subject (see n. to *Inf.* VII, 94). *zanca*: The term, like "shank" in English, is not necessarily derisive and its use is not comparable to the use of "zucca" for "head" in the preceding canto (see *Inf.* XVIII, 124). This is borne out

by the fact that "zanche" later is used to refer to Virgil's legs (*Inf.* XXXIV, 79).

46–47. *O qual che se' . . . commessa*: The opening phrase immediately reduces the sinner to the status of uncertain identity, to a "thing" with its upper side turned down, an object comparable to a stake thrust in a hole (as vs. 47 clearly implies).

47. *come pal commessa*: See "piantato," vs. 81. The simile anticipates that of vss. 49–51, and refers to a horrible punishment known as *propagginazione*, literally, "the planting of grapevines," by which assassins were stuck head downward in a hole, the hole was filled with dirt, and the criminal choked to death. Scartazzini (3rd edn.), commenting on vs. 49, quotes an old decree of Florence which refers to such punishment: "Assassinus . . . plantetur capite deorsum, ita quod moriatur." ("Let the assassin . . . be planted with his head down, so that he will die.")

48. *se puoi, fa motto*: The challenge continues the derisive focus on this upside-down "thing." Can it speak or not?

49–51. *Io stava come 'l frate . . . cessa*: On the punishment of assassins (here alluded to in the sense of hired murderers) and the calling back of the confessor, Benvenuto comments:

> Aliquando contingit . . . quod unus pessimus sicarius damnatus . . . ad plantationem corporis, postquam est positus in fossa cum capite deorsum, revocat confessorem suum ut confiteatur sibi aliquid peccatum, et dicat sibi aliquid de novo. Tunc confessor necessario inclinat aurem suam ad terram et attente auscultat illum.

> Sometimes it happens . . . that a wicked murderer, who has been condemned . . . to be planted with his head down, will, after he has been placed in the ditch head first, call back his confessor to confess some further sin. At such times, the confessor necessarily bends his ear toward the earth, and attentively listens to him.

51. *cessa*: "Delays." Here *cessare* is a transitive verb, having "morte" as object.

52. *costì*: "Up there"; the word refers to the position of the person spoken to. The speaker, as we learn in vss. 69–70 (though not explicitly), is Pope Nicholas III; see n. to vs. 69. He thinks he is addressing Pope Boniface VIII; see n. to vss. 53–57. *ritto*: "Standing," as if to say, "as I am not and as you shall not be for long." The word is repeated (vs. 53) with telling emphasis.

53–57. *Bonifazio . . . farne strazio*: Boniface VIII (Benedetto Caetani), born at Anagni *ca.* 1235, was created cardinal by Martin IV in 1281; elected pope at Naples in succession to Celestine V on December 24, 1294; and crowned at Rome on January 23, 1295. He died at Rome, October 11, 1303. Since Boniface died three years after the assumed date of Dante's journey through Hell, the poet by anticipation has assigned Boniface his place among the simonists. He has been referred to before (see *Inf.* VI, 69; *Inf.* XV, 112–14) and will be the object of many another bitter denunciation in the poem. Villani (who as a Guelph might have been expected to support the Church) says of him (VIII, 6, 64):

> Pecunioso fu molto per aggrandire la Chiesa e' suoi parenti, non faccendo coscienza di guadagno, che tutto dicea gli era licito quello ch'era della Chiesa. . . . Fece al suo tempo più cardinali suoi amici e confidenti, intra gli altri due suoi nipoti molto giovani, e uno suo zio fratello che fu della madre, e venti tra vescovi e arcivescovi suoi parenti e amici della piccola città d'Anagna di ricchi vescovadi, e l'altro suo nipote e figliuoli, ch'erano conti . . . lasciò loro quasi infinito tesoro.

> By aggrandizing the church and his relatives, he became very rich; nor did he have any scruples about making profits, for he said that everything that belonged to the church was lawfully his. . . . In his time he created several cardinals from among his friends and confidants, among them two very young nephews of his, and an

uncle who was his mother's brother. He also created
twenty bishops and archbishops from among his rela-
tives and friends in the small city of Anagni, giving
them rich dioceses; and, to his other nephew and to his
sons, who were counts . . . he left an almost infinite
fortune.

On the charge that Boniface was elected pope by fraud
(seized "by guile the beautiful lady," vss. 56–57), and on
Boniface's relations with his predecessor, Pope Celestine V,
see n. to *Inf.* III, 59–60, especially the passage from the
Cronica fiorentina there cited. See also Villani (VIII, 6):

Nel detto anno 1294, messer Benedetto Guatani cardi-
nale, avendo per suo senno e sagacità adoperato che
papa Celestino avea rifiutato il papato . . . seguì la
sua impresa, e tanto adoperò co' cardinali e col pro-
caccio del re Carlo, il quale avea l'amistà di molti
cardinali, spezialmente de' dodici nuovi eletti per
Celestino, e stando in questa cerca, una sera di notte
isconosciuto con poca compagnia andò al re Carlo, e
dissegli: "Re, il tuo papa Celestino t'ha voluto e potuto
servire nella tua guerra di Cicilia, ma non ha saputo;
ma se tu adoperi co' tuoi amici cardinali che io sia
eletto papa, io saprò, e vorrò, e potrò"; promettendogli
per sua fede e saramento di mettervi tutto il podere
della Chiesa. Allora lo re fidandosi di lui, gli promise
e ordinò co' suoi dodici cardinali che gli dessero le loro
boci . . . e per questo modo fu eletto papa nella città
di Napoli, la vilia della natività di Cristo del detto anno.

In that year 1294, Messer Benedetto Caetani, the car-
dinal, having shrewdly and sagaciously induced Pope
Celestine to renounce the papacy . . . pursued his plan.
He skillfully won over the cardinals, and the support
of King Charles, who enjoyed the friendship of many
cardinals, especially of the twelve newly elected by
Celestine. One night, in pursuit of his goal, he secretly
went with but a few companions to King Charles and
said to him: "King, your Pope Celestine wanted to
serve you and could have served you in your war in

Sicily, but he did not know how. If you influence your friends and cardinals to elect me pope I shall know how, I am willing, and I will be able to." And he promised him by his faith and by the sacrament that he would bring all the power of the church to bear on that war. The king believed him, made him the promise, and arranged to have his twelve cardinals give him their vote . . . and thus was he elected pope, in the city of Naples, on the eve of Christmas in the said year.

54. *Di parecchi anni mi mentì lo scritto*: "The writing [i.e., the 'Book of the Future'] lied to me by several years." The speaker, like all souls in Hell, can dimly see things in the future (see n. to *Inf.* X, 100–105). He thinks he is speaking to Boniface, not Dante; but he has "read" in the "Book of the Future" that Boniface will die in 1303 and accordingly does not yet expect him. Hence his surprise.

56. *a 'nganno = a inganno*. The reference may be both to Boniface's deceit of Celestine and to Boniface's fraudulent election as pope.

57. *la bella donna*: The Church, Bride of Christ and of His Vicar on earth (see "suo marito," vs. 111). See Eph. 5:25–27:

Viri, diligite uxores vestras, sicut et Christus dilexit ecclesiam, et seipsum tradidit pro ea, ut illam sanctificaret, mundans lavacro aquae in verbo vitae, ut exhiberet ipse sibi gloriosam ecclesiam, non habentem maculam aut rugam aut aliquid huiusmodi, sed ut sit sancta et immaculata.

Husbands, love your wives, just as Christ also loved the Church, and delivered himself up for her, that he might sanctify her, cleansing her in the bath of water by means of the word; in order that he might present to himself the Church in all her glory, not having spot or wrinkle or any such thing, but that she might be holy and without blemish.

57. *di farne strazio*: "To do her outrage" by practicing simony. The *Ottimo Commento* (n. to vs. 52) comments: "Nullo maggiore strazio puote uomo fare della sua donna, ch'egli ha sposata, che sottometterla per moneta a chi più ne dà." ("A man can do no greater outrage to the woman he has married than to subject her for money to whoever pays the most.")

62. *Non son colui, non son colui*: This repeated reply corresponds to Nicholas' repeated question in vss. 52-53 ("Se' tu già . . . se' tu già") and represents a kind of tit for tat.

64. *tutti storse i piedi*: "Tutti" has the value of "both" (adjective) and "all over" (adverb). Nicholas is writhing his feet in extreme vexation over having so needlessly revealed his identity by his "sudden question" (see vs. 78).

65. *pianto*: "Weeping" because of rage, more than anything else.

67. *ch'i' sia* = *chi io sia.   ti cal* = *ti cale*.

68. *che tu abbi però la ripa corsa*: The shade of Nicholas, "planted" head down as he is in his hole, has no way of knowing this on his own. The wayfarer may have said as much when he "answered as [he] was bidden" (vs. 63). Or perhaps he simply said he was not among those doomed to this *bolgia* and Nicholas concluded that he was passing by and came all the way "down the bank" in order to satisfy his curiosity.

69. *sappi ch'i' fui vestito del gran manto*: The speaker, Pope Nicholas III (Giovanni Gaetano Orsini), was a nobleman of Rome. He was created cardinal-deacon of San Nicola in Carcere Tulliano by Innocent IV in 1244; and was elected pope at Viterbo on November 25, 1277, in succession to John XXI, after a vacancy in the Holy See of more than six months. He died at his castle near Viterbo on August 22, 1280. The less than three years of Nicholas' pontificate were marked by nepotism (see vs. 71 and the note) and intrigue. On his nepotism, which led naturally to simony, Villani elaborates (VII, 54):

Poi che fu chiamato papa Niccola terzo, fu magnanimo,
e per lo caldo de' suoi consorti imprese molte cose per
fargli grandi, e fu de' primi o primo papa, nella cui
corte s'usasse palese simonia per gli suoi parenti; per
la qual cosa gli aggrandì molto di possessioni e di
castella e di moneta sopra tutti i Romani, in poco tempo
ch'egli vivette. Questo papa fece sette cardinali romani,
i più suoi parenti . . . . E tolse alla Chiesa castello
Santangiolo, e diello a messer Orso suo nipote. Ancora
il detto papa fecesi privilegiare per la Chiesa la contea
di Romagna e la città di Bologna a Ridolfo re de' Ro-
mani . . . . Incontanente che'l detto papa ebbe
privilegio di Romagna, sì ne fece conte per la Chiesa
messer Bertoldo degli Orsini suo nipote, e con forza di
cavalieri e di gente d'arme il mandò in Romagna, e con
lui per legato messer frate Latino di Roma cardinale
ostiense suo nipote, figliuolo della suora . . . .

After he became Pope Nicholas III his magnanimity
and his affection for his relatives caused him to do
many things for their aggrandizement. He was one of
the first, if not the first pope at whose court simony
was openly practiced for the benefit of relatives. In the
short time that he lived, he multiplied their possessions,
their castles, and their money, so that they had more
than all other Romans. This pope created seven cardi-
nals, most of them his relatives . . . . He took away
Castel Sant'Angelo from the Church and gave it to his
nephew Messer Orso. Furthermore, said pope made
Rudolph king of the Romans invest him, on behalf of the
Church, with the county of Romagna and the city of
Bologna . . . . As soon as the pope had Romagna, his
nephew Bertoldo degli Orsini was made count thereof
in the name of the Church. The pope sent him to Ro-
magna with knights and men at arms, and with him as
legate Messer Frate Latino of Rome, the cardinal of
Ostia, who was his nephew, the son of his sister.

On Nicholas' part in European intrigues of the time, see n.
to vss. 98–99. *del gran manto*: See "papale ammanto"
(*Inf.* II, 27) and "il gran manto" (*Purg.* XIX, 104).

70. *figliuol de l'orsa*: The Orsini were commonly referred to as *filii ursae*; see I. Del Lungo (1898), p. 469. H. Grundmann (1932, p. 252) notes that in the Pseudo-Joachist prophecy of the popes known as the *Papalisto* there is a reference to the Orsini as "genus nequam ursa catulos pascens" ("that nefarious species the bear, feeding its young"). The bear was known as a voracious animal, and the female was thought to be particularly fierce in guarding her young.

71. *cupido sì per avanzar li orsatti*: A reference to Nicholas' nepotism.

72. *che sù l'avere e qui me misi in borsa*: The *contrapasso* aspect of the punishment is evident here. Nicholas' words echo Peter's condemnation of Simon (Actus 8:20): "Pecunia tua tecum sit in perditionem." ("Thy money go to destruction with thee.") The hole in which the sinner is thrust is his "purse"; his "money" is there with him, and he is told to guard it well (vs. 98).

73. *tratti*: Each sinner remains "planted with his feet aglow" (vs. 81) until "thrust" lower by his successor. Apparently this hole is reserved exclusively for popes.

75. *piatti*: A predicate adjective after "son" (vs. 73). "Piatti" has something of the value of a past participle: "flattened," "mashed."

76–81. *Là giù cascherò io . . . coi piè rossi*: Nicholas, who died in 1280, has been in Hell twenty years and will not be supplanted by Boniface, who died in 1303, until three years hence. Boniface, in turn, will wait nearly eleven years to be replaced by the next pope (Clement V; see n. to vs. 83), who died in 1314. However, Nicholas' prediction cannot be taken as incontrovertible evidence that the present canto was composed after 1314, although G. Petrocchi (1957, pp. 660–61) has proposed that after 1314 Dante was able to retouch these verses and thus safely to "predict" the death of the Gascon pope.

78. *'l sùbito dimando*: Which he has already regretted (see vss. 64–65). *dimando = dimanda*; for this form see *Inf.* II, 97.

79–80. *Ma più è 'l tempo . . . sottosopra*: See n. to vss. 76–81.

83. *ver' = verso.* *un pastor sanza legge*: Clement V (Bertrand de Got) was born in Gascony *ca.* 1264. He was archbishop of Bordeaux before his election to the papacy on June 5, 1305, in succession to Benedict XI, and he was crowned on November 14 of that year. He died near Avignon, on April 20, 1314. It was during the pontificate of Clement V (who appears never to have entered Italy) that the papal see was removed to Avignon (1309), where it remained for over seventy years in what has been called the Babylonian Captivity. Clement owed his election to the influence of Philip the Fair ("chi Francia regge," vs. 87), and as pope was little more than a puppet of the French king. See Villani, VIII, 80; E. Gorra (1917).

Here in Canto XIX, Clement is judged only as a simoni-acal pope, who will take his place with Nicholas III and Boniface VIII in the third *bolgia* of the eighth circle. At other points in the poem, Clement will be denounced bit-terly on other grounds, though he is never mentioned by name. Villani (IX, 59) says of him: "Questi fu uomo molto cupido di moneta, e simoniaco, che ogni beneficio per danari s'avea in sua corte." ("He was a man very greedy for money, and a simoniac. At his court, any benefice could be had for money.")

85–87. *Nuovo Iasón . . . suo re*: Jason (born Joshua), second son of the high priest Simon, wrested the office of high priest from his own brother by promising the king, Anti-ochus IV Epiphanes, 360 talents of silver; see II Mach. 4:7–8. Antiochus (died *ca.* 164 b.c.) and Jason then endeavored to root out the Jewish religion and to introduce Greek customs and the worship of Greek divinities; see II Mach. 4:13–16. This attempt led to an uprising of the Jews under the Maccabees; see I Mach. 6:1–16.

87. *fia* = *sarà*.   *lui*: Dative.   *chi Francia regge*: Philip the Fair. Even as Antiochus favored Jason, so Philip will have Clement made pope; see n. to vs. 83.

88. *s'i' mi fui*: The reflexive in such constructions can hardly be translated, but it sets off the subject by reinforcing it with something of the suggestion of "on my part."   *s'i' mi fui qui troppo folle*: Freely, "whether I went too far." See *Inf.* II, 35; XXVI, 125.

89. *pur rispuosi*: Goes back to "troppo folle" (vs. 88) with the touch, "But I did reply to him so."   *a questo metro*: The phrase is obviously trenchant: "I sang him this tune."

91-92. *in prima . . . ch'* = *prima . . . che.*

92. *ch'ei ponesse le chiavi in sua balìa*: See Matt. 16:18-19: "Et ego dico tibi, quia tu es Petrus, et super hanc petram aedificabo Ecclesiam meam . . . . Et tibi dabo claves regni caelorum." ("And I say to thee, thou art Peter, and upon this rock I will build my Church . . . . And I will give thee the keys of the kingdom of heaven.")

93. *Viemmi* = *vienmi*. See Matt. 4:18-19:

Ambulans autem Iesus iuxta mare Galilaeae vidit duos fratres, Simonem qui vocatur Petrus, et Andream fratrem eius, mittentes rete in mare (erant enim piscatores). Et ait illis: Venite post me, et faciam vos fieri piscatores hominum.

As he was walking by the sea of Galilee, he saw two brothers, Simon, who is called Peter, and his brother Andrew, casting a net into the sea (for they were fishermen). And he said to them, "Come, follow me, and I will make you fishers of men."

94-96. *Matia . . . l'anima ria*: Matthias the Apostle was chosen by lot ("sortito") to fill the place of Judas Iscariot; see Actus 1:24-26.

97. *Però ti sta*: Again the pleonastic reflexive in its "distancing" function; freely, "Stay right here where you are." *ben*: "Justly."

98. *e guarda ben*: The "ben" echoes that of the preceding verse. The hole in which the pope is thrust is like a purse, where, with his head down, he should be able to guard the money with which he justly perished; see n. to vs. 72. *la mal tolta moneta*: See vs. 72.

98–99. *la mal tolta moneta . . . Carlo ardito*: This probably refers to Nicholas' part in an intrigue against Charles of Anjou, brother of St. Louis and king of Naples and Sicily, who had refused to marry Nicholas' niece. It was commonly believed that the Eastern emperor, Michael Palaeologus, supplied Pope Nicholas with funds to aid a Sicilian rebellion against Charles that led to an insurrection known as the Sicilian Vespers and to the eventual loss (after Nicholas' death) of Sicily by the house of Anjou (see Villani, VII, 54). This was, however, only one of a number of plots and counterplots with and against the royal houses of Europe which were part of Nicholas' brief career as pope.

104. *la vostra avarizia*: Passing to the plural *voi* at this point, Dante condemns all simoniacal popes and churchmen for their avarice (see *Inf.* VII, 46–48).

105. *calcando i buoni e sollevando i pravi*: Buti comments:

Li pastori simoniaci della santa Chiesa fanno tristo il mondo, per ch'ellino calcano i buoni non accettandoli a' benefìci, perchè non ànno che dare; e inalzino li rei per danari, accettandoli a' benefìci: e così danno materia a' cherici d'essere tristi, e non curare se non d'avere danari, sperando per quelli d'ottenere ogni grazia.

The simoniacal pastors of the Holy Church make the world wicked; for they put down good men, and do not give them benefices because they cannot pay; and they raise up bad men, and give them benefices. With that, they give clerics cause to be wicked, and to think of nothing but getting money, through which they can hope to obtain any favor.

106–11. *il Vangelista . . . al suo marito piacque*: See Apoc. 17:1–3, 7, 9, 12, 18:

342

Et venit unus de septem angelis qui habebant septem
phialas, et locutus est mecum dicens: Veni, ostendam
tibi damnationem meretricis magnae quae sedet super
aquas multas, cum qua fornicati sunt reges terrae . . . .
Et abstulit me in spiritu in desertum, et vidi mulierem
sedentem super bestiam coccineam plenam nominibus
blasphemiae, habentem capita septem et cornua decem.
. . . Et dixit mihi angelus: Quare miraris? Ego dicam
tibi sacramentum mulieris et bestiae quae portat eam,
quae habet capita septem et cornua decem. . . . Et hic
est sensus, qui habet sapientiam: septem capita, septem
montes sunt super quos mulier sedet: et reges septem
sunt. . . . Et decem cornua quae vidisti, decem reges
sunt, qui regnum nondum acceperunt . . . . Et mulier
quam vidisti, est civitas magna quae habet regnum
super reges terrae.

And there came one of the seven angels who had the
seven bowls, and he spoke with me, saying, "Come, I
will show thee the condemnation of the great harlot
who sits upon many waters, with whom the kings of
the earth have committed fornication . . . ." And he took
me away in spirit into a desert. And I saw a woman
sitting upon a scarlet-colored beast, full of names of
blasphemy, having seven heads and ten horns. . . . And
the angel said to me, "Wherefore dost thou wonder? I
will tell thee the mystery of the woman, and of the beast
that carries her which has the seven heads and the ten
horns. . . . And here is the meaning for him who has
wisdom. The seven heads are seven mountains upon
which the woman sits; and they are seven kings. . . .
And the ten horns that thou sawest are ten kings, who
have not received a kingdom as yet . . . . And the
woman whom thou sawest is the great city which has
kingship over the kings of the earth."

For the author of the Apocalypse, the "civitas magna" was
presumably imperial Rome; for Dante it is Christian Rome.
Dante, moreover, has combined woman and beast, and made
of the one figure the symbol of the corrupt Church, who
"whores" with kings.

343

---

108. *a lui* = *da lui*.

109. *le sette teste*: The Seven Gifts of the Holy Spirit; see *Purg.* XXIX, 73–78.

110. *e da le diece corna ebbe argomento*: The ten horns symbolize the Ten Commandments, from which the Church derived strength as long as the pope ("suo marito," vs. 111) governed virtuously.

112. *Fatto v'avete dio d'oro e d'argento*: "Gold and silver" are also paired earlier in this canto, in vss. 4 and 95. See Ps. 113B[115]:4: "Simulacra gentium argentum et aurum." ("Their idols are silver and gold.") See also Eph. 5:5: "aut avarus, quod est idolorum servitus" ("or covetous one—for that is idolatry"). And see Osee 8:4: "Argentum suum et aurum suum fecerunt sibi idola." ("Of their silver and their gold they have made idols to themselves.")

113. *idolatre*: Plural of *idolatra*; see the similar form, "omicide," in *Inf.* XI, 37.

114. *se non ch'elli uno, e voi ne orate cento*: This verse may be construed to mean: "For every idol they worship, you worship a hundred." Or, since the verse perhaps contains a reference to the Golden Calf of the Israelites, it may mean: "You worship not just one idol, but everything that is of gold."

115. *matre* = *madre* (see n. to vs. 117).

116. *non la tua conversion*: See *Par.* XX, 55–59.   *quella dote*: According to a legend universally accepted in the Middle Ages as historical fact, Constantine the Great (Roman Emperor 306-37), before he removed his government to Byzantium, abandoned to the Church his temporal power in the West. This so-called Donation of Constantine is said to have been made by the emperor in return for his having been cured of leprosy by Pope Sylvester I. Lorenzo Valla, who flourished more than a century after Dante's death, proved the Donation to be a forgery; it is now thought to have been composed at the papal court or in France in the

second half of the eighth century (see B. Nardi, 1944, pp. 109–59).

Dante did not doubt the authenticity of a document so widely accepted as genuine in his day, but he did deny that it had any juridical value (see *De mon.* III, x, 1–6). From the way in which Dante refers to it, Nardi (1944, pp. 144–45) concludes that he did not know directly the text of the Donation; he cites as evidence *De mon.* III, x, 1: "Dicunt adhuc quidam quod Constantinus imperator, mundatus a lepra intercessione Silvestri tunc summi pontificis, Imperii sedem, scilicet Romam, donavit Ecclesie cum multis aliis Imperii dignitatibus." ("It is further urged by some that the Emperor Constantine, when cleansed of his leprosy at the intercession of Sylvester, who was then supreme pontiff, granted the seat of empire, to wit Rome, to the church, together with many other dignities of the empire.")

117. *il primo ricco patre*: Sylvester I (pope 314–35). See n. to vs. 116.   *patre = padre*. See n. to vs. 115.

118. *cantava cotai note*: These words have the same trenchant tone as "metro" in vs. 89.

120. *forte*: The adjective is used for the adverb.   *piote*: "Feet" or "soles." According to E. G. Parodi (1957, p. 275), the word is still used in some parts of northern Italy. It is not necessarily a sarcastic or derisive term (see *Par.* XVII, 13).

121. *al mio duca piacesse*: What pleased Virgil was that Dante should sing him "such notes."

122. *labbia*: "Countenance." See *Inf.* VII, 7.   *attese*: "Heeded."

123. *espresse*: "Uttered" by Dante.

124. *con ambo le braccia*: This amounts to an embrace, for this time Virgil clasps Dante to his breast, whereas he had carried him down the bank on his hip (vss. 40–45).

128. *sì men portò* = *sì me ne portò*. On this construction see vs. 44 and the note.

129. *tragetto*: "Crossing"; see E. G. Parodi (1957), p. 272.

130. *spuose* = *depose*.

131. *soave*: The adjective is used for the adverb; "soave" repeats "soavemente," vs. 130.

CANTO XX

1. *nova*: "New," perhaps also "strange."   *mi conven far versi*: The voice of Dante the poet is much to the fore here, as at the beginning of *Inf.* XIX.

3. *canzon* = *cantica*. See *Purg.* XXXIII, 140; also Dante's *Letter to Can Grande* (*Epist.* XIII, 26): "Totum opus dividitur in tres canticas." ("The whole work is divided into three cantiche.")   *d'i* = *dei*.   *sommersi*: Those "sunk" within the earth and in Hell.

5. *scoperto fondo*: See *Inf.* XIX, 133.

7. *vallon*: See *Inf.* XIX, 133.

8. *tacendo*: It should be noted that not one of the sinners in this canto speaks—perhaps, for one thing, because their necks are twisted.

9. *letane* = *letanie* (pronounced *letànie*), Latin *litaniae*, modern Italian *litanie*. The reference is to slow-paced processions chanting litanies.

10. *'l viso mi scese in lor più basso*: "My eyes [or gaze] descended lower on them." The wayfarer was at first looking in the sinners' faces; he now lowers his eyes to their twisted necks.

347

13. *da le reni*: "Toward the reins," i.e., backward.   *tornato*: A transitive verb.

14. *li = gli*, "to each one" (see "ciascun," vs. 12).

15. *lor*: Dative, the verb *togliere* taking the preposition *a*.

16. *parlasia* (pronounced *parlasìa*) *= paralisia*, modern *paralisi*.

19–20. *Se Dio ti lasci . . . lezione*: The familiar formula of adjuration (see *Inf*. X, 82), whereby the reader is entreated by that which is, or ought to be, dear to him (here: "prender frutto / di tua lezione") to do what then is stated: "or pensa per te stesso."

20. *lezione = lettura*.

20–24. *or pensa per te stesso . . . per lo fesso*: The reader is asked to put himself in Dante's place and consider whether he too would not have wept. This entreaty on the part of Dante the poet anticipates Virgil's rebuke to the wayfarer, and its full import continues in the emphatic "Certo io piangea" (vs. 25), the overtone of which is "and so would you have wept."

22. *la nostra imagine*: "Our human image," which—since man was made in the image of God (Gen. 1:26)—is the essence of man's nobility and dignity as a creature.

24. *lo fesso = la fessura*, the "crack" between the buttocks.

25. *rocchi*: Plural of *rocchio*. See *Inf*. XXVI, 17.

27. *Ancor*: In the sense of "even now"; i.e., after all the wayfaring Dante has seen in this journey through Hell. See Matt. 15:16: "Adhuc et vos, sine intellectu estis?" ("Are you also even yet without understanding?")

29. *scellerato*: "Nefarious" or, in the context, "impious" in the extreme—strong language indeed for the "dolce duca" (*Inf*. XVIII, 44) to use.

30. *che al giudicio divin passion comporta?* Other editors have "passion porta" or "compassion porta." See examples of

passione in the sense of *compassione* and the discussions in M. Barbi (1934b), p. 272, and in Petrocchi's note to this verse and in his vol. I, *Introduzione*, pp. 181–82.

31. *Drizza la testa*: The wayfarer's head was bowed as he wept.   *a cui = a chi*.

31–32. *a cui . . . la terra*: This is Amphiaraus (vs. 34), a great prophet and hero of Argos. He was one of the seven kings who joined Adrastus, king of Argos, in the expedition against Thebes (see *Inf.* XIV, 68–69 and n. to *Inf.* XIV, 69). Foreseeing that he would perish in the war of the Seven against Thebes, Amphiaraus concealed himself to avoid going to battle; but his hiding place was revealed by his wife Eriphyle, sister of Adrastus, who had been bribed with a necklace. (For this betrayal Eriphyle was slain by Alcmaeon, her son by Amphiaraus; see *Purg.* XII, 50–51.) Amphiaraus met his death at Thebes when he and his chariot were swallowed up by the earth as he attempted to flee from his pursuers. The incident appears to have been borrowed from Statius (see *Theb.* VII, 690–823; VIII, 1–210).

32. *a li occhi = dinanzi a li occhi.   d'i = dei*.

33–36. *Dove rui . . . afferra*: The words "Dove rui" echo Pluto's words to Amphiaraus as he "ruins" to the nether-world in Statius' poem (see *Theb.* VIII, 84–85):

> "At tibi quos" inquit, "manes, qui limite praeceps
> non licito per inane ruis?" . . .

> "But what shall be thy doom," he cries, "who rushest headlong through the empty realm on a path for-bidden?"

But Statius does not present the scene of the prophet's plunge from the point of view of the Thebans, nor does he report any derisive words called out to him by them.

33. *rui*: Latin *ruis*. See *Par.* XXX, 82.

35. *non restò = non cessò.   ruinare*: See "rovinava," *Inf.* I, 61:   *a valle*: "Downward" (see *Inf.* XII, 46).

36. *fino a Minòs che ciascheduno afferra*: See *Inf.* V, 4–15.

38. *davante*: Into the future.

39. *fa retroso calle*: Cf. the Latin *retrorsum iter facit*.

40–45. *Vedi Tiresia . . . le maschili penne*: Tiresias, famous
soothsayer of Thebes, once separated with his staff two
serpents that he found coupled in a wood, whereupon he
was changed into a woman for seven years. At the end of
this period he found the same two serpents and struck them
again, whereupon he was changed back into a man. Sub-
sequently, when Jupiter and Juno differed as to which of
the two sexes experienced the greater pleasure in love, the
question was referred to Tiresias, because he had belonged
to both sexes. He decided in favor of woman, which coin-
cided with the opinion of Jupiter. Juno in anger struck him
with blindness, but Jupiter, by way of compensation, en-
dowed him with the gift of prophecy. Dante may well have
taken the story from Ovid; see *Metam.* III, 322–31.

43–45. *prima . . . che*: See *Inf.* XIX, 91–92.

43. *li = gli*.

45. *le maschili penne*: His beard (see *Purg.* I, 42) and by
implication his masculine characteristics generally.

46. *Aronta*: Aruns, Etruscan soothsayer who, according to
Lucan (*Phars.* I, 584–638), foretold the civil war that was
to end in the death of Pompey and the triumph of Caesar.
Lucan describes Aruns—with a different spelling—as fol-
lows (*Phars.* I, 584–88):

> Haec propter placuit Tuscos de more vetusto
> Acciri vates. Quorum qui maximus aevo
> Arruns incoluit desertae moenia Lucae,
> Fulminis edoctus motus venasque calentes
> Fibrarum et monitus errantis in aere pinnae . . .

Therefore it was resolved to follow ancient custom and
summon seers from Etruria. The oldest of these was
Arruns who dwelt in the deserted city of Luca; the
course of the thunderbolt, the marks on entrails yet

350

warm, and the warning of each wing that strays through
the sky, had no secrets for him.

Most editors of Lucan read "Lunae" for "Lucae"—i.e., Luna
(modern Luni) for Luca (modern Lucca).   *li = gli*.
s'atterga: "Backs up."

47. *Luni*: Ancient Luna, maritime town in Etruria on the
left bank of the Magra, on the boundary between Liguria
and Etruria. Modern Luni is west of Apuania, Tuscany,
near the famous white marble quarries of Carrara. It was
from Luni that the district of Lunigiana derived its name.

ronca: Buti comments: "Roncare è divegliere le piante."
("*Roncare* [to weed] means to uproot the plants.") "To
weed" or "to clear land" seems to be the first meaning of
the term here; freely translated, it means "to grub," "to
cultivate." "Scratches the soil" may possibly be the mean-
ing. H. D. Austin (1935, p. 83) notes that Uguccione da
Pisa has the entry "*Runco, -as*, herbas a terra evellere"
("*Runco, -as*, to tear the plants out of the soil"). Austin
points out that this is copied closely from Isidore of Seville,
Etym. XVII, ii, 5. Also see M. Barbi (1935), pp. 15–17.

48. *lo Carrarese*: The inhabitant "who lives below" and
comes into the mountains to engage in whatever meager
farming he can in the difficult terrain of these hills of
marble.

51. *li = gli*.   *tronca = troncata*, "cut off."

53. *con le trecce sciolte*: Benvenuto comments: "In hoc
tangit actum mulierum incantatricium, quae aliquando
vadunt de nocte nudae cum crinibus sparsis." ("Here he
hints at the witches who sometimes go about at night,
naked, with their hair loose.") For the image of loose hair,
see E. R. Dodds (1951), pp. 273–74; *Aen.* II, 403–6; VI,
48; *Phars.* V, 141–72.

54. *di là*: On her front side, which is turned away from
the wayfarer and is not visible.

55. *Manto*: Theban prophetess, daughter of Tiresias. Ac-
cording to some accounts, this Manto went to Italy and

married the god of the Tiber, by whom she had a son, Ocnus, who founded a town named Mantua in his mother's honor. According to others, the Italian Manto, mother of Ocnus, was a local nymph with the gift of prophecy. Dante's Manto is the Theban prophetess who settled in Italy, but he makes no mention of her marriage or of Ocnus. Ovid (*Metam.* VI, 157–62), Statius (*Theb.* IV, 463–592; VII, 758), and Virgil (*Aen.* X, 198–200) all mention Manto.

It is noteworthy that Dante here has Virgil state that Mantua (Virgil's native city) was founded by Manto, an account inconsistent with the version Virgil himself gives in the *Aeneid.* There it is stated that Mantua was founded by Ocnus, son of the river Tiber and of the prophetess Manto (but presumably not the Greek prophetess) and that it was so called by him after his mother's name (*Aen.* X, 198–200):

. . . Ocnus . . .
fatidicae Mantus et Tusci filius amnis,
qui muros matrisque dedit tibi, Mantua, nomen . . .

Ocnus . . . son of prophetic Manto and the Tuscan river, who gave thee, O Mantua, ramparts and his mother's name . . . .

It may be noted that Servius, who perhaps was Dante's authority, says in his commentary on *Aen.* X, 198 that Manto was the daughter of Tiresias and came to Italy after his death. Isidore of Seville says (*Etym.* XV, i, 59): "Manto Tiresiae filia post interitum Thebanorum dicitur delata in Italiam Mantuam condidisse." ("Manto, the daughter of Tiresias, is said to have been brought to Italy after the slaughter of the Thebans and there to have founded Mantua.") On the difference between Virgil's account and Dante's, and on the identification of Manto, see E. K. Rand (1916), pp. 8–10; E. Moore (1896), pp. 173–75. See also E. G. Parodi (1908a), cols. 194–95, 237–40.

56. *là dove nacqu' io*: Mantua, Virgil's birthplace. See *Inf.* I, 69, where Virgil affirms that his parents were "mantoani per patria ambedui"; also *Purg.* XVIII, 82–83.

58. *'l padre suo*: Tiresias.   *uscìo = uscì*.

59. *e venne serva la città di Baco*: According to tradition, Thebes, the capital of Boeotia, was the birthplace of Bacchus. After the war of the Seven against Thebes, the city fell ("venne serva") to the tyrant Creon.   *venne = divenne*.

    Baco: The god's name was often spelled Bachus in medieval Latin. See E. G. Parodi (1957), pp. 236, 354.

60. *gio = gì* (preterit of *gire*): *andò*.

61. *laco = lago*.

61–84. *Suso in Italia . . . nuda*: See Map 2, facing p. 354.

62. *l'Alpe*: The Venostian Alps, to the north of the castle of Tiralli (see n. to vs. 63).   *Lamagna* (or *La Magna*) *= Alemagna* (Germany).

63. *Tiralli*: Tirol, but the reference in this case is almost certainly not to the Tirol as a region (as understood today), but to the castle known as Tiralli, which was built in the twelfth century by the counts of Venosta and in fact gave its name to the region—that is, the *contea*. The counts were known thereafter as the counts of Tiralli or Tirolo. See A. Solmi (1933), pp. 110–12, 129–30; also Petrocchi's note.   *Benaco*: The Roman Lacus Benacus, modern Lago di Garda (Lake Garda). It is in east Lombardy, with its eastern shore on the Venezia Euganea boundary.

64–66. *Per mille fonti . . . stagna*: See Scartazzini-Vandelli, also Vandelli (1928), p. 68, for the view that the whole adverbial phrase "tra Garda e Val Camonica e Pennino" (vs. 65), in a construction common in early Italian, should be construed as the subject of "si bagna," in which case "Pennino" would indicate that section of the Alpine range that lies to the north of Lake Garda. Other editors prefer the reading "tra Garda e Val Camonica, Apennino," in which case "Apennino" is the subject and indicates the whole Alpine region between Lake Garda and the Val Camonica as that which is bathed by the "thousand springs and more" that flow into the lake. See Petrocchi's n. to vs. 65.

65. *Garda*: A town on the east shore of Lake Garda, about fifteen miles northwest of Verona.   *Val Camonica*: A valley, west of Garda, some fifty miles in length.

67–69. *Loco è nel mezzo . . . cammino*: Since a bishop (*pastore*) can give his blessing (*segnare*) only within the limits of his own diocese, the place Dante indicates would have to be where the three dioceses of Trent, Brescia, and Verona meet. The reference is probably to an islet in the middle of Lake Garda, where there was a chapel, which in fact was subject to the jurisdiction of the three bishops. See J. Ferrazzi, 1865, pp. 91–92; 1871, pp. 31–32, 389; 1877, pp. 344–46. Also see Map 2, facing.

69. *poria = potrebbe.   fesse = facesse.*

70. *Siede*: See *Inf.* V, 97.   *Peschiera*: Town and fortress (modern Peschiera del Garda) at the southeast shore of Lake Garda, about twenty miles southeast of Brescia and fifty miles southeast of Bergamo. It was a principal stronghold ("arnese") of the Scaligers of Verona in Dante's day (the verb *fronteggiare*, vs. 71, describes the matter of defense from their point of view). Benvenuto speaks of Peschiera as "satis novum, munitum multis turribus et arcibus, quasi tutela totius contratae" ("something quite new, armed with many towers and fortresses—the protector, as it were, of the whole area").

75. *fassi = si fa.*

76. *mette co = mette capo*, "has its head," i.e., "begins." On the form "co" (used again but not in rhyme in *Inf.* XXI, 64; *Purg.* III, 128; *Par.* III, 96), see E. G. Parodi (1957), pp. 274, 291–92.

77. *Mencio*: Mincio (ancient Mincius). Flowing out of Lake Garda near Peschiera del Garda, the river Mincio now forms a lake just above Mantua, its waters being dammed for the purpose, and enters the Po close to Governolo, about twelve miles southeast of Mantua. See Map 2, facing.

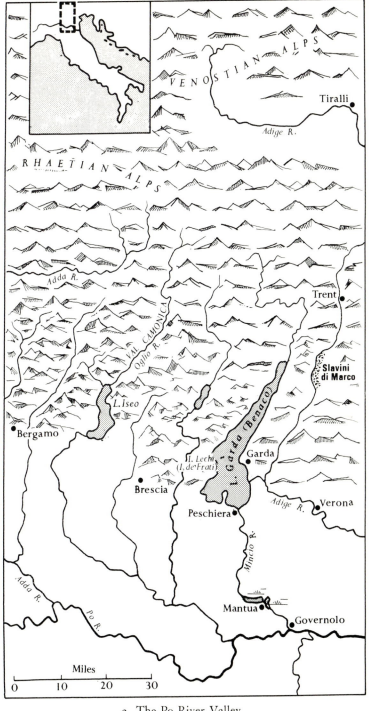

2. The Po River Valley

78. *Governol*: Governolo (pronounced *Govèrnolo*), a town about twelve miles from Mantua. See Map 2, facing p. 354.

79. *el*: The Mincio.   *lama*: A lowland flat, often (as here) bordering on a stream.

81. *grama*: A possible meaning is "scarce," scarce of water in this case; but the adjective also can mean "harmful," here referring to the malaria that infested the swamp.

82. *vergine*: Statius (*Theb.* IV, 463) refers to "innuba Manto" ("the virgin Manto").   *cruda*: See "Eritón cruda," *Inf.* IX, 23. The adjective may well have different meanings as applied to Erichtho and to Manto. In *Inf.* IX, 23, Erichtho is said to be "cruda" ("cruel," "savage," "untamed") because of the assistance she gave her father in the performance of his savage rites. Porena takes "cruda" here in Canto XX to mean "untamed" in the sense of "disinclined to marriage." The word *crudo* presumably might also be applied to one who sought "to avoid all human fellowship" (vs. 85).

86. *con suoi servi*: Some commentators, because of the phrase "fuggire ogne consorzio umano" in the preceding verse, understand the servants of Manto to be not men but devils. This would seem to be a misunderstanding. Dante does not mean that she shuns her own servants, her own people, but rather all strangers, all other human society.

87. *suo corpo vano*: Her dead body, "empty" of its soul.

89. *s'accolsero*: Preterit of *accogliersi*.

91. *Fer = fecero.   Fer la città sovra quell' ossa morte*: This was in accordance with ancient custom. Compare the following passages from the *Aeneid* (VI, 226–28, 232–35):

> postquam conlapsi cineres et flamma quievit,
> reliquias vino et bibulam lavere favillam,
> ossaque lecta cado texit Corynaeus aëno.
>
> . . . .
>
> at pius Aeneas ingenti mole sepulchrum
> imponit, suaque arma viro remumque tubamque,

> monte sub aërio, qui nunc Misenus ab illo
> dicitur, aeternumque tenet per saecula nomen.

After the ashes fell in and the flame died away, they washed with wine the remnant of thirsty dust, and Corynaeus, gathering the bones, hid them in a brazen urn. . . . But good Aeneas heaps over him a massive tomb, with the soldier's own arms, his oar and trumpet, beneath a lofty mount, which now from him is called Misenus, and keeps from age to age an ever-living name.

See also *Aen.* II, 293–97; Ovid, *Metam.* VIII, 235.

93. *appellar = appellarono.*   *sanz' altra sorte*: Lana comments: "Anticamente si usava quando si dovea ponere nome ad alcuno luogo, di gittarne sorte, e secondo quello che le sorti diceano, così avevano nome." ("In the olden days, when a place had to be named, they used to cast lots. And whatever the lot decreed, that was the name.")

94. *fuor = furono.*

95–96. *la mattia da Casalodi . . . ricevesse*: The commentators' accounts of the expulsion of Count Alberto da Casalodi from Mantua by Pinamonte de' Buonaccorsi (or Bonacolsi), lord of Mantua (1272–91), differ in detail, but agree as to the main facts. The Brescian counts of Casalodi, a family of Guelphs, made themselves masters of Mantua in 1272, incurring the hostility of the people. In order to appease the populace, Count Alberto da Casalodi, on what proved to be the treacherous advice of Pinamonte, expelled great numbers of the nobles, including his own adherents. When Alberto thus was left defenseless, Pinamonte, who wished to seize the government of Mantua, suddenly, and with the aid of the populace, compelled him to leave the city, confiscated all his possessions, and put to the sword or drove out nearly every remaining family of note in Mantua. According to Benvenuto, as many as fifty families were thus exterminated. Salimbene da Parma, a contemporary of Pinamonte, says of him in his *Cronica* (vol. II, p. 105): "Et timebatur sicut diabolus. Et erat homo senex et totus canus, et habebat filiorum maximam turbam." ("He was feared as the devil himself, this white-haired old man with his countless children.")

97. *Però = perciò.   t'assenno*: "I admonish you."

98. *originar la mia terra altrimenti*: In view of the fact that the *Aeneid* itself offers another account of the origin of Mantua, Virgil's "retractation" is most striking, and his admonition (vs. 99) the more emphatic: "Let no falsehood [including that told by me] defraud the truth." See n. to vs. 55.

102. *sarien = sarebbero.   carboni spenti*: A curious metaphor, though the meaning is plain enough.

105. *rifiede (rifedire)*: "Reverts to."

106–13. *Quel che da la gota . . . loco*: Dante seems to have confused two incidents here. When the Greeks departed for Troy from Aulis, Agamemnon, on the advice of Calchas, sacrificed Iphigenia (alluded to in *Par.* V, 67–72) in order to appease the goddess Diana. There is no mention in the *Aeneid* of Eurypylus in connection with this incident. When the Greeks were preparing to return home from Troy, however, they sent Eurypylus to consult the oracle of Apollo regarding the favorable time of their sailing. He brought back the reply that, because their departure from Greece had cost them a bloody sacrifice in the death of Iphigenia, they must also purchase their return by blood (*Aen.* II, 114–19). In describing this incident, Virgil does associate Eurypylus with Calchas. See *Aen.* II, 114–24 (possibly Dante took the word "placastis" to include both Eurypylus and Calchas):

> suspensi Eurypylum scitantem oracula Phoebi
> mittimus, isque adytis haec tristia dicta reportat:
> "sanguine placastis ventos et virgine caesa,
> cum primum Iliacas, Danai, venistis ad oras:
> sanguine quaerendi reditus animaque litandum
> Argolica." volgi quae vox ut venit ad auris,
> obstipuere animi, gelidusque per ima cucurrit

> ossa tremor, cui fata parent, quem poscat Apollo.
> hic Ithacus vatem magno Calchanta tumultu
> protrahit in medios; quae sint ea numina divum,
> flagitat. . . .

Perplexed, we send Eurypylus to ask the oracle of Phoebus, and he brings back from the shrine these gloomy words: "With blood of a slain virgin ye appeased the winds, when first, O Greeks, ye came to the Ilian coasts; with blood must ye win your return and gain favour by an Argive life." When this utterance came to the ears of the crowd, their hearts were dazed, and a cold shudder ran through their inmost marrow. For whom is fate preparing this doom? Whom does Apollo claim? On this the Ithacan with loud clamour drags the seer Calchas into their midst and demands what this is the gods will.

On Dante's interpretation of Virgil here, see E. G. Parodi (1908a), cols. 242–43. Servius (in his commentary on Virgil's *Eclog.* VI, 72) gives a complete account of Eurypylus.

107. *spalle brune*: Why "dark" shoulders, one wonders?

108. *quando Grecia fu di maschi vòta*: All adult males had gone to the Trojan War.

110–111. *diede 'l punto . . . la prima fune*: Determined the right moment for sailing.

110. *Calcanta*: On this Greek accusative form see E. G. Parodi (1957), pp. 247–48. Other examples of this form are "Aronta" (vs. 46), "orizzonta" (*Inf.* XI, 113), "Flegetonta" (*Inf.* XIV, 116). / Calchas, son of Thestor, was the soothsayer who accompanied the Greeks to Troy. See n. to vss. 106–13.

111. *Aulide*: Pronounced *Àulide*; Aulis, port in Boeotia, on the Euripus (modern Evripos), where the Greek fleet assembled before sailing for Troy.

112. *così*: By that name and as an augur.

113. *l'alta mia tragedìa*: See "comedìa," *Inf.* XVI, 128. On his reasons for calling Virgil's poem a "tragedy" and his own a "comedy," see Dante's *Letter to Can Grande* (*Epist.* XIII, 29); also see *De vulg. eloqu.* II, iv, 5–7.   *in alcun loco*: *Aen.* II, 114 (quoted in n. to vss. 106–13).

115. *poco*: "Thin," "lean." On this word see M. Barbi (1934b), p. 273.

116. *Michele Scotto*: Michael Scot, scholar and necromancer, probably was born at Balwearie, Scotland, *ca.* 1175 and died probably *ca.* 1235. He translated, from Arabic into Latin, Alpetragius' astronomical treatise, *De sphaera*; Aristotle's *De caelo*, probably the *De anima*, and several of his biological works; and the commentaries of Averroës on Aristotle. He probably served for many years as court astrologer to Frederick II at Palermo. His own works deal mainly with astrology and the other occult sciences. On Michael Scot's life and works see L. Thorndike (1965).

Villani, who speaks of Scot (XII, 19) as "il grande filosofo maestro Michele Scotto" ("the great philosopher, Master Michael Scot"), records prophecies of his about Can Grande (X, 101, 137) and about Florence (XII, 19, 92). Boccaccio introduces him into *Decam.* VIII, 9 (vol. II, p. 161, ll. 1–3) as "un gran maestro in nigromantìa il quale ebbe nome Michele Scotto, per ciò che di Scozia era" ("a great master of necromancy, whose name was Michael Scot, because he came from Scotland"). Benvenuto relates that Scot incorrectly prophesied that Frederick II would die in Florence (Florentia), which is in Tuscany, whereas he actually died in Castelfiorentino (Florentiola), which is in Apulia. Benvenuto also tells how Scot correctly predicted the manner of his own death:

> Michael tamen dicitur praevidisse mortem suam, quam vitare non potuit: praeviderat enim se moriturum ex ictu parvi lapilli certi ponderis casuri in caput suum: ideo providerat sibi, quod semper portabat celatam ferream sub caputeo ad evitandum talem casum. Sed semel cum intrasset in unam ecclesiam, in qua pulsabatur ad Corpus Domini, removit caputeum cum celata,

ut honoraret Dominum; magis tamen, ut credo, ne notaretur a vulgo, quam amore Christi, in quo parum credebat. Et ecce statim cecidit lapillus super caput nudum, et parum laesit cutim; quo accepto et ponderato, Michael reperit, quod tanti erat ponderis, quanti praeviderat; quare de morte sua certus, disposuit rebus suis, et eo vulnere mortuus est.

At any rate, it was said that Michael foresaw his own death, which he was unable to avoid. He foresaw that he would be killed by the blow of a small stone of a certain weight, which would fall on his head. To ward off that fate, he took the precaution of wearing an iron helmet under his hat. But one day, when he came into a church just at the moment of the consecration, he removed his hat and his helmet, to honor the Lord—or, in my opinion, so that he would not be noticed by the people, and not out of love of Christ, in whom he placed little faith. There, a little stone fell on his bare head, scarcely scratching the skin. Michael picked up the stone, weighed it, and found it weighed just as much as the one he had foreseen. Certain that he would die, he disposed of his goods. And then he died of that wound.

Many wonderful feats of magic are related of Scot by the commentators, feats which Benvenuto characterizes, however, as "potius ficta quam facta" ("more fiction than fact"). See A. Graf (1893), pp. 239–99; C. H. Haskins (1921–22).

117. *magiche frode*: See "froda," *Inf.* XVII, 7. Also see *Aen.* IV, 493: "Magicas invitam accingier artis." ("Against my will I arm myself with magic arts!") Torraca, in his note to *Inf.* XX, 86, quotes from *Novelle antiche* XXVIII, which reads: "Lo 'mperadore li pregò che giucassero cortesemente: quelli giucarono loro arti et loro incantamenti." ("The emperor asked them to play courteously; and they performed their arts and their enchantments.")

118. *Guido Bonatti*: This famous astrologer and soothsayer of Forlì (he may have been born in Florence), was a tiler

by trade (Villani VII, 81 refers to him as "ricopritore di tetti"—literally, a "coverer of roofs"). He appears to have served as domestic astrologer to Guido da Montefeltro. It is said to have been by his aid that the latter won his decisive victory over the French papal forces at Forlì, May 1, 1282 (see Villani, VII, 81). Bonatti's treatise on astrology enjoyed three editions, and that of 1550 (Basel) bears the title *Guidonis Bonati foroliviensis mathematici, de astronomia, tractatus X, universum quod ad iuditiariam rationem Nativitatum, Aeris, Tempestatum attinet comprehendentes.* In the course of this work the astrologer claims that in 1246 he unveiled the plot against Frederick II by astrological means; that he served the emperor for a time and was in the entourage of Ezzelino III da Romano, in Brescia in 1259; and that, as a follower of Guido Novello, he participated in the battle of Montaperti, the victory being ascribed partly to his calculations. Presumably, he moved to Florence after the Ghibelline victory and became official astrologer of the republic. A document published by G. Zaccagnini (1914, pp. 22–24) attests that Guido was still living on January 31, 1296. On Guido's life and works see B. Boncompagni (1851); D. Guerri (1915). *Asdente*: Maestro Benvenuto, nicknamed Asdente ("Toothless"), was a shoemaker of Parma who was famed as a prophet and soothsayer during the latter half of the thirteenth century. In *Conv.* IV, xvi, 6, Dante says that if notoriety constituted nobility, "Asdente, lo calzolaio da Parma, sarebbe più nobile che alcuno suo cittadino" ("Asdente the cobbler of Parma would be nobler than any of his fellow-citizens"). According to Benvenuto the commentator, Asdente foretold the defeat of Frederick II at the siege of Parma in 1248.

121. *le triste*: All are women, none worthy of being named.

121-22. *l'ago, la spuola e 'l fuso*: Sewing, weaving, and spinning.

122. *fecersi = si fecero. 'ndivine = indovine.*

123. *con erbe*: The reference is to juices or herbs with which the sorceresses made magic potions. Benvenuto notes that

at Venice such philters were called "herbariae."   *e con imago*: With waxen images, which were stuck full of needles or burned, in order to produce the desired effect—usually death—in the "imaged" person. See F. D'Ovidio (1901), pp. 113-14, for examples of such practices in Dante's time.

124. *vienne = vieni* (imperative) + ne (adverb).

124-26. *tiene 'l confine . . . le spine*: The moon ("Cain and his thorns"; see n. to vs. 126) is said to "hold the confines of both the hemispheres" (the hemisphere that has Jerusalem at its center and the hemisphere of water) and to touch "the waves below Seville" in setting in the West (i.e., for an observer ideally stationed at Jerusalem). E. Moore (1887, pp. 43-44) states that the time indicated here by moonset is approximately 6:00 A.M. Moore points out that although Dante naturally records the beginning of a new day in the pilgrimage, the poet seems to avoid mentioning the sun in the *Inferno*, preferring, for example, here to register the new day in terms of moonset rather than sunrise. See the latest time reference, in *Inf*. XI, 113-14, where it is said to be about two hours before sunrise, or 4:00 A.M.

126. *Sobilia = Siviglia.   Caino e le spine*: Cain, eldest son of Adam and Eve and murderer of his brother Abel, is here mentioned in connection with the old popular belief that the man in the moon was Cain with a bundle of thorns. According to the Italian tradition, Cain attempted to excuse himself for the murder of Abel and was condemned by God to be confined to the moon; see *Par*. II, 51. Thus "Cain and his thorns" here indicate the moon.

127. *iernotte*: "Last night" commonly is *stanotte* in Italian.
fu la luna tonda: A statement taken by many to be an essential factor in determining the exact time of Dante's imaginary journey through Hell.

128. *ten de' = te ne devi.   non ti nocque*: "Did you no harm," i.e., "helped you." But it is hard to see any allegorical meaning in this statement. Literally, of course, a

full moon would help one see one's way through a dark wood (*Inf.* I, 2), but the light that really helps in that initial scene is the light of the dawning sun, "the planet that leads men aright by every path," i.e., both a real and an allegorical sun. This full moon, which is said to have shone through the night, seems to bear no equivalent "other" meaning.

130. *introcque*: Latin *inter hoc*; "meanwhile." In *De vulg. eloqu.* I, xiii, 2, Dante cites the word as an example of the Florentine municipal vulgar tongue: "Locuntur Florentini et dicunt: *Manichiamo introque che noi non facciano atro.*" ("The Florentines open their mouths and say, 'Let's eat meanwhile—we haven't anything else to do.'")

CANTO XXI

1. *di ponte in ponte*: From the bridge over the fourth *bolgia* to that which spans the fifth.

2. *la mia comedìa*: See *Inf.* XVI, 128; see also the similar form "tragedìa," *Inf.* XX, 113, and the note.

3. *tenavamo = tenevamo*, "were holding"(i.e., "were standing on"). *'l colmo*: The summit of the bridge over the fifth *bolgia*, now called a "fessura" (vs. 4).

5. *pianti vani*: Depends on "per veder" in the preceding verse. The wayfarer expects to see such "lamentations," even as he has seen the bottom of the fourth *bolgia* bathed with "angoscioso pianto" (*Inf.* XX, 6). Instead, to his great surprise, he sees the fifth *bolgia* "marvelously dark" (vs. 6); no sinners are visible in it.

6. *e vidila mirabilmente oscura*: The verse registers great surprise and, with the long simile that follows, generates considerable suspense because there is no one moving around on this scene. The *bolgia* is naturally dark, as are the others in this eighth circle; but what creates the strange darkness that the wayfarer "sees" (we are then told) is black pitch, which becomes the subject of the simile in vss. 7–18. *vidila = la vidi*.

364

7–18. *Quale ne l'arzanà . . . parte*: This simile is neither digressive nor ornamental, as some commentators hold, but serves to build up the suspense and surprise already present in vs. 6. The first term (vss. 7–15) describes a scene of great activity around the boiling pitch in the Venetian Arsenal. The second term (a single *tercet*) contains nothing to match this, nothing except boiling pitch. This noncorrespondence of the two terms of the figure is the most effective feature of the whole; through the surprising difference thus brought out, the reader's eye dwells on the "tenace pece" and its viscous bubbling. / "Quale" (vs. 7) modifies "pece" (vs. 8); construe: *quale la tenace pece bolle l'inverno*. "Tal" (vs. 16) begins the second term of the simile and refers to the "pece," now called "pegola" (vs. 17).

7. *arzanà*: Venetian form for *arsenale*.   *l'arzanà de' Viniziani*: The Arsenal at Venice (built in 1104 and greatly enlarged in 1303–4 and 1325) was one of the most important shipyards in Europe in Dante's time. About two miles in perimeter, it was enclosed within high walls surmounted by battlements and flanked by towers. See F. C. Lane (1934), pp. 129-31.

9. *rimpalmare* = *rispalmare*; "to pay," in the sense of "to coat again with tar."

10. *navicar non ponno*: This is not to be taken literally, although winter certainly is not the best season for navigation and hence is a good time for building and repairing ships.   *ponno* = *possono*; the subject is "i Viniziani" (vs. 7).   *in quella vece*: "Instead of which."

11–15. *chi . . . chi . . . chi . . .* : The very movement of the eye over the busy scene reinforces the sense of animation.

11. *ristoppa*: "Recaulks."

13. *ribatte*: "Hammers away," the prefix *ri-* implying repeated blows.

365

14. *volge sarte*: The "sarte" are the ropes, the tackle of the vessel. They are made of twisted strands of hemp, hence "volge."

15. *terzeruolo e artimon*: A sailing ship's three principal sails are the mainsail, mizzen, and jib. *rintoppa = rattoppa*, "patches."

17. *bollia = bolliva.* *pegola*: A synonym of "pece," from the Latin *picula*, originally a diminutive of *pix*. The words "pegola spessa" correspond to the phrase "tenace pece" (vs. 8) in the first term of the simile.

18. *'nviscava = inviscava*; "was begluing," as with bird lime (*vischio*). See n. to *Inf.* XIII, 55–57.

19. *lei*: Refers to the "pegola" (vs. 17).

20. *mai che* (Latin *magis quam*) *= più che, altro che*. See *Inf.* IV, 26.

21. *gonfiar = gonfiarsi.* *riseder = risedersi.* See Virgil, *Georg.* II, 479–80: "unde tremor terris, qua vi maria alta tumescant / obicibus ruptis rursusque in se ipsa residant" ("whence come tremblings of the earth, the force to make deep seas swell and burst their barriers, then sink back upon themselves"). *compressa*: Suggests the bursting of the bubbles in boiling viscous liquid, and the settling back of the whole mass.

23. *Guarda = guardati* (pronounced *guàrdati*): "look out!"

24. *del loco dov' io stava*: From the edge of the bridge, where the wayfarer is standing in order to look down into the *bolgia*.

25. *cui tarda*: Literally, "to whom it is late"; i.e., "who longs."

26. *li = gli.*

28. *che, per veder, non indugia 'l partire*: The wayfarer looks and at the same time rushes to Virgil's side.

31. *fero = fiero.*

32. *acerbo*: "Fierce," "savage."

33. *con l'ali aperte e sovra i piè leggero*: The devil's out-spread (and no doubt batlike) wings make him "light of foot," as if he were just alighting.

34. *omero*: Pronounced *òmero*; the subject of "carcava" in the following verse. The object is "peccator" (also vs. 6).
   superbo: "High," "haughty."

35–36. *carcava un peccator . . . nerbo*: The figure, as Benvenuto observes, is that of a butcher carrying the carcass of some animal to be skinned:

> Quod iste daemon portabat unum peccatorem in spatula, et corpus pendebat per renes cum capite deorsum, et diabolus cum unguibus suis tenebat eum ante per pedes, sicut recte macellarius portat animal iugulatum nigrum ad macellum ad excoriandum et vendendum ipsum.

> For this demon carried a sinner on his back, with the body hanging from the loins, head down. In front, the devil held the sinner's feet with his claws, just as the butcher carries to the abattoir an animal with its throat cut, to have it skinned and to sell it.

35. *con ambo l'anche*: The sinner is slung over the devil's shoulder like the carcass of a slaughtered animal.   *ghermito*: Suggests "gripped by claws," which is literally true here, no doubt, since this devil is one of the Malebranche, or "Evil-claws" (see vs. 37).

36. *nerbo*: The strong sinew just above the hoof, by which butchers customarily hang or carry carcasses.

37. *Del = dal*.   *Malebranche*: "Evil-claws." The name suggests one of the more grotesque and terrifying features of these devils.

38. *anzian*: M. Barbi (1934b, p. 210) cites the unpublished commentary of Guido da Pisa, whose authority in this case is to be respected: "In lingua tuscia rectores et gubernatores populares anciani vocantur, ut est Pisis Pistorii et Luce." ("In the Tuscan language, the rectors and gov-

ernors of the people are called *anziani*, just as they are in Pisa, Pistoia, and Lucca.") V. Capetti (1913, p. 59) states that the *anziani* were ten citizens, two from each division of the city, who held office for two months. The office of "elder" in Lucca thus corresponded to the Florentine office of prior, in which Dante himself served; and the sinner condemned to punishment in this fifth *bolgia* of the eighth circle is guilty of corruption in public office (barratry), the very charge made against Dante when he was sentenced to exile. (Barratry, the buying and selling of public office, is the civil equivalent of simony, the buying and selling of church office, the sin punished in the third *bolgia*.)

In the same gloss referred to above, Guido da Pisa identifies the barrator in question as one Martino Bottaio, who died in Lucca on the same day that Virgil and Dante in Hell reached the *bolgia* of the barrators (see vss. 112–14 for the exact time reference). Barbi (1934b, p. 210) quotes Guido:

> Iste Martinus bottarius, qui propter peccatum baractarie hic ponitur ab auctore, fuit homo multum levis in moribus, sicut sunt omnes alii etiam sui cives. Nam re vera omnes lucani comuniter stulti sunt et fatui reputantur. Hic ergo Martinus adeo levis fuit quod cum quadam vice ad Romanam Curiam ex parte sui Comunis ambaxiator ivisset, et una die cum papa Bonifatio in camera se multum iactasset, ait ad dominum Papam: *Padre santo, crollami.* Quod cum papa causa ioci et recreationis illum crollasset, inquit Martinus: *Messa Lucca hai crollata.*

> This Martino Bottaio, who is placed here by the author because of his sin of barratry, was a very silly man, as are all his fellow citizens. As a matter of fact, the Lucchese are generally very foolish, and are known to be fatuous. Once, this Martino was sent to the Roman *curia* as ambassador of his commune. He was so silly that one day, at an audience with Pope Boniface at which he had boasted a great deal, he said: "Holy Father, shake me." To go along with the joke, the pope

shook him, whereupon Martino said: "You have just shaken half of Lucca."

38. *Santa Zita*: St. Zita (born 1218, died *ca.* 1278), the patron saint of Lucca, is also the patron saint of domestic servants, since she herself was a servant. Her tomb is in the church of San Frediano at Lucca (see the illustration given by C. Ricci, 1921b, p. 212).

39. *per anche*: "Again," and, by implication, "for another sinner," as is clear from what the devil goes on to say. The implication that the sinners are carried directly down into Hell from Lucca does not accord with the statement in *Inf.* III, 122-23 that all sinners first assemble at the river Acheron; but we may at least imagine that the devil hauls his prey before Minos for judgment (see *Inf.* V, 4–15) before bringing it to its allotted place, according to that judge's sentence.

40. *terra = città*, as elsewhere in the poem; here the word refers to Lucca.

41. *fuor che Bonturo*: The jeering sarcasm of this touch is evident. Bonturo is actually the worst barrator of all; and in Lucca every public official is corrupt, it seems.   *Bonturo*: Bonturo Dati, the head of the popular party in Lucca at the beginning of the fourteenth century, appears to have bought and sold public offices on so grand a scale that he controlled nearly all such traffic in the city. Benvenuto credits Bonturo with the remark to Boniface VIII that Guido da Pisa imputes to Martino Bottaio (see n. to vs. 38), but Guido's opinion is probably the more trustworthy in matters concerning Lucca. On Bonturo Dati see C. Minutoli (1865), pp. 211–20.

42. *del no, per li denar, vi si fa ita*: Buti comments: "In Lucca . . . a chi dè esser detto di no nelli offici è detto di sì; et a chi non à ragione è fatto che l'abbia per li denari." ("In Lucca . . . those who should be told 'no' in certain offices are told 'yes' and those who are in the wrong are made to be in the right, through money.")   *ita*: Latin

adverb, meaning "in this manner," "just so." As M. Barbi points out (1934b, p. 273), its use in Italian as an affirmative was not uncommon. Cf. *sì*, from the Latin *sic*.

44–45. *e mai non fu mastino . . . lo furo*: The devil is intent on his next prey, another barrator back there in Lucca, where barrators are so numerous that already another one has died unrepentant.

45. *furo*: "Thief"; see *Inf.* XII, 90.

47. *ma i demon*: Finally the suspense generated by the long simile of the Arsenal is resolved: there *are* guardians here, after all. The appearance of the creature who brought Martino Bottaio has suggested that the guardians might be devils, and now the true situation becomes clear. *demon*: Pronounced *demòn*.

48. *gridar* = *gridarono*.   *Qui non ha loco il Santo Volto*! The vulgar jeer is evident: the sinner's rear end turns up, all black with pitch.   *Santo Volto*: The "Volto Santo" ("Sacred Face") of Lucca is an ancient crucifix of great sanctity, carved in dark wood. According to tradition, this relic was carved by Nicodemus, who, while attempting to portray the divine features, fell asleep and on awaking found the work had been miraculously completed for him. The story of how it was transferred from the Holy Land to Lucca, where it is said to have been deposited in 742, is told by Benvenuto, who concludes his account with the remark, "Tu de hoc crede quod vis, quia hoc non est de articulis fidei." ("You can believe whatever you like about that matter; it is not an article of faith.") Benvenuto states that the Lucchese were accustomed to offer up prayers and oblations to the Volto Santo, particularly when they were in trouble. Its renown was such that even the impious William Rufus is said to have been in the habit of swearing by it. It is still an object of veneration, and is preserved in the nave of the cathedral of San Martino at Lucca, in a small marble chapel known as the Tempietto. For the legend itself, the miracles wrought by the holy image, and a bibliography, see G. Fallani (1961), pp. 117–23. (See Plate 5, facing.)

5. The Volto Santo ("Sacred Face"), an ancient crucifix carved of dark
wood, in the cathedral at Lucca

49. *si nuota altrimenti che nel Serchio*: Lana comments:
"La state comunemente ogni lucchese vi si bagna entro."
("In the summer all the Lucchese generally bathe there.")

Serchio: A river of Tuscany, which rises in the Apennines
of Lunigiana and flows south toward Lucca, a few miles to
the north of which it turns southwest and empties into the
Ligurian Sea between Viareggio and Pisa (it formerly
joined the Arno a short distance from its mouth).

51. *non far sopra la pegola soverchio*: This terrible warning
stresses the *contrapasso* aspect of the punishment: those
who sinned in barratry operated "under cover" and must
continue to do so here.

52. *addentar = addentarono*; literally, "bit into."   *raffi*:
"Hooked spears."

53–54. *Coverto convien . . . accaffi*: The stress on "under-
cover operation" continues, in the words "coverto," "nasco-
samente," and "accaffi." The sharpest taunt lies in the phrase
"se puoi."

54. *accaffi*: "Seize," "hook," a meaning easily applied to
the activity of barratry. On this word see E. G. Parodi
(1957), p. 277.

55–57. *Non altrimenti i cuoci . . . non galli*: Porena com-
ments that Dante has in mind the huge kitchen—equipped
with big kettles—of a court or great noble house, where a
cook directs and supervises the work of many subordinates.
The whole simile continues that of the butcher with his
carcass (vss. 34–36), the "meat" (vs. 57) now having been
brought to "pot" (vs. 56).

55. *cuoci* (archaic) = *cuochi*.   *vassalli*: "Kitchen boys."

58. *non si paia = non appaia, non apparisca*.

59. *t'acquatta = acquattati* (pronounced *acquàttati*);
"crouch," "squat down"; see "quatto quatto," vs. 89.

60. *dopo = dietro*.   *scheggio*: Literally, "splinter," but
here the word has the meaning of "rocchio" (see *Inf.* XX,

25), a "jag" or "jutting rock" of the rough reef. *aia =
abbia.*

62. *i' ho le cose conte*: "I have things under control here."

63. *altra volta*: Virgil may be referring to his difficulties
with the devils at the walls of Dis (see *Inf.* VIII, 82–130)
or to some skirmish that he had with these devils on his
previous journey to lower Hell (see *Inf.* IX, 22–30). The
first meaning seems more probable and more significant,
since Virgil appears to forget that his difficulties before Dis
were solved not by himself but by a messenger from Heaven.
Hence Virgil here exhibits the same self-confidence he
showed in the earlier encounter, before the devils shut the
gate in his face. *baratta*: "Skirmish," "wrangle"; see
E. G. Parodi (1957), p. 277. The term by its very form
brings barratry (*baratterìa*) to mind; see *Inf.* XI, 60.

64. *di là dal co del ponte*: Virgil advances beyond the far
head of the bridge. On the form "co," see n. to *Inf.* XX, 76.

65. *ripa sesta*: The wall dividing the fifth and sixth *bolge.*

66. *li = gli.*

68. *ch'escono = con cui escono.*

69. *che di sùbito chiede ove s'arresta*: When the dogs rush
out at him, the poor beggar ventures no nearer the house,
but asks for alms from where he has stopped, all fearful.
However, Virgil, neither suppliant nor frightened, gives a
command (vs. 72). For another interpretation (but one that
seems less acceptable), see M. Barbi (1928).

74. *traggasi = si tragga.*

75. *e poi d'arruncigliarmi si consigli*: The subject of "si
consigli" could be "l'un di voi" in the preceding verse, but
probably the whole group of devils is intended, as though
the phrase read: "si consigli tra voi." In that case, the verse
as a whole implies: "[After what I shall tell him,] then
take counsel [among yourselves] if I am to be gaffed."

76. *Malacoda*: "Evil-tail."

78. *Che li approda = che pro gli fa*: "What good will it do him?" *approda = fa pro*; cf. the Latin *prodesse*. As Malacoda advances toward Virgil, he addresses his comrades behind him, or perhaps only himself.

81-82. *sicuro già . . . e fato destro*: The reference in vs. 81, as in vs. 63 (see note), seems to be to the encounter at the walls of Dis (*Inf.* VIII, 82–130), where the devils (those who had "rained down from Heaven," *Inf.* VIII, 83) put up their most troublesome resistance (*schermo*). But now Virgil, with predictable effect, refers to the divine aid he was given in that encounter. The phrase "fato destro," in fact, seems to echo the words "le fata" of *Inf.* IX, 97.

83. *Lascian' = lasciane* (pronounced *làsciane; ne = ci*). Virgil's use of *ne* cannot be understood by the devils, since they presumably have not yet seen his companion, who is crouching behind a jut of rock (see vss. 58–60; 88–89). The reference to "altrui" in the following verse is equally obscure—deliberately so—for the moment.

83-84. *Lascian' andar . . . silvestro*: Virgil's words here are a variation on the formula of adjuration, "vuolsi così colà . . . si vuole," that he had used in upper Hell when his passage was challenged (see, for example, *Inf.* III, 95–96).

84. *silvestro*: See *Inf.* II, 142.

85. *li = gli.*

86. *si lasciò cascar l'uncino a' piedi*: An effective touch in the diabolical histrionics of this scene.

87. *Omai*: The little word, often so hard to translate, has in it a touch of "Well, in that case!" *feruto = ferito.*

90. *omai*: See n. to vs. 87, above.

93. *temetti ch'ei tenesser*: Scartazzini-Vandelli compares the Latin *vereor ut.* *patto*: Here used primarily in the sense of "assurance," "promise." Thus the Pisans, surrendering the fortress of Caprona and being given assurance of safe-conduct, were "patteggiati" (vs. 95). Here in vs. 93,

"patto" refers to Malacoda's order (vs. 87): "Let no one strike him."

95. *Caprona*: A castle in the territory of Pisa, about five miles from that city, on a hill close to the Arno. In August 1289, shortly after the death of Count Ugolino, head of the Guelph party in Pisa, and the expulsion of the Guelphs from that city, the Tuscan Guelphs, headed by the Lucchese and Florentines, invaded Pisan territory and captured several forts, including that of Caprona, as Villani records (VII, 137):

> Nel detto anno 1289 del mese d'Agosto, i Lucchesi feciono oste sopra la città di Pisa colla forza de' Fiorentini . . . e andarono insino alle porte di Pisa, e fecionvi i Lucchesi correre il palio per la loro festa di san Regolo, e guastarla intorno in venticinque dì che vi stettono ad oste, e presono il castello di Caprona, e guastarlo . . . .

> In the year 1289, in the month of August, the Lucchese, with the help of the Florentines, besieged Pisa . . . and while they were at the gates of Pisa, they celebrated their feast of San Regolo by playing the *palio* right there. During the twenty-five days the siege lasted, they laid waste the surrounding countryside, and they took and destroyed the castle of Caprona.

Benvenuto states that Dante himself took part in the siege: "Et hic nota quod autor fuit personaliter in isto exercitu; erat enim tunc iuvenis viginti quinque annorum, et ibi vidit istum actum; ideo libentius fecit talem comparationem, ut de se memoriam faceret, quia aliquando tractaverat arma." ("And note here that the author was in this army himself. He was then a young man of twenty-five, and there he witnessed this event. All the more willingly, then, did he make this comparison, to record the fact that, at one time, he had borne arms.") I. Del Lungo (1888, pp. 171-73) supports this view, on the ground that the campaign against Ghibelline Pisa took place soon after the battle of Campaldino (June 11, 1289), where Dante is known to have been.

98. *lungo*: See this usage in *Inf.* X, 53.

100. *Ei = essi.*

100–102. *Vuo' che 'l tocchi . . . accocchi*: The language of the devils is as low and vulgar as their actions.

102. *rispondien = rispondevano. gliel' = gliele. Le* is invariable and can represent *lo, li,* or *la*; in this case it is *la,* a form common to many idioms in Italian. Thus, *accoccarla ad uno* means "to let someone have it," "to deal someone an ugly blow."

103. *quel demonio*: Malacoda. *tenea sermone*: "Was speaking" with Virgil.

105. *Posa, posa*: It is easy to imagine such a command given to a watchdog: "Down, down!"

106–11. *Più oltre andar . . . face*: As the reader learns later (*Inf.* XXIII, 133–44), Malacoda deliberately tricks Virgil, but in this particular moment he is telling the truth: the sixth bridge is indeed broken down. The fact that he declares as much and does not simply point to the broken bridge ahead implies that they cannot see the next bridge, either because the bank on which they stand at the head of the fifth bridge is too wide, or because it is too dark for them to see so far.

107. *iscoglio = scoglio* (vs. 111); one of the several reefs which, like the spokes of a wheel, run from the surrounding wall of the eighth circle across the whole series of *bolge* (except for the sixth, where at least the bridge ahead is broken down). See the earlier description, *Inf.* XVIII, 14–18; also Fig. 6, p. 312.

110. *grotta*: Literally, "cliff"; see *Inf.* XIV, 114; *Purg.* I, 48. Here in Canto XXI "grotta" means the bank that divides the fifth from the sixth *bolgia*.

111. *presso = vicino. presso è un altro scoglio che via face*: As it turns out, the devil's lie is wholly in this verse, since actually *all* the bridges over the sixth circle are broken down, as will be evident. *face = fa.*

112–14. *Ier, più oltre cinqu' ore . . . fu rotta*: "Ier" is the subject of "compié" (vs. 114); the object is "anni" (vs. 114). / See the latest time reference, *Inf*. XX, 124–29. It was then a little after six o'clock in the morning of the second day of the journey; it is now seven o'clock in the morning. On the full symbolic and structural import of Malacoda's time-telling and the connection with Christ's death on the cross, see C. S. Singleton (1966).

112. *otta = ora.*

114. *la via fu rotta*: This breakdown of the rock bridge obviously is related to the "ruina" of *Inf*. V, 34 and to that of *Inf*. XII, 31–45, over which second ruin Virgil marveled. Like these two *ruine*, the breakdown over the sixth *bolgia*, referred to by Malacoda, occurred after Virgil's previous journey to lower Hell, and consequently he is easily deceived. Virgil does know, however (see *Inf*. XII, 45), that the rock of Hell collapsed at more than one point.

115–16. *Io mando . . . sciorina*: Malacoda states this as if he had been intending all along to send a squad of devils on just such a mission, but (as later becomes evident) this touch is part of a ruse designed to trap the wayfarers.

116. *s'alcun se ne sciorina*: *Sciorinare* commonly refers to the hanging out of clothes or other articles to dry; hence the expression means: "If any is drying himself."   *ne*: "Out" of the pitch.

117. *gite = andate.*

118. *Tra'ti = tràiti.*

118–23. *Alichino, e Calcabrina . . . Rubicante pazzo*: A good deal has been written about the possible meaning of these devils' names. Some, like Malacoda, are obvious; others can only be guessed at. (See Torraca; E. G. Parodi, 1957, pp. 354–56; A. Chiari, 1939, p. 20; L. Olschki, 1937, pp. 75–77; L. Spitzer, 1943, pp. 256–62; 1944.)

120. *la decina*: The squad is in fact a *decuria* (Latin for "decury," a division of ten men). Later (*Inf*. XXII, 74)

Barbariccia, the leader, is termed "decurio" ("decurion," the leader of a decury).

122. *sannuto*: "Tusked," i.e., "with *sanne*" (*zanne*).

124. *boglienti* = *bollenti*.   *pane* = *panie* (pronounced *pànie*); see in *Inf.* XX, 9 the similar form "letane" for *letanie* (pronounced *letànie*). "Pane" is "bird lime" or "glue"; see n. to vs. 18, above.

125–26. *costor sian salvi . . . tane*: This turns out to be another example of Malacoda's deliberate treachery, and the other devils know it. Since all the bridges across the sixth *bolgia* are down, Malacoda is guaranteeing the way-farers safe-conduct all the way to—nowhere!

128. *andianci* = *andiamoci*. *Ci* has the function of the pleonastic reflexive (see n. to *Inf.* VII, 94), setting off the subject; here it is reinforced by "soli."

129. *se tu sa' ir*: The words look back to Virgil's assurance (vs. 62) that he knows "about these things," and perhaps to his earlier statement (*Inf.* IX, 30) that he well knows the way.   *cheggio* = *chiedo*.

132. *ne* = *ci*.

135. *li lessi*: "The stewed ones," the souls in the boiling pitch. The term continues the figure of vss. 55–57; see also "i bolliti," *Inf.* XII, 102.

136. *Per l'argine sinistro*: The devilish squad turns left (with respect to the direction of the wayfarers' advance) along the far bank of the fifth *bolgia*.   *dienno* = *diedero*.

137–38. *la lingua stretta coi denti . . . per cenno*: The grotesque gesture (one has only to imagine what snouts these demons have) amounts to a "wink" of complicity and delight at the prospect of the adventure ahead, in which the devils are going to trick Virgil and Dante.

139. *elli avea del cul fatto trombetta*: The decurion's an-swer amounts to a "Let's be off!" quite worthy of a devil.

377

1. *muover campo*: Cf. the Latin *castra movere*.

4. *corridor*: Light cavalry, who scout ahead of the army.

   vidi: Dante probably saw such cavalry in the campaign against Arezzo that ended in the battle of Campaldino on June 11, 1289, between the Florentine Guelphs and the Aretine Ghibellines, in which the Ghibellines were totally defeated. Then, later in the same summer, he was probably at Caprona and may have seen similar cavalry there (see *Inf.* XXI, 95 and the note).

5. *gualdane*: Cavalry who make forays into enemy territory. On this word see A. Bassermann (1932), pp. 169–70.

6. *fedir = ferire*.

7. *campane*: See Villani, VI, 76:

> E quando l'oste era bandita uno mese dinanzi dove dovesse andare, si poneva una campana in sull'arco di porte sante Marie, ch'era in sul capo di Mercato nuovo, e quella al continuo era sonata di dì e di notte, e per grandigia di dare campo al nimico ov'era bandita l'oste, che s'apparecchiasse. E chi la chiamava Martinella, e chi la campana degli asini. E quando l'oste de' Fiorentini andava, si sponeva dell'arco, e poneasi in uno

castello di legname in su uno carro, e al suono di quella
si guidava l'oste.

And when the army was assembled, a month before it
was to march off, a bell was hung on the arch of the
Porta Santa Maria, which was at the head of the Mer-
cato Nuovo. And it rang constantly, day and night.
This was done out of pride, to give the enemy, against
whom the army was to fight, time to prepare itself.
Some called it the Martinella, others, the jackass bell.
And when the Florentine army marched off, the bell
was taken down, and placed on a cart, in a wooden
housing. And its peal guided the army.

The armies of many communes had such bells. Signals by
bell were also given from towers. Torraca quotes from *Tav.
riton.* CXXXV, p. 517: "Lo re Artù fa dare alle campane a
martello, e sonare le trombe e cennamelle; e a quello suono,
tutta la baronìa si prende ad armare." ("King Arthur has
the bells struck with hammers, and he has the trumpets
sound and the bagpipes play; whereupon all the barons
rush to arms.")

8. *cenni di castella*: See *Inf.* VIII, 5. Such signals were
given during the day by flags or smoke and at night by
lights or fires.   *castella*: Plural of *castello*.

10. *già*: "Indeed," "truly."   *cennamella*: A wind instru-
ment, possibly resembling the modern clarinet, commonly
used in military operations (see the passage from *Tav. riton.*
CXXXV quoted in n. to vs. 7, above). Cf. the OFr *chalemel*,
from the Latin *calamus, calamellus*.

12. *a segno di terra o di stella*: See *Aen.* VII, 215: "Nec
sidus regione viae litusve fefellit." ("Nor hath star or shore
misled us in our course.")

14-15. *ma ne la chiesa . . . ghiottoni*: No doubt this was a
popular proverb. Torraca calls attention to the following
passage from *Tav. riton.* XXVI, p. 96: "E quie sì si afferma
la parola usata che dice cosìe: 'Gli mercatanti ànno botteghe,
e gli bevitori ànno taverne, e' giucatori ànno i tavolieri; e

ogni simile con simile.' " ("And therewith the popular proverb is affirmed that says: 'The merchants have shops, the drinkers have taverns, the gamblers have card tables, and each has his own.' ") In the context of "tavern," "ghiottoni" could mean "gluttons" or "guzzlers," but "rascals" or "knaves" also is a common meaning of the word. See also Ps. 17:26[18:25]: "Cum sancto sanctus eris, et cum viro innocente innocens eris." ("Toward the faithful you are faithful, toward the wholehearted you are wholehearted.")

16. *Pur*: "Only," "entirely."

19–21. *Come i dalfini . . . legno*: M. Barbi (1934b, p. 242) quotes a relevant passage from Iacopo Passavanti. See Passavanti, *Lo specchio*, p. 322: "I dalfini, quando vengono notando sopra l'acqua del mare, appressandosi alle navi, significano che tosto dee venire tempesta." ("When the dolphins come swimming on the surface of the sea, drawing near to ships, it means there will soon be a storm.")

19. *dalfini = delfini*.

22. *alleggiar = alleggerire*, "to alleviate."

24. *nascondea*: The understood object is " 'l dosso" in the preceding verse.

28. *d'ogne parte*: All along both edges of the *bolgia*. The same phrase occurs in vs. 56.

30. *così*: Refers back to "in men che non balena," vs. 24. *ritraen = ritraevano*.

31. *anco = ancora*. See *Inf.* XIV, 78.

32. *elli 'ncontra*: "It happens" ("elli" is impersonal here).

33. *spiccia*: With the suggestion of a leap that is like a sudden spurt. See *Inf.* XIV, 76 (in rhyme with "raccapriccia").

34. *li = gli*, as also in the next verse. *più di contra*: The one who was nearest to being opposite him on the bank, hence the closest to him.

36. *trassel = lo trasse.   lontra*: The sinner, covered with black pitch, reminds Dante of an otter, which has long dense fur that sticks, matted and dripping, to its skin when it is hauled from the water. The otter, which lives on fish, is a fast swimmer—the connotation here is that the sinner has been caught even though he is a fast swimmer.

37–39. *I' sapea già . . . come*: The tercet accounts for the wayfarer's knowing Graffiacane's name, as well as the names of the others.

38. *fuorono = furono.*

39. *chiamaro = chiamarono.*

40. *metti = metta.*

41. *scuoi*: Subjunctive of *scuoiare*, "to flay." See *Inf.* VI, 18.

45. *a man de li avversari suoi*: See *Storie pistoresi* CXXIV: "Ordinarono che Parma venisse a mano di messer Luchino e Reggio venisse a mani de' marchesi da Ferrara e la città di Mantova alle mani di messer Mastino." ("They arranged to have Parma come into the hands of Messer Luchino, Reggio into the hands of the marquis of Ferrara, and the city of Mantua into the hands of Messer Mastino.") Part of this is quoted by Casini-Barbi.

46. *li = gli.*

47. *domandollo = lo domandò.*

48. *I' fui del regno di Navarra nato*: Nothing is known of this sinner, who is never named. The early commentators state that his name was Ciampolo (for Giampolo, i.e., Gian Paolo), but they supply nothing beyond a mere paraphrase of what he here tells of himself.   *nato = nativo.*

49. *a servo = al servizio.*

50. *che = la quale* (the mother).   *ribaldo*: "Good-for-nothing" is probably the meaning; see M. Barbi (1934b), pp. 212-13.

51. *distruggitor di sé e di sue cose*: This verse brings to mind the suicides and squanderers who are punished in the second *girone* of the seventh circle (see *Inf.* XIII).

52. *fui famiglia = fui della famiglia.*   *re Tebaldo*: Thibaut II, king of Navarre from 1253 to 1270 (as count of Champagne, Thibaut V). Benvenuto says of him: "Ultra reges Navarriae fuit vir singularis iustitiae et clementiae." ("He was a singularly just and clement man—more so than any other king of Navarre.")

54. *rendo ragione*: See Luc. 16:2: "Redde rationem." ("Make an accounting.")

55. *uscia = usciva.*

56. *d'ogne parte*: See vs. 28 and the note.   *sanna = zanna.* See *Inf.* VI, 23; XXI, 122.

57. *sdruscia = sdrucia*, i.e., *sdruciva*; literally, "opened the seams," "ripped open."

58. *sorco = sorcio*; see E. G. Parodi (1957), p. 284.

59–60. *il chiuse con le braccia . . . lo 'nforco*: Because the Navarrese is covered with hot pitch, Barbariccia no doubt puts his arms around him but holds them out from the sinner's "body," thereby nearly encircling him but not actually touching him. Hence he holds him enforked.

63. *altri*: Indefinite pronoun, meaning "any one of the devils."

64. *rii = rei.*

65. *latino*: The word frequently means "Italian" in the poem. See *Conv.* IV, xxviii, 8: "lo nobilissimo nostro latino Guido montefeltrano" ("our most noble Latin [i.e., Italian], Guido da Montefeltro").

67. *poco è = poco fa.*   *di là vicino*: Near Italy; i.e., Sardinia. See *De vulg. eloqu.* I, xi, 7: "Sardos . . . qui non Latii sunt, sed Latiis adsociandi videntur" ("the Sardinians

. . . who are not Italians, but are, it seems, to be associated with them").

70. *avem* = *abbiamo*.

72. *lacerto*: "Sinew." Buti comments: "Lacerto è propriamente congiunzione di più capi di nervi insieme." ("*Lacerto* means the juncture of several muscle ends.")

73. *i* = *gli*.   *dar di piglio*: This idiom means "to lay hold of"; see *Inf*. XII, 105.

74. *'l decurio*: Barbariccia, who guides the squad (see *Inf*. XXI, 120 and the note).

75. *mal piglio*: Like the word *cipiglio* (Latin *supercilium*), this phrase means "a frowning look." The sense of "piglio" here is different from that of "piglio" in vs. 73, and the word thus constitutes a legitimate rhyme.

76. *elli* = *essi*, the devils.   *rappaciati*: Literally, "pacified."   *fuoro* = *furono*.

78. *dimoro* = *dimora* (see *Inf*. X, 70).

79–80. *da cui mala partita di' che facesti*: See vss. 66–68.

80. *di'* = *dici*.

81. *frate Gomita*: Fra Gomita, a Sardinian friar (the order is not known) who, having been appointed chancellor or deputy of Nino Visconti of Pisa, judge of the judicial district of Gallura in Sardinia, abused his position in order to traffic in the sale of public offices. Nino turned a deaf ear to all complaints against Fra Gomita until he discovered that the friar had connived at the escape of certain prisoners who were in his keeping, whereupon Nino immediately had him hanged. On Fra Gomita see T. Casini (1913), pp. 109–17.

82. *Gallura*: One of the four judicatures into which Sardinia was divided at the time. The others were Logudoro (see vs. 89 and the note), Arborea, and Cagliari. Gallura

comprised the northeast portion of the island. See Map 3.
vasel = *vaso* (see "Vas d'elezione," *Inf.* II, 28).

83. *donno*: Latin *dominus*. This is Nino Visconti (see note
to vs. 81). Dante here intended to reflect Sardinian usage,
even though other dialects also employ this particular form
of address (see Boccaccio's *Decameron* IX, 10, vol. II, pp.
228–31).

85. *lasciolli* = *li lasciò*.   *di piano*: Latin *de plano*, Sar-
dinian (and other dialects) *di pianu*. M. Barbi (1934b, pp.
213, 242) cites two examples of the phrase, of which the
first will serve as illustration: "Qui, trattandosi di proscio-
glimento di persone da giudicare, *di piano* vorrà dire piut-
tosto con procedimento sommario, 'sine strepitu et figura
iudicii.'" ("This being a case of releasing persons about
to go to trial, *di piano* probably means with summary pro-
cedure, with neither the clamor nor the appearance of a
trial.") See also *Bullettino della Società Dantesca Italiana*
N.S. IX (1902): 257–58; A. Bassermann (1932), pp. 170–71.

87. *non picciol, ma sovrano*: See *Inf.* XVII, 72.

88–89. *Michel Zanche di Logodoro*: The accounts of this
man given by the early commentators are vague and con-
fused. Lana, for example, says of him:

Questo donno Michele Zanche, fu fattore della madre
del re Enzo, figliuolo naturale dello imperadore Fede-
rigo secondo. E dopo la morte del detto re Enzo, don
Michele tolse la ditta donna per moglie, la quale era
donna del giudicato di Logodoro di Sardigna; e seppe
fare avviluppamento per grande baratterìa. Ebbe dalla
ditta donna una figliuola, la quale in processo di tempo
elli diè per mogliere a messer Branca d'Oria da Genova.
E sicome apparirà nel penultimo capitolo di questa can-
tica, volendo lo detto messer Branca possedere la ric-
chezza del detto donno Michele, sì lo invitò un dìe a
disinare, poi per frutte lo fece tagliare a pezzi.

This Don Michel Zanche served as steward in the
household of the mother of King Enzio, natural son of

the Emperor Frederick II. After the death of King
Enzio, Don Michel took her for his wife. She was from
the district of Logudoro in Sardinia. He succeeded in
doing well through barratry. By her he had a daughter
whom, in the course of time, he married off to Messer
Branca d'Oria of Genoa. And, as will appear in the
penultimate chapter of this *cantica*, Messer Branca,
desirous of possessing the riches of Don Michel, invited
him to dinner one day and, as the fruit was served, had
him cut to pieces.

Little is known of Michel Zanche the historical personage,
except (as has lately been established) that he could not
have been the vicar of King Enzio in Sardinia, as was
commonly affirmed, or even a lesser official. Neither does
it appear that he was married either to King Enzio's
mother, as Lana implies, or to his divorced wife, Adelasia
di Torres, as some other commentators have believed. It is
probable that he was much involved in intrigues aimed at
gaining political power and that the date of his murder by
Branca d'Oria (see *Inf.* XXXIII, 137) was 1275.

The following account of Fra Gomita and Michel Zanche
is given in the *Chiose anonime*:

E frate Gomita fu cancelliere del Giudice di Gallura,
e fu molto malizioso e grande trabaldiere per danari;
e fra l'altre cose che fece di rivenderia, avendo cacciati
i Pisani il Giudice Nino di Gallura fuori di Pisa,
Giudice Nino scrisse che tutti i Pisani ch'erano nel
suo Giudicato fossero sostenuti: e così fu fatto. E, a
questo, Don Gomita per danari li lasciò fuggire; onde
Giudice Nino lo fece mettere in prigione, e in suo luogo
mise Don Michele Zanche. Don Michele Zanche, es-
sendo Cancelliere di Giudice Nino di Gallura, subita-
mente si cominciò a recare per le mani le tenute e fare
rivenderie peggio che Don Gomita.

And Fra Gomita was chancellor of the judge of Gallura.
He was a very wicked man, and a great shark for
money. Among his other acts of barratry was this one:
when the Pisans had expelled Judge Nino of Gallura

from Pisa, Judge Nino wrote that all the Pisans in his district were to be arrested, and that was done. Whereupon Don Gomita, for money, allowed them to escape. Judge Nino had him put in prison, and replaced him with Don Michel Zanche. Being chancellor of Judge Nino of Gallura, Don Michel Zanche at once began to take over certain properties and became an even worse barrator than Don Gomita.

Benvenuto sums up Ciampolo's account of himself and his two fellow barrators in these words: "Et vult dicere breviter: nos sumus tres boni socii, qui fuimus tres praecipui baratatores trium optimorum dominorum; sed Ciampolus sciebat plus caeteris, et tenuisset omnes ad scholam." ("And in brief, it means: we are three boon companions, and we were three outstanding barrators, serving three excellent lords. But Ciampolo knew more about it than the others, and could have given everyone lessons.")

On Michel Zanche and the history of Sardinia in his time, see P. L. Rambaldi (1896); F. Pintor (1905, 1914); T. Casini (1913), pp. 92–109.

89. *Logodoro*: Logudoro or Torres, largest of the four judicial districts into which Sardinia was divided at the time (see note to vs. 82). It comprised the northwest portion of the island. See Map 3.

92. *anche = ancora.   ello = egli.*

93. *la tigna*: See *Inf.* XV, 111.

94. *gran proposto*: Cf. the Latin *praepositus*. This "provost" in a mock-heroic style is Barbariccia.

95. *fedire = ferire* (see vs. 6).

96. *Fatti 'n costà*: The language of the devils here is characteristically vulgar (see n. to *Inf.* XXI, 100–102). As an example of *farsi in (a, verso)*, Torraca quotes S. Bongi (1890, p. 83): "Sosso vecchio leto, fact'in costà, levati dalla via." ("You filthy, stinking old man, stand aside, get out of the way.")   *uccello*: In the popular imagination of the

day, these devils would have been thought of as having
bat's wings. Such are the wings of Satan (see *Inf.* XXXIV,
46–50).

98. *lo spaurato*: "The frightened one."

99. *Toschi o Lombardi*: From his choice of these regions it
would seem that the Navarrese has recognized Dante as a
Tuscan and Virgil as a Lombard, and wishes to please them.
See *Inf.* I, 68, where Virgil's Lombardic parentage is men-
tioned; also *Inf.* XXVII, 20, where he is said to speak
Lombard.

100. *i Malebranche*: See *Inf.* XXI, 37.   *in cesso*: "Aside."
On this phrase see E. G. Parodi (1957), p. 262.

102. *seggendo*: If the devils will withdraw, the Navarrese
proposes to sit down and summon his friends by a secret
signal, as if there were no devils about.

103. *sette*: Actually an indefinite number, as in *Inf.* VIII,
97.

104. *suffolerò = zuffolerò*.

105. *fori = fuori*.

109. *divizia*: "Abundance."

112. *di rintoppo*: "In opposition." See *Inf.* XXXIII, 95 and
for the similar "s'intoppa," *Inf.* VII, 23.

116. *Lascisi = si lasci.   Lascisi 'l collo, e sia la ripa scudo*:
Since the whole expanse of Malebolge slopes toward the
center, the top of each bank between the *bolge* has a sloping
surface, the inner edge being somewhat lower than the
outer. Thus, if the devils draw back from the "collo," or
higher edge, of the inner bank of the fifth *bolgia* and go a
little down the slope toward the edge of the sixth, they will
be hidden from the sinners in the fifth *bolgia*.   *'l collo*:
The ridge of the bank, along which the wayfarers walk.

119. *ciascun da l'altra costa li occhi volse*: The devils turn
their backs on the fifth *bolgia*.

120. *quel*: Cagnazzo, who distrusted Ciampolo from the first and was more averse ("crudo") than the other devils to the whole idea of their retiring.

122. *fermò le piante*: As a diver does just before he plunges.

123. *proposto*: Barbariccia, who has somewhat relaxed his "enforking" of the sinner but has not yet withdrawn.   *si sciolse = si liberò.*

125. *quei*: Alichino.   *più = più compunto.*

126. *giunto = raggiunto.* See *Inf.* VIII, 18.

127. *i = gli.*

127-28. *l'ali al sospetto . . . avanzar*: Alichino's wings are no match for the sinner's frightened flight. See *Aen.* VIII, 224: "Pedibus timor addidit alas." ("Fear lent wings to his feet.")

128. *potero = poterono.*

130. *di botto = d'un subito.*

132. *rotto*: "Flouted."

133. *buffa = beffa.*

134. *li = gli.*

135. *quei*: Ciampolo.

139. *l'altro*: Alichino.   *sparvier grifagno*: A hawk taken when it is adult and therefore one that is fiercer than the *nidiace* (one taken in the nest) or the *ramingo* (one taken when it is beginning to fly).

142. *fue = fu.*

143. *però = perciò.*   *di levarsi era neente*: See *Inf.* IX, 57.

144. *avieno = avevano.*   *sue = loro.*

146-47. *quattro ne fé . . . raffi*: The marshal dispatches four devils to the other side, thereby equally dividing the devils who are out of the boiling pitch, in order that they may help rescue the fallen ones.

148. *a la posta*: To their appointed stations. See *Inf.* XIII, 113.

150. *dentro da la crosta*: The image of cooking (see *Inf.* XXI, 55-57) reappears to close the canto: the cooks them-selves are finally cooked.

CANTO XXIII

1. *Taciti*: "Silent," and "thoughtful," as is soon made plain. *soli, sanza compagnia*: The apparent tautology of these words carries a touch of irony in view of the "company" the wayfarers have just left behind.

2–3. *l'un dinanzi e l'altro dopo, come frati minor*: Francis of Assisi instructed his brethren always to travel in bands of two. Moreover, as the *Anonimo fiorentino* explains: "È usanza de' Frati minori più che degli altri frati, andando a cammino, andare l'uno innanzi, quello di più auttorità, l'altro dirietro et seguitarlo." ("Among the Friars Minor, more so than among other friars, it is customary, when walking, to have the one with more authority walk ahead, and the other follow behind him.")

3. *frati minor*: The Franciscans, who devoted their lives to poverty and humility, called themselves Friars Minor.

4–9. *Vòlt' era in su la favola d'Isopo . . . fissa*: Aesop, the reputed Greek author of *Aesop's Fables*, is said to have lived *ca.* 620–550 B.C., but it is doubtful that there was a historical Aesop who left any written works; scholars now believe that Aesop belongs solely in the oral tradition. Although fables bearing his name were known in Athens during the time of

Aristotle, several of these have been traced to sources considerably earlier than Aesop's alleged lifetime.

During the Middle Ages, Aesopean fables circulated in various Latin and French prose and verse collections. The fable of the mouse and the frog, to which Dante here alludes, was a favorite with medieval writers and appears, for example, in a collection attributed to Romulus, a writer of the Carolingian period (see fable I, 3 in L. Hervieux, 1894, p. 196), and in one by the late-twelfth-century French poet Marie de France (see fable III, 79–82 in K. Warnke, 1898, p. 16). Benvenuto says the fable was included in a small book of selections from Aesop used by students of Latin, and Buti describes such a book: "Isopo è uno libello che si legge a' fanciulli che imparano Grammatica, ove sono certe favole moralizzate per arrecarli a buoni costumi." ("Aesop is a book read to children learning grammar. It contains certain didactic fables to teach them good manners.") In the collection of Romulus (I, 3), the fable reads as follows:

Mus cum transire vellet flumen, a rana petiit auxilium. Illa grossum petiit linum, murem sibi ad pedem ligavit, et natare coepit. In medio vero flumine rana se deorsum mersit, ut miserrimo vitam eriperet. Ille validus dum teneret vires, milvus e contra volans, murem cum unguibus rapuit, simul et ranam pendentem sustulit.

Sic enim et illis contingit, qui de salute alterius adversa cogitant.

A mouse wanted to cross a river, and asked help of a frog. The frog took a long string, tied the mouse to his leg, and began to swim. But in the middle of the river, he dove down, to kill the poor mouse. While the mouse was resisting valiantly, a kite flew by, and grabbed him with his claws, lifting out the dangling frog at the same time.

That is what happens to those who want to bring harm to others.

In the version of Marie de France, the fable comes to a different conclusion, one that more closely parallels the incident in the *Commedia*: while the mouse and the frog are struggling in the water, the kite swoops down and carries off the frog, setting the mouse at liberty.

From the beginning, the commentators have puzzled over the application of the fable to the previous canto. The most widespread interpretation has been that Dante's phrase "presente rissa" (vs. 5) refers to the broil described in the closing verses of Canto XXII: the mouse equals Alichino; the frog, Calcabrina. However, N. M. Larkin (1962, pp. 97–99) sheds new light on the parallel by pointing out that the "beginning" referred to in vs. 9 is the moment when the two poets, having arrived at the sixth *bolgia*, find they cannot cross it without help—just as the mouse, arriving at the stream, asks the frog's assistance. The "end" referred to in vs. 9, Larkin avers, is the unhappy tumble of the devils into the pitch (the would-be tricksters in their malice are tricked by Ciampolo, as the frog in his malice is seized by the kite). Larkin stresses the complete innocence of the intended victim in all versions of the fable, which makes the gratuitousness of the treachery complete. He also points out that the equivalence (Dante + Virgil = mouse; demons = frog) is not precise, since in the poem sets of characters fill the roles played by individuals in the fable. He concludes (p. 99): "The fable, therefore, bears the same relation to its application in Inferno XXII as *mo* does to *issa* [vs. 7]: alike in significance but different in form."

Larkin's view of the application of the fable of the mouse and the frog seems correct on the whole, but it might be even more convincing if the author had respected the all-important distinction between Dante the character in the poem and Dante the poet which scholars are coming more and more to observe. Dante the character does not yet know that Malacoda has deceived Virgil in the matter of the bridge over the sixth *bolgia*, for he and his guide will know this only at the end of the present canto. Therefore the wayfarer cannot be comparing Malacoda's treachery with the frog's. But he can and does know the evil intent of the devils, since they are evil by their very nature; he is aware of their "ill-will" (vs. 16) and fears that they will also be wrathful, since they have been put to scorn; this suspicion must serve as sufficient evidence of their intent to deceive. Later Dante will have the proof of this evil intent. For another interpretation of the fable and Dante's allusion to it, see E. Mandruzzato (1955–56).

6. *el*: Aesop.

7. *"mo"* . . . *"issa"*: Both words mean "now." Cf. the Latin *modo* (and see vs. 28) and *ipsa hora*. For "issa," a Lucchese form, see *Purg.* XXIV, 55; E. G. Parodi (1957), p. 261.

8. *l'un con l'altro*: "The one thing with the other." M. Barbi (1934b, pp. 213–14, 242) points out that the pronouns are used in a neuter sense.   *s'accoppia*: "Is coupled," "is paired," "is compared."

9. *fissa* = *attenta*.

11. *quello*: The thought of the correspondence of the fable with the incident in Canto XXII.

12. *la prima paura*: The fear the wayfarer experienced when Malacoda offered to have his devils escort him and his guide (see *Inf.* XXI, 115–32).   *mi fé doppia*: This "double" fear is explained in vs. 16: "And if anger be added to ill-will . . . ."

13. *per noi*: "On our account," because of our wish to question Ciampolo.

14. *con danno e con beffa*: A standing phrase, frequent in Boccaccio and others, for example, in the expression "rimanere col danno e con le beffe" ("to end up with insult added to injury").

15. *assai credo che lor nòi* = *credo che lor nòi assai*.   *nòi*: Third person singular, present subjunctive, of *noiare*, "to vex."

16. *s'aggueffa*: "Is skeined," "is wound into the hank," "is added." Buti comments: "Aggueffare è filo a filo aggiugnere." ("*Aggueffare* means 'to join thread to thread.'")

17. *ei = essi*, the devils.   *ne = ci.*

18. *lievre = lepre.*

19. *sentia = sentiva.*

20. *de la paura = da la paura.*

22. *pavento = spavento.*

23. *d'i = dei.   avem = abbiamo.*

25. *piombato vetro*: "Mirror"; see *Conv.* III, ix, 8: "quasi
come specchio, che è vetro terminato con piombo" ("some-
thing like a mirror, which is glass with lead behind it").
See also *Par.* II, 89–90.

26. *trarrei*: "I should draw," i.e., "I should catch."

27. *quella dentro*: "Your inner [image]": your thoughts
and feelings.   *'mpetro = impetro*: "I obtain," "I receive."
See Prov. 27:19.

28. *mo*: See n. to vs. 7.   *venieno = venivano.   tra ' miei
= tra i miei.*

29. *con simile atto e con simile faccia*: The poets' thoughts
(see vss. 5, 28) are personified in this turn of phrase. And
now the opening word of the canto, "Taciti," acquires full
meaning: the two wayfarers were going along "silently"
with their thoughts turned "on what lay behind" (see vs.
20) and ahead of them.

30. *intrambi*: "Both" your thoughts and mine.   *un sol
consiglio*: The "sole resolve" is to escape.   *fei = feci.*

31. *elli*: Impersonal subject.   *destra costa*: Since Virgil
and Dante have turned to the left along the circular bank,
the slope to their right is the inner bank of the next, or
sixth, *bolgia.   giaccia = penda*; see *Inf.* XIX, 35; *Purg.*
III, 76. Evidently Virgil cannot yet see whether or not the
bank does slope in such a way that they can descend it to
the next ditch; see n. to *Inf.* XXI, 106–11.

32, 34, 36. *che noi . . . scendere . . . rendere . . . prendere*:
These *versi sdruccioli* are most effective in the context. For
a definition of this verse form, see n. to *Inf.* XV, 1, 3.

32. *l'altra bolgia*: The sixth.

33. *l'imaginata caccia*: The reference is to the devils' pur-
suit, which both Virgil and Dante are picturing to them-
selves.

35. *con l'ali tese*: Like the devil first seen (see *Inf.* XXI, 33).

36. *volerne = volerci*.

42. *solo una camiscia*: It was the custom of the time to sleep
naked.   *vesta*: Subjunctive of *vestire*, following "solo."

43. *collo*: The upper edge of the bank, as before (see *Inf.*
XXII, 116).

44. *si diede*: Cf. the Latin *se dedit*, as in *Aen.* XI, 565: "dat
sese fluvio" ("plunges into the flood").

45. *l'altra bolgia*: The sixth, as in vs. 32.   *tura*: "Closes."

46. *doccia*: "Canal," "conduit," "millrace." See *Inf.* XIV,
117.

47. *molin terragno*: The familiar "land mill" is one situ-
ated near a stream or other body of water; its paddles are
set in motion by water brought to it through a sluice. It
should be distinguished from the water mill, also common
in Dante's day, which was built on a raft set in a stream;
its paddles were turned by the current of the stream.

48. *approccia*: "Draws near" (see *Inf.* XII, 46). The water
flows faster as it nears the paddles.

49. *vivagno*: "Edge," "margin"; see *Inf.* XIV, 123.

51. *come suo figlio*: The phrase continues and completes
the simile (vss. 38–42) of the mother who takes up her
child and flees from danger. Virgil carried Dante in this
way before, when he climbed the bank of the third *bolgia*
(see *Inf.* XIX, 124–29).

52. *fuoro = furono*.

53. *e' = essi*, the devils. *colle*: The upper edge of the bank; see vs. 43 and the note.

54. *sovresso noi*: "Directly above us"; *-esso* is an intensive particle, originally the accusative form of the pronoun, or pronominal adjective, *ipse*. *non lì era sospetto*: "There was no [cause for] fear there."

57. *poder = potere*. *indi*: From the bank of the fifth *bolgia*. *tolle = toglie*.

58. *Là giù*: Down on the floor of the ditch. *gente dipinta*: The sense in which these people are "painted" is made clear in vs. 64. The phrase recalls the "sepulcris dealbatis" ("whited sepulchres") of Matt. 23:27.

59. *assai*: Probably this should be construed as modifying "lenti."

62. *taglia = taglio*, "style."

63. *Clugnì*: Cluny, the famous Benedictine abbey in Burgundy. It should be noted, however, that the early commentators followed the reading *Cologna*, as do some modern editors. / G. A. Venturi (1905, p. 239) refers to a letter of Bernard of Clairvaux to his nephew, who had left the Cistercian to enter the Cluniac order. In this letter (*Epistola* I, 11) Bernard observes ironically: "Si pelliciae lenes et calidae, si panni subtiles et pretiosi, si longae manicae et amplum caputium . . . sanctum faciunt; quid moror et ego quod te non sequor?" ("If sanctity is to be found in soft and delicate robes made of the finest and most expensive fabrics, with long sleeves and a full hood . . . then I do not see why I hold back and do not follow you.") *fassi = si fa*.

64. *elli*: The impersonal "it" refers to the effect of the bright gold of the robes.

65. *gravi = pesanti*.

66. *Federigo*: "The second Frederick" of *Inf.* X, 119. No incontrovertible evidence has been found to prove that Frederick actually employed such a method of torture, but the reference here reflects the widespread belief that he did. On this mode of punishment, see G. L. Hamilton (1921).

Although the exact nature of the *cappa plumbea*, or "leaden cloak," itself is uncertain, and may have varied, the punishment by which it was imposed was a recognized one in the Middle Ages. Du Cange (vol. II, p. 113), under the first "capa" entry, subentry "capa plumbea," quotes a document dated 1377 which refers to the punishment of a certain evildoer: "Se nostre saint pere le Pape savoit l'estat et la vie dont il vivoit, il le feroit mourir en la Chappe de plonc." ("If our Holy Father the pope knew the sort of life he lived, he would have him executed in the cape of lead.") Hamilton (1921, pp. 335–41) cites several earlier references to the punishment. Lana, whose account was copied by subsequent commentators, glosses as follows:

È da sapere che lo imperadore Federigo secondo usava di fare fare giustizia a quelli che sommo peccato commetteano contra la corona, in questo modo: elli facea fare di piombo una coverta al giudicato, la qual tutto lo covrìa, e questa era grossa circa un'oncia; poi facea mettere tal giudicato in una caldera, e questa cappa di piombo indosso a colui, poi facea fare fuoco sotto la detta caldera: per lo fuoco si liquefacea lo ditto piombo, e menava a pezzo a pezzo la carne di quello giuso, sì che infine bollìa lo piombo e 'l giudicato insieme: lo quale giudizio non era senza smisurata pena.

You must know that the Emperor Frederick II used to punish those who committed crimes against the crown in the following manner: he had a leaden cover made for the condemned man, to cover him entirely. The cover was about an inch thick. Then he had the man placed in a cauldron, and the leaden cape put over him. Then he had a fire made under the cauldron. The heat melted the lead, which took the skin off piece by piece. Finally, both the lead and the condemned man boiled. This punishment was not without immeasurable pain.

66. *le mettea di paglia*: The weight of Frederick's leaden capes was nothing ("like straw") compared to these.

68. *ancor pur*: "As usual," i.e., in the usual direction of turning; the two poets now fall in with these sinners—hypocrites all—who of course circle to the left.

71. *venìa = veniva*.

71-72. *sì pian, che noi eravam . . . ogne mover d'anca*: The sinners walk so slowly that the wayfarers come abreast of new ones at every step they take.

76. *la parola tosca*: Dante's Tuscan speech; see *Inf*. X, 22; XXII, 99.

77-79. *Tenete . . . correte . . . avrai . . .* : The sinner first addresses both wayfarers ("Tenete," "correte"), then only Dante ("avrai"), as the one who had asked Virgil to "find someone who may be known by deed or name" (vss. 73–74).

78. *voi che correte*: Typically the sinners notice the fact (the wayfarers' haste) that most contrasts to their own very slow pace (see *Inf*. XVI, 32–33). *aura = aria*.

80. *'l duca si volse*: As usual, Virgil is walking ahead of his charge and so must turn around to speak to him.

81. *poi*: I.e., "when he has reached you."

84. *tardavali = li tardava*. The verb has a compound subject, "carco" and "via." *via stretta*: The way is narrow because it is crowded with the slow-paced, heavy-clad sinners. See *Inf*. XIX, 42, where "fondo . . . arto" has a similar significance.

85. *fuor = furono*. *con l'occhio bieco*: The two sinners look askance at the wayfarer, first of all because their heavy cowls and capes make it difficult for them to turn their heads; such a glance is also quite descriptive of their hypocritical demeanor.

88. *atto de la gola*: Dante's breathing.

90. *grave*: The word here means both "heavy" and "grave."

91. *collegio*: The term was commonly used for assemblies of ecclesiastical persons, and in this sense fits the context very well. See Iob 15:34: "Congregatio enim hypocritae sterilis" ("for the breed of the impious shall be sterile"). Also see Ioan. 11:47 ("Collegerunt . . . facit," quoted in the key passage in n. to vss. 115–17, below).

92. *ipocriti tristi*: See Matt. 6:16: "Cum autem ieiunatis, nolite fieri sicut hypocritae tristes; exterminant enim facies suas, ut appareant hominibus ieiunantes." ("And when you fast, do not look gloomy like the hypocrites, who disfigure their faces in order to appear to men as fasting.")

94. *fui nato* = *nacqui*. See *Conv.* I, iii, 4: "Fiorenza . . . nel quale nato e nutrito fui in fino al colmo de la vita mia" ("Florence . . . wherein I was born, and nurtured until the culmination of my life"). See also *Inf.* V, 97.

95. *la gran villa*: Florence was the largest city on the Arno. *villa* = *città*.

97–98. *a cui tanto distilla quant' i' veggio dolor*: The subject of "distilla" is "tanto dolor"; the verb is intransitive here.

100. *rance*: "Orange" or "yellow."

102. *bilance*: The scales called "balances," which have a bar supported in the middle and two pans of equal weight suspended from the extremities, resemble the human figure, particularly the neck and shoulders. Such scales, if overweighted, as these sinners are in their heavy cloaks, do indeed creak, especially at the point of juncture of the cross-beam and its support, which in the comparison would be the necks of the hypocrites.

103. *Frati godenti*: The members of a military and conventual order called the Ordo Militiae Beatae Mariae ("Knights of the Blessed Virgin Mary") were popularly known as Frati Gaudenti, or Jovial Friars. The order was founded in 1261 by certain citizens of Bologna under the

sanction of Urban IV. Its object was to make peace between contending factions in the cities of Italy, to reconcile family feuds, and to protect the weak against their oppressors. The nickname Frati Gaudenti, which was in common use (as is proved by documentary evidence) within ten years of the foundation of the order, reputedly was bestowed upon the knights because of the laxity of their rules, which permitted them to marry and to live in their own homes, and merely required them to abstain from the use of gold and silver trappings, from attending secular banquets, and from encouraging actors. The knights bound themselves not to take up arms, except in defense of widows and orphans, and of the Catholic faith, or for the purpose of making peace between man and man. On the Frati Gaudenti see Giovanni Gozzadini (1851). Villani describes the order's habit and remarks on the aptness of its nickname (VII, 13):

> E' frati godenti erano chiamati cavalieri di santa Maria,
> e cavalieri si faceano quando prendeano quell'abito,
> che le robe aveano bianche e uno mantello bigio, e
> l'arme il campo bianco, e la croce vermiglia con due
> stelle, e doveano difendere le vedove e' pupilli, e intra-
> mettersi di paci, e altri ordini, come religiosi, aveano.
> . . . Ma poco durò, che seguiro al nome il fatto, cioè,
> d'intendere più a godere che ad altro.

> The Frati Gaudenti were called Knights of the Blessed
> Virgin Mary, and they were knighted when they took
> the habit, which had a white tunic and a gray cape; and
> their arms had a white field on which were a vermilion
> cross and two stars. They were to defend widows and
> orphans and to serve as peacemakers; and as religious
> men, they had other duties as well. . . . But within a
> short time, their deeds followed their name: that is,
> they were more intent upon enjoying themselves than
> upon anything else.

F. Torraca (1912, pp. 216–19) gives another interpretation of the nickname.

104. *Catalano*: Catalano di Guido di Ostia was born in Bologna *ca.* 1210 (for this form of his name see R. David-

sohn, 1908, pt. 1, p. 590). He served as *podestà* of various cities of Emilia and Lombardy; and in 1249 he commanded a division of the Bolognese infantry at the battle of Fossalta, in which King Enzio of Sardinia (the illegitimate son of Frederick II) was defeated and captured. In 1261, Catalano was associated with Loderingo degli Andalò in founding the Frati Gaudenti; and in 1265 and 1267, he and Loderingo shared the office of *podestà* in Bologna. Shortly after his last term of office, he retired to the monastery of the Frati Gaudenti at Ronzano near Bologna, where he died and was buried in 1285. *Loderingo*: Loderingo degli Andalò (born *ca.* 1210) belonged to a Ghibelline family of Bologna. His career paralleled that of Catalano: he served as *podestà* in several cities of Emilia and Tuscany, was among the founders of the Frati Gaudenti, and died at Ronzano in 1293. On these two sinners, see G. Gozzadini (1875), pp. 202–10; F. Torraca (1912), pp. 219-22.

After the defeat of Manfred and the Ghibellines at Benevento in February 1266, Pope Clement IV arranged for Catalano and Loderingo to share the office of *podestà* in Florence. This seemed conducive to the pope's ostensible purpose of securing peace between the Florentine Guelphs and Ghibellines: first, because Loderingo and Catalano jointly serving as *podestà* in Bologna in 1265 had managed to mediate between the two warring parties of that city; and second, because Loderingo was a Ghibelline and Catalano a Guelph. Clement's actual purpose, however, was to further the interests of the Florentine Guelphs, while ridding himself of the Ghibellines who remained in Florence with an army of German mercenaries and constituted a threat to his power. Since Catalano and Loderingo owed absolute obedience to the pope by virtue of their having taken religious orders, their previous political affiliations meant very little; in practice they were controlled by the pope. Thus, during their term of office there occurred an uprising of the Guelphs, who drove from Florence the most powerful Ghibelline nobles and the German mercenaries. By the spring of 1267, the houses of the most prominent Ghibelline families lay in ruins (see n. to vs. 108), and the remaining

Ghibelline leaders had been condemned to exile. / On the justice of Dante's charge of hypocrisy against Catalano and Loderingo, see F. Pintor (1903).

105. *tua terra*: Florence.

106. *un uom solingo*: The office of *podestà* was usually held by "one man alone."

107. *e fummo tali*: Ironically: "We conserved the peace so well that . . ."

108. *Gardingo*: A part of Florence in the neighborhood of the Palazzo Vecchio. In early times it appears to have been covered with ruins. According to Villani (I, 38):

> Alcuni dicono che fu ove oggi si chiama il Guardingo di costa alla piazza ch'è oggi del popolo dal palazzo de' Priori . . . . Guardingo fu poi nomato l'anticaglia de' muri e volte che rimasono disfatte dopo la di-struzione di Totile, e stavanvi poi le meretrici.

> Some people say [the Campidoglio of Florence] stood in what is now the Gardingo, next to what is now called the Piazza del Popolo, because of the Palace of the Priors . . . . Later, the name Gardingo was given to the ruins of walls and arches left by the destruction of Totila; and later, the prostitutes inhabited it.

There probably is no truth in the legend that Florence was destroyed by Totila (see n. to *Inf.* XIII, 150). Actually, Gardingo was first the name of a tower built by the Longobards to guard the city (see R. Davidsohn, 1896, pp. 21–22), and the name was then applied to the area around it (see M. Barbi, 1899, p. 211). The Uberti, who headed the Ghibelline party in Florence, built their houses there; and these houses, according to Benvenuto, were wrecked by the populace during the rising against the Ghibellines under the joint rule of Catalano and Loderingo (see n. to vs. 104).

109. *i vostri mali* ...: The broken-off sentence appears to leave "mali" ambiguous—the word can mean "sufferings"; but it is scarcely conceivable that Dante would have gone

on to speak words of commiseration to this pair; hence "mali" must refer to all the "ills" that the two had caused.

111. *con tre pali*: The sinner is staked to the ground, with one stake piercing each outstretched hand and the third his crossed feet.

112. *tutto si distorse*: See the description of Nicholas III, *Inf.* XIX, 64: "tutti storse i piedi." This sinner writhes in chagrin and rage for the same reason, that he should be seen and known here by this living man who can go back and report it to the world above.

115-17. *Quel confitto . . . martìri*: Caiaphas, the high priest, with surpassing hypocrisy "counseled the Pharisees that it was expedient to put one man to torture for the people." See Ioan. 11:45–52:

Multi ergo ex Iudaeis qui venerant ad Mariam et Martham, et viderant quae fecit Iesus, crediderunt in eum. Quidam autem ex ipsis abierunt ad pharisaeos, et dixerunt eis quae fecit Iesus. Collegerunt ergo pontifices et pharisaei concilium, et dicebant: Quid facimus? quia hic homo multa signa facit. Si dimittimus eum sic, omnes credent in eum; et venient Romani, et tollent nostrum locum et gentem. Unus autem ex ipsis, Caiphas nomine, cum esset pontifex anni illius, dixit eis: Vos nescitis quidquam; nec cogitatis, quia expedit vobis ut unus moriatur homo pro populo, et non tota gens pereat. Hoc autem a semetipso non dixit, sed cum esset pontifex anni illius, prophetavit quod Iesus moriturus erat pro gente, et non tantum pro gente, sed ut filios Dei qui erant dispersi, congregaret in unum.

Many therefore of the Jews who had come to Mary [and Martha], and had seen what he did, believed in him. But some of them went away to the Pharisees, and told them the things that Jesus had done. The chief priests and the Pharisees therefore gathered together a council, and said, "What are we doing? for this man is working many signs. If we let him alone as he is, all will believe in him, and the Romans will come and take away both our place and our nation." But one of them, Caiphas, being high priest that year, said to them, "You know nothing at all; nor do you reflect that it is expedient for us that one man die for the people, instead of the whole nation perishing." This, however, he said not of himself; but being high priest that year, he prophesied that Jesus was to die for the nation; and not only for the nation, but that he might gather into one the children of God who were scattered abroad.

Also see Ioan. 18:14.

116. *convenia* = *conveniva*.

118. *Attraversato*: See Isa. 51:23: "Et ponam illum in manu eorum qui te humiliaverunt, et dixerunt animae tuae: Incurvare, ut transeamus; et posuisti ut terram corpus tuum, et quasi viam transeuntibus." ("And I will put it in the hand of them that have oppressed thee and have said to thy soul: Bow down, that we may go over. And thou hast laid thy body as the ground and as a way to them that went over.") "Attraversato" probably means, not "crosswise" in the *bolgia*, but "placed as something to be traversed, walked on," as the following two verses make clear. See *Purg.* XXXI, 25: "quai fossi attraversati." *nudo*: A notable feature in this case, since if Caiphas does not wear a leaden cape, he is not shielded from the weight of the others who walk upon him, who weigh themselves upon him as upon a platform scale, each time they circle.

121. *il socero*: Annas, father-in-law of Caiphas. See Ioan. 18:13: "Et adduxerunt eum ad Annam primum. Erat enim socer Caiphae, qui erat pontifex anni illius." ("And they brought him to Annas first, for he was the father-in-law of Caiphas, who was the high priest that year.")

122. *dal concilio* = *del concilio*; the "pharisaei concilium" of Ioan. 11:47 (see quotation in n. to vss. 115–17).

123. *mala sementa*: An ironic echo of Ioan. 11:52, quoted in n. to vss. 115–17. Also see Matt. 27:25: "Et respondens universus populus dixit: Sanguis eius super nos, et super filios

nostros." ("And all the people answered and said, 'His blood be on us and on our children.'") The blood of Christ was thus the seed which bore evil fruit in the destruction of Jerusalem and the dispersal of the Jews. Dante refers to those events later in the *Commedia* as a "just vengeance" (*Par.* VII, 20). See *Purg.* XXI, 82–84; *Par.* VI, 91–93; VII, 16–51.

124. *Allor vid' io maravigliar Virgilio*: The crucified figures upon the floor of the ditch, Caiaphas, Annas, and the others, were not there when Virgil passed this way before. Virgil can marvel also at the particular form of their punishment and wonder what the reason for it may be, since he died before he could know that Christ was crucified. I. Della Giovanna (1901, p. 25) observed that this is the only time in Hell we see Virgil marvel.

126. *etterno essilio*: All sinners are exiled from Heaven, God's city. See *Inf.* I, 124–26; *Purg.* XXI, 18.

127–28. *drizzò al frate . . . Non vi dispiaccia*: Virgil speaks primarily to Fra Catalano (who then answers), but he includes, with his plural form of address, Fra Loderingo.

129. *a la man destra*: The two wayfarers, it should be remembered, proceed through Hell circling to the left: hence they have on their right hand the bank that divides the sixth *bolgia* from the seventh.   *foce*: An "opening" which might serve as exit.

130. *onde = per dove.   uscirci = uscire di qui. Ci* here has the meaning "hence"; see *Inf.* IV, 49, 55; VIII, 81.

131–32. *sanza costrigner . . . a dipartirci*: Virgil's words are ironical.

131. *angeli neri*: The devils, fallen angels, are all black.

132. *che vegnan d'esto fondo a dipartirci = che vegnano a dipartirci d'esto fondo*.

133. *adunque = allora*; see *Inf.* XXII, 64.

134. *un sasso*: One of the reefs that span the *bolge* like the spokes of a wheel, from the high rock wall ("gran cerchia") to the pit at the center. See *Inf.* XVIII, 4–18; Fig. 6, p. 312.

136. *'n questo è rotto*: As this stone bridge, which once spanned the sixth *bolgia*, has collapsed (contrary to Malacoda's assertion, *Inf.* XXI, 111, 125–26), it seems safe to conclude that Malacoda was telling the truth when, referring to the other reef on which the two wayfarers had been crossing the *bolge*, he said that the sixth arch (which formerly spanned this sixth *bolgia*) had also broken down. From this—although it is nowhere declared in so many words—it may be surmised that over the *bolgia* of the hypocrites *all* the rock bridges are broken down.

137. *ruina*: Like the other *ruine* of Hell ("ruina" has an emphatic position in this verse), this one was caused by the quake that shook the earth when Christ died on the Cross. Here, then, is a point from which we are able to understand much in retrospect: the special significance of this and the other two *ruine* (see *Inf.* V, 34; XII, 4, 32), Malacoda's time reference, and the true nature of his deception (on which see C. S. Singleton, 1966).

140. *contava*: "Set forth."   *la bisogna = la faccenda*.

141. *colui*: Malacoda.   *di qua*: Virgil is standing nearer the bank that separates the fifth and sixth *bolge*, with his back to it.

142–44. *Io udi' già dire . . . menzogna*: The trenchant irony of the friar's words is evident. See Christ's description of the devil (Ioan. 8:44): "Ille homicida erat ab initio et in veritate non stetit, quia non est veritas in eo. Cum loquitur mendacium, ex propriis loquitur, quia mendax est et pater eius." ("He was a murderer from the beginning, and has not stood in the truth because there is no truth in him. When he tells a lie he speaks from his very nature, for he is a liar and the father of lies.")

143–47. *del diavol vizi assai . . . mi parti'*: Vss. 143, 145, and 147 constitute what are called, in Italian prosody, *versi tronchi*. That is, they end in words accented on the final syllable ("udi'," "gì," "parti' ") and have one syllable less (in this case ten) than the normal measure (eleven).

147. *parti'* = *partii*.

CANTO XXIV

1–2. *In quella parte . . . tempra*: The sun is in the sign of Aquarius, "tempering his locks" (that is, warming his rays), between approximately January 21 and February 21.

2. *che* = *in cui.   i crin*: "His rays." See *Aen.* IX, 638: "crinitus Apollo" ("long-haired Apollo").   *tempra*: This can mean either "cools" or "warms." See Statius, *Silvae* I, ii, 14–15: "crinem temperat" ("tempers the tresses").

3. *e già le notti al mezzo dì sen vanno*: The line can have one of two meanings. M. A. Orr (1956, pp. 177–78) explains that if "mezzo dì" is translated as "half the day," the meaning is that the nights are growing shorter and will very soon—when the sun has reached the equinox—be twelve hours long. If "mezzo dì" is translated as "the south," the verse must be understood along with others in the *Commedia* in which Night is personified and considered always to be circling opposite to the sun (see, for instance, *Purg.* II, 1–6). In that case, Orr points out, the meaning of the verse is that the nights are going toward the south, since "the sun in Aquarius is not far from the point where he crosses the equator to the north, therefore Night circling opposite to him is nearing the point where she goes south." Orr avers that either interpretation is faithful to the text,

but suggests that the use of the plural noun "notti" favors the first meaning, "half the day."

4. *assempra = essempla* (from *exemplare*, "to copy"). The hoarfrost is personified as one who "copies"—i.e., likens herself to—her white sister, the snow, with a quill pen that soon loses its point ("tempra," vs. 6)—i.e., melts, because the weather gets warmer. See Lucan, *Phars.* IV, 52–53: "Urebant montana nives camposque iacentes / Non duraturae conspecto sole pruinae." ("The mountains were nipped by snow, and the lowlying plains by hoar frost that would vanish at first sight of the sun.") Dante uses *assemplare* also in *Vita nuova* I.

6. *tempra*: Cf. *temperino*, "penknife."

7. *villanello*: The diminutive suffix *-ello* introduces a modification of sentiment that is essentially pastoral. See "pecorelle," vs. 15. For the whole scene, see Orosius, *Hist.* IV, preface, 7.   *la roba*: "Provender," "forage" for his flock and perhaps also food for himself and his family.

8–9. *la campagna biancheggiar tutta*: See Horace, *Odes* I, iv, 4: "Nec prata canis albicant pruinis." ("Nor are the meadows longer white with hoary frost.")

9. *si batte l'anca*: An expression of despair, also in ancient times. Cf. the Latin *percutere femur, plangere femur*. J. Camus (1904) cites several examples of this gesture in Biblical, classical, and other literature.

11. *non sa che si faccia*: The so-called pleonastic reflexive is frequently found after *non sapere*.

12. *poi*: "After a short while," as vs. 14 and then vs. 18 (in the second term of the simile) make clear.   *riede*: This could mean either that the farmer goes back to the door to look out, or that he goes out again.   *ringavagna*: Literally, "puts back in his basket" (*gavagno*). The *Anonimo fiorentino* comments: "Gavagne sono certi cestoni che fanno i villani; sì che ringavagnare non vuole dire altro che incestare, ciò è insaccare speranza, avere maggiore speranza

che prima." ("*Gavagne* are certain baskets that the peasants make; *ringavagnare*, therefore, simply means 'to put into the basket'; in this case, to put hope into the basket means 'to have more hope than before.'") See the similar expression "fidanza non imborsa," *Inf.* XI, 54.

16. *mastro = maestro.*

17. *li = gli.*

18. *al mal*: Dante's fright.   *lo 'mpiastro = lo impiastro*, "medicine," "remedy"—the subject of "giunse."

20–21. *con quel piglio . . . monte*: This must refer to Virgil's reassuring manner when he first came to rescue Dante, although the poet's demeanor was not described in so many words at the time (*Inf.* I, 61–78). The first explicit mention of Virgil's tenderness occurs in *Inf.* III, 20. / See "mal piglio," *Inf.* XXII, 75.

21. *prima*: "First" in the sense of "the first time."

24. *diedemi di piglio*: See *Inf.* XII, 105; XXII, 73.   *diedemi = mi diede.*

25–30. *E come quei . . . reggia*: A pseudosimile.

26. *'nnanzi = innanzi.*   *proveggia = provegga.*

27. *ver' = verso.*

28. *ronchione*: See *Inf.* XX, 25.   *scheggia*: See "scheggion," *Inf.* XXI, 89.

29. *Sovra quella poi t'aggrappa*: The verse fairly pants, expressing Virgil's effort.   *t'aggrappa = aggràppati*, imperative.

30. *reggia = regga.*

31. *Non era via da vestito di cappa*: A reference to the hypocrites, the "costoro" of vs. 56.

32. *ei lieve*: Virgil is "light" because he is a spirit.

33. *potavam = potevamo.   chiappa*: A jut of the rock that can provide a hand or foot hold for the climbers.

34. *fosse = fosse stato.   da*: "On the side of."   *precinto = recinto*, the inner bank, which divides the sixth *bolgia* from the seventh.

35. *più che da l'altro era la costa corta*: Each *bolgia* has two *precinti* or "banks," an inner and an outer; thus "altro" refers to the outer bank of the sixth *bolgia* down which Virgil had slid, carrying his charge (see *Inf.* XXIII, 43–45). The slope of the inner bank is shorter than that of the other, for the reason given in n. to vss. 37–40, below.

36. *sarei ben vinto = sarei stato ben vinto.* See "fosse" as used for *fosse stato* in vs. 34.

37–40. *Ma perché Malebolge . . . scende*: The whole "field" of Malebolge, as it was called in *Inf.* XVIII, 4, slopes toward the pit at the center, and this causes the inner bank of each *bolgia* to be lower and shorter than the outer bank—assuming the bottoms to be level. (See Fig. 6b, p. 312.)

37. *inver' = inverso.   porta*: "Opening," but the metaphor suggests that the opening is also an entrance—as, in fact, it is—to the lowest level of Hell.

39. *valle = bolgia.   porta*: "Requires."

40. *l'una costa*: The outer bank.   *l'altra*: The inner bank.

41. *pur*: I.e., continuing to climb.   *punta*: See "la punta de la rotta lacca," *Inf.* XII, 11.

42. *l'ultima pietra*: The last rock that Virgil and Dante come to, at the summit of the ruin.   *si scoscende*: "Breaks away," that is, at the head of the broken bridge.

43. *munta*: Literally, "milked" (past participle of *mungere*). See *Inf.* XII, 135.

44. *ch'i' non potea più oltre*: The wayfarer is completely exhausted.

45. *ne la prima giunta*: At the top of the ruin.

46–48. *Omai convien . . . coltre*: Clearly Virgil's words re-
fer to Dante's (and our) journey here in this life, and its
"hard climbs," and in that sense are allegorical; for, as
Porena observes: "Certo non si conquista la fama arrampi-
candosi su per le salite erte!" ("Fame is certainly not con-
quered by climbing up steep hills!")

46. *così*: By such exertion as this.   *ti spoltre = ti spol-
trisca*.

48. *sotto coltre*: "Lying abed."

49. *sanza la qual*: "Without [fame]."

49–51. *sanza la qual . . . schiuma*: Virgil's words express
the very ethos of Hell, in this respect, as the reader well
knows by now. Cf. Beatrice's *exordium* addressed to Virgil
in *Inf.* II, 58–60; see also the note to those verses.

51. *fummo in aere*: See Ps. 36[37]:20: "Inimici vero
Domini . . . deficientes quemadmodum fumus deficient"
("And the enemies of the Lord . . . vanish; like smoke they
vanish"); Ps. 67:3[68:2]: "Sicut deficit fumus, deficiant"
("As smoke is driven away, so are they driven"); *Sapien.*
5:15, quoted below; *Aen.* V, 740: "et tenuis fugit ceu fumus
in auras" ("and passed like smoke into thin air").   *in
acqua la schiuma*: See Sapien. 5:15: "Quoniam spes impii
tamquam lanugo est quae a vento tollitur, et tamquam
spuma gracilis quae a procella dispergitur, et tamquam
fumus qui a vento diffusus est." ("Yes, the hope of the
wicked is like thistledown borne on the wind, and like
fine, tempest-driven foam; like smoke scattered by the
wind.") Also see Osee 10:7: "Transire fecit Samaria regem
suum quasi spumam super faciem aquae." ("Samaria hath
made her king to pass as froth upon the face of the water.")

52. *ambascia*: The wayfarer is panting from the exhausting
effort of his climb.

54. *s'accascia*: Scartazzini-Vandelli notes a relevant quota-
tion in Vincenzo Borghini. See Borghini, "Errori," p. 238:
"Chiamasi una persona accasciata, quando per vecchiezza o
infermità è molto mal condotta e quasi non si regge." ("A

person is called *accasciata* if, through old age or sickness, he is in a very bad way and can hardly stand on his feet.")

55. *Più lunga scala*: The "longer stair" proves to be the climb from the bottom of Hell up to the surface of the earth (*Inf.* XXXIV, 127–39); Virgil may also be referring to the climb to the top of Purgatory.

56. *costoro*: The hypocrites of the sixth *bolgia*.

58. *Leva'mi* = *mi levai*.

59. *sentia* = *sentiva*.

60. *forte e ardito*: Virgil exhorts the wayfarer with the same words as they are about to descend into Malebolge (see *Inf.* XVII, 81).

62–63. *ch'era ronchioso . . . di pria*: This reef is craggier and more difficult to climb than the one along which Dante and Virgil had come over the first five *bolge*, which may mean that all the reefs become increasingly so in the descent to the pit at the center. This reef is also higher here with respect to the banks it traverses. See "lo muro," vs. 73.

64. *andava* = *andavo*.

65. *l'altro fosso*: The seventh *bolgia*.

66. *a parole formar disconvenevole*: "Inept at forming words." The reason for this will soon be clear.

69. *ad ire parea mosso*: Some editors prefer the reading "ad ira" ("to anger") and believe this spirit to be the wrathful Vanni Fucci (vs. 125). But the souls of the thieves punished in this seventh *bolgia* are running here and there (for a reason that is soon evident), and Pietro di Dante explicitly defends the reading "ad ire" and rejects "ad ira." Scartazzini-Vandelli quotes the following from a manuscript of Pietro's commentary in the Vatican (Vaticano-Ottoboniano 2867, c. 71ᵛ): "Tamen qui eam [vocem] fecerat, videbatur motus non dicas *ad iram*, ut multi textus dicunt falso, sed dicas *ad ire*, idest ad iter." ("However, he who uttered that word

seemed, do not say, *moved to anger*, as many texts falsely read, but say seemed *to be moving*.") See M. Barbi (1934a), pp. 28–30, for a discussion of the two readings; see also Petrocchi's long note on this verse.

70. *li occhi vivi*: The meaning may be "my living eyes," i.e., "the eyes of my body," of a living man. But see *Inf.* XXIX, 54–55, which lines suggest that "my intent gaze" is the more probable meaning.

73. *da l'altro cinghio*: For this use of "da," see vs. 34 and the note. In vs. 34 the "cinghio" was termed "precinto," meaning the bank between the sixth and seventh *bolgia*.
    dismontiam lo muro: "Muro" here refers to the side of the bridgehead, which is a wall extending down from the top of the reef, on which the two now stand, to the bank that divides the seventh *bolgia* from the eighth, a bank that is much lower than the reef along which Dante and Virgil have been moving. The wall must have rough projections to enable the wayfarer to climb down it. See the description of the climb back up, *Inf.* XXVI, 13–15.

75. *affiguro = raffiguro*.

78. *si de' = si deve.*   *seguir*: "To carry out."

79–80. *Noi discendemmo . . . ripa*: The two wayfarers descend from the head of the bridge, where it abuts on the eighth bank, down the side of the bridgehead (which has been called a "wall" in vs. 73), and thus proceed to view the seventh *bolgia*, swarming with snakes, from the top of the bank.   *da la testa*: For this use of "da," see vs. 34 and the note.

82. *vidivi = vi vidi.*   *stipa*: See *Inf.* VII, 19; XI, 3. The *Anonimo fiorentino* comments: "Stipa è detta ogni cosa ch'è calcata et ristretta insieme, et questo è detto stipato." ("A thing is said to be a *stipa* when it is pressed and squeezed together [with other things]; and this is called *stipato*.")

83. *serpenti*: See Ecclus. 39:35–36: "Ignis, grando, fames et mors, omnia haec ad vindictam creata sunt; bestiarum

dentes et scorpii et serpentes, et romphaea vindicans in exterminium impios." ("In his treasury also, kept for the proper time, are fire and hail, famine, disease, ravenous beasts, scorpions, vipers, and the avenging sword to exterminate the wicked.")

84. *scipa*: The subject is "memoria." Buti comments: "La ricordanza di quelli serpenti ancora mi divide il sangue da' luoghi suoi, e fallo tornare al cuore come fa la paura." ("The memory of those snakes still drives my blood from its proper places, and makes it rush to my heart the way fear does.") See *Inf.* VII, 19, 21, where "scipa" is also rhymed with "stipa."

85. *Libia*: In ancient Greek geography, Libya was the name for North Africa, outside of Egypt. Later, divided into Marmarica and Cyrenaica, Libya became part of the Roman colony of Africa. See Lucan, *Phars.* I, 367; II, 417; IX, 711–14, 719–21 (quoted below); Ovid, *Metam.* IV, 617–20.

86–87. *chelidri, iaculi . . . anfisibena*: Dante apparently took his list of serpents from Lucan's description of the plagues of Libya (see *Phars.* IX, 711-14, 719-21):

> . . . tractique via fumante chelydri,
> Et semper recto lapsurus limite cenchris:
> Pluribus ille notis variatam tinguitur alvum
> Quam parvis pictus maculis Thebanus ophites.
>
> . . . .
> Et gravis in geminum vergens caput amphisbaena,
> Et natrix violator aquae, iaculique volucres,
> Et contentus iter cauda sulcare parias . . .

. . . the *chelydrus*, whose track smokes as it glides along; the *cenchris*, which moves ever in a straight line—its belly is more thickly chequered and spotted than the Theban serpentine with its minute patterns . . . the fell *amphisbaena*, that moves towards each of its two heads; the *natrix*, which pollutes waters, and the *iaculus*, that can fly; the *parias*, that is content to plough a track with its tail . . . .

88. *pestilenzie*: "Pestilential animals." Cf. the Latin *pestes*, the word used by Lucan (*Phars.* IX, 805) for the serpents of Africa ("Libycae pestes").

89–90. *l'Etiopia né . . . èe*: Ancient Ethiopia was a country west of the Red Sea, in northeast Africa, which included modern southern Egypt, the eastern Sudan, Eritrea, and modern northern Ethiopia—in other words, that part of Africa south from Egypt as far as Zanzibar. In vss. 85–90 Dante includes the desert areas that constituted Libya, Ethiopia, and the region near the Red Sea which some take to be Arabia and others Egypt.

90. *èe = è*. The form is found in prose in Dante's time.

91. *copia*: "Profusion" of serpents.

92. *nude*: Here as elsewhere Dante emphasizes the nakedness of the damned in order to heighten the reader's sense of their suffering. See n. to *Inf.* XIV, 19. The nude bodies of the thieves punished in this seventh *bolgia* are more exposed to punishment by snakes than they would be if they were clothed.

93. *sanza sperar pertugio o elitropia*: A taunting verse, particularly in its mention of the fact that there is no heliotrope here (why would there be?). The stone called heliotrope is meant, not the plant. See Pliny's description of the heliotrope (*Nat. hist.* XXXVII, lx, 165):

> Heliotropium nascitur in Aethiopia, Africa, Cypro, porraceo colore, sanguineis venis distincta. . . . Magorum inpudentiae vel manifestissimum in hac quoque exemplum est, quoniam admixta herba heliotropio, quibusdam additis precationibus, gerentem conspici negent.
>
> The heliotrope, which is found in Ethiopia, Africa and Cyprus, is leek-green in colour, but is marked with blood-red streaks. . . . Here, moreover, we have quite the most blatant instance of effrontery on the part of the Magi, who say that when the heliotrope plant is joined to the stone and certain prayers are pronounced over them the wearer is rendered invisible.

The meaning of the verse, then, is that these sinners have neither a hole into which they might crawl nor heliotrope to render them invisible. / Boccaccio based one of his most entertaining stories, *Decam.* VIII, 3 (vol. II, pp. 111–19), on the legendary power of the heliotrope to make the wearer invisible.

95. *quelle*: The serpents.

95–96. *quelle ficcavan . . . aggroppate*: The head and tail of the snake are thrust through the body of the sinner and tied in a knot in the front.

97. *da nostra proda*: The bank on which Dante and Virgil stand; see n. to vss. 79–80.

99. *là dove 'l collo a le spalle s'annoda*: The nape of the neck. The implication is that, in this instance, the serpent darts at the sinner furtively from behind.

100. *Né o sì tosto mai né ı si scrisse*: The *Anonimo fiorentino* comments: "Queste due lettere O et I si scrivono a uno tratto di penna; et pertanto si scrivono più velocemente che l'altre." ("These two letters, *O* and *I*, are written with one stroke of the pen; and therefore they can be written faster than the others.") But for this to be so, the *i* must be un-dotted (*ı*). Nor is there any reason to conceive the *i* as a capital *I*, which certainly could not be made with a single stroke of the pen; indeed, we should probably conceive it as a small *i*.

101–3. *com' el s'accese . . . distrutto*: See Lucan's description, *Phars.* IX, 761–88, of the miserable Sabellus (referred to in *Inf.* XXV, 95), who, after being bitten by a snake, melts completely away.

105. *e 'n quel medesmo ritornò*: See Virgil, *Georg.* IV, 444 (said of Proteus, after many transformations): "In sese redit." ("He returns to himself.")   *di butto = di botto* (see *Inf.* XXII, 130). On the form with *u* rather than *o*, see E. G. Parodi (1957), p. 223.

106. *per* = *da*.   *li gran savi*: Poets and others, one of whom is Ovid in this instance. See n. to vss. 107–11.   *si confessa*: "It is avowed."

107–11. *la fenice . . . fasce*: The phoenix is a mythical Arabian bird. Every five hundred years it burned itself on a pyre of incense and rose again from the ashes in the shape of a small worm, which on the third day developed into the full-grown bird. The phoenix often appears in ancient poetry, but Dante's account probably is taken from Ovid, *Metam.* XV, 392–402.

> una est, quae reparet seque ipsa reseminet, ales:
> Assyrii phoenica vocant; non fruge neque herbis,
> sed turis lacrimis et suco vivit amomi.
> haec ubi quinque suae conplevit saecula vitae,
> ilicet in ramis tremulaeque cacumine palmae
> unguibus et puro nidum sibi construit ore,
> quo simul ac casias et nardi lenis aristas
> quassaque cum fulva substravit cinnama murra,
> se super inponit finitque in odoribus aevum.
> inde ferunt, totidem qui vivere debeat annos,
> corpore de patrio parvum phoenica renasci . . .

But there is one bird which itself renews and repro-duces its own being. The Assyrians call it the phoenix. It does not live on seeds and green things, but on the gum of frankincense and the juices of amomum. This bird, you may know, when it has completed five cen-turies of its life, builds for itself a nest in the topmost branches of a waving palm-tree, using his talons and his clean beak; and when he has covered this over with cassiabark and spikes of smooth nard, broken cinnamon and yellow myrrh, he takes his place upon it and so ends his life amidst the odours. And from his father's body, so they say, a little phoenix springs up which is destined to attain the same length of years.

Also see Brunetto Latini (*Tresor* I, clxii, 1-3); Lactantius, "Carmen de ave Phoenice" (in E. Baehrens, 1881, pp. 253–62); Pliny, *Nat. hist.* X, ii, 3–5.

109. *pasce*: See Dante's use of this verb in *Inf.* XIII, 101, applied to the Harpies.

111. *l'ultime fasce*: The nest that the bird constructs for itself, in which to die. See Ovid, *Metam.* XV, 395-400, quoted in n. to vss. 107–11.

112-17. *quel che cade . . . sospira*: The epileptic was often said to be afflicted with the "falling sickness."

112. *como = come*, frequent in early Italian.

113. *per forza di demon*: "Possessed by a devil." See Mar. 1:26; 9:16–26[17–27]; Luc. 4:35.

114. *oppilazion*: "Stoppage" of the vital passages, particularly from the heart to the brain. See Giovanni Battista Gelli, *Letture* IX, 4, p. 446 (quoted also by Scartazzini-Vandelli):

> *Oppilare* è uno verbo latino, che significa serrare e chiudere. Laonde son chiamati dai medici quegli che hanno di sorte chiuse e serrate, per essere ripiene di vapori grossi, le vene, che gli spiriti e la virtù nutritiva non posson passare e andare per le parti del corpo dove fa di bisogno loro. E [se] si fa per sorte tale oppilazione in quelle vie che hanno a passare gli spiriti che vanno da 'l cuore al cervello, l'uomo cade subitamente senza sentirsi in terra; e da questo nasce il mal caduco e le sincope, chiamate da noi *venirsi meno*, e altri accidenti simili.

> *Oppilare* is a Latin word meaning "to close" or "to shut." Hence, that is what physicians call those people whose veins are somewhat closed or shut because they are filled with thick vapors, so that the spirits and the nutritive virtues cannot pass and go on to the parts of the body that need them. And [if] perchance such a stoppage should take place in the paths through which the spirits must pass in going from the heart to the brain, a man will immediately fall unconscious to the ground. And from this is born the falling sickness and

the syncopes, which we call fainting, and other similar ills.

114. *lega*: In the sense of restricting the vital functions.

116. *de la = per la*.

120. *croscia*: See Gelli, *Letture* IX, 4, p. 446 (quoted also by Scartazzini-Vandelli): "metafora tolta da le pioggie e da l'acque, che si dicono *crosciare*, quando piovono e si versono abbondantissimamente" ("a metaphor taken from rains and waters, which are said [to] *crosciare*, when they rain down and fall in great abundance"). The use of *crosciare* here also suggests the descent of a lightning bolt.

122. *Io piovvi*: See *Inf.* VIII, 83; XXX, 95.

123. *poco tempo è*: "A little before" 1300. See n. to vs. 125.
    gola: Literally, "throat"; the *bolgia*, as if it had swallowed the sinner. See *Inf.* XIII, 96 and the note.

125. *Vanni Fucci*: Illegitimate son ("mule") of Guelfuccio di Gerardetto de' Lazzari, of a noble family of Pistoia. Fucci was a violent partisan of the Neri. There are various accounts of the theft to which Dante here refers. According to one, in 1293, together with a notary by the name of Vanni della Monna and one Vanni Mironne, also of Pistoia, Vanni Fucci broke into and plundered the treasury of San Jacopo in the church of San Zeno at Pistoia, for which crime a namesake of his, with whom he had deposited the booty, was hanged, Vanni having revealed his name in order to save the life of a certain Rampino di Francesco Foresi, who was on the point of being executed as the culprit. Benvenuto, who tells the story at some length, says that although Fucci "bannitus saepe propter multa maleficia enormia, nequiter et nefarie perpetrata, tamen aliquando de nocte stabat in civitate, et cum pravissimis conversabatur" ("was often banned from the city on account of his enormous misdeeds, he nevertheless managed to slip in from time to time, to spend the night in town, and consort with wicked men"). See S. Ciampi (1810), pp. 57–67, for another version of the story; G. Fallani (1961), pp. 126–28, for a review of the case and

pertinent bibliography; P. Bacci (1892), p. 15, for a contemporary account from an old record of the miracles of the Virgin at Pistoia.

126. *bestia*: This appears to have been a true nickname. The *Anonimo fiorentino* comments: "Et perchè egli era bestiale, fu chiamato Vanni bestia." ("And because he was so bestial, he was called Vanni the beast.") / On the word "bestia," see M. Barbi (1934b), pp. 273-74.   *tana*: The "lair" of wild beasts. Matt. 21:13 may be relevant in this context: "Vos autem fecistis illam speluncam latronum." ("But you have made it a den of thieves.")

127. *Dilli = digli.   mucci*: "Slip away," "escape"; see E. G. Parodi (1957), p. 282. Scartazzini-Vandelli calls attention to Vincenzio Buonanni's definition of the word. See Buonanni, *Discorso*, p. 157: "Dicesi smucciare di una cosa, che per la liscezza esce di mano, e che non si può tenere forte, antzi quanto più si strigne, più sguscia, e scappa, e fugge di mano." ("*Smucciare* is used for things that slip out of one's hands because they are so slithery. They are things one cannot hold tight—in fact, the tighter you hold them, the more they slip, flee, and get out of your hands.") This is a fitting term for a thief.

128. *pinse = spinse.*

129. *ch'io 'l vidi omo di sangue e di crucci*: See n. to vs. 125. If Vanni Fucci had been condemned to Hell as "a man of blood and rages," he would have been relegated to the river of boiling blood—the first *girone* of the seventh circle— where bestiality in the form of violence is punished. (Rinier Pazzo, mentioned in *Inf.* XII, 137, is referred to in a contemporary document as a man of blood; see E. Regis, 1912, p. 1093, n. 2.) Dante might have seen and known Vanni Fucci in the war against Pisa, 1289-93, in which Fucci served among the soldiers of Florence. See the reference to Caprona in *Inf.* XXI, 95.

130. *s'infinse*: From *infingersi*, "to feign." The verb can also mean "to hesitate," but "to dissemble" or "to feign"

seems the preferable meaning here; see M. Barbi (1934b), p. 214.

131. *ma drizzò verso me l'animo e 'l volto*: See *Aen.* XI, 800–801: "Convertere animos acris oculosque tulere / cuncti ad reginam Volsci." ("All the Volscians turned their eager eyes and minds upon the queen.")

132. *e di trista vergogna si dipinse*: Vanni Fucci colors with dismal shame at being seen and known. A sense of shame at being recognized becomes more and more common among the sinners in lowest Hell.

135. *che quando fui de l'altra vita tolto*: "Tolto" does not necessarily imply that Vanni Fucci met a violent death. On the meaning of this word, see M. Barbi (1934b), p. 274.

136. *Io non posso negar quel che tu chiedi*: Vanni Fucci cannot deny that which the wayfarer is bound to learn—that those punished in this seventh *bolgia* were thieves. Accordingly he confesses to the thievery that put him there.

137. *in giù son messo tanto*: In saying "so far" Fucci means that he has been put farther down in Hell than might have been expected, since he might have been put in the seventh circle instead of the eighth. See n. to vs. 129.

138. *ladro*: The word comes in the initial position, which is emphatic. Only now does the wayfarer realize that thieves are punished in this *bolgia*. *a la sagrestia d'i belli arredi*: The treasury; see n. to vs. 125. / It is also possible to construe *d'i belli arredi a la sagrestia*. *d'i = dei*.

139. *altrui*: Rampino di Francesco Foresi; see n. to vs. 125.

140. *Ma perché di tal vista tu non godi*: Vanni Fucci assumes that as a White, Dante might rejoice at the sight of a member of the Black party—such as Vanni Fucci—being punished here. *godi = goda*.

141. *se mai sarai di fuor da' luoghi bui*: The sharp thrust in these words is evident; they imply that Dante may not be released from Hell but be kept there for his sins after all.

142. *annunzio*: "Prophecy."

143–50. *Pistoia in pria . . . feruto*: Vanni Fucci hastens to predict the downfall of the Bianchi, Dante's own party, foretelling how, after helping to expel the Neri from Pistoia, they will themselves be driven out of Florence and finally be defeated at Campo Piceno. This is the fourth such prophecy in the *Inferno* (see *Inf.* VI, 64–72; X, 79–81; XV, 64). See also notes to vss. 143, 144, 145–50, below.

143. *Pistoia in pria d'i Neri si dimagra*: The expulsion of the Neri from Pistoia came about in May 1301. Villani (VIII, 45) records the event as follows: "Negli anni di Cristo 1301, del mese di Maggio, la parte bianca di Pistoja coll'aiuto e favore de' bianchi che governavano la città di Firenze, ne cacciarono la parte nera, e disfeciono le loro case, palazzi e possessioni." ("In the year of Christ 1301, in the month of May, the Whites of Pistoia, with the help of the Whites who were governing Florence, expelled the Black faction, destroying their houses, palaces, and possessions.")   *d'i = dei*.

144. *poi*: "In consequence," implying a sort of just retribution.   *Fiorenza rinova gente*: On All Saints' Day 1301, Charles of Valois arrived in Florence, having been allowed to enter the city unopposed, on the strength of his promise to hold the balance between the two parties and to maintain peace. However, no sooner had he obtained command of the city than he treacherously espoused the cause of the Neri and threw the whole of Florence into confusion. In the midst of the panic Corso Donati, the exiled leader of the Neri, made his way back into the city ("Florence renovates her people"), broke open the prisons, and released the prisoners, who, together with his own adherents, attacked and pillaged the houses of the Bianchi for five days. Charles of Valois, meanwhile, in spite of his promises, made no attempt to interfere. During the following year, in a series of orders of banishment, the Bianchi were expelled from Florence, Dante being among those who were condemned to exile.

   modi: Her mode of government, when this passed to the Neri.

145–50. *Tragge Marte vapor . . . feruto*: Vanni Fucci's prophecy becomes very obscure, dealing now in meteorological terms. Torraca (1921, pp. 365–66) calls attention to a passage in Ristoro d'Arezzo which helps to explain these terms. See Ristoro d'Arezzo, *Della comp.* VII, 2, p. 229:

Stando su nell'aere vapori acquei e vapori aerei e terrestri, per la contrarietà ch'è in loro combatte insieme l'uno coll'altro; e se'l vapore acqueo moltiplica nell'aire e truova entro per esso delli vapori ignei, [questi] si raccolgono insieme; imperciò che ogni simile trae volentieri al suo simile: ed anco per forza del vapore acqueo, ch'è moltiplicato d'attorno a questo igneo dell'aere; e lo vapore acqueo, moltiplicandosi d'attorno a questo, combatte con esso e costrignelo insieme per forza, sì che questo non può patire in quello luogo, rompe lo valore acqueo dal lato più debole, e corre entro per esso; e infiammandosi e facendo fuoco e fuggendo, va facendo romore entro per lo vapore acqueo: come lo ferro infiammato, che va facendo romore entro per l'acqua, ed allora udimo quello romore, lo quale noi chiamiamo tuono, e vedemo la fiamma, la quale noi chiamiamo baleno.

Up in the air, there are watery vapors as well as airy and earthly vapors. Because of the contrariety that is in them, each fights with the other. Now, if the watery vapors multiply in the air, and find therein some igneous vapors, these latter gather together, for similar things move toward each other; besides, they are pressed by the force of the watery vapors, which have multiplied around these igneous vapors in the air. The watery vapors, multiplying about the igneous vapors, fight with these, and compress them by force, so that the igneous vapors cannot remain in that place, but break the watery vapors where they are weakest, and rush into them, and igniting and bursting into flames, and escaping, they make a noise within the watery vapor, just as hot iron makes noise in water. Then we hear that noise which we call thunder, and we see the flame, which we call lightning.

Literally, Fucci's prophecy is as follows: Mars, god of war, draws forth from Val di Magra a vapor (*igneo* being understood), which becomes enveloped in turbid clouds. Between the igneous vapor and the clouds there shall be combat in an impetuous and harsh storm over Campo Piceno, whereupon the igneous vapor will break through the mist (i.e., the enveloping clouds) with violence.

The commentators generally agree that by the "vapor" drawn by Mars from the Val di Magra is meant Moroello Malaspina, a Guelph leader who in 1288 acted as general of the Florentines in their campaign against the Ghibellines of Arezzo and thereafter held important offices in various cities. From 1301 to 1312 Moroello was constantly in arms on behalf of the Neri of Tuscany, and during the campaigns of the latter against the Ghibellines of Pistoia he added greatly to his military fame.

There is some doubt as to what particular battle is referred to here, since neither Villani nor Compagni makes mention of any battle on the Campo Piceno, a district near Pistoia. Some take the allusion to be to the siege and capture, in 1302, of the stronghold of Serravalle by the Florentine Neri and the Lucchese, under Moroello Malaspina, in the course of their attack upon Pistoia. See, for example, F. Torraca (commentary and 1903). Others hold that the reference is to the siege and final reduction, in 1305–6, of Pistoia itself by the Florentines and Lucchese, on which occasion Moroello also was a leader. See M. Barbi (1934b), pp. 214–15; A. Bassermann (1902), pp. 155–68. Ever since the expulsion of the Bianchi from Florence in 1302, Pistoia had remained the only stronghold in Tuscany of the Bianchi and the Ghibellines. After the capture of Pistoia on April 10, 1306, the fortifications were razed and the territory divided between Florence and Lucca. See Villani (VIII, 52 and 82) for descriptions of the respective battles.

It is not clear why the Campo Piceno was so called. It is at some distance from the ancient Picenum, which was a district on the Adriatic coast. As Butler and others have pointed out, the wrongful application of the name probably arose from a misunderstanding of a passage in Sallust (*Bellum Catilinae* LVII, 1–3) on the defeat of Catiline:

> Reliquos Catilina per montis asperos magnis itineribus in agrum Pistoriensem abducit eo consilio, uti per tramites occulte perfugeret in Galliam Transalpinam. At Q. Metellus Celer cum tribus legionibus in agro Piceno praesidebat, ex difficultate rerum eadem illa existumans quae supra diximus Catilinam agitare. Igitur ubi iter eius ex perfugis cognovit, castra propere movit ac sub ipsis radicibus montium consedit, qua illi descensus erat in Galliam properanti.

> The remainder Catiline led by forced marches over rugged mountains to the neighbourhood of Pistoria, intending to escape secretly by cross-roads into Transalpine Gaul. But Quintus Metellus Celer, with three legions, was on the watch in the Picene district, inferring from the difficulty of the enemy's position that he would take the very course which I have mentioned. Accordingly, when he learned through deserters in what direction Catiline was going, he quickly moved his camp and took up a position at the foot of the very mountains from which the conspirator would have to descend in his flight into Gaul.

Villani (I, 32), who expressly refers to Sallust as his authority, says that Catiline, on leaving Fiesole, "arrivò di là ov'è oggi la città di Pistoja nel luogo detto Campo a Piceno, ciò fu di sotto ov'è oggi il castello di Piteccio" ("arrived where today stands the city of Pistoia, at the place called Campo Piceno, which was below where today stands the castle of Piteccio"). Villani goes on to say: "Alla fine dell'aspra battaglia Catellina fu in quello luogo di Piceno sconfitto e morto con tutta sua gente." ("At the end of the bitter battle, at that place called Piceno, Catiline was defeated and killed, together with all his soldiers.") Some of the commentators on Dante hold this view, for the same reason. For example, Benvenuto says: "Picenum appellatus est ager apud Pistorium, in quo olim fuit debellatus Catilina, ut patet apud Sallustium." ("The countryside near Pistoia, where Catiline was defeated, is called Piceno, as Sallust attests.") And John of Serravalle states: "Ille campus, qui est prope Pistorium, in quo devictus fuit Cathellina, vocatur Picenum a Salustio." ("The field near Pistoia, where Catiline was defeated, is called Piceno by Sallust.")

145. *Tragge = trae.*

148. *fia combattuto = sarà combattuto.* This is an impersonal construction.

149. *repente*: On this word, see M. Barbi (1934b), p. 243.

151. *debbia = debba.*

CANTO XXV

2. *le fiche*: An obscene gesture made by thrusting out (up, at God, in this case) the fist with the thumb between the fore and middle finger. Apparently the gesture was often made with both hands; it would seem to have been used especially at Pistoia, as Villani records (VI, 5): "In su la rocca di Carmignano avea una torre alta settanta braccia, e ivi su due braccia di marmo, che faceano le mani le fiche a Firenze." ("Upon the stronghold of Carmignano there was a tower seventy *braccia* high, and up there two marble arms that made the *fiche* toward Florence with their hands.") Carmignano was a stronghold in Pistoiese territory which the Florentines had taken in 1228. A. Chiappelli (1905, p. 229) also mentions this statue. Tommaseo has pointed out a curious law in the Statute of Prato: "Chiunque *ficas fecerit vel monstraverit nates versus coelum vel versus figuram Dei* o della Vergine, paga dieci lire per ogni volta; se no, frustato." ("Whoever has made the *fiche* or has shown his buttocks toward the image of God or the Virgin must pay ten lire for each offense; otherwise he will be whipped.") Torraca cites *Il Fiore* CLXXVI, 14: "e facciagli sott'al mantel la fica" ("and make the *fiche* at him under his cloak").

4. *fuor = furono*, with all the force of a narrative tense, implying that "they were my friends for what they then did."

5. *li = gli*.

6. *vo' = voglio.   diche = dica.*

7. *rilegollo* (pronounced *rilegòllo*) *= lo rilegò*. The serpents now rebind Vanni Fucci as he had been bound before, like the others (see *Inf.* XXIV, 94–96); this time they mean especially to still his tongue and his arms so that he can no longer blaspheme God.

8. *ribadendo*: From *ribadire*, "to rivet."

9. *con esse = con le braccia*.

10. *ché = perché.   stanzi*: From *stanziare*, "to decree officially." G. Manuzzi (1865, p. 369), under the entry "stanziare," gives an example of the word's use: "Nel detto anno . . . si stanziaro per lo Comune di Firenze, e si cominciaro . . . le mura nuove della città di Firenze." ("In that year . . . the commune of Florence officially decreed and began work on . . . the new walls of the city of Florence.")

12. *il seme tuo*: Those who founded the city of Pistoia (Pistoria). It was near Pistoia that Catiline was defeated in 62 B.C. According to legend the town was founded by the survivors of Catiline's forces. Villani says (I, 32):

> I tagliati e' fediti della gente di Catellina scampati di morte della battaglia, tutto fossono pochi, si ridussero ov'è oggi la città di Pistoja, e quivi con vili abitacoli ne furono i primi abitatori per guerire di loro piaghe. E poi per lo buono sito e grasso luogo multiplicando i detti abitanti, i quali poi edificaro la città di Pistoja, e per la grande mortalità e pistolenza che fu presso a quel luogo e di loro gente e di Romani, le posero nome Pistoja; e però non è da maravigliare se i Pistolesi sono stati e sono gente di guerra fieri e crudeli intra loro e con altrui, essendo stratti del sangue di Catellina e del

rimaso di sua così fatta gente, sconfitta e tagliata in battaglia.

The wounded and maimed men in Catiline's army who had escaped death in battle, few though they were, repaired to where now is the city of Pistoia. Here, in vile habitations, while recovering from their wounds, they became its first inhabitants. Then, because of the good site and the fertile earth, the inhabitants multiplied; and later, they built the city of Pistoia. And because of the many deaths and the pestilences that took place in that area, killing many of their people as well as Romans, they called it Pistoia. We need not wonder, therefore, that the Pistoiese have been and are fierce and cruel fighters among themselves and against others; for they are descended from the blood of Catiline and of the remains of his army, which was defeated and cut down in battle.

However, it is also possible to interpret "seme" as "product," in which case the reference may be to the civil strife that began in Pistoia and came to Florence (see *Inf.* XXIV, 143–50 and the notes), but this reading seems less satisfactory.

14. *in Dio*: Cf. the Latin *in Deum*.

15. *quel che cadde a Tebe*: Capaneus, who is brought to mind by Vanni Fucci's irreverence (see *Inf.* XIV, 46–72). Though punished in Hell for entirely different crimes, both Capaneus and Vanni Fucci are seen as *superbi*, or "proud" (see *Inf.* XIV, 64; and in the present canto, vs. 14), hence as *acerbi* or "unripe" (see *Inf.* XIV, 48 and the note; in the present canto, see vs. 18). The proud soul is "green" like an unripened fruit and is "short of full formation" (see *Purg.* X, 128–29). In Canto XIV, Capaneus the blasphemer is punished by having to lie supine, looking toward God, on the burning sand under the rain of fire. Here in Canto XXV, the centaur with the fire-breathing dragon on his shoulders comes shouting after Vanni Fucci (vs. 18), "Where is the unripe one?" for he proposes to ripen him with his fire. Thus in both cases the proud sinner is "ripened"

(humbled) by fire for his blasphemy.   *muri*: Note in the episode of Capaneus (*Inf.* XIV, 44, 46, 48) the same rhyme in *-uri* as here in vss. 11, 13, 15.

16. *si fuggì*: "Fled" from the approaching centaur (vs. 17).
che non parlò più verbo: Indeed, the first snake had wrapped itself about his throat to prevent him from saying more.

19. *Maremma*: This region has been referred to already in the *Inferno* as a haunt of wild beasts (see *Inf.* XIII, 7–9). Buti comments that in the Maremma "abondano molte serpi, intanto che a Vada è uno monasterio bellissimo, lo quale per le serpi si dice essere disabitato." ("Snakes abound, so much so that at Vada there is a very beautiful monastery which is said to be uninhabited because of the snakes.")

20. *la groppa*: The snakes lie along "the croup," the equine part of the centaur.

21. *nostra labbia*: The dragon lies down over "our semblance," the human part of the centaur.

22. *dietro da = dietro a*.   *la coppa*: "The nape" of the human neck. The *Anonimo fiorentino* comments: "La coppa chiama quello concavo che fanno le spalle dirietro, sotto il nodo del collo." ("The *coppa* is that hollow which the shoulders form in the back, below the nape of the neck.")

23. *li = gli*.   *draco = drago* (see "laco" for *lago*, vs. 27).

24. *quello*: The dragon.   *affuoca*: See *Inf.* VIII, 74.
qualunque s'intoppa: "Whoever meets up [with it]"; *con esso* is understood.

25. *Caco*: Cacus, the son of Vulcan and Medusa, was a fire-breathing, half-human monster who lived in a cave on the Aventine hill and preyed on the inhabitants of the district. He stole from Hercules some of the cattle (four bulls and four heifers, according to Virgil) that Hercules had taken from the monster Geryon in Spain. So that Hercules would not be able to follow their tracks Cacus dragged them back-

ward into his cave by their tails; but their bellowing disclosed their hiding place to Hercules, who attacked Cacus and strangled him (see *Aen.* VIII, 193–267).

Dante's monster differs in two striking respects from that of Virgil and Ovid. First, probably due to a misunderstanding of Virgil, who calls Cacus "semihominis" or "half human" (*Aen.* VIII, 194), Dante makes his creature a centaur. Second, Dante's Cacus does not belch fire from his own mouth, but has a dragon on his shoulders which belches fire (for him).

Dante most likely borrowed other details of his description from Virgil (see *Aen.* VIII, 193–99):

> hic spelunca fuit, vasto summota recessu,
> semihominis Caci facies quam dira tenebat,
> solis inaccessam radiis; semperque recenti
> caede tepebat humus, foribusque adfixa superbis
> ora virum tristi pendebant pallida tabo.
> huic monstro Volcanus erat pater: illius atros
> ore vomens ignis magna se mole ferebat.

> Here was once a cave, receding to unfathomed depth, never visited by the sun's rays, where dwelt the awful shape of half-human Cacus; and ever the ground reeked with fresh blood, and, nailed to its proud doors, faces of men hung pallid in ghastly decay. This monster's sire was Vulcan; his were the black fires he belched forth, as he moved his mighty bulk.

With regard to the mode of Cacus' death, Dante apparently followed not Virgil but Livy (I, vii, 7): "Cum vadentem ad speluncam Cacus vi prohibere conatus esset, ictus clava . . . morte occubuit." ("When [Hercules] came towards the cave, Cacus would have prevented his approach with force, but received a blow from the hero's club, and . . . gave up the ghost.") It is possible that Dante also had in mind a passage in Ovid, in which Cacus is killed by four blows of Hercules' (Alcides') club (*Fasti* I, 575–78):

> occupat Alcides, adductaque clava trinodis
> ter quater adverso sedit in ore viri.

> ille cadit mixtosque vomit cum sanguine fumos
>   et lato moriens pectore plangit humum.

But Alcides was too quick for him; up he heaved the triple-knotted club, and brought it thrice, yea four times down full on the foeman's face. He fell, vomiting smoke mixed with blood, and dying beat the ground with his broad breast.

On the one hand, Cacus has the function here in Canto XXV of guardian, like "his brothers" (vs. 28) the centaurs who guard the first *girone* of the seventh circle (see Canto XII). He is also punished in Hell as a sinner. Like Vanni Fucci, he is covered with snakes, and like Fucci he is a creature of "blood and rages" (see *Inf.* XXIV, 129; in the present canto, vss. 17, 27), condemned to this seventh *bolgia* for fraudulent theft (see n. to vs. 29).

26. *'l sasso*: See Virgil's description of the Aventine hill, where Cacus had his cave (*Aen.* VIII, 190–92):

> iam primum saxis suspensam hanc aspice rupem,
> disiectae procul ut moles desertaque montis
> stat domus et scopuli ingentem traxere ruinam.

Now first look at this rocky overhanging cliff, how the masses are scattered afar, how the mountain-dwelling stands desolate, and the crags have toppled down in mighty ruin!

27. *di sangue fece spesse volte laco*: See *Aen.* VIII, 195–96: "Semperque recenti / caede tepebat humus." ("And ever the ground reeked with fresh blood.")

28. *fratei = fratelli*, the centaurs who guard Phlegethon in the first *girone* of the seventh circle.

29. *per lo furto che frodolente fece*: By its position and function as an adverb, "frodolente" is emphatic here, and serves to stress precisely the particular nature of the sin that has condemned Cacus to Malebolge. The reference is to the crafty way in which Cacus concealed his theft of Hercules' cattle, by dragging them backward, causing their tracks to

point in the wrong direction. Both Virgil and Ovid have this detail. See *Aen.* VIII, 205-11:

> at furiis Caci mens effera, ne quid inausum
> aut intractatum scelerisve dolive fuisset,
> quattuor a stabulis praestanti corpore tauros
> avertit, totidem forma superante iuvencas.
> atque hos, ne qua forent pedibus vestigia rectis,
> cauda in speluncam tractos versisque viarum
> indiciis raptos saxo occultabat opaco.

But Cacus, his wits wild with frenzy, that naught of crime or craft might prove to be left undared or unessayed, drove from their stalls four bulls of surpassing form, and as many heifers of peerless beauty. And these, that there might be no tracks pointing forward, he dragged by the tail into his cavern, and, with the signs of their course thus turned backwards, he hid them in the rocky darkness.

Note Virgil's use of "craft" ("doli," vs. 205) to describe the method of the crime. Also see Ovid, *Fasti* I, 550: "Traxerat aversos Cacus in antra ferox." ("Fierce Cacus had dragged the bulls backwards into his cave.")

30. *a vicino*: In *Aen.* VIII, 201-4, it is told how Hercules brought the herd of Geryon to the Aventine hill; hence the cattle were "near" Cacus' lair.

31. *cessar = cessarono.* *biece*: Archaic for *bieche*, "crooked," "evil."

33. *cento*: Signifies an approximate number. In any case, Dante has added considerably to the number of blows mentioned in his sources (see the accounts of Ovid and Livy quoted in n. to vs. 25). *e non sentì le diece*: Cacus was dead even before the tenth blow fell on him; but the phrase has a derisive ring to it, comparable to that of *Inf.* XVIII, 38-39.

34-35. *ed el trascorse, e tre spiriti venner*: The first "and" correlates the second action to the first, but with the special shade of meaning suggested by M. Barbi (1934a, p. 23), who points out that before Virgil has said more than a few words, Cacus has already disappeared. Then the second "and" coordinates another action in this same way.

35. *tre spiriti*: The spirits prove to be Agnello, Buoso, and Puccio (see vss. 68, 140, 148, respectively). *sotto noi*: Virgil and Dante are now on the bank above; the phrase serves as a further pointer to the fact that they do not descend into the bottom of the *bolgia* (see *Inf.* XXIV, 79-80).

36. *s'accorse*: A singular verb with a plural subject. The two poets have been watching Cacus so intently that they have not seen the three spirits who have come toward them.

37. *gridar = gridarono*. The spirits shout to the wayfarers, but then do not follow up their question, since other things soon claim all their attention.

38. *nostra novella*: "Our discourse," referring to Virgil's words about Cacus.

39. *intendemmo = attendemmo*.

40. *ei seguette*: Impersonal construction: "it came to pass."

42. *che l'un nomar un altro convenette*: The subject of "convenette" is the whole phrase "l'un nomar un altro."

43. *Cianfa*: According to the early commentators, Cianfa was a member of the Donati family of Florence. The *Chiose anonime* says: "Cianfa fu cavaliere de' Donati, e fu grande ladro di bestiame, e rompia botteghe e votare le cassette." ("Cianfa was a knight of the Donati family, and was a great cattle thief. He broke into shops and emptied out the strongboxes.") A Dominus Cianpha de Donatis, who is possibly the Cianfa referred to by Dante, is mentioned in a document published by A. Gherardi (1896, p. 135), from which it appears that he was a member of a council for the Sesto di Porta San Piero in 1283. He died before 1289 (see M. Barbi, 1899, p. 208; 1934b, p. 308). / When Dante hears the name, he knows that Cianfa is a Florentine and suspects that the other souls also may be his fellow towns-

men.   *fia = sarà*, the future tense used in the dubitative mode: "where ever can he be."

44. *per ch' = per il che.*

45. *mi puosi 'l dito su dal mento al naso*: Dante places his forefinger over his lips in the familiar gesture urging silence. From this point on, the two wayfarers become mere spectators.

46. *Se tu se' or, lettore*: A kind of address to the reader that signals some amazing thing (cf. *Inf.* XVI, 127–29) and generates suspense.

48. *il mi = me lo.*

49–50. *Com' io . . . e un serpente*: The "e" here has the value of *ed ecco.*

49. *levate in lor le ciglia*: This standard expression has lost its literal sense, "to raise the eyebrows," since the wayfarer is standing on the bank above the souls, and is looking down.

50. *un serpente*: This is Cianfa, whom his companions "lost" when he became just such a reptile.

52. *li = gli.*

54. *poi li addentò e l'una e l'altra guancia*: We should probably imagine that the snake does this by turning its head to one side and opening its mouth wide enough over the face of the other (Agnello) to sink its fangs into both cheeks simultaneously.

56. *miseli = gli mise.   tra 'mbedue*: Refers to "le cosce" (vs. 55).

60. *avviticchiò*: The verb is based on *viticcio*, a tendril of a vine, thus harmonizing with the image of the ivy (vss. 58–59).

61. *appiccar = appiccarono.*

62. *mischiar = mischiarono.*

63. *né l'un né l'altro*: The pronouns refer to "colore" in the preceding verse, thus preparing for the simile that follows. The *Anonimo fiorentino* comments: "Egliono si mischiorono sì i colori, il serpente collo spirito et lo spirito col serpente, che feciono uno terzo colore." ("The serpent and the spirit intermixed their colors in such a manner that they produced a third color.")

64–66. *come procede . . . 'l bianco more*: The image is exact, and with "procede" is made vivid, gradual, and progressive, as a good metamorphosis should be. Lana, the *Anonimo fiorentino*, and others understand *"papiro"* (vs. 65) to mean "cotton paper"; others take it to mean "wick," while Benvenuto is undecided between the two. But, precisely because of the verb "procede" and the qualifier "suso," "paper" would seem to be what Dante intends.

64. *innanzi da = innanzi a*.

68. *Agnel*: According to the early commentators, this first spirit (see vs. 35) is Agnello or Agnolo de' Brunelleschi (a Ghibelline family of Florence), who first joined the Bianchi and then went over to the Neri. Only the *Chiose anonime* gives pertinent details about him:

> Questo Agnello fu de' Brunelleschi di Firenze; e infino picciolo votava la borsa al padre e a la madre, poi votava la cassetta a la bottega, e imbolava. Poi da grande entrava per le case altrui, e vestiasi a modo di povero, e faciasi la barba di vecchio, e però il fa Dante così trasformare per li morsi di quello serpente come fece per furare.

> This Agnello was a member of the Brunelleschi family of Florence. Even as a boy, he used to empty the purses of his father and mother; later, he would empty the strongbox in the shop and steal other things. Then, as an adult, he broke into other people's houses. He would dress like a pauper and wear the beard of an old man. And for this reason, Dante has him transformed through the serpent's bites, as he was when he stole.

69–72. non se' né due né uno . . . ov' eran due perduti:
The story in Ovid's *Metamorphoses* that most closely re-
sembles this one of Cianfa the snake and Agnello the man
recounts the merging into one body of the nymph Salmacis
and Hermaphroditus, the son of Mercury (Hermes) and
Venus (Aphrodite)—hence the word "hermaphrodite." See
particularly the moment of the actual merging (*Metam.*
IV, 373–79):

> vota suos habuere deos; nam mixta duorum
> corpora iunguntur, faciesque inducitur illis
> una. velut, si quis conducat cortice ramos,
> crescendo iungi pariterque adolescere cernit,
> sic ubi conplexu coierunt membra tenaci,
> nec duo sunt et forma duplex, nec femina dici
> nec puer ut possit, neutrumque et utrumque videntur.

The gods heard her prayer. For their two bodies, joined
together as they were, were merged in one, with one
face and form for both. As when one grafts a twig on
some tree, he sees the branches grow one, and with com-
mon life come to maturity, so were these two bodies
knit in close embrace: they were no longer two, nor
such as to be called, one, woman, and one, man. They
seemed neither, and yet both.

A. Dobelli (1897) elucidates the parallel between the meta-
morphoses in Dante and in Ovid.

71. n' = ci.

73. Fersi = si fecero. quattro liste: "Four stripes," the
two arms of the man and the two front feet of the snake.

74. 'l casso: The chest.

75. fuor = furono.

76. primaio = primiero. casso = cassato, "destroyed,"
"blotted out." See *Inf.* XXVI, 130; XXX, 15.

78. e tal sen gio con lento passo: Note the slow rhythm of
the verse. *gio = gì (andò).*

79. *Come 'l ramarro sotto la gran fersa*: Lizards are a familiar sight in Italy and most Mediterranean countries, during the hot days of summer, along roads bordered with stone walls. *fersa = ferza, sferza*.

80. *dì canicular*: In Europe, the "dog days" fall between July 23 and August 11, when Sirius, the Dog Star, rises with the sun. *sepe*: Archaic for "siepe."

82. *sì pareva = tal pareva*.

83. *un serpentello*: This proves to be the soul of Francesco Guercio de' Cavalcanti (see n. to vs. 151). *acceso*: The meaning is uncertain. Some commentators take it to be that the little snake is literally afire or is breathing fire from its mouth, thus causing the smoke described in vss. 92–93. Others understand that the snake's eyes are flaming with anger. G. G. Ferrero and S. A. Chimenz (1954, p. 31, n. 16) discuss the various interpretations.

84. *livido e nero come gran di pepe*: Porena thinks that although the peppercorn is black, Dante is perhaps referring to grains of crushed pepper which, mixing the inside of the corn and fragments of the shell, result in a color that is "partly livid and partly black."

85–86. *quella parte . . . nostro alimento*: The navel.

86. *a l'un*: Buoso, named in vs. 140.

95. *Sabello*: Sabellus, a Roman soldier of Cato's army in Africa. Lucan relates that in the desert of Libya he was stung by a venomous serpent called a "seps," whose bite caused his body to putrefy and fall into a mass of corruption (see *Phars.* IX, 763–76):

> . . . in crure Sabelli
> Seps stetit exiguus; quem flexo dente tenacem
> Avolsitque manu piloque adfixit harenis.
> Parva modo serpens sed qua non ulla cruentae
> Tantum mortis habet. Nam plagae proxima circum
> Fugit rupta cutis pallentiaque ossa retexit;
> Iamque sinu laxo nudum sine corpore volnus.

439

Membra natant sanie, surae fluxere, sine ullo
Tegmine poples erat, femorum quoque musculus omnis
Liquitur, et nigra destillant inguina tabe.
Dissiluit stringens uterum membrana, fluuntque
Viscera; nec, quantus toto de corpore debet,
Effluit in terras, saevum sed membra venenum
Decoquit, in minimum mors contrahit omnia virus.

When a tiny *seps* struck in the leg of . . . Sabellus and
clung there with barbed fang, he tore it off and pinned
it to the sand with his javelin. Though this reptile is
small in size, no other possesses such deadly powers. For
the skin nearest the wound broke and shrank all round,
revealing the white bone, until, as the opening widened,
there was one gaping wound and no body. The limbs
are soaked with corrupted blood; the calves of the legs
melted away, the knees were stripped of covering, all
the muscles of the thighs rotted, and a black discharge
issued from the groin. The membrane that confines the
belly snapped asunder, and the bowels gushed out. The
man trickles into the ground, but there is less of him
than an entire body should supply; for the fell poison
boils down the limbs, and the manner of death reduces
the whole man to a little pool of corruption.

95. *Nasidio*: Nasidius, another Roman soldier who served
with Cato in Africa. According to Lucan, in the desert of
Libya he was stung by a poisonous serpent called a "prester,"
whose bite caused his body to swell up till his corselet burst
and he died (*Phars.* IX, 790–97):

Nasidium Marsi cultorem torridus agri
Percussit prester. Illi rubor igneus ora
Succendit, tenditque cutem pereunte figura
Miscens cuncta tumor; toto iam corpore maior
Humanumque egressa modum super omnia membra
Efflatur sanies late pollente veneno;
Ipse latet penitus congesto corpore mersus,
Nec lorica tenet distenti pectoris auctum.

Nasidius, once a tiller of Marsian soil, was smitten by
a burning *prester*. His face grew fiery red, and swelling

distended the skin till all shape was lost and all features
were confounded; then, as the strong poison spread, the
hurt, larger than the whole body or than any human
body, was blown out over all the limbs; the man himself
was buried deep within his bloated frame, nor could his
breast-plate contain the growth of his swollen chest.

96. *si scocca*: Literally, "is shot forth," as an arrow from a
bowstring. The tone of the expression adds to the note of
challenge; it means, freely, "what I now let fly." See *Purg.*
XXV, 17–18: "Scocca / l'arco del dir."

97. *Cadmo*: Cadmus, son of Agenor, king of Phoenicia,
and brother of Europa, was the founder of Thebes. As a
penalty for slaying a dragon sacred to Mars, he was trans-
formed into a serpent. Apparently Dante borrowed several
touches for his own description (vss. 103–38) from Ovid's
account (*Metam.* IV, 576–80, 586–89):

> . . . ut serpens in longam tenditur alvum
> durataeque cuti squamas increscere sentit
> nigraque caeruleis variari corpora guttis
> in pectusque cadit pronus, commissaque in unum
> paullatim tereti tenuantur acumine crura.
>
> . . . .
> . . . lingua repente
> in partes est fissa duas, nec verba volenti
> sufficiunt, quotiensque aliquos parat edere questus,
> sibilat . . .

He was stretched out in long snaky form; he felt his
skin hardening and scales growing on it, while irides-
cent spots besprinkled his darkening body. He fell prone
upon his belly, and his legs were gradually moulded
together into one and drawn out into a slender, pointed
tail. . . . His tongue was of a sudden cleft in two; words
failed him, and whenever he tried to utter some sad
complaint, it was a hiss.

Dante may also have had in mind Ovid's account of the
transformation by Ceres of a boy into a lizard (*Metam.* V,
453–58):

441

offensa est neque adhuc epota parte loquentem
cum liquido mixta perfudit diva polenta:
conbibit os maculas et, quae modo bracchia gessit,
crura gerit; cauda est mutatis addita membris,
inque brevem formam, ne sit vis magna nocendi,
contrahitur, parvaque minor mensura lacerta est.

She was offended, and threw what she had not yet
drunk, with the barley grains, full into his face.
Straightway his face was spotted, his arms were changed
to legs, and a tail was added to his transformed limbs;
he shrank to tiny size, that he might have no great
power to harm, and became in form a lizard, though
yet smaller in size.

97. *Aretusa*: Arethusa, one of the Nereids, was nymph of
the fountain of Arethusa in the island of Ortygia near
Syracuse; while bathing in the stream, she was seen by the
god Alpheus, who pursued her; on appealing to Diana she
was changed into the fountain of the same name, but Al-
pheus continued to pursue her under the sea and to mingle
his stream with the waters of the fountain. Dante alludes
to Ovid's account (*Metam.* V, 572–641).

100. *due nature*: "Two [different] natures," those of man
and serpent. See the reference to the breast of the centaur
(*Inf.* XII, 84) as the place "where the two natures are con-
joined."

101–2. *forme . . . matera*: The "form" is the soul, in the
Thomistic sense, which informs the *materia* or "substance"
of the body; see *Inf.* VI, 106–7 and the note.

104. *fesse = fendette*, past absolute of *fendere*; "split."

105. *feruto = ferito*; Buoso, who has been wounded in
the navel. *ristrinse = congiunse.* *orme*: "Footprints,"
"feet."

106. *seco stesse*: "Between them," "to each other."

107. *s'appiccar = s'appiccarono.*

108. *che si paresse* = *che apparisse*.

109. *Togliea* = *toglieva*. The subject is "la coda"; the object, "figura."

110. *che si perdeva là*: "Which was being lost there."   *là*: In the man.   *la sua pelle*: The serpent's skin.

111. *quella di là*: The skin of the man.   *dura*: "Hard" like a serpent's.

115. *li piè di rietro*: "The hind feet" of the snake.

116. *lo membro che l'uom cela*: The penis.

117. *del suo*: From his penis.   *porti*: Past participle of *porgere*; "extended" to form the two hind feet.

119. *'l pel*: The human hair.   *suso*: On the skin.

121. *l'un*: Guercio, who was first a serpent and is now almost a man.   *l'altro*: Buoso, who was first a man and will soon be a serpent.

122. *non torcendo però le lucerne empie*: Each continues to stare into the other's eyes. See Matt. 6:22: "Lucerna corporis tui est oculus tuus." ("The lamp of the body is the eye.")

123. *ciascun cambiava muso*: The *Anonimo fiorentino* comments: "La faccia dell'uomo divenìa muso di serpente, e 'l muso del serpente divenìa faccia d'uomo." ("The man's face became a serpent's face, and the serpent's face became a man's face.")

124. *il* = *lo*; his "muzzle." "Il" is the object of "trasse."   *ver'* = *verso*.

126. *uscir* = *uscirono*.   *le gote scempie*: The smooth cheeks, at first devoid of ears.

127-29. *ciò che non corse in dietro . . . quanto convenne*: From the part of the serpent's muzzle that is in excess the nose and lips are formed.

443

130. *Quel che giacea*: As in vs. 121, the reference is to Buoso, who had been a man and is now almost a full-formed snake.

131. *per = dentro*.

132. *face = fa.   lumaccia = lumaca*.

133–34. *la lingua . . . si fende*: To become the forked or "split" tongue of a serpent. See Ovid's description of the transformation of Cadmus into a snake (*Metam.* IV, 586–87): "Ille quidem vult plura loqui, sed lingua repente / in partes est fissa duas." ("He wanted to say much more, but his tongue was of a sudden cleft in two.")

135. *'l fummo resta*: "The smoke ceases," as does the metamorphosis, now complete in both figures.   *resta*: Cf. modern *ristà*.

138. *sputa*: Torraca observes that in antiquity and during the Middle Ages, it was believed that human saliva had power against serpents. He cites Fra Giordano da Rivalto, *Prediche inedite* LX (1867 edn., p. 307): "[Dicesi] dello sputo dell'uomo ch'è veleno del serpente, ed all'uomo non fa male." ("Wherefore it is said of human spittle that it is poisonous to the serpent, and it does not harm men.") Also see Lucretius, *De rerum natura* IV, 638–39: "Est itaque ut serpens, hominis quae tacta salivis / disperit ac sese mandendo conficit ipsa." ("For this case is like the serpent, which when touched by man's spittle perishes and gnaws itself to death.")

139. *li = gli.   le novelle spalle*: His newly formed shoulders.

140. *a l'altro*: To Puccio Sciancato; see vs. 148 and the note.

140–41. *I' vo' che Buoso . . . questo calle*: Buoso (see n. to vs. 140, below) is already doing precisely that. The phrase implies: "Let him run a while as I have had to do!"

140. *vo' = voglio.   Buoso*: The identity of this Buoso, the second of the three spirits (see vs. 35), is uncertain; the

commentators are not agreed even as to his family name. For a review of the documents, see M. Barbi (1934b), pp. 305–22, who argues that the Buoso in question was probably Buoso di Forese Donati, who died about 1285, and hence is not to be identified with the Buoso Donati referred to in *Inf.* XXX, 44, as some commentators believe.

141. *calle*: The bottom of the *bolgia*.

142. *zavorra*: The term serves to lump together all the sinners in this seventh *bolgia* (which by implication is compared to the hold of a ship) as so much "stuff," or worthless merchandise.

143. *mutare = mutarsi*; the word refers to the single or simple transformation of two forms (here Cianfa the snake and Agnello the man) into one.   *trasmutare = tramutarsi*; the word refers to the double metamorphosis of two forms which exchange their matter (here Buoso the man and Guercio the serpent). In *De mon.* II, vii, 10, Dante refers to the *Metamorphoses* of Ovid as "De Rerum Transmutatione" ("Transmutations of Things").

143–44. *e qui mi scusi . . . la penna abborra*: Regardless of the etymology of "abborra" (see n. to vs. 144, below), it seems reasonable to let the use of the verb by Dante in Canto XXXI serve as the controlling factor in determining its meaning here in Canto XXV. In the phrase "nel maginare abborri" (*Inf.* XXXI, 24), the verb clearly means "to go wrong," "to stray from the truth," and such is undoubtedly its connotation here. This sense, and the excuse of which it is a part, must be seen within a broader context to be fully understood, since it represents a passing apology on the part of the poet for indulging so long in spectacle for spectacle's sake. His pen may have "gone wrong," but if so then let the "novità," the strangeness of the entire drama in this *bolgia*, be his plea.

144. *fior*: Here used as an adverb: "somewhat," "a little"; see *Inf.* XXXIV, 26.   *abborra*: The meaning of this verb has long been debated by the commentators. Dante uses it

again in *Inf*. XXXI, 24, where its meaning is clearer from the context, and seems there to be "to wander," "to be confused." However, arguing from the alleged etymon *borra*, E. G. Parodi (1957, p. 357) observes that Dante's use of the word reflects the fact that in certain dialects *abborrare* is the equivalent of *abbarrucciare*, "to throw things around in confusion," "to do something poorly and hurriedly" (see n. to vss. 143–44, above).

146. *smagato*: "Distraught," "dismayed" (which is, in fact, the English cognate, from the OFr *esmaier*).

147. *poter = poterono. quei*: The souls of Puccio Sciancato and Guercio (see notes to vss. 148, 151). *fuggirsi*: "To run away," as souls do constantly in this *bolgia* (see "ad ire . . . mosso," *Inf*. XXIV, 69).

148. *Puccio Sciancato*: The third spirit (see vs. 35) is Puccio Galigai, nicknamed Sciancato ("lame"), of the Galigai family of Florence. As a Ghibelline he was banished with his children in 1268; in 1280, along with others of his party, he entered into a peace pact with the Guelphs. A gloss in a manuscript cited by M. Barbi (1899, p. 216) says: "Si novellano belli furti e legiadri." ("It is recounted that he committed beautiful and graceful thefts.") Though punished along with the others in this *bolgia* for thievery, Puccio undergoes no bodily change. According to the same manuscript, he was "cortese furo a tempo, e però non era trasmutato; overo perchè li suoi furti erano di die e non di notte, e s'era veduto, sì si gabava" ("a mannerly thief, and therefore he was not transformed; or, because his thefts were committed by day and not by night, and he cared nothing if he was seen").

151. *l'altr' era quel che tu, Gaville, piagni*: This spirit, who first came on the scene as a little snake (vs. 83), now, by the reference to Gaville, is identifiable as Francesco de' Cavalcanti, nicknamed Guercio ("squinting"). The *Ottimo Commento* refers to him as Guelfo. He was a member of the Cavalcanti family of Florence, and was murdered by the inhabitants of Gaville, a village in the Upper Val d'Arno not

far from Figline; the death was speedily avenged by the
Cavalcanti, who in their fury are said to have almost dis-
peopled Gaville. The *Anonimo fiorentino* says of Guercio:

> Questi è . . . messer Francesco Cavalcanti, che fu morto
> da certi uomini da Gaville, ch'è una villa nel Val d'Arno
> di sopra nel contado di Firenze, per la qual morte i con-
> sorti di messer Francesco molti di quelli da Gaville
> uccisono et disfeciono; et però dice l'Auttore che per
> lui quella villa ancor ne piagne, et per le accuse et
> testimonianze et condennagioni et uccisioni di loro, che
> per quella cagione ne seguitorono, che bene piangono
> ancora la morte di messer Francesco.

> This is . . . Messer Francesco Cavalcanti, who was
> murdered by certain men of Gaville, a town in the
> Upper Val d'Arno in the Florentine countryside. Be-
> cause of this murder, the relatives of Messer Francesco
> killed and tormented many of the inhabitants of Gaville.
> For that reason the author says that that town is still
> weeping on his [Francesco's] account. And, because of
> the accusations, the testimony, the sentences, and the
> murders perpetrated against them as a result of that
> act, they indeed still do weep for the death of Messer
> Francesco.

CANTO XXVI

1-3. *Godi, Fiorenza . . . spande*: The bitter irony of the
opening verses, sealed so powerfully by the third, is evident
enough. A. Chiappelli (1930) points out the possible echo
in vs. 2 of an inscription on the west front of the Palazzo
del Podestà in Florence that exalts the city with the words:
"que mare, que terram, que totum possidet orbem" ("who
rules the sea, the land, and, in fact, the whole world").

4-5. *Tra li ladron . . . vergogna*: The five Florentine thieves
whom the wayfarer has just encountered in the seventh
bolgia are all of noble or upper-class families. The stress
falls on "cotali" and again on "onde" ("wherefore").

6. *orranza* = *onoranza*. See *Inf*. IV, 74. The irony continues.

7. *Ma se presso al mattin del ver si sogna*: For the ancient
belief that dreams that come just before dawn are prophetic,
see Horace, *Satires* I, x, 33: "post mediam noctem . . . cum
somnia vera" ("after midnight, when dreams are true"). See
also Ovid, *Heroides* XIX, 195-96: "namque sub aurora, iam
dormitante lucerna, / somnia quo cerni tempore vera so-
lent" ("for, just before dawn, when my lamp was al-
ready dying down, at the time when dreams are wont to
be true"). Sapegno refers to Iacopo Passavanti's men-

448

tion of this belief; see Passavanti, *Lo specchio*, p. 351: "Quegli sogni che si fanno intorno all'alba del dì, secondo che dicono, sono i più veri sogni che si facciano." ("Those dreams we have at the dawn of day are, they say, the truest dreams one can have.") At just such an hour on three successive days in Purgatory, the wayfarer has a dream which proves to be true and prophetic. See *Purg.* IX, 13-20; XIX, 1-7; XXVII, 94-99.

9. *di quel*: *Male*, "disaster," is the noun understood.
Prato: Prato is a town in Tuscany, about eleven miles northwest of Florence, on the road to Pistoia. The allusion here is not altogether clear (having the obscurity proper to certain prophecies), for the people of Prato seem in the main to have been on friendly terms with the Florentines. Some interpreters, however, take this as a reference to the feeling of discontent and envy that a small state would naturally harbor against a powerful and overbearing neighbor. Or the meaning may be, as Butler suggests, that even Prato, generally her friend, is now wishing evil to Florence.

Others see an allusion to Cardinal Niccolò da Prato, who, after the failure of his attempt to make peace between the rival factions in Florence in the spring of 1304, departed in anger, leaving the city under an interdict and excommunicating the inhabitants. To this malediction of the cardinal were commonly attributed the terrible calamities that shortly after befell the city of Florence, calamities to which Dante's "prediction" (of events that had in fact already taken place) doubtless refers. Thus Villani (VIII, 69), in recording the cardinal's departure from Florence, says:

Il legato cardinale . . . subitamente si partì di Firenze a dì 4 Giugno 1304, dicendo a' Fiorentini: *Dappoichè volete essere in guerra e in maladizione, e non volete udire nè ubbidire il messo del vicario di Dio, nè avere riposo nè pace tra voi, rimanete colla maladizione di Dio e con quella di santa Chiesa,* scomunicando i cittadini, e lasciando interdetta la cittade, onde si tenne, che per quella maladizione, o giusta o ingiusta, non fosse sentenzia e gran pericolo della nostra cittade, per le avversità e pericoli che le avvennero poco appresso, come innanzi faremo menzione.

The cardinal legate . . . immediately left Florence, on the fourth of June 1304, saying to the Florentines: "Since you want to be at war and under a curse, and will neither hear nor obey the messenger of the Vicar of God, or have peace and quiet among yourselves, you will be left with the curse of God and of the Holy Church." He excommunicated the citizens and put the city under interdict. Wherefore it was believed that this curse, justly or unjustly, became a judgment and a great danger to our city, because of the adversities and dangers that befell it soon afterward, as I shall mention hereafter.

Villani (VIII, 70–71) then goes on to relate how in that same year the Ponte alla Carraia, which in those days was made of wood, suddenly gave way under the excessive weight of a great crowd of people who were watching a show on the river and a large number of them were drowned. According to Benvenuto they were watching a depiction of Hell and the torments of the damned:

Inter alios illi de burgo sancti Floriani fecerunt proclamari publice, quod quicumque vellet scire nova de alio mundo, deberet venire kalendis maii ad pontem Carrariae; et in Arno flumine ordinaverunt solaria super barcis et naviculis. Et fecerunt quamdam simulatam repraesentationem inferni cum ignibus et aliis poenis et suppliciis; et homines transfiguratos, et daemonia horribilia et alios nudos sub specie animarum. Et videbantur daemones iniicere animas inter ista varia et crudelia tormenta cum maximis clamoribus et horrendis stridoribus visu et auditu. Novitate cuius spectaculi totus populus concurrit ad videndum. Unde pons Carrariae, qui tunc erat de lignamine, onustus multitudine magna nimis, cecidit in Arnum cum his, qui erant desuper. Ex quo multi mortui sunt et suffocati, et multi destructi de persona . . . . Et hoc fuit augurium alterius maioris damni de proximo eventuri ipsi civitati.

The people of the St. Florian quarter had it publicly proclaimed that whoever wanted to have news of the other world should come to the Ponte alla Carraia at the beginning of May. They set up floats on boats and barges in the river Arno, and arranged a sort of representation of Hell, with fire and other pains and torments. There were men in disguises, horrible demons and naked people representing souls. Among other cruel torments, one could see the demons attacking the souls with great clamor and horrible screams, terrible to hear and behold. Because this kind of representation was new, everyone went to see it. Because of that, the Ponte alla Carraia, which was then made of wood, was so overloaded by the great crowd that it crashed into the Arno with all the people on it. Many were drowned and killed and many bodies were broken. . . . This was an augury of even greater harm that would come to the city in the near future.

Moreover, not long after, a great fire broke out in the heart of the city and burned down over seventeen hundred palaces, towers, and houses, destroying an immense amount of treasure and merchandise. / E. G. Parodi (1908b, p. 26), among others, takes the reference to be to the driving out of the Neri from Prato, April 6, 1309.

10. *saria* = *sarebbe*.

11. *Così foss' ei*: "So were it." The shift to a note of sadness is evident in what follows.

13-14. *su per le scalee . . . pria*: The wayfarers now climb back up what was termed a "muro" in *Inf.* XXIV, 73—i.e., the steep, rough side of the bridgehead—to the top of the bank that divides the seventh from the eighth *bolgia*.

14. *i borni*: Petrocchi's reading "iborni," instead of the usual reading *i borni*, reflected in the present translation, is explained in a long note of his with reference to A. Pagliaro (1961, pp. 201-9) and others. In this reading it would have the meaning "pale."

15. *mee = me*. See *èe* and other examples discussed by E. G. Parodi (1957), p. 243.

18. *lo piè sanza la man non si spedia*: Apparently the reef becomes rougher and steeper as the poets climb toward the crest of the arching bridge.   *non si spedia = non si spediva*, "was unable to make its way."

19–24. *Allor mi dolsi . . . nol m'invidi*: This fervent little prayer generates a certain suspense for the reader, who as yet has seen nothing. The verbs in the present tense following "ridoglio" ("drizzo," "affreno," "soglio") temporarily place the emphasis on Dante the poet, who has returned from his journey and is now recalling and relating what he saw in the eighth *bolgia*.

21. *'ngegno*: The poet's genius. On the use of "ingegno" here, see n. to *Inf*. II, 7. It may be recalled that at the beginning of his journey the poet invoked his own "alto ingegno" (*Inf*. II, 7). Later the father of Guido Cavalcanti referred to the poet's making the journey through Hell "per altezza d'ingegno" (*Inf*. X, 58–60). Moreover, at the summit of Mount Purgatory, Beatrice says of Dante that he was highly endowed both naturally and divinely (*Purg*. XXX, 109–12). And much later, in the *Paradiso*, when the wayfaring Dante reaches the constellation of Gemini, under which he declares he was born, he thanks those stars for giving him the "ingegno" he has (*Par*. XXII, 112–14).

22. *corra*: The verb suggests a journey.

23. *stella bona*: Singular for plural, the reference in this case being to Gemini (see n. to vs. 21).   *miglior cosa*: The "grazie divine" of *Purg*. XXX, 112.

24. *'l ben*: Dante's own genius.   *ch'*: The *che* is redundant in this construction, a repetition of the relative pronoun common in early Italian prose as well as in verse.   *io stessi nol m'invidi*: "I may not deny it to myself" (hence "deprive myself of it"). Cf. the Latin *invidere sibi*.   *stessi = stesso*.

25. *Quante*: Modifies "lucciole" (vs. 29), the object of "vede." The subject is "villan."

26-27. *nel tempo . . . ascosa*: In summertime, or, more precisely, during the summer solstice, when the sun ("colui che 'l mondo schiara") "hides his face least from us," i.e., when the nights are shortest.

28. *come la mosca cede a la zanzara*: At dusk.

30. *dov' e' vendemmia e ara*: Plowing is usually done in the spring, and grape harvest takes place in the fall. It is summertime now, and there is respite from such labors.

33. *là 've 'l fondo parea*: The summit of the arch of the bridge.   *'ve = ove.   parea = appariva.*

34-42. *E qual colui . . . invola*: Although the simile applies to all the flames in the *bolgia*, it characteristically singles one out now, thus preparing for the selection of one from among the many. See *Inf.* V, 40-49 and the note; also especially *Inf.* XV, 16-21.

34. *qual*: Modifies "carro," vs. 35.   *colui che si vengiò con li orsi*: The prophet Elisha. See IV Reg. 2:23-24:

> Ascendit autem inde in Bethel; cumque ascenderet per viam, pueri parvi egressi sunt de civitate et illudebant ei, dicentes: Ascende, calve, ascende, calve. Qui cum respexisset, vidit eos et maledixit eis in nomine Domini; egressique sunt duo ursi de saltu, et laceraverunt ex eis quadraginta duos pueros.

> And [Eliseus] went up from thence to Bethel. And as he was going up by the way, little boys came out of the city and mocked him, saying: Go up, thou bald head. Go up, thou bald head.
>   And looking back, he saw them, and cursed them in the name of the Lord: and there came forth two bears out of the forest, and tore of them two and forty boys.

34. *vengiò*: Past absolute of *vengiare* (= *vendicare*).

35. *vide 'l carro d'Elia*: See IV Reg. 2:11–12:

> Cumque pergerent et incedentes sermocinarentur, ecce currus igneus et equi ignei diviserunt utrumque; et ascendit Elias per turbinem in caelum.
>
> Eliseus autem videbat et clamabat: Pater mi, pater mi, currus Israel et auriga eius. Et non vidit eum amplius . . . .
>
> And as they went on, walking and talking together, behold a fiery chariot, and fiery horses parted them both asunder: and Elias went up by a whirlwind into heaven.
>
> And Eliseus saw him, and cried: My father, my father, the chariot of Israel, and the driver thereof. And he saw him no more.

The reference to an Old Testament episode serves to distance the narrative and remove it from the familiar everyday scene suggested by the simile of the peasant in vss. 25–33.

36. *erti*: Dante's description of the erect posture of the horses, an original detail, makes the image more vivid. (Cf. the poet's probable source, the Biblical passage quoted in n. to vs. 35.)   *levorsi = si levarono*.

39. *sì come nuvoletta*: Cf. "per turbinem" in the Biblical passage quoted in n. to vs. 35. For a "nuvoletta" as a conspicuous feature of an ascension, see *Vita nuova* XXIII, 25.

40. *tal*: The comparison is with the "carro d'Elia," vs. 35.   *ciascuna*: The "fiamma" of vs. 38.

40–41. *per la gola del fosso*: See "gola," *Inf.* XXIV, 123. Porena observes that this might even be an explanatory genitive: "that throat which is the ravine."

41. *nessuna*: The "flame" of vs. 38.   *'l furto*: "The theft," as is made clearer by the verb "invola" in the following verse. Such terms serve to point up the *contrapasso* of the punishment: the punishing flames are thus furtive, fraudulent. See "il foco furo," *Inf.* XXVII, 127.

42. *e ogne fiamma un peccatore invola*: The reader is told that the false counselors punished in this eighth *bolgia* are enveloped in flames, before Virgil explains this to his charge. When he does (vss. 47–48), Dante then indicates that he had already "judged it to be so" (vss. 50–51).

43. *surto = sorto*, past participle of *surgere* (see vs. 53). Dante is not only standing as erect as possible, in order to see into the *bolgia*, but he is also leaning forward, as the following two verses make clear.

45. *urto = urtato*. On this truncated form, see E. G. Parodi (1957), p. 260.

46. *atteso*: "Intent." See *Inf*. XIII, 109.

47. *Dentro*: The word comes in an emphatic position. *dai = ai*. See "dentro da" in vss. 58 and 64.

48. *catun = ciascuno.   di quel ch' = di quello da cui. inceso = acceso*. See *Inf*. XXII, 18.

50. *m'era avviso*: Cf. the Latin *mihi visum erat*.

52–54. *chi è . . . miso?* Here again is a simile which in its first part presents a human figure within a fire and by its classical aura distances the narrative, as did the Old Testament comparison in vss. 35–36 (see n. to vs. 35, above).

54. *miso = messo*.

54. *Eteòcle*: Eteocles was the son of Oedipus, king of Thebes, and Jocasta, and twin brother of Polynices. When the brothers compelled Oedipus to abdicate and leave Thebes, Oedipus prayed to the gods that the twins might be eternally at enmity with each other. Eteocles and Polynices agreed to reign in Thebes alternately year by year; but when Eteocles' term had expired, he refused to resign the throne to his brother. Polynices consequently invoked the aid of Adrastus, king of Argos, and thus originated the famous war of the Seven against Thebes (see *Inf*. XIV, 68–69 and n. to *Inf*. XIV, 69). The prayer of Oedipus was now answered, for in the course of the war Polynices and

Eteocles killed each other in single combat. Their bodies
were burned on the same funeral pyre, but so intense was
the hatred between them, even after death, that the flame
from the pyre divided in two as it ascended. For his descrip-
tion of the divided flame, Dante probably drew on Statius,
Theb. XII, 429-32, 441:

> Ecce iterum fratres: primos ut contigit artus
> ignis edax, tremuere rogi et novus advena busto
> pellitur; exundant diviso vertice flammae
> alternosque apices abrupta luce coruscant.
>
> . . . .
> . . . vivunt odia improba, vivunt.

Once more behold the brothers: as soon as the devour-
ing fire touched the body, the pile shook, and the new-
comer is driven from the pyre; a flame streams up with
double head, each darting tongues of flashing light. . . .
Alive, ay, alive is that impious hatred.

See also Lucan, *Phars.* I, 549-52:

> . . . Vestali raptus ab ara
> Ignis, et ostendens confectas flamma Latinas
> Scinditur in partes geminoque cacumine surgit
> Thebanos imitata rogos. . . .

From Vesta's altar the fire vanished suddenly; and the
bonfire which marks the end of the Latin Festival split
into two and rose, like the pyre of the Thebans, with
double crest.

56. *Ulisse*: Ulysses of Ithaca, son of Laertes and father by
Penelope of Telemachus, was one of the principal Greek
heroes in the Trojan War and the hero of Homer's *Odyssey*.
He undertook, with Diomedes, to decoy the youthful
Achilles away from the island of Skyros and to steal the
Palladium, a wooden image on the preservation of which
the safety of the city of Troy depended (see vs. 63 and the
note), and he is supposed to have been the originator of the
stratagem of the wooden horse by means of which Troy
was taken. / The source of Dante's account of the death of
Ulysses, which the hero himself relates in this canto, is un-

known. It is at variance with the prophecy of Tiresias in the *Odyssey* (XI, 134–37)—with which Dante had no direct acquaintance—whereby a peaceful death from the sea is predicted for Ulysses (see, however, A. T. Murray's translation, which reads "death shall come to thee thyself far from the sea," and his comment on the possible—and more natural—translation "from out the sea"). Dante's account varies also from the story, current in the Middle Ages, given by the so-called Dictys Cretensis in the *Ephemeris belli Troiani* (VI, 15), of how Ulysses met his death at the hand of Telegonus, his son by Circe. It is possible, as B. Nardi (1949, pp. 153–54) suggests, that Dante's idea was suggested to him by the voyage in 1291 of the Genoese brothers Vivaldi, who sailed out past Gibraltar and into the west, seeking a route to India, and were never heard of again.

Diomede: Diomedes, son of Tydeus and Deipyle, was king of Argos and one of the famous Greek heroes who fought against Troy.

56–57. *e così insieme . . . come a l'ira*: Even as Ulysses and Diomedes together incurred the wrath of God in committing the fraudulent deeds now to be named, so do they together incur His punishment by fire.

59. *l'agguato del caval*: The famous wooden horse which the Greeks constructed as a pretended atonement for the Palladium (see n. to vs. 63) which Ulysses and Diomedes had stolen from Troy. The Trojans, taken in by the treacherous story of Sinon, a Greek who let himself be captured (see *Inf.* XXX, 98), dragged the horse, which was full of armed Greeks, into the midst of the city. In the middle of the night Sinon let out his comrades, who fell suddenly upon the unsuspecting Trojans and thus made themselves masters of Troy. Virgil describes these events in the *Aeneid* (II, 13–290), but he makes no mention of Diomedes in connection with the strategy of the horse. Evidently Dante understood that Diomedes was involved with Ulysses in this as in the other events to which the shade of Ulysses now refers.

59–60. *che fé la porta . . . seme*: The stratagem of the wooden horse brought about the departure of Aeneas and his band from fallen Troy and ultimately the founding of Rome by him.

61. *Piangevisi = vi si piange.   entro*: Adverb, "within."

62. *Deidamìa*: Daughter of Lycomedes, king of Skyros, with whom Thetis left her son Achilles, disguised in woman's clothes, in order that he might not take part in the expedition against Troy. After Deidamia had become the mother of Pyrrhus (or Neoptolemus) by Achilles, the latter, yielding to the persuasion of Ulysses, who together with Diomedes had penetrated his disguise, abandoned her and sailed to Troy. Deidamia died of grief for him. Cf. *Inf.* V, 65, n. See Statius, *Achilleid* I, 536 to II, 26. In *Purg.* XXII, 114, Deidamia is said to be among those who are in Limbo; hence, since Virgil is himself consigned to Limbo, he may have knowledge of this story of Achilles directly from her.

63. *Palladio*: The Palladium was a wooden image of Pallas Athena, said to have been sent from heaven by Jupiter to Ilus, the legendary founder of Troy, as a gift. On its preservation within the walls of Troy was believed to depend the safety and prosperity of the city. The theft of the Palladium by Diomedes and Ulysses is recorded by Virgil (*Aen.* II, 162–70).

67. *facci = faccia.   niego*: "Denial."

69. *del disio*: The desire that Virgil, knowing Dante's thoughts, then renders articulate in his question to Ulysses, vs. 84.   *ver' = verso.*

72. *si sostegna = si astenga.*

73. *concetto = concepito.*

74–75. *ch'ei sarebbero schivi . . . detto*: The traditional pride and haughtiness of the Greek constitute part of the reason for Virgil's words here, no doubt; but the fact that Dante is a modern, of a time and culture remote from those of ancient Greece and such heroes as these, enters into the matter, too. Virgil, poet of ancient Rome, would be much closer to the two Greek heroes. Indeed, as Benvenuto observes in his comment on vs. 84: "Sic est verum quod autor devenerit in cognitionem istorum mediante Virgilio." ("Thus it is true that the author made their acquaintance through Virgil.") This understanding of the reason Virgil gives, which has puzzled many commentators, is borne out in *Inf.* XXVII, 33, where Dante is in fact encouraged to speak with another hero because he is an Italian, i.e., a modern. In short, Virgil's injunction accentuates the poetic distancing of the story to be told by Ulysses, helping to raise it to the loftiness associated with tragedy. See Virgil's "alta tragedìa," *Inf.* XX, 113; also his "alti versi" in vs. 82 of the present canto.

75. *fuor* = *furono:*

78. *audivi* = *udii.*

80–81. *s'io meritai . . . s'io meritai . . . :* The repetition of "s'io meritai" is highly rhetorical and raised toward the lofty style of tragedy, while the appeal in itself is an instance of *captatio benevolentiae* ("gaining the good will of another"—see *Inf.* II, 58–60 and the note), since it concerns the fame of these two shades in the world of the living, as immortalized by Virgil in his "alti versi" (vs. 82). See *Aen.* IV, 317 (Dido to Aeneas): "si bene quid de te merui" ("if ever I deserved well of thee").

84. *perduto:* The meaning of "perduto" can be understood on the purely literal level in the light of its use in medieval romance. As Scartazzini-Vandelli points out, a knight who has not returned from an adventurous voyage and is presumed dead is described as "lost." On this word see also P. Rajna (1920), pp. 224–27. Only in retrospect will the reader know that "perduto" can bear another meaning here (see *Purg.* I, 131–32). *gissi* = *si gì (si andò).*

85. *Lo maggior corno:* As elsewhere in the poem, greater moral stature is signified by greater physical size. Cf., for example, *Inf.* X, 33, 53; XIII, 32; XVIII, 83. *la fiamma*

antica: The adjective too serves to distance and remove to a focus of great antiquity the action to be narrated.

87. *come quella cui vento affatica*: When the reader learns that it is a whirlwind ("turbo," vs. 137) that sends the hero and his companions to their death, this simile acquires greater meaning. See Horace's use of "laborant" to describe a wind in the following passage from the *Odes* (II, ix, 6–8):

> . . . aut Aquilonibus
> querqueta Gargani laborant
> et foliis viduantur orni . . .

Nor are Garganus' oak groves always lashed by the blasts of the North and the ash trees reft of their leaves.

88. *menando = dimenando*.

89. *come fosse la lingua*: See *Inf.* XXVII, 16–18, where the manner in which the voice finds its way up through the flame is indicated more precisely. The principle of *contrapasso* is evident in the punishing flame's being likened to a tongue, for the sin punished in this *bolgia* is fraudulent counsel—false advice given by the tongue.

90–120. *Quando mi diparti' . . . canoscenza*: Among the possible sources for Dante's conception of Ulysses is a passage in Cicero, *De fin.* V, xviii, 48–49:

> Videamus animi partes, quarum est conspectus illustrior; quae quo sunt excelsiores, eo dant clariora indicia naturae. Tantus est igitur innatus in nobis cognitionis amor et scientiae ut nemo dubitare possit quin ad eas res hominum natura nullo emolumento invitata rapiatur. Videmusne ut pueri ne verberibus quidem a contemplandis rebus perquirendisque deterreantur? ut pulsi recurrant? ut aliquid scire se gaudeant? ut id aliis narrare gestiant? ut pompa, ludis atque eiusmodi spectaculis teneantur ob eamque rem vel famem et sitim perferant? Quid vero? qui ingenuis studiis atque artibus delectantur, nonne videmus eos nec valetudinis nec rei familiaris habere rationem omniaque perpeti ipsa cognitione et scientia captos et

cum maximis curis et laboribus compensare eam quam
ex discendo capiant voluptatem? Mihi quidem Homerus
huiusmodi quiddam vidisse videtur in iis quae de
Sirenum cantibus finxerit. Neque enim vocum suavitate
videntur aut novitate quadam et varietate cantandi
revocare eos solitae qui praetervehebantur, sed quia
multa se scire profitebantur, ut homines ad earum saxa
discendi cupiditate adhaerescerent. Ita enim invitant
Ulixem . . . . Vidit Homerus probari fabulam non posse
si cantiunculis tantus irretitus vir teneretur; scientiam
pollicentur, quam non erat mirum sapientiae cupido
patria esse cariorem. Atque omnia quidem scire cuius-
cumquemodi sint cupere curiosorum, duci vero maio-
rum rerum contemplatione ad cupiditatem scientiae
summorum virorum est putandum.

Let us consider the parts of the mind, which are of
nobler aspect. The loftier these are, the more unmis-
takable indications of nature do they afford. So great
is our innate love of learning and of knowledge, that
no one can doubt that man's nature is strongly at-
tracted to these things even without the lure of any
profit. Do we [not] notice how children cannot be
deterred even by punishment from studying and in-
quiring into the world around them? Drive them away,
and back they come. They delight in knowing things;
they are eager to impart their knowledge to others;
pageants, games and shows of that sort hold them
spell-bound, and they will even endure hunger and
thirst so as to be able to see them. Again, take persons
who delight in the liberal arts and studies; do we not
see them careless of health or business, patiently endur-
ing any inconvenience when under the spell of learning
and of science, and repaid for endless toil and trouble
by the pleasure they derive from acquiring knowledge?
For my part I believe Homer had something of this sort
in view in his imaginary account of the songs of the
Sirens. Apparently it was not the sweetness of their
voices or the novelty and diversity of their songs, but
their professions of knowledge that used to attract the

passing voyagers; it was the passion for learning that kept men rooted to the Sirens' rocky shores. This is their invitation to Ulysses . . . . Homer was aware that his story would not sound plausible if the magic that held his hero immeshed was merely an idle song! It is knowledge that the Sirens offer, and it was no marvel if a lover of wisdom held this dearer than his home. A passion for miscellaneous omniscience no doubt stamps a man as a mere dilettante; but it must be deemed the mark of a superior mind to be led on by the contemplation of high matters to a passionate love of knowledge.

Cicero continues with many illustrious examples of men who felt an overwhelming desire for knowledge. See also Horace, *Epistles* I, ii, 17-26:

> Rursus, quid virtus et quid sapientia possit,
> utile proposuit nobis exemplar Ulixen,
> qui domitor Troiae multorum providus urbes
> et mores hominum inspexit, latumque per aequor,
> dum sibi, dum sociis reditum parat, aspera multa
> pertulit, adversis rerum immersabilis undis.
> Sirenum voces et Circae pocula nosti;
> quae si cum sociis stultus cupidusque bibisset,
> sub domina meretrice fuisset turpis et excors,
> vixisset canis immundus vel amica luto sus.

Again, of the power of worth and wisdom he has set before us an instructive pattern in Ulysses, that tamer of Troy, who looked with discerning eyes upon the cities and manners of many men, and while for self and comrades he strove for a return across the broad seas, many hardships he endured, but could never be o'er-whelmed in the waves of adversity. You know the Sirens' songs and Circe's cups; if, along with his comrades, he had drunk of these in folly and greed, he would have become the shapeless and witless vassal of a harlot mistress—would have lived as an unclean dog or a sow that loves the mire.

Compare Seneca, *Epist. mor.* LXXXVIII, 7:

Quaeris, Ulixes ubi erraverit, potius quam efficias, ne
nos semper erremus? Non vacat audire, utrum inter
Italiam et Siciliam iactatus sit an extra notum nobis
orbem, neque enim potuit in tam angusto error esse
tam longus; tempestates nos animi cotidie iactant et
nequitia in omnia Ulixis mala inpellit.

Do you raise the question, "Through what regions did
Ulysses stray?" instead of trying to prevent ourselves
from going astray at all times? We have no leisure to
hear lectures on the question whether he was sea-tost
between Italy and Sicily, or outside our known world
(indeed, so long a wandering could not possibly have
taken place within its narrow bounds); we ourselves
encounter storms of the spirit, which toss us daily, and
our depravity drives us into all the ills which troubled
Ulysses.

91-93. *Circe . . . nomasse*: The enchantress Circe was the
daughter of Helios, god of the Sun, and Perse, a nymph.
According to legend, she dwelt on the island of Aeaea (in
Virgil's time Circaeum Promontorium, modern Mount
Circeo, a mountain and promontory on the north side of
the Gulf of Gaeta; see n. to vs. 92). She had the power to
transform men into beasts (see *Aen.* VII, 10–20, 189–91).
When Ulysses was cast up on her island (*Odyssey* X, 135),
she changed his men into swine. But Ulysses, protected
against enchantment by a magic root, forced her to change
them back. He then lived with Circe (by whom he had a
son, Telegonus) for a year before continuing on his voyage.

92. *Gaeta*: Gaeta, ancient Caieta, seaport of central Italy
in the south of Latium, is situated on a promontory at the
head of the Gulf of Gaeta, on the Tyrrhenian coast, about
forty-five miles northwest of Naples. It was named by
Aeneas for Caieta, his nurse, who had died there. See *Aen.*
VII, 1–4:

Tu quoque litoribus nostris, Aeneia nutrix,
aeternam moriens famam, Caieta, dedisti;

et nunc servat honos sedem tuus, ossaque nomen
Hesperia in magna, si qua est ea gloria, signat.

Thou, too, Caieta, nurse of Aeneas, hast by thy death
given deathless fame to our shores; and still thine
honour guards thy resting-place, and in great Hesperia,
if such glory be aught, thy name marks thy dust.

See also Ovid, *Metam.* XIV, 157: "Litora adit nondum
nutricis habentia nomen." ("[Aeneas] landed on a shore
which did not yet bear his nurse's name.")

94. *pieta*: Piety, "duty."

100. *l'alto mare aperto*: The western Mediterranean.

101. *sol con un legno = con un sol legno.   compagna =
compagnia.*

102. *diserto*: "Abandoned."

103. *L'un lito e l'altro*: The European and the African
shores of the western Mediterranean.

103–5. *infin la Spagna . . . bagna*: Ulysses looks first to the
traditional western boundary of the habitable world—to
Spain and Morocco—and then in his narrative comes back
to Sardinia ("l'isola d'i Sardi").   •

104. *d'i = dei.*

105. *e l'altre che quel mare intorno bagna*: Dante may have
believed that the western Mediterranean contained more
islands than it actually does. Several medieval *mappae
mundi* so represent it; see, for example, the Hereford Map
in K. Miller (1896), fold-out following p. 54.

106. *Io e ' compagni eravam vecchi e tardi*: The verse im-
plies that Ulysses' voyage of exploration was long and hard.
See Ovid, *Metam.* XIV, 436: "resides et desuetudine tardi"
("grown sluggish and slow through inactivity").

107. *quella foce stretta*: The Strait of Gibraltar. Note the
following passage from Orosius, *Hist.* I, ii, 7: "Europae in
Hispania occidentalis oceanus termino est, maxime ubi apud
Gades insulas Herculis columnae visuntur et Tyrrheni maris

faucibus oceani aestus inmittitur." ("The Western Ocean forms the boundary of Europe in Spain at the very point where the Pillars of Hercules stand near the Gades [Cadiz] Islands and where the Ocean tide comes into the straits of the Tyrrhenian Sea.")

108–9. *Ercule segnò li suoi riguardi . . . metta*: The Pillars of Hercules usually are considered to be the promontory of Abyla (in Arabic, Jebel Musa) in North Africa and that of Calpe (Gibraltar) in Spain, so called from the tradition that they were originally one mountain, which was torn asunder by Hercules. They were supposed to mark the western limit beyond which no one could sail and come back alive. Brunetto Latini (*Tresor* I, cxxiii, 23) says:

> Iki est la fins de la terre, selonc ce que les ancienes gens proverent; et meismement le tesmoignent li tertre de Calpe et de Albinna (ou Ercules ficha ses colombes quant il venki tote la terre), ou leu ou la nostre mer ist de la mer ocheaine, et s'en vient parmi ces .ii. mons (ou sont les illes Gades et les colombes Ercules) . . . .

> Here [in Spain] is the land's boundary, as the ancients proved; moreover, this is confirmed by Mount Calpe and Mount Abyla (where Hercules established his columns when he conquered the entire earth), at the place where our sea flows from the ocean and makes its way between these two mountains (where the Gades Islands and the Columns of Hercules are located) . . . .

See the *Tesoretto*, vss. 1043–52 (in G. Contini, 1960, vol. II, p. 212):

> E io, ponendo mente
> là oltre nel ponente
> apresso questo mare,
> vidi diritto stare
> gran colonne, le quale
> vi pose per segnale
> Ercolès lo potente,
> per mostrare a la gente
> che loco sia finata
> la terra e terminata . . .

And I turned my thoughts out there toward the west.
After this sea I saw standing straight great columns,
which were put there as signals by the mighty Hercules,
to show people that the earth ends there and terminates.

The Pillars of Hercules are actually shown on the Hereford
Map (see K. Miller, 1896, fold-out following p. 54).

109. *più oltre non*: This phrase echoes the familiar Latin
ne plus ultra. Moreover, the verb "si metta" is in the present:
the injunction holds good in the present, is addressed to
man now and always.

110. *Sibilia*: Seville (see the form "Sobilia" in *Inf.* XX,
126). As Porena points out, Villani (VII, 11) calls the
Strait of Gibraltar the "stretto di Sibilia" ("Strait of Se-
ville").

111. *Setta*: Ceuta (Latin Septa), city in North Africa, in
Morocco, opposite Gibraltar. It is situated on a peninsula
that juts out from the mainland, and it forms the eastern
extremity of the Strait of Gibraltar. Its name is derived
from its seven hills, the highest of which, Mount Acho,
often is identified with the ancient Abyla, the southernmost
of the two Pillars of Hercules. As B. Nardi (1949, p. 153)
points out, a chronicle of Dante's time mentions Ceuta in
connection with the expedition of the Vivaldi brothers re-
ferred to in n. to vs. 56: Jacopo d'Oria, *Annales Ianuenses*
for the year 1291, speaks of their journey as "versus strictum
Septe, ut per mare occeanum irent" ("toward the strait of
Septe, passing from the [Mediterranean] sea into the
ocean"). On the Vivaldi expedition, see F. M. Rogers
(1955), pp. 35–45.

112-20. *O frati . . . canoscenza*: See Aeneas' speech to
his company in *Aen.* I, 198–203:

O socii (neque enim ignari sumus ante malorum),
o passi graviora, dabit deus his quoque finem.
vos et Scyllaeam rabiem penitusque sonantis
accestis scopulos, vos et Cyclopia saxa
experti; revocate animos maestumque timorem
mittite . . .

466

O comrades—for ere this we have not been ignorant of evils—O ye who have borne a heavier lot, to this, too, God will grant an end! Ye drew near to Scylla's fury and her deep-echoing crags; ye have known, too, the rocks of the Cyclopes; recall your courage and put away sad fear.

See also Lucan, *Phars.* I, 299: "Bellorum o socii, qui mille pericula" ("men who have fought and faced . . . the peril . . . a thousand times") and Horace, *Odes* I, vii, 25–26: "Quo nos cumque feret melior fortuna parente, / ibimus, o socii comitesque!" ("Whithersoever Fortune, kinder than my sire, shall bear us, thither let us go, O friends and comrades!")

115. *d'i = dei.*   *ch'è del rimanente*: Cf. the Latin *quae de reliquo est.* E. G. Parodi (1957, p. 358) comments on Dante's use of this phrase and gives two examples of it in Old French.   *del rimanente*: Cf. the OFr *de remenant.*

116–17. *non vogliate negar . . . gente*: For an earlier expression of a similar aspiration, see the *Alexandreis* (X, 5307–12, col. 569) of Walter of Châtillon, a French poet of the twelfth century who wrote in Latin:

> Nunc quia nil mundo peragendum restat in isto,
> Ne tamen adsuetus armorum langueat usus;
> Eia, quaeramus alio sub sole iacentes
> Antipodum populos, ne gloria nostra relinquat
> Vel virtus quid inexpertum, quo crescere possit,
> Vel quo perpetui mereatur carminis odas.

Now since there is nothing more left of the world to be traversed, lest weapons so used to war should grow rusty, come, let us seek those who dwell under another sun, on the other side of the world, lest our glory should fade and our courage miss a chance to shine; this way, an immortal song will be our reward.

Torraca (1895, p. 154) notes that the poem was known to Arrigo da Settimello at the end of the twelfth century and the Faentine chronicler Tolosano in the first part of the thirteenth century; thus it was in circulation in Dante's time.

In the geography of Dante's *Commedia*, Jerusalem is at the center of the northern hemisphere, which is of land and has India at its eastern limit and Gibraltar at its western ("l'occidente," vs. 113). The other, southern hemisphere is composed entirely of water, except for the mountain-island of Purgatory, which rises directly opposite Jerusalem on the orb of the earth (as will be made clear in the poem). See Fig. 2, p. 35. Ulysses' use of the phrase "mondo sanza gente" (vs. 117) reflects the common belief that the hemisphere of water was uninhabited.

117. *di retro al sol*: Following after the sun in its westward course.

118. *la vostra semenza*: "Your [human] origin." Ulysses exhorts his companions to remember that they are men, endowed by nature with intellect and the possibility of gaining knowledge.

119. *fatti non foste*: The accent falls effectively on "foste." Ulysses, pagan though he is, speaks of man as created, quite as if he knew Genesis.

119–20. *fatti non foste . . . canoscenza*: See *De vulg. eloqu.* I, xii, 4: "Siquidem illustres heroes Federicus Cesar et benegenitus eius Manfredus, nobilitatem ac rectitudinem sue forme pandentes, donec fortuna permansit, humana secuti sunt, brutalia dedignantes." ("But those illustrious heroes Frederick Caesar and his happy-born son Manfred, displaying the nobility and righteousness of their character, as long as fortune remained favourable, followed what is human, disdaining what is bestial.") On "virtue and knowledge," see Horace, *Epistles* I, ii, 17 (quoted in n. to vss. 90–120). Also see *Conv.* I, 1, 1–2:

> Sì come dice lo Filosofo nel principio de la Prima Filosofia, tutti li uomini naturalmente desiderano di sapere. La ragione di che puote essere ed è che ciascuna cosa, da providenza di prima natura impinta, è inclinabile a la sua propria perfezione; onde, acciò che la scienza è ultima perfezione de la nostra anima, ne la quale sta

la nostra ultima felicitade, tutti naturalmente al suo desiderio semo subietti. Veramente da questa nobilissima perfezione molti sono privati per diverse cagioni . . . .

As saith the Philosopher in the beginning of the First Philosophy, "All men by nature desire to know"; the reason whereof may be, that each thing, impelled by its own natural foresight, inclines to its own perfection; wherefore, inasmuch as knowledge is the distinguishing perfection of our soul, wherein consists our distinguishing blessedness, all of us are naturally subject to the longing for it. Yet of this most noble perfection many are bereft, for divers causes.

As Chimenz points out, virtue and knowledge were pagan ideals that related to the practical and intellectual spheres of human activity.

120. *canoscenza = conoscenza.*

121–22. *aguti . . . al cammino*: "Keen on the journey" (cf. the Latin *acuere*, "to sharpen").

124. *volta nostra poppa nel mattino*: Their course is westward at first, hence the poop is turned to the east; but to phrase it as Dante does is to convey Ulysses' resolute turning of his back on all the known world, to face toward the unknown and follow "the course of the sun" (vs. 117).

125. *de' remi facemmo ali*: The ship is large enough to be worthy of the open sea and equipped with oarsmen (who are not mentioned among Ulysses' companions, but whose presence is taken for granted). Ulysses and his comrades, in their eagerness now to journey into the unknown, do not wait for favorable winds, but cause the oars to be plied. For *fare ali*, see *Aen.* III, 520: "Temptamusque viam et velorum pandimus alas." ("[We] venture on our way, and spread the wings of our sails.") Also see Propertius, *Elegies* IV, vi, 47: "Classis centenis remiget alis." ("Their fleet is winged, each ship, with an hundred oars.")   *al folle volo*: Ulysses is speaking in retrospect and with full knowledge of the disastrous end of his journey, which the reader does

not yet know; but, given the context, "folle" points back to the folly of disregarding Hercules' markers and the injunction of *ne plus ultra* represented by them. Later in the poem, Dante looks down upon Gibraltar from a lofty vantage point in the heavens, as he journeys upward with Beatrice, and again the adjective "folle" is used to describe Ulysses' journey. See *Par.* XXVII, 82–83.

126. *sempre acquistando dal lato mancino*: "Gaining always on the left" with respect to their original westward direction (vs. 124), hence sailing to the southwest, which will finally bring them to a point opposite Jerusalem on the orb of the earth—i.e., to the exact center of the southern hemisphere of water. See Fig. 2, p. 35.

127–28. *Tutte le stelle . . . basso*: "L'altro polo" is the Antarctic. The subject is "Night" (personified), the objects "all the stars" and "our [pole]"; the stars of our pole are understood, particularly the North Star. This means that the ship now has crossed the equator as it continues in its southwesterly course.

130–31. *Cinque volte racceso . . . luna*: The light on the underside—the earthward side—of the moon had five times been lighted and five times extinguished (the moon had waxed and waned that many times): five months had passed.

132. *che 'ntrati = che intrati*.   *alto passo*: See *Inf.* I, 26–27; II, 12.

133. *n'apparve = ci apparve*.   *una montagna*: What this unexpected land is, looming dark through the distance here in the hemisphere of water where there was thought to be no land, will be disclosed in the *Purgatorio*.

134-35. *parvemi alta tanto . . . alcuna*: The reason why this would be the highest mountain Ulysses had ever seen is not made evident until the *Purgatorio*.   *parvemi = mi parve*.

136. *e tosto tornò in pianto*: The subject of the verb is understood to be "our great joy."

138. *del legno il primo canto*: The prow of the ship.

139–42. *Tre volte il fé girar . . . richiuso*: See *Aen.* I, 114–17:

> . . . ingens a vertice pontus
> in puppim ferit; excutitur pronusque magister
> volvitur in caput; ast illam ter fluctus ibidem
> torquet agens circum et rapidus vorat aequore
>   vertex . . .

A mighty toppling wave strikes astern. The helmsman is dashed out and hurled head foremost, but the ship is thrice on the same spot whirled round and round by the wave and engulfed in the sea's devouring eddy.

140–41. *levar la poppa . . . ire*: "Fé" (*fece*) is understood with the verbs "levar" and "ire."

141. *com' altrui piacque*: "Altrui" is dative (with the verb *piacere*) and here, in English usage, may bear a capital initial letter to denote the Deity. This (see "folle volo," vs. 125) is uttered in retrospect. Ulysses now knows what he did not know at the time.

CANTO XXVII

2. *per non dir più*: "Having stopped speaking." See *Inf.* XVI, 101 for "per" meaning, as here, "on account of," "through." *sen gia = se ne giva (se ne andava)*.

5. *ne = ci.*

6. *uscia* (pronounced *uscìa*) *= usciva*. See the rhyme word *venìa (= veniva)*, vs. 4.

7-12. *Come 'l bue cicilian . . . trafitto*: The victims of Phalaris, tyrant of Agrigentum in Sicily, are said to have been shut up and roasted alive in a brazen bull invented by the Athenian artisan Perillus. The contrivance was so fashioned that the shrieks of those inside sounded like the bellowing of a bull. According to legend, Perillus was the first to perish by his own invention. Dante could have known the story from any of several sources; it is told by Orosius (*Hist.* I, xx, 1–4); Ovid (*Tristia* III, xi, 39–54 and *Ars amat.* I, 653–56); Pliny (*Nat. hist.* XXXIV, xix, 89); and Valerius Maximus (*Fact. dict. memor.* IX, ii, 9), whose account follows:

Saevus etiam ille aenei tauri inventor, quo inclusi subditis ignibus longo et abdito cruciatu mugitus resonantem spiritum edere cogebantur, ne eiulatus eorum humano

sono vocis expressi Phalaridis tyranni misericordiam
implorare possent. quam quia calamitosis deesse voluit,
taeterrimum artis suae opus primus inclusus merito
auspicatus est.

There was a savage fellow who invented a brazen bull
in which victims were enclosed and a fire kindled be-
neath; they suffered a long and a hidden torture for he
so arranged it that the moans that were torn from them
sounded like the lowing of a bull, since if they sounded
at all like human voices, they might plead for mercy
from the tyrant, Phalaris. Now, since he was so anxious
to torment the unfortunate, the artisan himself was the
first to experience the efficiency of his hideous invention.

7. *cicilian* = *siciliano*, as also "Cicilia" is used in the poem
for *Sicilia*.

8. *e ciò fu dritto*: See Ovid, *Ars amat.* I, 655–56: "Iustus
uterque fuit: neque enim lex aequior ulla est, / Quam necis
artifices arte perire sua." ("Both were just; for there is no
juster law than that contrivers of death should perish by
their own contrivances.") Pliny also describes Perillus' pun-
ishment as "cruciatum eum iustiore saevitia" ("a cruelty
more just than the one he proposed").

12. *el*: The brazen bull.   *pareva dal dolor trafitto*: See
Ovid, *Tristia* III, xi, 48: "Et veri vox erit illa bovis." ("And
that will be the voice of a true bull.")

14. *dal principio* = *da principio*; "at first."   *in suo lin-
guaggio*: Just as the shrieks of the victims roasted alive in
the brazen bull had no outlet and were thus incoherent, so
the voice of the shade enclosed within the flame at first has
no outlet and is indistinct.

17–18. *dandole . . . lor passaggio*: Giving to the tip of the
flame the movement made by the speaker's tongue as it
uttered the words.   *quel guizzo che dato avea la lingua*:
The expression is *dare un guizzo*, "to give a twist."

19–20. *udimmo dire . . . la voce*: The shade who begins to speak here, who is never named, is the great Ghibelline leader Guido da Montefeltro, nicknamed "the Fox." Villani (VII, 80) calls him "il più sagace e il più sottile uomo di guerra ch'al suo tempo fosse in Italia" ("the shrewdest and finest soldier that there was in Italy at that time") and (VII, 44) "savio e sottile d'ingegno di guerra più che niuno che fosse al suo tempo" ("wise, possessing a more refined military talent than anyone in his time"). Salimbene, the thirteenth-century chronicler, calls him (vol. II, p. 224) "homo nobilis et sensatus et discretus et morigeratus, liberalis et curialis et largus, strenuus miles et probus in armis et doctus ad bellum" ("a nobleman, intelligent, discreet, and gracious, generous, courtly, and openhearted, and a very ardent soldier, able in arms and versed in the art of war").

Guido was born *ca.* 1220. In June 1275, commanding a combined force of Romagnole Ghibellines and exiled Ghibellines from Bologna and Florence, he defeated a Guelph army led by Malatesta da Rimini (Villani, VII, 48). In September 1275, Guido defeated the Guelphs at Reversano, near Cesena, and took possession of Cesena, from which he expelled Malatesta da Rimini, and of Cervia. In 1282, he held Forlì against the combined French and Italian troops of Pope Martin IV, commanded by the French knight and mercenary, Jean d'Eppes, on whom he inflicted severe losses (see n. to vss. 43–44).

The following year, however, Guido was driven out by the inhabitants of Forlì, who had come to terms with the pope, and nearly all of Romagna submitted to the Church (Villani, VII, 80–82). In 1286 Guido himself made his submission to the new pope, Honorius IV, and was reconciled to the Church but banished to Piedmont (Villani, VII, 108). Probably in March 1288, upon his election as leader of the Pisan Ghibellines, he returned from exile. The pope punished this act of disobedience by excommunicating Guido and his family and by laying Pisa, where Count Ugolino had just been murdered, under an interdict (Villani, VII, 128). Under Guido's leadership, the Pisan Ghibellines won several victories against the Florentine Guelphs; but in 1293, when Florence and Pisa made peace, Guido was dismissed (Villani, VIII, 2).

In 1292 Guido made himself master of Urbino, which he held against Malatestino da Rimini, at that time *podestà* of Cesena. Shortly afterward, he was once more reconciled to the Church, and late in 1296 he joined the Franciscan order. It is said that in 1298 Pope Boniface VIII induced Guido to advise him how to reduce the stronghold of Palestrina, then held by the Colonna family. It is on the basis of this story—whether real or invented—that Dante places Guido in the *bolgia* of the fraudulent counselors (see n. to vs. 67).

Guido died in September 1298 at the age of seventy-five. According to some, he died and was buried in the Franciscan monastery at Assisi. Benvenuto, however, has a different account; he says, with reference to Guido's supposed conversion:

> Dominus Malatesta, cum narraretur sibi a quodam familiari, quod comes Guido erat factus frater minor, respondit: caveamus ergo ne fieret guardianus Arimini. . . . devote assumpsit habitum, humiliter servavit regulam, et patienter tulit paupertatem; unde saepe visus est ire publice mendicando panem per Anconam, in qua mortuus est et sepultus; et multa audivi de eo, per quae poterat satis sperari de eius salute.

> When Dominus Malatesta was told by one of his entourage that Count Guido had become a Franciscan, he announced, "Let us beware lest he become the guardian of Rimini." . . . He assumed the monk's habit with sincerity, hewed to the clerical regimen with humility, and endured poverty patiently. And so he could often be seen publicly begging for bread in the city of Ancona, where he died and was buried. I have heard many things about him that would allow one to be of good hope for his salvation.

20. *che parlavi mo lombardo*: Strange as it may seem, Virgil is said to have been speaking in the Lombard dialect to Ulysses, and this serves to drop the pitch of the episode from high tragedy to the everyday. Most readers will come

to this with some surprise; but, as Grandgent comments, Dante believed that the Italian dialects dated from antiquity and had always existed simultaneously with Latin. Hence Virgil, who came from Lombardy, might appropriately enough speak his local dialect. (For Virgil's Lombard origins, see *Inf.* I, 68–69.) B. Terracini (1954, pp. 9–10) reviews the various interpretations of this verse.

21. *dicendo "Istra ten va, più non t'adizzo"*: Guido has evidently understood these parting words addressed to Ulysses. Hence Virgil's "lombardo" must indeed resemble contemporary Lombard.

23. *restare = fermarti.*

24. *e ardo*: The value of "e" is that of Latin *et* in the expression *et tamen.*

25. *pur mo*: "Just now"; Guido's shade thinks it is addressing one who has just fallen into Hell.   *in questo mondo cieco*: Hell can always be so designated because of its darkness, but in view of Guido's burning desire to know about present conditions in his native Romagna and his evident blindness to present events, the words take on special meaning. In *Inf.* X, 58–59, Hell is called a "cieco carcere" for similar reasons. On the "blindness" of all souls in Hell, see n. to *Inf.* X, 100–105.

It is not clear whether the souls inside the flames can see or not. In this case Guido evidently does not see that the wayfarer is present in the flesh.

27. *latina = italiana.* See vs. 33; also *Inf.* XXII, 65.

28. *Romagnuoli*: For Romagna in general and the many places referred to now, including Montefeltro, which is denoted by the next two verses, see Map 3.

29. *d'i = dei.*

30. *e 'l giogo di che Tever si diserra*: The Apennines, where the Tiber rises, at the foot of Mount Fumaiolo.

32. *mi tentò di costa*: "Nudged my side"; see *Inf.* XII, 67.

33. *Parla tu; questi è latino*: This plainly connects with Virgil's speaking Lombard (vss. 20–21) and serves to drop the pitch to something less than high tragedy. Compare the moment in the preceding canto when Virgil enjoined Dante not to speak, since the souls there addressed were Greeks (see *Inf.* XXVI, 73–75). / In *Conv.* IV, xxviii, 8, Dante calls Guido "lo nobilissimo nostro latino" ("our most noble Italian").

36. *là giù*: The flame is obliged to stay down in the "gullet of the ditch" (*Inf.* XXVI, 40). *nascosta*: "Hidden" within the flame.

37. *mai*: Benvenuto comments: "Postquam coepit habere tyrannos." ("After which, it began to have tyrants.")

38. *tiranni*: The petty tyrants of Romagna seized rule by force, generally without legitimate claim. Machiavelli called them "princes," of course.

39. *'n palese nessuna or vi lasciai*: At this time, spring 1300, there was peace, or at least no open warfare, in Romagna. Torraca comments that after twenty-five years of continuous war, in April 1299 the political parties, the tyrants, and the communes agreed to a general and perpetual peace, which apparently was still in force in 1300.

40–41. *Ravenna . . . l'aguglia da Polenta*: Polenta was a castle near Brettinoro (modern Bertinoro), a few miles south of Forlì (see Map 3), from which the Guelph Polenta family took its name. The Polenta acquired authority over Ravenna toward the end of the thirteenth century and relinquished it to Venice in 1441. The head of the house at the time of which the wayfarer is speaking was Guido da Polenta the elder (died 1310), father of Francesca da Rimini, and grandfather of Guido Novello, Dante's host at Ravenna in 1321. The arms of the Polenta family displayed an eagle, "half argent on a field azure, half gules on a field or." Benvenuto says that Dante's metaphor implies, as was the fact, that the rule of the Polenta was beneficent:

Nunc autor descripturus specialiter statum Romandiolae, incipit a Ravenna, et sententialiter vult dicere, quod nobilis et antiqua prosapia istorum de Polenta dominatur Ravennae et Cerviae. Unde debes scire, quod eo tempore regnabat Ravennae quidam dominus Guido Novellus de Polenta, vir quidem satis magnae intelligentiae et eloquentiae; qui multum honoravit Dantem in vita et in morte . . . ideo loquitur de eo valde honeste, describens ipsum ab insignio suae domus . . . . Vult enim dicere, quod iste Guido Novellus fovet et protegit ravennates sub umbra alarum suarum, sicut aquila filios suos. Et de rei veritate Ravenna tunc erat in florenti statu, quae nunc est in languido.

Now the author, about to describe in detail the conditions in Romagna, begins at Ravenna, and he means to say, sententiously, that the noble and ancient race of these Polenta ruled in Ravenna and Cervia. Now, you must know that in those days Ravenna was ruled by a certain Guido Novello da Polenta, a man of truly great intelligence and eloquence. He honored Dante highly, both in life and in death . . . and Dante therefore speaks of him in the highest terms, describing him by reference to the escutcheon of his house . . . . He means to say that this Guido Novello nourishes and protects the citizens of Ravenna under the shadow of his wings, just as the eagle does its young. And in truth, Ravenna flourished in those days, whereas now it languishes.

41. *la si cova* = *se la cova.*

42. *Cervia*: Cervia, a town on the Adriatic, about fourteen miles southeast of Ravenna, was a place of some importance in the Middle Ages because of its salt monopoly, which appears to have yielded a considerable revenue. It had been under the dominion of Ravenna for some years. Benvenuto says: "Habet haec civitas praerogativam salis; unde cardinalis ostiensis dominus Bononiae et Romandiolae erat solitus dicere: Plus habemus de Cerviola parvula, quam de tota Romandiola." ("This city had the monopoly on salt; where-

fore the cardinal of Ostia, lord of Bologna and Romagna, was wont to say, 'We receive more from dear little Cervia than we do from all of Romagna.' ")

43–44. *La terra . . . sanguinoso mucchio*: This is Forlì, of which Dante speaks in *De vulg. eloqu.* (I, xiv, 3) as the central town of Romagna. Under the direction of Guido da Montefeltro (whose very shade the wayfarer is addressing, though he does not know it yet), the city successfully withstood a year-long siege laid by the French and Italian troops of Pope Martin IV under Jean d'Eppes, who were finally repulsed with heavy losses ("sanguinoso mucchio"). Villani says (VII, 81): "I Franceschi e la gente della Chiesa ricevettono grande sconfitta e dammaggio, e morirvi molti buoni cavalieri Franceschi." ("The French and the soldiers of the Church were roundly defeated and suffered many casualties. Many good French knights were killed.") / We may imagine that Guido hears the wayfarer's account with some satisfaction.

44. *Franceschi = francesi.* The form was common in early Italian.   *sanguinoso mucchio*: On the meaning of this phrase, see F. Torraca (1912), pp. 109–21.

45. *sotto le branche verdi*: The family thus designated is the Ordelaffi, who in Dante's time ruled Forlì. Its escutcheon bore on the upper half "on a field or a lion rampant vert"; or, as the *Anonimo fiorentino* describes it, it was "uno scudo dal mezzo in giù addogato, da indi in su uno mezzo leone verde nel campo giallo" ("an escutcheon, the lower half divided by vertical bands, and in the upper, a half lion vert on a field or"). / It is probable that Dante was at Forlì early in his years of exile, in 1303, as aide and secretary to Scarpetta degli Ordelaffi, who was head of the family at the time and leader of the Bianchi forces there in 1302–3.   *branche*: Here the word implies "paws" rather than "claws."

46. *'l mastin vecchio*: Malatesta da Verrucchio (died 1312), who, after defeating Montagna de' Parcitati and the Ghibelline party of Rimini in 1295 (see n. to vs. 47), became the

first Malatesta lord of Rimini. He retained the lordship until his death at the age of one hundred. Malatesta had four sons: Malatestino, who succeeded his father as lord of Rimini in 1312; Gianciotto, husband of Francesca da Rimini; Paolo, her lover; and Pandolfo, who succeeded his eldest brother as lord of Rimini in 1317, since both Gianciotto and Paolo predeceased their father. / The family originally came from Montefeltro to Verrucchio, a castle and village some ten miles southwest of Rimini, and from that place took their name. *'l nuovo*: Malatestino, the "Young Mastiff," lord of Rimini 1312–17.

47. *Montagna*: Montagna de' Parcitati was head of the Ghibelline party in Rimini. When Malatesta overpowered Montagna and the Ghibellines of the city in 1295, Montagna was taken prisoner and entrusted to the charge of Malatestino. Benvenuto tells of Malatestino's harsh dealing with Montagna:

> Nobilis miles di Parcitatis de Arimino, princeps partis ghibellinae; quem captum cum quibusdam aliis Malatesta tradidit custodiendum Malatestino filio. Postea petivit ab eo, quid factum esset de Montagna. Cui iste respondit: Domine, est sub fida custodia; ita quod si vellet se suffocare, non posset, quamvis sit iuxta mare. Et dum iterum et iterum peteret, et replicaret, dixit: Certe dubito, quod nescies ipsum custodire. Malatestinus, notato verbo, fecit Montagnam mactari cum quibusdam aliis.

> The noble knight of the Parcitati of Rimini, head of the Ghibelline faction, was captured together with some other men by Malatesta, who turned him over to his son Malatestino. Later, the father asked him what he had done with Montagna, whereupon the son replied: "My lord, he is so well guarded that although he is near the sea, he could not drown himself even if he wanted to." Malatesta, after several times making the same inquiry and receiving the same reply, at last said: "I see that you do not know how to guard him." Mala-

testino, taking the hint, had Montagna and several others killed.

48. *là dove soglion*: At Rimini. *fan d'i denti succhio*: "They make an auger [*succhiello*] of their teeth,"—i.e., they govern cruelly. See Prov. 30:14: "Generatio quae pro dentibus gladios habet, et commandit molaribus suis, ut comedat inopes de terra, et pauperes ex hominibus." ("There is a group whose incisors are swords, whose teeth are knives, devouring the needy from the earth, and the poor from among men.") *d'i = dei*.

49. *Le città di Lamone e di Santerno*: Faenza, nineteen miles southwest of Ravenna, is on the Lamone River; and Imola, about twenty-one miles southeast of Bologna, is on the Santerno River (see Map 3).

50. *il lioncel*: Maghinardo, or Mainardo, Pagano da Susinana, head of the Pagani family in Dante's time, was lord of Faenza in 1290, of Forlì in 1291, and of Imola in 1296. Dante's designation of him as the "Little Lion" refers to his coat of arms, "on a field argent a lion azure." Maghinardo was also called "the Demon" (see *Purg.* XIV, 118). He died at Imola in 1302.

51. *che muta parte*: Although a Ghibelline by birth and a staunch supporter of that party in Romagna, Maghinardo was loyal to the Florentine Guelphs, in gratitude for the care they had taken of him and his property when his father, at his death, entrusted him to their protection as a minor. Documents show that the richest Florentine bankers later underwrote his activities. Instances of his political inconsistency are numerous. Villani gives the following account of him (VII, 149):

> Il detto Maghinardo fu uno grande e savio tiranno, e della contrada tra Casentino e Romagna grande castellano, e con molti fedeli; savio fu di guerra e bene avventuroso in più battaglie, e al suo tempo fece grandi cose. Ghibellino era di sua nazione e in sue opere, ma co' Fiorentini era guelfo e nimico di tutti i loro nimici, o

guelfi o ghibellini che fossono; e in ogni oste e battaglia
ch'e' Fiorentini facessono, mentre fu in vita, fu con sua
gente a loro servigio, e capitano; e ciò fu, che morto il
padre, che Piero Pagano avea nome, grande gentile
uomo, rimanendo il detto Maghinardo picciolo fanciullo
e con molti nimici, conti Guidi, e Ubaldini, e altri
signori di Romagna, il detto suo padre il lasciò alla
guardia e tuteria del popolo e comune di Firenze, lui e
le sue terre; dal qual comune benignamente fu cresciuto,
e guardato, e migliorato suo patrimonio, e per questa
cagione era grato e fedelissimo al comune di Firenze
in ogni sua bisogna.

This Maghinardo was a great and wise tyrant, and a
great chatelain in the region between Casentino and
Romagna, where he had many faithful followers. He
knew a great deal about war, and had fought very
boldly in many battles. In his time he did great things.
He was a Ghibelline by birth and by deed; but with the
Florentines he was a Guelph and the enemy of all their
enemies, whether they were Guelphs or Ghibellines. For
as long as he lived, whenever the Florentines were en-
gaged in a siege or a battle, he supported them with his
troops, and served as their captain. And the reason was
that at the death of his father, Piero Pagano, a great
gentleman, Maghinardo was left a small boy among
many enemies—the Conti Guidi, the Ubaldini, and
other lords of Romagna; wherefore his father left him
and all his lands under the guardianship and tutelage
of the people and the commune of Florence. The com-
mune raised him with gentle care, guarded him, and
increased his patrimony; and for that reason, he was
grateful and thoroughly faithful to the commune when-
ever it was in need.

Benvenuto, who copies Villani's account almost verbatim,
says of Maghinardo:

Maghinardus Paganus . . . fuit nobilis castellanus in
montibus supra Imolam; qui sua probitate et felicitate
ex parvo castellano factus est magnus dominus in

Romandiola, ita quod habuit tres civitates, scilicet
Forlivium, Faventiam et Imolam.

Maghinardo Pagano . . . was the noble lord of a castle
in the mountains above Imola. His probity and his good
fortune caused him to rise from [the status of] a small
chatelain to great lordship in Romagna, to the point
where he had three cities under him, Forlì, Faenza,
and Imola.

52. *quella cu' il Savio bagna il fianco*: This is Cesena, on
the Savio River, midway between Forlì and Rimini, at the
foot of the hills belonging to the Tuscan Apennine range
(see Map 3).

53. *così com' ella sie' tra 'l piano e 'l monte*: Torraca com-
ments that although Cesena now is almost completely on a
plain, in Dante's time it rose toward the hills. The Savio
River, which washed the base of these hills, also washed
the edge of the city.   *sie' = siede.*

54. *tra tirannia si vive e stato franco*: Cesena appears to have
been to some extent a free municipality about the time of
which Dante is speaking (1300). It was legally a free com-
mune but was bossed by Galasso da Montefeltro, Guido's
cousin, who was *capitano del popolo* from 1296 and *podestà*
from 1298 until his death in 1300, despite the fact that the
office of *podestà* normally changed every year. Thus Cesena
enjoyed more freedom than the other cities Dante mentions;
although it did not enjoy self-government, it was not en-
tirely in the hands of a tyrant either.   *si vive*: The pleo-
nastic reflexive sets the subject off to itself; see n. to *Inf.*
VII, 94.

55. *che ne conte*: "That you tell us."   *ne = ci.   con-
te = conti.*

56. *altri*: The indefinite pronoun refers to Dante himself;
on this usage see M. Barbi (1920).

57. *se 'l nome tuo nel mondo tegna fronte*: For this fa-
miliar formula of adjuration, see also, for example, *Inf.*
X, 82. *tegna fronte*: Literally, "holds its head" high.

58-59. *'l foco . . . al modo suo*: See vss. 14-15.

60. *diè cotal fiato*: "Gave forth this breath"—i.e., spoke these
words. See Ovid, *Metam.* IX, 584: "Linguaque vix tales
icto dedit aere voces." ("And then with choked and feeble
utterance you spoke.")

61. *S'i' credesse = se io credessi.*

61-66. *S'i' credesse . . . ti rispondo*: These words follow
naturally upon Dante's entreaty based on Guido's enduring
fame in the world (see vss. 55-57); and Guido's pride in his
fame is evident (see vss. 77-78). Even Vanni Fucci, "bestia"
that he was, could suffer embarrassment over being seen
where he was in Hell.

63. *staria = starebbe.*

67. *Io fui uom d'arme*: Did Dante invent the story that is
told now, or did he find it already recorded in some con-
temporary chronicle? No conclusive answer to the question
has been found. Although it was long debated, chiefly by
Francesco D'Ovidio and Francesco Torraca, probably no
definitive evidence is forthcoming. The whole matter hinges
on whether the Ferrarese chronicler Riccobaldo, writing be-
fore 1313, knew this canto of the *Inferno* and based his
account on it, or whether he wrote independently. In any
case, Riccobaldo gives the story as follows (quoted by E. G.
Parodi, 1911b, p. 266):

> Erat eo tempore in ordine beati Francisci Guido qui,
> comes olim de Monte Feretro, dux fuerat bellorum pro
> Gibilinis. Hunc ad se vocavit papa Bonifacius. Persuadet,
> ut dux belli sit contra cardinales adversos. Cum omnino
> talia abnueret constanter, tum ait: —Saltem me instruas
> quonam modo eos subigere valeam—. Tum ille: —
> Multa promittite, pauca servate de promissis—.

At that time there was a Franciscan named Guido, a former count of Montefeltro, who was a general of the Ghibellines. Pope Boniface called him in and urged him to become leader in the war against the rebellious cardinals. And when he persisted in refusing to have any part in it, the pope said, "At least you can advise me how to get the better of them." To which Guido replied: "Promise much but fulfill little that you promise."

Clearly Dante learned of Guido's fraudulent counsel after he had written of him so glowingly in the *Convivio* (see the quotation in n. to vs. 33, above). The story is also told by Francesco Pipino, a Bolognese chronicler who wrote shortly after Riccobaldo. For the controversy in detail, see E. G. Parodi (1911b); Porena, "Nota finale," pp. 245–46; F. Torraca (1912), pp. 305–46; F. D'Ovidio (1901), pp. 27–75. For the corresponding version of Francesco Pipino and for the relation of the two chroniclers, see A. F. Massèra (1915); G. Petraglione (1903).

69. *venìa* = *veniva*, a common use of the imperfect tense for the conditional perfect; hence "venìa" = *sarebbe venuto*.

70. *se non fosse* = *se non fosse stato*.   *il gran prete*: Boniface VIII. The phrase is derisive and sarcastic.

71. *ne le prime colpe*: "In the old ruses," stratagems, the "coperte vie" of vs. 76.

72. *quare*: Latin, "why."

73–74. *Mentre ch'io forma fui . . . madre mi diè*: The soul speaks in keeping with scholastic doctrine, which held that the soul is the form of the body ("of the flesh and bones the mother gave me"); see n. to *Inf.* VI, 106–7.

74–75. *l'opere mie . . . leonine, ma di volpe*: See Cicero, *De officiis* (I, xiii, 41), for the metaphor of the lion and the fox. On force or fraud as distinguishing elements in the sins of malice punished in lower Hell, see n. to *Inf.* XI, 23–24. If Guido's deeds had been "leonine"—that is, sins of violence—he would have fallen instead to the seventh circle of Hell. / The anonymous *Cronica di Pisa* (col. 981C) relates: "Quando il detto Conte Guido usciva fuore di Pisa con la gente, sonandoli innanzi una Cennamella, li Fiorentini fuggiano e diceano: *ecco la Volpe*." ("When this count went forth from Pisa with his troops, with the bagpipes playing before them, the Florentines fled, saying: 'Here comes the Fox.'")

78. *al fine de la terra il suono uscie*: See Ps. 18:5 [19:4]: "In omnem terram exivit sonus eorum, et in fines orbis terrae verba eorum." ("Through all the earth their voice resounds, and to the ends of the world, their message.")
  uscie = uscì.

79–80. *quella parte di mia etade*: Old age. Dante also speaks of Guido in the context of old age in *Conv.* IV, xxviii, 8.

81. *calar le vele e raccoglier le sarte*: In *Conv.* IV, xxviii, 8, as here, Dante uses a nautical metaphor to describe old age; here it calls to mind that other voyager, Ulysses, who with his companions was old and slow when he reached the western limits of the inhabited world (see *Inf.* XXVI, 106–8). Unlike Guido, Ulysses sailed forth on unknown seas. Horace uses a similar metaphor in the *Odes* (I, xxxiv, 3–5): "Nunc retrorsum / vela dare atque iterare cursus / cogor relictos." ("[I] am now compelled to spread my sails for the voyage back, and to retrace the course I had abandoned.")

83. *pentuto e confesso mi rendei*: The *Anonimo fiorentino*, commenting on vs. 43, says: "Pentutosi et confessatosi, si arrendè a Dio." ("Having repented and confessed, he surrendered to God.") See *Purg.* XX, 54, where "un renduto" denotes a monk.

85. *Lo principe d'i novi Farisei*: Boniface VIII. The word "principe" is used ambiguously. As pope, Boniface was chief among the cardinals and other ecclesiastics, here termed the "new Pharisees," of the Catholic Church; he was also, in Dante's view, the greatest Pharisee of all.   *d'i = dei*.

86. *guerra presso a Laterano*: The war between Boniface VIII and the Colonna family and faction, who contested the validity of the abdication of Celestine V (see n. to *Inf.* III, 59–60) and charged that Boniface had entered the papacy by fraud. The struggle existed throughout Boniface's reign but came to a head in 1297, when it appears that Stefano Colonna stole part of the papal treasure. The pope in consequence (in May 1297) deprived the two Colonna cardinals, Jacopo and Pietro, of their rank, excommunicated them and the rest of their house, and demanded the surrender of certain castles. The Colonna left Rome and openly defied Boniface from their stronghold at Palestrina, not far from the city, where they held out against the papal forces until September 1298.   *presso a Laterano*: Refers to the Colonna stronghold. Palestrina is twenty miles southeast of Rome; see n. to vs. 102.   *Laterano*: In Dante's day "Laterano" was equivalent to the modern "Vaticano," since the Lateran palace was the usual residence of the pope. "Laterano" is used here to denote Rome.

89. *e nessun era stato a vincer Acri*: Acre (French, Saint-Jean-d'Acre, called Accho in the Old Testament and Ptolemaïs in the New Testament), now a city and seaport of Israel, is situated on a low promontory of Mount Carmel on the northern extremity of the Bay of Acre. It is about eighty miles northwest of Jerusalem and twenty-seven miles south of Tyre. After having been in the possession of the Saracens since the middle of the seventh century (638), Acre was taken in 1104 by the crusaders under Baldwin I, who made it their principal port and retained it until 1187, when it was recovered by Saladin. In 1191, after a long siege, it was retaken by Philip Augustus of France and Richard Coeur de Lion, who gave the town to the Knights of St. John of Jerusalem, from whom it received the name of Saint-Jean-d'Acre. It remained in the possession of the Christians for a hundred years and, in spite of frequent Saracen attacks, grew into a large and populous city, protected on the land side by a double line of fortifications. In the spring of 1291, however, it was besieged by the Sultan

al-Ashraf Khalil because Christian mercenaries within the city had violated a truce with the Saracens. After holding out for a few weeks, the city was taken by assault. With the defeat of Acre, the last of the Christian possessions in the Holy Land reverted to the Saracens, and the Latin kingdom of Jerusalem came to an end.

90. *né mercatante in terra di Soldano*: On receiving news of the fall of Acre, Pope Nicholas IV at once attempted to organize a crusade for the recovery of the city and called on all Christians under pain of excommunication to abstain from any further commerce with Egypt, the seat of Moslem power.

92. *quel capestro*: The Franciscan girdle or "corda" (see vs. 67).

93. *che solea fare i suoi cinti più macri*: Many times Dante deplores the decline and corruption of religious orders.

94. *Ma come Costantin chiese Silvestro*: The legend of Constantine's conversion by Sylvester I (pope 314–35) is narrated by Jacobus de Varagine (or Voragine), archbishop of Genoa 1292–98, in his *Legenda aurea* XII, 2–3. According to this account, Constantine, stricken with leprosy in punishment for persecuting Christians, was advised by the heathen priests to wash himself in a bath of infants' blood. Three thousand infants were collected, but Constantine was touched by the lamentations and prayers of the mothers and ordered the children to be restored to their parents, saying that it was better for him to die than to sacrifice so many innocent lives. The same night St. Peter and St. Paul appeared to him in a vision and told him to send for Sylvester, who had taken refuge in a cave on Mount Soracte. Constantine did as he was bidden and after receiving baptism at Sylvester's hands was immediately cured; he then determined to convert his mother Helena and finally succeeded in bringing her and all of Rome to Christianity. Other accounts add that Constantine, to prove his gratitude still further and to leave the Church completely at liberty, bestowed upon Pope Sylvester the city of Rome and his

temporal power in the West. As the legend goes, he then
retired to Byzantium, which he rebuilt and renamed Con-
stantinople. This story, widely accepted in the Middle
Ages, later proved baseless. On the so-called Donation of
Constantine, see n. to *Inf.* XIX, 116. G. Fallani (1958)
comments on the legend of Constantine and its iconography.

95. *Siratti*: Soracte (in medieval Latin, *Siraptis*), a moun-
tain near the Tiber about twenty-four miles north of Rome,
where Pope Sylvester I is said to have taken refuge in a
cave during the persecutions of Constantine. On its summit
now stands the church of San Silvestro.

95. *guerir = guarire.   lebbre = lebbra*; for this form see
E. G. Parodi (1957), p. 244.

96. *maestro*: The title for a physician.

98. *domandommi = mi domandò.*

99. *ebbre*: The pope seemed "drunken," "raving," to be
asking a corded friar for such counsel.

100. *ridisse*: "Went on to say."   *Tuo cuor non sospetti*:
"Let your heart not mistrust," "have no fear." The specific
reassurance is then given in vs. 103.

101. *finor = fin da ora.* This is a most important point, for
the word means that absolution is given in advance. "Finor"
also anticipates that the counsel requested will be fraudulent
and therefore sinful.   *t'assolvo*: The formal words of
absolution in Latin are "Ego te absolvo."   *e tu m'in-
segna = e tu insegnami* (imperative); "e" has the value
of "and now," "in return."

102. *Penestrino*: The ancient Praeneste, now Palestrina, a
town situated on a steep hill about twenty miles southeast
of Rome. It was the stronghold of the Colonna, who man-
aged to hold out there against the papal forces until Sep-
tember 1298, when it was surrendered on a promise from
the pope of complete amnesty (the "lunga promessa" of
vs. 110). No sooner did Boniface get possession of Palestrina

than he razed it to the ground (see "l'attender corto," vs. 110). For Villani's account, see VIII, 23, quoted in n. to vs. 110.

103-4. *Lo ciel poss' io . . . chiavi*: See Matt. 16:19: "Et tibi dabo claves regni caelorum; et quodcumque ligaveris super terram, erit ligatum et in caelis; et quodcumque solveris super terram, erit solutum et in caelis." ("And I will give thee the keys of the kingdom of heaven; and whatever thou shalt bind on earth shall be bound in heaven, and whatever thou shalt loose on earth shall be loosed in heaven.") See also *De mon.* III, viii.

105. *che 'l mio antecessor non ebbe care*: It was commonly believed that Pope Celestine V was induced to make "the great refusal" by Benedetto Caetani, who then succeeded him as Pope Boniface VIII (see n. to *Inf.* III, 59-60). The words, in the light of this belief, are cynical and ironical in the extreme.

106. *pinser = spinsero.*   *argomenti gravi*: The pope argues from his own authority, delegated to him by Christ; Guido finds these arguments weighty, for, as a corded friar, he is bound by an oath of obedience to higher authority.

107. *là 've = là ove.*   *'l tacer mi fu avviso 'l peggio*: As a Franciscan, bound by oath to strict obedience, Guido would have good reason to fear the wrath of Boniface if he did not yield to the latter's request (see *Par.* IV, 109-11). Not to obey seems a worse sin than giving false counsel, though by his words Guido clearly admits to an awareness that in giving the counsel requested he will be committing a grave sin, and he declares as much in the following verses. Benvenuto observes: "Sic comes, dum nititur se excusare, accusat; quia voluit potius contra conscientiam complacere Bonifacio, quam displicere illi pro salute animae suae." ("And thus the count, in trying to excuse himself, accuses himself. For he would rather please Boniface against his conscience than displease him for the good of his soul.")

108. *da che = poichè.   mi lavi*: See Ps. 50:4 [51:2]: "Amplius lava me ab iniquitate mea, et a peccato meo munda me." ("Thoroughly wash me from my guilt and of my sin cleanse me.")

109. *di quel peccato ov' io mo cader deggio*: "Since you wash me of that sin which I must now incur." Guido consents to sin on the assurance that he is absolved in advance.   *mo cader deggio*: Guido solemnly repeats the conditions of the pact, and in so doing shows his confidence in its full validity; for this reason he never bothered later to repent.

110. *lunga promessa con l'attender corto*: An account of the pope's treachery at Palestrina is given by Villani (VIII, 23):

> Nel detto anno del mese di Settembre, essendo trattato d'accordo da papa Bonifazio a' Colonnesi, i detti Colonnesi cherici e laici vennero a Rieti ov'era la corte, e gittarsi a piè del detto papa alla misericordia, il quale perdonò loro . . . ma fece disfare la detta città di Pilestrino del poggio e fortezze ov'era, a fecene rifare una terra al piano, alla quale puose nome Civita Papale; e tutto questo trattato falso e frodolente fece il papa per consiglio del conte da Montefeltro, allora frate minore, ove gli disse la mala parola: *lunga promessa coll'attender corto.*

> In the same year, in the month of September, Pope Boniface offered peace terms to the Colonna. Members of that family, both priests and laymen, came to the papal court at Rieti to throw themselves at the pope's feet and ask for mercy. He forgave them . . . but he had the city of Palestrina, which was strongly fortified on top of a hill, destroyed and had it rebuilt on the plain and called it Città Papale. The pope committed all these false and fraudulent acts on the advice of the count of Montefeltro, who was then a Franciscan, and who spoke the evil words, "a long promise and a short fulfillment."

It is possible that Villani took the words "lunga promessa coll'attender corto" from Dante and that they do not represent an independent view. On the historicity of the incident, see n. to vs. 67.   *attender*: G. Manuzzi (1859, p. 364), under the entry "attender," par. 16, gives another example of this meaning: "Il castello s'arrendè a patti, salve le persone, i quali non furono loro attesi." ("The castle surrendered on the condition that the people not be harmed; and the condition was not observed.")

111. *ne l'alto seggio*: "On your lofty throne."

112. *Francesco venne poi*: The transition is the more effective for being so abrupt. Guido in fact did die in September 1298, the month in which Boniface tricked the Colonna. / St. Francis, in coming for one of his order, replaces the angel that sometimes comes to struggle against a devil for the possession of a soul; see *Purg.* V, 104.

113. *un d'i neri cherubini*: See the reference to "angeli neri" in *Inf.* XXIII, 131; but Dante may well have chosen one of the fallen cherubim in particular, since (according to Pseudo-Dionysus) among the nine orders of angels they are second in rank and the most learned, and even a fallen cherub presumably would keep some of this special power. Thomas Aquinas (*Summa theol.* I, q. 63, a. 7, ad 1) says: "Cherubim interpretatur *plenitudo scientiae*." ("Cherubim is interpreted *fulness of knowledge*.") See also *Par.* XI, 38–39.   *d'i = dei*.

114. *li = gli*.   *Non portar = non lo portar*; the omission of the object with the imperative form of the verb is common in early Italian.

115. *Venir se ne dee = se ne deve venire*.

117. *dal quale = dal quale consiglio*.   *in qua*: "Down to this moment."   *stato li sono a' crini*: The cherub has been waiting to seize him the moment he died.   *li = gli*.

118–20. *ch'assolver . . . per la contradizion*: "He cannot be absolved [of a sin] who does not repent [of it]." To repent is to will not to do. Hence it is not possible to repent in advance of a sin which one is about to commit willingly.

Nevertheless, Guido, thinking himself absolved, never bethought himself to repent later.

118. *ch'* = *chè* in the sense of *perchè*.   *assolver non si può*: This impersonal construction may be taken passively: "He may not be absolved." The subject is "chi non si pente."   *si pente*: From *pentirsi*, "to repent." See *De mon.* III, viii, 7: "Unde cum dicitur 'quodcunque ligaveris,' si illud 'quodcunque' sumeretur absolute, verum esset quod dicunt . . . . Posset etiam solvere me non penitentem: quod etiam facere ipse Deus non posset." ("Wherefore when it is said 'Whatsoever thou hast bound,' if this 'whatsoever' were to be taken absolutely their contention would be true . . . . He would also be able to absolve me while I am not penitent, which even God himself could not do.")

119. *pentere*: Pronounced *pentère*; archaic for *pentire* (from the Latin *paenitere*).   *puossi* = *si può*, impersonal.

121. *mi riscossi*: "I awakened with a start." See *Inf.* IV, 2. Only now does Guido realize how he erred by believing in the fraudulent absolution promised by Boniface. He knows that the charge against him is valid: he has given false counsel and has never repented.

123. *io loico*: The expressed subject pronoun is emphatic. *loico* = *logico*.

124. *Minòs*: For Minos' role in Hell, see *Inf.* V, 4-12.

125. *otto volte*: Thus sentencing him to the eighth circle of Hell.

126. *per gran rabbia la si morse*: For this characteristic expression of wrath, see the descriptions of Filippo Argenti turning upon himself with his teeth (*Inf.* VIII, 61-63) and of the Minotaur gnawing himself (*Inf.* XII, 14). See also Giotto's conception of *Ira* (Plate 6, facing p. 502).

127. *Questi è d'i rei del foco furo*: These words condemn the soul to the eighth *bolgia*.   *d'i* = *dei*.   *foco furo*: See *Inf.* XXVI, 41-42: "il furto . . . invola."

128. *per ch'*: "For which reason," i.e., for which sin and for which judgment against me [I am damned].

129. *sì vestito*: With the flame that encloses him.   *mi rancuro* = *mi dolgo*, but with the suggestion of bitter remorse, thereby throwing into relief the great contrast between his suffering and that of Ulysses.

131-32. *la fiamma dolorando . . . aguto*: Ulysses' flame no longer waved as in *Inf.* XXVI, 86, but became "erect and still" (vs. 1) after he told his tale; Guido's flame goes off as it came, "grieving . . . twisting and tossing its sharp horn."

131. *partio* = *partì*.

135. *'l fosso*: The ninth *bolgia*.   *il fio*: "That which is due," the penalty.

136. *scommettendo*: The opposite of *commettendo* ("putting together").   *acquistan carco*: "Take on their burden" of guilt.

CANTO XXVIII

1. *poria = potrebbe.* *con parole sciolte*: I.e., in prose. "Sciolte" means "loose" in the sense of "unbound"—in this case unbound by rhyme. Cf. the Latin *prosa oratio* and *oratio soluta*; and see Ovid's "verba soluta modis" ("words freed from rhythm"), *Tristia* IV, x, 24.

2. *dicer = dire.* *a pieno*: Depends on "dicer."

3. *per narrar più volte*: "For telling many times"—that is, "though one should tell many times."

4–6. *Ogne lingua . . . seno*: See *Aen.* VI, 625–27:

> non mihi si linguae centum sint oraque centum,
> ferrea vox, omnis scelerum comprendere formas,
> omnia poenarum percurrere nomina possim.

Nay, had I a hundred tongues, a hundred mouths, and voice of iron, I could not sum up all the forms of crime, or rehearse all the tale of torments.

See also *canzone* II, 14–18 (*Conv.* III):

> Però, se le mie rime avran difetto
> ch'entreran ne la loda di costei,
> di ciò si biasmi il debole intelletto
> e'l parlar nostro, che non ha valore
> di ritrar tutto ciò che dice Amore.

495

Wherefore if defect shall mark my rhymes, which shall enter upon her praises, for this let our feeble intellect be blamed, and our speech which hath not power to tell again all that love speaketh.

And see the gloss on these verses, *Conv.* III, iv, 4: "E dico che se difetto fia ne le mie rime, cioè ne le mie parole che a trattare di costei sono ordinate, di ciò è da biasimare la debilitade de lo'ntelletto e la cortezza del nostro parlare." ("And I say that if there be defect in my rhymes, that is to say, in my words, which are ordained to treat of her, the blame must fall upon the weakness of intellect and the scant power of our speech.")

4. *verria = verrebbe.*

6. *seno*: Literally, "hollow."

7. *S'el s'aunasse = se egli si radunasse.*

7–21. *S'el s'aunasse ancor tutta la gente . . . sozzo*: Apropos of this comparison, V. Crescini (1907, p. 55) credits M. Scherillo (1897, pp. 477–78) with pointing to a striking stylistic resemblance with verses commonly attributed to the Provençal poet Bertran de Born on the death of the "Young King" (Prince Henry, son of Henry II of England; see n. to vs. 135, below). In view of the fact that there are other echoes of Bertran in this canto (see vss. 24, 37, and the notes) and his very appearance at the end (see vss. 118–35), the resemblance is of particular interest. See the following lines by Bertran (sec. XLIII, i, 1–5, in C. Appel, 1932, p. 98):

> Si tuit li dol e·lh plor e·lh marrimen
> E las dolors e·lh dan e·lh chaitivier
> Qu'om anc auzis en est segle dolen
> Fossen ensems, sembleran tot leugier
> Contra la mort del jove rei engles . . .

If all the sorrow, tears, sadness, pain, loss, and suffering which were ever heard of in this grieving world were combined, they would all seem light when weighed against the death of the young English king.

7. *el*: A redundant subject pronoun, anticipating "gente."

ancor: We are asked to imagine that all the maimed and dead named in the following verses might be brought together.

8. *fortunata*: "Storm-tossed," said of Apulia because of the many wars that took place there.

9. *Puglia*: Modern Apulia is the compartment of southeast Italy that forms the heel of the peninsula and extends along the coast of the Adriatic Sea to Abruzzi e Molise; but in the Middle Ages the name was often used to indicate the whole of the southern extremity of continental Italy, including ancient Apulia. It is in the latter sense that Dante uses it here.

10. *li Troiani*: The Romans, descendants of Aeneas and his men. The Trojans are referred to as the "noble seed" of the Romans in *Inf.* XXVI, 60. The allusion here is to the wars with the Tarentines and Samnites. See Livy, especially Book X.   *la lunga guerra*: The second·Punic War, against Hannibal (218–201 B.C.). See Livy, XXII.

11. *che de l'anella fé sì alte spoglie*: The reference is to a heap of gold rings taken from the bodies of Romans killed in the battle of Cannae (216 B.C.) during the second Punic War and produced in the senate house at Carthage by Hannibal's envoy as proof of his victory. Cannae was a village in Apulia. In vs. 12, Dante mentions Livy as his authority for this incident. See Livy, XXIII, xii, 1–2:

Ad fidem deinde tam laetarum rerum effundi in vesti-bulo curiae iussit anulos aureos, qui tantus acervus fuit ut metientibus dimidium supra tris modios explesse sint quidam auctores; fama tenuit, quae propior vero est, haud plus fuisse modio. Adiecit deinde verbis, quo maioris cladis indicium esset, neminem nisi equitem, atque eorum ipsorum primores, id gerere insigne.

Then in evidence of such successes he ordered the golden rings to be poured out at the entrance of the Senate House. And so great was the heap of them that, when measured, they filled, as some historians assert, three pecks and a half. The prevailing report, and nearer the truth, is that there was not more than one peck. Then, that it might be proof of a greater calamity, he added in explanation that no one but a knight, and even of the knights only those of the higher class, wore that token.

E. Moore (1896, pp. 274–75) has suggested that Dante's epithet "alte" as applied to "spoglie" is explained by "acervus" in the above passage from Livy and would thus mean "high-heaped." It seems possible, however, that "alte" refers to the fact mentioned by Livy that only knights "wore that token."

It is interesting to note that in *Conv.* IV, v, 19, Dante probably had accepted the account of Orosius (IV, xvi, 5), which put the number of pecks of rings at three. Augustine also has three (*De civ. Dei* III, 19). *anella*: Plural of *anello*.

12. *Livio*: The Roman historian Livy (Titus Livius) was born in 59 B.C. and died in A.D. 17. Only part of his great work *Ab urbe condita*, the history of Rome from the foundation of the city to the death of Drusus (9 B.C.), is now extant. Dante probably was not acquainted with any part of the work that has not been preserved to the present time.

13. *con quella*: The "people" referred to in vs. 7. *sentio = sentì*.

14. *contastare = contrastare*, "to oppose," "to resist." *Ruberto Guiscardo*: The Norman adventurer Robert Guiscard, duke of Apulia and Calabria, fought the Greeks and Saracens in southern Italy and Sicily during the last half of the eleventh century. Dante places Guiscard in the heaven of Mars, among the Christian warriors who fought for the faith; see *Par.* XVIII, 48.

15. *l'altra*: The "people," vs. 7. *ossame*: "Scattered bones." *ancor*: Thirty-four years or more after the battle (see n. to vs. 16, below).

16. *Ceperan*: Modern Ceprano; a town in southeast Latium on the banks of the Liri. The allusion is to the betrayal of Manfred by the Apulians just before the fatal battle of Benevento, February 26, 1266. Villani (VII, 5) gives the following account:

Lo re Manfredi sentendo la loro venuta, del detto Carlo, e poi della sua gente . . . incontanente mise tutto suo studio alla guardia de' passi del regno, e al passo al ponte a Cepperano mise il conte Giordano e quello di Caserta . . . con gente assai a piè e a cavallo . . . . Avvenne che giunto il re Carlo con sua oste a Fresolone in Campagna, scendendo verso Cepperano, il detto conte Giordano che a quello passo era a guardia, veggendo venire la gente del re per passare, volle difendere il passo; il conte di Caserta disse ch'era meglio a lasciarne prima alquanti passare, sì gli avrebbono di là dal passo sanza colpo di spada. Il conte quando vide ingrossare la gente, ancora volle assalirli con battaglia; allora il conte di Caserta il quale era nel trattato, disse che la battaglia era di gran rischio, imperciocchè troppi n'erano passati. Allora il conte Giordano veggendo sì possente la gente del re, abbandonarono la terra e il ponte, chi dice per paura, ma i più dissono per lo trattato fatto dal re al conte di Caserta, imperciocch'egli non amava Manfredi . . . e volle fare questa vendetta col detto tradimento. E a questo diamo fede, perocchè furono de' primi egli e' suoi che s'arrenderono al re Carlo, e lasciato Cepperano, non tornaro all'oste del re Manfredi a san Germano, ma si tennero in loro castella.

King Manfred, hearing about the approach of Charles and his soldiers . . . immediately turned all his attention to guarding the passes to the kingdom. He posted Count Giordano and the count of Caserta at the pass at the bridge of Ceprano . . . with many soldiers, both horse and foot . . . . When King Charles arrived with his army in Fresolone in the Campagna, and was descending toward Ceprano, Count Giordano, who was on guard at that pass, saw the king and his army drawing

closer, and wished to defend it. The count of Caserta
said it was better to let some of them get through,
that they might be captured this side of the pass with-
out striking a blow. The count [Giordano], seeing the
army get larger and larger [this side of the pass],
wanted to attack; but then the count of Caserta, who
was in league with the enemy, said that the battle
would be too dangerous because too many had got
through. When Count Giordano realized how power-
ful the king's army was, they abandoned the town and
the bridge—some say out of fear, but most say it was
because of the understanding between the king and the
count of Caserta, who did not love Manfred . . . and
wanted to get his revenge through this betrayal. And
that is what we believe; for he and his men were among
the first to surrender to King Charles. And when they
left Ceprano, they did not return to the army of King
Manfred at San Germano, but stayed instead in their
castles.

Dante implies that there was a battle at Ceprano, but as a
matter of fact no engagement took place at the bridge. He
perhaps confused what happened there with the action at
San Germano, which was besieged and taken a few days
later (see Villani, VII, 6). Or possibly, since the context
seems to point to an engagement in which there was great
loss of life, his words (taken somewhat loosely) refer to
the decisive battle at Benevento itself, during which, at a
critical moment, as Villani (VII, 9) relates, "la maggiore
parte de' baroni pugliesi, e del Regno . . . o per viltà di
cuore, o veggendo a loro avere il peggiore, e chi disse per
tradimento . . . si fallirono a Manfredi, abbandonandolo
e fuggendosi." ("The majority of the barons of Apulia and
of the kingdom . . . either out of cowardice, or because they
thought they would be beaten—some said through be-
trayal . . . failed Manfred, abandoning him and fleeing.")

17. *Pugliese*: Soldier of Apulia (see n. to vs. 9, above).
  da Tagliacozzo: Near Tagliacozzo, town of central Italy
in Abruzzi e Molise, about twenty-one miles south south-
west of Aquila.

18. *dove sanz' arme vinse il vecchio Alardo*: Érard (or Érart) de Valéry, lord of Saint-Valérien and of Marolles and constable of Champagne, was born about 1200 and died in 1277. In 1268, returning from Palestine to France, he passed through Italy, as Villani (VII, 26) records: "[Il] buono messer Alardo di Valleri, cavaliere francesco di grande senno e prodezza . . . di quegli tempi era arrivato in Puglia tornando d'oltremare dalla terra santa." ("The good Messer Érard de Valéry, a French knight of great good sense and bravery . . . arrived in those days in Apulia, returning from the Holy Land, beyond the sea.") Charles of Anjou, being engaged in a battle with Conradin, nephew of Manfred and grandson of Frederick II, at Tagliacozzo, was advised by Érard to keep his reserves in the background until Conradin's troops, who at the beginning of the day had routed his opponents, were disordered by pursuit and scattered over the field in search of plunder. Charles then advanced with fresh troops and completely routed the enemy. It is to Charles' victory by means of this stratagem of Érard's that Dante alludes here.

19-20. *e qual . . . mostrasse*: These verses continue the imagined gathering that begins at vs. 7, and now add to the scene the condition that these warriors display their wounds.

19. *suo membro*: The object of "mostrasse," vs. 20. *mozzo = mozzato*.

20. *d'aequar sarebbe nulla*: The Latinism "aequar" points to the possibility that the whole imagined scene and this conclusion were in some sense inspired by Virgil. See *Aen.* II, 361-62: "Quis cladem illius noctis, quis funera fando / explicet aut possit lacrimis aequare labores?" ("Who could unfold in speech that night's havoc? Who its carnage? or who could match our toils with tears?") Also see n. to vss. 4-6 above.

22. *Già*: The word reinforces the whole negation that follows. *mezzul*: The midboard or middle piece of the three that make up the end of a cask. *lulla*: One of the

two crescent-shaped boards of the end of a cask, properly termed "cant" in English. Lana comments: "Li fondi delle botti sono di tre pezzi: quello di mezzo è ditto *mezule*[OI], e li estremi hanno nome *lulle*." ("The ends of casks are made of three pieces: the middle piece is called *mezzule* [midboard] and the other two are called *lulle* [cants].")

22-23. *Già veggia . . . si pertugia*: The broken construction effectively renders the broken object described. See the separation of "modo" and "sozzo" in vs. 21. A whole clause now intervenes between "veggia" and "così non si pertugia."

24. *rotto dal mento infin dove si trulla*: The language is violent for the same stylistic reason that the construction discussed in the preceding note is broken. Also see vs. 27. M. Scherillo (1897, p. 459), as V. Crescini (1907, p. 56) notes, has called attention to the echo in this verse of Bertran de Born's description of a hoped-for battlefield on which he seems to see warriors lying "de fendutz per bustz tro als braiers" ("cleft through the chest right down to the waist"); see sec. XXXVII, ii, 12 in C. Appel (1932), p. 89.

26. *la corata*: The pluck—the heart, liver, lungs, and windpipe of a slaughtered animal.   *pareva = appariva*.
  'l tristo sacco: The stomach, which is "tristo" (in the familiar sense of "sorry") when seen thus and in its (alleged) function as stated in the next verse.

28. *m'attacco*: Even this verb implies a certain vehemence in Dante's gaze and contributes to the vocabulary of violence in this canto, wherein the punishments of the sowers of discord and division are described.

29. *guardommi = mi guardò.   e con le man s'aperse il petto*: Following on Dante's intent gaze comes this violent rending gesture, as much as to say: "So you want to see? Well, I'll show you something." (See Giotto's conception of *Ira*, Plate 6, facing.)

30. *mi dilacco*: V. Crescini (1907, p. 14) observes:

  "Lacca" è "anca," "coscia" . . . "di-laccare" è "separare,

6. Ira ("Wrath"), a fresco by Giotto

dividere, divaricare, aprire le cosce"; e quindi, in genere, "divaricare, aprire."

Nè spiaccia ch'io avverta come il suono stesso della parola, con quell'apertissimo *a* tonico ("io mi dilàcco") compia anche musicalmente l'atto e l'aspetto di quello squarciato in se stesso crudele. Ed è rima insolita "io mi dilacco"; una di quelle che i provenzali dicevano *caras rimas*: e son qui tutte, ne' tre terzetti, che ora chioso, *caras rimas*, ma in un senso scabro e spregiativo: -ùlla: -ùgia: -àcco . . . .

Lacca is the "haunch," the "thigh" . . . *di-laccare* means "to separate, divide, spread, open the thighs"; and there-fore it generally means "to spread," "to open."

It may also be noted that the very sound of the word, with that completely open tonic *a* ("io mi dilàcco"), renders musically the act and aspect of him who so cruelly tears himself open. And it is an unusual rhyme, "io mi dilacco," one of those rhymes the Provençals called *caras rimas*. And all of them, in the three tercets that I am now glossing, are *caras rimas*, but in a scabrous and pejorative sense, *-ùlla, -ùgia, -àcco* . . . .

31. *Maometto*: Mohammed, founder of the Mohammedan re-ligion, was born at Mecca *ca.* 570. In 630 he was recognized as chief and prophet, and before his death in 632 at Medina he had extended his power to include all of Arabia. There was a belief current in the Middle Ages that Mohammed was an apostate Christian, perhaps even a cardinal, and it may have been for this reason that Dante placed him in this ninth *bolgia* along with other great sowers of religious dissent. Or, as Sapegno points out, the poet may have placed Mohammed here because he considered the founding of Islam a divisive factor in religious unity. On Dante's atti-tude toward Mohammed, see J. S. P. Tatlock (1932); on the legend of Mohammed in the West, see the lengthy dis-cussion of A. D'Ancona (1889).

32. *Alì*: 'Ali ibn-abi-Ṭālib, fourth of the caliphs, or suc-cessors of Mohammed, was born at Mecca *ca.* 600. He was one of the first followers of Mohammed and married his

daughter Fatima. In 656 he assumed the caliphate, which he held until his assassination in 661. The question of Ali's right to succeed to the caliphate divided the Mohammedans into two great sects, the Sunnites and the Shiites or Fatimites. It is to be noted that both Mohammed and Ali are described as split, the former—sower of discord among nations—from the chin down, the latter—sower of discord among the heads of the Mohammedan sect—from the chin up, thus completing a total schism.

33. *fesso*: Past participle of *fendere*, "to cleave." See "fessi" in vs. 36.

35. *seminator di scandalo e di scisma*: A single verse serves to label the sinners of this ninth *bolgia*. "Scandalo" is to be understood in the Scriptural sense of the term as discussed and defined in the theology of Dante's day. See Thomas Aquinas, *Summa theol.* II-II, q. 43, a. 1, resp.:

> Respondeo dicendum, quod, sicut Hieronymus ibidem dicit, quod graece σχάνδαλον dicitur, nos, *offensionem*, vel *ruinam*, vel *impactionem pedis* possumus dicere. Contingit enim quod quandoque aliquis obex ponitur alicui in via corporali, cui impingens disponitur ad ruinam; et talis obex dicitur scandalum.

> *I answer that*, As Jerome observes [in his commentary on Matt. 15:12], the Greek σχάνδαλον may be rendered offense, downfall, or a stumbling against something. For when a body, while moving along a path, meets with an obstacle, it may happen to stumble against it, and be disposed to fall down: such an obstacle is a σχάνδαλον.

On schism, see *Summa theol.* II-II, q. 39, a. 1, resp.:

> Respondeo dicendum, quod sicut Isidorus dicit in lib. 8 Etymolog., cap. 3, *nomen schismatis a scissura animorum vocatum est*, scissio autem unitati opponitur; unde peccatum schismatis dicitur quod directe et per se opponitur unitati. . . . Et ideo peccatum schismatis proprie est speciale peccatum, ex eo quod intendit se ab unitate separare, quam charitas facit.

I answer that, As Isidore says (*Etym.* viii. 3), schism takes its name *from being a scission of minds,* and scission is opposed to unity. Wherefore the sin of schism is one that is directly and essentially opposed to unity. . . . Hence the sin of schism is, properly speaking, a special sin, for the reason that the schismatic intends to sever himself from that unity which is the effect of charity.

Aquinas goes on to distinguish between schism and heresy as sins (*Summa theol.* II-II, q. 39, a. 1, ad 3):

Haeresis et schisma distinguuntur secundum ea quibus utrumque per se et directe opponitur. Nam haeresis per se opponitur fidei; schisma autem per se opponitur unitati ecclesiasticae charitatis. Et ideo sicut fides et charitas sunt diversae virtutes, quamvis quicumque caret fide, careat charitate; ita etiam schisma et haeresis sunt diversa vitia, quamvis quicumque est haereticus, sit etiam schismaticus; sed non convertitur. Et hoc est quod Hieronymus dicit in Epist. ad Tit. (sup. illud cap 3: *Haereticum hominem,* etc.): *Inter schisma et haeresim hoc interesse arbitror, quod haeresis perversum dogma habet, schisma ab Ecclesia separat.*

Heresy and schism are distinguished in respect of those things to which each is opposed essentially and directly. For heresy is essentially opposed to faith, while schism is essentially opposed to the unity of ecclesiastical charity. Wherefore just as faith and charity are different virtues, although whoever lacks faith lacks charity, so too schism and heresy are different vices, although whoever is a heretic is also a schismatic, but not conversely. This is what Jerome says in his commentary on the Epistle to [Titus 3:10]: *I consider the difference between schism and heresy to be that heresy holds false doctrine while schism severs a man from the Church.*

36. *fuor vivi = furono vivi,* "while they lived."   *e però = e perciò.   son fessi così:* Thus observing what will be called, in the last verse of this canto, the *contrapasso* (see vs. 142).

37. *n'accisma = ci accisma*. Cf. the OFr *acesmer*, Provençal *acesmar*. V. Crescini (1907, p. 22) comments that the Italian word retains its original significance and here means "adorns." He notes that mutilated prisoners are described with similar irony in a twelfth-century poem as *lah acesmat* ("adorned in an ugly way"). Crescini suggests that Dante might not have known this poem. He goes on to say:

> La diabolica spada orna davvero, "accisma": ed ecco perchè, oltre che per la rima, Dante adoperi con ricercata, squisita ironia, l'esotica voce, usata spesso a indicare, nella letteratura cavalleresca, acconciamenti, adornamenti, abbigliamenti di signori e di dame. La conscia spada fa una specie di *toilette* miserevole e bizzarra, che imbruttisce con arte, con un, direi quasi, dileggio chirurgico.

> The diabolical sword truly adorns, *accisma*. And that is why, aside from the rhyme, Dante uses this exotic word, with unusual, exquisite irony. In chivalresque literature, it is often used to indicate the ornaments, the adornments, and the dress of gentlemen and of ladies. The conscious sword performs a sort of pitiable and bizarre toilette, one which skillfully renders them ugly—with what I might almost call a surgical mockery.

M. Fubini (1962, p. 21, n. 1) observes, in approving of Crescini's interpretation given above, that "accisma" is not only a Provençalism but an echo of Bertran de Born's "chascus deu esser acesmatz." ("Everyone must be adorned.") See sec. XL, iii, 27 in C. Appel (1932), p. 93. / For the ironical use of the verb, compare the use of *acconciare* and *governare* in *Vita nuova* IV, 2; *Purg.* XXIII, 35. On the verb's origin and significance, see A. Schiaffini (1931).

38–39. *al taglio de la spada rimettendo ciascun*: In connection with these verses, Torraca quotes a similar passage in the *Tavola ritonda*, a version of the Tristan and Arthurian legends. See *Tav. riton.* XCVII (p. 383): "E Tristano disse: Se io troverrò la porta serrata, io metteròe al taglio della spada quanti cavalieri vi troverrò." ("And Tristan said:

'If I find the door shut, I will put to the sword all the knights I find there.' ")

39. *risma*: "Lot," literally "ream" (as of paper), which in fact is the English cognate. Here the word is used ironically.

40. *avem = abbiamo*.   *volta*: Past participle of *volgere*.

41. *però che = perciò che*.

42. *li = gli*.

43. *muse = musi*. Cf. the OFr *muser* (also mod. French *amuser*), Provençal *muzar*, and English *muse*, "to loiter," "to trifle," "to reflect." E. G. Parodi (1957, p. 282) comments on this word and offers several examples of its use; V. Crescini (1907, p. 23) discusses its meaning.

45. *ch'è giudicata in su le tue accuse*: Before Minos, where the soul "confesses all" (*Inf.* V, 8).

46. *giunse = raggiunse*.

46–47. *né colpa 'l mena . . . a tormentarlo*: The subject of "tormentar" is "colpa."

48. *lui*: Dative.   *esperienza piena*: See *Inf.* XVII, 37–38.

52. *Più fuor di cento = furono più di cento*.   *udiro = udirono*.

54. *martiro = martirio*.

55–60. *Or dì a fra Dolcin . . . leve*: Dolcino Tornielli of Novara, born in the second half of the thirteenth century, was known as Fra Dolcino because of his connection with the sect of the Apostolic Brothers, founded in Parma by Gherardo Segarelli with the object of bringing the Church back to the simplicity of apostolic times. After the death of Segarelli *ca.* 1300, Fra Dolcino became the acknowledged head of the sect and was accused by his opponents of holding heretical doctrines, including the community of goods and women. His biographer, L. Mariotti, says, however (1853, p. 297), that he simply wished to reform the Church and destroy the temporal power of the clergy. Following the promulgation in 1305 of a bull of Clement V for the extirpation of his sect, Fra Dolcino with thousands of followers in the hills between Novara and Vercelli defied the repeated attacks of the Church authorities. They finally were reduced by starvation, large numbers were massacred on the mountains, and others were burned. Fra Dolcino and his companion, the beautiful Margaret of Trent, who was said to be his mistress, were taken prisoner and burned alive in June 1307. The tone of the prophecy here, as of other prophecies in the canto, is ironical. For a review of the literature on Fra Dolcino, see A. Zenatti (1903); see also *Historia fratris Dulcini*.

56. *forse*: Modifies "in breve."

58. *sì di vivanda*: Connects with "s'armi," vs. 55.

59. *al Noarese*: Singular for plural, *Novaresi*.

60. *ch'altrimenti acquistar non saria leve*: See *Historia fratris Dulcini* (p. 6, ll. 13–14): "A nemine expugnari poterant nec aliquem hominem timebant, dummodo tamen haberent victualia." ("Nobody could defeat them and they feared no man, at least as long as they were supplied with food.")
saria = sarebbe.

61–63. *Poi che l'un piè . . . distese*: The meaning of these verses has been well explained by F. D'Ovidio (1923, p. 26), who points out that the poet has not conceived of Mohammed as standing with one foot up in the air all the while he makes this long prophecy, but has focused on him at the moment when the step is not yet complete:

> Maometto per ripigliare il cammino aveva incominciato il primo passo, aveva mosso un piede, ed era giunto all'attimo in cui il piede rimane appoggiato sul calcagno epperò sospeso; e in quell'atteggiamento si soffermò ad avventare la profezia, finita la quale se ne partì davvero distendendo il piede a terra, compiendo cioè il passo già incominciato. E non è solo affare di buona fisica, ma di buona lingua: se il poeta avesse voluto dire che

rimise a terra un piede tenuto tutto in aria, avrebbe detto così, e non già che lo *distese in terra*.

To start walking again, Mohammed had taken the first step, had moved a foot, and had reached the moment in which the foot was pressing on the heel, but was still suspended. In that attitude, he stopped to shout his prophecy; and when he had finished, he started off again, putting his foot on the ground—that is, finishing the step he had begun. This is not only a matter of good physics, but of good language as well. If the poet had wanted to say that he "put down" a foot completely suspended in mid-air, he would have said that; and not that he "extended it on the ground."

62. *esta parola* = *questa parola*, "these words." See *Inf.* II, 67; VII, 126.

64. *Un altro*: One Piero da Medicina, about whom little or nothing is known, beyond what the early commentators report. He must have seen Dante somewhere in Italy (see vss. 71–72), which excludes the possibility that the reference is to a Piero da Medicina of Bologna (the family was originally from Medicina) who died about 1271. A relative of this first Piero, one Piero di Aimo di Medicina, who is cited in a document of 1271 (quoted by G. Zaccagnini, 1914) as "nepos quondam domini Petri de Medicina" ("nephew of the late Messer Piero da Medicina") is thought by some possibly to be the Piero in question. The younger Piero is further mentioned in documents of 1272 and 1277, in which his city too is given as Bologna. However, nothing is known of the misdeeds for which he would have been placed in this *bolgia*. See G. Zaccagnini (1914), pp. 8–14, and C. Ricci (1921a), pp. 28–29, for the view that the younger man was the one Dante had in mind. Benvenuto, in his gloss on vs. 72, says that Dante and Piero had met at Medicina:

> Medicina est villa grossa et pinguis inter Bononiam et Imolam; et est territorium per se, et habebat olim arcem fortem. Et ibi regnaverunt olim quidam nobiles

et potentes, qui vocati sunt Catanei de Medicina, quorum hodie nullus extat. De ista domo fuit Petrus praedictus. Ad domum istorum pervenit semel Dantes, ubi fuit egregie honoratus. Et interrogatus quid sibi videretur de curia illa, respondit, se non vidisse pulcriorem in Romandiola, si ibi esset modicum ordinis.

Medicina is a large, prosperous village between Imola and Bologna, and forms a territory unto itself. It once had a strong fortress, and for some time was ruled by powerful noblemen, the lords of Medicina, of whom at present there are no descendants left. The aforementioned Piero was of that house. Dante once visited his home and was highly honored. When he was asked what he thought of that court, he replied that if only it were a little more orderly, he could say that he had never seen a more beautiful one in Romagna.

The early commentators describe Piero as a persistent mischief-maker and sower of discord. Benvenuto says of him:

Fuit pessimus seminator scandali, in tantum quod se aliquandiu magnificavit et ditavit dolose ista arte infami. Et ecce modum gratia exempli: si sensisset Petrus de Medicina, quod dominus Malatesta de Arimino tractabat contrahere affinitatem vel societatem cum domino Guidone de Ravenna, invenisset ergo Petrus a casu quemdam familiarem domini Malatestae, et petivisset affectuose: Quomodo valet Dominus meus? Et post longam confabulationem dixisset in fine: Dicas domino Malatestae, ut mittat mihi fidum nuntium, cum quo loqui possim, sicut secum, aliqua non spargenda in vulgo. Et veniente tali nuntio petito, dicebat Petrus: Vide, carissime, male libenter dicam, quia de honore meo esset forte tacere; sed sincera affectio, quam habeo ad dominum meum dominum Malatestam, non permittit me amplius dissimulare. Res ita se habet: Caveat sibi dominus Malatesta ab illo de Ravenna, alioquin inveniet se deceptum. Et statim remittebat istum nuntium sic informatum: et deinde illud idem falso fingebat apud dominum Guidonem de Ravenna, persuadens, ut

caveret sibi ab illo de Arimino. Tunc ergo dominus
Malatesta concepta suspicione ex verbis Petri, incipiebat
remissius agere cum domino Guidone, et paulatim in-
cipiebat revocare quod conceperat. De quo perpendens
dominus Guido, dicebat: Bene dicebat mihi verum
Petrus de Medicina. Et e contrario dicebat dominus
Malatesta. Et uterque deceptus mittebat Petro equos,
iocalia, munera magna, et uterque habebat ipsum in
amicum, qui erat familiaris inimicus, quo nulla pestis
est efficacior ad nocendum, ut ait Boetius.

He was a wicked troublemaker who for a while became
very important and very rich through fraud and in-
famous acts. Here is an example of how he did it: Piero
da Medicina would hear that Messer Malatesta da Ri-
mini was negotiating a matrimony or an alliance with
Messer Guido da Ravenna [i.e., Guido da Polenta]; then
he would come across some friend of Messer Malatesta,
and would ask him affectionately: "How is my lord?"
And after a long conversation, he would finally say to
him: "Tell Messer Malatesta to send me a completely
trustworthy messenger, with whom I may talk as freely
as though I were talking to him, about matters which
should not generally be known." And when such a
messenger came, Piero would say: "You see, my dear
friend, I tell you this very reluctantly, for my honor
requires that I be silent. But the genuine affection I feel
for my lord Messer Malatesta does not allow me to dis-
semble any longer. Things are this way: let Messer
Malatesta beware of the lord of Ravenna, or he will find
himself deceived." And he would immediately send
forth the messenger with that information. Later, he
would make the same false statements to Guido da
Ravenna, urging him to beware of the lord of Rimini.
Meanwhile, Messer Malatesta, made wary by Piero's
words, would begin to act somewhat coldly toward
Messer Guido and gradually to change his plans. And
Messer Guido, perceiving that, would believe that Piero
da Medicina had given him good advice. Messer Mala-
testa, in turn, thought the same thing. And both dupes

would send Piero horses, playthings, and rich gifts. Both the one and the other considered him a friend, whereas in fact he was an intimate enemy. And, as Boethius says, no plague is more efficacious in doing harm than that.

The *Anonimo fiorentino* says that Piero used similar tactics to try to divide the lords of Romagna as well as the citizens of Bologna.

66. *mai ch'* = *più che*. See *Inf.* IV, 26.

68. *aprì la canna*: Piero pulled open his throat to speak; the word "canna" focuses on his slit throat, all bloody outside.

71. *terra latina*: Italy. See *Inf.* XXVII, 26–27.

73. *rimembriti* = *ti rimembri*, impersonal third person construction with the pronoun in the dative; literally, "may it remember you of." See "ricorditi," the same construction, in *Purg.* V, 133. *Medicina*: See the first quotation from Benvenuto in n. to vs. 64.

75. *Vercelli*: Town in Piedmont, about forty miles northeast of Turin. *Marcabò*: A castle built by the Venetians in the territory of Ravenna on the Po di Primaro in order to protect the navigation of the river toward Ravenna and Ferrara, so that all merchandise coming in from the sea might pass through their hands. By 1270 it had become a considerable stronghold. In 1309, after the defeat of the Venetians by the forces of Clement V at Ferrara, it was destroyed. On the history of the castle and the form of its name, see A. Solmi (1914), pp. 4–10. Dante's mention of Vercelli and Marcabò serves to indicate the whole extent of the Po Valley.

76–90. *E fa sapere . . . preco*: Guido del Cassero and Angiolello di Carignano, two noblemen of Fano, of opposite parties, were invited by Malatestino, lord of Rimini (whom Dante calls the "Young Mastiff" in *Inf.* XXVII, 46), to a conference at La Cattolica on the Adriatic coast. On their way to the rendezvous (or perhaps as they were returning) they were surprised in their boat by Malatestino's men, thrown overboard, and drowned off the promontory of Focara. This event is thought to have taken place soon after 1312, the year in which Malatestino succeeded his father as lord of Rimini; and according to the *Anonimo fiorentino*, Malatestino's object in perpetrating the crime ("enorme facinus," or "violent act," Benvenuto calls it) was to prepare the way to seize the lordship of Fano. An earlier date than 1312 has been claimed by some; on which dispute see E. G. Parodi (1920), p. 373; G. Petrocchi (1957), pp. 659–60. I. Del Lungo (1888, p. 426, n. 1) says of Dante's epithet "due miglior da Fano" that we should attribute to "miglior" ("betters") the political meaning it shared with "buoni" ("good") as applied to important citizens.

78. *l'antiveder*: If the murder of Guido and Angiolello took place in 1312 or soon after, and if the time of the poem is 1300, that foresight extends some twelve years into the future. On the foresight of the damned in Hell, see *Inf*. X, 100–108.

80. *mazzerati*: Buti says of this word: "Mazzerare è gittare l'uomo in mare in uno sacco legato con una pietra grande, o legate le mani et i piedi et uno grande sasso al collo." ("*Mazzerare* means to throw a man into the sea in a sewn sack, with a large stone; or, with his hands and feet bound and a large stone around his neck.") Grandgent points out that *mazzera* indicates stones attached to a tunny net.   *la Cattolica*: Small town on the Adriatic, between Rimini and Pesaro.

81. *fello*: See *Inf*. VIII, 18; XI, 88.

82. *Tra l'isola di Cipri e di Maiolica*: Between the island of Cyprus in the east and the island of Majorca in the west—in other words, from one end of the Mediterranean to the other.

84. *pirate* = *pirati*.   *gente argolica*: The people of Argolis or Argos, i.e., the Greeks, perhaps with an allusion to the

Argonauts. See *Aen.* II, 78, "Argolica de gente" ("of Argive birth"), and Statius, *Achilleid* I, 775–76, "decora inclita gentis / Argolicae" ("ye famous heroes of the Argolic race"). Buti, however, understands the phrase to mean simply "[gente] di mare o vero naviganti" ("people of the sea, or navigators"), because "Argos [*sic*] fu chiamata la prima nave de' Greci ch'andò per mare." ("*Argo* was the name of the first Greek ship that took to the sea.")

85. *Quel traditor che vede pur con l'uno*: Malatestino had only one eye, and he was therefore known as Malatestino dell'Occhio. See *Cronaca riminese* MCCXCV (col. 896A).
  pur = solamente.   *con l'uno*: That is, *con un occhio.*

86–87. *la terra . . . digiuno*: Rimini.

87. *vorrebbe di vedere esser digiuno*: Literally, "could wish he had fasted of the sight thereof." See *Inf.* XVIII, 42. Rimini, near which the crime was committed, is termed a "bitter sight" in vs. 93.

88. *farà venirli = li farà venire.*

88–89. *farà venirli . . . poi farà sì*: If "farà venirli" is understood to mean "will send for them to come," then Guido and Angiolello may have been thrown into the sea on their way *to* the parley and may never have reached Rimini. Torraca understands the "poi" of vs. 89 to indicate that the two were murdered as they were returning *from* the parley; but if vs. 88 is interpreted as suggested, "poi" refers simply to time subsequent to the summons, not subsequent to the actual meeting. There is, however, no certain evidence one way or the other.

89–90. *poi farà sì . . . preco*: The whole tone is ironical: as Grandgent points out, Guido and Angiolello will not need to offer up prayers against the fear of shipwreck, because they will have been drowned anyway. Focara, a lofty headland on the Adriatic, between La Cattolica and Fano in the Marches, was dreaded by sailors because of the violent squalls that swept down from it. It was the custom to offer vows for a safe passage around the point, from which, says

Benvenuto, arose a proverbial saying: "Deus custodiat te a vento focariensi." ("God preserve you from the wind of Focara.")

90. *preco = preghiera*.

91. *Dimostrami e dichiara*: This is, in fact, exactly what Piero does (vss. 95–96); he pulls open the mouth of Curio (see n. to vss. 97–102) and declares: "Questi è desso."

93. *colui da la veduta amara*: Literally, "he of the bitter sight," i.e., he who rues the sight of Rimini (see vss. 86–87 and n. to vs. 87).

95. *li = gli*.

96. *desso*: Emphatic, for *quel proprio*, formed on the Latin *id ipsum*.

97–102. *Questi, scacciato . . . ardito*: Gaius Scribonius Curio the Younger originally was an adherent of the Pompeian party, and by its influence was made tribune of the plebs in 50 B.C. But he was bought over by Caesar, and employed his power as tribune against his former friends. When civil war broke out and Caesar was proclaimed by the senate an enemy of the republic, Curio fled from Rome and joined him. Caesar sent him to Sicily with the title of propraetor. Curio drove Cato from the island, then crossed over to Africa, where he was defeated and slain in 49 B.C. in battle against Juba I of Numidia.

Dante apparently drew several details of his description of Curio from Lucan. For example, compare vss. 97–99 with *Phars.* I, 280–81: "Dum trepidant nullo firmatae robore partes, / Tolle moras; semper nocuit differre paratis." ("While your foes are in confusion and before they have gathered strength, make haste; delay is ever fatal to those who are prepared.") Dante also quotes these lines from Lucan in his *Letter to the Emperor Henry VII* (*Epist.* VII, 16). Dante follows Lucan in making Curio responsible for Caesar's crossing of the Rubicon (see n. to vss. 97–98, below), though it appears that Caesar already had taken the decisive step when Curio joined him. The term "scacciato" (vs. 97)

as applied to Curio is reminiscent of *Phars.* I, 278–79:
"Pellimur e patriis laribus patimurque volentes / Exilium;
tua nos faciet victoria cives." ("And we have been driven
from our country. We suffer exile willingly, because your
victory will make us citizens again.") The reference to
Curio's boldness of speech (vs. 102) also probably derives
from Lucan (*Phars.* I, 269): "Audax venali comitatur Curio
lingua." ("With them came Curio of the reckless heart and
venal tongue.")

97–98. *il dubitar sommerse in Cesare*: Curio quenched
Caesar's hesitation over crossing the Rubicon (according to
Lucan and Dante).

100. *sbigottito*: The adjective is plainly the opposite of
"ardito" in vs. 102.

101. *strozza*: A strong term. See *Inf.* VII, 125.

103. *mozza = mozzata.*

105. *sì che 'l sangue facea la faccia sozza*: Dante, describing
the shades in upper Hell as empty, speaks of their having
"the appearance of bodies" (*Inf.* VI, 36). But how dense,
substantial, and real shades have become in lower Hell!

106. *Ricordera'ti = ti ricorderai.   anche*: Harks back to
"rimembriti" in vs. 73.   *Mosca*: Mosca de' Lamberti was
a passionate Ghibelline at whose instigation the Amidei
murdered Buondelmonte de' Buondelmonti, a crime that
led to the beginning of the Guelph and Ghibelline feuds in
Florence. The following account of the murder, and of the
incident which led to it, is given by Villani (V, 38):

> Negli anni di Cristo 1215 . . . avendo uno messer
> Bondelmonte de' Bondelmonti nobile cittadino di Fi-
> renze, promessa a torre per moglie una donzella di
> casa gli Amidei, onorevoli e nobili cittadini; e poi
> cavalcando per la città il detto messer Bondelmonte,
> ch'era molto leggiadro e bello cavaliere, una donna di
> casa i Donati il chiamò, biasimandolo della donna
> ch'egli avea promessa, come non era bella nè sofficiente

a lui, e dicendo: io v'avea guardata questa mia figliuola: la quale gli mostrò, e era bellissima; incontanente per *subsidio diaboli* preso di lei, la promise e isposò a moglie, per la qual cosa i parenti della prima donna promessa raunati insieme, e dogliendosi di ciò che messer Bondelmonte aveva loro fatto di vergogna, sì presono il maladetto isdegno, onde la città di Firenze fu guasta e partita; che di più casati de' nobili si congiuraro insieme, di fare vergogna al detto messer Bondelmonte, per vendetta di quelle ingiurie. E stando tra loro a consiglio in che modo il dovessero offendere, o di batterlo o di fedirlo, il Mosca de' Lamberti disse la mala parola: cosa fatta, capo ha; cioè che fosse morto: e così fu fatto; che la mattina di Pasqua di Risurresso, si raunaro in casa gli Amidei da santo Stefano, e vegnendo d'oltrarno il detto messere Bondelmonte vestito nobilemente di nuovo di roba tutta bianca, e in su uno palafreno bianco, giugnendo appiè del ponte Vecchio dal lato di qua, appunto appiè del pilastro ov'era la 'nsegna di Marti, il detto messere Bondelmonte fu atterrato del cavallo per lo Schiatta degli Uberti, e per lo Mosca Lamberti e Lambertuccio degli Amidei assalito e fedito, e per Oderigo Fifanti gli furono segate le vene e tratto a fine; e ebbevi con loro uno de' conti da Gangalandi. Per la qual cosa la città corse ad arme e romore; e questa morte di messer Bondelmonte fu la cagione e cominciamento delle maladette parti guelfa e ghibellina in Firenze, con tuttochè dinanzi assai erano le sette tra' nobili cittadini e le dette parti, per cagione delle brighe e questioni dalla Chiesa allo 'mperio; ma per la morte del detto messere Bondelmonte, tutti i legnaggi de' nobili e altri cittadini di Firenze se ne partiro, e chi tenne co' Bondelmonti che presono la parte guelfa e furonne capo, e chi con gli Uberti che furono capo de' ghibellini, onde alla nostra città seguì molto di male e ruina, come innanzi farò menzione; e mai non si crede ch'abbia fine, se Iddio nol termina. E bene mostra che 'l nemico dell'umana generazione per le peccata de' Fiorentini avesse podere nell'idolo di Marti, ch'e' Fiorentini pagani anticamente adoravano, che appiè della sua figura si commise sì fatto micidio, onde tanto male è seguito alla città di Firenze.

In the year of Christ 1215 . . . Messer Buondelmonte de' Buondelmonti, a noble citizen of Florence, had promised to marry a damsel of the house of the Amidei, honorable and noble citizens. Later, while riding through the city, Messer Buondelmonte, who was a very gracious and handsome knight, was called by a lady of the house of the Donati, who reproached him for having promised himself to that woman, saying she was not beautiful enough for him nor worthy of him. "I had saved this daughter of mine for you," she said; and she showed her to him, and she was indeed very beautiful. Immediately, by the work of the devil, he was taken with her; he promised himself to her, and then married her. The relatives of the first woman gathered together and complained of the shame Messer Buondelmonte had brought upon them. They were filled with the accursed anger that ruined and divided Florence; for many noble houses conspired to bring shame upon Messer Buondelmonte to avenge that offense. They were discussing the manner in which they would attack him—whether to beat him, or to draw blood— when Mosca de' Lamberti spoke the evil words: "A thing done has an end," that is, he should be killed. And that was done. On the morning of Easter of the Resurrection, they gathered in the house of the Amidei at Santo Stefano. Messer Buondelmonte, nobly dressed in new white garments, was returning from Oltrarno, riding a white palfry. When he arrived at the foot of the Ponte Vecchio, this side of the river, precisely at the foot of the pillar where was the statue of Mars, Messer Buondelmonte was thrown from his horse by Schiatta degli Uberti. Mosca Lamberti and Lambertuccio degli Amidei assaulted and stabbed him, Odarrigo Fifanti cut his veins and killed him. One of the counts of Gangalandi was with them. The city rushed to arms and a tumult arose; and this murder of Messer Buondel-

monte became the reason and the beginning of the ac-
cursed Guelph and Ghibelline factions in Florence,
even though the nobles had adhered to these factions
before, on account of the trouble and strife between the
Church and the emperor; but the death of Messer
Buondelmonte caused all the noble houses and all the
other citizens to take sides: some sided with the
Buondelmonti, who joined the Guelph side and be-
came its leaders, and some sided with the Uberti, who
were heads of the Ghibellines. Whence came great evil
and ruin to our city, as I shall relate below. Nor will
it ever end, unless God put an end to it. This shows
very well that the enemy of mankind, on account of
the sins of the Florentines, exercised power through the
idol of Mars, whom the pagan Florentines worshiped
in ancient times. For it was at the foot of his statue that
this murder was committed which brought such great
harm to the city of Florence.

Mosca is one of the five Florentines about whom Dante in-
quires of Ciacco in the third circle of Hell (*Inf.* VI, 80).
On Mosca see P. Santini (1923), pp. 29–30.

107. *Capo ha cosa fatta*: I. Del Lungo, in his edition of
Dino Compagni's *Cronica*, has interpreted this famous pro-
nouncement as follows (see I, 2, n. 20): "Cosa fatta non può
disfarsi; riesce ad un capo, ad un fine, ad un effetto: e perciò
si uccida addirittura Buondelmonte, senza pensar troppo
com'andrà a finire; basta ch'e' muoia." ("A thing done
cannot be undone. It comes to one end, one goal, one
effect. Let Buondelmonte be killed outright, without think-
ing too much about the consequences. The important thing
is that he die.")

109. *E io li aggiunsi: "E morte di tua schiatta"*: This is a
sharp and telling thrust at Mosca, who then goes off (vs.
110) "accumulando duol con duolo." (See Dante's exchange
with Farinata, *Inf.* X, 49–51.) The reference is to the fact
that the Lamberti family, as Ghibellines, were expelled from
Florence in 1258, and in 1268 were sentenced as *ribelli*

("rebels," "enemies") and exiled, this sentence being then renewed in 1280. Thereafter they no longer figure on the Florentine scene. *li = gli.*

110. *per ch'*: "Wherefore."

111. *sen gio = se ne andò.   gio* (pronounced *gìo*) *= gì.*
matta: "Demented."

112. *stuolo*: See *Inf.* XIV, 32.

113–26. *e vidi cosa . . . governa*: The familiar strategy of creating suspense. See *Inf.* XVI, 124–27, before the appearance of Geryon.

113–14. *e vidi . . . di contarla solo*: The "la" is redundant.

114. *sanza più prova*: M. Barbi (1934b, p. 275) interprets this phrase as meaning "without proof other than that I saw it."   *solo = solamente,* or perhaps, as Sapegno suggests, the meaning is "I alone, without witnesses."

115. *coscienza*: "Conscience," in the sense of knowledge that one is telling the truth.

117. *asbergo = usbergo.* Cf. the Provençal *ausberc.* See Horace, *Epistles* I, i, 60–61: "Hic murus aeneus esto, / nil conscire sibi, nulla pallescere culpa." ("Be this our wall of bronze, to have no guilt at heart, no wrongdoing to turn us pale.")

121. *tronco = troncato.*

122. *pesol = penzoloni* (adjective for adverb).

127. *diritto al piè*: "Right under." See *Inf.* XVIII, 4.   *fue = fu.*

128. *con tutta la testa*: See similar phrases in *Inf.* XXII, 147; XXVI, 139.

129. *appressarne = appressarci.*

130. *fuoro = furono.*

131. *spirando = respirando.*

132. *vedi s'alcuna è grande come questa*: See Lam. 1:12: "O vos omnes qui transitis per viam, attendite et videte, si est dolor sicut dolor meus." ("O all ye that pass by the way, attend, and see if there be any sorrow like to my sorrow.") Also see Dante's sonnet "O voi che per la via," *Vita nuova* VII, 3-6.

134. *Bertram dal Bornio*: Bertran de Born, lord of Haute-fort near Périgueux, was a soldier and one of the earliest and most famous of the troubadours. He was born *ca.* 1140 and died probably in 1215, as a monk in the Cistercian monastery of Dalon, near Hautefort. One of the most famous of Bertran's poems is his lament, "Si tuit li dol" (see n. to vss. 7-21), on the death of the "Young King," Prince Henry, son of Henry II of England. Of the part played by Bertran in the rebellion of the Young King against his father, for which role Dante places him in Hell, little or nothing is known historically, and not much is to be gathered from Bertran's own poems. The sources of Dante's information upon the subject were the old Provençal biographies of the troubadour and the *razos*, or arguments, to his poems. In one of these it is related that the king of England hated Bertran as the evil counselor of his son and the cause of the strife between them. Dante mentions Bertran as an example of munificence in *Conv.* IV, xi, 14 and as the poet of arms par excellence in *De vulg. eloqu.* II, ii, 9. For the works of Bertran de Born, see C. Appel (1932); for a defense of Bertran as a patriot, see J. L. Perrier (1920, 1921).

135. *re giovane*: Prince Henry of England, second son of Henry II, was born in 1155 and died in 1183. Because he was crowned twice during his father's lifetime (at Westminster in June 1170 and at Winchester in August 1172), he was known at home and abroad as the "Young King." Shortly after his second coronation, he and his brothers Geoffrey and Richard went to the French court. With the backing of his mother, Queen Eleanor, and of the French king, Louis VII, he demanded from Henry II that part of the lands that were his heritage be handed over to him. The refusal of this demand occasioned open hostilities, car-

ried on at intervals until Prince Henry died of fever at Martel in Périgord on June 11, 1183. On Prince Henry, see O. H. Moore (1925).

136. *in sé = fra loro.   ribelli*: "Enemies."

137-38. *Achitofèl . . . punzelli*: In the Bible Ahithophel (Achitophel) the Gilonite encouraged Absalom in his rebellion against his father, King David. When Ahithophel's counsel was overthrown by David's emissary, Ahithophel hanged himself (see II Reg. 15:7-17:23).

138. *punzelli*: "Instigations."

142. *lo contrapasso*: This is Dante's only use of the term that is so often cited in discussion of the principle on which he conceived the punishments of Hell, that is, the law of retribution, the *lex talionis* of the Old Testament (see Exod. 21:24; Deut. 29:21; Lev. 24:20; Matt. 5:38, 7:2). The term itself comes out of the medieval translation of Aristotle's *Nicomachean Ethics*, the term employed by the *Ethics— contrapassum*—being the Latin translation of the Greek τὸ ἀντιπεπονθός. Note the following passage from *Eth. Nicom*. V, 5, 1132^b (in Aquinas, *Opera omnia*, vol. XXI, p. 169; also in R. M. Spiazzi, 1964, p. 266):

> Videbitur autem aliquibus, et contrapassum esse simpliciter iustum, ut Pythagorici dixerunt. Determinabant enim simpliciter iustum contrapassum alii.
>
> Contrapassum autem non congruit, neque in distributivum iustum.
>
> Neque in directivum: quamvis voluerit hoc dicere et Rhadamantis iustum: Si patiatur quae fecit, vindicta recte sit.

> Some philosophers seem to think that, generally speaking, justice is reciprocation, as the Pythagoreans held; in this way they defined justice without qualification.
>
> However, reciprocation does not belong to distributive justice.
>
> Likewise, it is not suited to the justice that regulates all transactions, although Rhadamantus wished to say

that it was, holding that if a man suffers what he him-
self did to another, justice is attained.

Thomas Aquinas and the many other commentators on
Aristotle's *Ethics* comment on the term *contrapassum* of this
translation. And Aquinas, like others, applied the term from
Aristotle to the discussion of the Old Testament texts that
deal with the *lex talionis*. See *Summa theol.* II-II, q. 61,
a. 4, resp.:

> Respondeo dicendum, quod hoc quod dicitur *contra-*
> *passum* importat aequalem recompensationem passionis
> ad actionem praecedentem; quod quidem propriissime
> dicitur in passionibus et actionibus iniuriosis, quibus
> aliquis personam proximi laedit, puta si percutit, quod
> repercutiatur. Et hoc quidem iustum determinatur in
> lege, Exod. 21, 23: *Reddet animam pro anima, oculum*
> *pro oculo,* etc. Et quia etiam auferre rem alterius est
> quoddam iniustum facere, ideo secundario etiam in his
> dicitur *contrapassum*, prout scilicet aliquis qui damnum
> intulit, in re sua etiam ipse damnificatur. Et hoc quidem
> iustum damnum continetur in lege, Exod. 22.

> *I answer that,* Retaliation (*contrapassum*) denotes equal
> passion repaid for previous action; and the expression
> applies most properly to injurious passions and actions,
> whereby a man harms the person of his neighbor; for
> instance if a man strike, that he be struck back. This
> kind of justice is laid down in the Law (Exod. xxi. 23,
> 24): *He shall render life for life, eye for eye,* etc. And
> since also to take away what belongs to another is to
> do an unjust thing, it follows that secondly retaliation
> consists in this also, that whosoever causes loss to an-
> other, should suffer loss in his belongings. This just
> loss is also found in the Law (Exod. xxii. 1).

See F. D'Ovidio's discussion of the term (1923), pp. 27–34,
especially p. 29:

> Chi aveva allora domestichezza con la terminologia
> etica d'Aristotele e del suo chiosatore san Tommaso,
> sapeva, come sa oggi chi per amor di Dante se ne
> impratichisca, e come dal Segni fu già reso notorio, che

il sostantivo dantesco mette capo all'aristotelico τὸ ἀντιπεπονθός, che latinamente veniva esemplato col participio neutro *contrapassum*. Il maschile o il femminile del participio greco significa *chi ha patito qualcosa alla sua volta* o *a vicenda*, e poteva quindi all'occorrenza significare *chi ha patito un danno*, o *una pena, in ricambio*, o *in isconto, di un danno arrecato altrui* o *di una colpa*. La forma neutrale del participio servì al gergo filosofico per indicare tale idea in astratto: *il patimento in isconto, il risarcimento della colpa mediante la pena*. Innanzi a un tal vocabolo lo scolastico latino non seppe far di meglio che renderselo con *contrapassum*. Se in latino ci fosse stato un sostantivo *passus*, di quarta declinazione, dalla radice stessa di *patior*, sarebbe stato probabilmente messo sù un *contrapassus*; ma il *passus* di quarta è quel che significa il *passo*, che è dalla radice di *pando*. Al più dunque si sarebbe potuto foggiare un *contrapassio*: che avrebbe detto *la passione* (il patimento da sopportare) in contraccambio dell'*azione* fatta, dell'*azione* colpevole. Ma il neutro *contrapassum* non è niente di peggio del termine greco esemplato. Quel che importa è solo di stabilir bene che nel prefisso, cioè tanto nell'*ἀντί* come nel *contra*, non c'è punto l'idea del *contrario*, dell'*opposto*, ma solo dell'*in cambio, in ricambio, in isconto*.

Those who were then acquainted with the ethical terminology of Aristotle and of his commentator St. Thomas knew, just as those who become expert in these matters through love of Dante now know—Segni had already made it very clear—that the Dantesque noun derives from the Aristotelian τὸ ἀντιπεπονθός, which in Latin was expressed with the neutral participle *contrapassum*. The masculine or the feminine of the Greek participle means "he who has suffered something in turn": and thus, if need be, it could signify "he who has suffered harm, or a punishment, in return, or as retribution for harm done to others, or for a fault." The neutral form of the participle served the philosophical jargon to indicate that idea in the abstract: "suffering as retribution,

the compensation for a fault through punishment."
Faced with such a word, Scholastic Latin could do no
more than render it with *contrapassum*. If there had
been the Latin noun *passus*, of the fourth declension,
from the same root as *patior*, there would probably
have been created a *contrapassus*. But the fourth de-
clension *passus* is the one that means *passo*, from the
root of *pando*. At best, therefore, a *contrapassio* might
have been fashioned, which would have signified the
"passion" (the suffering to be undergone), in requital
for the *action* taken, for the culpable *action*. But the
neuter *contrapassum* is no worse than the Greek term
on which it is patterned. The important thing is to
establish firmly that in the prefix, in the ἀντί as well
as in the *contra*, there is no notion whatsoever of "con-
trary," of "opposite," but only of "in return, in ex-
change, in retribution."

CANTO XXIX

1. *diverse*: "Strange."

2. *luci*: Other examples of the meaning "eyes" are *Purg.* XV, 84; XXXI, 79. *inebriate*: See Isa. 16:9: "Super hoc plorabo in fletu Iazer vineam Sabama: inebriabo te lacrima mea Hesebon et Eleale." ("Therefore I will lament with the weeping of Jazer the vineyard of Sabama: I will water thee with my tears, O Hesebon and Eleale.")

3. *che de lo stare a piangere eran vaghe*: See Dante's *Rime* CV, 1: "Se vedi li occhi miei di pianger vaghi" ("If thou seest mine eyes fain to weep"). Dante is on the verge of weeping over "our image so contorted," as he did at first sight of the shades of the diviners in the fourth *bolgia* (see *Inf.* XX, 22–23); but Virgil, ever aware of his charge's thoughts, reproaches him (vss. 4–6), even as he did on that earlier occasion (see *Inf.* XX, 27–30).

4. *Che pur guate?* "What are you lingering to gaze at?" *guate* = *guati*.

5. *si soffolge*: The exact meaning of the verb is not clear; it apparently expresses the notion of dwelling or resting; see *Par.* XXIII, 130. On the meaning see E. G. Parodi (1957), p. 284.

6. *smozzicate*: "Maimed."

7. *sì = così*.

8. *pensa, se tu annoverar le credi*: Virgil's irony in attributing any such absurd desire to his charge is plain.

9. *miglia ventidue la .valle volge*: This is the first exact measurement Dante gives of any part of Hell. If the circumference of this ninth *bolgia* is twenty-two miles, and if that of the next or tenth *bolgia* is, as we learn in *Inf.* XXX, 86, eleven miles, then apparently the great cavity of Hell is shaped like an inverted cone, becoming narrower in circumference as the wayfarers descend toward the bottom. Grandgent observes that the number twenty-two was one that would naturally occur in reference to a circle, since the ratio of circumference to diameter is roughly twenty-two to seven.   *volge*: "Circles about" in its circumference.

10. *E già la luna è sotto i nostri piedi*: Dante continues to indicate the passage of time by reference, not to the sun, but to the position of nocturnal bodies. In the last such reference to time (see *Inf.* XX, 124–27 and n. to vss. 124–26), the moon, which only the night before had been full, was said to be setting in the western horizon. It was then around 6:00 A.M. If the moon is now beneath the wayfarers' feet, the sun must be over their heads; thus, it is about 1:00 P.M.

11. *lo tempo è poco omai che n'è concesso*: This is the first indication that a definite amount of time has been allotted for the descent through Hell, but the reader must wait until the end of that descent to know the total time. The words serve also to signal that the end of the journey through this first realm is fast approaching.   *n' = ci*.

13–15. *Se tu avessi . . . dimesso*: Virgil, who always can read Dante's thoughts, does know the reason; but the wayfarer is concerned to justify himself and with a circumspect "forse" puts it so.

15. *dimesso*: From Latin *dimittere*, "to permit," "to allow." For this meaning, see M. Barbi (1934b), p. 275.

16. *Parte*: "Meanwhile."

16–17. *Parte sen giva, e io . . . risposta*: A more normal word order would be: "Parte sen giva lo duca, e io retro li andava già faccendo la risposta."

16. *li = gli.*

19. *a posta*: Suggests also *appostare*, "to spy out."

20. *del mio sangue*: "Of my family."

22. *si franga*: Literally, "break upon," i.e., "strike upon."

23. *ello = lui.*

27. *udi' 'l = lo udii.   nominar*: "Named" by other spirits in the *bolgia.   Geri del Bello*: Geri del Bello degli Alighieri, the grandson of Alighiero I, was first cousin to Dante's father, Alighiero II. He is mentioned in documents of 1269 and 1276. Lana says of this fomenter of discord: "Fu sagacissima persona, piacevole e conversevole: dilettossi di commettere male tra le persone, e sapealo fare sì acconciamente, che pochi se ne poteano guardare da lui." ("He was a very sagacious person, very likable and easy to talk to. He enjoyed making trouble among people, and he did it so skillfully that few people could guard themselves against him.") The early commentators differ as to the details of Geri's story. Lana, Buti, and the *Anonimo fiorentino* say that he murdered one of the Geremei (Guelphs of Bologna) and was killed in retaliation by one of them. Benvenuto and the *Ottimo Commento*, on the other hand, believe that Geri was killed by one of the Sacchetti family. Benvenuto says:

> Gerius iste vir nobilis fuit frater domini Cioni del Bello de Aldigheriis; qui homo molestus et scismaticus fuit interfectus ab uno de Sacchettis nobilibus de Florentia . . . quia seminaverat discordiam inter quosdam; cuius mors non fuit vindicata per spatium triginta annorum. Finaliter filii domini Cioni et nepotes praefati Gerii,

fecerunt vindictam, quia interfecerunt unum de Sacchettis in ostio suo.

This Geri was a nobleman, brother of Messer Cione del Bello degli Alighieri. He was a troublesome and factious man, and he was murdered by one of the Sacchetti, nobles of Florence . . . because he had sown discord among them. His death was not avenged for about thirty years. Finally, the sons of Messer Cione and the nephews of this Geri took their revenge, for they killed one of the Sacchetti in his own house.

There can be little doubt that the Sacchetti were the family with whom Geri was feuding, for Pietro di Dante, in one version of his commentary (unpublished MS, Laurentian Library, Ashburnham 841), names Geri's murderer as one of the Sacchetti. P. Toynbee (1968, p. 88) quotes this version of Pietro: "Occiso olim per quemdam Brodarium de Sacchettis de Florentia." ("He was murdered some time ago by a certain Brodarius de Sacchetti of Florence.") Like Benvenuto, Pietro states that Geri was avenged by his nephews: "Nepotes dicti Gerii in eius ultione quemdam de dictis Sacchettis occiderunt." ("In revenge for Geri's murder, his nephews killed one of the Sacchetti.") The existence of a blood feud between the Alighieri and the Sacchetti is attested to further by the fact that in 1342 the two families entered into an act of reconciliation. The guarantor on the part of the Alighieri was Dante's half brother Francesco, who appeared on behalf of himself, his two nephews (the poet's sons Pietro and Jacopo), and the rest of the family.

28. *del tutto impedito*: "Completely absorbed," and thus "impeded" in his awareness of anything else.

29. *Altaforte*: Hautefort, a castle in the Limousin belonging to Bertran de Born (see *Inf.* XXVIII, 134 and the note) and his brother. It was located in the bishopric of Périgueux, in what is the modern department of the Dordogne. Hautefort was a first-class fortress, worthy of its name ("High Fort"), but otherwise unimportant. Today a small town has grown up around the castle.

30. *che non guardasti in là, sì fu partito*: For this construction, common in early Italian prose and verse, see *Inf.* XIX, 44, 127. The subject of "fu partito" is "Geri."

31-36. *la violenta morte . . . pio*: On family feuding and the private vendetta, which in Dante's time was sanctioned by law, see I. Del Lungo (1898), pp. 65-145, and P. Santini (1886). The custom enjoyed Old Testament sanction; see Num. 35:19: "Propinquus occisi homicidam interficiet; statim ut apprehenderit eum interficiet." ("The avenger of blood may execute the murderer, putting him to death on sight.") See also II Reg. 14:5-6; and Dante's *Rime* CIII, 83: "Chè bell'onor s'acquista in far vendetta." ("For fair honor is acquired in accomplishing revenge.")

32. *li* = *gli*.

33. *per alcun* = *da nessuno*.

34. *ond'*: "Wherefore." *sen gio* = *se ne andò*. *gio* = *gì*.

36. *in ciò*: "By that," "for that reason," i.e., by his show of disdain and outrage at being still unavenged (at the time of the poem). For other examples of this expression, see M. Barbi (1934b), p. 216. *in ciò m'ha el fatto a sé più pio*: Dante recognizes that Geri has a just grievance against him, and this causes him to feel more compassionate. "Pio" here seems to carry some of the meaning of the Latin *pietas* or *pius*, which express respect for family ties.

38. *de lo* = *da lo*. *l'altra valle*: The tenth *bolgia*.

40. *sor* = *sopra*. *chiostra*: "Enclosure" (from the Latin *claustrum*) but with the suggestion of "chiostro," "cloister" or "monastery." This suggestion in turn reinforces "conversi," vs. 41; see *Par.* III, 107.

42. *parere* = *apparire*.

44. *che di pietà ferrati avean li strali*: The laments are said, in this curious conceit, to be as arrows tipped or barbed with compassion, that strike upon the wayfarer and wound him with pity.

46. *Qual*: Connects with "tal," vs. 50.   *fora = sarebbe.*

47. *Valdichiana*: The Val di Chiana, the valley of the Chiana River, extends from near Chiusi to the Arno near Arezzo. In Dante's time it was notoriously infested with malaria, especially in the summer.

48. *Maremma*: The Tuscan Maremma (see n. to *Inf.* XIII, 9; *Inf.* XXV, 19).   *Sardigna*: The island of Sardinia. Both Sardinia and the Maremma were marshy and malarial in Dante's time.

49. *in una fossa*: Like the souls here in the tenth *bolgia*.   *'nsembre = insieme*; cf. the Latin *insimul* and French *ensemble*.

50. *tal*: I.e., "dolor," correlative to "Qual dolor," vs. 46.

51. *de le = da le.   membre = membra.* For this irregular plural, see E. G. Parodi (1957), p. 249.

52-53. *Noi discendemmo . . . sinistra*: The wayfarers now climb down from the reef to the farther, or inner, bank of the tenth *bolgia*. They turn along it, proceeding as usual to the left.

53. *lungo*: Indicates the whole extent of the reef, which spans all the *bolge*.

54. *e allor fu la mia vista più viva*: See "occhi vivi" *Inf.* XXIV, 70.

55. *ver' = verso.   've = ove.*

57. *qui*: "Here" in this world, in the sense that the sins were committed here.   *registra*: See *Par.* XIX, 113-14; also Apoc. 20:12: "Et libri aperti sunt, et alius liber apertus est, qui est vitae: et iudicati sunt mortui ex his quae scripta erant in libris secundum opera ipsorum." ("And scrolls were opened. And another scroll was opened, which is the book of life; and the dead were judged out of those things that were written in the scrolls, according to their works.")

58–59. *Non credo . . . infermo*: A normal prose order for
the construction would be "Non credo che il popolo tutto
infermo in Egina fosse maggior tristizia a vedere."

58–64. *Non credo . . . di seme di formiche*: According to
legend the nymph Aegina, daughter of the river god Asopus,
was carried to the island of Oenone by Jupiter, to whom she
bore a son, Aeacus. Aeacus eventually renamed the island
in honor of his mother; but Juno, jealous of her rival, nearly
depopulated the island by infesting it with a pestilence.
Aeacus then appealed to Jupiter, who restored the popula-
tion by changing the ants on the island into men, thereafter
called Myrmidons (from the Greek μύρμηξ, "ant"). Dante
directly echoes Ovid, *Metam.* VII, 523–657.

59. *Egina*: Aegina is an island off the coast of Greece in the
Saronic Gulf between Argolis and Attica.

63. *che i poeti hanno per fermo*: The qualification indicates
a view of the story as poetic myth or "favola," as Dante
explicitly terms it in *Conv.* IV, xxvii, 17:

> N'ammaestra Ovidio nel settimo Metamorfoseos, in
> quella favola dove scrive come Cefalo d'Atene venne
> ad Eaco re per soccorso . . . . Mostra che Eaco vecchio
> fosse prudente, quando, avendo per pestilenza di cor-
> rompimento d'aere quasi tutto lo popolo perduto, esso
> saviamente ricorse a Dio e a lui domandò lo ristoro de
> la morta gente; e per lo suo senno, che a pazienza lo
> tenne e a Dio tornare lo fece, lo suo popolo ristorato
> li fu maggiore che prima.

> Ovid instructs us in the seventh of the *Metamorphoses*,
> in the story where he tells how Cephalus of Athens
> came to King Aeacus for help . . . . He shows that the
> old Aeacus was prudent, when, having lost by pesti-
> lence, through corruption of the air, almost all his
> people, he wisely had recourse to God, and asked from
> him the restoration of his dead people; and by his wit,
> which held him to patience and made him turn to God,
> his people were restored to him greater than before.

See also *Inf.* II, 13, 25.

64. *si ristorar = si ristorarono.   di seme di formiche*:
"From the seed of ants," meaning "species ant."

66. *languir*: See Ovid, *Metam*. VII, 547–48: "Omnia languor
habet: silvisque agrisque viisque / corpora foeda iacent, vitian-
tur odoribus aurae." ("Lethargy holds all. In woods and
fields and roads foul carcasses lie; and the air is defiled by
the stench.")   *biche*: "Shocks," sheaves of grain piled one
upon another, once a familiar scene at harvest time. See n.
to *Inf*. IX, 78. The image is graphic, in that each sheaf,
bound around the middle, rests upon another with a certain
limpness.

70. *Passo passo*: "Slowly."

72. *levar = sollevare.*

74. *com' a scaldar si poggia tegghia a tegghia*: As one pan
is leaned against another on the stove to dry—evidently an
everyday sight in Dante's time. The homely quality of this
simile serves to drop the tone of the narrative to one of
banality, which then continues in the comparisons of vss.
77–78, 83–84.   *tegghia = teglia.*

76. *stregghia = striglia.*

77. *ragazzo*: A common term for "stable boy."   *segnorso
= signor suo*. For the position of the possessive, see E. G.
Parodi (1957), p. 251; also compare such forms as *signormo*
("signor mio"), *mammata* ("mamma tua"), all common in
early Italian.

78. *vegghia = veglia.*

79. *morso*: Literally, "bite," here from the sharp edge of the
fingernails.

81. *che non ha più soccorso*: "Which has no other succor"
than scratching. But the relief, in this case, must be very
painful.

83. *scardova*: Scartazzini-Vandelli identifies this as the fish
called *Cyprinus latus* by Linnaeus, in which case the trans-

lation "bream" would not be exact. One may imagine the
common carp or any fish with larger scales.

84. *o d'altro pesce che più larghe l'abbia*: Within the con-
text, this concession is clearly ironic and amounts to saying:
"Or you name the fish." The derisive tone continues through
the adjuration of vss. 89–90.

85. *dismaglie = dismagli*. The scabs are so thick on the
bodies of these shades—those of falsifiers—that they may be
compared to a coat of mail, which the sinners are said to
pick to pieces, link by link.

88. *dinne = dicci.   Latino = italiano*. See *Inf.* XXII, 65;
XXVII, 27, 33.

89. *quinc' entro*: "Here within" this *bolgia;* see *Inf.* X, 17.

89–90. *se l'unghia ti basti . . . lavoro*: Certainly one of the
most amusing instances of the familiar formula of adjura-
tion. Nothing else can be so much desired by these spirits,
since their sharp nails provide their only relief.

97–98. *Allor si ruppe lo comun rincalzo; e tremando*: The
two spirits break "their mutual support" and try to sit up
straight, but they are so weak that this causes them to
tremble.

99. *di rimbalzo*: Literally, "on the rebound," as if the words
addressed to the two spirits bounced off them and struck
other spirits nearby.

100. *Lo buon maestro a me tutto s'accolse*: Virgil's gesture
is reassuring as he urges his charge to take time to speak
with these spirits.   *s'accolse = si accostò*; from *accogliersi*.

101. *vuoli = vuoi*.

102. *volse = volle*.

103. *Se la vostra memoria*: The formula of adjuration, re-
peated in vs. 105.   *imboli = involi* (see *Inf.* XXVI, 42).

534

106. *di che genti*: "From what cities." The wayfarer already
knows that they are Italian (see vs. 91); hence the reply
"Io fui d'Arezzo" (vs. 109). See vs. 122 for another instance
of this meaning of "gente."

108. *spaventi*: "Deter."

109. *Io fui d'Arezzo*: The speaker, not otherwise named, is
identified by the early commentators as one Griffolino, an
alchemist of Arezzo, but little is known of him beyond
what they report. According to the commentators, Griffolino
pretended that he could teach Albero da Siena (see vs. 109
and the note) how to fly, in order to get money from him.
Albero's indignation at having been fleeced led him to de-
nounce Griffolino as a magician, and Griffolino was subse-
quently burned to death according to a widespread custom
of the day. Benvenuto says:

> Est breviter sciendum rem iocosam: fuit igitur in nobili
> civitate Senarum circa tempora autoris quidam magister
> Grifolinus de Aretio, magnus naturalis et alchimicus,
> qui astutissimus contraxit familiaritatem magnam cum
> quodam filio episcopi senensis, cui nomen erat Albarus,
> a quo sagaciter emungebat pecuniam et munera multa,
> quia ille cum lingua sua mirabili promittebat illi simplici
> et fatuo facere mirabilia magna. Inter alia, dum Albarus
> iste levissimus miraretur et laudaret Grifolinum, dicens:
> o quale est ingenium tuum! dixit Grifolinus: certe
> scirem facere impossibilia per naturam. Quid diceres,
> si videres me patenter volare more avis per aerem?
> Albarus pinguis et pecuniosus expensis Crucifixi, coepit
> rogare, ut doceret eum artem volandi artificialiter, qui
> tamen erat per naturam levissimus ad volandum cum
> sua mente vanissima. Multa ergo dicebat, et plura
> promittebat. Sed Grifolinus ludificabatur eum, et dabat
> illi verba in solutum. Tandem Albarus videns se de-
> lusum et deceptum, conquestus est episcopo patri suo;
> qui accensus indignatione magna fecit formari unam
> inquisitionem contra eum, qualiter exercebat magicam,
> quam tamen ille ignorabat; et sub isto colore fecit eum
> digne cremari.

Let me briefly tell you a funny story: in the noble city of Siena, at about the time of our author, there lived a certain master Griffolino d'Arezzo, a man very well versed in the science of nature and in alchemy. He very astutely became a close friend of Albero, the son of the bishop, from whom he shrewdly knew how to squeeze money and large gifts. With this extraordinary gift of speech, he promised to enable that simple fool to accomplish great prodigies. Among other things, once, while this lightheaded Albero was admiring and praising Griffolino, and telling him what a great genius he was, Griffolino said: "Indeed, I do know how to do things which cannot be done by natural means. What would you say if you clearly saw me fly through the air, like a bird?" The rich Albero, who was wealthy at the expense of the Crucifix, begged him to teach him that art of flying—teach him who by nature was so disposed to flying with his empty head! Therefore he said a great deal and promised more. But Griffolino was making fun of him and only treated him to words. Finally, realizing he had been deluded and tricked, Albero went to complain to his father the bishop, who became highly indignant. He set up an inquiry against Griffolino for practicing magic, of which in fact he was ignorant. And as a practitioner of magic, he was duly burned.

The *Anonimo fiorentino* says that Griffolino pointed out to his dupe one of the particular advantages of being able to fly: "Vedi, Albero, e' sono poche cose ch'io non sappia fare: s'io volessi, io t'insegnerei volare; et s'egli ha in Siena veruna donna a cui tu voglia bene, poterai intrare in casa per le finestre volando." ("You see, Albero, there are few things I cannot do. If I wanted to, I could teach you to fly. Then, if there were any woman in Siena you liked, you could fly into her house through the window.")

A somewhat different account is given in the *Ottimo Commento*:

Dice l'Aretino . . . ch'elli fu d'Arezzo, e uno Sanese, nome Alberto, il fece ardere non per archimia, ma perocchè li appuose ch'elli fosse ingiuratore di demonii, ed eretico in fede; e ciò si mosse a fare, perocchè 'l detto Aretino disse un die al detto Alberto: s'i' voless'io, volerei come uno uccello. Il Sanese volle che Griffolino glie le insegnasse: l'Aretino disse, che glie l'aveva detto per sollazzo; quelli indegnò, e poi in Firenze ad uno inquisitore de' Paterini, ch'era Sanese di nazione, e tenea che Alberto fosse suo figliuolo, il fece ardere. . . . Alcuni dicono che 'l fe' ardere al Vescovo di Siena, ch'era suo padre.

The Aretine says . . . he was from Arezzo. A Sienese named Albero had him burned not for alchemy, but by accusing him of being a conjurer of devils and a heretic. Albero did this because the Aretine said to him one day: "If I wanted, I could fly like a bird." Albero wanted Griffolino to teach him how to fly, but Griffolino answered that he had just said it as a joke. Albero got angry; and later, in Florence, he had him burned by an inquisitor of the Patarines [heretics], who was from Siena and claimed that Albero was his son. . . . Some people say he had him burned by the bishop of Siena, who was his father.

109. *Albero da Siena*: Albero is said to have been the son or protégé of a bishop of Siena. The simplicity of a certain Alberto da Siena, supposed to be the same person here mentioned, forms the subject of several stories by Sacchetti (see *Novelle* XI–XIV). The early commentators identify the bishop as one Bonfiglio, bishop of Siena from 1216 to 1252, and an ardent persecutor of heretics; but this identification is unlikely since Griffolino, supposedly put to death by the bishop, was still living in 1259. On the date of Griffolino's death, see G. Zaccagnini (1914), pp. 20–22.

112. *lui = a lui.*

115. *li = gli.*

116. *Dedalo*: See n. to *Inf.* XVII, 109.

117. *a tal = da tale*, i.e., by the bishop of Siena. *che l'avea per figliuolo*: See n. to vs. 109, above.

120. *fallar non lece*: "Cannot err"; see *Inf.* XIII, 54.

123. *francesca = francese*; see *Inf.* XXVII, 44. Benvenuto comments on the vanity of the French:

> Galli sunt genus vanissimum omnium ab antiquo, sicut patet saepe apud Iulium Celsum, et hodie patet de facto . . . . Portant enim catenam ad collum, circulum ad brachium, punctam ad calceum, pannos breves . . . et ita de multis vanitatibus.

> Since antiquity, the French have been the vainest of people. Julius Caesar remarked it often; and today, it is proved by the facts . . . . They wear a chain around their necks, a bracelet on the arm, pointed footwear, short clothing . . . and many other vanities.

123. *sì d'assai*: The "sì" reinforces the negation; hence, "not by far."

125. *Tra'mene = traimene* (pronounced *tràimene*). Literally, "take away of them for me"; i.e., "grant me the exception of." Stricca was actually a lavish spender. For a similar irony, see *Inf.* XXI, 41 and the note. *Stricca*: The early commentators know nothing of this man's identity; he is supposed to be the Stricca di Giovanni de' Salimbeni of Siena (brother of Niccolò, mentioned in vs. 127) who was *podestà* of Bologna in 1276 and again in 1286. On the other hand, some think he belonged to the Tolomei family; others, to the Marescotti. The name itself is said to be an abbreviation for Baldastricca.

127. *Niccolò*: Niccolò de' Salimbeni (or, according to some, de' Bonsignori) of Siena, was said by the early commentators to have been a member of the Brigata Spendereccia, or "Spendthrift Club," of Siena (see n. to vs. 130). It was formerly believed that he was the Niccolò of whom Folgore da San Gimignano speaks in his opening sonnet to the Brigata Spendereccia (in G. Contini, 1960, vol. II, p. 405, vss. 7-8): "In questo regno Nicolò incorono, / perch'elli

è 'l fior della città sanese." ("In this realm I crown Niccolò, for he is the flower of the city of Siena." The complete poem is quoted in n. to vs. 130.) This view, however, is no longer seriously held; for the identification of Niccolò, see Contini, vol. II, p. 403; M. Barbi (1899), p. 215.

Niccolò probably was a son of Giovanni de' Salimbeni of Siena. He has been identified with the Niccolò de' Salimbeni mentioned by Dino Compagni as having been appointed imperial vicar in Milan in 1311 by the Emperor Henry VII; but the vicar Dino was speaking of in this connection probably was Niccolò de' Bonsignori. The two Niccolòs were nearly contemporary, both came from large Sienese families and led similar lives; hence it is not surprising that someone who knew them or knew of them both might confuse them. For Compagni's knowledge of Niccolò, see I. Del Lungo (1879), pp. 596–604.

127–28. *la costuma ricca del garofano*: The commentators differ as to the precise use of the clove that Niccolò introduced; some say it was the roasting of pheasants and other birds over fires made with cloves; others, with less extravagance, say that it was the serving of cloves and spice with roast meats; others conjecture that it was a subtle method of growing spices in proximity to one another so that the various flavors were intermingled and modified.

129. *ne l'orto dove tal seme s'appicca*: Siena is the "garden" where such fashions take root and thrive.

130. *la brigata*: The Brigata Spendereccia of Siena, an organization of extravagant young men that flourished for a short time during the second half of the thirteenth century. Benvenuto gives an account of this club, which he says was composed of twelve wealthy young men, bent on doing something to make themselves talked about. Accordingly, they each contributed a large amount to a common fund, which the members were bound to spend lavishly under pain of expulsion from the society. They then hired a magnificent palace, where they met once or twice a month and gave sumptuous banquets, entertaining and loading with

gifts anyone of distinction who happened to come to Siena. They prided themselves on having all sorts of exotic dishes and flung the gold and silver utensils and table ornaments out the window as soon as each banquet was over. In this way they ran through their means in less than two years and became a public laughingstock, while some of them were reduced to living on charity. Benvenuto adds that two sets of poems were composed about them, one describing their magnificent beginning, the other their miserable ending. The poems mentioned by Benvenuto are probably those of Folgore da San Gimignano (supposedly a member of the club) and Cenne da la Chitarra of Arezzo. Folgore addressed to the "brigata nobile e cortese" (see below) a series of twelve sonnets, one for each month of the year, celebrating their merry life, while Cenne wrote a series in parody of the other, giving a picture of the miserable condition to which they were reduced by their folly. In his opening sonnet, Folgore names six other members of the club, making up, with the five mentioned by Dante, and Folgore himself, the complete number of twelve (in G. Contini, 1960, vol. II, p. 405):

> Alla brigata nobile e cortese,
> in tutte quelle parti dove sono,
> con allegrezza stando sempre dono,
> cani, uccelli e danari per ispese,
>
> ronzin portanti e quaglie a volo prese,
> bracchi levar, correr veltri a·bbandono:
> in questo regno Nicolò incorono,
> perch'elli è 'l fior della città sanese;
>
> Tingoccio e Min di Tingo ed Ancaiano,
> Bartolo e Mugàvero e Fainotto,
> che pariano figliuol' de·re Prïàno,
>
> prodi e cortesi più che Lancilotto,
> se bisognasse, con le lance in mano
> farian tornïamenti a Camellotto.

To this noble and courteous company, wherever it may be, I always happily give dogs, birds, and money for expenses, packhorses and quail caught in flight; leaping

foxhounds and unleashed greyhounds: in this realm I
crown Niccolò, for he is the flower of the city of Siena;
Tingoccio and Min di Tingo and Ancaiano, Bartolo and
Mugàvero and Fainotto, who looked like sons of King
Priam, more heroic and more courteous than Lancelot—
if need be, with lance in hand they could fight tourna-
ments at Camelot.

Dante places one member of the "Spendthrift Club" in the
second *girone* of the seventh circle (see *Inf.* XIII, 118 and
the note).

131. *Caccia d'Ascian*: Caccia of Asciano, or Caccianemico,
was the son of Messer Trovato of Asciano. His name appears
in documents dated 1250, 1288, 1291, and 1293. His family
was a branch of the Scialenghi. On Caccia see A. Massèra,
1920, pp. 211–13. Apparently he squandered a vineyard and
his great possessions in land.   *Ascian*: Asciano is a small
town on the Ombrone River about fifteen miles southeast
of Siena.   *fonda*: The word can mean "purse"—that is,
"riches." Some manuscripts give "fronda," which would
have the meaning "forest" here. On the variant, see Petroc-
chi's long note in his vol. I, *Introduzione*, pp. 185–86.

132. *l'Abbagliato*: The nickname (literally, "dazed") of a
spendthrift who has been identified as one Meo (i.e., Bar-
tolommeo), son of Rainieri de' Folcacchieri of Siena. Meo
was a member of the Brigata Spendereccia and held high
office in Siena and other Italian towns between 1277 and
1300. It is recorded that he was fined, in 1278, for drinking
in a tavern. He is referred to as "Meo dicto Abbagliato filio
quondam Ranerii Folcalchieri" ("Meo, called Abbagliato,
son of the late Rainieri Folcalchieri") in a document pub-
lished by A. Vannini (1914), a clear indication that he was
generally known by that nickname. On Meo see C. Mazzi
(1894), p. 31. It is not known just how he "demonstrated
his wit"—which is said in irony.

133. *ti seconda = ti asseconda*.

134. *ver' = verso*.

135. *sì che la faccia mia ben ti risponda*: The face, we are
not to forget, is covered with scabs and therefore hard to
make out; but if Dante will only "sharpen his eye," the face
will tell him who he is and of what people (see vs. 106).

136. *Capocchio*: Capocchio was a Florentine (or, according
to some, a Sienese) who was burned alive at Siena in 1293
as an alchemist, as is proved by a document dated August 3,
1292, preserved in the Archivio di Stato at Siena: "Item
pagati xxxviii sol. dicta die in uno floreno de auro tribus
ribaldis qui fecerunt unam iustitiam, ideo quod fecerunt
comburi Capocchium." ("On this day thirty-eight soldi in
the form of a gold florin were paid to three ruffians who
jointly carried out an act of justice; namely, they burned
Capocchio.")

Benvenuto tells an amusing incident about Capocchio and
Dante:

> Iste . . . fuit quidam magister Capochius florentinus,
> vir ingeniosus ad omnia, maxime ad transnaturandum
> metalla; qui ob hoc, ut quidam dicunt, fuit combustus
> in civitate Senarum . . . . Semel die quodam Veneris
> sancti cum staret solus abstractus in quodam claustro,
> effigiavit sibi totum processum passionis Domini in
> unguibus mira artificiositate; et cum Dantes super-
> veniens quaereret: quid est hoc quod fecisti? iste subito
> cum lingua delevit quidquid cum tanto labore ingenii
> fabricaverat. De quo Dantes multum arguit eum, quia
> istud opus videbatur sibi non minus mirabile, quam opus
> illius, qui totam Iliadem tam subtiliter descripsit, quod
> intra testam nucis claudebatur; et alius fecit formicas
> eburneas.

> He was Master Capocchio, a Florentine, very ingenious
> in all things, especially in counterfeiting metals. For
> which reason, according to some people, he was burned
> in the city of Siena . . . . Once, on Good Friday, while
> he was off to himself in a cloister, he depicted, with
> extraordinary skill, the whole story of Christ's passion
> on his fingernails. Dante arrived and said, "What is that
> you have done?" Whereupon he quickly erased with

his tongue all that he had so painstakingly and in-
geniously wrought. Dante scolded him severely, for he
thought that this work was no less admirable than that of
the man who had transcribed the whole *Iliad* so minutely
that it fit into a nutshell, or the work of another man
who made ants in ivory.

The *Anonimo fiorentino* says that Capocchio was also a
wonderful mimic:

> Capocchio fu da Firenze, et fu conoscente dell'Auttore,
> et insieme studiorono; et fu uno che, a modo d'uno
> uomo di corte, seppe contraffare ogni uomo che volea,
> et ogni cosa, tanto ch'egli parea propriamente la cosa
> o l'uomo ch'egli contraffacea in ciascuno atto: diessi
> nell'ultimo a contraffare i metalli, come egli facea gli
> uomini.

> Capocchio was from Florence, and he was acquainted
> with the author, for they had been students together.
> He was a person who, like the performers at court,
> could mimic anyone or anything he liked, so much so
> that he looked just like the thing or the man he was
> imitating. Later he began to counterfeit metals, just
> as he had done people.

138. *te dee ricordar*: The construction is impersonal; see
Inf. XXVIII, 73. "Te" is the object of the verb.   *dee =
deve*.

139. *di natura*: Probably to be understood as *di mia natura*,
"by nature."   *scimia = scimmia*.

CANTO XXX

2. *Semelè*: Semele was the daughter of Cadmus, king of Thebes, and Harmonia and the sister of Ino, Agave, Autonoë, and Polydorus (not the same Polydorus mentioned in vs. 18; see n. to vss. 16–21). She was beloved by Jupiter, by whom she became the mother of Bacchus. Juno, in order to avenge herself upon Jupiter for his unfaithfulness to her, appeared to Semele in the guise of her aged nurse Beroë and induced her to ask Jupiter to show himself to her in the same splendor and majesty in which he appeared to Juno. Jupiter, knowing the danger, reluctantly complied with Semele's request and appeared before her as the god of thunder, whereupon she was struck by lightning and consumed to ashes (see *Par.* XXI, 6; Ovid, *Metam.* III, 259–309). / For the accent on the final syllable of Greek names, as in Semele, see *Inf.* V, 4 and the note; XIV, 131 and the note; and E. G. Parodi (1957), pp. 233–34.

3. *una e altra fiata*: Compare the wording in *Inf.* X, 50. / With this phrase Dante may be alluding to more than the two victims of Juno's wrath against the Theban blood here specified, Semele and Athamas. Another instance may be the destruction of Pentheus, son of Semele's sister Agave.

4-12. *Atamante . . . carco*: Athamas, king of Orchomenus in Boeotia, was the son of Aeolus and Enarete. At the command of Juno, Athamas married Nephele; but he was secretly in love with Semele's sister, the mortal Ino, by whom he had two sons, Learchus and Melicertes. Possibly because he was unfaithful to Nephele, or because Ino was the nurse of Bacchus, son of Semele and Jupiter, Athamas incurred the wrath of Juno, who afflicted him with madness. He mistook Ino and her two sons for a lioness and cubs and, seizing Learchus, dashed him against a rock. Ino flung herself with Melicertes into the sea. Dante's allusion to this story, especially his vss. 7-12, closely follows Ovid (see *Metam*. IV, 512-30):

Protinus Aeolides media furibundus in aula
clamat "io, comites, his retia tendite silvis!
hic modo cum gemina visa est mihi prole leaena"
utque ferae sequitur vestigia coniugis amens
deque sinu matris ridentem et parva Learchum
bracchia tendentem rapit et bis terque per auras
more rotat fundae rigidoque infantia saxo
discutit ora ferox; tum denique concita mater,
seu dolor hoc fecit seu sparsi causa veneni,
exululat passisque fugit male sana capillis
teque ferens parvum nudis, Melicerta, lacertis
"euhoe Bacche" sonat: Bacchi sub nomine Iuno
risit et "hos usus praestet tibi" dixit "alumnus!"
inminet aequoribus scopulus: pars ima cavatur
fluctibus et tectas defendit ab imbribus undas,
summa riget frontemque in apertum porrigit aequor;
occupat hunc (vires insania fecerat) Ino
seque super pontum nullo tardata timore
mittit onusque suum; percussa recanduit unda.

Straightway cried Athamas, the son of Aeolus, madly raving in his palace halls: "Ho! my comrades, spread the nets here in these woods! I saw here but now a lioness with her two cubs"; and madly pursued his wife's tracks as if she were a beast of prey. His son, Learchus, laughing and stretching out his little hands

in glee, he snatched from the mother's arms, and whirl-
ing him round and round through the air like a sling,
he madly dashed the baby's head against a rough rock.
Then the mother, stung to madness too, either by grief
or by the sprinkled poison's force, howling wildly, and,
quite bereft of sense, with hair streaming, she fled
away, bearing thee, little Melicerta, in her naked arms,
and shouting "Ho! Bacchus!" as she fled. At the name
of Bacchus, Juno laughed in scorn and said: "So may
your foster-son ever bless you!" A cliff o'erhung the
sea, the lower part of which had been hollowed out by
the beating waves, and sheltered the waters underneath
from the rain. Its top stood high and sharp and stretched
far out in front over the deep. To this spot—for mad-
ness had made her strong—Ino climbed, and held by
no natural fears, she leaped with her child far out above
the sea. The water where she fell was churned white
with foam.

8. *al varco*: See the same expression in *Inf.* XII, 26. This
can be translated freely, "as they pass by."

11. *rotollo = lo rotò*. See Ovid's use of "rotat" in *Metam.*
IV, 518, quoted in n. to vss. 4–12, above.   *percosselo =
lo percosse*.

12. *quella*: Ino.   *l'altro carco*: This is the other son,
Melicertes, with whom Ino had fled. See "andar carcata" in
vs. 6.   *carco = carico*.

13. *la fortuna volse in basso*: In the familiar image of For-
tune turning her wheel. See *Inf.* VII, 73–96.

14. *l'altezza de' Troian che tutto ardiva*: See *Inf.* I, 75,
"superbo Ilión"; *Purg.* XII, 61–63. The "all-daring loftiness
of the Trojans" had been manifested in the rash refusal of
Laomedon, king of Troy and father of Priam, to pay Nep-
tune and Apollo the wages they had earned in serving him,
and in the abduction of Helen by Paris, son of Priam.

15. *sì che 'nsieme col regno il re fu casso*: See Ovid, *Metam.*
XIII, 403–4: "Inposita est sero tandem manus ultima bello. /

546

Troia simul Priamusque cadunt." ("The final blow was at
last given to the longdrawn war. Troy fell and Priam with
it.")   *il re*: Priam.   *casso*: See *Inf.* XXV, 76; also *Aen.*
XI, 104: "Nullum cum victis certamen et aethere cassis."
("No war, they plead, is waged with vanquished men, bereft
of air of heaven.")

16–21. *Ecuba trista . . . torta*: After the fall of Troy, Hecuba,
widow of Priam, king of Troy, and her daughter Polyxena
were taken captive by the Greeks. On their way to Greece,
Polyxena was torn from Hecuba and sacrificed on the tomb
of Achilles (see n. to vs. 17); and soon after, the lifeless body
of Hecuba's son Polydorus, who had been murdered by Poly-
mestor, king of Thrace, was washed up on the shore. Mad
with grief, Hecuba was changed into a dog and in this
state leaped into the sea at a place thenceforward called
Cynossema, or "tomb of the dog." Dante's account here
apparently derives from Ovid (*Metam.* XIII, 404–571). Com-
pare, for example, Hecuba's grief at the death of Polyxena
in *Metam.* XIII, 494–95:

> nata, tuae—quid enim superest?—dolor ultime matris,
> nata, iaces, videoque tuum, mea vulnera, vulnus . . .

> O child, your mother's last cause for grief—for what
> else is left me—my child, low you lie, and I see your
> wound, my wound.

And note Hecuba's discovery of Polydorus' body as told
by Ovid (*Metam.* XIII, 536–37, 539–40):

> adspicit eiectum Polydori in litore corpus
> factaque Threiciis ingentia vulnera telis;
> . . . .
> et pariter vocem lacrimasque introrsus obortas
> devorat ipse dolor . . .

And there she saw the body of Polydorus, cast up upon
the shore, covered with gaping wounds made by Thrac-
ian spears. . . . Her very grief engulfed her powers of
speech, her rising tears.

See *Metam.* XIII, 404–6, where Ovid tells of Hecuba's trans-
formation into a dog:

. . . Priameia coniunx
perdidit infelix hominis post omnia formam
externasque novo latratu terruit auras . . .

The poor wife of Priam after all else lost her human form
and with strange barking affrighted the alien air . . . .

Ovid also describes Hecuba's metamorphosis in *Metam.*
XIII, 568–70:

. . . rictuque in verba parato
latravit, conata loqui: locus exstat et ex re
nomen habet . . .

And, though her jaws were set for words, [she] barked
when she tried to speak. The place still remains and
takes its name from this incident . . . .

See also Seneca, *Agamemnon*, vs. 708: "Circa ruinas rabida
latravit suas." ("Around her ruined walls madly she
barked.")

17. *Polissena*: Polyxena was the daughter of Priam and
Hecuba. After the fall of Troy, when the Greeks were on
their voyage home, bearing Hecuba and Polyxena as cap-
tives, the shade of Achilles, who had been enamored of
Polyxena, appeared and demanded that she be sacrificed to
him. She was thereupon slain by Pyrrhus (Neoptolemus),
Achilles' son, on the tomb of his father. The incident is
related by Ovid (*Metam.* XIII, 439–52).

18. *Polidoro*: Polydorus was the son of Priam and Hecuba.
Just before Troy fell into the hands of the Greeks, Priam
entrusted Polydorus, together with a large sum of money,
to Polymestor, a Thracian king, but after the destruction of
Troy Polymestor killed Polydorus for the sake of the
treasure and cast his body into the sea. Subsequently the
body was washed up on the shore and was found and recog-
nized by Hecuba, who avenged her son's murder by putting
out Polymestor's eyes and killing his two children. The story
of Polydorus' murder is told by Ovid (*Metam.* XIII, 429–
38).

21. *fé = fece.*   *torta*: "Wrenched" out of her mind.

22. *Ma né di Tebe furie né troiane*: Not such raging madness as was seen in Athamas, king of Thebes, and in Hecuba, queen of Troy.

23. *in alcun*: "Against anyone."

24. *punger*: Literally, "to goad," hence "to wound" (*si videro* is understood).   *bestie*: As in the case of Athamas, who in his madness saw his wife as a lioness.   *nonché membra umane*: The reference is probably to the fact that Hecuba in her fury tore out the eyes of Polymestor (see Ovid, *Metam.* XIII, 561-64).

25. *quant'*: That is, *quanto crude*.   *due ombre*: These two shades are to be seen as two furies in terms of the simile.   *smorte*: These souls, for all their furious running here and there about this tenth *bolgia*, are sick and pale like the rest.

26-27. *mordendo correvan di quel modo . . . si schiude*: The comparison clearly suggests that these souls run on all fours. The hog, when let out from the sty to pasture, runs hungrily here and there, biting at grass or at anything it can devour. The animal has its own peculiar way of running, with a kind of rocking motion from front to back, an image that the verses are no doubt intended to evoke.

28-29. *nodo del collo*: The nape of the neck.

29. *l'assannò = l'azzannò*. See the use of "sanna" ("tusk") in *Inf.* XXII, 56. The verb thus keeps the image of the hog or boar.

30. *grattar li fece*: An ironical, derisive touch. See *Inf.* XXIX, 79-84.   *li = gli.*

31. *l'Aretin*: Griffolino (see *Inf.* XXIX, 109-20).   *che rimase, tremando*: Deprived as he is of "mutual support" (*Inf.* XXIX, 97), he is still trembling.

32. *folletto*: Possible meanings are "pixy," "goblin." Note the following passage from Gervase of Tilbury (*Otia imperialia* I, 18):

Sunt et alii, quos *Folletos* vulgus nominat, qui domos simplicium rusticorum inhabitant, et nec aqua, nec exorcismis arcentur, et quia non videntur, ingredientes lapidibus, lignis et domestica supellectile affligunt, quorum verba utique humano more audiuntur, et effigies non comparent.

There are other [spirits] commonly called *Folletos* [goblins], which inhabit the houses of simple peasants and cannot be removed by [holy] water or exorcisms, and because they cannot be seen, they throw stones, pieces of wood, or household objects at anyone who enters. Their words sound like human words; but they do not show themselves.

Torraca points out that in quite a few parts of Italy this belief still persists. *Gianni Schicchi*: A Florentine (died *ca.* 1280) of the Cavalcanti family, noted for his powers of mimicry. On the sin of impersonation for which Gianni Schicchi is punished here, see vss. 42-45. The *Anonimo fiorentino* describes the circumstances of the fraud in detail:

Questo Gianni Sticchi fu de' Cavalcanti da Firenze, et dicesi di lui che, essendo messer Buoso Donati aggravato d'una infermità mortale, volea fare testamento, però che gli parea avere a rendere assai dell'altrui. Simone suo figliuolo il tenea a parole, per ch'egli nol facesse; et tanto il tenne a parole ch'elli morì. Morto che fu, Simone il tenea celato, et avea paura ch'elli non avessi fatto testamento mentre ch'egli era sano; et ogni vicino dicea ch'egli l'avea fatto. Simone, non sappiendo pigliare consiglio, si dolse con Gianni Sticchi et chiesegli consiglio. Sapea Gianni contraffare ogni uomo, et colla voce et cogli atti, et massimamente messer Buoso, ch'era uso con lui. Disse a Simone: Fa venire uno notajo, et di' che messer Buoso voglia fare testamento: io enterrò nel letto suo, et cacceremo lui dirietro, et io mi fascerò bene, et metterommi la cappellina sua in capo, et farò il testamento come tu vorrai: è vero che io ne voglio guadagnare. Simone fu in concordia con lui: Gianni entra nel letto, et mostrasi appenato, et contraffà la

voce di messer Buoso che parea tutto lui, et comincia
a testare et dire: Io lascio soldi xx all'opera di santa
Reparata, et lire cinque a' Frati Minori, et cinque
a' Predicatori, et così viene distribuendo per Dio, ma
pochissimi danari. A Simone giovava del fatto: et lascio,
soggiunse, cinquecento fiorini a Gianni Sticchi. Dice
Simone a messer Buoso: Questo non bisogna mettere
in testamento; io gliel darò come voi lascerete—Simone,
lascerai fare del mio a mio senno: io ti lascio sì bene,
che tu dèi essere contento—Simone per paura si stava
cheto. Questi segue: Et lascio a Gianni Sticchi la mula
mia; chè avea messer Buoso la migliore mula di Toscana.
Oh, messer Buoso, dicea Simone, di cotesta mula si cura
egli poco et poco l'avea cara: io so ciò che Gianni Sticchi
vuole meglio di te. Simone si comincia adirare et a con-
sumarsi; ma per paura si stava. Gianni Sticchi segue:
Et lascio a Gianni Sticchi fiorini cento, che io debbo
avere da tale mio vicino: et nel rimanente lascio Simone
mia reda universale con questa clausula, ch'egli dovesse
mettere ad esecuzione ogni lascio fra quindici dì, se
non, che tutto il reditaggio venisse a' Frati Minori del
convento di Santa Croce; et fatto il testamento, ogni
uomo si partì. Gianni esce del letto, et rimettonvi messer
Buoso, et lievono il pianto, et dicono ch'egli è morto.

This Gianni Schicci was of the Cavalcanti of Florence,
and the story is told of him that when Messer Buoso
Donati was stricken with a fatal illness, he wanted to
make a will, for he knew he had a great many things
to give back to others. His son Simone put him off
with words, to prevent his doing it; and he put him
off so long that he finally died. When he was dead,
Simone kept him hidden, afraid he might have made
a will while he was healthy. Indeed, all the neighbors
said he had made one. Not knowing what to do,
Simone unburdened himself to Gianni Schicchi and
asked his advice. Gianni knew how to imitate the voice
and actions of everyone, and especially of Messer Buoso,
whom he knew very well. He said to Simone: "Have a
notary come, and tell him that Messer Buoso wants to

make a will. I will get into the bed, and we'll shove him behind it. I will cover myself well, put on his nightcap, and will make a will just as you want it. Of course, I want to get something out of it myself." Simone agreed. Gianni gets into the bed, pretends to be in great pain, and imitates the voice of Messer Buoso so well that it seems to be he. Then he begins to dictate the will, saying: "I leave twenty soldi to the *opera* of Santa Reparata, five lire to the Friars Minor, five to the Dominicans," and so on, giving for God, but in small amounts. This was what Simone wanted. "And," he adds, "I leave five hundred florins to Gianni Schicchi." Simone says to Messer Buoso: "You needn't put that in the will. I'll give them to him, just as you say." "Simone, you will let me dispose of my own property as I see fit. I am leaving you so well off that you will be satisfied." Simone kept quiet, out of fear. And then the other continues: "I leave Gianni Schicchi my mule"—for Messer Buoso had the best mule in Tuscany. "Oh, Messer Buoso," said Simone, "he cares little about that mule, and never prized it particularly. I know what Gianni Schicchi wants better than you do." Simone began to get angry and to fume; but out of fear, he kept quiet. Gianni Schicchi goes on: "And I leave Gianni Schicchi one hundred florins, which my neighbor so-and-so owes me. And all the rest I leave to my heir Simone, on this condition: that he carry out each of my bequests within the next fifteen days. If not, the whole estate is to go to the Friars Minor of the convent of Santa Croce." When the will was finished, everyone left. Gianni gets out of the bed, and they put Messer Buoso back in. Then they begin to wail, and say he just died.

33. *rabbioso*: In the context of the animal similes here this adjective implies that the spirit is rabid in the sense of being affected with rabies (as in vss. 46 and 79).   *conciando*: The word means "dressing," "bedecking," hence its use here is ironical. See *Inf.* XXVIII, 37 and the note for another word used with similar irony.

34-35. *se l'altro . . . a dosso*: The familiar formula of adjuration.

38. *Mirrà*: Myrrha was the daughter of Cinyras, king of Cyprus. Seized with a fatal passion for her father, she contrived, with the aid of her nurse, to introduce herself in disguise into his chamber during the absence of her mother. When Cinyras discovered the deception, he attempted to slay Myrrha, but she escaped and wandered to Arabia, where she was transformed into a myrrh tree and gave birth to Adonis. In his *Epist.* VII, 24, Dante describes her as "hec Myrrha scelestis et impia in Cinyre patris amplexus exestuans" ("the foul and impious Myrrha that burns for the embraces of her father Cinyras"). Ovid tells the story in *Metam.* X, 298-513; also see his *Ars amat.* I, 285-88.

42. *sostenne*: "Ventured," "dared"; the verb "falsificare" (vs. 44) depends on this verb.

43. *la donna de la torma*: The lead mule, queen of the herd.

44. *Buoso Donati*: The Buoso Donati whom Gianni Schicchi is said to have impersonated was probably the son of Vinciguerra di Donato del Pazzo. He lived from the last decades of the twelfth century to about the middle of the thirteenth century and appears to have died a widower without direct heirs. Collusion in the crime by a nephew of his named Simone is related by some of the early commentators. Buoso di Vinciguerra did have a nephew by that name who was the father of Corso Donati, the leader of the Neri faction of the Florentine Guelphs. For this identification and supporting documents, see M. Barbi (1934b), pp. 305-22. The *Anonimo fiorentino* refers to Simone as the son of Buoso Donati (see n. to vs. 32).

45. *dando al testamento norma*: "Giving due form to the will," which may mean due legal form or simply the form calculated to serve his fraudulent purpose.

46. *fuor = furono*.

48. *rivolsilo = lo rivolsi.*   *mal nati*: See *Inf.* V, 7; XVIII, 76. Among the ill-born shades to whom the wayfarer now turns his attention are the falsifiers of money.

49. *fatto a guisa di leuto*: With his swollen belly and emaciated head and neck, Master Adam (named in vs. 61), if he had had his legs cut off, would have looked like a lute. The image is precise, for the belly of the lute swells toward the bottom. Adam's legs are apparently so dwarfed by the huge paunch that they can be counted out of the picture; he may be sitting cross-legged or in some other way so that they are covered by his enormous paunch.

50. *l'anguinaia = l'inguinaia, l'inguine.*

51. *tronca = troncata.*   *altro*: On this use of the word, see N. Zingarelli (1906), pp. 368–74.

52. *La grave idropesì*: Benvenuto says of the dropsy that "reddit hominem gravem, ita ut moveri non possit." ("It renders a man heavy, so that he cannot move.") See Fra Giordano da Rivalto, *Prediche inedite* LIX (1867 edn., p. 303): "L'idropico, quanto più mangia e bee, quegli omori si corrompono tutti e convertonsi in mali omori flemmatici; e però quanto più bee e mangia, più enfia e cresce il male, e più ha sete." ("When someone with dropsy eats and drinks more and more, those humors are corrupted and convert themselves into bad phlegmatic humors. And therefore the more he eats and drinks, the more the illness grows and swells, and he becomes thirstier.")   *idropesì = idropisia.*

56. *l'etico*: One affected with hectic fever, a wasting disease attended by flushed cheeks and a hot, dry skin.

58–59. *O voi che . . . perché*:   Evidently Master Adam overheard what Virgil said to Griffolino and Capocchio in the previous canto (see *Inf.* XXIX, 94–96) and hence knows that Virgil and Dante are not souls going to their punishment in lower Hell; but in his passing puzzlement over this fact there is an unmistakable note of sarcasm.

58–61. *O voi che . . . maestro Adamo*: See Lam. 1:12: "O vos omnes qui transitis per viam, attendite et videte, si est dolor sicut dolor meus." ("O all ye that pass by the way, attend, and see if there be any sorrow like to my sorrow.") Also see *Inf.* XXVIII, 130–32; *Vita nuova* VII, 3.

61. *maestro Adamo*: According to the *Anonimo fiorentino*, Master Adam was from Brescia, but this is now seriously questioned (see G. Livi, 1921; G. Contini, 1953, pp. 7–8, n. 1). At the instigation of the Conti Guidi of Romena, Master Adam counterfeited the gold florin of Florence, in coins containing twenty-one carats of gold instead of the legal standard of twenty-four carats (see vss. 89–90). The fraud was soon detected, and the Florentines, jealous of the purity of their coinage, which had become a standard throughout Christendom, caused the false coiner to be burned alive in 1281 (see n. to vs. 75, below).

62. *assai di quel ch'i' volli*: Money, principally, the fruit of his clever counterfeiting. Given the context, there is something of the notion of a thirst for gold in the turn of phrase.

63. *un gocciol = una gocciola*, but *gocciolo* may denote an even smaller droplet than *gocciola*. Compare the rich man in Luke 16:23–24.

64–66. *Li ruscelletti . . . molli*: Master Adam fairly caresses the image (note "imagine," vs. 68), which, as he says, adds to his torment. This is evident in the suffix *-etti*; and the phrase "faccendo i lor canali freddi e molli" is especially expressive, since clearly he craves coolness and moistness for his own parched throat. Many little streams do rise in the Casentino, a beautiful region of the upper valley of the Arno and Tuscan Apennines, dominated in Dante's day by several branches of the family of the Conti Guidi. / For the use of "freddi" and "molli" in conjunction, see Virgil, *Eclog.* X, 42: "Hic gelidi fontes, hic mollia prata." ("Here are cold springs, here soft meadows.")

64. *d'i = dei*.

71. *tragge = trae.* *tragge cagion del*: "Draws on," "makes use of."

72. *a metter più li miei sospiri in fuga*: Scartazzini (1st edn.) explains that the phrase means "a farmi sospirare più spesso. Quanto più frequenti escono i sospiri, tanto più velocemente essi fuggono, l'uno spingendo l'altro e quasi mettendolo in fuga" ("to make me sigh more often—the more frequently sighs come forth, the quicker they flee, the one pushing the other, putting it, as it were, to flight").

73. *Ivi*: In the Casentino. *Romena*: A castle in the village of Romena in the Casentino, near Pratovecchio, which in Dante's time belonged to the Conti Guidi. The ruins of the castle are still standing. One line of the family (to which the three brothers named in vs. 77 belonged) took its name from Romena.

74. *la lega suggellata del Batista*: The Florentine gold florin was stamped on one side with the flower of the lily (the name *fiorino*, "florin," comes from *fiore*, "flower") and on the other with the image of John the Baptist, patron saint of Florence. The florin was first minted in 1252, according to Villani (VI, 53): "E allora si cominciò la buona moneta d'oro fine di ventiquattro carati, che si chiamano fiorini d'oro." ("And then they began to make good coins of fine twenty-four-carat gold, which are called *fiorini d'oro* [gold florins].")

75. *il corpo sù arso*: Burning alive at the stake was a customary punishment for counterfeiting, a crime against the state. Paolino di Piero in his *Cronica* (MCCLXXXI), says: "Nel milledugentottantuno . . . si trovaro Fiorini di oro falsi in quantitade per un fuoco, che si apprese in Borgo San Lorenzo . . . e dissesi, che li facea fare uno de' Conti da Romena, e funne preso un loro spenditore, e per cose, che confessò, sì fu arso." ("In 1281 . . . a large number of counterfeit gold florins was discovered because of a fire that broke out in the Borgo San Lorenzo . . . and it is said that one of the counts of Romena had them made. One

who disbursed on their behalf was seized, and because of the things he confessed, he was burned.")

77. *Guido . . . Alessandro . . . lor frate*: Guido II da Romena, his brother Alessandro, and—since the brothers were four—either Aghinolfo or Ildebrandino. On the genealogy of the Conti Guidi, particularly the counts of Romena, see F. Torraca (1904).

78. *Fonte Branda*: Perhaps the reference here is to the celebrated fountain at Siena (mention of which occurs as early as 1081), situated at the foot of the hill upon which the church of San Domenico stands; the fountain was so called after the Brandi family, to whom the site at one time belonged. However, another fountain of the same name (now almost dry, but the existence of which is attested to by its mention in ancient documents), near the castle of Romena and thus much closer than Siena to the scene of Master Adam's crime, may be the one alluded to. The early commentators take the reference to be to the Fonte Branda at Siena, but this may be because it was better known. On this question, see E. Londi (1908), pp. 115-17; A. Bassermann (1902), p. 91.

79. *Dentro c'è l'una già*: This has to be Guido, who died before 1300, the year in which the action of the poem takes place. The other brothers were still alive in 1300.

79-80. *se l'arrabbiate ombre . . . dicon vero*: These shades—of the falsifiers of persons—apparently run around the whole *bolgia* and occasionally carry news, though this hardly befits their mad condition and antics.

81. *le membra legate*: The limbs are "bound" by dropsy and the heaviness caused by that malady.

82-87. *S'io fossi . . . ci ha*: Greater hate hath no man, nor any soul in Hell! Porena has calculated that it would take Master Adam seven hundred thousand years to make his way around the whole circle of the *bolgia*—yet it should be remembered that he has all eternity before him!

84. *io sarei messo = io mi sarei messo.*

85. *sconcia = sconciata.* "Disfigured," "deformed."

86. *ella*: The unexpressed antecedent is *bolgia.*

86–87. *volge undici miglia . . . ha*: Exactly half the circumference of the ninth *bolgia* (see *Inf.* XXIX, 9). Such precise measurements are calculated to add realism to the description of Hell, but they in fact show a curious indifference to reality; for if the *bolgia* is half a mile or more across, it is hard to conceive the size of the bridge that would be required to span it.

87. *non ci ha*: To be read *nòncia* so as to rhyme with "oncia" (vs. 83) and "sconcia" (vs. 85). For comparable rhymes, see *Inf.* VII, 28; XXVIII, 123.   *ci ha*: "There is."

89. *e' = ei.* The three Conti Guidi mentioned in vs. 77.

90. *tre carati di mondiglia*: The *Anonimo fiorentino* (in the gloss on vs. 73) comments: "Erono buoni di peso ma non di lega; però ch'egli erano di xxi carati, dove elli debbono essere di xxiiii: sì che tre carati v'avea dentro di rame o d'altro metallo." ("They were of good weight but not of good composition, for they were only twenty-one carats instead of twenty-four. The other three carats were made up of copper or some other [base] metal.") For the statutory composition of the florin, see the quotation from Villani in n. to vs. 74, above.

92. *fumman = fumano.   fumman come man bagnate 'l verno*: Wet hands "smoke" when exposed to the cold air of winter. These spirits, however, steam because of the burning fever they suffer, as vs. 99 indicates.   *verno = inverno.*

93. *stretti*: The adjective may be understood to mean that the two are lying close together or that they are close to Master Adam's right "frontier." The latter sense seems preferable.

94. *volta non dierno*: They have not moved or turned over in any way.   *dierno (dierono) = diedero*.

95. *greppo*: Literally, a precipitous slope.

96. *che dieno*: I.e., *che dieno volta   dieno = diano*.

97. *la falsa ch'accusò Gioseppo*: The wife of Potiphar, who, after trying in vain to seduce Joseph, made the false accusation that he had sought to lie with her. See Gen. 39:6–20.
   Gioseppo: This form, or *Giuseppo*, was common in Dante's day.

98. *Sinon*: Sinon, the treacherous Greek who during the siege of Troy allowed himself to be taken prisoner by the Trojans and then by a lying tale persuaded them to admit within their walls the famous wooden horse. See n. to *Inf.* XXVI, 59.   *greco di Troia*: Note what Priam, who believed the lying Sinon, had said to him (*Aen.* II, 148–49): "Quisquis es, amissos hinc iam obliviscere Graios; / noster eris." ("Whoever thou art, from henceforth forget the Greeks thou hast lost; thou shalt be ours.")

99. *febbre aguta*: See Fra Giordano da Rivalto, *Prediche inedite* XLIV (1867 edn., p. 238): "Quando la febbre è *intra vasa*, dentro alle veni, nel sangue, or questa è la mala febbre, questa è detta febbre aguta." ("When the fever is *intra vasa*, in the veins, in the blood, it is a bad fever, what is called a *febbre aguta* [acute fever].")   *leppo*: Buti comments: "Leppo è puzza d'arso unto, come quando lo fuoco s'appiglia alla pentola o alla padella." ("*Leppo* means the stench of burnt grease—for instance, when the pot or pan begins to burn.")

100. *l'un*: Sinon.

101. *nomato sì oscuro*: I.e., called "false" and a "Greek from Troy" (vs. 98).

102. *li = gli.   epa*: See vs. 119 and *Inf.* XXV, 82.   *croia*: "Hard," apparently always used in a pejorative

sense. See E. G. Parodi (1957), p. 279, who cites the
Piedmontese *invern croj*, meaning a "hard winter."

103. *Quella sonò come fosse un tamburo*: G. Contini (1953,
p. 11) quotes Bartholomaeus Anglicus, who, in his *De
proprietatibus rerum*, speaks of a kind of dropsy in which
"extenditur venter et sonat sicut tympanum . . . collum
et extrema efficiuntur gracilia." ("The stomach is distended
and resounds like a drum . . . the neck and the extremities
become very thin.") V. Cian (1902, p. 113, n. 1) also
quotes this passage.

104. *li = gli.*

110. *avei = avevi.   presto*: "Ready," "quick" to strike
out. This is a taunt, since Master Adam went to the stake
bound.

112–14. *Tu di' ver . . . richesto*: The repetition of "ver" is
notably emphatic.

112. *di' = dici.*

115. *e*: The value of this conjunction in such a construction
is evident in a sonnet by Cecco Angiolieri addressed to
Dante (see M. Marti, 1956, p. 231):

> Dante Alighier, s'i' so' bon begolardo,
> tu mi tien' bene la lancia a le reni;
> s'eo desno con altrui, e tu vi ceni;
> s'eo mordo'l grasso, e tu vi suggi'l lardo;
> s'eo cimo'l panno, e tu vi freghi il cardo . . .

Dante Alighieri, if I am a writer of nonsense, you are
not far behind me. If I dine with others, you eat supper
there. If I bite the fat, you suck the lard. If I shear the
cloth, you card it.

117. *e tu per più ch'alcun altro demonio*: As if every
florin Master Adam falsified had counted as a sin.

118. *Ricorditi*: The impersonal *ricordare* with the pronoun
in the dative.   *spergiuro*: Sinon had sworn by the gods.
His oath-taking is described in *Aen.* II, 152–59:

. . . ille, dolis instructus et arte Pelasga,
sustulit exutas vinclis ad sidera palmas:
"vos, aeterni ignes, et non violabile vestrum
testor numen," ait, "vos arae ensesque nefandi,
quos fugi, vittaeque deum, quas hostia gessi:
fas mihi Graiorum sacrata resolvere iura,
fas odisse viros atque omnia ferre sub auras,
si qua tegunt . . ."

The other, schooled in Pelasgian guile and craft, lifted
to the stars his unfettered hands: "Ye, O everlasting
fires," he cries, "and your inviolable majesty, be ye my
witness; ye, O altars, and accursed swords which I
escaped, and chaplets of the gods, which I wore as
victim! rightly may I break my solemn obligations to
the Greeks, rightly hate them and bring all things to
light if they hide aught."

120. *sieti = ti sia.*   *reo*: A torment to you.   *tutto il
mondo sallo*: The *Aeneid* relates it, hence "the whole world
must know of it."   *sallo = lo sa.*

121. *te*: Dative.

121-22. *ti crepa . . . la lingua*: The subject in this construc-
tion is "lingua."

123. *t'assiepa*: Hedges (*siepi*) commonly mark boundaries
in Italy, hence this touch connects with the derisive "confini"
of vs. 93.

125. *per tuo mal come suole*: "To your own hurt, as is [was]
its wont" in the world.

126. *rinfarcia = infarcisca. Ri* serves to intensify the verb.

127. *l'arsura*: G. Contini (1953, p. 11) quotes from Bar-
tholomaeus Anglicus, *De proprietatibus rerum*, the symp-
toms of *febris putrida*: "dolor capitis, malicia anhelitus, sitis
et similia" ("headaches, shortness of breath, thirst, and
such things").

128. *Narcisso*: Narcissus, Greek youth, of whom the nymph Echo became enamored. Finding him insensible to love, she pined away in grief and was reduced to nothing but a voice. To punish Narcissus for his insensibility, the goddess Nemesis caused him to see his own image reflected in a fountain, whereupon he became so enamored of it that he too pined away gradually, until he was changed into the flower that bears his name. Ovid relates the story in *Metam.* III, 351–510.

134. *volsimi = mi volsi.*

136. *dannaggio = danno.*

138. *come non fosse = come se non fosse.*

139–41. *tal mi fec' io . . . fare*: By his speechlessness and his blushing (see *Inf.* XXXI, 2), Dante gives ample evidence of his sense of shame (see vs. 130), but it should also be remembered that Virgil can read Dante's every thought and so knows his inner as well as his outer state.

142. *Maggior difetto men vergogna lava*: The subject is "vergogna," the object "difetto."

144. *ti disgrava = disgràvati* (imperative).

145. *E fa ragion*: "And know that." Allegory comes to the fore in this turn of phrase, for if Virgil can be at Dante's side simply by his being concerned that it be so, then Virgil must be Reason, or some such guide.

CANTO XXXI

1. *Una medesma lingua*: Virgil's.   *pria = prima.   mi morse*: With his angry rebuke (see *Inf.* XXX, 131–32). For the choice of verb, compare the expression *lingua mordace* ("biting tongue").

2. *mi tinse l'una e l'altra guancia*: "Brought blushes to both my cheeks."

3. *la medicina*: Virgil's comforting words (see *Inf.* XXX, 142–48).

4. *od' io*: The verb suggests that the healing power of Achilles' lance is poetic myth (see n. to vss. 4–5, below). For another such suggestion of poetic myth, see *Inf.* XXIX, 63.   *solea = soleva.*

4–5. *la lancia d'Achille*: According to legend, Achilles' spear could heal the wounds it inflicted. Early in the Trojan War, Telephus, son of Hercules and king of Mysia, was wounded by Achilles. Since the wound did not heal, Telephus consulted an oracle and was told that only he who inflicted the wound could cure it. Accordingly Telephus sought out Achilles, who applied some of the rust from his spear to the wound and thereby healed it. In the Provençal and early Italian versions of this myth the spear's healing property was altered. Instead of healing by means of its own rust, the spear was said to effect a cure by wounding again. See, for example, Bernard de Ventadour (*Chanso* I, in M. Raynouard, 1818, p. 43):

> Cum fo de Peleus la lansa,
> Que de son colp non podi'hom guerir,
> Si per eys loc no s'en fezes ferir.

. . . as Peleus' spear whose wound no man could be cured of unless he had himself wounded by it again.

5. *e del suo padre*: Peleus, the father of Achilles, was the son of Aeacus and king of the Myrmidons of Phthia in Thessaly (see n. to *Inf.* XXIX, 58–64). His wife was the Nereid, Thetis. / Dante follows the Homeric tradition (*Iliad* XVI, 143–44) in stating that Achilles' spear formerly belonged to his father. But since there does not appear to be any Latin authority from whom Dante could have derived this knowledge, it is probable that his statement is based upon a misunderstanding of Ovid (*Remedia amoris*, vss. 47–48), possibly due to a textual variant of "Pelias": "Vulnus in Herculeo quae quondam fecerat hoste, / Vulneris auxilium Pelias hasta tulit." ("The Pelian spear which wounded once its Herculean foe, bore relief also to the wound.") Dante evidently took "Pelias hasta" to mean "the spear of Peleus," instead of "the spear from Mount Pelion," the abode of the centaur Chiron, who gave the spear to Peleus. As P. Toynbee (1902, pp. 137–41) points out, this association of Peleus with the miraculous spear of Achilles was a commonplace with medieval poets.

6. *prima di trista e poi di buona mancia*: See Ovid, *Remedia amoris*, vss. 43–44: "Discite sanari, per quem didicistis amare: / Una manus vobis vulnus opemque feret." ("Learn healing from him through whom ye learnt to love: one hand alike will wound and succour.") *mancia*: "Gratuity."

7–8. *Noi demmo il dosso . . . dintorno*: The wayfarers turn away from the tenth and last *bolgia* (the "misero vallone") and proceed across the apparently wide area between it and the central pit.

11. '*l viso* = *la vista*.

14. *che, contra sé la sua via seguitando*: "Seguitando" has here the value of a participle and refers to "li occhi miei" of the following verse, as if the sequence were "li miei occhi seguitanti."

17. *Carlo Magno*: Charlemagne, or Charles the Great (742–814), king of the Franks, was crowned Emperor of the West on Christmas Day 800, by Pope Leo III in Rome. In the year 1165 Charlemagne was canonized.   *perdé la santa gesta*: "Gesta" here means "band," "guard," "company," specifically "rear-guard," since Dante is referring to the destruction of Charlemagne's rear-guard led by Roland. In the traditional account, preserved in the OFr *Chanson de Roland* (late eleventh or early twelfth century), Roland is betrayed by his stepfather Ganelon, to the Saracen king Marsile, whose vast army annihilated the French forces at Roncesvalles.

18. *non sonò sì terribilmente Orlando*: Dante probably derived his knowledge of Roland's horn from the *Chanson de Roland*; see especially vss. 1753–67:

Rodlanz at mis l'olifant a sa boche,
Empeint lo bien, par grant vertut lo sonet.
Halt sont li pui e la voiz est molt longe,
Granz .xxx. liwes l'odirent il respondre.
Charles l'odit e ses compaignes totes.
Ço dist li reis: "Bataille font nostre home."
E li quens Guenles li respondiét encontre:
"S'altre·l desist, ja semblast grant mençonge."

   Li quens Rodlanz par peine e par ahans,
Par grant dolor sonet son olifant.
Par mi la boche en salt fors li clers sans,
De son cervel li temples est rompant.
De·l corn qu'il tient l'odide en est molt grant,
Charles l'entent ki est as porz passant,
Naimes l'odit si·l escoltent li Franc.

Roland put the horn to his lips; he gripped it firmly and blew with all his strength. The mountains are high

and the horn's note carries far; a full thirty leagues away
its prolonged note is heard. Charles heard it as did all
his companions. The king said, "Our men are joined in
battle." And Ganelon replied in disagreement, "Had
another said this, it would certainly seem great non-
sense."

Count Roland with much effort and in great agony
very painfully sounds his horn. Bright blood spurts from
his mouth. His temple bursts. The sound of the horn
he is holding is exceedingly loud. Charles hears it while
going through the pass. Duke Naimon hears it and so
do all the Franks.

A similar account is given in a work attributed to the
Archbishop Turpin (see Pseudo-Turpin, the *Historia Karoli
Magni*, XXVI, 35–39):

> Tunc tanta virtute tuba sua eburnea insonuit quod
> flatu oris eius tuba per medium scissa et vene colli eius
> et nervi rupti fuisse feruntur. Cuius vox usque ad aures
> Karoli, qui in valle que Karoli dicitur cum exercitu
> suo tentoria fixerat, loco scilicet qui distabat a Roth-
> lando .viii. miliariis versus Gasconiam, angelico ductu
> pervenit.

> At that point he blew on his ivory horn with such force
> that it was split down the middle, and the veins and
> nerves of his neck were said to have burst. Charlemagne,
> who was encamped with his army in the valley called
> Charles', eight miles away toward Gascony, heard the
> sound, borne by an angel.

20. *me = a me*.

21. *terra*: "City," as before, notably in referring to the city
of Dis (for example, in *Inf.* VIII, 130).

22. *Però che = perciò che*.   *trascorri*: "Pass on," i.e.,
with your eyes.

24. *maginare = imaginare*, in the sense of "to perceive."
abborri: "You go astray." For the meaning of this verb,
see n. to *Inf.* XXV, 144.

25. *se tu là ti congiungi* = *se tu arrivi colà*.

26. *'l senso*: "The sense" of sight.

27. *pungi*: Imperative, "spur yourself."

32. *intorno da la ripa*: The giants are standing in the pit and against its perpendicular wall; it is possible that they are standing on some sort of ledge (see n. to vs. 145).

33. *umbilico* (pronounced *umbilìco*) = *ombelico*.

36. *ciò che cela 'l vapor*: The subject is "vapor." *che l'aere stipa*: The vapor is said to "pack" or "thicken" the air; see *Inf*. VII, 19.

37. *forando*: Literally, "boring through." *l'aura* = *l'aria*; see "aere" in the preceding verse.

38. *appressando* = *appressandosi*. *ver'* = *verso*.

39. *fuggiemi* = *mi fuggiva*. *crescémi* = *mi crescé*. As the wayfarer realizes that he is looking not at towers but at giants, his terror increases.

41. *Montereggion*: Dante likens the giants to the towers of Montereggioni (*castrum Montis regionis*), a strongly forti-fied castle, situated on the crown of a low hill about eight miles northwest of Siena. The fortress is surrounded by a massive wall surmounted by fourteen towers placed at regu-lar intervals (these are no longer as tall as they were in Dante's time). (See Plate 7, facing p. 568.) The castle was built by the Sienese in 1213, and the wall with its massive towers was added some time between 1260, when the Sienese were victorious over the Florentine Guelphs at Montaperti, and 1270. Villani states (VI, 55) that in 1254 Montereggioni was besieged by the Florentines, who, hav-ing attempted to bribe the garrison of German mercenaries, would have taken it, had not the Sienese come to terms with Florence.

42. *così la proda*: "Proda" is the direct object of "torreg-giavan," vs. 43. On *torreggiare* as a transitive verb, see Petrocchi's note.

44–45. *cui minaccia Giove . . . quando tuona*: Jove still thunders because of the giants' defiant attack on heaven; see *Inf.* XIV, 52–60.

49–50. *Natura . . . quando lasciò l'arte di sì fatti animali*: "When Nature stopped producing such creatures." For *animale* in the sense of "animate being," see *Inf.* II, 2.

51. *per tòrre tali essecutori a Marte*: By ceasing to produce giants, Nature takes them out of warfare. For the warlike qualities of the Biblical giants, see Bar. 3:26–28: "Ibi fuerunt gigantes nominati illi, qui ab initio fuerunt, statura magna, scientes bellum; non hos elegit Dominus, neque viam disciplinae invenerunt, propterea perierunt. Et quoniam non habuerunt sapientiam, interierunt propter suam insipientiam." ("There were the giants, those renowned men that were from the beginning, of great stature, expert in war. The Lord chose not them: neither did they find the way of knowledge. Therefore did they perish. And because they had not wisdom, they perished through their folly.") Gmelin, commenting on vs. 49, notes that Augustine cites this passage in *De civ. Dei* (XV, xxiii, 4). *tòrre* = *togliere*. *essecutori* = *esecutori*.

53. *non si pente*: I.e., continues to create.

55. *l'argomento de la mente*: "The faculty of the mind," reason.

55–56. *l'argomento de la mente . . . possa*: Pietro di Dante recalls Aristotle's *Politics*: "Sicut homo, si sit perfectus virtute, est optimus animalium, sic si sit separatus a lege et iustitia, pessimus omnium, cum homo habeat arma rationis." ("Just as a man, if he is advanced in virtue, is the noblest of all animals, so if he departs from the path of justice, he is the most dangerous of all, since he is armed with reason.") For the exact quotation, see Aristotle, *Polit.* I, 1, 1253ᵃ, in Thomas Aquinas, *Opera omnia*, vol. XXI, p. 366. E. Proto (1912, p. 231) cites a relevant passage from Aquinas (*Exp. Eth. Nicom.* VII, lect. 6, n. 1403): "Unus homo malus decies millies potest mala facere quam

7. Montereggioni, a fortified castle northwest of Siena

bestia, propter rationem quam habet ad excogitandum diversa mala." ("An evil man can do ten thousand times more harm than a beast by his reason which he can use to devise very diverse evils.") See also *Purg.* V, 112-14.

57. *la gente*: "Mankind."

59. *la pina di San Pietro*: Dante compares the face of the giant Nimrod to the huge bronze pine cone which is said to have stood originally near the Campus Martius in Rome. The cone, which is over four yards high, was transferred by Pope Symmachus (pope 498-514) to the old basilica of St. Peter's and centuries later was put in its present location in the formal gardens of the papal palace. (See Plate 8, facing p. 570.)

60. *a sua proporzione*: The proportion of the face.   *l'altre ossa*: "The other bones"—i.e., the other parts of his body.

61. *la ripa, ch'era perizoma*: "Perizoma" (Greek περίζομα) is used in this sense to describe how Adam and Eve covered themselves with fig leaves. See Gen. 3:7: "Fecerunt sibi perizomata." ("[They] made themselves coverings.")

64. *tre Frison*: Frisians or Frieslanders (the inhabitants of Friesland) were noted for their great stature. This giant— Nimrod—is so tall that three Frisians standing on one another's shoulders would not have reached from his waist to his hair. From this it is possible to calculate approximately the giant's height. Butler says that if we estimate the height of the Frisians at six feet six inches and allow two feet for the reach of the topmost, we find that the distance from the giant's waist to his neck—i.e., to the lower ends of the giant's hair—is twenty-one and a half feet. If we add a few feet for his neck and twelve feet for his head—the height of the bronze pine cone mentioned in vs. 59 (see note)—we arrive at a figure of thirty-five feet for half the giant.

65. *trenta gran palmi*: About seven meters. Scartazzini-Vandelli quotes G. Antonelli, who mentions a calculation of the height of the giants based on this figure:

Dicendo Dante *trenta gran palmi* . . . conviene pren-
dere il palmo architettonico; e ponendo che dalla
clavicola . . . al vertice del capo corra uno spazio che
sia circa 1/6 dell'umana statura, si trova che Nembrotto
sarebbe di braccia fiorentine 45 9/10 alto, ossia di m.
26 e mm. 806.

Since Dante says "thirty large *palmi*" . . . one should
understand this to mean the architectural *palmo*, and
assuming that from the clavicle . . . to the top of the
head the distance is about one sixth of the human
stature, we find that Nimrod was forty-five and nine-
tenths Florentine *braccia* tall, or 26.806 meters.

Note that this calculation differs from Butler's (see n. to
vs. 64) by about ten feet.

66. *dal loco in giù dov' omo affibbia 'l manto*: From the
neck down to the waist.

67. *Raphèl maì amècche zabì almi*: Numerous unsuccess-
ful attempts have been made to interpret this jargon. But
Dante, doubtless alluding to the confusion of tongues which
struck the builders of the Tower of Babel, expressly states
(vss. 80–81) that Nimrod's language is intelligible to no
one. The early commentators regard the words as meaning-
less. Benvenuto, for example, says:

Est hic notandum, quod ista verba non sunt signifi-
cativa, et posito quod in se aliquid significarent, sicut
aliqui interpretari conantur, adhuc nihil significarent
hic, nisi quod ponuntur ad significandum quod idioma
istius non erat intelligibile alicui, quia propter eius
superbiam facta est divisio labiorum. Et haec est intentio
autoris quam expresse ponit in litera.

It must be noted that these words are without meaning.
Even if they did mean something, as some are at great
pains to prove, they would not mean anything here.
They have been used here only to show that his lan-
guage was not intelligible to anyone, for the division
of tongues took place as a result of his pride. That is the
author's intention, to which he thus gives literal ex-
pression.

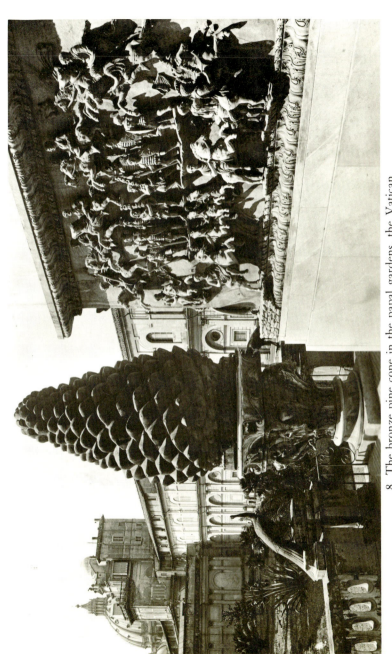

8. The bronze pine cone in the papal gardens, the Vatican

Similarly Buti says: "Queste sono voci sanza significazione: altrimenti, chi ci volesse dare significazione, mosterrebbe che l'autore avesse contradetto a sè medesimo." ("These words are without meaning. To attribute any meaning to them would amount to saying that the author contradicted himself.") Apparently the first to suggest an interpretation of Nimrod's words was Landino (1424–1504), who thought they might be explained by means of the Chaldean language. On the basis of this hint futile attempts have been made to read the words into Hebrew, Arabic, Greek, and so on; some of these are given in G. A. Scartazzini (1899), p. 1618, under "Rafel mai amech zabi almi." See also D. Guerri (1909), pp. 69–76. For the precise metrical reading of this unintelligible verse, see Petrocchi's note and G. Vandelli (1921c), pp. 64–67.

69. *cui non si convenia più dolci salmi*: The phrase is clearly ironical.

70. *ver'* = *verso*.

71. *ti disfoga* = *sfògati*.

73. *soga*: "Rope."

74. *anima confusa*: The adjective is most appropriate for Nimrod and recalls the confusion of tongues which afflicted those who (according to tradition), under Nimrod's direction (see n. to vs. 77), attempted to build the Tower of Babel. See Gen. 11:7, 9: "Descendamus et confundamus ibi linguam eorum, ut non audiat unusquisque vocem proximi sui. . . . Et idcirco vocatum est nomen eius Babel, quia ibi confusum est labium universae terrae." ("Let us go down, and there confuse their language so that they will not understand one another's speech. . . . For this reason it was called Babel, because there the Lord confused the speech of all the earth.") See also *De vulg. eloqu.* I, viii, 1: "confusione linguarum" ("confusion of tongues"); and the Brunetto Latini quotation in n. to vs. 77.

75. *lui*: The horn itself.   *che 'l gran petto ti doga*: In heraldic terminology, a "doga" is a band running diagonally

across a shield; the verb here echoes the noun and ironically connotes "decorate."

77. *Nembrotto*: Nimrod, the son of Cush (Nemrod, Chus in the Douay version of the Bible), was, according to Gen. 10:9, "robustus venator coram Domino" ("a mighty hunter before the Lord"); hence he is equipped in Hell with a hunter's horn. According to a medieval and patristic tradition that probably arose from Genesis, Nimrod was the deviser of the Tower of Babel on the plain of Shinar. See Gen. 10:10: "Fuit autem principium regni eius Babylon et Arach et Achad et Chalanne in terra Senaar." ("The beginning of his kingdom was Babylon, Arach and Acchad [and Chalanne], all of them in the land of Sennaar.") For "Babylon" the Authorized Version of the Bible gives "Babel"; the Akkadian word is the same for both forms. The tradition connecting Nimrod with the Tower of Babel is mentioned by Josephus (*Jewish Antiquities* I, 113–18), by Augustine (*De civ. Dei* XVI, 4), and by Orosius (*Hist.* II, vi, 7). Isidore of Seville (*Etym.* XV, i, 4) and Petrus Comestor (*Hist. schol.*, commenting on Gen. 38) refer to him as founder either of the tower or of the city of Babylon, as do some other medieval writers. Brunetto Latini says of him (*Tresor* I, 24): "Cil Nembrot edefia la tor Babel en Babilone, ou avint la diversités des parleures et de la confusion des langues." ("Nimrod built the Tower of Babel in Babylon, where the mixture of languages and the confusion of tongues occurred.")

Nothing in the Bible suggests that Nimrod was a giant. It appears only (from Gen. 6:4) that the Biblical giants were extinct before the flood; but both Orosius (*Hist.* II, vi, 7) and Augustine (*De civ. Dei* XVI, iii, 1; XVI, 4; XVI, xi, 3), who probably were Dante's authorities, represent Nimrod as a giant. Dante mentions him as a giant also in *De vulg. eloqu.* I, vii, 4.   *coto*: From *cogitare* ("to think").

79. *Lasciànlo = lasciamolo.*   *a vòto*: See *Inf.* VIII, 19.

80–81. *ché così è a lui ciascun linguaggio . . . altrui*: Virgil must know that the giant cannot understand him, but he speaks to him anyway (vss. 70–75), either for the way-farer's sake or as one might speak to an animal that cannot understand. For a discussion of Virgil's address to Nimrod, see E. G. Parodi (1902), p. 100.

83. *al trar d'un balestro*: I.e., *alla distanza di un tiro di balestra*.

84. *l'altro*: The next giant.   *maggio = maggiore*, as in *Inf.* VI, 48.

85. *qual che fosse 'l maestro*: See *Inf.* XV, 12.

86. *soccinto = succinto*, past participle of *succingere*, "to bind up." The word suggests that the giant's left arm is bent up across his chest and bound above the waist, where the wayfarers can see it.

88. *d'una catena = con una catena*.   *avvinto*: Past participle of *avvincere*, "to bind around." The chain is coiled spirally around the giant's torso.

89. *lo scoperto*: The uncovered or visible part of the giant's body, from the waist up.

91. *Questo superbo*: The adjective points to the fact that the giants are punished for the sin of pride. See the description of another giant, Capaneus, *Inf.* XIV, 46–72.

91–92. *volle esser esperto di sua potenza*: "Wished to try his strength."

93. *merto = merito*, "reward."

94. *Fialte*: Ephialtes, the son of Neptune and Iphimedia. He and his brother Otus were known as the Aloidae (by which name Statius refers to them in *Theb.* X, 850 and Virgil in *Aen.* VI, 582), after their foster-father, Aloeus, the husband of Iphimedia. At the age of nine the two brothers, who were marvelously strong, made war upon the Olympian gods and attacked Olympus itself, but according to the Homeric account of the legend were killed during the attempt.

95. *quando i giganti fer paura a' dèi*: See Horace, *Odes*
III, iv, 42–52:

>   . . . scimus, ut impios
>   Titanas immanemque turbam
>   fulmine sustulerit caduco,
>
>   qui terram inertem, qui mare temperat
>   ventosum et urbes regnaque tristia,
>   divosque mortalesque turmas
>   imperio regit unus aequo.
>
>   magnum illa terrorem intulerat Iovi
>   fidens iuventus horrida bracchiis
>   fratresque tendentes opaco
>   Pelion imposuisse Olympo.

Full well we know how the impious Titans and their
frightful horde were struck down with the descending
bolt by him who rules the lifeless earth, the wind-swept
sea, cities, and the gloomy realms below, who alone with
righteous sway governs the gods and throngs of men.
Mighty terror had been brought on Jove by that insolent
crew bristling with hands, and by the brothers who
strove to set Pelion on shadowy Olympus.

95. *fer = fecero*.

97. *puote = può*.

98. *Briareo*: Briareus, or Aegaeon, son of Uranus and Earth,
was one of the giants who warred against Olympus. Ac-
cording to some accounts, he was slain by Jupiter with a
thunderbolt and buried under Mount Etna. Virgil repre-
sents him with a hundred arms and fifty heads (*Aen*. X,
565–68):

>   Aegaeon qualis, centum cui bracchia dicunt
>   centenasque manus, quinquaginta oribus ignem
>   pectoribusque arsisse, Iovis cum fulmina contra
>   tot paribus streperet clipeis, tot stringeret ensis . . .

Even as Aegaeon, who, men say, had a hundred arms
and a hundred hands, and flashed fire from fifty mouths
and breasts, what time against Jove's thunders he

clanged with as many like shields, and bared as many swords . . . .

Dante's description of the giant as "lo smisurato Briareo" recalls the "immensus Briareus" ("Briareus vast in bulk") of Statius (*Theb.* II, 596).

100. *Anteo*: Antaeus, the son of Neptune and Earth, was a mighty giant and wrestler of Libya, invincible as long as he remained in contact with his mother, Earth. Hercules discovered the source of his strength, lifted him from the ground, and crushed him while he held him so (see Lucan, *Phars.* IV, 593-660).

Dante represents Antaeus as unbound ("disciolto," vs. 101), since unlike the giants who are in chains (vss. 87-88, 104), he was born after the war against the gods (vss. 119-21). Dante's account of Antaeus owes much to Lucan. For the geographical details of the struggle with Hercules (mentioned in vss. 115-17), see *Phars.* IV, 585-90:

> Inter semirutas magnae Carthaginis arces
> Et Clipeam tenuit stationis litora notae,
> Primaque castra locat cano procul aequore, qua se
> Bagrada lentus agit siccae sulcator harenae.
> Inde petit tumulos exesasque undique rupes,
> Antaei quas regna vocat non vana vetustas.

He gained the shore of famous anchorage between Clipea and the half-ruined citadels of great Carthage. His first camp he pitched at some distance from the hoary sea, where the Bagrada slowly pushes on and furrows the thirsty sand. From there he marched to the rocky eminence, hollowed out on all sides, which tradition with good reason calls the realm of Antaeus.

For Lucan's account of the lions slain by Antaeus (vs. 118) see *Phars.* IV, 601-2: "Haec illi spelunca domus; latuisse sub alta / Rupe ferunt, epulas raptos habuisse leones." ("Yonder cave was his dwelling; men say that he hid beneath the towering cliff and feasted on the lions he had carried off.") The opinion that if Antaeus had helped the other giants in the war against Olympus, the gods would

have lost (vss. 119–20) evidently is also borrowed from
Phars. IV, 595–97:

> Nec tam iusta fuit terrarum gloria Typhon
> Aut Tityos Briareusque ferox; caeloque pepercit,
> Quod non Phlegraeis Antaeum sustulit arvis.

She [Earth] had more cause to boast of him than of
Typhon or Tityos and fierce Briareus; and she dealt
mercifully with the gods when she did not raise up
Antaeus on the field of Phlegra.

102. *ne = ci. nel fondo d'ogne reo*: The ninth and last
circle of Hell. *reo*: "Sin"; the adjective is used in place
of the noun. See "rio," *Inf.* IV, 40.

104. *e fatto come questo*: That is, with only one head and
two arms; not, as Virgil had represented him (see n. to vs.
98), with fifty heads and a hundred arms.

105. *par = appare.*

106. *già*: The word serves to reinforce the affirmation.
   rubesto: "Fierce," an adjective that would be appropriate
for an earthquake, or a giant.

108. *Fialte a scuotersi fu presto*: Ephialtes is furious that
Briareus should be proclaimed "more savage in his look"
than he (vs. 105).

110. *dotta = paura.*

111. *ritorte*: Properly, "ropes," as in *Inf.* XIX, 27; here,
"chains."

112. *allotta = allora*; see *Inf.* V, 53.

113. *alle*: "Ells." As a measure of length the ell varied from
country to country, the English ell being forty-five inches,
the Flemish twenty-seven inches. The *Anonimo fiorentino*
comments: "Alla è una misura in Fiandra . . . ch'è intorno
di braccia II e mezzo." ("The ell is a measurement used in
Flanders . . . which is about two and one half *braccia*." Reck-
oning the *braccio fiorentino* at sixty centimeters, five ells
would equal seven and one half meters. For the correspond-

ence of this with the measure of thirty *palmi* for Nimrod
from navel to neck, see n. to vs. 65.

114. *uscia = usciva.*   *grotta*: The rock wall of the pit in
which he is standing.

115-21. *O tu che ne la fortunata valle . . . terra*: This is
plainly intended as a *captatio benevolentiae* ("gaining the
good will of another"), appealing as it does, in vss. 119-
21, to fame on earth as that which the souls in Hell hold
dearest. See *Inf.* II, 58-60 and the note.

115. *fortunata valle*: The "fateful valley" of the Bagradas
River (modern Medjerda River), in north central Tunisia,
near Zama, where Scipio won the decisive victory over
Hannibal in 202 B.C. For a similar use of "fortunata," see
Inf. XXVIII, 8-9.

116. *che fece Scipion di gloria reda*: After the battle of
Zama, Scipio returned to Italy and entered Rome in tri-
umph, receiving the surname Africanus to commemorate his
victory over Hannibal. See *Purg.* XXIX, 115-16.   *reda =
erede.*

117. *quand' Anibàl co' suoi diede le spalle*: Hannibal lived
for some years after the battle of Zama, from which he had
"retreated" in defeat; he then committed suicide, probably
in 183 B.C.

118. *recasti già mille leon per preda*: Virgil flatters Antaeus
so that the giant will fulfill his request. The flattery is
extended by the word "mille," which Dante has added to
Lucan's account of Antaeus' strength. See Lucan's descrip-
tion, quoted in n. to vs. 100.

119. *e che, se fossi stato*: For this touch, see n. to vs. 100.

121. *i figli de la terra*: According to legend, the giants were
the offspring of Gaea, or Earth.

122. *mettine = mettici.*   *ten = te ne.*

123. *dove Cocito la freddura serra*: The object of "serra" is "Cocito." The meaning of this phrase will become clearer in the next canto. *Cocito*: Cocytus, the frozen lake of the ninth circle of Hell.

124. *Tizio*: According to legend the giant Tityus was the son of Jupiter and Elara. For having attempted to violate Latona, he was killed by her children Apollo and Diana and hurled down to Tartarus, where he lay outstretched on the ground covering nine acres. Vultures eternally preyed on his liver. Virgil mentions the punishment of Tityus (*Aen.* VI, 595–600), as does Ovid (*Metam.* IV, 456–58). *Tifo*: Typhon, or Typhoeus, the son of Earth (Gaea) and Tartarus, was a tremendous monster, who is sometimes described as having a hundred heads, sometimes as breathing fire, and sometimes as having a body made of snakes from the hips down and arms with serpents' heads instead of hands. In-cited by his mother, Typhon attacked the Olympian gods, but was eventually defeated by Jupiter. According to some accounts, he was buried under Mount Etna, which he caused to erupt by his struggles to free himself.

In mentioning Tityus and Typhon together here, Dante evidently had in mind a passage in which Lucan also speaks of them together and implies that Antaeus was mightier than both of them (Virgil's reference consequently is meant as a compliment to Antaeus); see Lucan, *Phars.* IV, 593–97 (vss. 595–97 are quoted in n. to vs. 100).

126. *ti china = chìnati.* *grifo*: "Snout"; in this context the word does not bear any strong pejorative sense. See Brunetto Latini, *Tesoretto*, vss. 2591–92 (in G. Contini, 1960, vol. II, p. 265): "o s'hai tenuto a schifo / la gente, o torto 'l grifo" ("if you have loathed people, or made a wry face").

130. *in fretta*: The *captatio benevolentiae* (vss. 114–21) proves effective. Antaeus does indeed desire fame on earth.

132. *ond'*: Refers to "le man" (vs. 131). For the struggle with Hercules, see n. to vs. 100.

133. *sentio = sentì.*

134. *Fatti*: Second person singular imperative.

136. *la Carisenda*: The Garisenda, one of the leaning towers of Bologna, was built in 1110 by Filippo and Oddo dei Garisendi. It is 163 feet high and ten feet out of the perpendicular. The tower was higher in Dante's time, but, according to Benvenuto, was partially destroyed in the mid-fourteenth century. At its side stands the Asinelli Tower, erected in 1109 by Gherardo degli Asinelli, which is 320 feet high and four feet out of the perpendicular. (See Plate 9, facing p. 580.) One of Dante's sonnets (*Rime* LI) mentions the tower.

137. *'l chinato*: The "leaning side," or overhang, of the tower.

139. *che stava a bada*: "Who stood expectant."

142–43. *al fondo che divora Lucifero con Giuda*: The exact sense of the verb will be made clearer later when we see how Lucifer and Judas are punished in Cocytus.

143. *ci sposò = ci depose. Sposare* in this case equals *posare* with an initial *s* added.

145. *come albero in nave*: See the end of *Inf.* XVII, where Geryon sets the wayfarers down on the bottom of the eighth circle. Such a last glance, taking in the departure or return of someone, is typical, particularly at the end of a canto. See also *Inf.* XII, 139.

Here Antaeus is seen after he has raised himself upright; he towers over the wayfarer, who is standing on the floor of the ninth circle, as the mast of a ship towers over someone standing on the deck. The question of where Antaeus and the other giants stand—whether on the bottom of the pit or on a ledge—has been long debated and cannot be clearly settled, since the poet chose to leave the matter ambiguous. It seems hard to believe that Dante intended the pit to be only about thirty-five feet deep, as it would be if the giants stand on its floor and are visible from the waist up. It has been suggested that they stand on some sort of ledge which is considerably higher than the bottom. But in that case it is difficult to see how Antaeus could stoop so low as to set the two wayfarers gently on the bottom, then rise "like the mast of a ship." There seems to be a contradiction here, comparable to that implied in the measure of "half a mile across" given for the tenth *bolgia*: see n. to *Inf*. XXX, 86–87.

9. The leaning towers of Bologna

CANTO XXXII

1. *S'io avessi le rime aspre e chiocce*: "Rime" here does not mean "rhymes," even though many of the harsh and clucking effects that the poet proceeds to create are indeed made up of words that rhyme. It means, rather, "verses" (hence, in general usage, *rimatore* for poet and *rime* for poems). For another example of "chioccia," see *Inf.* VII, 2, where Pluto with clucking words begins to speak mysteriously of Satan.

2. *buco*: The pit, or "pozzo" as it was termed when first mentioned (*Inf.* XVIII, 18). Here the reference is to the bottom of the pit, Cocytus, the frozen lake which constitutes the ninth and last circle of Hell.

3. *pontan*: "Thrust in upon." *tutte l'altre rocce*: All the rocky cliffs of Hell, and indeed all the rocks of the earth, since this is the very "bottom of the whole universe" (vs. 8) and the center of gravity.

4. *premerei = spremerei*. The verb retains the material sense of "squeeze," as one might a lemon, in order to extract all the "juice" ("suco"). *concetto*: What the poet, having returned from his journey and endeavoring now to recount in verse, remembers to have been his experience.

5. *abbo* (from Latin *habeo*) = *ho*. On this form, found fre-
quently in prose—or out of rhyme—see E. G. Parodi (1957),
p. 257.

6. *tema* = *timore*.   *dicer*: In this context the verb takes
on the meaning of "write verses." Compare the phrases *dir
per rima, dicitore per rima*.

7–9. *ché non è impresa . . . babbo*: As Rossi comments, this
is said with a light spirit of irony, just as we say, for ex-
ample, that a difficult and dangerous mountain pass cannot
be crossed with eyes closed. "Pigliare a gabbo" and "che
chiami mamma o babbo" are examples of extreme litotes.
Cf. *Par.* XXXIII, 106–8.

7. *da pigliare a gabbo*: "To be taken in jest" or "to be made
light of." Cf. *Par.* XXIII, 64–69.

8. *discriver fondo*: In early Italian the article is frequently
omitted, as it is here, but the omission is especially expressive
in this case, as if the poet were building the bottom of Hell
in describing it. / The bottom of Hell is near the center of
the earth, which in the Ptolemaic conception is the central
point of the whole material universe. See Seneca, *Hercules
furens*, vs. 831: "iusserat mundi penetrare fundum" ("had
bidden thee explore the world's foundations").

9. *né da lingua* = *né impresa da lingua*.

10. *Ma quelle donne aiutino il mio verso*: Dante's appeal
to the Muses ("quelle donne") for help in describing the
bottom of Hell amounts to a fresh invocation and marks, as
it were, a new beginning, serving to set off the ninth circle
as a new area, now entered upon. See the poet's first such
entreaty, *Inf.* II, 7.   *donne*: From the Latin *dominae*.

11. *Anfione a chiuder Tebe*: Amphion, son of Jupiter and
Antiope, with the help of the Muses built the walls of
Thebes; charmed by the magic skill with which he played
the lyre, the stones came down from Mount Cithaeron and
placed themselves of their own accord. Horace refers to the
story in the *Ars poetica* (vss. 394–96):

dictus et Amphion, Thebanae conditor urbis,
saxa movere sono testudinis et prece blanda
ducere quo vellet. . . .

. . . hence too the fable that Amphion, builder of
Thebes's citadel, moved stones by the sound of his
lyre, and led them whither he would by his supplicating
spell.

See Statius, *Theb.* X, 873–77.

12. *sì che dal fatto il dir non sia diverso*: "So that my words
be not different from the reality that I saw." See *Inf.* IV,
147.   *il dir*: Cf. the word "dicer," vs. 6.

13. *mal creata*: See "mal nata" in *Inf.* V, 7; and "mal nati"
in *Inf.* XVIII, 76; XXX, 48.   *plebe*: "Plebs." Morally and
geographically, these are the lowest of the low in Hell—
traitors, murderers, the worst sinners of all.

14. *onde = del quale luogo.*

15. *mei = meglio* (see *Inf.* XIV, 36).   *qui*: On earth;
the word is spoken from the point of view of the poet, who
has returned to earth. See Matt. 26:24: "Bonum erat ei si
natus non fuisset homo ille." ("It were better for that man
if he had not been born.")   *pecore o zebe*: "Sheep or
goats" do not have intellects subject to perversion or im-
mortal souls capable of sinning. / The subject has shifted to
the plural, to agree with the verb "foste."   *zebe*: Lana
comments: "[Zebe] sono li capretti saltanti, e sono dette
zebe, perchè vanno zebellando cioè saltando." ("*Zebe* are
jumping goats. And they are called *zebe* because they go
about *zebellando*, that is, jumping.")

16. *nel pozzo scuro*: See the description of this circle in *Inf.*
IX, 28.

17–18. *sotto i piè del gigante . . . muro*: With these verses
the problem of where Antaeus and the other giants are
standing (see n. to *Inf.* XXXI, 145) is brought into sharp
focus. The wayfarer is said to be looking up at the high
wall, which suggests that he and his guide are still more or

less in the place where Antaeus had set them down. The giant is not described as standing with his feet on the icy floor of Cocytus; therefore, it makes sense that he and the others may be standing on some sort of ledge high above that floor. But are we to conceive of Antaeus as being able to bend so far beneath his own feet as to set Dante and Virgil down on the ice? The mystery remains. The wayfarer certainly would seem to be looking up at the wall as if in wonder still at the surprising and frightening means of descent provided him in his "fated journey" (*Inf.* V, 22).

19. *dicere udi'mi = udii dirmi.*

19–21. *Guarda come passi . . . lassi*: Commentators are not agreed as to who utters this plea. Torraca believes that Virgil utters it; others that some unnamed soul frozen in the ice does so; and still others think that one or both of the two Alberti (not identified until vs. 57) speak thus of "brothers," which seems the most plausible interpretation. Against the last explanation is the argument that so many verses intervene before the relationship between the two shades is revealed. But this scarcely refutes such a reading. It may be argued that this gap in the narrative simply creates suspense.

22. *vidimi davante = mi vidi davante.*

23. *un lago*: Cocytus, as it has been termed already (in *Inf.* XIV, 119, where it was called a "stagno," or pond, and in *Inf.* XXXI, 123). The water originates from the crack in the statue of the "veglio" (see *Inf.* XIV, 103) within Mount Ida in Crete, and forms Acheron, Styx, and Phlegethon, all circular bodies of still water, before it flows down to form this bottommost pool. See *Inf.* XIV, n. to vss. 121–38. As the subsequent cantos will show, Cocytus is divided into four concentric areas, in which are punished four categories of traitors. We should probably imagine the ice as blood-colored (see *Inf.* XVI, 104), though nothing is made of this here.

25. *sì grosso velo*: "So heavy a veil" or crust of ice.

26.· *la Danoia*: The Danube, which flows from southwest
Germany through central Europe to the Black Sea. "Danoia"
corresponds to the German Donau. In *Par.* VIII, 65, Dante
uses the more common form "Danubio."   *Osterlicchi*:
Austria. See E. G. Parodi (1957), pp. 271–72, who gives
this and other forms that approximate the German Öster-
reich.

27. *Tanai*: The river Don (also called Tana by the Italians
in the Middle Ages; the classical Tanaïs), which rises
southeast of Tula, Russia, and flows first southeast and then
southwest, discharging into the Sea of Azov. It was once
regarded as the boundary between Europe· and Asia. For
example, Orosius (*Hist.* I, ii, 4) says of the Don: "Europa
incipit ut dixi sub plaga septentrionis, a flumine Tanai, qua
Riphaei montes Sarmatico aversi oceano Tanaim fluvium
fundunt." ("Europe begins, as I have said, in the north at
the Tanaïs River, where the Riphaean Mountains, standing
back from the Sarmatian Sea, pour forth the Tanaïs
flood.")   *là sotto 'l freddo cielo*: In Russia, farther north
and therefore colder than Austria.

28. *Tambernicchi*: There is considerable uncertainty as to
which mountain is intended. Many early commentators
locate it in Slavonia or thereabouts, while Buti claims it
for Armenia. More probably it is Mount Tambura in the
Apuan Alps (see Torraca and the review of A. Fiammazzo
in G. Vandelli, 1932b). Mount Tambura is called "Stamber-
licche" in certain early texts. A "Stambernicchi" is also to
be noted in Luigi Pulci's *Morgante* XXIV, 88. A point in
favor of Mount Tambura is that it is in the same mountain
range as Pietrapana, mentioned in the following verse as
part of the same image. On the identification of the moun-
tain, see B. Guyon (1903).

29. *Pietrapana*: Commonly identified with one of the peaks,
known as Pania della Croce, of the Apuan Alps, a group of
peaks in the northwest corner of Tuscany that lie west of
the valley of the Serchio and are loosely connected with the
Apennine range. The Latin name, Petra Apuana, probably

derived from the Apuani, a Ligurian tribe that formerly
inhabited the neighboring district. Benvenuto says: "Est
montanea altissima omnium Tusciae, quae olim vocata est
Petra Appuana, sicut saepe patet apud Titum Livium,
et est prope Petram sanctam non longe a civitate lucana in
confinibus Tusciae." ("It is the highest mountain in Tus-
cany and was once called Petra Apuana, as we know from
Titus Livy. It is in the vicinity of Pietrasanta, not far from
the city of Lucca, on the borders of Tuscany.") Landino
comments: "Pietrapana è in Toscana in Carfagnana sopra
Lucca; da' Latini è detta Pietra Apuana." ("Pietrapana is
in Tuscany, in the Garfagnana, above Lucca. The Latins
called it Petra Apuana.") E. Repetti (1833, p. 69, under the
entry "Alpe Apuana, Pania") understands Dante's refer-
ence to be to this group of mountains.

30. *avria = avrebbe.   pur da l'orlo*: The ice on ponds
usually thaws first near the edge and consequently is
weakest there. For a special reason, which we learn later,
it is colder nearer the center of Cocytus, and the ice would
be thicker there.

31-36. *E come a gracidar si sta la rana . . . cicogna*: See
the description of the froglike positions of the barrators in
the fifth *bolgia*, in *Inf*. XXII, 25-27. The comparison here
is more terrible in that these "frogs" cannot move, but are
frozen in ice up to their necks. Note, moreover, the contrast
between summer in the first term of this simile and deep
winter in the second.

32-33. *quando sogna . . . la villana*: The time of gleaning
in Italy is early summer. The peasant woman is said to
dream of this work because gleaning is primarily woman's
work (one thinks of Ruth in the Bible) and because she
stands to gain from such labor.

34-35. *livide . . . ghiaccia*: The ice is transparent enough
for the submerged part of the shades to be visible (see *Inf*.
XXXIV, 12). Apparently the bodies are livid. The verses
make the point that the shades are set in the ice up to where
shame appears—i.e., up to their necks (like the frogs in

water)—which must be above the ice, since the souls are able to move their heads.

35. *ghiaccia*: Archaic for *ghiaccio*.

36. *in nota di cicogna*: The clack of the stork's beak is (one imagines) brittle, metallic, hard, and this suggested sound adds markedly to the stylistic effect. See Ovid, *Metam.* VI, 97: "ipsa sibi plaudat crepitante ciconia rostro" ("and claps her rattling bill, a stork"), and Brunetto Latini, *Tresor* I, clx, 1: "Cygoine est .i. oisiau sans lengue; et por ce dient les genz que ele ne chante pas, mais bat son bec et fait grand tumulte." ("The stork is a bird without a tongue; and for this reason people say that it does not sing, but clacks its beak and makes a loud noise.")

37. *Ognuna in giù tenea volta la faccia*: The position of these souls, "each [keeping] his face turned downward," distinguishes them from the souls immersed in the next area of ice, whose heads are erect. This downward-turned position of the sinners' heads allows the tears to fall immediately from the sinners' eyes (as vs. 46 suggests) instead of accumulating in the eye sockets and freezing there. Thus these souls are afforded relief from pain at least to that extent.

38. *da bocca il freddo*: The cold is attested by the chattering of the sinners' teeth.   *e da li occhi il cor tristo*: The "sad [or sorry] heart" is attested to by the tears in the sinners' eyes. / Thus "freddo" and "cor tristo" each serve as subject of "si procaccia," of which "testimonianza" is the object.

41. *volsimi* = *mi volsi*.

41–42. *due sì stretti . . . misto*: The two, who prove to be brothers (see vs. 58), face each other, their heads bent forward and pressed so hard against each other that their hair is mingled.

42. *avieno* = *avevano*.

44. *piegaro i colli*: In order to raise their heads as much as possible, as the following verse makes clear.

46-47. *li occhi lor . . . le labbra*: As long as these souls hold their heads bent downward, the tears do not freeze in the eye sockets and hence up to this moment their eyes have been wet only within, but now, as they raise their heads, the tears overflow their eyes and run down to and over their lips. Some commentators would understand "le labbra" as metaphorical for "the eyelids," and construe "su per" as meaning "up over" rather than simply "over." But it seems best to take "labbra" in its usual meaning of "lips" and bear in mind how tightly pressed together the heads of the two are said to be. One imagines them with chins and mouths still touching, even after they have bent back their heads as far as they can to see who the new-comers are.

47. *gocciar = gocciarono*.

47-51. *e 'l gelo strinse le lagrime tra essi . . . li vinse*: Different interpretations of these verses have been advanced. If "labbra" is taken to mean "lips" (see n. to vss. 46-47), then it seems reasonable to understand that the attention of the narrative here focuses on the lips, over which the tears have run and have congealed. The cold is thus said to bind the tears "tra essi" ("between them")—that is, between the two brothers—freezing them together in a grotesque icy "kiss"; and since these brothers hated each other and slew each other (see n. to vs. 57), their icy fate now stirs them to such rage that they butt one another like two goats, each being capable of a forward movement of the forehead. This interpretation is adopted by Sapegno, who gives credit to Casini.

48. *riserrolli = li riserrò*.

49. *spranga*: An iron clamp. "Spranga" here is the subject of the verb.

50. *ei = essi*.

51. *cozzaro = cozzarono.   tanta ira li vinse*: The ice-locked "kiss" stirs such rage in them that they butt each other, ramming their foreheads together.

53. *pur col viso in giùe*: Keeping his face turned down, this shade (named in vs. 68) avoided the awkward situation of the other two and thus remained able to speak.

54. *in noi ti specchi*: In this case *specchiarsi in* probably implies nothing more than "to gaze on," as it is far from clear how the wayfarer could be said to "mirror himself" in any more literal sense.

55. *Se vuoi saper chi son cotesti due*: The pleasure this soul takes in disclosing the names of his comrades is evident. Malice and treachery, "squealing" on one's companions in misery, are notable characteristics of these vilest of sinners.

56. *Bisenzo*: The Bisenzio River flows close to Prato and Campi Bisenzio and falls into the Arno at Signa, approximately ten miles west of Florence. The Conti Alberti (see n. to vs. 57) had castles in the Val di Bisenzio and the Val di Sieve.

57. *del padre loro Alberto e di lor fue*: This, along with the foregoing mention of the Bisenzio Valley (vs. 56), is enough to identify the father as Alberto degli Alberti, count of Mangona, and the two sons as Alessandro and Napoleone, who killed each other in a dispute over their inheritance.

Villani (VI, 68) states that the castle of Mangona belonged by right to Alessandro, a Guelph and the younger of the two brothers, and was unjustly seized by Napoleone, who was a Ghibelline. Villani does not mention the subsequent fatal quarrel between the two brothers (which took place some time after 1282 and before 1286). Benvenuto, however, in his gloss on vs. 54, says: "Venientes ad discordiam propter hereditatem, se invicem interfecerunt." ("As a result of disagreements over the inheritance, they killed each other.") On the feud between the two Alberti, see M. Barbi (1899), pp. 204–5.

57. *fue = fu.*

58. *D'un corpo usciro*: They were born of the same mother, i.e., were blood brothers, hence their crime is the more terrible. *la Caina*: Caina, as we are soon to understand, is the first subdivision of Cocytus, where those are punished who betrayed (and murdered) their kinsmen—and so it is well named after Cain, the first such murderer. / The name of the place was uttered by Francesca in *Inf.* V, 107 as that which awaited her husband, Gianciotto, murderer of her lover, Paolo (Gianciotto's brother), and of herself.

60. *fitta in gelatina*: It is difficult to judge the semantic flavor of the phrase, but it seems ironical and derisive (as it certainly would be in modern parlance). See a similarly ironic use of "broda" in *Inf.* VIII, 53 and of "la gelata" in *Inf.* XXXIII, 91. "Gelatiňa" could be construed as "cold consommé" or the whole phrase simply, as Rossi suggests, as "set in (or on) ice" or "placed in the cooler."

61-62. *quelli a cui fu rotto il petto . . . per la man d'Artù*: Mordred, the traitorous nephew (or son, according to some versions) of King Arthur, whom he slew and by whom he was slain. The incident referred to by Dante is narrated in the romance *La Morte d'Arthur*. For the OFr manuscript version, see P. Toynbee (1968), p. 68, under the entry "Artù":

Et Mordret, qui bien voit que li rois ne baiot s'a lui non ochire, nel refuse pas, ains li adrece la teste del ceval; et li rois, qui li vient al plus droit qu'il puet, le fiert de toute sa force si durement qu'il li ront les mailles del hauberc, et li met parmi le cors le fer de son glaive. Si dist l'estoire qu'apres l'estors del glaive passa parmi la plaie uns rais de soleil si apertement que Girflet le vit. Dont cil del pais distrent que ce avoit fait Nostre Sires par coros qu'il avoit a lui.

And Mordred, who clearly saw the king glaring at him with murder in his eye, did not hesitate, but straightened his horse's head; and the king, who came at him as directly as he could, struck him with all his strength so hard that he broke the chain mail of his hauberk

and split his body with the steel of his sword. The story
recounts that after the sword thrust, a ray of sunlight
passed through the wound so visibly that Girflet saw it.
Whence the people of the region said that Our Lord
did this because of the anger He bore him.

62. *esso* (Latin *ipse*): With one and the selfsame blow. Cf.
"sovresso," *Inf.* XXIII, 54.

63. *Focaccia*: Vanni de' Cancellieri, nicknamed Focaccia,
of Pistoia, was guilty of murdering (October 1293), not his
uncle, as many early commentators have it, but a cousin,
one Detto di Sinibaldo Cancellieri. M. Barbi (1934b, pp.
299–300) calls attention to the following passage from the
Storie pistoresi III:

> Uno dì venendo messer Detto alla ditta piazza e en-
> trando in una bottega d'uno che li facea uno farsetto di
> zendado presso a casa de' figliuoli di messer Ranieri, lo
> Focaccia e Freduccio con certa quantità di fanti en-
> trarono nella ditta bottega e quivi l'uccisono, e parti-
> ronsi . . . .

> One day, Messer Detto came to that square and went
> into the shop of someone who was making a sendal
> doublet for him. The shop was near the house of the
> sons of Messer Ranieri. Focaccia and Freduccio, with
> a number of others, entered the shop, killed him, and
> then fled.

65. *Sassol*: Pronounced *Sassòl*.   *Sassol Mascheroni*: A
Florentine, said by the commentators to have belonged to
the Toschi family, who murdered a kinsman (variously
recorded as brother, nephew, uncle, or cousin), for the sake
of his inheritance. On the discovery of the crime, he was
rolled through the streets of Florence in a cask full of nails
and afterward beheaded. According to the *Anonimo fioren-
tino*: "Fu questa novella sì palese, che per tutta Toscana se
ne parlò: et però dice l'Auttore: Se tu se' di Toscana, tu il
dei sapere." ("This story was so well known that all Tus-
cany spoke of it. And that is why the author says: 'If you
are from Tuscany, you must know about it.'")

67. *metti* = *metta*.

68. *il Camiscion de' Pazzi*: Alberto (or Uberto) Camicione de' Pazzi of Val d'Arno, of whom nothing is known except that he treacherously killed his kinsman Ubertino. The *Anonimo fiorentino* gives as the motive for the deed the fact that Camicione desired certain fortresses which he and Ubertino held in common.

69. *Carlin*: Carlino de' Pazzi of Val d'Arno, who, while the Neri of Florence and the Lucchese were besieging Pistoia in 1302, held the castle of Piantravigne in the Val d'Arno for the Bianchi of Florence, but for a bribe betrayed it into the hands of the Neri. Villani (VIII, 53) gives the following account:

> Nella stanza del detto assedio di Pistoia si rubellò a' fiorentini il castello di Piantrevigne in Valdarno, per Carlino de' Pazzi di Valdarno, e in quello col detto Carlino si rinchiusono de' migliori nuovi usciti bianchi e ghibellini di Firenze grandi e popolani, e faceano grande guerra nel Valdarno: la qual cosa fu cagione di levarsi l'oste da Pistoia, lasciando i fiorentini il terzo della loro gente all'assedio di Serravalle in servigio de' Lucchesi, come detto avemo, e tutta l'altra oste tornata in Firenze, sanza soggiorno n'andarono del mese di Giugno in Valdarno e al detto castello di Piano, e a quello stettono e assediarono per ventinove dì. Alla fine per tradimento del sopraddetto Carlino, e per moneta che n'ebbe, i Fiorentini ebbono il castello. Essendo il detto Carlino di fuori, fece a' suoi fedeli dare l'entrata del castello, onde molti vi furono morti e presi pure de' migliori usciti di Firenze.

When the siege of Pistoia was going on, Carlino de' Pazzi of Val d'Arno caused the castle of Piantravigne in Val d'Arno to rebel against the Florentines. Carlino and some of the best of the recent Ghibelline and White exiles of Florence—both noblemen and commoners— shut themselves in the castle and waged a great war in the Val d'Arno. On account of this, the Florentines had

to remove their army from Pistoia. Leaving a third of
their men in the service of the Lucchese at the siege
of Serravalle, as we have said, the rest of the army was
returned to Florence; and then, without resting, they
went to the Val d'Arno, in the month of June, to that
castle of Piano. They besieged it for twenty-nine days.
Finally, through the treachery of Carlino, who received
a bribe, the Florentines took the castle. While Carlino
was outside, he had some of his trusted men give the
Florentines access to the castle. Many of the best
Florentine exiles were captured or killed.

Dino Compagni says in his *Cronica* (II, 28):

A Parte bianca e ghibellina accorsono molte orribili
disaventure. Egli aveano in Valdarno un castello in
Pian di Sco, nel quale era Carlino de' Pazi con LX
cavalli e pedoni assai. I Neri di Firenze vi pòssono
l'assedio. Dissesi che Carlino li tradì per danari ebbe:
il perchè i Neri vi misono le masnade loro, e presono
gli uomini, e parte n'uccisono, e il resto feciono ricom-
perare.

The White and Ghibelline faction suffered many hor-
rible misfortunes. They had a castle in the Val d'Arno,
at Pian di Sco; inside it, there was Carlino de' Pazzi,
with sixty knights and many infantrymen. The Blacks
of Florence besieged the castle. Carlino was said to have
betrayed it for money. The Blacks threw in their
soldiers and captured the men. Some they killed, others
they held for ransom.

On the payment of the bribe to Carlino and others involved,
see R. Davidsohn (1912), pp. 227–28.

When Carlino dies, he will go to the next or second ring
of Cocytus for this crime against his party, which is so much
worse than Camicione's crime that Camicione expects it to
make his own deed seem less heinous by comparison. Since
at the time of the poem Carlino's crime has not yet been
committed, Camicione's statement exemplifies the ability of
souls in Hell to "prophesy" future events (see *Inf.* X, 100–
102).

70–72. *Poscia vid' io . . . guazzi*: The transition to the second subdivision of the ninth circle of Hell is here very subtly suggested, by the sight now of the many faces in a new position (erect, else the poet could not so readily describe their color) and by the use of the word "guazzi" ("fords"), which serves to signal a crossing over from one area to another.

70. *cagnazzi*: "Purple" from the cold, a deeper color than the "livide" of vs. 34. That "cagnazzi" here denotes a color and not "doglike" is argued by F. Maggini (1920, pp. 142–43), with a persuasive example from Franco Sacchetti.

71. *riprezzo = ribrezzo*.

72. *guazzi = guadi*. See *Inf.* XII, 139.

73. *inver' = inverso*.

73–74. *lo mezzo al quale ogne gravezza si rauna*: The "bottom of the whole universe" (vs. 8) is, in the Ptolemaic system, just such a place where all gravity converges. See *Inf.* XXXIV, 111.

74. *rauna = raduna*.

76. *se voler fu*: Some commentators interpret "voler" to refer to the wayfarer's will and understand that now, out of cold indifference, he does not remember or is uncertain that he kicked a shade in the face. Surely "voler" here refers to Another's will, the Divine Will, which often "increases the vengeance" (vs. 80; also see *Inf.* IX, 94–96). On the relationship between destiny and will, see *Inf.* IX, 97.

78. *nel viso ad una*: This shade proves to be Bocca degli Abati (named in vs. 106), who, while ostensibly fighting on the side of the Florentine Guelphs at the battle of Montaperti, at the moment when the latter were hard pressed by Manfred's German cavalry, treacherously cut off the hand of the Florentine standard-bearer, thus creating a panic, which ended in the disastrous defeat of the Guelphs. On the identity of Bocca, see A. Della Torre (1905), pp. 171–72, n. 4.

79. *peste = pesti.*

80. *a crescer = ad accrescere.   vendetta*: The punishment, for his crime at Montaperti (see n. to vs. 78). Compare *Inf.* VIII, 52–60, where the wayfarer, acting with *bona ira*, caused the punishment of Filippo Argenti to be increased, wishing to see him ducked in the Styx.

81. *Montaperti*: Montaperti is a village in Tuscany, a few miles east of Siena, on a hill near the Arbia. The famous battle between the Ghibellines of Siena and Florence and the Florentine Guelphs took place at Montaperti on September 4, 1260, resulting in the total defeat of the Guelphs, to which Dante refers in *Inf.* X, 85–86 as "the havoc and great slaughter that dyed the Arbia red."   *moleste = molesti.*

84. *quantunque vorrai = quanto ti piacerà.* See *Inf.* V, 12.

87. *altrui*: This indefinite pronoun used for a definite pronoun is the direct object of the verb. See similar cases in *Inf.* VIII, 87; XXVII, 56; and vs. 89 of the present canto.

88. *Antenora*: The name of the second of the four subdivisions of the ninth circle of Hell, in which are punished those who betrayed their country or their party—political traitors—is derived from the Trojan Antenor, who in the Middle Ages was believed to have betrayed Troy to the Greeks. In the twelfth-century *Roman de Troie* of Benoît de Sainte-Maure, for example, he is spoken of in vs. 26135 as "Antenor, li coilverz Judas" ("Antenor, the treacherous Judas") and in vs. 25842 as "li vieuz Judas" ("the old Judas"). Among other acts of treachery, Antenor was thought to have been involved with the theft of the Trojan Palladium (mentioned by Dante in *Inf.* XXVI, 63) and the stratagem of the Trojan horse—Aeneas, in some versions, being implicated in these betrayals. The medieval belief was no doubt derived from the histories of Dictys Cretensis and Dares Phrygius, which, through the medium of Latin versions, were widely read in the Middle Ages (see

Ephemeris belli Troiani V, 4–17 and *De excidio Troiae* XXXIX–XLIV).

The Homeric account (*Iliad* III, 146–60; VII, 345–53), that Antenor tried to save his country by advising the surrender of Helen, was apparently lost sight of at the time. There is no hint of his treachery in Virgil, but Servius (who lived in the late fourth and early fifth centuries) makes mention of it in his note on *Aen.* I, 242, and refers for confirmation to Livy (I, i, 1): "Iam primum omnium satis constat Troia capta in ceteros saevitum esse Troianos: duobus, Aeneae Antenorique, et vetusti iure hospitii et quia pacis reddendaeque Helenae semper auctores fuerunt, omne ius belli Achivos abstinuisse." ("First of all, then, it is generally agreed that when Troy was taken vengeance was wreaked upon the other Trojans, but that two, Aeneas and Antenor, were spared all the penalties of war by the Achivi, owing to long-standing claims of hospitality, and because they had always advocated peace and the giving back of Helen.")

89. *altrui*: Dative, referring to "gote" and echoing the "altrui" of the question in vs. 87.

90. *se fossi vivo, troppo fora*: Since the subject of "fossi" is either *tu* or *io* (understood), one of two interpretations is possible: if *you* were alive, it would be too hard a kick for a living foot to give; or, if *I* were alive, it would be too much to bear and already I would have made you pay for it. The first meaning seems preferable. The reply in the next verse, echoing the "vivo," makes sense in either case.

93. *tra l'altre note*: In the book of my memory where this journey is recorded.

94. *Del contrario*: What Bocca most desires is *not* to be remembered on earth.

95. *quinci = di qui.   lagna*: "Annoyance," "cause for complaint."

96. *lama*: See *Inf.* XX, 79, where the term refers to the low-lying swamp on which Mantua was built. Here it indicates the pond of Cocytus, the lowest place of all.

97. *cuticagna*: Scalp at the nape of the neck or the hair of the nape, as in vs. 103. Bocca, to hide his face, bends his head down and refuses to raise it.

100. *Perché = per quanto.*

101. *né mosterrolti = né te lo mostrerò*, i.e., by raising my head and showing my face. The soul does not know that Dante would not recognize him in any case (the battle of Montaperti took place five years before the poet's birth). / *Mosterrò* is very common as a form of the future tense in early Italian.

102. *tomi*: *Tomare = cadere.* See *Inf.* XVI, 63. The meaning here is "to fall upon" or "to jump on."

105. *latrando lui*: A construction on the model of an ablative absolute.   *raccolti*: "Turned down fixedly." Porena believes that the looking down fixedly is a concentration of effort on Bocca's part, so that he will not be overcome by pain and give in.

106. *Bocca*: This name, together with the mention of Montaperti (vs. 81), is quite enough to suggest to the wayfarer who this traitor may be.

109. *vo' = voglio.   favelle = favelli.*

110. *a la tua onta*: The phrase can mean either "in spite of you" or "to your shame." In this context, it might well have both meanings.

113. *se tu di qua entro eschi*: This can hardly be the formula of adjuration, even though "eschi" might stand for the subjunctive *esca* here, a possible colloquialism. The phrase seems rather to contain a thrust, suggesting a certain doubt that the wayfarer will ever get out of Hell.

114. *la lingua pronta*: "Quick to speak."

115. *piange*: "Pays the penalty for." *argento*: Given the context, perhaps this is intended as a Gallicism, echoing the French *argent*, but not necessarily (see, for example, *Par.* XVII, 84). *Franceschi = Francesi*. See *Inf.* XXVII, 44.

116. *quel da Duera*: Buoso da Duera was a Ghibelline leader of Cremona. When the army of Charles of Anjou entered Italy in 1265, on its way to encounter Manfred and take possession of the kingdom of Naples, the French troops were able to advance through Lombardy and make their way into Parma unmolested, although Manfred had ordered the force of Cremonese and other Ghibellines of Lombardy to block their passage. This neglect of Manfred's instructions was due to some act of treachery, not clearly specified, on the part of the Cremonese leader Buoso da Duera, who was believed to have been bribed by the French—by Charles' wife, according to Benvenuto: "Uxor Caroli veniens cum Guidone de Monforte portabat secum magnam pecuniam, cum qua venenavit avaram mentem Bosii." ("The wife of Charles, who came with Guy de Montfort, brought a great deal of money with her, which she used to corrupt the greedy mind of Buoso.") Villani is less specific (VII, 4):

> Il conte Guido di Monforte colla cavalleria che'l conte Carlo gli lasciò a guidare, e colla contessa moglie del detto Carlo, e co' suoi cavalieri, si partirono di Francia del mese di Giugno del detto anno. . . . E coll'aiuto de' Milanesi, si misono a passare la Lombardia tutti in arme, e cavalcando schierati, e con molto affanno di Piemonte infino a Parma, perocchè'l marchese Pallavicino parente di Manfredi, colla forza de' Chermonesi e dell'altre città ghibelline di Lombardia ch'erano in lega con Manfredi, era a guardare i passi con più di tremila cavalieri, che Tedeschi e che Lombardi; alla fine, come piacque a Dio . . . i Franceschi passarono sanza contasto di battaglia, e arrivarono alla città di Parma. Bene si disse che uno messer Buoso della casa di que' da Duera di Chermona, per danari ch'ebbe dai Franceschi, mise consiglio per modo, che l'oste di Manfredi non fosse al

contasto al passo, com'erano ordinati, onde poi il popolo
di Chermona a furore distrussono il detto legnaggio di
quegli da Duera.

In the month of June of that same year [1265], Count
Guy de Montfort left France with the cavalry put under
his charge by Count Charles. With him went Charles'
wife, the countess, and his knights. . . . With the help
of the Milanese, they passed through Lombardy, com-
pletely armed and riding in formation. They had great
difficulty from Piedmont all the way to Parma, for the
Marquis Pallavicino, a relative of Manfred, was guard-
ing the passes with more than three thousand knights,
some Germans, some Lombards, and with the help of
Cremona and the other Ghibelline cities in Lombardy
allied with Manfred. Finally, it pleased God . . . to have
the French pass through without a contest of arms, and
they arrived in the city of Parma. It was rightly said that
a certain Messer Buoso, of the house of the Duera of
Cremona, having received a bribe from the French,
arranged things in such a way that Manfred's army
did not contest the pass, as it had been ordered to do.
For this reason, the infuriated people of Cremona later
destroyed the line of the Duera.

117. *là dove i peccatori stanno freschi*: This might well be
the origin of the modern idiomatic expression *stare fresco*,
"to be in a pickle." In any case it seems extremely ironical,
given the context, and in tone resembles the phrase "esser
fitta in gelatina" of vs. 60.

118. *Se fossi domandato "Altri chi v'era?"* Bocca's purely
gratuitous malice continues.

119. *quel di Beccheria*: Tesauro de' Beccheria of Pavia, abbot
of Vallombrosa and legate in Tuscany of Alexander IV.
After the expulsion of the Ghibellines from Florence in
1258, he was seized by the Florentines on a charge of in-
triguing with the Ghibellines, and beheaded in the same
year. Benvenuto points out that Tesauro was a Florentine
not by birth but by adoption: "Poterat dici florentinus,

ratione incolatus, quia erat ibi beneficiatus." ("He could be called a Florentine, since, as a resident, he enjoyed its privileges.")

120. *gorgiera*: "Gorget," the piece of armor that defended the throat. Porena suspects this is a Lombardism, used by Bocca as a way of alluding to the fact that Tesauro was a Lombard.

121. *Gianni de' Soldanier*: A Florentine Ghibelline. After the defeat and death of Manfred at Benevento in 1266 the Florentine commons rose against the government of Guido Novello and the Ghibelline nobles. On this occasion Gianni de' Soldanieri, though a Ghibelline, placed himself at the head of the populace in opposition to his own party, his motive being, according to Villani (VII, 14), his own aggrandizement:

> Il popolo si ridusse tutto nella via larga di santa Trinita, e messer Gianni de' Soldanieri si fece capo del popolo per montare in istato, non guardando al fine, che dovea riuscire a sconcio di parte ghibellina, e suo dammaggio, che sempre pare sia avvenuto in Firenze a chi s'è fatto capo di popolo.

> The people all gathered in the broad street of Santa Trinita, and Messer Gianni de' Soldanieri became their head, in an attempt to get power, not thinking of the outcome, which was to be so ruinous to the Ghibelline cause, nor the harm to himself, which, it seems, always befalls those in Florence who become heads of the people.

Elsewhere, however, Villani mentions Gianni among those who had done good service to the state and had been treated with ingratitude (XII, 44).

122. *Ganellone*: Ganelon, the traitor who brought about the destruction of Charlemagne's rear guard at Roncesvalles, where Roland, Oliver, and the rest of the twelve peers were slain. His name, like that of Antenor, became a byword for treachery in the Middle Ages. See *Inf.* XXXI, 16–18 and notes to *Inf.* XXXI, 17, 18.

122–23. *Tebaldello . . . si dormia*: Tebaldello, called by some chroniclers and commentators Tribaldello, was a member of the Ghibelline Zambrasi family of Faenza. In order to avenge a private grudge against some of the Lambertazzi (the Ghibellines of Bologna), who after their expulsion from Bologna had taken refuge in Faenza, he treacherously opened the gates of that city in the early morning of November 13, 1280, to their Guelph opponents, the Geremei of Bologna. Villani (VII, 81) states that Tebaldello was killed in 1282 during the assault on Forlì, which was repulsed by Guido da Montefeltro. This is the battle referred to in *Inf.* XXVII, 43–44.

124. *da ello = da lui*, i.e., Bocca degli Abati. See "con elle," *Inf.* III, 27.

125. *ch'io = quand'io*.

127. *si manduca = si mangia*.

128. *pose*: Dante sometimes in rhyme uses a past absolute tense which cannot be understood in the usual sense. The soul did not sink its teeth into the other at just that moment, as such a narrative tense might suggest, but had already done so, and long since.

129. *là 've 'l cervel s'aggiugne con la nuca*: B. Nardi (1944, pp. 249–57) has shown that *nuca*, in Dante's time, had the precise meaning of "spinal marrow," which was held by some to be part of the brain.   *s'aggiugne = si congiunge*.

130–31. *non altrimenti Tideo . . . Menalippo per disdegno*: Tydeus, king of Calydon, was one of the seven kings who joined Adrastus, king of Argos, in the expedition against Thebes (see *Inf.* XIV, 68–69 and n. to *Inf.* XIV, 69). In this war Tydeus was mortally wounded by the Theban, Menalippus (or Melanippus), whom, however, he managed to slay in turn. According to Statius, Tydeus, in a fury of madness, seized on the head of Menalippus, and, fixing his teeth in it, gnawed through the skull and ate part of the brain. See Statius' account (*Theb.* VIII, 739–62):

". . . caput, o caput, o mihi si quis
adportet, Melanippe, tuum! nam volveris arvis,
fido equidem, nec me virtus suprema fefellit.
i, precor, Atrei si quid tibi sanguinis umquam,
Hippomedon, vade, o primis puer inclyte bellis
Arcas, et Argolicae Capaneu iam maxime turmae."
   Moti omnes, sed primus abit primusque repertum
Astaciden medio Capaneus e pulvere tollit
spirantem laevaque super cervice reportat,
terga cruentantem concussi vulneris unda:
qualis ab Arcadio rediit Tirynthius antro
captivumque suem clamantibus intulit Argis.
   Erigitur Tydeus voltuque occurrit et amens
laetitiaque iraque, ut singultantia vidit
ora trahique oculos seseque adgnovit in illo,
imperat abscisum porgi, laevaque receptum
spectat atrox hostile caput, gliscitque tepentis
lumina torva videns et adhuc dubitantia figi.
infelix contentus erat: plus exigit ultrix
Tisiphone; iamque inflexo Tritonia patre
venerat et misero decus immortale ferebat,
atque illum effracti perfusum tabe cerebri
aspicit et vivo scelerantem sanguine fauces—
nec comites auferre valent . . .

"Thy head, thy head, O Melanippus, could one but
bring me that! for thou art grovelling on the plain, so
indeed I trust, nor did my valour fail me at the last.
Go, Hippomedon, I beg, if thou hast aught of Atreus'
blood, go thou, Arcadian, youth renowned in thy first
wars, and thou, O Capaneus, mightiest now of all the
Argive host!"
   All were moved, but Capaneus first darts away, and
finding the son of Astacus lifts him still breathing from
the dust, and returns with him on his left shoulder,
staining his back with blood from the stricken wound:
in such wise did the Tirynthian return from the
Arcadian lair, when he brought home to applauding
Argos the captive boar.

Tydeus raises himself and turns his gaze upon him,
then mad with joy and anger, when he saw them drag
the gasping visage, and saw his handiwork therein, he
bids them cut off and hand to him his foe's fierce head,
and seizing it in his left hand he gazes at it, and glows
to see it still warm in life and the wrathful eyes still
flickering ere they closed. Content was the wretched
man, but avenging Tisiphone demands yet more. And
now, her sire appeased, had Tritonia come, and was
bringing immortal lustre to the unhappy hero: when
lo! she sees him befouled with the shattered brains'
corruption and his jaws polluted with living blood—
nor can his comrades wrest it from him . . . .

130. *si rose*: The "si" (which is untranslatable) adds a spe-
cial touch. Cf. the English "I'm going to have me a good
meal." See also the "ti" in vs. 134.

131. *le tempie*: Used here for the skull (see "teschio" in
the next verse). Cf. "caput" in *Theb.* VIII, 739, 755, quoted
in n. to vss. 130–31.

132. *il teschio e l'altre cose*: See Statius, *Theb.* VIII, 760–
61, quoted in n. to vss. 130–31.

135. *per tal convegno* = *a tal patto*, "on condition that."

137. *sappiendo* = *sapendo*, i.e., *sapendo io.   chi voi
siete*: The two are addressed with "voi."   *pecca* =
peccato (see *Inf.* XXXIV, 115).

138. *te ne cangi*: "I may make up for it," "I may repay you
for it," i.e., by rehabilitating the memory of you and de-
nigrating his. This phrase depends on "per tal convegno,
che . . ." (vss. 135–36).   *cangi* = *cambi*.

139. *quella con ch'io parlo*: My tongue.   *non si secca*:
Porena comments that this means "if my tongue is not struck
with paralysis" and points out that the adjective *secco*
("dry"), meaning "crippled by paralysis," is still current
in Tuscany. As Rossi says, this is a sinister oath to keep

the promise and translated into a more vulgar but no less energetic phrase would sound like this: "May I drop dead if I don't keep my promise." Torraca suggests that the image arises from the pain of Cocytus itself and notes that it is still customary to say that great cold withers the skin, the ears.

CANTO XXXIII

3. *guasto* = *guastato*. "Spoiled," in this case "gnawed away."

4–6. *Tu vuo' ch'io rinovelli . . . favelli*: See the beginning of Aeneas' tale of the disaster that befell Troy (*Aen.* II, 3–6):

> Infandum, regina, iubes renovare dolorem,
> Troianas ut opes et lamentabile regnum
> eruerint Danai, quaeque ipse miserrima vidi
> et quorum pars magna fui. . . .

> Beyond all words, O queen, is the grief thou bidst me revive, how the Greeks overthrew Troy's wealth and woeful realm—the sights most piteous that I myself saw and whereof I was no small part.

One thinks, by contrast, of Francesca's words (*Inf.* V, 121–23): "There is no greater sorrow than to recall a happy time in a time of wretchedness."

5. *preme*: "Presses," "wrings."

6. *pur pensando*: "Only to think of it."

7. *dien* = *devono*. Cf. the forms *dienno* and *denno*, also equivalent to *devono*.   *seme*: See *Conv.* IV, ii, 8: "Per che le parole, che sono quasi seme d'operazione, si deono

molto discretamente sostenere e lasciare, perchè bene siano ricevute e fruttifere vegnano." ("Wherefore words, which are like the seed of activities, must be very discreetly retained and let go . . . in order that they may be well received and brought to fruit.") For the metaphor, see the parable of the sower, especially Luc. 8:11: "Semen est verbum Dei." ("The seed is the word of God.")

Ugolino is referring to the wayfarer's promise (*Inf.* XXXII, 137–39) to "requite [him] in the world above."

9. *parlare e lagrimar vedrai insieme*: Another echo of Francesca's words (see *Inf.* V, 126): "I will do as one who weeps and speaks."

11–12. *fiorentino mi sembri veramente quand' io t'odo*: Like Farinata (*Inf.* X, 25), Ugolino recognizes the wayfarer as a Florentine because of his speech. Since Dante is Florentine, he must certainly know about the whole series of tragic events that led to Ugolino's death, since Nino Visconti, Ugolino's grandson (see n. to vss. 17–18), who played a large part in these events, fled to Florence shortly before Ugolino's imprisonment.

13. *fui conte Ugolino*: Ugolino della Gherardesca, Conte di Donoratico, also known as Ugolino da Pisa, was born *ca.* 1220 and belonged to a noble and traditionally Ghibelline family that controlled vast territories in the Pisan Maremma and in Sardinia. In 1275, he conspired with the Guelph leader Giovanni Visconti to seize control of Pisa, traditionally a Ghibelline city, but when the plot was discovered he was banished and his property was confiscated. He returned to Pisa the following year and in a short time again acquired great power and prestige. After the defeat of Pisa in the battle of Meloria (1284), a defeat which some accounts accuse him of contriving, he was made *podestà* of Pisa and the next year entered into the negotiations referred to by his opponents as the "tradimento de le castella" ("betrayal of the castles"; see vs. 86 and n. to vss. 17–18). For this supposed treachery he was put in prison, where he died of starvation in 1289.

14. *l'arcivescovo Ruggieri*: Ruggieri degli Ubaldini, son of Ubaldino dalla Pila (mentioned in *Purg.* XXIV, 29), nephew of the famous Ghibelline cardinal Ottaviano degli Ubaldini (see *Inf.* X, 120), and first cousin of Ugolino d'Azzo (see *Purg.* XIV, 105), was archbishop of Pisa from 1278 to 1295. For the details of his betrayal of Ugolino, see n. to vss. 17–18.

15. *i = gli, a lui.*   *i son tal vicino*: There is a gruesome irony in this phrase, since the two are in one hole and the speaker, Ugolino, is gnawing the other's skull.

16. *mai = mali.*

17–18. *fidandomi di lui . . . morto*: Villani's account of Ugolino's intrigue with the Ghibellines and his subsequent betrayal by the Archbishop Ruggieri doubtless is taken in part from Dante (see Villani, VII, 121):

> Negli anni di Cristo 1288, del mese di Luglio, essendo creata in Pisa grande divisione e sette per cagione della signoria, che dell'una era capo il giudice Nino di Gallura de' Visconti con certi guelfi, e l'altro era il conte Ugolino de' Gherardeschi coll'altra parte de' guelfi, e l'altro era l'arcivescovo Ruggeri degli Ubaldini co' Lanfranchi, e Gualandi, e Sismondi, con altre case ghibelline: il detto conte Ugolino per esser signore s'accostò coll'arcivescovo e sua parte, e tradì il giudice Nino, non guardando che fosse suo nipote figliuolo della figliuola, e ordinarono che fosse cacciato di Pisa co' suoi seguaci, o preso in persona. Giudice Nino sentendo ciò, e non veggendosi forte al riparo, si partì della terra, e andossene a Calci suo castello, e allegossi co' Fiorentini e' Lucchesi per fare guerra a' Pisani. Il conte Ugolino innanzi che il giudice Nino si partisse, per coprire meglio suo tradimento, ordinata la cacciata di giudice, se n'andò fuori di Pisa a uno suo maniero che si chiamava Settimo. Come seppe la partita di giudice Nino, tornò in Pisa con grande allegrezza, e da' Pisani fu fatto signore con grande allegrezza e festa; ma poco stette in sulla signoria, che la fortuna gli si rivolse al

contrario . . . . E certo l'ira di Dio tosto gli sopravvene, come piacque a Dio, per gli suoi tradimenti e peccatii che come era conceputo per l'arcivescovo di Pisa e suoi seguaci di cacciare di Pisa giudice Nino e' suoi, col tradimento e trattato del conte Ugolino, scemata la forza de' guelfi, l'arcivescovo ordinò di tradire il conte Ugolino, e subitamente a furore di popolo il fece assalire e combattere al palagio, faccendo intendere al popolo ch'egli avea tradito Pisa, e rendute le loro castella a' Fiorentini e a' Lucchesi; e sanza nullo riparo rivoltoglisi il popolo addosso, s'arrendeo preso, e al detto assalto fu morto uno suo figliuolo bastardo e uno suo nipote, e preso il conte Ugolino, e due suoi figliuoli, e tre nipoti figliuoli del figliuolo, e misergli in pregione, e cacciarono di Pisa la sua familia e suoi seguaci, e Visconti, e Ubizinghi, Guatani, e tutte l'altre case guelfe. E così fu il traditore dal traditore tradito.

In the year of Christ 1288, in the month of July, great dissension and faction broke out in Pisa because of the government. One faction was headed by the judge, Nino di Gallura de' Visconti, together with certain Guelphs; another by Count Ugolino della Gherardesca with the rest of the Guelphs; and still another by the Archbishop Ruggieri degli Ubaldini together with the Lanfranchi, the Gualandi, the Sismondi, and other Ghibelline families. To gain power, this Count Ugolino allied himself with the archbishop and his faction, thus betraying Judge Nino, though he was the count's grandson, the son of his daughter. They decreed that the judge was either to be driven out of Pisa together with his followers or captured. When Judge Nino heard about this, he realized he was not strong enough to stop them; whereupon he left Pisa and repaired to his castle at Calci. He allied himself with the Florentines and the Lucchese, to make war on Pisa.

Before Judge Nino left, Count Ugolino, after having ordered the expulsion of the judge, tried to cover his betrayal by leaving Pisa and going to one of his manors called Settimo. As soon as he heard that the judge had departed, he returned to Pisa very happy, and the Pisans made him their lord amidst great feasting and rejoicing. But he remained lord for only a short time, for fortune turned against him . . . . And surely the wrath of God soon fell upon him, as it pleased God, for his betrayals and his sins . . . for just as the archbishop and his followers had planned to drive Judge Nino and his men from Pisa through the treachery and intrigue of Count Ugolino, they now planned—since the strength of the Guelphs was diminished—to betray Count Ugolino. The archbishop gave the people to understand that Count Ugolino had betrayed Pisa by surrendering its castles to the Florentines and the Lucchese, whereupon the infuriated people immediately attacked the palace and waged a battle there. Since there was no way to escape them, he surrendered. In that attack, a bastard son of his was killed, as well as a grandson. Count Ugolino was captured, together with two sons and three grandsons, sons of his son, and all were imprisoned. His family was driven from Pisa, as were his followers, the Visconti, the Upezzinghi, the Guatani, and all the other Guelph families. Thus was the traitor by the traitor betrayed.

Villani's account and estimate of the treachery for which Ugolino is condemned to Antenora, the second subsection of the ninth circle of Hell, appears to be substantially correct in the light of modern scholarship. A scrutiny of the available documents and chronicles of the time suggests the following line of events leading to the final downfall of the count.

Following her disastrous defeat by Genoa in the naval battle of Meloria (1284), the traditionally Ghibelline city of Pisa found itself threatened on all sides by an alliance of powerful Guelph forces, particularly Genoa, Florence, and Lucca. At this time of crisis, Ugolino was elected *podestà* of the city for a period of ten years; he was chosen for the office not only for the competence he had already shown in public affairs, but because as a Guelph he could better negotiate with the hostile Guelph powers, Florence especially, now threatening the city.

The so-called "tradimento de le castella," with which Ugolino was later charged, took place in the spring and summer of 1285, when he ceded to Lucca the castles of Ripafratta and Viareggio and to the Guelph party of Florence the stronghold of Pontedera, which was later officially conveyed to the city itself. Given the danger in which Pisa found herself and the necessity of propitiating the hostile Guelph powers surrounding her, Ugolino's action was entirely in line with the new policy of conciliation and was in no sense an act of treachery or betrayal. The negotiations had to be shrouded in secrecy because, among other reasons, Ugolino was attempting to damage relations between Florence and her Guelph allies; however, the clandestine nature of the count's actions was later taken as evidence of treason.

In the year when Ugolino was taking part in these negotiations, his grandson, Nino Visconti, was emerging upon the scene as a young man who aspired to replace his late father, Giovanni Visconti, as leader of the Guelph party in Pisa. Nino was giving every promise of doing so when toward the end of the year he was called to share with his grandfather high offices in Pisa. But the personal ambitions of grandfather and grandson soon led to dissension and armed strife between them and their factions, so that the two were finally induced to relinquish their offices for the good of the city. They continued to clash, however, until February 1288, when the two men, equally desirous of regaining power, came to a temporary accord. In March, taking advantage of riots deliberately provoked by Ugolino, they stormed the "Palazzo del governo" by armed force and seized control of the city.

Meanwhile the Ghibellines in Tuscany and throughout Italy generally were enjoying better fortunes and achieving some important military victories. The party was accordingly showing new strength in Pisa itself. In June 1288, following the victory of Ghibelline Arezzo over Guelph Siena in the battle of the Pieve del Toppo, Count Ugolino, aware that the Pisan Ghibellines might again gain control of the city, began conniving with them and their leader, the Archbishop Ruggieri, in this way aspiring to better his own political fortunes and to rid himself of further interference from his grandson and political rival, Nino Visconti.

It appears that the count came to secret terms with Archbishop Ruggieri and the leaders of prominent Ghibelline families (Dante mentions the Gualandi, Lanfranchi, and Sismondi), agreeing among other things that Nino was to be driven from the city. At this point Ugolino withdrew to his estate at Settimo so that the plan might be carried out in his absence. Nino, sensing the threat, turned to his grandfather for assistance, but when he got none, fled the city.

The archbishop, now acclaimed *podestà*, took over control of Pisa and sent word to the count that he might return, which Ugolino did on June 30, 1288. But he came to the city gates with some thousand armed men, such a large force that he was not allowed to enter until he agreed to come in with only a few of them. Outraged that the archbishop should have seized the office and power he had aspired to gain by betraying his party and his grandson, the count managed, on the following day, to bring all his forces into the city. The archbishop and his Ghibelline followers then incited the people against the count and his guard, accusing Ugolino of the "betrayal of the castles." The count and two of his sons and two grandsons were taken captive and imprisoned for more than a fortnight, whence they were removed to the Torre della Fame (see n. to vs. 22), the tower in which they were to die.

It was a complete triumph for the Ghibellines of Pisa. Within a few months the archbishop resigned the office of *podestà* in favor of another, who in turn yielded to Guido da Montefeltro.

The Archbishop Ruggieri may seem to belong to Ptolomea, the next and third division of Cocytus, to which those who have betrayed their guests and associates are assigned, since he invited Ugolino to return to Pisa. However, Ruggieri is punished also for treachery against a member of his own party, since Ugolino, who was Ghibelline by tradition, returned to the party after the Guelph interval and was invited as a Ghibelline to return to Pisa; for this reason the archbishop belongs here in Antenora.

Thus the deed of treachery for which Count Ugolino is condemned to Antenora is his betrayal of his own party, the Guelph party which first entrusted him with the rule of the city, and of his Guelph grandson Nino Visconti. The reason for his consignment to Antenora is not the "tradimento de le castella," with which he was falsely charged, nor is it, as another view would have it, for any treachery against his native city in the defeat of Pisa at Meloria.

For Ugolino's dealings with Nino Visconti, see I. Del Lungo (1888), pp. 271–369. U. Dorini (1927) discusses the "tradimento de le castella."

18. *morto*: "Killed"; past participle of "morire," here used as a transitive verb. *dir non è mestieri*: "There is no need to tell" you, a Florentine, about such things.

21. *e saprai s'e' m'ha offeso*: Francesca, too, is referred to as an "anima offensa" (*Inf.* V, 109; see also *Inf.* V, 102). Here, in the light of the terrible events to be recounted, the word "offeso" bears a grim irony in its understatement. The phrase harks back to *Inf.* XXXII, 136: "che se tu a ragion di lui ti piangi." Ugolino now proposes to show the wayfarer that he does indeed have "reason to complain."

22. *pertugio*: A little slit, perhaps a small window.
Muda: Literally, "mew," a loft where birds are kept for moulting (*muda*), probably a small, dark place. Some early commentators claim that the eagles of the city were kept here to moult. This Mew, or tower, became known as the Torre della Fame or "Tower of Hunger" (originally the Torre dei Gualandi; see vs. 32); it stood in what is now the Piazza dei Cavalieri. After 1318, according to Torraca, the tower was no longer used as a prison; apparently it had exuded a terrible stench and the lack of both space and facilities had caused prisoners to die before their time.

23. *la qual per me ha 'l titol de la fame*: This statement is repeated by the author of the *Fragmenta historiae Pisanae* (col. 655E): "E da inde inansi la dicta pregione si chiamò la Pregione e Torre della fame." ("And from then on, that prison was called the Prison and Tower of Hunger.")

24. *altrui*: The subject of "si chiuda," vague in its dire prophecy, which no doubt was fulfilled more than once before 1318, when the tower ceased to be used as a prison.

26. *più lune già*: The count and his "sons" were imprisoned in the tower in late July and died there in early February; hence over six months passed before their death.
    sonno = sogno. See also vs. 38.

27. *che del futuro mi squarciò 'l velame*: If Ugolino's bad dream came to him just before dawn, as vs. 37 suggests, it was likely to be truly prophetic (see n. to *Inf.* XXVI, 7).

28. *Questi*: Ruggieri.   *pareva*: The verb *parere* is commonly used in narrating the events of a dream.   *maestro e donno*: "Master" of the hunt and "leader" of the party. For "donno" in another acceptation, see *Inf.* XXII, 83 and 88.

28-36. *Questi pareva a me . . . fianchi*: The ominous dream is recounted in three tercets, of which the first two allegorically recount the events that led up to the imprisonment of the count and his "sons," while the third bears the presage of their death.

29. *cacciando il lupo e ' lupicini al monte*: The true meaning of the allegory is suggested by the use of the definite article here. Torraca points out that wolves were commonly hunted in this and neighboring regions in Dante's day; thus the allegory has a basis in reality.

29-30. *al monte . . . non ponno*: Monte San Giuliano, a long flat mountain northeast of Pisa. Rossi remarks that it is no accident that the wolf and the whelps flee toward Lucca, where the count had friends and political connections.

30. *ponno* = *possono.*

31. *cagne*: These, as Buti observes, represent the *popolo minuto* or rabble, incited against Ugolino by the archbishop and his fellow Ghibellines.   *conte*: "Trained," or perhaps "accustomed to the terrain," hence "keen" ("studiose") in this sense.

32. *Gualandi . . . Sismondi . . . Lanfranchi*: All prominent Ghibelline families of Pisa, who joined the archbishop in the uprising against the count.

33. *messi dinanzi da la fronte*: The Ghibelline families appear here in Ugolino's dream as "beaters" of the hunt, employed in rousing and driving the quarry.

34. *corso* = *corsa.*   *parieno* = *parevano.*

35. *lo padre e ' figli*: The allegory of the dream becomes transparent as the terms "padre" and "figli" are applied to the wolves.   *scane*: Buti comments: "Scane sono li denti pungenti del cane, ch'elli à da ogni lato coi quali elli afferra." ("*Scane* are the dog's incisor teeth, which he has on both sides and which he uses to bite into things.")

36. *mi parea lor veder fender li fianchi*: "Lor" is dative, indicating possession, in this case of a part of the body.

37. *la dimane*: For other examples of this usage see E. G. Parodi (1957), p. 280.

38. *i miei figliuoli*: See the separate notes on the four "sons" (notes to vss. 50, 68, 89). In fact, two of the prisoners were Ugolino's grandsons, and all four were older than the poet represents them. Dante is not alone, however, in calling them all "figliuoli," for both the *Cronica di Pisa* (col. 979C) and Buti, lecturing on Dante in Pisa around 1385, do so. F. Romani (1901, p. 19) points out the inconsistency of the early commentators in this matter.

39. *ch'eran con meco*: Torraca observes that someone who did not know the story of Ugolino, reading it here in Canto XXXIII for the first time, would learn only at this point

that his sons were with him in the Mew. Thus they come
upon the scene, as it were, at the hour of their common
catastrophe. However, the sons have already figured as
the "lupicini" (vs. 29) in Ugolino's dream; moreover, the
story of their imprisonment in the tower with Ugolino was
so well known that any contemporary reader would have
assumed their presence all the while.   *dimandar del
pane*: Thus we are given to understand that each of the
children also had an ominous dream, in some way pro-
phetic of death by starvation (see "per suo sogno," vs. 45).
Although hunger had not figured in the count's dream, it
is now added to his fears.

44. *ne = ci.   solea = soleva.*

46. *chiavar = inchiodare* (see *Purg.* VIII, 137). The verb
chiavare can signify "to lock with a key" (*chiave*), but
this meaning seems unlikely here, since the door of the
tower must surely have been kept locked all the time,
though not at first nailed shut. As the door was being nailed
closed, the hammer blows were clearly audible to the count;
and, because of his sons' dreams and because it was being
sealed at the hour when food was usually brought, he felt
that his worst fears were confirmed.

49. *sì dentro impetrai*: For a similar use of this expression,
see Villani VIII, 63: "il dolore impetrato nel cuore di papa
Bonifazio" ("the pain that turned to stone in the heart
of Pope Boniface").

50. *Anselmuccio mio*: The suffix *-uccio* connotes endear-
ment. Anselmuccio was the younger brother of Nino il
Brigata (vs. 89), and the two actually were grandchildren
of Ugolino, sons of his eldest son Guelfo. Anselmuccio ap-
pears to have been born some time after 1272, since his
name is omitted from a document of that date in which the
other sons of Guelfo are mentioned as having claims in
Sardinia in their mother's right. Consequently he must
have been about fifteen at the time of his death.

52. *Perciò*: In consequence of his turning "to stone within"
(vs. 49).

54. *infin che l'altro sol nel mondo uscìo*: This means, given the time of day, a silence of some twenty-four hours. *uscìo = uscì.*

57. *per quattro visi il mio aspetto stesso*: All four faces were gaunt with fear and hunger, as the father knew his own must be.

59. *fessi = facessi.*

60. *manicar = mangiare.* In *De vulg. eloqu.* I, xiii, 2, Dante cites the expression "manichiamo" as typically Florentine, which suggests the colloquial tone of the verb in its present context.   *levorsi = si levarono* (see *Inf.* XXVI, 36).

62. *ne = ci.*

63. *e tu le spoglia*: Imperative. Torraca appropriately recalls Iob 1:21: "Nudus egressus sum de utero matris meae, et nudus revertar illuc. Dominus dedit, Dominus abstulit." ("Naked I came forth from my mother's womb, and naked shall I go back again. The Lord gave and the Lord has taken away.")

64. *Queta'mi = mi quetai.*

65. *lo dì = quel dì.* In early Italian, the definite article (derived from the Latin demonstrative *ille*) often preserves its original demonstrative force. The days here indicated are the second and third following the nailing shut of the door.

66. *ahi dura terra, perché non t'apristi?* See *Aen.* X, 675–76: "Aut quae iam satis ima dehiscat / terra mihi?" ("What earth could now gape deep enough for me?") See also *Aen.* XII, 883–84: "O quae satis ima dehiscat / terra mihi" ("O what deepest earth can gape enough for me"). And see Seneca, *Thyestes*, vss. 1006–9:

> . . . sustines tantum nefas
> gestare, Tellus? non ad infernam Styga
> tenebrasque mergis rupta et ingenti via
> ad chaos inane regna cum rege abripis?

Canst thou endure, O Earth, to bear a crime so monstrous? Why dost not burst asunder and plunge thee down to the infernal Stygian shades and, by a huge opening to void chaos, snatch this kingdom with its king away?

68. *Gaddo*: Count Ugolino's fourth son. The exact date of Gaddo's birth is unknown, but he was surely a grown man by 1288.   *mi si gittò disteso a' piedi*: We should conceive of the prisoners as shackled. The Pisan commentator Buti claims to have seen the bodies "coi ferri in gamba" ("in leg-irons") when they were removed from the tower.

69. *Padre mio, ché non m'aiuti?* An echo of Christ's words from the Cross (Matt. 27:46): "Eli, eli, lamma sabacthani? hoc est: Deus meus, Deus meus, ut quid dereliquisti me?" (" 'Eli, Eli, lema sabacthani,' that is, 'My God, my God, why hast thou forsaken me?' ") In this connection the reader should note the expression "porre a tal croce" (vs. 87).

74. *fur = furono*.

75. *Poscia, più che 'l dolor, poté 'l digiuno*: Some commentators have held the curious view that by this last line of Ugolino's narrative Dante meant to imply that the count, in the extremity of starvation, did actually attempt to prolong his life by feeding upon the bodies of his sons, as they had begged him to do while they were yet alive (vss. 61–63)—that "hunger" prevailed over "grief" in that sense. But such a view of the meaning here is hardly worth a serious rebuttal; see F. D'Ovidio (1907), pp. 63–116; R. Murari (1898).

76. *con li occhi torti*: See Statius, *Theb.* VIII, 756: "lumina torva" ("wrathful eyes").

78. *furo = furono*.

79–80. *de le genti del bel paese*: "Of the peoples of Italy," in the sense of those belonging to this or that city or state. For this use of "gente," see *Inf.* XXIX, 106.

617

80. *del bel paese là dove 'l sì suona*: For the traditional classification of the Romance languages according to the affirmative adverb of each, see *De vulg. eloqu.* I, viii, 6:

> Totum autem quod in Europa restat ab istis, tertium tenuit ydioma, licet nunc tripharium videatur; nam alii *oc*, alii *oïl*, alii *sì* affirmando locuntur; ut puta Yspani, Franci et Latini.

> But a third idiom prevailed in all that part of Europe which remains from the other two, though it now appears in a threefold form. For of those who speak it, some say in affirmation *oc*, others *oïl*, and others *sì*, namely the Spaniards, the French, and the Italians.

81. *i vicini*: Especially Florence and Lucca.

82. *la Capraia e la Gorgona*: Two small islands in the Mediterranean, east of the northern tip of Corsica. Both islands, which belonged to Pisa in Dante's time, lie fairly close to the mouth of the Arno. A nephew of Count Ugolino, the Count Anselmo, took his title from Capraia.

82-84. *muovasi la Capraia . . . persona*: For the imprecation as such, see Lucan, *Phars.* VIII, 827-30:

> Quid tibi, saeva, precer pro tanto crimine, tellus?
> Vertat aquas Nilus quo nascitur orbe retentus,
> Et steriles egeant hibernis imbribus agri,
> Totaque in Aethiopum putres solvaris harenas.

> What curse can I invoke upon that ruthless land in reward for so great a crime? May Nile reverse his waters and be stayed in the region where he rises; may the barren fields crave winter rains; and may all the soil break up into the crumbling sands of Ethiopia.

85-87. *Che se 'l conte . . . tal croce*: Villani, who may well be following Dante, makes a similar point, qualifying the justice of Ugolino's death with "per avventura" (VII, 128):

> Di questa crudeltà furono i Pisani per lo universo mondo, ove si seppe, forte biasimati, non tanto per lo conte, che per gli suoi difetti e tradimenti era per

avventura degno di sì fatta morte, ma per gli figliuoli
e nipoti, che erano giovani garzoni e innocenti.

For this cruel deed, the Pisans were strongly condemned
throughout the entire world, wherever it became
known—not so much for the count, who perhaps de-
served such a death on account of his faults and be-
trayals, but for the sons and grandsons, who were
young boys and innocent.

86. *d'aver tradita . . . castella*: Specific reference to the
"betrayal of the strongholds" with which the archbishop
and his faction charged the count in their final betrayal;
see n. to vs. 17.

87. *dovei = dovevi.*   *croce*: See n. to vs. 69.

88. *Innocenti facea l'età novella*: The subject is "età."

89. *novella Tebe*: Pisa has renewed the horrors of Thebes,
a city notorious for crimes and bloodshed (see *Inf.* XXVI,
53–54; *Inf.* XXX, 4).   *Uguiccione*: The fifth and young-
est son of Count Ugolino and brother of Gaddo (vs. 68).
    'l Brigata: Nino, known as "il Brigata," was the son of
Guelfo, eldest son of Ugolino and brother of Anselmuccio
(vs. 50). He would have been in his late teens, or possibly
older, in 1288; he is said to have been married, and not
long before his death the Ghibellines wished to associate
him with his grandfather in the government of Pisa.

90. *appella*: "Names."

91. *Noi passammo oltre*: The transition to Ptolomea, the
next and third division of Cocytus (not named until vs.
124), is indicated with these words.   *la gelata*: Cf.
"gelatina," *Inf.* XXXII, 60.

93. *non volta in giù*: As in the first division, Caina.   *tutta
riversata*: Suggesting perhaps that the souls lie supine. The
phrase may also mean that their heads are thrown back
while they stand upright in the ice like the others in Caina
and Antenora.

95. *rintoppo*: "Opposition."

97. *groppo*: "Knot," i.e., a solid block of ice.

98. *visiere*: "Visor," the piece of armor that covers the face but allows the wearer to see through, as do the veils of ice (vs. 112) over the eyes of these sinners. *di cristallo*: Again suggests the transparency of the ice.

99. *il coppo*: Literally a vase or jar of terra cotta, here the socket of the eye. For this meaning, see E. G. Parodi (1957), p. 246.

102. *stallo*: "Stay"; every feeling had ended its stay in the face.

104. *questo*: Object of "move."

105. *non è qua giù ogne vapore spento*: In other words, how can there be wind in this ice-locked place, to which the heat of the sun—which causes wind—never penetrates? Scartazzini quotes Vitruvius (*De architectura* I, vi, 2): "Ventus autem est aeris fluens unda cum incerta motus redundantia. Nascitur cum fervor offendit umorem et impetus factionis exprimit vim spiritus flatus." ("Now the wind is a wave of air flowing with uncertain currents of motion. It rises when heat strikes moisture and the onrush of the force presses out the power of the breath of the blast.")

106. *Avaccio*: "Soon"; see *Inf*. X, 116.

108. *piove*: The verb is transitive; "fiato" is the object. The wind "drives down" from above, for a reason yet to be disclosed; meanwhile this touch generates suspense.

110–11. *O anime crudeli . . . posta*: The assumption that the wayfarer is so cruel that he has been assigned to the last section of Cocytus is a grave insult to him and stirs his wrath. See Filippo Argenti's question (*Inf*. VIII, 33), "Who are you who come before your time?" which, bearing a similar implication, also provoked the wayfarer's anger.

115. *ti sovvegna*: From *sovvenire*, "to help"; see *Inf.* XVII,
94.

117. *al fondo de la ghiaccia ir mi convegna*: The wayfarer
does not yet know that he will actually go to the bottom
of the ice in the sense that he will climb down the body of
Satan and pass through the center of the earth. Here the
phrase "to go to the bottom of the ice" seems to suggest
that the ice of Cocytus slopes toward the center. The
"fondo," then, is its lowest place, and the wayfarer knows
that he is moving toward it and is bound to go there in any
case. This, then, is his betrayal: when he does not keep
his promise, he does indeed go to the bottom of the ice,
that is, to its lowest point.

118. *frate Alberigo*: Friar Alberigo belonged to the order
of the Frati Gaudenti ("Jovial Friars"), which he joined
in or before 1267. He was a member of the Manfredi fam-
ily, the Guelph lords of Faenza (to which also belonged
Tebaldello; see *Inf.* XXXII, 122). The circumstances of
Alberigo's crime, which took place in 1285, are narrated by
Benvenuto, who states that Manfred, a close relative
("consanguineus"), plotted against Alberigo to obtain the
lordship of Faenza. In the consequent dispute, Manfred
struck Alberigo, who pretended to forgive the insult as an
act of impetuous youth. A reconciliation took place, and
later when he thought the matter had been forgotten,
Alberigo invited Manfred and one of his sons to a banquet
(at his house at Cesate). When dinner was finished, he
called out, "Bring the fruit," and at this signal assassins,
concealed behind the tapestry, rushed out and dispatched
father and son before Alberigo's eyes. Hence, "le male
frutta di frate Alberigo" passed into a proverb. In recording
the murder of a brother of Alberigo by his nephew in 1327,
Villani says (X, 27): "Così mostrò che non volesse tra-
lignare e del nome e del fatto di frate Alberigo suo zio,
che diede le male frutta a' suoi consorti, faccendogli tagliare
e uccidere al suo convito." ("Thus he showed that he
wanted, in name and deed, to be like his uncle, Friar

Alberigo, who gave the evil fruit to his relatives, having
them stabbed and killed at his banquet.")

119–20. *le frutta del mal orto . . . figo*: Friar Alberigo turns
his infamous signal to the assassins into an ironical meta-
phor—"fruit from a garden of evil"—playing further on his
words with the phrase "dattero per figo." He is saying
that he receives more than good measure, since a date is
worth more than a fig.

121. *ancor*: The exact date of Friar Alberigo's death is
unknown, but apparently he was still living in the spring
of 1300.

122. *stea = stia*.

123. *nulla scienza porto*: For some reason Friar Alberigo
cannot foresee when his body will finish its time on earth.
Nor can he see or know the present facts of its continuing
existence above; see *Inf.* X, 103–5.

124. *vantaggio*: Obviously ironical. *Tolomea*: Ptolomea.
The name of this division of Cocytus, in which are pun-
ished those who murdered their guests and friends, is
derived, according to some, from Ptolemy XII, king of
Egypt (51–47 B.C.), who murdered Pompey; see Lucan,
Phars. VIII, 536–712 and *De mon.* II, viii, 9. But it is more
probably named after Ptolemy, son of Abubus, the captain
of Jericho, who treacherously murdered Simon the Maccabee
and two of his sons at a banquet he gave for them in 134
B.C. The incident is related in I Mach. 16:11–17:

> Et Ptolemaeus filius Abobi constitutus erat dux in campo
> Iericho, et habebat argentum et aurum multum; erat
> enim gener summi sacerdotis. Et exaltatum est cor eius;
> et volebat obtinere regionem, et cogitabat dolum ad-
> versus Simonem et filios eius ut tolleret eos. Simon
> autem perambulans civitates quae erant in regione
> Iudaeae, et sollicitudinem gerens earum, descendit in
> Iericho, ipse et Mathathias filius eius et Iudas, anno
> centesimo septuagesimo septimo, mense undecimo: hic
> est mensis Sabath. Et suscepit eos filius Abobi in

munitiunculam quae vocatur Doch cum dolo, quam
aedificavit; et fecit eis convivium magnum, et abscondit
illic viros. Et cum inebriatus esset Simon et filii eius,
surrexit Ptolemaeus cum suis; et sumpserunt arma sua,
et intraverunt in convivium, et occiderunt eum et duos
filios eius et quosdam pueros eius. Et fecit deceptionem
magnam in Israel et reddidit mala pro bonis.

Now Ptolemee the son of Abobus was appointed cap-
tain in the plain of Jericho: and he had abundance of
silver and gold, For he was son-in-law of the high
priest. And his heart was lifted up and he designed
to make himself master of the country: and he pur-
posed treachery against Simon, and his sons, to destroy
them. Now Simon, as he was going through the cities
that were in the country of Judea and taking care for
the good ordering of them, went down to Jericho,
he and Mathathias and Judas his sons, in the year
one hundred and seventy-seven, the eleventh month:
the same is the month of Sabath. And the son of
Abobus received them deceitfully into a little fortress
that is called Doch, which he had built: and he made
them a great feast and hid men there. And when Simon
and his sons had drunk plentifully, Ptolemee and his
men rose up and took their weapons and entered into
the banqueting place and slew him and his two sons
and some of his servants. And he committed a great
treachery in Israel and rendered evil for good.

126. *Atropòs*: Atropos ($\dot{a} + \tau\rho\acute{\epsilon}\pi\omega$, i.e., "inexorable"), one
of the three Fates (Parcae). At the birth of every mortal,
Clotho, the spinning Fate, was supposed to wind a certain
amount of yarn on the distaff of Lachesis, the allotting Fate;
the duration of the life of the individual was the length
of time occupied in spinning the thread, which, when com-
plete, was severed by Atropos, the inevitable Fate.   *dea =
dia.*

127. *rade = rada.   le 'nvetriate = le invetriate.*

129. *sappie = sappi.   trade = tradisce* (see *Inf.* XI, 66).

131. *il* = *lo*.

133. *Ella*: The soul.   *ruina*: For this meaning, see "rovinava," *Inf.* I, 61.

134. *pare* = *appare*.   *suso*: "Up" on earth.

135. *verna*: "Is spending the winter." The irony continues.

136. *dei* = *devi*.   *pur mo*: See *Inf.* X, 21; *Inf.* XXVII, 20. This "present" fact would also be concealed from Friar Alberigo (see n. to vs. 123).

137. *Branca Doria*: Member of the famous Ghibelline house of Doria (or d'Oria) at Genoa (born *ca.* 1233, died *ca.* 1325). With the aid of a relative, either a nephew or cousin, he treacherously murdered his father-in-law, Michel Zanche, governor of Logudoro in Sardinia, at a banquet to which he had invited him. Some commentators date the murder *ca.* 1275, while others prefer *ca.* 1290.

140. *unquanche*: "Never yet"; cf. the Latin *unquam*.

141. *e mangia e bee e dorme e veste panni*: This he apparently continued to do for some twenty-five years, until his death *ca.* 1325.

142. *Nel fosso sù . . . de' Malebranche*: The fifth *bolgia* of the eighth circle, where the souls guilty of barratry are confined.

143. *là dove bolle la tenace pece*: See *Inf.* XXI, 8: "bolle l'inverno la tenace pece."

146. *un suo prossimano*: The relative, nephew or cousin, who assisted Branca d'Oria in the murder of Michel Zanche. "Prossimano" is the second subject of "lasciò" (vs. 145).

148. *oggimai* = *oramai*; i.e., "now" that I have told you so much.

150. *e cortesia fu lui esser villano*: Not to keep a solemn promise is to be "villano." For the apparent paradox, see *Inf.* XX, 28: "Here pity lives when it is altogether dead."

The reader will also recall the "courtesy" which the way-farer wished to see (and did see) shown to Filippo Argenti (*Inf.* VIII, 52–60). Torraca gives examples of the "ethics" of such dealing with a traitor. See Lanfranco Cigala, "Ges eu non vei," vss. 35–38 (in F. Branciforti, 1954, p. 215):

> Que segon dreg non es ges traimenz
> Trair traichor; qu'eu dic tot engalmenz
> Con es trair son amic malvestatz,
> Es son trachor trair pretz e bontatz.

For, by right, it is not at all treachery to betray a traitor, and with reason I affirm that, just as it is wicked to betray a friend, so is it worthy and good to betray one who betrays you.

See also *I nobili fatti di Alessandro Magno* (p. 99): "E anche li antichi nostri dicono, che a traditore non se de' tenere leanza." ("Our old people say that no loyalty is due a traitor.")   *lui = a lui*, dative.

151–52. *diversi d'ogne costume = diversi d'ogni buon costume.*

152. *magagna*: "Blemish," or as here, "vice," "corruption."

153. *spersi = dispersi.*

154. *col peggiore spirto di Romagna*: Friar Alberigo.

155. *un tal*: Branca d'Oria.   *opra = opera*, "deed."

157. *par = appare.*   *di sopra*: In the world above.

CANTO XXXIV

1. *Vexilla regis prodeunt*: The first verse of the first stanza of a well-known hymn by Venantius Fortunatus (*ca.* 530–610):

> Vexilla Regis prodeunt:
> Fulget Crucis mysterium,
> Qua vita mortem pertulit,
> Et morte vitam protulit.

> Abroad the regal banners fly,
> Now shines the Cross's mystery;
> Upon it Life did death endure,
> And yet by death did life procure.

The full text of the hymn, with a translation, is printed in M. Britt (1955), pp. 115–16. Fortunatus composed the hymn at Poitiers for the reception of a fragment of the so-called True Cross on November 19, 569 (see J. Julian, 1892, p. 1220). The hymn, primarily processional, is sung, in the Divine Office, from Vespers of the Saturday before Passion Sunday until Maundy Thursday. The hymn at Vespers is sung after the reading of the five psalms and the Capitulum, and before the Magnificat. During Passiontide the hymn has the following versicle and response: *v.*: Eripe me, Domine, ab homine malo. *r.*: A viro iniquo eripe me. In the light of the time reference here in vs. 68 of Canto XXXIV,

626

the allusion in vs. 1 is thus especially appropriate. *inferni*: Dante has strikingly added this word to the hymn to fill out his verse and to introduce the ironic and derisive tone which attends his use of the "Vexilla regis" to announce what will be revealed to the wayfarers at the bottom of Hell. See C. S. Singleton (1954), pp. 33–39.

2. *verso di noi*: Depends on "prodeunt" (vs. 1). The "banners of the king" are thus said to "advance"; in this connection it is necessary to remember that the hymn is a processional or triumphal hymn. Actually the notion that these "banners" can advance is plainly derisive in the light of what they are revealed to be. "Advance" is precisely what they cannot do (see n. to vs. 46 below).

2-3. *mira . . . se tu 'l discerni*: "Look and see if you can make him out."

4. *grossa nebbia*: See *Inf.* XVI, 130.

5. *emisperio* = *emisfero*.   *nostro*: The inhabited or northern hemisphere of land where windmills are found.

6. *par* = *appare*.   *un molin che 'l vento gira*: A windmill in operation.

7. *dificio* = *edificio*. The term was used especially of a machine, such as a siege tower, or a vehicle (see *Purg.* XXXII, 142); here, in metaphor, it refers to the windmill. See the quotation from Lana, n. to vs. 56, in which he refers to the heckle or hemp brake as "uno edificio da tritare."
    allotta = *allora* (see *Inf.* V, 53).

8. *poi*: "Then," meaning as Dante advances farther.   *per lo vento*: See *Inf.* XXXIII, 103, where Dante first felt this cold wind. Virgil's promise there (*Inf.* XXXIII, 106–8) is now beginning to be realized.
    We may pause to reflect that this is a curious windmill indeed if it "blows"—gives forth a wind—instead of being turned by the wind: a grotesque reversal in itself.

9. *grotta*: A wall behind which to take shelter. Porena comments that one of the word's many meanings is that of a wall against which plants are cultivated in order to protect them from cold winds; hence the word may mean "protection from the wind."

10. *Già era* = *già ero venuto.   e con paura il metto in metro*: See *Aen.* II, 204: "Horresco referens." ("I shudder as I tell the tale.") See also *Inf.* XXII, 31.

11. *là dove l'ombre tutte eran coperte*: Once again the position and posture of the sinners in the ice serves to mark off a subdivision of Cocytus, the fourth and last—Judecca (named in vs. 117).   *tutte*: For this word in the sense of "completely," see also *Inf.* XIX, 64; XXXI, 15.

12. *trasparien* = *trasparevano*.

16. *fummo fatti* = *ci fummo fatti*. See *Inf.* XXII, 96; XXXI, 134.

18. *la creatura ch'ebbe il bel sembiante*: The full force of the past absolute tense in Italian can be felt in this "ch'ebbe"—"who once was." Thus a single verse focuses on Satan (before he is named—see vs. 20) and precisely on his present ugliness as contrasted to his former beauty. Lucifer was the "light-bearing" seraph, most beautiful of all angelic creatures, but now how fallen! See *Purg.* XII, 25–26; *Par.* XIX, 47–48.

19. *mi*: Here in the dative.   *fé restarmi* = *mi fece ristare*.

20. *Ecco Dite*: Satan has already been referred to by this classical name in *Inf.* XI, 65 and XII, 39. For the classical use of the name, see *Aen.* VI, 127, 269, 397.

23. *nol* = *non lo*.

26. *oggimai* = *oramai.   fior*. For the same use of the word, see *Inf.* XXV, 144; *Purg.* III, 135.

27. *d'uno e d'altro privo*: Deprived of the one thing (staying alive) and the other (dying).

28. *Lo 'mperador del doloroso regno*: See *Inf.* I, 124.

29. *da mezzo 'l petto*: Similarly the giants, prefigurations
of Satan, their master in pride, "betowered [the bank]
with half their bodies" (*Inf.* XXXI, 43).   *uscia = usciva*.

31. *i giganti*: Probably a specific reference to Nimrod and
the other giants of Canto XXXI.

32. *dee = deve*.

33. *così fatta parte*: I.e., one of the arms of Satan.   *si
confaccia*: "Is proportionate to," "answers to."

34. *fu*: Again one feels the full force of the past absolute
tense, as with "ebbe" in vs. 18.

35. *e contra 'l suo fattore alzò le ciglia*: The gesture ex-
presses the act of pride which was Lucifer's sin. See Isa.
14:12–15, quoted in n. to vs. 121. See also Aquinas (*Summa
theol.* I, q. 63, a. 3, resp.), who cites Anselm (*De casu
diaboli* VI).

36. *ben dee da lui procedere ogni lutto*: See Apoc. 12:9:
"Et proiectus est draco ille magnus, serpens antiquus qui
vocatur diabolus et Satanas, qui seducit universum orbem."
("And that great dragon was cast down, the ancient ser-
pent, he who is called the devil and Satan, who leads astray
the whole world.") And since, according to Isaiah, Lucifer
in his pride aspired to rule (Isa. 14:13) "in lateribus
aquilonis" ("in the sides of the north"), Ier. 1:14 is also
relevant to this verse: "Ab aquilone pandetur malum super
omnes habitatores terrae." ("From the north shall an evil
break forth upon all the inhabitants of the land.") Guittone
d'Arezzo, in *Lettere* XXXVII, remarks that "superbia
l'Angielo fecie cadere, unde tucti mali preseno commincio,
e tucte cose ruina." ("Pride made the angel fall, whence
began all ills and the ruin of all things.") See *Inf.* I, 111;
also Sapien. 2:24: "Invidia autem diaboli mors introivit in
orbem terrarum." ("But by the envy of the devil, death
entered the world.")   *dee = deve*.

38. *quand' io vidi tre facce a la sua testa*: The gradual disclosure of the monstrous figure continues, and creates considerable suspense. Satan's three faces are the grotesque counterpart of the triune God. On three-faced or three-headed Satans in popular lore and iconography, see A. Graf (1893), pp. 92–93.

40. *s'aggiugnieno = s'aggiungevano.* *sovresso 'l mezzo*: See *Inf.* XXIII, 54. / The two lateral heads perhaps should be imagined as turned at right angles to the face in front and thus seen in profile, although no specific point is made of this.

42. *sé giugnieno = sé giungevano.* *al loco de la cresta*: "Cresta," for example in the expression "rizzare la cresta" ("to take courage"), can signify pride. This monstrous feature affirms unity in trinity and is thus a part of the grotesque distortion of the seraph who aspired to be as the triune God and has had his wish fulfilled.

43. *la destra*: "Faccia" is understood. *tra bianca e gialla*: "Yellowish," "sallow."

45. *di là onde 'l Nilo s'avvalla*: Ethiopia.

46. *Sotto ciascuna uscivan due grand' ali*: Lucifer has kept the six wings which he had as a seraph, but now they are monstrously joined to the three necks instead of being as Isaiah had seen them. See Isa. 6:2: "Seraphim stabant super illud: sex alae uni et sex alae alteri; duabus velabant faciem eius, et duabus velabant pedes eius, et duabus volabant." ("Upon it stood the seraphims: the one had six wings, and the other had six wings: with two they covered his face, and with two they covered his feet, and with two they flew.") Also see *Par.* IX, 78. These wings, like huge sails (vs. 48), are the "banners" of the "Emperor" who is stuck in the ice and who cannot possibly advance (see n. to vs. 2).

47. *convenia = conveniva.* *tanto uccello*: Plainly ironical and derisive.

49. *Non avean penne*: I.e., they were not like his seraphic wings, before his fall.   *vispistrello* (Latin *vespertilio*) = *pipistrello*. The image of "sails" had suggested as much.

50. *svolazzava*: The verb is transitive and singular because of the unity in trinity.

51. *da ello*: From Satan (see *Inf*. III, 27).

52. *quindi Cocito tutto s'aggelava*: A backward glance over the whole frozen ninth circle.

53. *Con sei occhi piangea*: Satan weeps for rage and impotence, but is so reduced to a slobbering, witless monster that his weeping seems almost a purely physical phenomenon, and does not convey any inner feeling.

54. *gocciava 'l pianto e sanguinosa bava*: The by now familiar construction in which a singular verb serves a plural subject.   *sanguinosa bava*: The foam is bloody because of the three sinners chewed in the three mouths (and they are shades!).

56. *maciulla*: An instrument for breaking up hemp or flax. Lana comments: "Maciulla è uno edificio di tritare lino, il quale volgarmente ha nome gramola, sì che si dice al lino, quando il fusto è ben trito, gramolato." ("*Maciulla* is a structure in which flax is pounded. It is commonly called *gramola* [a place for scutching flax]; hence, when the stalk is well pounded, flax is said to be *gramolato* [scutched].")

61. *là sù*: By this touch we are reminded of Satan's towering height and now understand the downward blast from the wings (see *Inf*. XXXIII, 108).

62. *Giuda Scariotto*: Judas Iscariot, the betrayer of Christ, who thus occupies the position of "honor" in Hell, and for whom this last subdivision of the ninth circle is named (see vs. 117). See *Inf*. XIX, 96, where Judas is called "the guilty soul."

63. *mena* = *dimena*.

64. *hanno il capo di sotto*: The other two sinners dangle by the feet from the other two mouths of Satan, their heads hanging down. This apparently is a lesser punishment than that suffered by Judas, who has his head in the mouth and his feet hanging down.

65. *Bruto*: Marcus Junius Brutus (*ca.* 85–42 B.C.), the so-called tyrannicide. As a young man, he was known for his devotion to the ideals of the Roman republic and for his personal honesty. When the civil war broke out in 49 B.C., he sided with Pompey, even though Pompey was responsible for the death of his father. After the battle of Pharsalia (48 B.C.), in which Pompey was defeated, Brutus was pardoned by Caesar and admitted into confidence and favor; he was made governor of Cisalpine Gaul (46 B.C.) and then praetor (44 B.C.). But in spite of his obligations to Caesar, he was persuaded by Cassius to murder him for the good of the republic. After Caesar's death, Brutus remained for a time in Italy, and then went to Greece and Asia Minor, where he joined forces with Cassius, who commanded in Syria, to oppose Caesar's heir, Octavian (afterward called Augustus), and Antony. In 42 B.C. two battles were fought in the neighborhood of Philippi in Macedonia. In the first, Brutus was victorious over Octavian, though Cassius was defeated; but in the second, Brutus was defeated and he put an end to his own life.

66. *e non fa motto*: With this touch Dante has allowed the Roman Brutus a certain dignity. See the description of Jason as "that great one who comes there, and who does not seem to shed a tear for pain" in *Inf.* XVIII, 83–84.

67. *Cassio*: Gaius Cassius Longinus, one of the murderers of Julius Caesar. In 49 B.C. he was tribune of the plebs, joined the aristocratic party in the civil war, and fled with Pompey from Rome. After Pompey's defeat at the battle of Pharsalia, Cassius surrendered to Caesar, who not only pardoned him but in 44 B.C. made him praetor and promised him the province of Syria for the next year. But he never ceased to look upon Caesar as his enemy, and it was he

who formed the conspiracy against the life of the dictator and convinced Brutus to take part in it. After the murder of Caesar (March 15, 44 B.C.), Cassius went to Syria, which he claimed as his province, although the senate had assigned it to Dolabella and had conferred Cyrene on Cassius in its stead. After defeating Dolabella he crossed over to Greece with Brutus to oppose Octavian and Antony at Philippi. Cassius was defeated by Antony, while Brutus, who commanded the other wing of the army, drove Octavian off the field. Cassius, ignorant of the success of Brutus, would not survive his defeat, and commanded one of his freedmen to put an end to his life (42 B.C.). *che par sì membruto*: Cassius seems so muscular because his skin has been stripped from the muscles of his body, leaving them starkly visible.

68. *Ma la notte risurge*: Time in Hell continues to be told by reference to night and to nocturnal bodies. It is nightfall (with respect to the meridian of Jerusalem). Since Virgil and Dante entered Hell at dusk on Good Friday, it is now clear, looking back to Malacoda's words (*Inf.* XXI, 112) that the journey through Hell takes them twenty-four hours. Thus it is now 6:00 P.M. on Holy Saturday evening.

69. *avem = abbiamo*.

70. *li = gli*; dative with "collo."

71. *prese di tempo e loco poste*: "He seized opportunity of time and place." Cf. *appostare*, "to spy out."

72. *fuoro = furono*.

75. *tra 'l folto pelo e le gelate croste*: The frozen tufts of hair apparently leave some space between Satan's body and the ice, even though the monster is squeezed into the ice as in a vise.

76–77. *là dove la coscia . . . l'anche*: Where the thigh curves out to form the hip—i.e., at the exact center of Satan's body, also the exact center of the earth and of the universe in the Ptolemaic conception.

79. *volse la testa ov' elli avea le zanche*: Virgil turns his head to where he had his feet. The experience of passing through the center of gravity is narrated from the bewildered point of view of the wayfaring Dante, who rides down on Virgil's back, his arms clasped about his master's neck. In this position he knows, of course, where Virgil's head and feet are and can feel that he turns about, but then thinks, since Virgil seems to climb, that he must be returning to Hell. Actually Virgil starts down feet first as one would on a ladder, and when he reaches the center of gravity must turn around to climb *up* the "ladder." Dante truly loses his bearings with respect to Satan's position in the ice and does not know which direction is up and which is down, but he never is confused with respect to Virgil's position and posture.

Some commentators would understand "elli" as referring to Lucifer and take the term "zanche" to be derisive and therefore inapplicable to Virgil. This hardly seems acceptable, because of vss. 88–89 and vss. 103–4. See also *Inf.* XIX, 45, where "zanca" may be derisive but is not necessarily so. For a discussion of the precise meaning of "zanche" and its significance here, see C. S. Singleton (1965b), pp. 94–96.

80. *aggrappossi* = *si aggrappò*.

81. *anche* = *ancora*.

82. *cotali scale*: The phrase is plainly ironical. See *Inf.* XVII, 82.

84. *conviensi* = *si conviene*. *da tanto male*: Deriving from Lucifer, first of all, and from his whole woeful realm.

85–87. *Poi uscì fuor per lo fóro . . . passo*: All is dark and mysterious here. The "cleft," it would seem, is fairly large if the wayfarer can be placed on its edge in a sitting position and Virgil can then step into it from Satan's shaggy thigh.

88–93. *Io levai li occhi . . . passato*: In his bewilderment the wayfarer has completely lost his sense of direction. Since he first thought (see n. to vs. 79) that Virgil was carrying him back into Hell, he now quite consistently looks up from the edge of the opening on which he sits and expects to see Lucifer "as he had left him"—head up—since Virgil seemed to have climbed part way back up toward Lucifer's head. Instead, having passed the center of the earth (as the wayfarer will soon understand) Virgil climbed toward Lucifer's legs and this direction is now up. Since the wayfarer has never lost his bearings with respect to his guide, the "elli" of vs. 79 must refer to Virgil, not Lucifer, and "zanche" cannot be a derisive term here because it applies to Virgil's legs.

90. *vidili = gli vidi*.

92. *la gente grossa il pensi*: "Let ignorant folk consider." *Pensare* has here something of its original meaning of "to weigh."

93. *quel punto*: The center of the earth and of gravity; see vs. 111.

94-96. *Lèvati sù . . . riede*: See *Aen*. VI, 628-30: "Haec ubi dicta dedit Phoebi longaeva sacerdos, / 'sed iam age, carpe viam et susceptum perfice munus, / acceleremus,' ait." ("So spake the aged priestess of Phoebus; then adds: 'But come now, take thy way and fulfil the task in hand. Let us hasten.'")

95. *la via è lunga*: Quite an understatement if one considers that the two wayfarers must climb up half the diameter of the earth. V. Rossi (1955, p. 664) remarks that it has been calculated that it would take a train traveling at a hundred kilometers an hour four days and four nights to cover the distance the wayfarers must travel. As will be evident, they traverse the distance in approximately twenty-four hours.

96. *e già il sole*: Time references in the descent through Hell have always been given with reference to night and to nocturnal bodies, never with respect to the position of the sun. Thus the present reference to the sun is most striking, since it signals that the two wayfarers, having passed

the center, must now be under the southern celestial hemisphere. Henceforth in their journey in this hemisphere, time will be told with respect to positions of the sun; the specific point of reference will be the mountain directly opposite Jerusalem on the globe, where they will soon find themselves. *a mezza terza riede*: See *Conv.* IV, xxiii, 15–16:

> Intorno a le parti del giorno è brievemente da sapere che, sì come detto è di sopra nel sesto del terzo trattato, la Chiesa usa, ne la distinzione de le ore, [ore] del dì temporali, che sono in ciascuno die dodici, o grandi o piccole, secondo la quantitade del sole; e però che la sesta ora, cioè lo mezzo die, è la più nobile di tutto lo die e la più virtuosa, li suoi offici appressa quivi da ogni parte, cioè da prima e di poi, quanto puote. E però l'officio de la prima parte del die, cioè la terza, si dice in fine di quella; e quello de la terza parte e de la quarta si dice ne li principii. E però si dice mezza terza, prima che suoni per quella parte; e mezza nona, poi che per quella parte è sonato.

> And briefly be it known that, as said above in the sixth chapter of the third treatise, the church in distinguishing between the hours of the day makes use of the temporal hours, of which there are twelve in each day, long or short according to the measure of the sun; and because the sixth hour, which is midday, is the most noble of the whole day, and the most virtuous, she approximates her offices thereto from each direction, that is to say before and after, as much as she may. And therefore the office of the first part of the day, that is tierce, is called after its close, and that of the third part and of the fourth after their beginnings; and therefore we speak of "mid-tierce" before the bell rings for that division, and of mid-nones after the bell has rung for that division.

Terza ("tierce") was the name either for the third hour of the day or for the period of the first three hours, 6:00 A.M. to 9:00 A.M. "Mezza terza" is thus about 7:30 A.M. "southern hemisphere" time, or, more precisely, with reference to the zenith of the celestial hemisphere which is directly oppo-site that of Jerusalem. This will prompt Dante's question of vss. 104–5, and does indeed present a puzzle for the mo-ment, since Virgil has only just declared that "night is rising again" (vs. 68).

97. *camminata di palagio*: The "palace hallway," so called because of its fireplace ("camino"), was usually the largest and finest room of all, and the one in which guests were received. Thus there is clearly a touch of irony in such a reference here.

98. *natural burella*: A "natural cellar" (as opposed to an artificial or man-made one). "Burella," said to be derived from *buio*, originally meant "cellar" or "subterranean vault"; that the term should also have served to indicate a dungeon or prison was understandable enough. But M. Barbi (1925a) has argued convincingly against any such meaning here.

99. *di lume disagio*: "A scarcity of light."

100. *abisso*: The term refers to the entire cavity of Hell; see *Inf.* IV, 8 and 24; XI, 5.   *mi divella*: Literally, "up-root myself" (cf. "disvelta," *Inf.* XIII, 95). The verb sug-gests the difficulty of the journey out of the abyss. It seems unlikely that any allegorical meaning attaches to the term or to the difficulty of the climb.

101. *dritto*: "Standing up," as Virgil had directed. See *Inf.* IV, 5.

102. *erro = errore*, in the sense of "doubt" or "puzzlement" (see *Inf.* X, 114).   *mi favella = favellami* (pronounced *favèllami*).

103. *la ghiaccia = il ghiaccio* (as before), the ice of the whole circle of Cocytus.   *questi*: Lucifer.

104. *in sì poc' ora*: Between 6:00 and 7:30 A.M., not reckoning the puzzling fact of the change from evening (vs. 68) to morning (vs. 96) mentioned in the following verse.

105. *da sera a mane ha fatto il sol tragitto*: See n. to vs. 104, above. "Tragitto" here means the sun's diurnal revolution about the earth. The wayfarer's question is answered in vs. 118.

107–8. *mi presi al pel*: Cf. "appigliò sé," vs. 73.

108. *vermo*: The term was applied to Cerberus in *Inf.* VI, 22.   *che 'l mondo fóra*: Inevitably one has the image here of some fruit, perhaps an apple, with a great worm at the core.

109. *cotanto quant'*: "For as long as."

110–11. *quand' io mi volsi . . . pesi*: See vs. 79 and the note.   *'l punto al qual si traggon d'ogne parte i pesi*: The "punto" mentioned in vs. 93 is now defined. It is the center of the earth, which, in the Aristotelian-Ptolemaic conception, is the center of gravity of the whole universe. See Aristotle, *De caelo* II, 14, 296[b]. See also Cicero, *De re publica* VI, 17: "Nam ea, quae est media et nona, tellus, neque movetur et infima est, et in eam feruntur omnia nutu suo pondera." ("For the ninth and central sphere, which is the earth, is immovable and the lowest of all, and toward it all ponderable bodies are drawn by their own natural tendency downward.") For the conception of the "center" as also the "bottom" see Macrobius, commenting on this passage (*Comm. in somn. Scip.* I, xxii, 4, 8):

> nam quod centron est medium est; in sphaera vero hoc solum constat imum esse quod medium est. et si terra ima est, consequitur ut vere dictum sit in eam ferri omnia. semper enim pondera in imum natura deducit, nam et in ipso mundo ut esset terra, sic factum est. . . . in hanc igitur, quae et ima est et quasi media et non movetur quia centron est, omnia pondera ferri necesse est . . . .

For that which is the center is in the middle, and in a
sphere only that which is in the middle can be at the
bottom. Now if the earth is at the bottom, it follows
that all things must gravitate towards it. Nature
always draws weights towards the bottom; obviously
this was done that there might be an earth in the uni-
verse. . . . To this point which is the bottom and
middle, so to speak, and is stationary because it is the
center, all weights must be drawn . . . .

112. *E se' or sotto l'emisperio giunto*: From "sotto" in this
verse and "coverchia" and "sotto 'l cui colmo" in vs. 114
it is clear that Virgil is speaking of the celestial hemisphere.
emisperio = emisfero.

113-15. *ch'è contraposto a quel . . . pecca*: On medieval
maps of the world Jerusalem is represented as being at the
center of the "hemisphere" of land. This conception is based
on scriptural authority; see Ezech. 5:5: "Haec dicit Dominus
Deus: Ista est Ierusalem, in medio gentium posui eam, et in
circuitu eius terras." ("Thus saith the Lord God: This is
Jerusalem. I have set her in the midst of the nations and the
countries round about her.") To mark this fact, such maps
frequently show Christ at the center hanging on the Cross.
Dante's verses clearly reflect this feature. For "la gran secca"
denoting the hemisphere of land, see Gen. 1:9–10: "Dixit
vero Deus: Congregentur aquae quae sub caelo sunt in
locum unum, et appareat arida. Et factum est ita. Et
vocavit Deus aridam terram, congregationesque aquarum
appellavit maria." ("Then God said, 'Let the waters be-
low the heavens be gathered into one place and let the
dry land appear.' And so it was. God called the dry land
Earth and the assembled waters Seas.")

Jerusalem, being at the center of the dry land, is directly
over the cavity of Hell. Dante and Virgil will now climb
to a point on the surface of the globe directly opposite
Jerusalem. (See Fig. 3, p. 43, and Fig. 7, p. 640.)

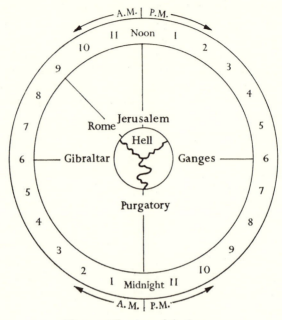

Figure 7. The time of the journey

115. *l'uom*: Christ, never named in Hell.   *che naque . . . sanza pecca*: Without original sin.   *e visse sanza pecca*: Without actual or personal sin.

116. *picciola spera*: A relatively small "disc" of stone corresponding ("l'altra faccia," vs. 117) to the fourth circular subdivision ("disc") of Cocytus, which finally receives its name in the next verse.

117. *la Giudecca*: Judecca, the innermost zone of Cocytus, is named, first of all, for the arch-sinner Judas who dangles from the central mouth of Satan. But the name was also commonly used, in Dante's time as later, for the ghetto in which Jews were confined in European cities.

118–20. *Qui . . . sì come prim' era*: These verses answer the questions the wayfarer asked in vss. 103–5.

640

118. *Qui*: Virgil speaks as one who stands beneath the zenith of the hemisphere opposite Jerusalem (referred to as "di là").   *è da man, quando di là è sera*: There is thus a difference of twelve hours between the two hemispheres, with respect to the meridian of Jerusalem and to the other directly opposite to it. But by assigning evening to the meridian of Jerusalem and morning to the other one, Dante makes it twelve hours earlier in the hemisphere opposite to Jerusalem, even as the time reference above has already suggested. This arrangement is completely arbitrary on the part of the poet, but by setting the clock back twelve hours he gains an entire Saturday (Holy Saturday at that) for the climb from center. From what we are told in vs. 68 (see n. to that verse), we know it was then 6:00 P.M. We know (from Malacoda and the time reference of *Inf.* XXI, 112–14) that it is the evening of Holy Saturday. From what we are then told in vs. 96 we know that it is 7:30 of the previous morning, or ten and one half hours earlier. (About an hour and a half was required to climb down and then up Satan's body to the point where the two pilgrims now find themselves.) Thus, we realize now, looking back, that the descent through Hell has required twenty-four hours—the night of Good Friday and the day of Holy Saturday. And now a whole new Saturday lies before the wayfarers for their ascent to the surface of the earth, which, like the descent to the center, takes twenty-four hours (beginning the ascent at the center of the earth).

119. *questi*: Lucifer.   *ne = ci.*

121. *Da questa parte*: Cf. "qui," vs. 118. Virgil now speaks as if he were actually standing on the surface of the earth in the hemisphere opposite Jerusalem.   *cadde giù dal cielo*: That Satan should fall to earth at a point directly antipodal to Jerusalem is Dante's own grandiose myth. In creating this myth Dante is exercising his privilege as a poet in no way bound by doctrine or by Aristotelian science (see J. Freccero, 1961b). For the fall itself there is good scriptural authority, even for a fall to a "lacus" (Cocytus is termed a "lago" in *Inf.* XXXII, 23) and to the

cold part of the earth (in "lateribus aquilonis"); see Isa. 14:12–15:

> Quomodo cecidisti de caelo lucifer, qui mane oriebaris? Corruisti in terram, qui vulnerabas gentes, qui dicebas in corde tuo: In caelum conscendam, super astra Dei exaltabo solium meum, sedebo in monte testamenti in lateribus aquilonis; ascendam super altitudinem nubium, similis ero Altissimo. Verumtamen ad infernum detraheris, in profundum laci.

> How art thou fallen from heaven, O Lucifer, who didst rise in the morning? How art thou fallen to the earth, that didst wound the nations?
>   And thou saidst in thy heart: I will ascend into heaven. I will exalt my throne above the stars of God. I will sit in the mountain of the covenant, in the sides of the north.
>   I will ascend above the height of the clouds. I will be like the most High.
>   But yet thou shalt be brought down to hell, into the depth of the pit.

Also see Apoc. 12:9.

122–24. *e la terra . . . nostro*: Myth on the grandest scale thus continues. Before Satan's fall, dry land stood forth ("si sporse") from the waters of the hemisphere opposite the future site of Jerusalem; but the land, shrinking to avoid being touched by the arch-sinner as he fell, removed itself to the other hemisphere, causing the land there to rise higher above the waters than it had done previously.

124. *emisperio nostro*: The hemisphere inhabited by us.

124–26. *e forse . . . ricorse*: Now the myth, qualified with "forse," passes to another notable occurrence, another displacement of earth which, in order to flee Satan, "ran up" itself to the surface of the earth, directly opposite Jerusalem ("di qua"), to form what is here referred to as "quella [i.e., terra] ch'appar di qua," a feature the reader is not in a position to understand as yet, but which will prove to be the mountain of Purgatory and the only land in this hemisphere of water. The "empty place" ("loco vòto") left by the displacement of earth has already been termed a "natural burella" (vs. 98) and will now be called (vs. 128) "la tomba." Thus the earth which flees to form Satan's "grave" as he falls forms the mountain of Purgatory. See Isa. 14:9: "Infernus subter conturbatus est in occursum adventus tui." ("Hell below was [disturbed in meeting] thee at thy coming.")

127. *Luogo è là giù da Belzebù remoto*: The reader can easily lose his bearings as he passes from Virgil's words of explanation to these which return to the narrative. We must realize, of course, that "là giù" is now spoken (written) by the poet as one who has returned to "our hemisphere," the hemisphere with Jerusalem at its center, and that the words point down from there, point through the earth and down to the place where the wayfarer was standing when his guide told him about the displacement of earth and the formation of Satan's tomb. Accordingly "da Belzebù remoto" indicates (looking down along Satan's body now, from head to foot) that point at which the "burella" or "tomba" terminates as an "empty space." At that terminus is the "hollow" (vs. 131) in the rock, formed by the erosive action of a little stream. The two pilgrims are guided now by sound to the "hollow," through which they then enter a hidden passageway through the rock, formed by erosion.

On the view that "tomba" is the same space which was called "burella" before, and for a refutation of other views, see M. Barbi (1934b), pp. 244–46. *Belzebù*: Beelzebub, the "prince of devils" (see Matt. 12:24–27), is identified with Satan.

130–32. *un ruscelletto . . . pende*: All continues to be dark and mysterious. We are never told what this "little stream" is. Does it flow down from Purgatory, perhaps from the river Lethe? Nothing of the sort is anywhere affirmed. All we are ever told is that this is a stream which, having worn away by erosion a winding and gently sloping course, offers a passageway through which the two way-farers can climb from Satan's "tomb" to the surface of the earth, a way which nobody except just such a pilgrim as Dante (so exceptional a pilgrim as Dante) would ever use. Indeed, in vs. 133, it is said to be "ascoso" (i.e., found by few—few indeed!). No allegory or symbolism seems to be implied in this; all is strictly within the literal dimension of the narrative. This is simply the way which they found, and which they took.

Perhaps the most striking part of the whole invention is the poet's determination that the journey from Hell to Purgatory should be made under normal and natural phys-ical conditions, when he might perfectly well have had him-self transported to the next realm in a more mysterious or supernatural way; but the latter means of transport he has long since abandoned (cf. the crossing of Acheron, *Inf.* III, 130–36).

137–38. *de le cose belle che porta 'l ciel*: See *Inf.* I, 37–40.

138. *per un pertugio tondo*: This seems to be the exit of the passageway through which the two wayfarers have climbed.

139. *a riveder le stelle*: Each of the three *cantiche* closes with the word "stelle"; this ending serves to point elo-quently to the upward way of the journey from now on and seems to exhort the reader to look up also, on *his* journey in this life.

NOTE

The spider's touch, how exquisitely fine!
Feels at each thread, and lives along the line.

POPE, Essay on Man

THE lines of Dante's great poem number 14,233. The web, to keep Pope's figure, is vast indeed; and well nigh any commentator who sets about to feel at every thread and live along these lines could easily produce a gloss on that experience which would fill many more volumes of commentary than the three that are planned in the present edition.

Many are the problems that cry for comment—indeed the problems that remain unsolved in our understanding of this great poetic structure are still many, despite the centuries-old exegetical labor that has been expended on it. One thing seems certain: Dante scholars will always find new problems, and continue to propose new solutions to the old problems.

A vast *glossa ordinaria* has grown up around the *Commedia* over the years. In this regard I wish here to declare my own very special debt to one reference work in particular, to Paget Toynbee's *Dante Dictionary*, a work which in its newly revised version may now be found on almost all library shelves, bearing still its original leisurely title: *A Dictionary of Proper Names and Notable Matters in the Works of Dante* by Paget Toynbee, Revised by Charles S. Singleton, Oxford, 1968.

Since in the making of the present commentary I have drawn so extensively on Toynbee's work, it seems proper here to quote from my own Preface to my revision of it:

Paget Toynbee's *Dictionary of Proper Names and Notable Matters* first appeared in print in 1898 and was soon acclaimed, as among the several such reference works on Dante then in existence, quite the best of them all. As E. G. Gardner was to say later in a *Memoir* on Toynbee, this *Dictionary* was "a work on a grand scale, illustrated with copious extracts from original sources, which is still [in 1932] invaluable to every student of the poet."

Toynbee was a passionate compiler of "facts." One might alter a familiar phrase and say that he truly had the *fonction compilatrice* as a great passion, to the point that, for the *Dictionary*, he had the patience, for instance, to count every reference to God in the works of Dante and every reference to Aristotle—and both not only in actual name but in *pronoun* reference!

By the year of Toynbee's death (1932) this, his *magnum opus* (which he never revised in its unabridged form), was clearly showing the familiar signs of being out of date—having been, by Toynbee's own admission, out of print since 1913. For one thing, the critical edition in one volume of Dante's works sponsored by the Società Dantesca Italiana of Florence had come out in 1921, in observance of the sixth centenary of the poet's death, and had readily been accepted as the standard critical text which any student of Dante would turn to—yet here was Toynbee's unrevised *Dictionary* with its thousands of references to the works of Dante, all to the *Oxford Dante* which Edward Moore and Toynbee had brought out long before the Italians achieved their own one-volume edition.

This was symptomatic of a widening gap which naturally increased in the first decades of our century, with Dante scholarship, particularly in its philological and historical phases, flourishing greatly in just those years. Obviously, with so many new facts and historical perspectives on Dante coming to light during that time, no such work as Toynbee's *Dictionary* could possibly continue to be entirely useful to readers and students of the poet. Still, it may be noted that as late as 1934, for instance, the year in which G. Busnelli and G. Vandelli published their two-volume commentary of Dante's *Convivio*, the *Dictionary* was still serving Dante scholars in Italy remarkably well, as is abundantly evident from their many references to Toynbee.

All of which may serve to suggest why it is that now, thirty-four years after Toynbee's death and sixty-eight years after the publication of his *Dictionary*, this work has seemed worth all the effort it has cost to bring it up to date in every possible respect and to incorporate, even as Toynbee had said in his Preface, "such information as had become available concerning the various persons and places mentioned or referred to in the works of Dante," as well as some additional "Notable Matters," as he had termed them. . . .

This revision of Toynbee's *Dictionary* amounted, finally, to a re-scrutiny of over sixty years of Dante scholarship (and Dante studies had rather flourished, particularly in the historical sense, during the better part of that time!); and as I think back now over the years of patient work this has required, I feel prompted to echo words which Toynbee set down about himself in his own Preface, where he wrote: "I am not sanguine enough to suppose that I have succeeded in every instance in bringing all the articles wholly up to date"; as I am also tempted to echo the plea he voiced regarding "the wide extent of the field which had to be explored, and the 'quel d'Adamo,' as Dante puts it, *l'incarco della carne d'Adamo*, beneath which the energies of even the most ardent explorers will sometimes flag."

Toynbee's *Dante Dictionary*, thus revised, constitutes the vast storehouse of information ("in a convenient and concise form") concerning persons and places and notable matters in the works of Dante that he intended it to be. Let it be said that, of course, a discerning student of Dante will soon realize, in using the work, that he will turn to it in vain for critical insights into the structure of Dante's poetry as such, or for elucidation in matters of allegory or symbolism. This is a dictionary of "the facts." Hence one readily conceives that a proper and fruitful use might be made of it by at least two kinds of readers, one of whom would turn to this volume, as to any reference work, simply to find out whether a given person or place figures anywhere in Dante's works, and if so, how and where. For such a reader Toynbee's patient account of the context in which that name appears will be much appreciated, this being surely a part of the information desired. On the other hand, there will be the reader who comes directly to the *Dictionary* from his study of the *Comedy*, say, and who does not need to be told how a given person or place enters into the action or the argument, and will pass over that portion to come to the historical sources in direct quotation which Toynbee offers him, from Villani or from Benvenuto, and which, in most instances, will constitute the most comprehensive gloss in this sense that he is likely to find on the item in question.

To this I need only add that my revision of the *Dictionary* was undertaken, in the first place, mainly as a necessary re-scrutiny of all the pertinent "facts" that predictably would come into this my present commentary. The *Dictionary*, I told myself, would serve as a vast storehouse of information, now re-examined and certified in its contents, a store on which (having *earned* the privilege, so to say) I might freely draw with familiarity and assurance. And this has indeed been done, so that nearly every gloss on the hundreds of persons and places named in the course of this long poem has been taken, in part at least, from the revised *Dictionary*. At times, no doubt, I have exceeded due measure for the "average" reader, at least. But then, as I always told myself, let each reader choose according to the scope of his own interests and his own sense of relevance. Or as Dante puts it:

> Or ti riman, lettor, sovra 'l tuo banco,
> dietro pensando a ciò che si preliba,
> s'esser vuoi lieto assai prima che stanco.
> Messo t'ho innanzi: omai per te ti ciba . . .
>
> *(Par.* X, 22–25)

Stay now, reader, on your bench, thinking over this of which you have a foretaste, if you would have joy long before you are weary. I have set before you; now feed yourself . . . .

A final remark on what I would term a *reader's respect* for the unfolding form of this great structure, and on the way in which I have sought to observe that respect. Take the case of the three beasts, the wolf, the lion, the leopard, which come to beset the wayfarer in the very first canto. We glimpse the *possible* significance of this famous trio, but glimpse it only dimly in the rapid narrative at this point; but retrospectively, *as the poem develops*, we see less dimly what the full meaning of the three beasts can be. Now, shall the commentator attempt to tell the reader at this point, in Canto I, all that he is finally to understand about the beasts when he has finished his thoughtful reading of the whole poem? Surely that would be a sad mistake in exegesis, would even defeat the proper reading of this (or many another) poetic structure. The *experience* of poetry which this *Comedy* holds potentially, for every reader who will make the effort, is precisely the experience of a gradual revelation of meaning, an *unveiling* (which happens to be the literal meaning of *revelatio*). Emerging meanings build on to what has gone before, and when this happens, *then* it is the commentator's duty to note it, but not before. Dante built his structure to contain its "mystery," to be big with mystery, until such time, such *times* within the poem, as it may be delivered of those

NOTE

meanings. It is the proper business of a commentator to respect that principle and to observe those times of delivery.

Many a problem in understanding awaits reader and commentator down the long unfolding line of this poem, hard problems indeed, in allegory, in symbolism, in patterns of meaning broad in nature and visible only from great pivotal points in this journey to God. Solutions to such problems will be attempted only in a supplementary volume which may well bear the title *Essays and Excursuses*. Meanwhile the reader will have to bear with patience an ever-growing burden of unresolved meanings until he himself has won to the vantage ground of a fuller experience of the whole and to those vistas in retrospect through which a full, or a fuller, understanding of the total meaning may be had.

C.S.S. ☐

List of Works Cited
and of Abbreviations

ABBREVIATIONS

a.   articulus

Aen.   Aeneid (Virgil)

*Anonimo fiorentino   Commento alla Divina Commedia
d'anonimo fiorentino del secolo XIV*

Ars amat.   Ars amatoria (Ovid)

*Comm. in somn. Scip.   Commentariorum in somnium
Scipionis* (Macrobius)

Conf.   Confessiones (Augustine)

Consol. philos.   Consolatio philosophiae (Boethius)

Conv.   Convivio (Dante Alighieri)

Decam.   Il Decameron (Giovanni Boccaccio)

*De civ. Dei   Ad Marcellinum De civitate Dei contra
paganos* (Augustine)

De fin.   De finibus bonorum et malorum (Cicero)

Della comp.   Della composizione del mondo (Ristoro
d'Arezzo)

De mon.   De monarchia (Dante Alighieri)

De nat. deor.   De natura deorum (Cicero)

De reg. prin.   De regimine principum ad regem Cypri
(Thomas Aquinas)

De vulg. eloqu.   De vulgari eloquentia (Dante Alighieri)

Eclog.   Eclogues (Virgil)

Enar. in Ps.   Enarrationes in Psalmos (Augustine)

Epist.   *Epistolae* (Dante Alighieri)

Epist. mor.   *Ad Lucilium Epistulae morales* (Seneca)

Eth. Nicom.   *Ethica Nicomachea* (Aristotle)

Etym.   *Etymologiarum sive Originum libri viginti* (Isidore of Seville)

Exp. Eth. Nicom.   *In decem libros Ethicorum ad Nicomachum expositio* (Thomas Aquinas)

Exp. Metaphys.   *In duodecim libros Metaphysicorum expositio* (Thomas Aquinas)

Exp. Phys.   *In octo libros Physicorum expositio* (Thomas Aquinas)

Exp. Polit.   *In octo libros Politicorum expositio* (Thomas Aquinas)

Exp. I super Apoc.   *Expositio I super Apocalypsim* (Thomas Aquinas)

Fact. dict. memor.   *Factorum et dictorum memorabilium libri novem* (Valerius Maximus)

Geneal. deor. gent.   *Genealogie deorum gentilium* (Giovanni Boccaccio)

Georg.   *Georgics* (Virgil)

Hist.   *Historiarum adversum paganos libri septem* (Orosius)

Hist. schol.   *Historia scholastica eruditissimi viri Magistri Petri Comestoris* (Petrus Comestor)

In Cat.   *In Catilinam I-IV* (Cicero)

Inf.   *Inferno* (Dante Alighieri)

In Ioan.   *In Ioannis evangelium tractatus CXXIV* (Augustine)

In Ioan. evangel.   *In Ioannem evangelistam expositio* (Thomas Aquinas)

LCL   Loeb Classical Library

lect.   lectio

Metam.   *Metamorphoses* (Ovid)

Metaphys.   *Metaphysica* (Aristotle)

MLN   *Modern Language Notes*

MLR   *Modern Language Review*

mod.   modern

Moral.   *Moralium libri, sive Expositio in librum b. Iob* (Gregory I)

Nat. hist.   *Naturalis historia* (Pliny)

obj.   objectio

OFr   Old French

OI   Old Italian

Par.   *Paradiso* (Dante Alighieri)

Phars.   *Pharsalia* (Lucan)

Phys.   *Physicorum libri octo* (Albertus Magnus)

P.L.   *Patrologiae cursus completus: Series Latina*, ed. J.-P. Migne. Paris, 1844–64 (with later printings).

PMLA   *Publications of the Modern Language Association of America*

Polit.   *Politica* (Aristotle)

Purg.   *Purgatorio* (Dante Alighieri)

q.   quaestio

resp.   respondeo

RIS   *Rerum Italicarum scriptores ab anno aerae Christianae quingentesimo ad millesimum quingentesimum*, ed. L. A. Muratori. Milan, 1723–51. New edn.: *Rerum Italicarum scriptores; Raccolta degli storici italiani dal cinquecento al millecinquecento*, rev. under the direction of G. Carducci, V. Fiorini, P. Fedele. Città di Castello, Bologna, 1900– (in progress).

Summa theol.   *Summa theologica* (Thomas Aquinas)

Suppl.   Supplementum

Tav. riton.   *La tavola ritonda o l'istoria di Tristano*

Theb.   *Thebaid* (Statius)

Tusc. disp.   *Tusculanae disputationes* (Cicero)

LIST OF WORKS CITED

Unless specifically and otherwise stated, all classical Greek and Latin texts cited in the *Commentary* to the *Inferno* are available in the Loeb Classical Library, to which the reader should refer.

Aesop. *Favole d'Esopo volgarizzate per uno da Siena.* Florence, 1864.

Albertus Magnus. *Opera omnia,* ed. Auguste and Émile Borgnet. Paris, 1890–99: *De animalibus,* vol. XI; *De meteoris,* vol. IV; *Physicorum libri VIII,* vol. III.

Alighieri, Dante. *La Commedia secondo l'antica vulgata,* ed. Giorgio Petrocchi. Vol. I: *Introduzione*; vol. II: *Inferno.* Milan, 1966.

———. *Le opere di Dante: Testo critico della Società Dantesca Italiana.* 2d edn. Florence, 1960:

    Convivio, ed. Ernesto Giacomo Parodi and Flaminio Pellegrini, pp. 143–293.

    De vulgari eloquentia, ed. Pio Rajna, pp. 295–327.

    La Divina Commedia, ed. Giuseppe Vandelli, pp. 443–798.

    Epistole, ed. Ermenegildo Pistelli, pp. 383–415.

    Monarchia, ed. Enrico Rostagno, pp. 329–81.

Rime; Rime dubbie, ed. Michele Barbi, pp. 51–142.

Vita nuova, ed. Michele Barbi, pp. 1–49.

————. TRANSLATIONS

The Convivio of Dante Alighieri, trans. Philip H. Wicksteed. The Temple Classics. London, 1903.

A Translation of the Latin Works of Dante Alighieri. The Temple Classics. London, 1940:

> *The De monarchia*, trans. Philip H. Wicksteed, pp. 125–280.

> *The De vulgari eloquentia*, trans. A. G. Ferrers Howell, pp. 1–115.

> *Epistolae*, trans. Philip H. Wicksteed, pp. 293–368.

The Vita Nuova and Canzoniere of Dante Alighieri. The Temple Classics. London, 1906:

> *Canzoniere*, ed. Thomas Okey, trans. Philip H. Wicksteed, pp. 155–323.

> *Vita nuova*, ed. and trans. Thomas Okey, pp. 2–153.

Ancona, Alessandro d'. "La leggenda di Maometto in Occidente." *Giornale storico della letteratura italiana* XIII (1889): 199–281.

Andreas Capellanus. *De amore*, ed. E. Trojel. Copenhagen, 1892.

————. *The Art of Courtly Love*, trans. John Jay Parry. New York, 1941.

Angiolieri, Cecco. *See* Marti, Mario (1956).

Anselm. *Dialogus de casu diaboli*. In Migne, *P.L.* CLVIII.

Antonelli, Giovanni. *Di alcuni studi speciali risguardanti la meteorologia, la geometria, la geodesia e la Divina Commedia*. Florence, 1871.

Appel, Carl (ed.). *Die Lieder Bertrans von Born*. Halle, 1932.

Aquinas, Thomas. *Opera omnia*. Parma, 1852–73. Photolithographic reimpression, with Introduction by Vernon J. Bourke, New York, 1948–50:

> *De malo*, vol. VIII

> *De regimine principum ad regem Cypri*, vol. XVI

> *De veritate Catholicae fidei contra Gentiles seu Summa philosophica*, vol. V

Expositio I super Apocalypsim, vol. XXIII
In X libros Ethicorum ad Nicomachum expositio,
vol. XXI
In XII libros Metaphysicorum expositio, vol. XX
In Ioannem evangelistam expositio, vol. X
In VIII libros Physicorum expositio, vol. XVIII
In VIII libros Politicorum expositio, vol. XXI
Summa theologica, vols. I–IV.

————. MARIETTI PUBLICATIONS

In decem libros Ethicorum Aristotelis ad Nicomachum expositio, ed. Raimondo M. Spiazzi, O.P. 3rd edn. Turin, 1964.

In duodecim libros Metaphysicorum Aristotelis expositio, ed. Raimondo M. Spiazzi, O.P. Turin, 1964.

In libros Politicorum Aristotelis expositio, ed. Raimondo M. Spiazzi, O.P. Turin, 1951.

In octo libros Physicorum Aristotelis expositio, ed. P. M. Maggiòlo, O.P. Turin, 1954.

————. TRANSLATIONS

Commentary on Aristotle's Physics, trans. Richard J. Blackwell, Richard J. Spath, and W. Edmund Thirlkel. New Haven, 1963.

Commentary on the Metaphysics of Aristotle, trans. John P. Rowan. 2 vols. Chicago, 1961.

Commentary on the Nicomachean Ethics, trans. C. E. Litzinger, O.P. 2 vols. Chicago, 1964.

On the Truth of the Catholic Faith, Summa contra Gentiles, Book III: Providence, trans. Vernon J. Bourke. 2 vols. Garden City, N.Y., 1956.

Summa theologica, trans. Fathers of the English Dominican Province. 3 vols. New York, 1947–48.

Aristotle. "Antiqua Translatio" in Thomas Aquinas, *Opera omnia,* Parma, 1852–73. Photolithographic reimpression, with Introduction by Vernon J. Bourke, New York, 1948–50:

De anima, vol. XX
De caelo, vol. XIX
Ethica Nicomachea, vol. XXI
Metaphysica, vol. XX

Physica, vol. xviii

Politica, vol. xxi

————. MARIETTI PUBLICATIONS

De anima. In Thomas Aquinas, *In Aristotelis librum De anima commentarium*, ed. Angelo M. Pirotta, O.P. 2d edn. Turin, 1936.

De caelo. In Thomas Aquinas, *In Aristotelis libros De caelo et mundo, De generatione et corruptione, Meteorologicorum expositio*, ed. Raimondo M. Spiazzi, O.P. Turin, 1952.

Ethica Nicomachea. In Thomas Aquinas, *In decem libros Ethicorum Aristotelis ad Nicomachum expositio*, ed. Raimondo M. Spiazzi, O.P. 3rd edn. Turin, 1964.

Metaphysica. In Thomas Aquinas, *In duodecim libros Metaphysicorum Aristotelis expositio*, ed. Raimondo M. Spiazzi, O.P. Turin, 1964.

Politica. In Thomas Aquinas, *In libros Politicorum Aristotelis expositio*, ed. Raimondo M. Spiazzi, O.P. Turin, 1951.

————. TRANSLATIONS

Metaphysics. In Thomas Aquinas, *Commentary on the Metaphysics of Aristotle*, trans. John P. Rowan. Vol. ii. Chicago, 1961.

Nicomachean Ethics. In Thomas Aquinas, *Commentary on the Nicomachean Ethics*, trans. C. I. Litzinger, O.P. 2 vols. Chicago, 1964.

Augustine. *Ad Marcellinum De civitate Dei contra paganos*. In Migne, *P.L.* xli.

————. *The City of God, Books XVII–XXII*, trans. Gerald G. Walsh, S.J. and Daniel J. Honan. New York, 1954.

————. *Enarrationes in Psalmos*. In Migne, *P.L.* xxxvi.

————. *In Ioannis evangelium tractatus CXXIV*. In Migne, *P.L.* xxxv.

————. *St. Augustine's Confessions*, trans. William Watts (1631), preface by W. H. D. Rouse. 2 vols. LCL, 1912.

Austin, H. D. "Gleanings from 'Dante's Latin Dictionary.'" *Italica* xii (1935): 81–90.

Bacci, Peleo. *Dante e Vanni Fucci secondo una tradizione ignota.* Pistoia, 1892.

Baehrens, Emil (ed.). Lactantius, "Carmen de ave Phoenice." In *Poetae Latini minores.* Vol. III, pp. 247–62. Leipzig, 1881.

Barbi, Michele. Review of Paget Toynbee, *A Dictionary of Proper Names and Notable Matters in the Works of Dante,* 1898. In *Bullettino della Società Dantesca Italiana* N.S. VI (1899): 201–17.

———. Review of Dante Alighieri, *La Divina Commedia riveduta nel testo e commentata da G. A. Scartazzini,* 4th edn., revised by G. Vandelli, 1903. In *Bullettino della Società Dantesca Italiana* N.S. X (1903): 1–8.

———. " 'Non esser duro più ch'altri sia stato,' *Inf.* XXVII, 56." *Studi danteschi* I (1920): 137–42.

———. "Ancora delle 'cerchie eterne' (*Inf.* XVIII, 72)." *Studi danteschi* IV (1921): 130–33.

———. "Il canto di Farinata." *Studi danteschi* VIII (1924a): 87–109.

———. "Le 'cerchie eterne.' " *Studi danteschi* VIII (1924b): 164.

———. " 'Sozza e scapigliata fante' (*Inf.* XVIII, 130)." *Studi danteschi* IX (1924c): 159–60.

———. " 'Burella' e 'cammino ascoso' (*Inf.,* XXXIV, 98 e 133)." *Studi danteschi* X (1925a): 81–91.

———. " 'Vegna il cavalier sovrano . . . ' (*Inf.,* XVII, 72)." *Studi danteschi* X (1925b): 55–80.

———. "Per due similitudini dell'*Inferno* (*Inf.* III 112–17; V 40–45)." *Studi danteschi* XI (1927): 121–28.

———. "Inf. XXI, 67–69." *Studi danteschi* XIII (1928): 62–63.

———. "Con Dante e coi suoi interpreti: II. Francesca da Rimini." *Studi danteschi* XVI (1932): 5–36.

———. *Dante: Vita, opere, e fortuna.* Florence, 1933.

———. "Ancora sul testo della *Divina Commedia.*" *Studi danteschi* XVIII (1934a): 5–57.

———. *Problemi di critica dantesca: Prima serie (1893–1918).* Florence, 1934b.

———. "Per un nuovo commento della *Divina Commedia.*" *Studi danteschi* xix (1935): 5–55.

———. "Ancora per un nuovo commento della *Divina Commedia.*" *Studi danteschi* xxi (1937): 93–156.

———. "Nuovi problemi della critica dantesca." *Studi danteschi* xxiii (1938): 5–77.

——— and Duro, A. "Peccatrici o pectatrici?" *Studi danteschi* xxviii (1949): 11–43.

Bassermann, Alfred. *Orme di Dante in Italia,* trans. from the 2d German edn. by Egidio Gorra. Bologna, 1902.

———. "Auslese aus einem Dante-Kommentar." *Deutsches Dante-Jahrbuch* xiv (N.S. v) (1932): 139–84.

Benoît de Sainte-Maure. *Le Roman de Troie,* ed. Léopold Constans. Vol. iv. Paris, 1908.

Bernard de Ventadour. *See* Raynouard, M. (1818).

Bernard of Clairvaux. *Epistolas numero CDLXXXII.* In Migne, *P.L.* clxxxii.

Bertoni, Giulio. *Cinque "letture" dantesche.* Modena, 1933.

Bianchi, Enrico. "Le 'cerchie eterne' (*Inf.*, XVIII, 72)." *Studi danteschi* iii (1921): 137–39.

Biscaro, Gerolamo. "Dante e il buon Gherardo." *Studi medievali* N.S. i (1928): 74–113.

Boccaccio, Giovanni. *Il Decameron,* ed. Charles S. Singleton. 2 vols. Bari, 1955.

———. *Genealogie deorum gentilium,* ed. Vincenzo Romano. Vol. i. Bari, 1951.

———. *Teseida,* ed. Salvatore Battaglia. Florence, 1938.

Boethius. *The Consolation of Philosophy.* In *The Theological Tractates,* ed. and trans. H. F. Stewart and E. K. Rand; *The Consolation of Philosophy,* trans. "I.T." (1609). Revised by H. F. Stewart, pp. 128–411. LCL, 1962.

Boffito, Giuseppe. "La circolazione del sangue secondo Cecco d'Ascoli"; "La circolazione del sangue secondo Dante Alighieri." *Rivista di fisica, matematica e scienze naturali* ser. 2, vi (1932): 182–88, 287–92, 448–55.

Boncompagni, Baldassarre. *Della vita e delle opere di Guido Bonatti, astrologo ed astronomo del secolo decimoterzo.* Rome, 1851.

Bongi, S. "Ingiurie, improperi, contumelie ecc. Saggio di lingua parlata del Trecento cavato dai libri criminali di Lucca." *Il Propugnatore* N.S. III (1890), pt. 1: 75–134.

Borghini, Vincenzo. "Errori di alcuni commentatori di Dante e principalmente di un falso Vellutello; Sensi e voci dichiarate nelle lor proprietà, e valore." In *Studi sulla Divina Commedia di Galileo Galilei, Vincenzo Borghini ed altri*, ed. Ottavio Gigli, pp. 227–67. Florence, 1855.

Born, Bertran de. *See* Appel, Carl (1932).

Bosco, Umberto. "Particolari danteschi." *Annali della R. Scuola Normale Superiore di Pisa, lettere, storia e filosofia* ser. 2, XI (1942): 131–47.

———. *Lectura Dantis scaligera: Il canto XV dell'Inferno.* Florence, 1961.

Branciforti, Francesco (ed.). *Il canzoniere di Lanfranco Cigala.* Florence, 1954.

Britt (O.S.B.), Matthew (ed.). *The Hymns of the Breviary and Missal.* Rev. edn. New York, 1955.

Bullettino della Società Dantesca Italiana N.S. IX (1902): 257–58. Review of J. Kohler, "Der summarische Strafprozess zu Dantes Zeit," *Archiv für Strafrecht und Strafprozess* XLVIII (1901): 109–10.

Busnelli, Giovanni. *L'Etica Nicomachea e l'ordinamento morale dell'Inferno di Dante.* Bologna, 1907.

Butler, H. E. *The Sixth Book of the Aeneid.* Oxford, 1920.

Camilli, Amerindo. "I fiumi infernali nel canto XIV dell'*Inferno.*" *Studi danteschi* XXVII (1943): 135–40.

Camus, Jules. "L'Expression de Dante 'ei si batte l'anca.' " *Giornale storico della letteratura italiana* XLIII (1904): 166–68.

Capetti, Vittorio. *Illustrazioni al poema di Dante.* Città di Castello, 1913.

Casella, Mario. "Questioni di geografia dantesca." *Studi danteschi* XII (1927): 65–77.

Casini, Tommaso. Review of Francesco Cipolla, "La lonza di Dante," *Rassegna bibliografica della letteratura italiana* III (1895): 103–14. In *Bullettino della Società Dantesca Italiana* N.S. II (1895): 116–20.

———. *Scritti danteschi*. Città di Castello, 1913.

Cavalcanti, Guido. *See* Monaci, Ernesto (1955).

———. *See* Contini, Gianfranco (1960).

Cessi, Roberto. "Jacopo da Sant'Andrea." *Bollettino del Museo Civico di Padova* XI (1908): 49–53.

La Chanson de Roland, ed. T. Atkinson Jenkins. Boston, 1924.

Chaucer, Geoffrey. *The Works of Geoffrey Chaucer*, ed. F. N. Robinson. 2d edn. London, 1957.

Chiappelli, Alessandro. *Dalla trilogia di Dante*. Florence, 1905.

———. "Un ricordo, non avvertito, della 'Firenze antica' nella *Divina Commedia*." *Il Marzocco* (Florence), Nov. 23, 1930, p. 3.

Chiari, Alberto. *Letture dantesche*. Florence, 1939.

Chisholm, A. R. "The Prototype of Dante's Geryon (*Inferno*, XVI and XVII)." *MLR* XXIV (1929): 451–54.

Chistoni, Paride. "La lonza dantesca." In *Miscellanea di studi critici edita in onore di Arturo Graf*, pp. 817–48. Bergamo, 1903.

Ciacci, Gaspero. *Gli Aldobrandeschi nella storia e nella Divina Commedia*. Vol. I. Rome, 1935.

Ciampi, Sebastiano. *Notizie inedite della sagrestia pistoiese de' belli arredi, del Campo Santo pisano, e di altre opere di disegno dal secolo XII al XV*. Florence, 1810.

Cian, Vittorio. "Vivaldo Belcalzer e l'enciclopedismo italiano delle origini." *Giornale storico della letteratura italiana*, supplement V (1902).

———. *Oltre l'enigma dantesco del Veltro*. 2nd edn. Turin, 1945.

Cigala, Lanfranco. *See* Branciforti, Francesco (1954).

Cipolla, Carlo. "Sulla descrizione dantesca delle tombe di Arles." *Giornale storico della letteratura italiana* XXIII (1894): 407–15.

Cipolla, Francesco. "Il Gerione di Dante." *Atti del R. Istituto Veneto di Scienze, Lettere ed Arti* ser. 7, VI (1894–95): 706–10.

Compagni, Dino. *La cronica di Dino Compagni delle cose occorrenti ne' tempi suoi*, ed. Isidoro Del Lungo. In *RIS* ix, pt. 2. New edn.

Comparetti, Domenico. *Virgilio nel Medio Evo*, ed. Giorgio Pasquali. Vol. 1. Florence, 1955.

Conner, Wayne. "*Inferno* XVIII, 66 ('femmine da conio') and 51 ('pungenti salse')." *Italica* xxxii (1955): 95–103.

Contini, Gianfranco. "Sul XXX dell'*Inferno*." *Paragone* xliv (1953): 3–13.

——— (ed.). *Poeti del Duecento* (2 vols.; Milan, 1960):
Cavalcanti, Guido, vol. ii, pp. 487–567.
Folgore da San Gimignano, vol. ii, pp. 403–19.
Guinizelli, Guido, vol. ii, pp. 447–85.
Latini, Brunetto, vol. ii, pp. 169–284.
Pier della Vigna, vol. i, pp. 119–28.

Cosmo, U. "Le mistiche nozze di frate Francesco con madonna Povertà." *Giornale dantesco* vi (1898): 49–82, 97–118.

Crescini, Vincenzo. *Lectura Dantis: Il canto XXVIII dell'Inferno letto da Vincenzo Crescini nella Sala di Dante in Orsanmichele*. Florence, 1907.

Cronaca riminese dall'anno 1188 fino all'anno 1385. In *RIS* xv, 893–926.

Cronica di Pisa. In *RIS* xv, 973-1088.

Cronica fiorentina compilata nel secolo XIII. In *Testi fiorentini del Dugento e dei primi del Trecento*, ed. Alfredo Schiaffini, pp. 82–150. Florence, 1926.

Curtius, Ernst Robert. *Kritische Essays zur europäischen Literatur*. Bern, 1950.

Dalla Vedova, Giuseppe. "Gli argini della Brenta al tempo di Dante." In *Dante e Padova, Studj storico-critici*, pp. 75–100. Padua, 1865.

Dares Phrygius. *De excidio Troiae historia*, ed. Ferdinand Meister. Leipzig, 1873.

Davidsohn, Robert. *Forschungen zur älteren Geschichte von Florenz*. Vol. 1. Berlin, 1896.

————. "I campioni nudi ed unti." *Bullettino della Società Dantesca Italiana* N.S. vii (1900): 39–43.

————. "I campioni 'nudi ed unti' (*Inf.* XVI, 19)." *Bullettino della Società Dantesca Italiana* N.S. ix (1902): 185–87.

————. *Geschichte von Florenz.* Vol. ii: *Guelfen und Ghibellinen,* 2 parts, 1908. Vol. iii: *Die letzten Kämpfe gegen die Reichsgewalt,* 1912. Berlin.

Debenedetti, Santorre. "Dante e Seneca filosofo." *Studi danteschi* vi (1923a): 5–24.

————. "Gli ultimi versi del canto di Brunetto Latini (*Inf.* XV, 121–24)." *Studi danteschi* vii (1923b): 83–96.

Della Giovanna, Ildebrando. *Lectura Dantis: Il canto XXIII dell'Inferno letto da Ildebrando Della Giovanna nella Sala di Dante in Orsanmichele.* Florence, 1901.

Della Torre, Arnaldo. "L'epistola all' 'amico fiorentino.'" *Bullettino della Società Dantesca Italiana* N.S. xii (1905): 121–74.

Del Lungo, Isidoro. *Dino Compagni e la sua Cronica.* Vol. ii. Florence, 1879.

————. "Alla biografia di ser Brunetto Latini, contributo di documenti." In Thor Sundby (1884), pp. 199–277.

————. *Dante ne' tempi di Dante.* Bologna, 1888.

————. *Dal secolo e dal poema di Dante.* Bologna, 1898.

————. "Canto decimoquarto." In *"Lectura Dantis" genovese.* Vol. ii: *I canti XII-XXIII dell'Inferno,* pp. 77–120. Florence, 1906.

————. *Lectura Dantis: Il canto VI dell'Inferno letto da Isidoro Del Lungo nella Sala di Dante in Orsanmichele.* Florence, 1908.

Dictys Cretensis. *Ephemeridos belli Troiani libri,* ed. Werner Eisenhut. Leipzig, 1958.

Dobelli, Ausonio. "Intorno ad una fonte dantesca." *Bullettino della Società Dantesca Italiana* N.S. iv (1897): 16–17.

Dodds, E. R. *The Greeks and the Irrational.* Berkeley, 1951.

Dorini, Umberto. "Il tradimento del conte Ugolino alla luce di un documento inedito." *Studi danteschi* xii (1927): 31–60.

Du Cange, Charles du Fresne. *Glossarium mediae et infimae Latinitatis*, ed. Léopold Favre. Vols. ii, v. Niort, 1883, 1885.

Fallani, Giovanni. " 'D'entro Siratti': Il paragone della lebbra di Costantino." *Lettere italiane* x (1958): 55–60.
———. *Poesia e teologia nella Divina Commedia*. Vol. ii: *Purgatorio*. Milan, 1961.
Fazio degli Uberti. *Il Dittamondo e le Rime*, ed. Giuseppe Corsi. Vol. i: *Il Dittamondo*. Bari, 1952.
Ferrazzi, Jacopo. *Manuale dantesco*. Vol. iii (1865); vol. iv (1871); vol. v (1877). Bassano.
Ferrero, Giuseppe Guido, and Chimenz, Siro A. *Nuova "Lectura Dantis": Il canto XXV dell'Inferno*. Rome, 1954.
Ferretti, Giovanni. *Saggi danteschi*. Florence, 1950.
Il Fiore. In *Il Fiore e il Detto d'amore*, ed. E. G. Parodi, pp. 1–119. Florence, 1922.
Folgore da San Gimignano. *See* Contini, Gianfranco (1960).
Fragmenta historiae Pisanae, Pisana dialecto conscripta ab anno MCXCI usque ad MCCCXXXVII. In *RIS* xxiv, 643–72.
Freccero, John. "Dante's Firm Foot and the Journey without a Guide." *The Harvard Theological Review* lii (1959): 245–81.
———. "Dante and the Neutral Angels." *The Romanic Review* li (1960): 3–14.
———. "Dante's Pilgrim in a Gyre." *PMLA* lxxvi (1961a), no. 3: 168–81.
———. "Satan's Fall and the *Quaestio de aqua et terra*." *Italica* XXXVIII (1961b): 99–115.
———. "Dante's 'per sé' Angel: the Middle Ground in Nature and in Grace." *Studi danteschi* xxxix (1962): 5–38.
Fubini, Mario. *Lectura Dantis scaligera: Il canto XXVIII dell'Inferno*. Florence, 1962.

Garver, Milton Stahl, and McKenzie, Kenneth. "Il *Bestiario toscano* secondo la lezione dei codici di Parigi e di Roma." *Studj romanzi* viii (1912): 1–100.

Gervase of Tilbury. *Otia imperialia ad Ottonem IV imperatorem.* In *Scriptores rerum Brunsvicensium,* ed. Gottfried Wilhelm Leibniz. I, 881–1005. Hanover, 1707.

Gherardi, Alessandro. *Le consulte della repubblica fiorentina dall'anno MCCLXXX al MCCXCVIII.* Vol. I. Florence, 1896.

Giamboni, Bono. [*Trattati morali*] *Della miseria dell'uomo, Giardino di consolazione, Introduzione alle virtù,* ed. Francesco Tassi. Florence, 1836.

Gibb, Hamilton A. R. *Studies on the Civilization of Islam,* ed. Stanford J. Shaw and William R. Polk. Boston, 1962.

Gilson, Étienne. *Études de philosophie médiévale.* Strasbourg, 1921.

Giordano da Rivalto. *Prediche del beato f. Giordano da Rivalto.* Florence, 1739.

———. *Prediche del beato fra Giordano da Rivalto.* 2 vols. Florence, 1831.

———. *Prediche inedite del b. Giordano da Rivalto dell'ordine de' Predicatori,* ed. Enrico Narducci. Bologna, 1867.

Gorra, Egidio. "Dante e Clemente V." *Giornale storico della letteratura italiana* LXIX (1917): 193–216.

Gozzadini, Giovanni. *Cronaca di Ronzano e memorie di Loderingo d'Andalò, Frate Gaudente.* Bologna, 1851.

———. *Delle torri gentilizie di Bologna e delle famiglie alle quali prima appartennero.* Bologna, 1875.

Graf, Arturo. *Miti, leggende e superstizioni del Medio Evo.* Vol. II. Turin, 1893.

Grandgent, Charles H. *"Quid ploras?" Annual Reports of the Dante Society* XLII–XLIV (1926): 8–18.

Grazzini, Antonio Francesco. *Le Cene di Antonfrancesco Grazzini detto Il Lasca.* Vol. I. Milan, 1815.

Gregory I. *Moralium libri, sive Expositio in librum b. Iob.* In Migne, *P.L.* LXXV.

Grundmann, Herbert. "Dante und Joachim von Fiore zu *Paradiso* X-XII." *Deutsches Dante-Jahrbuch* XIV (N.S. V) (1932): 210–56.

Guerri, Domenico. "'Papé Satan, Papé Satan aleppe!' *(Inf.,* VII, 1)." *Giornale dantesco* XII (1904): 138–42.

———. "Il nome di Dio nella lingua di Adamo secondo il

XXVI del *Paradiso* e il verso di Nembrotte nel XXXI dell'*Inferno*." *Giornale storico della letteratura italiana* LIV (1909): 65–76.

————. "Un astrologo condannato da Dante. Guido Bonatti." *Bullettino della Società Dantesca Italiana* N.S. XXII (1915): 200–54.

Guinizelli, Guido. *See* Contini, Gianfranco (1960).

Guittone d'Arezzo. *Le lettere di frate Guittone d'Arezzo*, ed. Francesco Meriano. Bologna, 1922.

Guyon, Bruno. "Il *Tabernik* di Dante." *Giornale dantesco* XI (1903): 49–59.

Hamilton, George L. "The Gilded Leaden Cloaks of the Hypocrites (*Inferno*, XXIII, 58–66)." *The Romanic Review* XII (1921): 335–52.

Hardie, Colin. "*Inferno* XV, 9: 'Anzi che Chiarentana il caldo senta.'" *MLN* LXXIX (1964): 47–57.

Harting, J. E. "Brunetto Latini in France." *The Athenaeum* No. 3655 (Nov. 13, 1897): p. 674.

Hartmann, Johannes. *Die Persönlichkeit des Sultans Saladin im Urteil der abendländischen Quellen*. Berlin, 1933.

Haskins, Charles H. "Michael Scot and Frederick II." *Isis* IV (1921-22): 250–75.

Hauvette, Henri. *Études sur la Divine Comédie, la composition du poème et son rayonnement*. Paris, 1922.

Haywood, Richard M. "*Inferno*, I, 106-108." *MLN* LXXIV (1959): 416–18.

Hervieux, Léopold (ed.). "Romuli vulgaris fabularum libri quatuor." In *Les Fabulistes latins depuis le siècle d'Auguste jusqu' à la fin du moyen âge*. Vol. II: *Phèdre et ses anciens imitateurs, directs et indirects*, pp. 195–233. 2d edn. Paris, 1894.

Historia fratris Dulcini heresiarche di anonimo sincrono and *De secta illorum qui se dicunt esse de ordine Apostolorum di Bernardo Gui*, ed. Arnaldo Segarizzi. In *RIS* IX, pt. 5. New edn.

Holbrook, Richard Thayer. *Dante and the Animal Kingdom*. New York, 1902.

Hopper, Vincent Foster. "Geryon and the Knotted Cord (Dante, *Inferno*, XVI, XVII)." *MLN* LI (1936): 445–49.

Huillard-Bréholles, A. *Vie et correspondance de Pierre de la Vigne, ministre de l'empereur Frédéric II*. Paris, 1865.

Isidore of Seville. *Etymologiarum sive Originum libri* XX, ed. W. M. Lindsay. 2 vols. Oxford, 1911.

Jacobus de Varagine. *Legenda aurea vulgo historia lomberdica dicta*, ed. T. Grässe. 2d edn. Leipzig, 1850.

Julian, John. *A Dictionary of Hymnology*. New York, 1892.

Kaske, R. E. "Dante's 'DXV' and 'Veltro.'" *Traditio* XVII (1961): 185–254.

Kuen, Heinrich. "Dante in Reimnot?" *Germanisch-Romanische Monatsschrift* XXVIII (1940): 305–14.

Lactantius. *See* Baehrens, Emil (1881).

Lane, Frederic Chapin. *Venetian Ships and Shipbuilders of the Renaissance*. Baltimore, 1934.

Larkin, Neil M. "Another Look at Dante's Frog and Mouse." *MLN* LXXVII (1962): 94–99.

Latini, Brunetto. *See* Contini, Gianfranco (1960).

———. *Li livres dou tresor de Brunetto Latini*, ed. Francis J. Carmody. Berkeley, 1948.

Lazzari, Alfonso. "Il marchese Obizzo II d'Este signore di Ferrara nel poema di Dante e nella storia." *Giornale Dantesco* XXXIX (1938): 127–50.

Livi, Giovanni. "Un personaggio dantesco: Maestro Adamo e la sua patria." *Giornale dantesco* XXIV (1921): 265–70.

Londi, Emilio. Review of Fabio Bargagli-Petrucci, *Le fonti di Siena e i loro acquedotti* (2 vols.), 1906; Ella Noyes, *The Casentino and Its Story*, 1905. In *Bullettino della Società Dantesca Italiana* N.S. XV (1908): 115–19.

Lorenzi, E. *La ruina di qua da Trento*. Trent, 1896.

———. *La leggenda di Dante nel Trentino*. Trent, 1897.

Luiso, F. P. "Su le tracce di un usuraio fiorentino del secolo XIII." *Archivio storico italiano* ser. 5, XLII (1908): 3–44.

LIST OF WORKS CITED

McKenzie, Kenneth. *See* Garver, Milton Stahl, and Mc-Kenzie, Kenneth (1912).

Macrobius. *Commentariorum in somnium Scipionis.* In *Macrobius,* ed. Franz Eyssenhardt, pp. 465–641. Leipzig, 1868.

———. *Commentary on the Dream of Scipio,* trans. William Harris Stahl. New York, 1952.

Maggini, F. Review of R. Davidsohn, *Forschungen zur älteren Geschichte von Florenz* (4 vols.), 1896–1908. In *Bullettino della Società Dantesca Italiana* N.S. XVII (1910): 120–30.

———. "Note lessicali." *Studi danteschi* I (1920): 142–45.

Mandruzzato, Enzo. "L'apologo 'della rana e del topo' e Dante *(Inf.* XXIII, 4–9)." *Studi danteschi* XXXIII, fasc. 2 (1955–56): 147–65.

Manuzzi, Giuseppe. *Vocabolario della lingua italiana.* 2d edn. Vols. I, IV. Florence, 1859, 1865.

Marie de France. *See* Warnke, Karl (1898).

Mariotti, L., *pseud.* [Antonio Gallenga]. *A Historical Memoir of Frà Dolcino and His Times; Being an Account of a General Struggle for Ecclesiastical Reform, and of an Anti-heretical Crusade in Italy, in the Early Part of the Fourteenth Century.* London, 1853.

Marti, Berthe M. "A Crux in Dante's *Inferno.*" *Speculum* XXVII (1952): 67–70.

Marti, Mario (ed.). "Cecco Angiolieri." In *Poeti giocosi del tempo di Dante,* pp. 111–250. Milan, 1956.

Martin of Dumio. *Formula honestae vitae.* In Migne, *P.L.* LXXII.

Masi, Gino. Review of Roberto Ridolfi, "La espiazione di Guido da Monforte," *Rivista storica degli archivi toscani* I (1929): 141–54. In *Archivio storico italiano* ser. 7, XIII (1930): 169.

———. "Fra savi e mercanti suicidi del tempo di Dante." *Giornale dantesco* XXXIX (1938): 199–238.

Massèra, Aldo Francesco. "Dante e Riccobaldo da Ferrara." *Bullettino della Società Dantesca Italiana* N.S. XXII (1915): 168–200.

————. "Per la storia letteraria del Dugento." *Giornale storico della letteratura italiana* LXXV (1920): 209–33.

Mazzi, Curzio. "Documenti senesi intorno a persone o ad avvenimenti ricordati da Dante Alighieri." *Giornale dantesco* I (1894): 31–32.

Mazzoni, Francesco. Review of L. Caretti, "Una interpretazione dantesca," in *Studi e ricerche di letteratura italiana*, pp. 4–14, 1951. In *Studi danteschi* XXX (1951): 286–87.

Mazzoni, Guido. *Lectura Dantis: Il canto XII dell'Inferno letto da Guido Mazzoni nella Sala di Dante in Orsanmichele.* Florence, 1906.

————. *Almae luces malae cruces. Studii danteschi.* Bologna, 1941.

Miller, Konrad (ed.). *Mappaemundi. Die ältesten Weltkarten.* Vol. IV: *Die Herefordkarte.* Stuttgart, 1896.

Minutoli, Carlo. "Gentucca e gli altri lucchesi nominati nella *Divina Commedia.*" In *Dante e il suo secolo*, ed. Mariano Cellini and Gaetano Ghivizzani, pp. 203–31. Florence, 1865.

Monaci, Ernesto (ed.). "Canzone di Guido Cavalcanti." In *Crestomazia italiana dei primi secoli*, pp. 573-75. New edn., revised by Felice Arese. Rome, 1955.

Moore, Edward. *The Time-References in the Divina Commedia.* London, 1887.

————. *Studies in Dante. First Series: Scripture and Classical Authors in Dante.* Oxford, 1896. *Second Series: Miscellaneous Essays*, 1899. *Third Series: Miscellaneous Essays*, 1903.

Moore, Olin H. *The Young King, Henry Plantagenet (1155-1183) in History, Literature and Tradition.* Columbus, Ohio, 1925.

Morpurgo, Emilio. "I prestatori di danaro al tempo di Dante." In *Dante e Padova, Studj storico-critici*, pp. 193–233. Padua, 1865.

Murari, Rocco. "Per la tecnofagìa del conte Ugolino ma non pel verso 75 del canto XXXIII dell'*Inferno.*" *Giornale dantesco* VI (1898): 491–97.

Nadiani, Pompeo. *Interpretazione dei versi di Dante sul fiume Montone.* Milan, 1894.

Nardi, Bruno. *Saggi di filosofia dantesca.* Milan, 1930.

———. *Nel mondo di Dante.* Rome, 1944.

———. *Dante e la cultura medievale: Nuovi saggi di filosofia dantesca.* 2d edn. Bari, 1949.

———. *Nuova "Lectura Dantis": Il canto XI dell'Inferno.* 2d edn. Rome, 1955.

I nobili fatti di Alessandro Magno, ed. Giusto Grion. Bologna, 1872.

Le novelle antiche, ed. Guido Biagi. Florence, 1880.

Olschki, Leonardo. "Dante, i barattieri e i diavoli." *Giornale dantesco* xxxviii (1937): 61–81.

———. *The Myth of Felt.* Berkeley, 1949.

Oria, Jacopo d'. *Annales Ianuenses a. 1280–1294.* In *Monumenta Germaniae historica inde ab anno Christi quingentesimo usque ad annum millesimum et quingentesimum, Scriptores,* xviii, ed. Georg Heinrich Pertz, 288–356. Hanover, 1863.

Orosius. *Historiarum adversum paganos libri VII,* ed. Karl Zangemeister. Leipzig, 1889.

———. *Seven Books of History against the Pagans: The Apology of Paulus Orosius,* trans. Irving Woodworth Raymond. New York, 1936.

Orr, M. A. *Dante and the Early Astronomers.* Rev. edn. London, 1956.

Ottokar, Niccolò. "La condanna postuma di Farinata degli Uberti." *Archivio storico italiano* ser. 6, ii for 1919 (1921): 155–63.

Ovidio, Francesco d'. *Studii sulla Divina Commedia.* Milan, 1901.

———. *Nuovi studii danteschi: Ugolino, Pier della Vigna, i simoniaci, e discussioni varie.* Milan, 1907.

———. "Sette chiose alla *Commedia.*" *Studi danteschi* vii (1923): 5–82.

Padoan, Giorgio. " 'Colui che fece per viltà il gran rifiuto.' " *Studi danteschi* xxxviii (1961): 75–128.

Pagliaro, Antonino. *Saggi di critica semantica*. Messina, 1953.

———. *Altri saggi di critica semantica*. Messina, 1961.

Palandri (O.F.M.), Eletto. "Il vescovo Andrea de' Mozzi nella storia e nella leggenda dantesca." *Giornale dantesco* XXXII (1931): 93–118.

Paolino di Piero. *Cronica di Paolino di Piero fiorentino dall'anno MLXXX al MCCCV.* In *Rerum Italicarum scriptores ab anno aerae Christianae millesimo ad millesimum sexcentesimum*, ed. Giuseppe Maria Tartini. II, 1–70. Florence, 1770.

Paris, Gaston. Review of A. Fioravanti, *Il Saladino nelle leggende francesi e italiane del medioevo*, 1891. In *Journal des savants*, 1893, pp. 284–99, 354–65, 428–38, 486–98.

Parodi, E. G. "La lettura di Dante in Orsanmichele." *Bullettino della Società Dantesca Italiana* N.S. IX (1902): 97–107.

———. "La critica della poesia classica nel ventesimo canto dell'*Inferno*." *Atene e Roma* XI (1908a): 183–95, 237–50.

———. Review of Egidio Gorra, "Quando Dante scrisse la *Divina Commedia*," *Rendiconti dell' R. Istituto Lombardo di Scienze e Lettere* ser. 2, XXXIX (1906): 666–89, 827–52; XL (1907): 202–38; "I 'nove passi' di Beatrice," *Mélanges Chabaneau, Romanische Forschungen* XXIII (1907): 585–90. In *Bullettino della Società Dantesca Italiana* N.S. XV (1908b): 1–51.

———. Review of Stanislao De Chiara, *Dante e la Calabria*, 2d edn., 1910. In *Bullettino della Società Dantesca Italiana* N.S. XVIII (1911a): 68–70.

———. Review of Girolamo Golubovich, O.F.M., "Una pagina dantesca: Notizie inedite sul conte frate Guido da Montefeltro (c. 1222–1298)," extracted from *Archivum Franciscanum historicum*, fasc. II, anno III (1910): 214ff.; et al. In *Bullettino della Società Dantesca Italiana* N.S. XVIII (1911b): 262–74.

———. Review of Giacomo Surra, *Studi su Dante. I: La conoscenza del futuro e del presente nei dannati danteschi*, 1911. In *Bullettino della Società Dantesca Italiana* N.S. XIX (1912): 169–83.

Parodi, E. G. *Poesia e storia nella Divina Commedia*. Naples, 1920.

————. *Lingua e letteratura: Studi di teoria linguistica e di storia dell'italiano antico*, ed. Gianfranco Folena, pt. 2. Venice, 1957.

Passavanti, Iacopo. *Lo specchio della vera penitenza di Iacopo Passavanti*, ed. F.-L. Polidori. Florence, 1856.

Perrier, Joseph Louis. "Bertran de Born, Patriot, and His Place in Dante's *Inferno*." *The Romanic Review* XI (1920): 223–38; XII (1921): 21–43.

Petraglione, G. "Una 'cronaca' del Trecento e l'episodio dantesco di Guido da Montefeltro." *Giornale dantesco* XI (1903): 136–42.

Petrocchi, Giorgio. "Intorno alla pubblicazione dell'*Inferno* e del *Purgatorio*." *Convivium* N.S. XXV (1957): 652–69.

Petrus Comestor. *Historia scholastica*. In Migne, *P.L.* CXCVIII.

Pier della Vigna. *See* Contini, Gianfranco (1960).

Pintor, Fortunato. Review of Giulio Vitali, "I Cavalieri Godenti e Guittone d'Arezzo," *Rassegna nazionale* CXXVI (1902): 369–89; "Per una pagina di storia fiorentina e per una chiosa dantesca," *Rassegna nazionale* CXXVII (1902): 579–603. In *Bullettino della Società Dantesca Italiana* N.S. X (1903): 356–57.

————. Review of Arturo Ferretto (ed.), *Codice diplomatico delle relazioni tra la Liguria, la Toscana e la Lunigiana ai tempi di Dante (1265-1321)*, pt. 2 (*Atti della Società Ligure di Storia Patria* XXXI [II], CXV-501). In *Bullettino della Società Dantesca Italiana* N.S. XII (1905): 54–56.

————. Review of Raffaello Piccoli, *La Sardegna di Dante*, 1912. In *Bullettino della Società Dantesca Italiana* N.S. XXI (1914): 74–76.

Piton, C. *Les Lombards en France et à Paris*, vol. I. Paris, 1892.

Proto, Enrico. "Gerione (la corda—la sozza imagine di froda)." *Giornale dantesco* VIII (1900): 65–105.

————. "La lonza dantesca." *Giornale dantesco* XV (1907): 1–16.

————. "I giganti." *Giornale dantesco* XX (1912): 225–43.

Pseudo-Callisthenes. *Epistola Alexandri ad Aristotelem, magistrum suum, de itinere suo et de situ Indiae*. In *Iuli Valeri Alexandri Polemi Res gestae Alexandri Macedonis translatae ex Aesopo Graeco*, ed. Bernhard Kübler, pp. 190–221. Leipzig, 1888.

Pseudo-Turpin. *The Pseudo-Turpin*, ed. H. M. Smyser. Cambridge, Mass., 1937.

Pulci, Luigi. *Il Morgante*, ed. George B. Weston. 2 vols. Bari, 1930.

Rajna, Pio. "Dante e i romanzi della *Tavola Rotonda*." *Nuova Antologia di lettere, scienze ed arti* ser. 6, ccvi (1920): 223–47.

Rambaldi, P. L. Review of Tommaso Casini, "Ricordi danteschi di Sardegna," extracted from *Nuova Antologia di scienze, lettere ed arti* ser. 3, lviii (1895): 75–93, 259–79. In *Bullettino della Società Dantesca Italiana* N.S. iii (1896): 185–95.

Rand, Edward Kennard. "Dante and Servius." *Annual Report of the Dante Society* xxxiii (1916): 1–11.

Raynouard, M. (ed.). "Bernard de Ventadour." In *Choix des poésies originales des troubadours*. Vol. iii, pp. 42–93. Paris, 1818.

Reade, W. H. V. *The Moral System of Dante's Inferno*. Oxford, 1909.

Regis, Emilia. "Una legge fiorentina inedita contro Rinier de' Pazzi." *Atti della R. Accademia delle Scienze di Torino* xlvii (1912): 1092–1110.

Repetti, Emanuele. *Dizionario geografico fisico storico della Toscana, contenente la descrizione di tutti i luoghi del Granducato, Ducato di Lucca, Garfagnana e Lunigiana*. Vol. i. Florence, 1833.

Ricci, Corrado. *Ore ed ombre dantesche*. Florence, 1921a.

——— (ed.). *La Divina Commedia illustrata nei luoghi e nelle persone*. Milan, 1921b.

Ristoro d'Arezzo. *Della composizione del mondo di Ristoro d'Arezzo*, ed. Enrico Narducci. Milan, 1864.

Rogers, Francis M. "The Vivaldi Expedition." *Annual Report of the Dante Society* lxxiii (1955): 31–45.

Romani, Fedele. *Lectura Dantis: Il canto XXXIII dell'Inferno letto da Fedele Romani nella Sala di Dante in Orsanmichele*. Florence, 1901.

Romulus. *See* Hervieux, Léopold (1894).

Rossi, Vittorio. "Il canto XXXIV dell'*Inferno*." In *Letture dantesche*, ed. Giovanni Getto. Vol. i: *Inferno*, pp. 651–65. Florence, 1955.

Sacchetti, Franco. *Delle novelle di Franco Sacchetti cittadino fiorentino*. Florence, 1724.

Salimbene da Parma. *Cronica*, ed. Ferdinando Bernini. 2 vols. Bari, 1942.

Salvagnini, Enrico. "Jacopo da Sant'Andrea e i feudatarii del padovano." In *Dante e Padova, Studj storico-critici*, pp. 29–74. Padua, 1865.

Salvemini, G. Review of G. Arias, *Le istituzioni giuridiche medievali nella Divina Commedia*, 1901. In *Bullettino della Società Dantesca Italiana* N.S. ix (1902): 112–22.

Sanesi, Emilio. "Del trasferimento di messer Andrea dei Mozzi da Firenze a Vicenza." *Studi danteschi* xxii (1938): 115–22.

Santini, Pietro. "Appunti sulla vendetta privata e sulle rappresaglie in occasione di un documento inedito." *Archivio storico italiano* ser. 4, xviii (1886): 162–76.

———. "Sui fiorentini 'che fur sì degni.'" *Studi danteschi* vi (1923): 25–44.

Sàntoli, Quinto. "La potesteria pistoiese di Venètico Caccianemici." *Bullettino storico pistoiese* xxiii (1921): 110–31.

Scartazzini, G. A. *Enciclopedia dantesca: Dizionario critico e ragionato di quanto concerne la vita e le opere di Dante Alighieri*. Vol. ii. Milan, 1899.

Scherillo, Michele. "Bertram dal Bornio e il Re giovane." *Nuova Antologia di scienze, lettere ed arti* ser. 4, lxx (1897): 452–78.

Schiaffini, A. Review of Leo Spitzer, "Altfrz. 'acesmer,' aprov. '(a)sesmar,' '(a)sermar' 'herrichten,'" *Archivum Romanicum* xii (1928): 323–24. In *Studi danteschi* xv (1931): 137–38.

———. Review of Paul Aebischer, "Précisions sur les origines lointaines du fr. 'plage,' " *Vox Romanica* 1 (1936): 225–34. In *Studi danteschi* XXI (1937a): 180–82.

————. Review of Ferdinando Neri, "La voce *lai* nei testi italiani," *Atti della R. Accademia delle Scienze di Torino, classe di scienze morali, storiche e filologiche* LXXII (1937): 105–19. In *Studi danteschi* XXI (1937b): 182–83.

————. Review of Leo Spitzer, "Altit. 'riviera,' " *Zeitschrift für romanische Philologie* LVII (1937): 90–91. In *Studi danteschi* XXI (1937c): 183–84.

Schick, Carla. "Per la lezione di un verso famoso." *Paideia* X (1955), Suppl.: 473–75.

Scott, Edward J. L. "Brunetto Latini's Home in France A.D. 1260–6." *The Athenaeum* No. 3654 (Nov. 6, 1897): 635.

Sepulcri, Alessandro. "Dante e 'li Tedeschi lurchi.' " *Rendiconti del R. Istituto Lombardo di Scienze e Lettere* ser. 2, XLIX (1916): 171–82.

Servius. *Commentarii in Virgilium Serviani; sive Commentarii in Virgilium, qui Mauro Servio Honorato tribuuntur,* ed. H. Albrecht Lion. 2 vols. Göttingen, 1826.

Shakespeare, William. *The Complete Works of Shakespeare,* ed. George Lyman Kittredge. Boston, 1936.

Silverstein, Theodore. "Dante and Vergil the Mystic." *Harvard Studies and Notes in Philology and Literature* XIV (1932): 51–82.

————. "*Inferno,* XII, 100–126, and the *Visio Karoli Crassi.*" *MLN* LI (1936): 449–52.

————. "Did Dante Know the Vision of St. Paul?" *Harvard Studies and Notes in Philology and Literature* XIX (1937): 231–47.

Simeoni, Luigi. "L'elezione di Obizzo d'Este a signore di Ferrara," *Archivio storico italiano* ser. 8, 1 (1935): 165–88.

Singleton, Charles S. " 'Sulla fiumana ove'l mar non ha vanto,' (*Inferno,* II, 108)." *The Romanic Review* XXXIX (1948): 269–77.

————. *An Essay on the Vita Nuova.* Cambridge, Mass., 1949; Baltimore, Md., 1977.

————. *Dante Studies 1: Commedia, Elements of Structure.* Cambridge, Mass., 1954; Baltimore, Md., 1977.

Singleton, Charles S. "Virgil Recognizes Beatrice." *Annual Report of the Dante Society* LXXIV (1956): 29–38.

———. *Dante Studies 2: Journey to Beatrice*. Cambridge, Mass., 1958; Baltimore, Md., 1977.

———. "*Inferno* X: Guido's Disdain." *MLN* LXXVII (1962): 49–65.

———. "In Exitu Israel de Aegypto." In *Dante: A Collection of Critical Essays*, ed. John Freccero, pp. 102–21. Englewood Cliffs, N.J., 1965a.

———. "*Inferno* XIX: O Simon Mago!" *MLN* LXXX (1965b): 92–99.

———. "The Vistas in Retrospect." *MLN* LXXXI (1966): 55–80.

Soldati, Benedetto. "La coda di Gerione." *Giornale storico della letteratura italiana* XLI (1903): 84–88.

Solinus, Gaius Julius. *Collectanea rerum memorabilium*, ed. T. Mommsen. Berlin, 1864.

Solmi, Arrigo. Review of Tommaso Casini, *Scritti danteschi*, 1913. In *Bullettino della Società Dantesca Italiana* N.S. XXI (1914): 1–10.

———. *Discorsi sulla storia d'Italia*. Florence, 1933.

Spiazzi, Raimondo M. (ed.). *See* Aquinas, Thomas (Marietti publications); Aristotle (Marietti publications).

Spitzer, Leo. "Two Dante Notes: I. An Autobiographical Incident in *Inferno* XIX; II. Libicocco." *The Romanic Review* XXXIV (1943): 248–62.

———. "The Farcical Elements in *Inferno*, Cantos XXI-XXIII." *MLN* LIX (1944): 83–88.

Storie pistoresi (MCCC–MCCCXLVIII), ed. Silvio Adrasto Barbi. In *RIS* XI, pt. 5. New edn.

Sundby, Thor. *Della vita e delle opere di Brunetto Latini*. Trans. from the Danish and ed. Rodolfo Renier. Florence, 1884.

Tatlock, J.S.P. "Mohammed and his Followers in Dante." *MLR* XXVII (1932): 186–95.

La tavola ritonda o l'istoria di Tristano, ed. Filippo-Luigi Polidori. Pt. 1. Bologna, 1864.

LIST OF WORKS CITED

Terracini, Benvenuto. "Il canto XXVII dell'*Inferno*." *Lettere italiane* VI (1954): 3–35.

Thorndike, Lynn. *Michael Scot*. London, 1965.

Tocco, Felice. *Quel che non c' è nella Divina Commedia, o Dante e l'eresia*. Bologna, 1899.

Todeschini, Giuseppe. *Scritti su Dante di Giuseppe Todeschini*, collected by Bartolommeo Bressan. Vol. II. Vicenza, 1872.

Torraca, Francesco. Review of Dante Alighieri, *La Divina Commedia di Dante Alighieri con commento del prof. Giacomo Poletto*, 1894. In *Bullettino della Società Dantesca Italiana* N.S. II (1895): 129–57, 168–90, 194–211.

———. " 'Sopra Campo Picen.' " *Rassegna critica della letteratura italiana* VIII (1903): 1–10.

———. "A proposito di Aghinolfo da Romena." *Bullettino della Società Dantesca Italiana* N.S. XI (1904): 97–108.

———. *Studi danteschi*. Naples, 1912.

———. *Nuovi studi danteschi nel VI centenario della morte di Dante*. Naples, 1921.

———. "Nuova chiosa ai vv. 20-27 del II canto dell'*Inferno*." *Studi danteschi* X (1925): 43–54.

Toynbee, Paget. "Brunetto Latini's *Trésor*." *The Athenaeum* No. 3656 (Nov. 20, 1897): 710.

———. *Dante Studies and Researches*. London, 1902.

———. "Boccaccio's Commentary on the *Divina Commedia*." *MLR* II (1907): 91–120.

———. *A Dictionary of Proper Names and Notable Matters in the Works of Dante*, revised by Charles S. Singleton. Oxford, 1968.

Valerius Maximus. *Factorum et dictorum memorabilium libri novem*, ed. Karl Halm. Leipzig, 1865.

Vallone, Aldo. *Lectura Dantis siciliana: Del Veltro dantesco*. Trapani, 1955.

———. *La critica dantesca nel Settecento ed altri saggi danteschi*. Florence, 1961.

Vandelli, G. " ' "Usciteci" gridò: "qui è l'entrata" ' (*Inf.*, VIII, 81)." *Studi danteschi* III (1921a): 129–31.

———. " 'E sè continuando al primo detto' (*Inf.*, X, 76)." *Studi danteschi* III (1921b): 132–37.

———. "Note sul testo critico della *Commedia.*" *Studi danteschi* IV (1921c): 39–84.

———. Review of Dante Bianchi, "Chiosa dantesca (*Inf.* XV, 78 segg.)." *Giornale storico della letteratura italiana* LXXXV (1925): 212–13. In *Studi danteschi* X (1925): 162–63.

———. "Di un antico uso sintattico dei complementi di luogo." *Studi danteschi* XIII (1928): 65–68.

———. Review of Manfredi Porena, "Noterelle dantesche," extracted from *Studj Romanzi* XX (1930): 201–15. In *Studi danteschi* XVI (1932a): 195–97.

———. Review of Antonio Fiammazzo, "Ortografia dantesca: slovena o italiana?" *Rivista letteraria* anno II (1930): fasc. 4–5, pp. 18–20. In *Studi danteschi* XVI (1932b): 191.

———. " 'E questo sia suggel ch'ogn'uomo sganni' (*Inf.* XIX, 21)." *Studi danteschi* XIX (1935): 117–20.

Vannini, Armando. "La brigata spendereccia e Bartolomeo Folcacchieri (per una nuova interpretazione del v. 132 del Canto XXIX dell'*Inferno*)." *Giornale dantesco* XXII (1914): 63–66.

Venturi, Giovanni Antonio. Review of Felice Delfino, "La bolgia degl'ipocriti," extracted from *Rivista d'Italia*, April 1905. In *Bullettino della Società Dantesca Italiana* N.S. XII (1905): 237–40.

Villani, Filippo. *Le vite d'uomini illustri fiorentini*, ed. Giammaria Mazzuchelli. Florence, 1847.

Villani, Giovanni. *Cronica di Giovanni Villani*, ed. F. Gherardi Dragomanni. 4 vols. Florence, 1844–45.

Walter of Châtillon. *Alexandreis sive Gesta Alexandri Magni libris X comprehensa*. In Migne, *P.L.* CCIX.

Warnke, Karl (ed.). *Die Fabeln der Marie de France.* Halle, 1898.

Wolfson, Harry A. "Plan for the Publication of a *Corpus Commentariorum Averrois in Aristotelem.*" *Speculum* VI (1931): 412–27.

Zaccagnini, Guido. "Personaggi danteschi in Bologna." *Giornale storico della letteratura italiana* LXIV (1914): 1–47.

———. "Il testamento di Venetico Caccianimici." *Giornale storico della letteratura italiana* LXV (1915): 51–54.

———. "Personaggi danteschi a Bologna e in Romagna." *Atti e memorie della R. Deputazione di Storia Patria per le Provincie di Romagna* ser. 4, XXIV (1934): 19–71.

Zenatti, Albino. Review of Arnaldo Segarizzi, "Fonti per la storia di fra' Dolcino," extracted from *Tridentum* III, fasc. V–VI; Arnaldo Segarizzi, "Contributo alla storia di fra' Dolcino e degli eretici trentini," extracted from *Tridentum* III, fasc. VII–X; Orsini Begani, *Fra' Dolcino nella tradizione e nella storia*. In *Bullettino della Società Dantesca Italiana* N.S. X (1903): 383–88.

Zingarelli, N. "Un serventese di Ugo di Sain Circ." In *In memoria di Napoleone Caix e Ugo Angelo Canello: Miscellanea di filologia e linguistica*, pp. 243–53. Florence, 1886.

———. "Appunti lessicali danteschi." *Giornale storico della letteratura italiana* XLVIII (1906): 368–80.

———. Review of F. D'Ovidio, *Opere*: IV, *Nuovo volume di studii danteschi*, 1926; V, *L'ultimo volume dantesco*, 1926. In *Studi danteschi* XII (1927): 90–100.

EARLY COMMENTATORS

Anonimo fiorentino. Commento alla Divina Commedia d'anonimo fiorentino del secolo XIV, ed. Pietro Fanfani. Vol. I. Bologna, 1866.

Bambaglioli, Graziolo de'. *Il commento più antico e la più antica versione latina dell'Inferno di Dante*, ed. Antonio Fiammazzo. Udine, 1892.

Benvenuto da Imola. *Comentum super Dantis Aldigherij Comoediam*, ed. Giacomo Filippo Lacaita. Vols. I, II. Florence, 1887.

Boccaccio, Giovanni. *Il comento alla Divina Commedia e gli altri scritti intorno a Dante*, ed. Domenico Guerri. 3 vols. Bari, 1918.

Buonanni, Vincenzio. *Discorso di Vincentzio Buonanni, sopra la prima cantica del divinissimo theologo Dante d'Alighieri del bello nobilissimo fiorentino, intitolata Commedia.* Florence, 1572.

Buti, Francesco da. *Commento di Francesco da Buti sopra la Divina Comedia di Dante Allighieri,* ed. Crescentino Giannini. Vol. I. Pisa, 1858.

Chiose anonime alla prima cantica della Divina Commedia di un contemporaneo del poeta, ed. Francesco Selmi. Turin, 1865.

Gelli, Giovanni Battista. *Letture edite e inedite di Giovan Batista Gelli sopra la Commedia di Dante,* ed. Carlo Negroni. Vol. II. Florence, 1887.

John of Serravalle. *Translatio et comentum totius libri Dantis Aldigherii,* ed. Marcellino da Civezza, M.O., and Teofilo Domenichelli, M.O., Prato, 1891.

Lana, Jacopo della. *Comedia di Dante degli Allagherii col commento di Jacopo della Lana bolognese,* ed. Luciano Scarabelli. Vol. I. Bologna, 1866.

Landino, Cristoforo. *Dante con l'espositioni di Christoforo Landino et d'Alessandro Vellutello. Sopra la sua Comedia dell'Inferno, del Purgatorio, e del Paradiso.* Venice, 1596.

L'Ottimo Commento della Divina Commedia, ed. Alessandro Torri. Vol. I. Pisa, 1827.

Pietro di Dante. *Super Dantis ipsius genitoris Comoediam commentarium,* ed. Vincenzio Nannucci. Florence, 1845.

MODERN COMMENTATORS

Butler, Arthur John. *The Hell of Dante Alighieri.* London, 1892.

Casella, Mario. *La Divina Commedia.* Bologna, 1964.

Casini, Tommaso and Barbi, S. A. *La Divina Commedia di Dante Alighieri,* comm. Tommaso Casini. 6th edn. revised by S. A. Barbi. Florence, 1926.

Chimenz, Siro A. *La Divina Commedia di Dante Alighieri.* Turin, 1962.

Del Lungo, Isidoro. *La Divina Commedia.* Florence, 1944.

Gmelin, Hermann. *Die göttliche Komödie.* Vol. I: *Die Hölle.* Stuttgart, 1954.

Grandgent, C. H. *La Divina Commedia di Dante Alighieri*. Rev. edn. Boston, 1933.

Petrocchi, Giorgio. *La Commedia secondo l'antica vulgata*. Vol. I: *Introduzione*. Vol. II: *Inferno*. Milan, 1966.

Porena, Manfredi. *La Divina Commedia di Dante Alighieri*. Vol. I: *L'Inferno*. Bologna, 1946.

Rossi, Vittorio. *La Divina Commedia di Dante Alighieri*. Vol. I: *L'Inferno*. 3rd edn. Rome, 1947.

Sapegno, Natalino. *La Divina Commedia*. Milan, 1957.

Scartazzini, G. A. *La Divina Commedia di Dante Alighieri*. Vol. I: *L'Inferno*. Leipzig, 1874.

————. *La Divina Commedia di Dante Alighieri*. 3rd edn. Milan, 1899.

———— and Vandelli, Giuseppe. *La Divina Commedia: Testo critico della Società Dantesca Italiana*, comm. G. A. Scartazzini. 17th edn. revised by Giuseppe Vandelli. Milan, 1958.

Tommaseo, Niccolò. *Commedia di Dante Allighieri*. Vol. I: *L'Inferno*. Milan, 1869.

Torraca, Francesco. *La Divina Commedia*. 12th edn. Vol. I: *Inferno*. Rome, 1951.

Vandelli, Giuseppe. *La Divina Commedia*. In *Le opere di Dante: Testo critico della Società Dantesca Italiana*, ed. M. Barbi, E. G. Parodi, F. Pellegrini, E. Pistelli, P. Rajna, E. Rostagno, G. Vandelli, pp. 443–798. 2d edn. Florence, 1960.

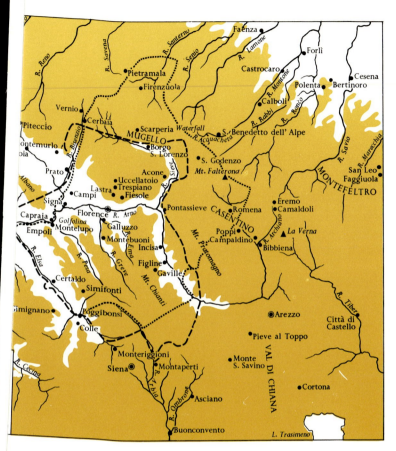

4. Tuscany